PATHFINDER
ROLEPLAYING GAME

BESTIARY 2

PATHFINDER
ROLEPLAYING GAME
BESTIARY 2

CREDITS

Designers: Wolfgang Baur, Jason Bulmahn, Adam Daigle, Graeme Davis, Crystal Frasier, Joshua J. Frost, Tim Hitchcock, Brandon Hodge, James Jacobs, Steve Kenson, Hal Maclean, Martin Mason, Rob McCreary, Erik Mona, Jason Nelson, Patrick Renie, Sean K Reynolds, F. Wesley Schneider, Owen K.C. Stephens, James L. Sutter, Russ Taylor, and Greg A. Vaughan
Developers: Jason Bulmahn, James Jacobs, and Sean K Reynolds

Cover Artist: Wayne Reynolds

Interior Artists: Eric Belisle, Branko Bistrovic, Christopher Burdett, Anna Christenson, Concept Art House, Mike Corriero, Alberto Dal Lago, Eric Dechamps, Julie Dillon, Matt Dixon, Mariusz Gandzel, John Gravato, Kelly Harris, Andrew Hou, Imaginary Friends, Kekai Kotaki, Peter Lazarski, Eric Lofgren, Jorge Maese, Damien Mammoliti, Hector Ortiz, Jim Pavelec, Drew Pocza, Scott Purdy, KyuShik Shin, Craig J Spearing, Dean Spencer, Florian Stitz, Sarah Stone, Christophe Swal, Adam Vehige, Tyler Walpole, Eva Widermann, Ben Wootten, Kevin Yan, and Kieran Yanner

Creative Director: James Jacobs
Senior Art Director: Sarah E. Robinson
Managing Editor: F. Wesley Schneider
Editing: Judy Bauer, Christopher Carey, Rob McCreary, Erik Mona, Mark Moreland, Lisa Stevens, F. Wesley Schneider, James L. Sutter, and Vic Wertz
Editorial Interns: Kelley Frodel and Patrick Renie
Graphic Designer: Andrew Vallas
Production Specialist: Crystal Frasier

Publisher: Erik Mona
Paizo CEO: Lisa Stevens
Vice President of Operations: Jeffrey Alvarez
Corporate Accountant: Dave Erickson
Director of Sales: Pierce Watters
Financial Analyst: Christopher Self
Technical Director: Vic Wertz
Marketing Director: Hyrum Savage
Events Manager: Joshua J. Frost

Special Thanks: The Paizo Customer Service, Warehouse, and Website Teams, Ryan Dancey, Clark Peterson, and the proud participants of the Open Gaming Movement.

This game is dedicated to Gary Gygax and Dave Arneson.

Based on the original roleplaying game rules designed by Gary Gygax and Dave Arneson and inspired by the third edition of the game designed by Monte Cook, Jonathan Tweet, Skip Williams, Richard Baker, and Peter Adkison.

This game would not be possible without the passion and dedication of the thousands of gamers who helped playtest and develop it. Thank you for all of your time and effort.

Paizo Publishing, LLC
7120 185th Ave NE, Ste 120
Redmond, WA 98052-0577
paizo.com

TABLE OF CONTENTS

ALPHABETICAL LISTING OF MONSTERS

Illustration by Andrew Hou

INTRODUCTION

Welcome to the *Pathfinder Roleplaying Game Bestiary 2*! Within the pages of this tome you will encounter a wide range of monsters to pit against your players as they explore your world. The creatures featured herein have been drawn from a wide range of sources, from real-world legends and myths (where we get our chupacabras and wendigos, our charybdises and scyllas), to the traditions of the RPG's rich history (such as the blink dog and the hellcat), to the inventions of writers old and new (such as Frank Belknap Long's hounds of Tindalos, Lewis Carroll's jabberwock, or H. P. Lovecraft's Leng spiders, gugs, and more). In order to fully use the creatures in the *Pathfinder RPG Bestiary 2*, you'll need a copy of the *Pathfinder RPG Core Rulebook* and the *Pathfinder RPG Advanced Player's Guide*. Additional monsters can be found in the first *Pathfinder RPG Bestiary*.

While each monster is a unique creature, many possess similar special attacks, defenses, and qualities. Unique abilities are described below the monster's stat block. Many abilities common to several monsters appear in the universal monster rules in Appendix 3. If a monster's listed special ability does not appear in its description, you'll find it there. Check pages 294–303 of this book for the complete universal monster rules.

This book's appendices also contain a wealth of other information—you'll find charts organizing the monsters into several different categories, new templates and variants, and more.

Each monster description on the following pages is presented in the same format, split into three specific areas: Introduction, Stat Block, and Description.

Introduction

Each monster is presented alphabetically. In the case of a group of monsters sharing similar traits (such as outsider races and some animals or vermin), the monster's basic name is listed first.

Stat Block

This is where you'll find all of the information you need to run the monster in an encounter. A stat block is organized as follows. Note that in cases where a line in a stat block has no value, that line is omitted.

Name and CR: The monster's name is presented first, along with its challenge rating (CR) and three icons you can use to quickly identify the creature's role in the game. Challenge rating is a numerical indication of how dangerous a monster is—the higher the number, the deadlier the creature. Challenge rating is detailed on page 397 of the *Pathfinder RPG Core Rulebook*.

XP: Listed here are the total experience points that PCs earn for defeating the monster.

MONSTER ICONS

Each monster in this book is presented with three visual cues to help you quickly identify the monster's role and niche in the game. The first of these icons indicates the monster's type. The second indicates the terrain where the creature can normally be encountered. The third shows what sort of climate the creature prefers. More precise notes on each monster's type (and subtypes), preferred terrain, and climate appear elsewhere in its stat block, but these three icons can help you recognize this basic information at a glance.

Creature Type

- Aberration
- Animal
- Construct
- Dragon
- Fey
- Humanoid
- Magical Beast
- Monstrous Humanoid
- Ooze
- Outsider
- Plant
- Undead
- Vermin

Terrain

- Desert
- Forest/Jungle
- Hill
- Mountain
- Plain
- Ruins/Dungeon
- Sky
- Swamp
- Underground
- Urban
- Water

Climate

- Cold
- Extraplanar
- Temperate
- Tropical

Race, Class, and Level: Some monsters do not possess racial Hit Dice and are instead defined by their class levels. For these monsters, their race, class, and level appear here. Unless otherwise noted, the first class listed is the class chosen by the monster as its favored class.

Alignment, Size, and Type: While a monster's size and type remain constant (unless changed by the application of templates or other unusual modifiers), alignment is far more fluid. The alignments listed for the monsters in this book represent the norm for those monsters—they can vary as you require them to in order to serve the needs of your campaign. Only in the case of relatively unintelligent monsters (creatures with an Intelligence of 2 or lower are almost never anything other than neutral) and planar monsters (outsiders with alignments other than those listed are unusual and typically outcasts from their kind) is the listed alignment relatively unchangeable.

Init and Senses: The creature's initiative modifier followed by any special senses and its Perception check modifier.

Illustration by Andrew Hou

Aura: If the creature has a particular magical or exceptional aura, it is listed here along with its radius from the creature and, as applicable, a save DC to resist the aura's effects.

AC: The creature's Armor Class, touch Armor Class, and flat-footed Armor Class. The modifiers that generate its AC are listed parenthetically at the end of this entry.

hp: The creature's hit points, followed by its Hit Dice (including modifiers from Constitution, favored class levels, creature type modifiers, and the Toughness feat). Creatures with PC class levels receive maximum hit points for their first HD, but all other HD rolls are assumed to be average. Fast healing and regeneration values, if any, follow the creature's HD.

Saving Throws: The creature's Fortitude, Reflex, and Will saves, followed by situational modifiers to those rolls.

Defensive Abilities/DR/Immune/Resist/SR: All of the creature's unusual defensive abilities. Damage reduction, immunities, resistances, and spell resistance are called out separately as necessary.

Weaknesses: All of the creature's unusual weaknesses are listed here.

Speed: The creature's land speed, and additional speeds as necessary for the creature.

Melee: The creature's melee attacks are listed here, with its attack roll modifier listed after the attack's name, followed by the damage in parentheses.

Ranged: As Melee above, but for ranged attacks.

Space/Reach: The creature's space and reach—if the creature's space and reach are standard (one 5-foot square and a reach of 5 feet), this line is omitted.

Special Attacks: The creature's special attacks. Full details for these attacks are given at the end of the stat block or in the universal monster rules appendix.

Spell-Like Abilities: After listing the caster level of the creature's spell-like abilities, this section lists all of the creature's spell-like abilities, organized by how many times per day it can use the abilities. Constant spell-like abilities function at all times but can be dispelled. A creature can reactivate a constant spell-like ability as a swift action.

Spells Known/Prepared: If the creature can actually cast spells, its caster level is indicated here, followed by the spells it knows or typically has prepared. Unless otherwise indicated, a spellcasting creature does not receive any of a spellcasting class's other abilities, such as a cleric's ability to spontaneously convert prepared spells to cure or inflict spells.

Ability Scores: The creature's ability scores are listed here. Unless otherwise indicated, a creature's ability scores represent the baseline of its racial modifiers applied to scores of 10 or 11. Creatures with NPC class levels have stats in the standard array (13, 12, 11, 10, 9, 8), while creatures with character class levels have the elite array (15, 14, 13, 12,

10, 8); in both cases, the creature's ability score modifiers are listed at the end of its description.

Base Atk/CMB/CMD: These values give the creature's base attack, its Combat Maneuver Bonus, and its Combat Maneuver Defense score.

Feats: The creature's feats are listed here. A bonus feat is indicated with a superscript "B."

Skills: The creature's skills are listed here. Racial modifiers to skills are indicated at the end of this entry.

Languages: The languages most commonly spoken by the creature are listed here. For unusual creatures, you can swap out the languages known for other choices as needed. A creature with a higher than normal Intelligence score receives the appropriate number of bonus languages.

SQ: Any special qualities possessed by the creature.

Environment: The regions and climates in which the creature is typically encountered are listed here; these often present wider ranges than the icons at the top of the stat block indicate. In this case, the icon listed at the top of the stat block indicates the creature's preferred terrain.

Organization: This lists how the creature is organized, including number ranges as appropriate.

Treasure: The exact value of the creature's treasure depends on whether you're running a slow, medium, or fast game, as summarized on Table 12–5 on page 399 of the *Pathfinder RPG Core Rulebook*. In cases where a creature has specific magical gear assigned to it, the assumption is a medium game—if you play a fast or slow game, you'll want to adjust the monster's gear as appropriate. "Standard" treasure indicates the total value of the creature's treasure is that of a CR equal to the average party level, as listed on Table 12–5 on page 399 in the *Pathfinder RPG Core Rulebook*. "Double" or "triple" treasure indicates the creature has double or triple this standard value. "Incidental" indicates the creature has half this standard value, and then only within the confines of its lair. "None" indicates that the creature normally has no treasure (as is typical for an unintelligent creature that has no real lair, although such creatures are often used to guard treasures of varying amounts). "NPC gear" indicates the monster has treasure as normal for an NPC of a level equal to the monster's CR (see page 454 of the *Pathfinder RPG Core Rulebook*).

Special Abilities: Finally, any of the creature's more unique special abilities are detailed in full here.

Description

Here you'll find information on how the monster fits into the world, notes on its ecology and society, and other bits of useful lore and flavor that will help you breathe life into the creature when your PCs encounter it. Some monsters have additional sections that cover variant creatures, notes on using the monsters as PCs, methods of constructing the creature, and so on.

ACHAIERAI

This bird-like beast is mostly head, lunging forward on four scaly legs. Wisps of noxious black vapor trail from its hooked beak.

ACHAIERAI	CR 5

XP 1,600
LE Large outsider (evil, extraplanar, lawful)
Init +1; **Senses** darkvision 60 ft.; Perception +12

DEFENSE

AC 20, touch 11, flat-footed 18 (+1 Dex, +1 dodge, +9 natural, −1 size)
hp 52 (7d10+14)
Fort +7, **Ref** +6, **Will** +4
SR 20

OFFENSE

Speed 50 ft.
Melee bite +10 (2d6+4), 2 claws +10 (1d6+4)
Space 10 ft.; **Reach** 10 ft. with claw
Special Attacks black cloud

STATISTICS

Str 19, **Dex** 13, **Con** 14, **Int** 11, **Wis** 14, **Cha** 16
Base Atk +7; **CMB** +12; **CMD** 24 (28 vs. trip)
Feats Combat Reflexes, Dodge, Mobility, Spring Attack
Skills Acrobatics +11 (+19 jump), Climb +14, Perception +12, Sense Motive +12, Stealth +7, Swim +14
Language Infernal

ECOLOGY

Environment any land (Hell)
Organization solitary or flock (5–8)
Treasure standard

SPECIAL ABILITIES

Black Cloud (Su) An achaierai can exhale a cloud of choking, toxic smoke three times per day. All creatures within 10 feet of the achaierai immediately take 2d6 points of damage as their flesh melts and rots away. The cloud erodes sanity as well as flesh, and anyone who takes damage from the black cloud must also make a DC 15 Fortitude save or become confused. Every round, the victim may attempt another DC 15 Fortitude save to recover from the confusion; otherwise it persists, lasting indefinitely until the condition is removed or the victim eventually makes her saving throw. The confusion element of a black cloud is a mind-affecting effect. The save DC is Constitution-based. This is a poison effect. Achaierais are immune to this ability.

An achaierai is a predator and scavenger of the lower planes that looks like a 15-foot-tall flightless bird, though its head and body are fused into one large unit, with four legs and atrophied wings. The thick, oily plumage covering its body all but conceals these tiny wings. An adult achaierai weighs roughly 750 pounds.

Though not devils themselves, achaierais live and hunt on the scorched and blasted plains of Hell, where they make excellent use of their long, stilt-like legs in running down any lost souls or lesser devils who stumble into their feeding grounds. Once it has closed with its target, an achaierai attacks with its two front legs, punching or slashing, as well as biting with its powerful beak. Far smarter than their animalistic form might suggest, achaierais prefer to hunt in shrieking packs and use their prey's confusion and their own reach to their advantage, circling their quarry and darting in to attack as soon as the victim becomes distracted, then retreating again before the prey has a chance to retaliate. They have been known to wander through battlefields in the lower planes, picking over dying and regenerating creatures and souls, which has earned them the nickname "Hell's vultures." As achaierais are immune to the toxic clouds of others of their kind, they often work in conjunction to use these clouds to herd or scatter enemies, form long lines of black clouds to protect their retreat, or merely panic opponents in large melees. Achaierais are fond of disemboweling their targets and feasting on the hot entrails while their mortally wounded prey screams itself to death. Of course, as outsiders, achaierais have no need to eat, and their elaborate hunting routines are simply the bird-beasts' sick form of entertainment.

Illustration by Tyler Walpole

7

Aeon

Beyond passion, beyond mercy, beyond reason, the faceless caretakers of reality toil without end, silently struggling to preserve the tenuous balance upon which all existence depends. These voiceless forces are the aeons, inscrutable shapers and eliminators of the multiverse. They exist beyond the understanding of most mortals, endlessly striving toward goals unfathomable even to many of the planes' eldest inhabitants. Aeons build order from the chaos of the Maelstrom, seed new life upon barren worlds, and halt the rampages of forces grown overbold. They rend nations to vapor, dismantle planets into cosmic dust, and pave the way for calamities. Their ways are at one moment beneficent and in the next utterly devastating, but always without ardor, compassion, or malice. Every aeon dispassionately but determinedly strives toward the same objective—an ever changing, amending, and readjusting pursuit of multiplanar equilibrium. United in this eternal and perhaps impossible pursuit, aeons embody the planes-spanning hand of a metaphorical omnipotent clockmaker, endlessly tuning and adjusting the myriad gears of reality in pursuit of ultimate perfection.

The balance aeons seek in all things begins with themselves. Most aeons embody a powerful dichotomy sustained in equilibrium. From the potency of birth and death meeting in akhanas to the philosophies of fate and freedom embodied by theletos, the workings of existence take on form and will within their living manifestations. Even the lesser paracletus unite diverse elements of creation in their intricate orbits. Such stability reaches beyond the shapes of aeons to inspire and direct their minds, imbuing each with a singular purpose and area of control. Thus, each embodies the realm of reality it would seek to balance, attempting to enforce a harmony as perfect as that of its physical form upon all things. The forms of various types directly suggest their abilities and objectives, with pleroma aeons, for example, exhibiting the power to create or annihilate, and using such influence to alter that which has grown either too abundant or sterile.

While aeons are not malicious creatures, they care nothing for individual beings or the struggles and emotions central to most life. The ruin of an entire city or burning of a vast forest means equally little in their manipulation of symmetry. By the same right, creating new life or constructing defenses against impending calamities are equally characteristic acts. For aeons, only the final tally matters, and a land overpopulated by humanoids is just as much in need of culling as a land overrun by ravenous fungi. Just as a body's natural defenses have neither mercy nor malice for invading parasites, aeons don't muddy their objectives with emotion. Such impartiality

extends to the interactions between aeons as well. Without culture, society, or even memory beyond the immediate needs of the multiverse, they build no relationships and, in general, have no personalities beyond an automaton-like directness. A vague caste system exists, with aeons that hold influence over greater multiversal principles acknowledged as superior by their lesser brethren. This caste system rarely translates to actual direction and obedience, though. Should the acts of a greater aeon jeopardize the works or even lives of a multitude of lesser aeons, the efforts of the more potent aeon proceed without hesitation. Only in matters of great existential concern do multiple aeons cooperate, directed into doing so by the united consciousness of their race and the multiverse itself, and even then rarely for long.

Many mistake aeons for friends or allies of nature and its creatures. While this might be true at times—and is definitely true if reality as a whole is considered a vast, united organism—aeons care no more for the trees of the forest than for the towers of civilization. For them, all life is life and all death is death, to be preserved or scoured regardless of its arbitrary shape.

In rare cases, aeons have been known to deviate from the whims of the multiverse. Such rogue aeons typically arise from interacting with other races excessively, living beyond their intended times, being exposed to unusual ideas, or being forced to perform acts they otherwise wouldn't contemplate. These aeons typically take on extreme personalities, coming to favor one aspect of their being over the other—an akhana is just as likely to become an artist of life as a mass murderer. Normal aeons perceive their rogue brethren as high-priority disturbances in the balance of the multiverse and seek the destruction of such rarities with all haste.

MONAD, THE CONDITION OF ALL

All aeons are bound in a state they know as "the condition of all" or "monad," a supreme oneness with all members of their race and the multiverse itself. Therefore, aeons exist as an extension of the multiverse; in a fashion similar to the way bones, muscle, and the various humors create a mortal, they exist as part of a greater being. When destroyed or upon accomplishing specific goals, their energies simply dissipate and become reabsorbed into the monad. They do not die, but are instead recycled. They have no discernible memories and seem to exist only in the present, arriving to repair balance. Relationships with non-aeons are generally nonexistent, and they feel no sense of affection, remorse, vengeance, or similar emotions. Aeons deal with each task as its own action, independent from all other tasks. Thus, an individual once at violent odds with an aeon may, upon their next encounter, have the aeon's full and undaunted support.

AEON, AKHANA

Four gray arms project from a swirling mass resembling a giant eye, from which a tail-like appendage dangles.

AKHANA	CR 12	

XP 19,200

N Medium outsider (aeon, extraplanar)

Init +10; **Senses** darkvision 60 ft., *deathwatch*; Perception +19

DEFENSE

AC 27, touch 18, flat-footed 21 (+2 deflection, +6 Dex, +9 natural)

hp 148 (11d10+88); fast healing 5

Fort +17, **Ref** +11, **Will** +14

Immune cold, critical hits, poison; **Resist** electricity 10, fire 10; **SR** 23

OFFENSE

Speed 30 ft., fly 40 ft. (poor)

Melee 4 claws +16 (1d4+5 plus grab)

Special Attacks soul siphoning

Spell-Like Abilities (CL 11th; concentration +15)

Constant—*deathwatch*

At will—*cure serious wounds, gentle repose, inflict serious wounds* (DC 17), *sanctuary* (DC 15)

3/day—*restoration, slay living* (DC 19)

1/day—*raise dead*

STATISTICS

Str 21, **Dex** 23, **Con** 26, **Int** 16, **Wis** 21, **Cha** 18

Base Atk +11; **CMB** +16 (+20 grapple); **CMD** 34 (38 vs. trip)

Feats Combat Reflexes, Great Fortitude, Hover, Improved Initiative, Iron Will, Lightning Reflexes

Skills Bluff +18, Fly +2, Heal +19, Intimidate +18, Knowledge (planes) +22, Knowledge (religion) +22, Perception +19, Sense Motive +19, Spellcraft +17, Stealth +20

Languages envisaging

SQ extension of all, void form

ECOLOGY

Environment any (Outer Planes)

Organization solitary, pair, or collective (3–6)

Treasure none

SPECIAL ABILITIES

Soul Siphoning (Su) As a swift action, an akhana can use its tail to siphon life essence from a grappled foe. At the start of the aeon's turn, the victim gains 1d4 negative levels (a DC 23 Fortitude save negates and grants immunity to this akhana's soul siphoning ability for 24 hours). When the number of negative levels equals the target's Hit Dice, the target's soul tears from its mortal body and gets stored within the body of the akhana as a *trap the soul* spell. The victim's body remains preserved as if via a *gentle repose* spell for as long as the soul is held by the akhana. The akhana can keep the soul indefinitely, or can release it as a full-round action. Upon doing so, the released soul immediately returns to its body if the body is within 300 feet, at which point the body returns to life and any negative levels imparted to it by the akhana are removed. If the body is not within 300 feet (or if it has been destroyed), then the creature dies when its soul is released. A *miracle, limited wish,* or *wish* can force a displaced soul to return to its proper body. If an akhana is slain, any soul it contains is released automatically. An akhana can only hold one soul at a time. The save DC is Constitution-based.

Akhanas bear charge over the duality of birth and death. They perceive the existence of living things as crucial to maintaining cosmic balance. They also understand the profound influence living things have on the cosmos, and if left untended, its ability to create terrible consequences. In this circumstance, life must give way to death.

Akhanas wander the byways of the multiverse, constantly on the hunt for imbalances in life. How they judge these imbalances is not well-understood by non-aeons, and the aeons are singularly unmotivated to justify akhanas' decisions when inquired about them. As a result, the focus of akhanas' attacks and attentions usually seems arbitrary or even random to most creatures—they do not always focus their attentions on the strongest or the weakest members of a group.

An akhana stands 5 feet in height and weighs 120 pounds. Its strange central body seems vaporous, but is weirdly solid (and slimy) to the touch.

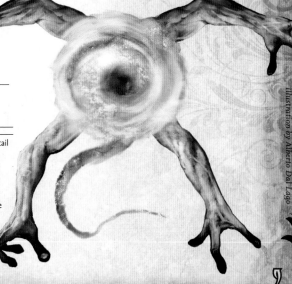

Illustration by Alberto Dal Lago

Aeon, Bythos

A shimmering, colorless mass congeals to form a four-armed humanoid shape with an eye-like pattern in its torso.

BYTHOS	CR 16

XP 76,800

N Large outsider (aeon, extraplanar)

Init +8; **Senses** blindsense 60 ft., darkvision 90 ft., low-light vision; Perception +30

DEFENSE

AC 31, touch 18, flat-footed 26 (+4 deflection, +4 Dex, +1 dodge, +13 natural, –1 size)

hp 207 (18d10+108); fast healing 10

Fort +18, **Ref** +12, **Will** +20

Immune cold, critical hits, poison; **Resist** electricity 10, fire 10; **SR** 27

OFFENSE

Speed fly 40 ft. (good)

Melee 4 slams +23 (1d6+6 plus 1d6 cold and aging strike)

Space 10 ft.; **Reach** 10 ft.

Special Attacks confusion gaze, temporal strike

Spell-Like Abilities (CL 18th; concentration +23)

At will—
> augury,
> greater
> teleport,
> slow (DC 18)

3/day—
> dimensional
> anchor,
> haste, plane
> shift (DC 20)

1/day—dimensional
> lock, moment of prescience,
> temporal stasis (DC 23)

STATISTICS

Str 22, **Dex** 19, **Con** 21, **Int** 24, **Wis** 28, **Cha** 21

Base Atk +18; **CMB** +25; **CMD** 44 (can't be tripped)

Feats Combat Casting, Combat Reflexes, Dodge, Great Fortitude, Hover, Improved Initiative, Lightning Reflexes, Mobility, Toughness

Skills Bluff +26, Fly +6, Heal +30, Intimidate +26, Knowledge (arcana, nature, religion) +33, Knowledge (history, planes) +36, Perception +30, Sense Motive +30, Spellcraft +28, Stealth +21, Use Magic Device +23

Languages envisaging

SQ extension of all, void form

ECOLOGY

Environment any (Outer Planes)

Organization solitary, pair, or tribunal (3 bythos)

Treasure none

SPECIAL ABILITIES

Aging Strike (Su) If a bythos strikes a living target with two slam attacks in a single round, the bythos ages the creature, causing it to advance to the next age category (*Pathfinder RPG Core Rulebook* 169) if it fails a DC 24 Fortitude save. The victim gains all of the penalties from this aging and none of the bonuses. A venerable victim targeted by this ability dies if it fails a DC 24 Fortitude save. This process is reversible with *greater restoration, limited wish, miracle,* or *wish.* The save DC is Constitution-based.

Confusion Gaze (Su) Confusion for 1d4 rounds, 30 feet, Fortitude DC 24 negates. The save DC is Charisma-based.

Temporal Strike (Su) As a standard action, a bythos can touch a creature or object to displace it from time. If the target fails a DC 24 Fortitude save, it disappears from the present moment and reappears in the same location 1d4 rounds later as if no time had passed. If an object occupies that space, the creature appears in the closest available space to its original location—this displacement does not cause the creature any additional harm. The save DC is Charisma-based.

The bythos are guardians of time and planar travel—indeed, to bythos, the act of aging is nothing more than a highly specialized method of travel. Although bythos themselves have no additional method of traveling through time, they scour the multiverse, hunting for creatures that do have the ability to time-travel and may have abused this ability. Far more often, though, bythos seek out abuses of planar travel, such as tears in reality, regions where planes overlap, or creatures that abuse the use of planar travel. In some cases, such distortions are ignored, but in others, a bythos or even a full tribunal comes to assess and repair the damage. In most cases, "repair" is analogous to the death of the creature responsible for the distortions, but placing such creatures in temporal stasis can also solve the problem.

While a bythos's body may seem to be made of smoke and vapor, it is strangely solid to the touch, feeling not dissimilar to dry stone. A bythos is 13 feet tall and weighs 600 pounds.

Illustrations by Alberto Dal Lago

Aeon, Paracletus

A small cluster of shimmering lights floats in the air, orbited by multiple vibrant crystals and gemstones.

PARACLETUS   **CR 2**

XP 600

N Small outsider (aeon, extraplanar)

Init +2; **Senses** darkvision 60 ft.; Perception +7

Aura emotion aura (DC 12, 30 ft.)

DEFENSE

AC 14, touch 13, flat-footed 12 (+2 Dex, +1 natural, +1 size)

hp 13 (3d10–3)

Fort +4, **Ref** +3, **Will** +6

Immune cold, critical hits, poison; **Resist** electricity 10, fire 10; **SR** 7

OFFENSE

Speed fly 40 ft. (good)

Melee slam +3 (1d3–1 plus 1d6 electricity)

Spell-Like Abilities (CL 3rd; concentration +4)

  At will—*sanctuary* (DC 12)

  3/day—*calm emotions* (DC 13)

  1/week—*commune* (6 questions, CL 12th)

STATISTICS

Str 8, **Dex** 14, **Con** 9, **Int** 11, **Wis** 13, **Cha** 12

Base Atk +3; **CMB** +1; **CMD** 13 (can't be tripped)

Feats Great Fortitude, Iron Will

Skills Fly +8, Intimidate +7, Knowledge (arcana) +7, Knowledge (planes) +7, Perception +7, Sense Motive +7, Stealth +12

Languages envisaging

SQ extension of all, void form

ECOLOGY

Environment any (Outer Planes)

Organization solitary, pair, or commune (3–12)

Treasure none

SPECIAL ABILITIES

Emotion Aura (Sp) Each paracletus exists as the embodiment of a specific emotive duality. Three times per day, a paracletus can create an aura representing one of its two programmed emotions. Creatures in the area must make a DC 12 Will save to resist the aura. A creature that makes its save against the aura is unaffected by that aeon's aura for the next 24 hours. The paracletus can choose one creature in the area to ignore its effects. The effect of the aura lasts for 10 minutes, and ends if a creature moves more than 30 feet from the aeon. The aura is a mind-affecting compulsion effect. The save DC is Charisma-based. Specific emotive dualities and their powers follow—any single paracletus can only use one of these three dualistic options and cannot change to a different one.

Courage/Fear: The aura acts as *bless* or *bane*.

Empathy/Apathy: The aura gives creatures a +2 bonus or a –2 penalty on Bluff, Diplomacy, and Intimidate checks.

Hope/Despair: The aura gives creatures a +2 morale bonus on Will saving throws or a –2 penalty on Will saving throws.

While mortals possess the gift of free will, both logic and emotion influence their decisions. The paracletus serve the aeons as agents who connect with mortals and study the influence of emotions (particularly the dualistic nature of raw emotion) upon mortal behavior. They wander the planes seeking mortals with particularly strong emotional or logical capabilities (characters with high Charisma or Intelligence scores). Once a paracletus locates such a creature, the paracletus remains nearby, studying the target's relationship with emotional and logical input and choices. Often, the paracletus will use its emotion aura on the target in order to study how outside influences affect the subject. Unfortunately for the target creature, whether or not the paracletus uses a helpful or harmful effect is, for all intents and purposes, a matter of random chance—even though to the paracletus's complex reasoning, nothing is left to actual random chance.

If presented the option, a paracletus avoids direct combat, and uses its emotion aura to influence situations. If pressed to defend itself, it flies at opponents, slamming into them and discharging an electrical jolt of energy in addition to buffeting with its crystalline components. The crystals that orbit a paracletus are solidified aspects of logic, while the swirling vapors and lights that make up its central mass are manifestations of raw emotion—when a paracletus is slain, both the crystals and vapors fade away into nothingness.

A paracletus can be chosen as a familiar by a 7th-level neutral spellcaster who has the Improved Familiar feat. A paracletus familiar does not abandon its mission to observe emotions and logic at play, but it does follow its master's orders—this is one situation where the application of a paracletus's emotion aura need not be random.

Although the central mass of a paracletus's body appears to be made of light and energy, it is in fact solid, and feels strangely like electrified flesh to the touch.

III

Aeon, Pleroma

Within the shadows of this vaguely humanoid figure stir swirling colors and spheres, as if it encompassed all the night sky.

PLEROMA	CR 20	

XP 307,200

N Large outsider (aeon, extraplanar)

Init +12; **Senses** blindsight 120 ft., darkvision 120 ft., *true seeing*; Perception +41

DEFENSE

AC 36, touch 24, flat-footed 27 (+6 deflection, +8 Dex, +1 dodge, +12 natural, −1 size)

hp 324 (24d10+192); fast healing 10

Fort +24, **Ref** +18, **Will** +26

Immune cold, critical hits, poison; **Resist** electricity 10, fire 10; **SR** 31

OFFENSE

Speed 0 ft., fly 60 ft. (perfect)

Melee touch +30 (20d8 energy)

Space 10 ft.; **Reach** 10 ft.

Special Attacks sphere of creation, sphere of oblivion

Spell-Like Abilities (CL 20th; concentration +27)

At will—*create food and water, mending, rusting grasp* (DC 21), *stone shape, wood shape* (DC 19)

7/day—*fabricate, plant growth, sculpt sound, shout* (DC 21)

5/day—*break enchantment, daylight, deeper darkness, freedom of movement, major creation*

3/day—*disintegrate* (DC 23), *horrid wilting* (DC 25)

1/day—*mage's disjunction* (DC 26), *wish* (DC 26)

Cleric Spells Prepared (CL 20th; concentration +30)

9th—*astral projection, gate, implosion* (3, DC 29)

8th—*cloak of chaos* (DC 28), *holy aura* (DC 28), *shield of law* (DC 28), *summon monster VII, unholy aura* (DC 28)

7th—*blasphemy* (DC 27), *destruction* (DC 27), *dictum* (DC 27), *holy word* (DC 27), *word of chaos* (DC 27)

6th—*banishment* (DC 26), *forbiddance* (DC 26), *geas, legend lore, repulsion* (DC 26), *veil* (DC 26)

5th—*contact other plane, dispel chaos* (DC 25), *dispel evil* (DC 25), *dispel good* (DC 25), *dispel law* (DC 25), *teleport*

4th—*chaos hammer* (DC 24), *holy smite* (DC 24), *order's wrath* (DC 24), *restoration, scrying* (DC 24), *unholy blight* (DC 24)

3rd—*clairaudience/clairvoyance, magic circle against chaos, magic circle against evil, magic circle against good, magic circle against law, suggestion* (DC 23)

2nd—*align weapon, detect thoughts* (DC 22), *enthrall* (DC 22), *make whole, see invisibility, undetectable alignment, zone of truth* (DC 22)

1st—*detect chaos, detect evil, detect good, detect law, identify, magic aura, true strike*

0—*create water, detect magic, guidance, read magic*

STATISTICS

Str 24, **Dex** 27, **Con** 26, **Int** 26, **Wis** 31, **Cha** 25

Base Atk +24; **CMB** +32; **CMD** 57 (can't be tripped)

Feats Alertness, Combat Casting, Combat Reflexes, Dodge, Great Fortitude, Improved Initiative, Improved Iron Will, Iron Will, Lightning Reflexes, Lightning Stance, Mobility, Wind Stance

Skills Appraise +30, Bluff +32, Fly +16, Heal +30, Intimidate +27, Knowledge (arcana) +47, Knowledge (dungeoneering) +44, Knowledge (engineering) +44, Knowledge (nature) +47, Knowledge (planes) +47, Knowledge (religion) +47, Perception +41, Sense Motive +39, Spellcraft +30, Stealth +27, Use Magic Device +27

Languages envisaging

SQ extension of all, void form

ECOLOGY

Environment any (Outer Planes)

Organization solitary or tribunal (1 pleroma, 3 akhanas, and 2–5 theletos)

Treasure none

SPECIAL ABILITIES

Energy Touch (Su) A pleroma's touch deals 20d8 points of damage from positive or negative energy, depending upon which type of energy would harm the creature touched. A pleroma's touch never heals damage.

Spells A pleroma casts spells as a 20th-level cleric, but does not have access to domains. A pleroma can cast certain sorcerer/wizard spells as divine spells.

Sphere of Creation (Su) Three times per day, the pleroma can manifest a 2-foot-diameter sphere of white energy that hovers above its left hand. By concentrating, the pleroma can control this sphere, causing it to fly slowly at a speed of 10 feet per round. The sphere can travel in any direction, but must remain within 300 feet of the pleroma or it immediately dissipates. Wherever the sphere travels, it leaves behind a 5-foot-wide path of new matter, creating either new terrain (such as swamp, tundra, desert, or forest) or a 10-foot-square wall composed of a single natural substance (such as clay, wood, or stone). Any existing matter, either living or nonliving that comes in contact with the sphere must make a DC 30 Fortitude save or be absorbed and incorporated into the new substance (only *freedom, miracle,* or *wish* can rescue creatures so trapped). Creatures that save are pushed to the nearest unoccupied location adjacent to the newly created substance. The sphere is highly unstable and only lasts 1d4 minutes before exploding with a blinding flash. All creatures within 30 feet of the flash must make a DC 30 Fortitude save or be permanently blinded. The save DCs are Constitution-based.

Sphere of Oblivion (Su) Three times per day, the pleroma can manifest a 2-foot-diameter sphere of complete and utter darkness that hovers above its right hand. The sphere is an empty void similar to a *sphere of annihilation.* Any matter (living or nonliving) that touches the sphere must succeed on a DC 30 Fortitude save or be sucked into the sphere and destroyed. Larger objects (such as ships or

Illustration by Alberto Dal Lago

buildings) are destroyed at a rate of one 10-foot cube per round of contact with the sphere. By concentrating, the pleroma can control this sphere, causing it to fly slowly at a speed of 10 feet per round. The sphere can travel in any direction, but must remain within 300 feet of the pleroma or it immediately dissipates. The sphere is highly unstable and only lasts 1d4 minutes before harmlessly imploding upon itself. Alternatively, the pleroma may hurl the sphere as a ranged touch attack (with a 10-foot range increment) against a single creature. When thrown in this manner, the sphere implodes immediately after the attack is resolved. The save DCs are Constitution-based.

The pleroma is the most powerful of all the aeons. As a manifestation of the opposing acts of creation and destruction, a pleroma exists in a state of flux, its very form shifting between creation and oblivion within the ebon folds of its vaporous cloak. One who gazes upon a pleroma could spend days studying the continual changes of its form, which most resemble the shifting of celestial bodies within the universe sped up to a pace at which the swirling of galaxies and the tumble of planets form a strange dance.

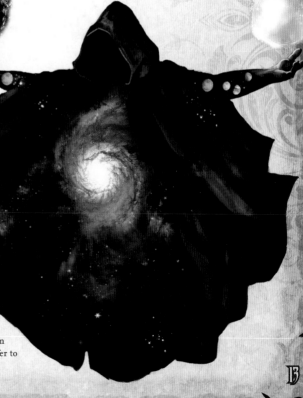

Pleromas view the concepts of creation and oblivion not so much as separate processes, but rather as two parts of a cyclical passage that everything in existence must explore. Pleromas guide this progression, ensuring everything remains balanced, such that whatever is created can be destroyed, and that nothing becomes so static that these two processes slow to a halt. For everything that attains a state of semi-permanence, there must be many more things that do not, or rather that cannot ever be reformed into a state of permanence. While pleromas believe in eternity, they understand that eternity is cyclical and infinity is something that repeats itself. Therefore, eternity and infinity are states that can be changed, or altered, if only slightly. Pleromas maintain such changes are necessary to keep the cosmos from becoming static and unbalanced, a state they refer to as apocalypse, or the end of everything.

Of all the aeons, pleromas possess the strongest connection to the entity or concept they refer to as Monad. All aeons believe themselves to be extensions of this entity, and while they act freely and independently of the entity, they always act within the constricts of its will or needs. This behavior is not so much a state of servitude as a symbiosis in which the actions of the pleromas are universally beneficial to both themselves and the entity they are part of. Pleromas describe Monad as the sentience of the multiverse, from which all things are created through the recycling of everything that ever existed.

Pleromas typically travel alone. Their arrival in a region almost always heralds some sort of dramatic change. They pay little mind to the wants and needs of other creatures, and remain entirely focused upon their primary task. They avoid conflicts of ethics, wars, and similar pursuits, save when manipulating such events would help to restore the balance between creation and oblivion. Should any be so foolish as to attempt to interfere with or sway their work, pleromas immediately retaliate by bringing all of their significant powers and devastating abilities to bear until the intervention is destroyed.

PATHFINDER
ROLEPLAYING GAME

AEON, THELETOS

Four bandy limbs, each splitting at the elbow into two three-fingered forearms, emerge from this creature's crystalline body.

THELETOS	CR 7

XP 3,200

N Medium outsider (aeon, extraplanar)

Init +6; **Senses** darkvision 60 ft.; Perception +16

DEFENSE

AC 20, touch 15, flat-footed 17 (+2 deflection, +2 Dex, +1 dodge, +5 natural)

hp 76 (9d10+27); fast healing 5

Fort +9, **Ref** +5, **Will** +12

Immune cold, critical hits, poison; **Resist** electricity 10, fire 10; **SR** 18

OFFENSE

Speed 30 ft., fly 30 ft. (poor)

Melee 2 slams +13 (1d6+4), 2 tentacles +8 (1d4+2 plus fate drain)

Space 5 ft.; **Reach** 5 ft.

Special Attacks wreath of fate

Spell-Like Abilities (CL 9th; concentration +10)

At will—*augury, command* (DC 12), *doom* (DC 12), *sanctuary* (DC 12)

3/day—*bestow curse* (DC 14), *enthrall* (DC 13), *touch of idiocy* (DC 13), *dispel magic, remove curse, suggestion* (DC 14)

1/day—*charm monster* (DC 15), *lesser geas* (DC 15)

STATISTICS

Str 18, **Dex** 14, **Con** 17, **Int** 11, **Wis** 19, **Cha** 12

Base Atk +9; **CMB** +13; **CMD** 28 (can't be tripped)

Feats Dodge, Hover, Improved Initiative, Improved Iron Will, Iron Will

Skills Fly –2, Intimidate +13, Knowledge (planes) +16, Perception +16, Sense Motive +16, Spellcraft +12, Stealth +14

Languages envisaging

SQ extension of all, void form

ECOLOGY

Environment any (Outer Planes)

Organization solitary, pair, or collective (3–12)

Treasure none

SPECIAL ABILITIES

Fate Drain (Su) A theletos possesses a pair of flexible crystalline tentacles with which it can drain a creature's sense of fate and destiny. Whenever it strikes a foe with these tentacles, the creature struck must make a DC 17 Will save or take 1d4 points of Charisma damage. Until a creature's Charisma damage from this ability is healed, the victim takes a –2 penalty on all saving throws (regardless of the actual total amount of Charisma damage it takes). The save DC is Constitution-based.

Wreath of Fate (Su) As a full-round-action every 1d4 rounds, a theletos can release a 60-foot cone of energy from its chest. Any intelligent creature struck by this cone must make a DC 15 Will save or become nearly overwhelmed with the knowledge of various fates that destiny has in store for him—there is no way to make sense of these myriad dooms and boons, and as a result, the victim is staggered. As long as this condition persists, the victim may choose to make two rolls when attempting an attack roll, a saving throw, or a skill check—he must accept the worse of the two rolls, but in so doing the wreath of fate passes from his soul and he is no longer staggered by this ability. Wreath of fate is a curse effect, and as such can be affected by *remove curse* or *break enchantment*—the effective caster level of this curse is equal to the theletos's HD (CL 9th in most cases). The save DC is Charisma-based.

The strange theletos is the guardian of the duality between freedom and fate. Slavery is no more of an issue to a theletos than is true freedom, but without one, the other cannot exist. In areas where slavery is rife, a theletos might aid in freeing some slaves, while in regions where slavery has been abolished, this strange being works to subjugate many creatures with its own mind-controlling spell-like abilities—often encouraging them to further undertake acts of slavery themselves. The theletos is also a guardian of fate and prophecy, and while for some creatures it might allow glimpses of futures, others who peer into the future almost seem to cause the aeon physical pain. The theletos cannot explain why one seer might be allowed to divine futures while another should not—it knows only that some prophets should be denied this pursuit.

A theletos is 5 feet tall and weighs 100 pounds.

AGATHION

Agathions are a race of beast-aspect outsiders native to the plane of Nirvana, a realm of pure good unconcerned with the dogma of law (represented by Heaven) or chaos (represented by Elysium). Though Nirvana is a place of rest where blessed souls seek enlightenment, agathions are aggressive and interventionist in the mortal world when it comes to dealing with evil. Created from the souls of good mortals who have managed to achieve the enlightenment they sought in life (or in some cases, after death), agathions embody the principles of a peaceable kingdom while marshaling their strength to defend that kingdom from any who would despoil it. Because they strike an ethical balance between the chaotic, fey-like azatas and the lawful, rigid process of the archons, agathions are often liaisons between the celestial races, soothing hot tempers and working toward mutual goals of vanquishing evil and protecting good.

All agathions have an animal-like aspect. Some are more humanoid in appearance, while others spend their entire existence in a form nearly identical to that of a true animal. Each type of agathion serves a particular role in Nirvana, and their duties on other planes echo these responsibilities: leonals watch over Nirvana's portals and have a guardian-like aspect in other worlds, draconals carry the wisdom of the ages and observe and guide exceptional mortals, vulpinals are bards and messengers and bear important news to celestial generals and mortal heroes, and so on. Agathions are proud of their feral aspects and don't take kindly to the suggestion that they are cursed folk like lycanthropes or nothing more than magical talking beasts. Every agathion was once a mortal who aspired to goodness and was rewarded in the afterlife with a form suiting her talents and personality; suggesting that an agathion's form is a kind of punishment is a terrible insult.

The following pages describe only a few of the best-known kinds of agathions, but other types exist, corresponding to other conventional animals (bears, dinosaurs, fish, wolves, and so on), with a few having shapes that resemble insects (particularly beetles, butterflies, and mantises); a handful resemble stranger creatures (such as basilisks and owlbears) or unique "animals" native to extreme environments on distant worlds. Certain animals, particularly those associated with scavenging activities (such as hyenas, buzzards, or jackals) or parasitism (like lampreys or ticks) specifically do not have agathions associated with them—these animals are not intrinsically evil, but their habits and ecological niches are far from the noble and proud traditions that most of the souls who seek enlightenment upon Nirvana would associate with themselves.

Individual agathions may be male or female, but they do not reproduce among their own kind—every agathion is a unique individual made from the soul of a good mortal. This does not prevent them from falling in love or having affairs with mortals, and a few aasimar and celestial sorcerer bloodlines derive from past contact with agathions, particularly among communities not averse to anthropomorphic humanoids. Indeed, many mythologies tie numerous races of this kind to the inevitable result of human tribes forming strong emotional attachments to visiting agathions.

Agathions speak Celestial, Draconic, and Infernal, though they can communicate with any intelligent creature because of their truespeech ability. They can also communicate with animals using a similar, silent ability. Even the weakest agathion is able to heal itself or others using a power similar to a paladin's ability to lay on hands. All agathions have a number of similar traits, as detailed in Appendix 3 of this book.

Agathions serving a particular deity or empyreal lord may have additional abilities depending on the role their deity assigns them. For example, a cetaceal serving a goddess of volcanic islands may be able to change shape into a more human-like form to walk on land, and may be immune to fire to tolerate and tend to the life-rich thermal vents at the ocean floor.

AGATHION LEADERS

Though agathions lack an organized hierarchy, each type of agathion has a few individuals invested with power by the gods of Nirvana or the plane itself. Common agathions look to these exceptional examples for leadership, wisdom, and inspiration; these enlightened folk do not openly claim any responsibilities or rank over their fellows, but welcome the obligations this added power places upon them and do not deny their status or shirk their duties. Part of a category of powerful outsiders known collectively as empyreal lords, these leaders are often significantly larger than common agathions (up to double the normal size, in some cases), and have unusual coloration (such as iron-gray fur) or unique sensory manifestations associated with their presence (such as illusory birds, a constant melody, the scent of oranges, or a calming aura). No agathion fails to recognize their presence when not disguised. Agathion leaders can serve as heralds for deities, although they tend not to encourage religions based on their teachings. The following is but a selection of notable agathion leaders.

Chavod Broken-Spear (cetaceal)
Kelumarion the King Over the Mountain (leonal)
Korada of the Dream Lotus (avoral)
Lady Taramyth the Singing Flame (vulpinal)
Sixlife the Violet Fury (silvanshee)
Walks with Golden Stars (draconal)

PATHFINDER

AGATHION, AVORAL

Great feathers sweep back from this fierce bird-man's brow, and long, clawed hands grow from the end of his wings.

AVORAL	CR 9

XP 6,400

NG Medium outsider (agathion, extraplanar, good)

Init +6; **Senses** darkvision 60 ft., *detect magic*, low-light vision, *see invisibility*, *true seeing*; Perception +23

Aura fear aura (20 ft., DC 17)

DEFENSE

AC 25, touch 17, flat-footed 18 (+6 Dex, +1 dodge, +8 natural)

hp 94 (9d10+45)

Fort +11, **Ref** +12, **Will** +6; +4 vs. poison

DR 10/evil or silver; **Immune** electricity, petrification; **Resist** cold 10, sonic 10; **SR** 20

OFFENSE

Speed 40 ft., fly 90 ft. (good)

Melee 2 claws +16 (2d6+3), 2 wings +10 (2d6+1)

Spell-Like Abilities (CL 9th; concentration +12)

Constant—*detect magic*, *see invisibility*, *speak with animals*

At will—*aid*, *blur* (self only), *command* (DC 14), *detect magic*, *dimension door*, *dispel magic*, *gust of wind* (DC 15), *hold person* (DC 16), *light*, *magic circle against evil* (self only)

3/day—*lightning bolt* (DC 16), empowered *magic missile*

STATISTICS

Str 17, **Dex** 23, **Con** 20, **Int** 15, **Wis** 16, **Cha** 16

Base Atk +9; **CMB** +12; **CMD** 29

Feats Dodge, Empower Spell-Like Ability (*magic missile*), Flyby Attack, Weapon Finesse, Weapon Focus (claw)

Skills Bluff +10, Diplomacy +7, Fly +22, Handle Animal +9, Intimidate +15, Knowledge (any one) +14, Perception +23, Ride +7, Sense Motive +15, Spellcraft +11, Stealth +18; **Racial Modifiers** Perception +8

Languages Celestial, Draconic, Infernal; *speak with animals*, truespeech

SQ lay on hands (4d6, 7/day, as a 9th-level paladin)

ECOLOGY

Environment any air (Nirvana)

Organization solitary, pair, or squad (3–6)

Treasure standard

SPECIAL ABILITIES

True Seeing (Su) This ability works like the spell (caster level 14th), except it only affects the avoral, the avoral must concentrate for 1 full round before it takes effect, and it remains as long as the avoral concentrates.

Avorals are generally human-shaped, but their upper limbs are great wings with a human-like hand at the end of each, allowing avorals to use tools and weapons, though in battle they prefer to attack from the air and slash with the large claws on their feet and buffets from their great wings. An avoral's head has a feathery cowl instead of hair, typically brown, white, gray, or golden, and its facial features are bird-like, with a large nose and piercing eyes. Its bones are hollow but strong, making it ideal for flying. Like eagles, avorals have phenomenal vision, and can see fine details even at great distances.

Though on their home plane they are content to soar among the clouds and challenge each other to diving contests among the mountain peaks, in war avorals are the scouts, spies, and messengers of the agathions. With their incredible speed, phenomenal eyesight, and magical powers, they can sneak into an area, spy on whatever lives there, silently converse with the local fauna for additional information, and fly or teleport out again with a comprehensive report. They are experts at hit-and-run attacks and are often responsible for ferrying other celestial soldiers to battle.

A typical avoral is 7 feet tall but weighs only 120 pounds.

Illustrations by Eva Widermann

16

AGATHION, CETACEAL

This mermaid-like creature has the torso and head of a long-haired woman and the lower half of a sleek killer whale.

CETACEAL	CR 15

XP 51,200

NG Medium outsider (agathion, aquatic, extraplanar, good)

Init +8; **Senses** blindsense 60 ft., darkvision 60 ft., low-light vision; Perception +28

Aura protective aura (20 ft.)

DEFENSE

AC 30, touch 15, flat-footed 25 (+4 Dex, +1 dodge, +15 natural; +4 deflection vs. evil)

hp 212 (17d10+119); regeneration 5 (evil weapons and spells)

Fort +17, **Ref** +16, **Will** +9; +4 vs. poison, +4 resistance vs. evil

DR 10/evil and silver; **Immune** cold, electricity, petrification; **Resist** sonic 10; **SR** 26

OFFENSE

Speed 10 ft., swim 80 ft.

Melee +1 *shocking burst* shortspear +28/+23/+18/+13 (1d6+14 plus 1d6 electricity), tail slap +22 (1d6+4 plus push and stun)

Special Attacks shockwave, push (tail slap, 10 ft.)

Spell-Like Abilities (CL 15th; concentration +18)

Constant—*speak with animals*

At will—*detect thoughts* (DC 15), *light, lightning bolt*

(DC 16), *hold monster* (DC 18), *message, greater teleport* (self plus 50 lbs. of objects only)

7/day—*break enchantment, cure serious wounds, neutralize poison, remove disease*

3/day—*cone of cold* (DC 18), *cure critical wounds, greater restoration, heal*

1/day—*awaken, summon monster VIII* (water elementals only)

STATISTICS

Str 29, **Dex** 19, **Con** 24, **Int** 14, **Wis** 18, **Cha** 17

Base Atk +17; **CMB** +26; **CMD** 41 (can't be tripped)

Feats Combat Casting, Dodge, Improved Initiative, Lightning Reflexes, Mobility, Spell Penetration,

Weapon Focus (shortspear, tail slap), Wind Stance

Skills Diplomacy +12, Handle Animal +14, Heal +21, Knowledge (arcana) +22, Knowledge (nature) +19, Knowledge (planes) +22, Perception +28, Sense Motive +24, Stealth +24, Swim +17; **Racial Modifiers** +4 Perception

Languages Celestial, Draconic, Infernal; *speak with animals,* truespeech

SQ amphibious, lay on hands (8d6, 11/day, as a 17th-level paladin)

ECOLOGY

Environment any water (Nirvana)

Organization solitary, pair, or pod (3–6)

Treasure double (+1 *shocking burst* shortspear, other treasure)

SPECIAL ABILITIES

Protective Aura (Su) Against attacks made or effects created by evil creatures, this ability provides a +4 deflection bonus to AC and a +4 resistance bonus on saving throws to anyone within 20 feet of the cetaceal. Otherwise, it functions as a *magic circle against evil* effect and a *lesser globe of invulnerability*, both with a radius of 20 feet (caster level equals cetaceal's HD). The defensive benefits from the circle are not included in the above stat block.

Shockwave (Su) Once per day, a cetaceal can release a 100-foot-radius burst of energy. All creatures in the area take 17d6 damage; half of this damage is cold, and half is electricity (DC 25 Reflex save halves). The save DC is Constitution-based.

Stun (Ex) Any creature moved by a cetaceal's push attack must make a DC 25 Fortitude saving throw or be stunned for 1 round. The DC is Constitution-based.

Cetaceals are great water-dwelling agathions who swim the planar seas and commune with the creatures of the deeps. Rarely seen by landwalkers, they defend the waters against aquatic evils such as aboleths. Their spirits usually were those of great mortal leaders of aquatic or coastal tribes, or good folk who died underwater serving some great cause, reborn in a celestial form that is part humanoid, part orca. They are social beings and develop close friendships with other celestials and marine creatures.

A cetaceal is 8 feet long and weighs 400 pounds, although some grow quite a bit larger than that.

AGATHION, DRACONAL

This noble creature seems to be part serpent, part humanoid, and part dragon, with great wings and a crown of horns.

DRACONAL	CR 20	

XP 307,200

NG Large outsider (agathion, extraplanar, good)

Init +6; **Senses** blindsense 60 ft., darkvision 120 ft., low-light vision; Perception +48

Aura protective aura (20 ft.)

DEFENSE

AC 36, touch 18, flat-footed 33 (+2 Dex, +1 dodge, +6 insight, +18 natural, −1 size) (+4 deflection vs. evil)

hp 324 (24d10+192); regeneration 10 (evil weapons and spells)

Fort +22, **Ref** +16, **Will** +17; +4 vs. poison, +4 resistance vs. evil,

DR 15/evil and silver; **Immune** one energy type (see Celestial Focus), electricity, petrification; **Resist** cold 10, sonic 10; **SR** 31

OFFENSE

Speed 40 ft., fly 120 ft. (average)

Melee bite +36 (2d6+13 plus 1d6 energy), 2 claws +31 (1d8+6 plus 1d6 energy)

Space 10 ft.; **Reach** 10 ft.

Special Attacks breath weapon (120-ft. line, 20d6 energy damage, Reflex DC 30 half, usable once every 1d4 rounds)

Cleric Spells Prepared (CL 17th; concentration +23)

9th—*implosion* (DC 26), *storm of vengeance*^D (DC 26)

8th—*demand*^D, *earthquake*, quickened *holy smite* (DC 21)

7th—empowered *breath of life*, empowered *flame strike* (DC 22), *holy word* (DC 24), quickened *invisibility purge*, *repulsion*^D (DC 24)

6th—*animate objects*, *blade barrier*^D (DC 23), *find the path*, *heal*, *heroes' feast*, quickened *remove paralysis*

5th—*breath of life*, *dispel evil*^D (DC 22), *flame strike* (DC 22), *greater command* (DC 22), *spell resistance*, *true seeing*

4th—*cure critical wounds* (3), *freedom of movement*, *holy smite*^D (DC 21), *repel vermin* (DC 21)

3rd—*bestow curse* (DC 20), *daylight*, *dispel magic*, *helping hand*, *magic vestment*^D, *prayer*, *protection from energy*

2nd—*align weapon*^D (good only), *calm emotions* (DC 19), *enthrall*, *hold person* (DC 19), *lesser restoration* (2), *shield other*

1st—*bless*, *detect undead*, *divine favor*^D, *obscuring mist*, *remove fear*, *sanctuary* (DC 18), *shield of faith*

0—*detect poison*, *guidance*, *purify food and drink*, *stabilize*

D domain spell; **Domains** Good, Nobility

Spell-Like Abilities (CL 24th; concentration +30)

Constant—*speak with animals*

At will—*beast shape II*, *command* (DC 17), *detect thoughts*, *elemental body III* (air or water elementals only), *greater teleport* (self plus 50 lbs. of objects only), *gust of wind*, *hold monster* (DC 20), *identify*, *light*, *lightning bolt* (DC 19), *mage hand*, *message*

7/day—*break enchantment*, *cure serious wounds*, *neutralize poison*, *remove disease*

3/day—*control water*, *control weather*, *control winds*, *heal*, *plane shift* (DC 23)

STATISTICS

Str 36, **Dex** 15, **Con** 27, **Int** 24, **Wis** 24, **Cha** 23

Base Atk +24; **CMB** +38; **CMD** 57 (can't be tripped)

Feats Alertness, Combat Casting, Dodge, Empower Spell, Greater Spell Penetration, Improved Initiative, Iron Will, Mobility, Power Attack, Quicken Spell, Skill Focus (Perception), Spell Penetration

Skills Acrobatics +25, Bluff +29, Diplomacy +26, Escape Artist +22, Heal +31, Intimidate +29, Knowledge (arcana) +30, Knowledge (nature) +27, Knowledge (planes) +34, Knowledge (religion) +31, Perception +48, Sense Motive +34, Spellcraft +27, Stealth +21, Use Magic Device +26; **Racial Modifiers** +4 Perception

Languages Celestial, Draconic, Infernal; *speak with animals*, truespeech

SQ celestial focus, divine insight, lay on hands (10d6, 16/day, as a 20th-level paladin)

ECOLOGY

Environment any air (Nirvana)

Organization solitary, pair, or flight (3–6)

Treasure double

SPECIAL ABILITIES

Celestial Focus (Ex) A draconal's color indicates aspects of its power and attunement to the powers of the good planes. These determine the draconal's breath weapon, the additional energy damage of its claw and bite attacks, additional resistances and immunities, and its additional domain choices (see Spells, below).

Divine Insight (Su) A draconal adds its Charisma bonus as an insight bonus to Armor Class.

Protective Aura (Su) Against attacks made or effects created by evil creatures, this ability provides a +4 deflection bonus to AC and a +4 resistance bonus on saving throws to anyone within 20 feet of the draconal. Otherwise, it functions as a *magic circle against evil* effect and a *lesser globe of invulnerability*, both with a radius of 20 feet (caster level equals draconal's HD). (The defensive benefits from the circle are not included in a draconal's stat block.)

Spells Draconals cast spells as 17th-level clerics. Like clerics, they have access to two domains, selecting from the following list: Air, Good, Nobility, Weather, and two additional domain options based on their color (see facing page). The majority of draconals choose Good and Nobility as their domains (as represented by this stat block). Draconals have a domain spell slot at each spell level but do not gain the granted powers of their chosen domains, nor do they gain access to other cleric abilities.

Draconals are mighty agathion lords, few in number and greatly removed from mortal affairs. They watch over powerful magic and are direct agents of the gods and

Illustration by Eva Widermann

the needs of the good planes. Patient and ageless, they plan for the long term, which often frustrates mortal creatures who seek to gain their assistance with a threat in the here and now. A draconal would rather support or enhance a group of heroes than tackle a problem directly, maintaining its focus on planar matters.

Draconals are attuned to nature and believe in cycles of life and death. Though they are good, they understand that the presence of evil gives good creatures something to strive against, preventing stagnation and complacency. This means their outlook sometimes appears almost neutral, though they hate suffering and needless death.

DRACONAL COLORS

A draconal's coloration represents mystical elements relating to energy, life, and the natural world. These colors are normally chromatic rather than metallic, and an ignorant person seeing a draconal's colors may mistake her for an evil half-dragon. However, some draconals have metallic or gem-like coloration; for example, a yellow draconal may appear mustard yellow or metallic gold, while a white draconal may be chalk white, pearlescent white, or metallic silver. Draconals can change their coloration after a lengthy period of meditation, but normally only do this in response to some horrible evil that requires their direct intervention. This change affects the draconals' personality, and may alter their physical shape or apparent gender.

Black: Black is a balance between male and female energy, and represents the sky, stars, immortality, and leadership. Black draconals are immune to fire damage, and their breath weapon is fire. A black draconal adds Fire, Glory, and Luck to its list of possible domains.

Green: Green is slightly skewed toward masculinity. It represents wood, plants, and flowers. Green draconals are immune to cold damage, and their breath weapon is cold. A green draconal adds Animal, Plant, and Water to its list of possible domains.

Red: Red is a strongly masculine color, and most red draconals are male or have aggressive or gregarious personalities. Red represents fire, light, and warding against bad luck. Red draconals are immune to fire damage, and their breath weapon is fire. A red draconal adds Fire, Protection, and Sun to its list of possible domains.

White: White is slightly skewed toward femininity, and most white draconals are female or have protective or serene personalities. White represents brightness, fulfillment, metal, mourning, and purity. White draconals are immune to cold damage, and their breath weapon is cold. A white draconal adds Artifice, Liberation, and Repose to its list of possible domains.

Yellow: Like black, yellow is a balance between male and female energy. Yellow represents earth, oracles, stone, and luck. Yellow draconals are immune to acid, and their breath weapon is acid. A yellow draconal adds Earth, Glory, and Luck to its list of possible domains.

AGATHION, LEONAL

This lion-headed humanoid has golden fur, sharp teeth, and long cat-like claws on its hands and feet.

LEONAL	CR 12

XP 19,200

NG Medium outsider (agathion, extraplanar, good)

Init +7; **Senses** darkvision 60 ft., low-light vision, scent; Perception +19

Aura protective aura (20 ft.)

DEFENSE

AC 27, touch 14, flat-footed 23 (+3 Dex, +1 dodge, +13 natural) (+4 deflection vs. evil)

hp 147 (14d10+70)

Fort +14, **Ref** +12, **Will** +6; +4 vs. poison, +4 resistance vs. evil

DR 10/evil and silver; **Immune** electricity, petrification; **Resist** cold 10, sonic 10; **SR** 23

OFFENSE

Speed 60 ft.

Melee bite +23 (1d8+8 plus grab), 2 claws +23 (1d6+8)

Special Attacks roar, pounce, rake (2 claws +23, 1d6+8)

Spell-Like Abilities (CL 14th; concentration +16)

Constant—*speak with animals*

At will—*detect thoughts, fireball* (DC 15), *hold monster* (DC 17)

3/day—*cure critical wounds, neutralize poison, remove disease, wall of force*

1/day—*heal*

STATISTICS

Str 27, **Dex** 17, **Con** 20, **Int** 14, **Wis** 14, **Cha** 15

Base Atk +14; **CMB** +22 (+26 grapple); **CMD** 36

Feats Ability Focus (roar), Dodge, Improved Initiative, Mobility, Spring Attack, Weapon Focus (bite, claw)

Skills Acrobatics +24 (+36 jump), Handle Animal +19, Intimidate +19, Knowledge (any one) +19, Perception +19, Sense Motive +19, Spellcraft +16, Stealth +24; **Racial Modifiers** +4 Acrobatics, +4 Stealth

Languages Celestial, Draconic, Infernal; *speak with animals*, truespeech

SQ lay on hands (7d6, 9/day, as a 14th-level paladin)

ECOLOGY

Environment any land (Nirvana)

Organization solitary, pair, or pride (3–8)

Treasure standard

SPECIAL ABILITIES

Protective Aura (Su) Against attacks made or effects created by evil creatures, this ability provides a +4 deflection bonus to AC and a +4 resistance bonus on saving throws to anyone within 20 feet of the leonal. Otherwise, it functions as a *magic circle against evil* effect and a *lesser globe of invulnerability*, both with a radius of 20 feet (caster level equals leonal's HD). The defensive benefits from the circle are not included in a leonal's stat block.

Roar (Su) Up to three times per day, a leonal can emit a powerful roar as a standard action. Each roar affects a 60-foot cone with the effects of a *holy word* spell and also deals 2d6 points of sonic damage to all creatures in the area (DC 21 Fortitude negates). This is a sonic effect. The save DC is Charisma-based.

A leonal is a lion-like agathion, noble and fierce. Though gentle with their families and patient with strangers on their home plane, in battle leonals are deadly foes of evil and cruelty. They hunt fiends and other evil monsters, silently tailing their prey until they find the right time to leap and slash. Leonals pride themselves on their hunting prowess, and few land creatures can match their speed. Although capable of using weapons, the majority of leonals prefer to battle evil with tooth and claw.

Leonals like their battles to be straightforward affairs. They begin with a roar to put their foes off balance, then follow up with claw and bite attacks. They closely coordinate with others in their pride, watching one another's flanks and setting up devastating attacks. They mainly use their magical abilities against large numbers of weaker foes and against those they need to capture or incapacitate without dealing harm to them.

Leonals stand 6 feet tall and weigh 270 pounds on average. Males usually have manes of either dark gold or black hair, which may only surround the head or may extend onto the shoulders and chest. Female leonals do not have manes, but may have longer hair on the back of the neck.

Illustrations by Eva Widermann

AGATHION, SILVANSHEE

This black cat has gray stripes, violet eyes, and an unusual white blaze on its chest.

SILVANSHEE	CR 2

XP 600

NG Tiny outsider (agathion, extraplanar, good)

Init +6; **Senses** darkvision 60 ft., low-light vision; Perception +10

DEFENSE

AC 15, touch 14, flat-footed 13 (+2 Dex, +1 natural, +2 size)

hp 13 (2d10+2)

Fort +5, **Ref** +6, **Will** +2; +4 vs. poison

DR 5/evil or silver; **Immune** electricity, petrification; **Resist** cold 10, sonic 10; **SR** 13

OFFENSE

Speed 30 ft., fly 90 ft. (good)

Melee bite +6 (1d3–4), 2 claws +6 (1d2–4)

Special Attacks heroic strength, pounce

Spell-Like Abilities (CL 2nd; concentration +3)

Constant—*know direction, speak with animals*

At will—*dancing lights, prestidigitation, stabilize*

1/day—*dimension door* (self plus 5 lbs. of objects only)

1/week—*commune* (6 questions, CL 12th)

STATISTICS

Str 3, **Dex** 15, **Con** 12, **Int** 10, **Wis** 12, **Cha** 13

Base Atk +2; **CMB** +2; **CMD** 8 (12 vs. trip)

Feats Improved Initiative, Weapon Finesse^B

Skills Acrobatics +11, Climb +7, Fly +6, Knowledge (arcana) +5, Knowledge (planes) +5, Perception +10, Stealth +19; **Racial Modifiers** +4 Acrobatics, +4 Perception, +4 Stealth

Languages Celestial, Draconic, Infernal; *speak with animals*, truespeech

SQ cat's luck, flight, lay on hands (1d6, 1/day, always as a 2nd-level paladin), spectral mist

ECOLOGY

Environment any land (Nirvana)

Organization solitary, pair, or clowder (3–10)

Treasure standard

SPECIAL ABILITIES

Cat's Luck (Su) A silvanshee adds its Charisma modifier as a luck bonus on all its saving throws. Once per day as a standard action, it can also grant this bonus to one ally within 30 feet for 10 minutes.

Heroic Strength (Su) Once per day, a silvanshee can grant itself a +8 enhancement bonus to Strength for 1 minute.

Spectral Mist (Su) A silvanshee can assume an eerie, mist-like form roughly the size and shape of a cat. This ability has the same effect as a *gaseous form* spell, except the silvanshee retains its own DR and supernatural abilities and can move at its normal speed. It can remain in mist form up to 5 minutes per day. This duration does not have to be consecutive, but it must be used in 1-minute increments.

Silvanshees are curious but reclusive cat agathions. Unobtrusive and able to blend in among normal animals (unlike the more anthropomorphic agathions), they are the eyes and ears of the good planes in the mortal world. Most roam hills, forests, and plains, keeping an eye out for evil influences. They can be taken as familiars by 7th-level good spellcasters with the Improved Familiar feat who meet the proper prerequisites. As familiars, silvanshees act as moral guides and steer their mortal allies toward corruptive forces that must be eliminated. In some mortal lands, they are called cat sìth or cath sìdhe, and are believed to be disguised witches or fairies—and not necessarily benign creatures, which only encourages silvanshees to avoid strangers.

Silvanshees are not fond of open combat, even against demons, devils, or other fiendish threats, and they're likely to run away if confronted. When they must fight, they prefer greater numbers and the element of surprise, using their magic to temporarily overcome their physical weaknesses, and melting away into mist if the battle turns against them.

A silvanshee is the size of a large domestic cat, though almost always sleek rather than fat, and weighs 20 pounds on average.

AGATHION, VULPINAL

This bright-eyed, anthropomorphic fox is dressed in simple traveling clothes and carries a musical instrument in one hand.

VULPINAL	CR 6

XP 2,400

NG Small outsider (agathion, extraplanar, good)

Init +7; **Senses** darkvision 60 ft., *detect evil*, low-light vision; Perception +12

Aura calm emotions (30 ft.)

DEFENSE

AC 22, touch 14, flat-footed 19 (+4 armor, +3 Dex, +4 natural, +1 size)

hp 59 (7d10+21)

Fort +5, **Ref** +10, **Will** +7; +4 vs. poison

DR 10/evil or silver; **Immune** electricity, petrification; **Resist** cold 10, sonic 10; **SR** 17

OFFENSE

Speed 30 ft.

Melee bite +11 (1d4+1), 2 claws +11 (1d3+1)

Special Attacks pounce

Spell-Like Abilities (CL 7th; concentration +10)

Constant—*detect evil, mage armor, speak with animals*

At will—*invisibility* (self only)

3/day—*charm monster* (DC 17), *dispel evil* (DC 18), *flame arrow, holy smite* (DC 17), *dimension door* (self plus 50 lbs. of objects only), *remove disease*

1/day—*major image* (DC 16)

STATISTICS

Str 12, **Dex** 16, **Con** 17, **Int** 19, **Wis** 15, **Cha** 16

Base Atk +7; **CMB** +7; **CMD** 20

Feats Combat Reflexes, Improved Initiative, Lightning Reflexes, Weapon Finesse

Skills Acrobatics +10 (+18 jump), Bluff +13, Knowledge (any one) +21, Knowledge (arcana) +21, Knowledge (planes) +21, Perception +12, Perform (any one) +13, Spellcraft +14, Stealth +17, Use Magic Device +10; **Racial Modifiers** +8 Acrobatics when jumping

Languages Celestial, Common, Draconic, Infernal; *speak with animals*, truespeech

SQ bardic knowledge +7, lay on hands (3d6, 6/day, as a 7th-level paladin)

ECOLOGY

Environment any land (Nirvana)

Organization solitary, pair, or team (3–12)

Treasure standard (masterwork musical instrument, other treasure)

SPECIAL ABILITIES

Calm Emotions Aura (Su) A vulpinal's aura acts like a *calm emotions* spell with a radius of 30 feet. Any creature entering this area must make a Will save (DC 16) to resist the effect. A creature that makes its save is immune to that vulpinal's aura for 24 hours. The save DC is Charisma-based.

Among the smallest of the agathions, vulpinals tend to be the most outspoken and friendly of their kind, and also the most far-ranging across the planes. A vulpinal looks like a humanoid fox, often with brilliantly colored fur (usually red or red-brown, though silver is not uncommon) and a tail as long as its height. As the bards and sages of the agathions, they dress in functional clothing, typically embellishing a single article to show their creativity and personality. Most appear to be adults, though others look more like fox kits (with shorter stature and larger eyes) while some look much older (leaner, with gray fur on the muzzle, chest, and tail). Their hands are humanoid in shape, with tiny clawed fingers.

A typical vulpinal prefers a life of solitary travel, though they have been known to pair up or travel in groups if they find like-minded individuals who have much to teach and share. They are particularly fond of lillends, and these winged azatas can easily carry the child-sized vulpinals, giving vulpinals many opportunities to share stories. Indeed, for a vulpinal, there are few greater pleasures than sharing their knowledge—acting as sages of the planes, teaching songs and dances from exotic places, and composing poems about beautiful places in the natural world. Though they are gentle by nature, they fight to defend beauty, especially if their magic can bolster the more martial celestial races.

A vulpinal stands about 3 feet in height and weighs 50 pounds.

Akata

This hairless blue lion has twin tentacular tails. Dozens more thick tentacles quiver and twitch where its mane should be.

AKATA   **CR 1**

XP 400

N Medium aberration

Init +6; **Senses** darkvision 120 ft., scent; Perception +1

DEFENSE

AC 13, touch 12, flat-footed 11 (+2 Dex, +1 natural)

hp 15 (2d8+6)

Fort +3, **Ref** +2, **Will** +4

Defensive Abilities no breath; **Immune** cold, disease, poison; **Resist** fire 30

Weaknesses deaf, vulnerable to salt water

OFFENSE

Speed 40 ft., climb 20 ft.

Melee bite +2 (1d6+1 plus void bite), 2 tentacles –3 (1d3)

STATISTICS

Str 12, **Dex** 15, **Con** 16, **Int** 3, **Wis** 12, **Cha** 11

Base Atk +1; **CMB** +2; **CMD** 14 (18 vs. trip)

Feats Improved Initiative

Skills Acrobatics +6 (+10 jump), Climb +9, Stealth +10; **Racial Modifiers** +4 Stealth

SQ hibernation

ECOLOGY

Environment any

Organization solitary, pair, or pack (3–30)

Treasure standard

SPECIAL ABILITIES

Deaf (Ex) Akatas cannot hear. They are immune to spells and effects that rely on hearing to function, but they also cannot make Perception checks to listen.

Hibernation (Ex) Akatas can enter a state of hibernation for an indefinite period of time when food is scarce. When an akata wishes to enter hibernation, it seeks out a den and surrounds itself in a layer of fibrous material excreted from its mouth—these fibers quickly harden into a dense, almost metallic cocoon. While hibernating, an akata does not need to drink or eat. The cocoon has hardness 10 and 60 hit points, and is immune to fire and bludgeoning (including falling) damage. As long as the cocoon remains intact, the akata within remains unharmed. The akata remains in a state of hibernation until it senses another living creature within 10 feet or is exposed to extreme heat, at which point it claws its way to freedom in 1d4 minutes as its cocoon degrades to fragments of strange metal.

Salt Water Vulnerability (Ex) Salt water acts as an extremely strong acid to akatas. A splash of salt water deals 1d6 points of damage to an akata, and full immersion in salt water deals 4d6 points of damage per round.

Void Bite (Ex) Akatas hold hundreds of invisibly small larval young within their mouths, spreading these parasitic creatures to hosts through their bite. Only humanoids make suitable hosts for akata young—all other creature types are immune to this parasitic infection. The disease itself is known as void death.

Disease (Ex) *Void Death:* Bite—injury; *save* Fort DC 12; *onset* 1 hour; *frequency* 1/day; *effect* 1d2 Dex and 1d2 Con damage; an infected creature who dies rises as a void zombie 2d4 hours later (see below); *cure* 2 consecutive saves.

Akatas hail from a strange, distant planet that long ago succumbed to a cataclysmic end. Countless akatas clung to fragments of the dead planet, entering hibernation and riding these asteroids until they eventually crashed upon a new planet—akatas' cocoons protected them from the impact, and they soon awoke to seek out suitable hosts to spawn their young. Left untended, an akata scourge can quickly grow into a significant threat. A typical akata stands 3-1/2 feet tall and weighs 400 pounds.

VOID ZOMBIE (CR +1)

A humanoid killed by void death becomes a void zombie. A void zombie is a fast zombie (*Pathfinder RPG Bestiary* page 289) that gains a secondary "tongue" attack (actually the larval akata's feeding tendril), dealing 1d6 points of damage. A void zombie also gains the following special attack.

    Blood Drain (Ex) If a void zombie hits a living creature with its tongue attack, it drains blood, dealing 2 points of Strength damage before the tongue detaches.

Illustration by Andrew Hou

AMOEBA, GIANT

This blob of protoplasm is somewhat transparent, allowing the bones of undigested meals and a dark nucleus to be seen within.

AMOEBA, GIANT	CR 1	

XP 400

N Small ooze (aquatic)

Init –5; **Senses** blindsight 30 ft.; Perception –5

DEFENSE

AC 6, touch 6, flat-footed 6 (–5 Dex, +1 size)

hp 15 (2d8+6)

Fort +3, **Ref** –5, **Will** –5

Defensive Abilities ooze traits

OFFENSE

Speed 10 ft., climb 10 ft., swim 20 ft.

Melee slam +3 (1d3+1 plus 1d3 acid and grab)

Space 5 ft.; **Reach** 5 ft.

Special Attacks constrict (1d3+1 plus 1d3 acid)

STATISTICS

Str 12, **Dex** 1, **Con** 16, **Int** —, **Wis** 1, **Cha** 1

Base Atk +1; **CMB** +1 (+5 grapple); **CMD** 6 (can't be tripped)

Skills Climb +9, Swim +9

SQ amphibious

ECOLOGY

Environment any land or underground

Organization solitary or colony (2–9)

Treasure none

A giant amoeba is a shapeless mass of living, liquid protoplasm. Though naturally translucent with darker interior spots, its surface is slightly sticky and tends to collect dirt and other debris from its environment; therefore, a moving giant amoeba looks like muddy water. A weaker cousin of creatures such as the gray ooze and black pudding, a giant amoeba is actually a mutated version of a harmless creature too small to be seen by the naked eye, grown dangerously large in size. Although happy to prey on creatures smaller than it, the giant amoeba's constant hunger often drives it to attack larger prey, such as humanoids.

AMOEBA SWARM

Thousands of tiny gelatinous clots of animate ooze swarm in a wet mound, surrounded by a cloying stink of rancid vinegar.

AMOEBA SWARM	CR 1	

XP 400

N Fine ooze (swarm)

Init –5; **Senses** blindsight 30 ft.; Perception –5

DEFENSE

AC 13, touch 13, flat-footed 13 (–5 Dex, +8 size)

hp 9 (2d8)

Fort +0, **Ref** –5, **Will** –5

Defensive Abilities ooze and swarm traits; **Immune** weapon damage

OFFENSE

Speed 10 ft., climb 10 ft., swim 20 ft.

Melee swarm (1d6 acid plus distraction)

Space 10 ft.; **Reach** 0 ft.

Special Attacks distraction (DC 11)

STATISTICS

Str 1, **Dex** 1, **Con** 10, **Int** —, **Wis** 1, **Cha** 1

Base Atk +1; **CMB** —; **CMD** —

Skills Climb +3, Swim +3

SQ amphibious

ECOLOGY

Environment any land or underground

Organization solitary or colony (2–5)

Treasure none

An amoeba swarm is a mobile group of amoebas, each about the size of a coin. Giant amoebas may cleave off tiny portions of their substance, which can then become amoeba swarms. At other times, a giant amoeba can spontaneously transform into a swarm, usually if the giant amoeba is starving or in an area with a high concentration of magic. Likewise, a well-fed amoeba swarm may fuse into a single giant amoeba.

When an amoeba swarm is found in the vicinity of a giant amoeba, the two oozes ignore each other. A giant amoeba in the space of an amoeba swarm takes no damage from the swarm's attacks and does not run the risk of becoming distracted as a result of being in the swarm.

Illustration by Kieran Yanner

AMPHISBAENA

This large snake has two heads, one at each end of its long, coiling body. Both display large sets of fangs.

AMPHISBAENA	CR 4	

XP 1,200

N Large magical beast

Init +2; **Senses** all-around vision, darkvision 60 ft., low-light vision, scent; Perception +11

DEFENSE

AC 19, touch 11, flat-footed 17 (+2 Dex, +8 natural, −1 size)

hp 45 (6d10+12)

Fort +6, **Ref** +7, **Will** +3

Defensive Abilities split; **Immune** petrification; **Resist** cold 10

OFFENSE

Speed 20 ft., climb 20 ft., swim 20 ft.

Melee 2 bites +8 (1d8+2 plus poison)

Space 10 ft.; **Reach** 5 ft.

STATISTICS

Str 14, **Dex** 15, **Con** 13, **Int** 2, **Wis** 13, **Cha** 4

Base Atk +6; **CMB** +9; **CMD** 21 (can't be tripped)

Feats Skill Focus (Stealth), Toughness, Weapon Focus (bite)

Skills Acrobatics +10 (+6 jump), Climb +10, Perception +11, Stealth +11, Swim +10; **Racial Modifiers** +8 Acrobatics, +4 Perception, +4 Stealth

ECOLOGY

Environment temperate hills or underground

Organization solitary or pack (2–5)

Treasure incidental

SPECIAL ABILITIES

Poison (Ex) Bite—injury; *save* Fort DC 14; *frequency* 1/round for 6 rounds; *effect* 1d3 Con; *cure* 1 save.

Split (Su) An amphisbaena functions normally even if cut in half. If dealt a critical hit with a slashing weapon, the creature is cut in half but continues to function as two separate creatures, each with half the original amphisbaena's current hit points (rounded down) after the damage from the critical hit is applied. Once split, an amphisbaena cannot be split again. If left alone for 1 minute, the split amphisbaena can rejoin its two halves and become a single whole creature again (add the two creatures' hit points together). If one of the split creatures is slain, the amphisbaena can regrow the lost portion over the course of 1d3 weeks.

The reclusive amphisbaena is a dreaded viper with a head at either end of its thick, serpentine coils. It travels in a strange, undulant crawl akin to that of a sidewinder, looping the coils of its long body back and forth and keeping both of its heads at the alert. Amphisbaenas are said to have formed from the blood of medusas, and while such stories are highly suspect, the creatures possess a natural immunity to petrification, which make them favored pets of medusas or other creatures with the petrification ability.

Adult amphisbaenas can grow up to 14 feet in length and weigh as much as 250 pounds. While their thick coils twitch and ripple with muscle, they are not constrictors; their attacks rely on speed and their deadly venom. Most amphisbaenas have dark, bluish-black scales with lighter bands; however, they can be encountered in a variety of colors appropriate to their habitats. Some reports even claim lizard-like versions of this beast exists, with short legs and long curved talons.

The amphisbaena's two heads can act independently, and the creature can move freely in either direction. In combat, it uses this ability to its utmost advantage, constantly spinning about to change up the direction of its strikes and guarding against enemies attempting to sneak closer or flank it. Unlike most snakes, amphisbaenas are aggressive, attacking anything that enters their territory. While they prefer smaller prey, they have been known to hunt gnomes, halflings, and other Small humanoids, and will sometimes attack larger foes if they're starving or preparing to shed.

Amphisbaenas reproduce infrequently, laying small clutches of up to a dozen dark onyx eggs at a time. Avidly sought by animal trainers and collectors, amphisbaena eggs can fetch between 300 to 500 gp on the market. Despite minimal intelligence, amphisbaenas are driven primarily by their instincts and are extremely difficult and dangerous to train. All attempts to train an amphisbaena take a −8 penalty on any Handle Animal checks as a result.

Illustration by Jim Pavelec

ANGEL, CASSISIAN

This finely crafted golden helm is decorated with intricate filigree, and flutters gracefully through the air on feathered wings.

CASSISIAN	CR 2

XP 600

NG Small outsider (angel, extraplanar, good)

Init +0; **Senses** darkvision 60 ft., *detect evil*, low-light vision; Perception +5

Aura lesser protective aura

DEFENSE

AC 14, touch 11, flat-footed 14 (+3 natural, +1 size) (+2 deflection vs. evil)

hp 13 (2d10+2)

Fort +4, **Ref** +3, **Will** +2; +4 vs. poison; +2 resistance vs. evil

DR 5/cold iron or evil; **Immune** acid, cold, petrification; **Resist** electricity 10, fire 10

OFFENSE

Speed fly 60 ft. (perfect)

Melee slam –1 (1d3–4)

Special Attacks breath weapon (15-ft. line, 1d6 cold or 1d6 fire, Reflex DC 12 half, usable every 1d4 rounds)

Spell-Like Abilities (CL 3rd; concentration +3)

Constant—*detect evil, know direction*

1/day—*aid, daylight*

1/week—*commune* (six questions, CL 12th)

STATISTICS

Str 3, **Dex** 11, **Con** 12, **Int** 6, **Wis** 11, **Cha** 10

Base Atk +2; **CMB** –3; **CMD** 7 (can't be tripped)

Feats Iron Will

Skills Diplomacy +2, Fly +10, Knowledge (planes) +2, Knowledge (religion) +2, Perception +5, Sense Motive +4, Stealth +8

Languages Celestial, Draconic, Infernal; truespeech

SQ change shape (2 of the following forms: Small human-like angel, dove, dog, or Tiny fish, *polymorph*), perfect memory

ECOLOGY

Environment any good-aligned plane

Organization solitary, pair, or squad (3–6)

Treasure none

SPECIAL ABILITIES

Perfect Memory (Ex) Though they are not particularly intelligent, cassisians have perfect memories and remember everything they see or hear. They can faultlessly recite conversations they heard hundreds of years before. They also have the power to erase portions of their own memories, which they do (usually under orders from superior angels) to protect sensitive information.

Lesser Protective Aura (Su) A cassisian has a lesser form of the protective aura possessed by more powerful angels.

This protective aura grants the cassisian a +2 deflection bonus to its AC against evil foes, and a +2 resistance bonus on all saving throws made against evil effects or spells cast by evil creatures. This aura extends to a radius of 5 feet, but can only benefit one additional creature other than the cassisian at any one time. A cassisian's protective aura is fragile, and as soon as an evil creature successfully strikes the cassisian, or as soon as the cassisian fails a saving throw against an evil source, its protective aura fades away and is no longer applicable. The cassisian can reactivate its protective aura by spending 1 minute concentrating upon the task.

Cassisians are the weakest sort of angel, but are absolutely dedicated to the cause of good. They serve as messengers for more powerful angels, and on the Material Plane they are often bound to good mortals to serve as familiars, acting as spiritual guides, reciting platitudes and quoting scripture from various benign faiths and philosophies (some forgotten for centuries). A 7th-level lawful good spellcaster with the Improved Familiar feat can select a cassisian as a familiar.

A cassisian's true form is a helmet possessing a pair of bird's wings. The exact style of helmet varies by the deity the angel serves—most appear to be steel with angular cheek-plates, though some resemble bascinets, skullcaps, great helms, or even samurai helmets, and a few older cassisians appear to be bronze or even leather. Though cassisians can assume other forms (that of a child-sized angelic humanoid wearing a proportional helmet matching the cassisians' true form, a dove, a dog, or a fish), they find it strange and rarely stay in that form for more than a few minutes.

Typically formed from the souls of trustworthy and pious soldiers, some cassisians arise spontaneously from the spiritual fragments of great angels destroyed while defending the celestial planes against fiendish incursions. In many cases, the lowly cassisian retains fragments of its previous life's memories, and friends of that old soul may visit with the cassisian to reminisce with what remains. Unfortunately, the reincarnated angel's memories are more like something memorized from a book, and lack the character and camaraderie the friends expect.

Illustrations by Kekai Kotaki

ANGEL, MONADIC DEVA

This angelic being has smooth skin, a muscular body, and large golden wings, and wields a large mace.

MONADIC DEVA	CR 12

XP 19,200

NG Medium outsider (angel, aquatic, extraplanar, good)

Init +8; **Senses** darkvision 60 ft., *detect evil*, low-light vision; Perception +29

Aura protective aura

DEFENSE

AC 27, touch 14, flat-footed 23 (+4 Dex, +13 natural; +4 deflection vs. evil)

hp 147 (14d10+70)

Fort +15, **Ref** +13, **Will** +10; +4 vs. poison; +4 resistance vs. evil

DR 10/evil; **Immune** acid, cold, electricity, fire, death effects, energy drain, petrification; **SR** 23

OFFENSE

Speed 40 ft., fly 90 ft. (good)

Melee +3 *morningstar* +22/+17/+12 (1d8+10 plus solid blow)

Spell-Like Abilities (CL 10th; concentration +14)

Constant—*detect evil*

At will—*aid, charm monster* (DC 18, elementals only), *discern lies* (DC 18), *dispel evil* (DC 19), *dispel magic, holy smite* (DC 18), *invisibility* (self only), *plane shift* (DC 19), *remove curse, remove disease, remove fear*

3/day—*cure serious wounds, holy word* (DC 21), *mirror image*

1/day—*heal, hold monster* (DC 19), *holy aura* (DC 22)

STATISTICS

Str 21, **Dex** 19, **Con** 18, **Int** 19, **Wis** 18, **Cha** 19

Base Atk +14; **CMB** +19; **CMD** 33

Feats Alertness, Cleave, Great Fortitude, Improved Initiative, Iron Will, Power Attack, Toughness

Skills Diplomacy +21, Fly +25, Intimidate +21, Knowledge (planes) +21, Knowledge (religion) +21, Perception +29, Sense Motive +25, Stealth +21, Survival +21, Swim +27; **Racial Modifiers** +4 Perception

Languages Celestial, Draconic, Infernal; truespeech

SQ amphibious

ECOLOGY

Environment any good-aligned plane

Organization solitary, pair, or squad (3–6)

Treasure double (+3 *morningstar*, other treasure)

SPECIAL ABILITIES

Solid Blow (Su) If a monadic deva strikes an opponent twice in 1 round with its mace, that creature takes an extra 1d8+10 points of damage.

Monadic devas are stoic watchers of the Ethereal Plane and the Elemental Planes. They search those planes for fiendish enclaves, battle evil planar monsters such as xills, and act as celestial liaisons to the genies and elementals. They have been known to broker temporary peace between warring elemental factions, often using their inherent magic to end hostilities long enough for negotiations to take place. In the armies of the good planes, they are leaders and officers, and after centuries of service to a deity, they may be transformed into astral devas.

Monadic devas like giving their maces names and proudly announcing them in battle with evil foes. Many of these weapons have seen battle for thousands of years and are quite battered. Younger devas may lend their weapons to good churches on the Material Plane so they can be used by great mortal heroes, though the angels eventually reclaim them after no more than a year and a day.

A monadic deva is 7 feet tall and weighs 220 pounds.

ANGEL, MOVANIC DEVA

This angel is all sharp lines and angles, muscular but lean, with large wings and a mighty flaming greatsword.

MOVANIC DEVA	CR 10

XP 9,600

NG Medium outsider (angel, extraplanar, good)

Init +7; **Senses** darkvision 60 ft., *detect evil*, low-light vision; Perception +26

Aura protective aura

DEFENSE

AC 24, touch 13, flat-footed 21 (+3 Dex, +11 natural; +4 deflection vs. evil)

hp 126 (12d10+60)

Fort +12, **Ref** +11, **Will** +9; +4 vs. poison, +4 resistance vs. evil

Defensive Abilities nature's pacifism, protected life force; **DR** 10/evil; **Immune** acid, cold, electricity, fire, death effects, energy drain, petrification; **SR** 21

OFFENSE

Speed 40 ft., fly 60 ft. (good)

Melee *+1 flaming greatsword* +17/+12/+7 (2d6+7/19–20 plus 1d6 fire)

Spell-Like Abilities (CL 8th; concentration +12)

Constant—*detect evil*

At will—*aid, discern lies* (DC 18), *dispel evil* (DC 19), *dispel magic, holy smite* (DC 18), *invisibility* (self only), *plane shift* (DC 19), *remove curse, remove disease, remove fear*

7/day—*cure serious wounds*

1/day—*antimagic field, awaken, holy aura* (DC 22)

STATISTICS

Str 19, **Dex** 17, **Con** 18, **Int** 17, **Wis** 17, **Cha** 19

Base Atk +12; **CMB** +16; **CMD** 29

Feats Cleave, Improved Initiative, Iron Will, Power Attack, Toughness, Vital Strike

Skills Diplomacy +19, Fly +22, Intimidate +19, Knowledge (planes) +18, Knowledge (religion) +18, Perception +26, Sense Motive +22, Stealth +18, Survival +18; **Racial Modifiers** +4 Perception

Languages Celestial, Draconic, Infernal; truespeech

ECOLOGY

Environment any good-aligned plane

Organization solitary, pair, or squad (3–6)

Treasure double (*+1 flaming greatsword*, other treasure)

SPECIAL ABILITIES

Nature's Pacifism (Ex) Animals and plant creatures do not willingly attack a movanic deva, though they can be forced to do so by magic. If the deva attacks a plant or animal, its protection against that creature ends.

Protected Life Force (Ex) Movanic devas are never harmed by positive-dominant or negative-dominant planar traits.

Movanic devas serve as infantry in the celestial armies, though they spend most of their time patrolling the Positive, Negative, and Material Planes. On the Positive Plane, they watch over wandering good souls, which sometimes puts them into conflict with the jyoti. On the Negative Plane, they battle undead, the sceaduinar, and the other strange things that hunt in the hungry void. Their rare visits to the Material Plane are usually to help powerful mortals when a great menace threatens to plunge an entire realm into evil.

Illustration by Kekai Kotaki

ANIMATE DREAM

This indistinct figure suddenly takes on a nightmarish shape, not quite human or animal or fiend.

ANIMATE DREAM	CR 8

XP 4,800

NE Medium outsider (extraplanar, incorporeal)

Init +4; **Senses** darkvision 60 ft.; Perception +17

DEFENSE

AC 20, touch 20, flat-footed 15 (+5 deflection, +4 Dex, +1 dodge)

hp 90 (12d10+24)

Fort +10, **Ref** +8, **Will** +12

Defensive Abilities incorporeal; **SR** 19

OFFENSE

Speed fly 40 ft. (perfect)

Melee incorporeal touch +16 (6d8 negative energy plus nightmare curse)

Spell-Like Abilities (CL 12th; concentration +17)

3/day—*deep slumber* (DC 18), *dimension door*, *nightmare* (DC 20)

1/day—*confusion* (DC 19), *fear* (DC 19), *phantasmal killer* (DC 19)

STATISTICS

Str —, **Dex** 18, **Con** 15, **Int** 10, **Wis** 15, **Cha** 21

Base Atk +12; **CMB** +16; **CMD** 32

Feats Blind-Fight, Combat Casting, Dodge, Flyby Attack, Iron Will, Mobility

Skills Bluff +20, Fly +12, Intimidate +20, Knowledge (planes) +15, Perception +17, Sense Motive +17, Stealth +19

Languages telepathy 100 ft.

ECOLOGY

Environment any (Ethereal Plane)

Organization solitary

Treasure none

SPECIAL ABILITIES

Nightmare Curse (Ex) An animate dream's touch puts horrifying visions in the target's mind. Curse—incorporeal touch; *save* Will DC 21; *frequency* 1/day; *effect* 1d4 Wisdom drain and target is fatigued; *cure* 3 consecutive saves or *dispel evil*, *dream*, or *remove curse*.

From time to time, when a powerfully imaginative sleeper wakes from a particularly vivid or unusual dream, a fragment of that dream lingers on the Ethereal Plane. To survive, this animate dream needs the power of living will, imagination, and emotion to sustain it. An animate dream seeks out mortal minds, appearing as a shadowy and often frightful dream figure. Its true appearance is vague and nebulous, but it reacts to the fears and emotions of those around it, taking on a nightmarish appearance that differs for each viewer.

An animate dream can find satisfaction and sustenance by passing one of its ghostly limbs through a mortal's body—the act infusing the mortal with negative energy that sates the animate dream's unnatural hunger. But by forcing a creature into a state of sleep, terror, or both, the animate dream can gain a much more satisfying meal, feeding on the emotions released in such states. It uses its spell-like abilities to this end, for each creature it harms with its nightmares, drives temporarily insane with *confusion* or *fear*, or outright slays with *phantasmal killer* provides the monster with more nourishment. An animate dream forced to go for a long period of time without feeding does not starve to death, but does grow increasingly feral and violent in nature.

Animate dreams sometimes associate with other creatures from the Ethereal Plane or that have associations with dreams and nightmares, such as night hags, phase spiders, and xills. Sometimes these alliances are mutually beneficial, but in many cases the animate dreams are treated as slaves. Night hags in particular like enslaving animate dreams, and sometimes use their essence as a component in creating heartstones.

Illustration by Kieran Yanner

ARANEA

This bloated spider has a hunchbacked body and a gleam of intelligence in its multiple eyes.

ARANEA	CR 4

XP 1,200

N Medium magical beast (shapechanger)

Init +7; **Senses** darkvision 60 ft., low-light vision; Perception +9

DEFENSE

AC 20, touch 13, flat-footed 17 (+4 armor, +3 Dex, +3 natural)

hp 37 (5d10+10)

Fort +6, **Ref** +7, **Will** +4

OFFENSE

Speed 50 ft., climb 30 ft.

Melee bite +8 (1d6 plus poison)

Special Attacks web (+8 ranged, DC 14, hp 5)

Sorcerer Spells Known (CL 5th; concentration +8)

 2nd (5/day)—*invisibility, mirror image*

 1st (7/day)—*charm person* (DC 14), *mage armor* (1 already cast), *silent image* (DC 14), *sleep* (DC 14)

 0 (at will)—*daze* (DC 13), *detect magic, ghost sound* (DC 13), *light, mage hand, resistance*

STATISTICS

Str 11, **Dex** 17, **Con** 14, **Int** 14, **Wis** 13, **Cha** 16

Base Atk +5; **CMB** +5; **CMD** 18

Feats Eschew Materials[B], Improved Initiative, Iron Will, Weapon Finesse

Skills Acrobatics +9 (+17 jump), Climb +14, Escape Artist +8, Knowledge (arcana) +7, Perception +9, Stealth +9; **Racial Modifiers** +2 Acrobatics, +2 Perception

Languages Common, Sylvan

SQ change shape (humanoid; *alter self*)

ECOLOGY

Environment tropical forests

Organization solitary or colony (2–6)

Treasure standard

SPECIAL ABILITIES

Change Shape (Su) An aranea can take the form of a Small or Medium humanoid or spider-humanoid hybrid. In humanoid form, an aranea cannot use its bite, web, or poison. In spider-humanoid hybrid form, an aranea looks like a humanoid with spidery fangs and spinnerets, with the latter typically located at the small of its back. The aranea retains its bite attack, webs, and poison in this form, and can wield weapons and wear armor. When in humanoid or hybrid form, an aranea's speed is 30 feet and it has no climb speed.

Poison (Ex) Bite—injury; *save* Fort DC 14; *frequency* 1/round for 6 rounds; *effect* 1d3 Strength; *cure* 1 save.

Spells An aranea casts spells as a 5th-level sorcerer, but does not gain any additional abilities, such as a sorcerous bloodline.

An aranea is an intelligent, shapechanging spider with sorcerous powers. In its natural form, an aranea resembles a humpbacked spider a little bigger than a human, and weighs about 150 pounds. The hump on its back houses the aranea's brain. All araneas have a single alternate form as well—this alternate form is that of a Small or Medium humanoid. Although an aranea can assume a spider-hybrid variant of this form, it cannot use its change shape ability to assume multiple humanoid forms—this additional shape is locked into one unique appearance.

Araneas typically gather in small colonies of two to six individuals, making webbed nests high in trees. These colonies work together to research magic, and may change membership many times over as individuals leave to pursue their own studies and are replaced by newer members. A single aranea may take on humanoid form and live for years in a humanoid community, never revealing its true nature. Though araneas generally prefer to be left alone, they often prove quite knowledgeable about the ways of magic, and if approached peacefully may be willing to share their expertise for the right price (typically a magic item or some service).

Skilled spellcasters, araneas try to avoid physical combat and use their webs and spells when they can. Rather than kill their enemies, araneas often subdue opponents and hold them for ransom.

Illustration by Jim Pavelec

ARCHON, SHIELD

This armored giant is sheathed in metal from head to toe. One arm ends in a spear-like blade, the other in a massive shield.

SHIELD ARCHON	CR 10

XP 9,600

LG Large outsider (archon, extraplanar, good, lawful)

Init +5; **Senses** darkvision 60 ft., low-light vision; Perception +15

Aura aura of menace (DC 18), *magic circle against evil*

DEFENSE

AC 29, touch 10, flat-footed 28 (+9 armor, +1 Dex, +4 natural, +6 shield, –1 size) (+2 deflection vs. evil)

hp 112 (9d10+63)

Fort +13, **Ref** +7, **Will** +8; +4 vs. poison

DR 10/evil; **Immune** electricity, petrification; **SR** 21

OFFENSE

Speed 40 ft., fly 90 ft. (good); 30 ft., fly 60 ft. in armor

Melee +3 *shortspear* +16/+11 (1d8+10)

Space 10 ft.; **Reach** 10 ft.

Special Attacks transpose ally

Spell-Like Abilities (CL 9th; concentration +11)

　Constant—*magic circle against evil*

　At will—*aid, greater teleport* (self plus 50 lbs. of objects only), *message*

　1/day—*disrupting weapon, divine power, shield other*

STATISTICS

Str 20, **Dex** 13, **Con** 25, **Int** 14, **Wis** 16, **Cha** 15

Base Atk +9; **CMB** +15; **CMD** 26 (30 vs. bull rush and trip)

Feats Combat Reflexes, Improved Initiative, Iron Will, Shield Focus, Stand Still, Weapon Specialization (shortspear)[B]

Skills Diplomacy +14, Fly +0, Intimidate +14, Knowledge (religion) +14, Perception +15, Sense Motive +15, Stealth –6, Survival +15

Languages Celestial, Draconic, Infernal; truespeech

SQ spear and shield, stability

ECOLOGY

Environment any (Heaven)

Organization solitary, pair, or squad (3–5)

Treasure standard (full plate, other treasure)

SPECIAL ABILITIES

Spear and Shield (Su) At will as a free action, a shield archon can transform his hands into a +1 *tower shield* and a +3 *shortspear*, or either individually, or back to hands again. He cannot transform both hands into shields or both into shortspears. A shield archon never takes the typical –2 penalty on attack rolls while wielding a tower shield. A shield archon's weapons cannot be disarmed, but they can be sundered. If a shield archon loses his spear or shield, he can manifest a new one as a full-round action. When a shield archon is slain, these two items fade away—they cannot be looted or wielded by any other creature.

Stability (Ex) Shield archons receive a +4 racial bonus to CMD when resisting a bull rush or trip attempt.

Transpose Ally (Su) Once per day as a standard action, a shield archon can teleport to the location of a willing (or unconscious) ally and immediately teleport that ally to the archon's previous position, in effect switching places with the ally. The archon must have line of effect to the target.

Shield archons are the mighty rocks of celestial armies, withstanding waves of demons and devils without complaint. Though more than capable of tearing apart lesser demons and devils, their true strength lies in their ability to shrug off deadly attacks from superior opponents, giving their offense-oriented allies time to flank and overwhelm their mutual foes. Shield archons are 9 feet tall and weigh 800 pounds.

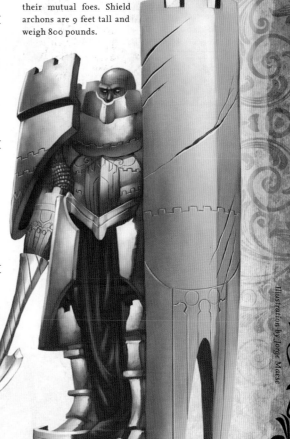

Illustration by Jorge Maese

31

Archon, Star

This powerful humanoid floats in the air on a nimbus of pearly light. He grips a golden starknife in one hand.

STAR ARCHON	CR 19	

XP 204,800

LG Large outsider (archon, extraplanar, good, lawful)

Init +8; **Senses** darkvision 60 ft., low-light vision, *detect evil, true seeing*; Perception +29

Aura aura of courage, aura of menace (DC 27), *magic circle against evil*

DEFENSE

AC 34, touch 11, flat-footed 32 (+9 armor, +1 Dex, +1 dodge, +12 natural, +2 shield, –1 size) (+2 deflection vs. evil)

hp 294 (19d10+190); regeneration 10 (evil weapons and effects)

Fort +21, **Ref** +17, **Will** +15; +4 vs. poison

Defensive Abilities explosive rebirth; DR 10/evil; **Immune** electricity, fire, charm, compulsion, fear, petrification; SR 30

OFFENSE

Speed 40 ft., fly 120 ft. (good); 30 ft. (fly 90 ft.) in armor

Melee +5 *holy starknife* +29/+24/+19/+14 (1d6+12/×3)

Space 10 ft.; **Reach** 10 ft.

Special Attacks smite evil 1/day (+6 attack and AC, +19 damage)

Spell-Like Abilities (CL 19th; concentration +25)

Constant—*detect evil, magic circle against evil, true seeing*

At will—*aid, continual flame, greater teleport* (self plus 50 lbs. of objects only), *message, sunbeam* (DC 23)

1/day—*meteor swarm* (DC 25), *polar ray* (DC 24), *prismatic spray* (DC 23), *sunburst* (DC 24)

Cleric Spells Prepared (CL 19th; concentration +26)

9th—*implosion* (DC 26), *mass heal, miracle*

8th—*dimensional lock, fire storm* (DC 25), *holy aura* (DC 25)

7th—*destruction* (2, DC 24), *holy word* (2, DC 24), *resurrection*

6th—*greater dispel magic, heal, mass cure moderate wounds* (3)

5th—*break enchantment* (2), *breath of life* (2), *flame strike* (DC 22)

4th—*cure critical wounds* (3), *death ward, divine power*

3rd—*cure serious wounds* (3), *dispel magic* (2), *invisibility purge*

2nd—*cure moderate wounds* (4), *eagle's splendor, status*

1st—*cure light wounds* (4), *divine favor, sanctuary* (DC 18)

0—*guidance, resistance, stabilize, virtue*

STATISTICS

Str 24, **Dex** 19, **Con** 31, **Int** 20, **Wis** 24, **Cha** 23

Base Atk +19; **CMB** +27; **CMD** 42

Feats Blind-Fight, Cleave, Combat Reflexes, Dodge, Improved Initiative, Iron Will, Lightning Reflexes, Mobility, Power Attack, Stand Still

Skills Diplomacy +28, Fly +20, Heal +16, Intimidate +28, Knowledge (arcana and engineering) +14, Knowledge (history and nature) +18, Knowledge (religion) +24, Perception +29, Sense Motive +29, Spellcraft +24, Stealth +14, Survival +17

Languages Celestial, Draconic, Infernal; truespeech

ECOLOGY

Environment any (Heaven)

Organization solitary or pair

Treasure double (full plate, heavy steel shield, +5 *holy starknife*)

SPECIAL ABILITIES

Explosive Rebirth (Su) When killed, a star archon explodes in a blinding flash of energy that deals 50 points of damage (half fire, half holy damage) to anything within 100 feet (Reflex DC 29 half). The save DC is Constitution-based. The slain archon reincarnates 1d4 rounds later as an advanced shield archon.

Spells Star archons cast divine spells as 19th-level clerics. They do not gain access to domains or other cleric abilities.

Star archons are the tacticians and strategists of Heaven. Gifted with insight and powerful magic, they spend much of their time steering long-term plans for Heaven's armies and good folk in the world.

ATHACH

This giant's maw contains a pair of dripping tusks, but it is its gangly third arm that makes its appearance truly bizarre.

ATHACH		CR 12	

XP 19,200

CE Huge humanoid (giant)

Init +1; **Senses** darkvision 60 ft., low-light vision; Perception +12

DEFENSE

AC 26, touch 9, flat-footed 25 (+2 armor, +1 Dex, +15 natural, −2 size)

hp 161 (14d8+98)

Fort +16, **Ref** +5, **Will** +7

Resist cold 10

OFFENSE

Speed 50 ft.

Melee 2 slams +19 (1d8+11), bite +19 (2d6+11 plus poison) or heavy mace +19/+14 (3d6+11), bite +17 (2d6+5 plus poison)

Ranged rock +10/+5 (2d6+16)

Space 15 ft.; **Reach** 15 ft.

Special Attacks rock throwing (140 ft.), swift claw

STATISTICS

Str 32, **Dex** 13, **Con** 25, **Int** 7, **Wis** 12, **Cha** 6

Base Atk +10; **CMB** +23; **CMD** 34

Feats Cleave, Improved Iron Will, Iron Will, Lunge, Multiattack, Power Attack, Vital Strike

Skills Acrobatics +1 (+9 jump), Climb +20, Perception +12, Stealth −7

Languages Giant

ECOLOGY

Environment cold or temperate hills

Organization solitary, gang (2–4), or tribe (7–12)

Treasure standard (leather armor, heavy shield, heavy mace, other treasure)

SPECIAL ABILITIES

Poison (Ex) Bite—injury; *save* Fort DC 24; *frequency* 1/round for 6 rounds; *effect* 1d4 Str; *cure* 2 consecutive saves.

Swift Claw (Ex) An athach can attack with its claw as a swift action, even when the creature's movement would normally restrict it to one attack. This attack is made at a +19 bonus and deals 1d10+11 points of damage, regardless of what other attacks are made on the athach's turn.

An athach is a twisted kind of giant, cruel and thuggish. It lives to bring misery, ruin, and terror to weaker creatures. An individual may be nearly any human color, though its arms are often a darker color or even grayish. Its upper fangs are long, extending from its mouth like those of a ferocious beast, and it constantly drools a weakness-inducing poison. A group of athachs is usually a family unit, with gangs typically consisting of a group of siblings and full tribes consisting of parents and young.

Athachs thrive upon the fear of their victims, preferring to play with their prey for some time before indulging their vile and murderous natures. Tales tell of how athachs cut down orchards and ruin crops by night, leaving the ruins to be discovered by innocent villagers at the dawning of the following day. Further tales tell of how athachs desecrate graveyards by exhuming graves and scattering the bones of the dead about. The motivation behind these games seems to be sheer entertainment— some athachs are unusually creative in their antics, displaying ingenuity beyond their normal capacity, as if an athach in the throes of desecration and cruelty were prone to some form of divine inspiration.

An athach is 18 feet tall and weighs 5,000 pounds. Athachs dislike other giants (and other monsters of their size) and either attack or flee from them, depending on whether the odds are in their favor.

Illustrations by Eric Belisle

Attic Whisperer

This thing resembles a gray, emaciated child, with cobwebs and dust for clothes and a fox skull for a head.

ATTIC WHISPERER	CR 4

XP 1,200

NE Small undead

Init +8; **Senses** darkvision 60 ft.; Perception +12

Aura sobs (10 ft.)

DEFENSE

AC 19, touch 16, flat-footed 14 (+4 Dex, +1 dodge, +3 natural, +1 size)

hp 45 (6d8+18)

Fort +5, **Ref** +6, **Will** +8

Immune undead traits

OFFENSE

Speed 20 ft.

Melee bite +9 (1d4–1 plus steal breath), touch +4 melee touch (steal voice)

STATISTICS

Str 9, **Dex** 19, **Con** —, **Int** 14, **Wis** 16, **Cha** 17

Base Atk +4; **CMB** +2; **CMD** 17

Feats Dodge, Improved Initiative, Weapon Finesse

Skills Bluff +9, Climb +8, Knowledge (history) +8, Knowledge (local) +8, Perception +12, Stealth +17

Languages Common (plus any 2d4 from victims)

ECOLOGY

Environment any urban or ruins

Organization solitary, pair, or chorus (3–8)

Treasure incidental

SPECIAL ABILITIES

Aura of Sobs (Su) All of the voices that an attic whisperer steals linger around it in an invisible but audible aura of unnerving childlike whimpers, songs, and sobs. Any living creature that enters this area loses the benefit of all bardic performances affecting it and takes a –1 penalty on all attack rolls, damage rolls, and Will saving throws. The attic whisperer can suppress or reactivate its aura as a free action. This aura is a sonic, mind-affecting effect.

Steal Breath (Su) A creature bit by an attic whisperer must make a DC 16 Will save or become fatigued for 1 hour. A fatigued creature that is bitten is instead exhausted for 1 hour, and an exhausted creature falls asleep for 1 hour if bitten. The sleeper can only be roused by killing the attic whisperer or by using *dispel magic*, *remove curse*, or similar effects. The save DC is Charisma-based.

Steal Voice (Su) Any creature hit by an attic whisperer's touch must make a DC 16 Will save or lose its ability to speak for 1 hour. During that time, the creature cannot talk, cast spells with verbal components, use auditory bardic performances, or use any other ability that requires speech. Once an attic whisperer has stolen a creature's voice, it can perfectly mimic that voice at any time, even after its victim's voice has returned, and while using that voice can speak any languages the victim knew. Those familiar with an individual's voice can make a Sense Motive check opposed by the attic whisperer's Bluff check to realize a mimicked voice is inauthentic. The save DC is Charisma-based.

An attic whisperer spawns as the result of a lonely or neglected child's death. Rather than animating the body of the dead youth, the creature rises from an amalgam of old toys, clothing, dust, and other objects associated with the departed—icons of the child's neglect. The widely varying materials that fuse together to form these creatures lead to attic whisperers with vastly different appearances. Attic whisperers linger in the places where they were formed, typically old homes, orphanages, schools, debtors' prisons, workhouses, and similar places where children might be discarded. When an attic whisperer first forms, it does so without a skull—this does not impact the creature's abilities in any way, but it usually seeks out a small animal's skull as a form of decoration soon after it manifests.

An attic whisperers haunts shadowy, forgotten places like old buildings and dilapidated institutions, places that were once homes to both young children and subtle evils. Hiding in drafty attics and moldy basements, an attic whisperer might lie dormant for decades while the quick go about their lives—often a scant floor away. The coming of a new child, though, rekindles some hope in the creature, its animating spirits motivated by loneliness, and ever seeking comfort and companionship. Once an attic whisperer finds a potential playmate, it does all it can to ensure it will never be lonely again by attempting to lure its friend to it, singing nursery rhymes, leaving trails of old toys, or calling out in the stolen voices of other children.

Destroying an attic whisperer reduces it to its component parts, usually consisting of dusty junk left to molder in the attics of old houses, though a few items, such as china dolls, small lockets, music boxes, precious marbles, fine teacups, sculpted metal soldiers, or the like, may have some value.

Illustration by Andrew Hou

AURUMVORAX

Powerful muscles ripple beneath the golden fur of this small yet fearsome eight-legged beast.

AURUMVORAX	CR 9

XP 6,400

N Small magical beast

Init +8; **Senses** darkvision 60 ft., low-light vision, scent; Perception +13

DEFENSE

AC 23, touch 15, flat-footed 19 (+4 Dex, +8 natural, +1 size)

hp 114 (12d10+48)

Fort +14, **Ref** +12, **Will** +7

Defensive Abilities ferocity; **DR** 10/piercing or slashing; **Immune** poison; **Resist** fire 10

OFFENSE

Speed 30 ft., burrow 10 ft.

Melee bite +18 (1d6+5 plus grab), 4 claws +18 (1d4+5 plus grab)

Special Attacks rake (4 claws +18, 1d4+5)

STATISTICS

Str 21, **Dex** 18, **Con** 18, **Int** 2, **Wis** 13, **Cha** 11

Base Atk +12; **CMB** +16 (+24 grapple); **CMD** 30 (42 vs. trip)

Feats Bleeding Critical, Critical Focus, Great Fortitude, Improved Initiative, Iron Will, Skill Focus (Perception)

Skills Perception +13, Stealth +17

ECOLOGY

Environment temperate plains, hills, or forests

Organization solitary or pair

Treasure standard

SPECIAL ABILITIES

Grab (Ex) An aurumvorax can grab a foe of up to one size category larger than itself (Medium size for most aurumvoraxes). It gains a +8 racial bonus on grapple attempts rather than the normal +4 racial bonus afforded by the grab ability.

Aurumvoraxes are very aggressive creatures, and lead solitary lives except when they mate. Adults typically claim the hunting area within a mile of their warrens, ruthlessly driving away other predators. In addition to fresh meat, aurumvoraxes are fond of gnawing on metals (particularly gold and copper), though whether they do this to sharpen their teeth or because of some nutritional need is unknown. Aurumvorax warrens can stretch for thousands of feet, often winding deep into the earth. The avaricious appetite of aurumvoraxes has earned them the appellation "golden gorger" among dwarves, who have lost more than a few miners to the dangerous beasts.

In battle, an aurumvorax latches onto its victim with its jaws and gouges savage wounds with its claws. It rarely looses its grip before it or its foe is dead. It typically attacks the nearest living creature regardless of size, and ignores any wounds it suffers at the hands of others until its prey is dead.

A typical aurumvorax is only 3 feet long but weighs more than 200 pounds, for it is densely packed with muscle and thick, sturdy bones. Its fur is golden, while its claws are black and sharp. Its weight relative to its body size makes it a poor swimmer, and most dislike crossing water, though they can trundle along the bottom of still or slow water if necessary.

Adult aurumvoraxes are impossible to train, but their offspring are valued for training as guard beasts. A healthy aurumvorax kit can be sold for 5,000 gp or more to a discerning buyer. Female aurumvoraxes rarely give birth to more than one offspring at a time, and are ferociously protective of their young.

An aurumvorax drags its prey back to its lair to consume at its leisure, and its bone-midden often contains valuable belongings from past kills. Uneaten precious metals, discarded gems, and well-chewed metal items can also be found in its warrens. Despite its metallic coloration, an aurumvorax is not vulnerable to attacks that target metal, such as *heat metal* or the touch of a rust monster—in fact, aurumvoraxes easily kill and eat rust monsters, and some dwarf clans use aurumvorax pets to protect their storehouses against them.

Illustration by Eric Belisle

AXIOMITE

As this lithe humanoid moves, its flesh shimmers and wavers, temporarily breaking apart into motes of shimmering light.

AXIOMITE	CR 8

XP 4,800

LN Medium outsider (extraplanar, lawful)

Init +8; **Senses** darkvision 60 ft.; Perception +18

DEFENSE

AC 21, touch 15, flat-footed 16 (+4 Dex, +1 dodge, +6 natural)

hp 85 (10d10+30); regeneration 5 (chaotic or magic)

Fort +6, **Ref** +11, **Will** +14

DR 10/chaotic; **Immune** disease, electricity, mind-affecting effects; **Resist** cold 10, fire 10; **SR** 19

OFFENSE

Speed 30 ft., fly 30 ft. (good)

Melee +1 longsword +16/+11 (1d8+7/19–20)

Spell-Like Abilities (CL 9th; concentration +14)

3/day—*dispel chaos, haste, hold monster* (DC 20), *lightning bolt* (DC 18), empowered *order's wrath* (DC 19), *telekinesis* (DC 20), *true strike*

1/day—*summon inevitable* (level 6, 1 zelekhut, see below), *true seeing*

STATISTICS

Str 21, **Dex** 19, **Con** 16, **Int** 21, **Wis** 20, **Cha** 20

Base Atk +10; **CMB** +15; **CMD** 30

Feats Dodge, Empower Spell-Like Ability (*order's wrath*), Improved Initiative, Iron Will, Mobility

Skills Craft (any one) +18, Diplomacy +18, Fly +8, Knowledge (any three) +15, Knowledge (planes) +18, Perception +18, Sense Motive +18, Spellcraft +18, Stealth +17, Survival +18

Languages Abyssal, Celestial, Common, Draconic, Infernal

SQ crystalline dust form

ECOLOGY

Environment any (lawful plane)

Organization solitary, pair, or team (3–12)

Treasure standard (+1 longsword, other treasure)

SPECIAL ABILITIES

Crystalline Dust Form (Su) An axiomite can shift between its solid body and one made

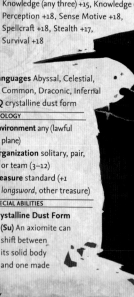

of golden, crystalline dust as a free action once per round. In dust form, the axiomite looks like a shifting mass of glowing mathematical symbols and equations. In this form it can fly and gains the incorporeal quality; it can use spell-like abilities but cannot make physical attacks. In its solid form, an axiomite cannot fly. Both shapes are the axiomite's true form, and it does not revert to a different form if killed. A *true seeing* spell reveals both forms simultaneously.

Summon Inevitable (Sp) Once per day, four axiomites may join hands to summon a single zelekhut inevitable as a full-round action.

Stewards of ancient, colossal cities on lawful planes, axiomites represent the fundamental search for order. According to their own history, the first axiomites sprang from the raw mathematical underpinnings of the cosmos long before the first gods began to stir—they are personifications of a primordial reality made flesh in an attempt to understand itself. New axiomites are formed from souls much like celestials or fiends, with spirits drawn across the planes to one of the axiomites' humming crystal monoliths, emerging later as purified creatures of law and theory.

A particular axiomite may look like any humanoid-shaped creature, though the particular form does not affect its abilities in any way. Beneath this form, all axiomites are the same—clouds of glowing, crystalline dust that constantly swirl and congeal into complex tangles of symbols and equations, making them literally creatures of pure mathematical law.

Axiomite society is broken into three divisions, each with its own duty and purpose. One devotes itself to the construction and maintenance of inevitables, another to the expansion and construction of their capital city, and the third to continuing the exploration and calculation of the laws and constants that underlie all of reality. Their leader is a gestalt mind formed by the greatest individuals of their race, forming when needed and then dispersing into its component axiomites to put the god-mind's plans into action.

AZATA, BRIJIDINE

This beautiful woman has flesh made of lava. She soars through the sky on a trail of fire.

BRIJIDINE	CR 17

XP 102,400
CG Medium outsider (azata, chaotic, earth, extraplanar, fire, good)
Init +5; **Senses** darkvision 60 ft., low-light vision, tremorsense 60 ft.; Perception +26
Aura flaming body, *holy aura*

DEFENSE
AC 32, touch 19, flat-footed 27 (+4 deflection, +5 Dex, +13 natural)
hp 256 (19d10+152)
Fort +22, **Ref** +15, **Will** +21
DR 10/cold iron and evil; **Immune** electricity, fire, petrification; **Resist** cold 10; **SR** 28
Weaknesses vulnerable to cold

OFFENSE
Speed 40 ft., fly 60 ft. (good)
Melee +1 *flaming burst keen longsword* +25/+20/+15/+10 (1d8+8/17–20 plus 1d6 fire and burn)
Ranged lava blast +24 (16d6 fire plus burn and entrap)
Special Attacks entrap (DC 26, instantaneous, hardness 8, hp 30), burn (2d6, DC 26), trample (1d8+7, DC 24)
Spell-Like Abilities (CL 19th; concentration +25)
Constant—*holy aura* (DC 24)
At will—*flaming sphere* (DC 18), *heat metal* (DC 18), *meld into stone* (self only), *soften earth and stone*, *stone shape*
5/day—*cure serious wounds*, *flame strike* (DC 21), *move earth*, *spike stones* (DC 20), *stone tell*, *summon nature's ally V* (earth and fire elementals only), *wall of stone* (DC 22)
3/day—*earthquake*, *fire storm* (DC 23), *heal*, *stoneskin*, *wall of fire*

STATISTICS
Str 20, **Dex** 21, **Con** 24, **Int** 15, **Wis** 18, **Cha** 23
Base Atk +19; **CMB** +24; **CMD** 43
Feats Cleave, Combat Expertise, Combat Reflexes, Critical Focus, Improved Bull Rush, Iron Will, Lunge, Power Attack, Staggering Critical, Toughness
Skills Craft (any one) +24, Escape Artist +27, Fly +9, Heal +26, Knowledge (nature) +24, Knowledge (planes) +24, Perception +26, Perform (oratory) +25, Sense Motive +26
Languages Celestial, Draconic, Ignan, Infernal, Terran; truespeech
SQ heat stone, obsidian blade

ECOLOGY
Environment any (Elysium)
Organization solitary or team (2–5)
Treasure double (no flammable items)

SPECIAL ABILITIES
Flaming Body (Su) A brijidine's body is molten rock covered in dancing flames. Anyone striking a brijidine with a natural weapon or unarmed strike takes 1d6 points of fire damage. A creature that grapples a brijidine or is grappled by one takes 6d6 points of fire damage each round the grapple persists.

Heat Stone (Su) Whenever a brijidine uses her *meld into stone*, *soften earth and stone*, *spike stones*, *stone shape*, or *wall of stone* spell-like abilities, she can have the affected stone radiate intense heat for 1 minute. Any creature within 5 feet of the stone takes 1d6 fire damage per round.

Lava Blast (Su) A brijidine can hurl a glob of lava at a target as a standard action. This attack has a range increment of 30 feet.

Obsidian Blade (Ex) At will as a free action, a brijidine can create a blade of jagged volcanic glass that functions as a +1 *flaming burst keen longsword*. One round after it leaves the brijidine's grasp, the weapon decays into useless powder.

Brijidines are passionate, powerful azatas attuned to the powers of earth and fire. They love basking in volcanoes, writing poetry, tending to sick creatures, and pursuing spicy recipes. The quickest way to befriend a brijidine is to present her with a fireproof copy of an exotic poem or a bag of rare peppers. Though their power is tied to primal destruction, they are quick-witted and love clever wordplay, whether in a sonnet or a dirty limerick.

The brijidine sees fire as a form of purity, a marked difference from its classical association with devastation and destruction. To a brijidine, the existence of hellfire is the rankest blasphemy, and while many azatas look to the demons of the Abyss as their greatest enemies, it is among the devils of Hell that most brijidines find focus for their anger. The fact that devils are immune to fire, the brijidine's greatest strength, frustrates and angers these azatas all the more, forcing them to become far more imaginative and creative in their tactics when facing such foes. A brijidine stands 5-1/2 feet tall and weighs 150 pounds.

Illustration by Jorge Maese

Azata, Lyrakien

This tiny woman has a lithe form with delicate butterfly wings. She is surrounded by sparkling lights and gentle rainbow arcs.

LYRAKIEN	CR 2

XP 600

CG Tiny outsider (azata, chaotic, extraplanar, good)

Init +8; **Senses** darkvision 60 ft., *detect evil, detect magic*, low-light vision; Perception +9

DEFENSE

AC 16, touch 16, flat-footed 12 (+4 Dex, +2 size)

hp 19 (3d10+3)

Fort +2, **Ref** +7, **Will** +6

DR 5/evil; **Immune** electricity, petrification; **Resist** cold 10, fire 10

OFFENSE

Speed 30 ft., fly 80 ft. (perfect)

Melee slam +2 (1d2–3)

Space 2-1/2 ft.; **Reach** 0 ft.

Special Attacks starlight blast

Spell-Like Abilities (CL 3rd; concentration +8)

Constant—*detect evil, detect magic, freedom of movement*

At will—*dancing lights, daze* (DC 15), *summon instrument, ventriloquism* (DC 16)

1/day—*cure light wounds, lesser confusion* (DC 16), *silent image* (DC 16)

1/week—*commune* (6 questions, CL 12th)

STATISTICS

Str 5, **Dex** 19, **Con** 12, **Int** 14, **Wis** 17, **Cha** 20

Base Atk +3; **CMB** +5; **CMD** 12

Feats Agile Maneuvers, Improved Initiative

Skills Acrobatics +10, Bluff +11, Diplomacy +11, Fly +16, Knowledge (any one) +8, Perception +9, Perform (any one) +11, Spellcraft +5, Stealth +18

Languages Celestial, Draconic, Infernal; truespeech

SQ traveler's friend

ECOLOGY

Environment any (Elysium)

Organization solitary, band (2–5), or company (6–24)

Treasure none

SPECIAL ABILITIES

Starlight Blast (Su) As a standard action once every 1d4 rounds, a lyrakien can tap into the divine power of Elysium, unleashing a blast of holy starlight in a 5-foot burst. All creatures in this area take 1d4 points of holy damage, plus 1 point for each step their alignment deviates from chaotic good. For example, a chaotic neutral or neutral good creature would take 1d4+1 points of damage, a neutral creature would take 1d4+2 points of damage, and a lawful evil creature would take 1d4+4 points of damage. A DC 12 Reflex save negates this damage. Chaotic good creatures are unaffected by this ability. The save DC is Constitution-based.

Traveler's Friend (Su) The performances and company of a lyrakien ease the burden of travel. Once per day, a creature may spend a minute listening to a lyrakien's performance—doing so removes the effects of exhaustion and fatigue from the listener.

Lyrakien are divine musicians and messengers, mainly in the employ of deities of travel and natural wonders. They love to explore and visit beautiful places, especially locations with excellent views of rainbows, moonlight, and the stars. Whimsical and joyous, they love contests of song, dance, and knowledge, and keep journeys happy by distracting their companions from weary feet and stale food. Mortals who please them with excellent tales and new songs may be rewarded with elaborate maps, forgotten shortcuts, or rambling directions to hidden locations that hold lost magic.

Lyrakien are light-hearted creatures, but they are very protective of breathtaking natural locations. Often called "glistenwings" by gnomes and halflings, lyrakien are frequently mistaken for fey—while they are generally friendly with true fey, their origin is the plane of Elysium. Like other azatas, they grow restless if they stay in one place too long. A chaotic good 7th-level spellcaster can gain a lyrakien as a familiar if she has the Improved Familiar feat.

Illustration by Jorge Maese

AZER

Heat ripples the air near this squat, brass-skinned humanoid. Its head and shoulders blaze with a mane of fire.

AZER	CR 2

XP 600

LN Medium outsider (extraplanar, fire)

Init +1; **Senses** darkvision 60 ft.; Perception +6

DEFENSE

AC 18, touch 11, flat-footed 17 (+5 armor, +1 Dex, +2 natural)

hp 15 (2d10+4)

Fort +5, **Ref** +1, **Will** +4

Immune fire; **SR** 13

Weaknesses vulnerability to cold

OFFENSE

Speed 30 ft. (20 ft. in armor)

Melee mwk warhammer +4 (1d8+1/×3 plus 1d6 fire)

Ranged light hammer +3 (1d4+1 plus 1d6 fire)

Special Attacks heat (1d6 fire)

STATISTICS

Str 13, **Dex** 12, **Con** 15, **Int** 12, **Wis** 12, **Cha** 9

Base Atk +2; **CMB** +3; **CMD** 14

Feats Power Attack

Skills Acrobatics +0, Appraise +6, Climb +3, Craft (any two) +6, Knowledge (nobility) +6, Perception +6

Languages Common, Ignan

ECOLOGY

Environment any land (Plane of Fire)

Organization solitary, pair, team (3–6), squad (11–20 plus 2 sergeants of 3rd level and 1 leader of 3rd–6th level), or clan (30–100 plus 50% noncombatants plus 1 sergeant of 3rd level per 20 adults, 5 lieutenants of 5th level, and 3 captains of 7th level)

Treasure standard (masterwork scale mail, masterwork warhammer, light hammer, other treasure)

A proud and hardworking race from the Plane of Fire, azers toil in their bronze and brass fortresses, always ready for their long, simmering war against the efreet. Azers live in a society where every member knows his place. Born into a particular duty, usually the trade of his father or mother, an azer continues this task his entire life. A caste system further keeps azer society in line. Nobles, ruling without question, wear decorated brass kilts as their symbol of caste, while merchants and business proprietors wear stout bronze. Copper kilts designate the working class, made up of servants, artisans, and laborers.

Able to channel heat through metal weapons and tools, azers almost never use nonmetallic weapons, and usually engage in close melee rather than using ranged attacks. Azers frequently take prisoners, bringing them back to their fortresses and forcing them to labor for a year and a day.

The legendary City of Brass boasts an azer population over half a million strong. Most of these unfortunate azers live a life of servitude to their efreet masters. Azers subjected to this slavery still perform their duties without question, preferring to wait out their contracts or hoping their masters die or get overthrown. A dedication to order burns strong in this race, to the extent that some enslaved azers act as taskmasters over their own kin. Beyond the City of Brass, azers are free to live their own lives, often in other planar metropolises crafting goods, selling wares, and running taverns.

Azers look strikingly similar to one another to the unfamiliar eye. They are 4 feet tall, but weigh 200 pounds.

Illustration by Mike Corriero

39

BADGER

The squat, waddling badger trudges forth. Thrusting its flattened nose about the ground, it sniffs incessantly.

BADGER	CR 1/2	

XP 200

N Small animal

Init +1; **Senses** low-light vision, scent; Perception +5

DEFENSE

AC 13, touch 12, flat-footed 12 (+1 Dex, +1 natural, +1 size)

hp 9 (1d8+5)

Fort +4, **Ref** +3, **Will** +1

OFFENSE

Speed 30 ft., burrow 10 ft.

Melee bite +1 (1d3), 2 claws +1 (1d2)

Special Attacks blood rage

STATISTICS

Str 10, **Dex** 13, **Con** 15, **Int** 2, **Wis** 12, **Cha** 6

Base Atk +0; **CMB** −1; **CMD** 10 (14 vs. trip)

Feats Toughness

Skills Escape Artist +5, Perception +5; **Racial Modifiers** +4 Escape Artist

ECOLOGY

Environment temperate forests

Organization solitary, pair, or clan (3–6)

Treasure incidental

The squat, burrowing badger is plentiful in most temperate forests. Most species are carnivorous, though some eat a variety of meat, insects, and vegetables. The badger possesses a fierceness and natural tenacity, while its stubby legs and wide, seemingly portly stature belie the creature's actual strength and speed.

A typical badger has dark brownish-gray fur highlighted with white markings, such as bands or striped masks about the eyes. These markings are distinct and vary by species. While generally friendly, if threatened or otherwise provoked, badgers can become fierce combatants. Once engaged with an opponent, they typically fight until slain. In combat, they fight with their sharp, needle-like teeth and long, curved claws, which they otherwise use for digging.

BADGER, DIRE

A tremendous badger snarls and scrapes its wicked, shovel-like claws. Stocky muscles ripple beneath its streaked and shaggy fur.

BADGER, DIRE	CR 2	

XP 600

N Medium animal

Init +6; **Senses** low-light vision, scent; Perception +10

DEFENSE

AC 14, touch 12, flat-footed 12 (+2 Dex, +2 natural)

hp 22 (3d8+9)

Fort +6, **Ref** +5, **Will** +2

Defensive Abilities ferocity

OFFENSE

Speed 30 ft., burrow 10 ft.

Melee bite +4 (1d4+2), 2 claws +4 (1d3+2)

Special Attacks blood rage

STATISTICS

Str 14, **Dex** 15, **Con** 17, **Int** 2, **Wis** 12, **Cha** 9

Base Atk +2; **CMB** +4; **CMD** 16 (20 vs. trip)

Feats Improved Initiative, Skill Focus (Perception)

Skills Escape Artist +6, Perception +10; **Racial Modifiers** +4 Escape Artist

ECOLOGY

Environment temperate forests

Organization solitary, pair, or clan (3–5)

Treasure incidental

A relentless predator, the violent and territorial dire badger hunts frequently, killing and devouring a variety of easy prey such as rabbits, deer, and occasionally livestock. These creatures are unafraid of attacking creatures larger than they are, drawing upon an almost legendary tenacity that has won them honor and respect among many races, particularly forest-dwelling gnomes.

Dire badgers reside in deep burrows and warrens dug with their monstrous claws—but unlike typical badgers, a dire badger's claws are capable of tunneling through solid rock. Dire badgers possess little patience for disturbances or interruptions. Utterly fearless creatures, when confronted they attack brutally, and if injured, they violently erupt into a killing frenzy.

Dire badgers stand 4 feet tall at the shoulder, and weigh 500 pounds.

Illustration by Christopher Bardett

BANSHEE

This beautiful, ghostly elven woman glides through the air, her long hair flowing around a face knotted into a mask of rage.

BANSHEE	CR 13

XP 25,600

CE Medium undead (incorporeal)

Init +15; **Senses** darkvision 60 ft., hear heartbeat; Perception +31

DEFENSE

AC 26, touch 26, flat-footed 14 (+4 deflection, +11 Dex, +1 dodge)

hp 161 (19d8+76)

Fort +10, **Ref** +19, **Will** +18

Defensive Abilities incorporeal; **Immune** undead traits

Weaknesses sunlight powerlessness

OFFENSE

Speed fly 60 ft. (perfect)

Melee incorporeal touch +26 (14d6 negative energy plus terror)

Special Attacks wail

STATISTICS

Str —, **Dex** 32, **Con** —, **Int** 5, **Wis** 20, **Cha** 19

Base Atk +14; **CMB** +25; **CMD** 40

Feats Alertness, Combat Reflexes, Dodge, Improved Initiative, Iron Will, Lightning Reflexes, Mobility, Step Up, Weapon Focus (touch), Wind Stance

Skills Fly +19, Perception +31, Sense Motive +7

Languages Common, Elven

ECOLOGY

Environment any

Organization solitary

Treasure standard

SPECIAL ABILITIES

Hear Heartbeat (Ex) A banshee can sense the beating hearts of living creatures within 60 feet, as if it had the blindsight ability.

Terror (Su) A creature damaged by the banshee's touch attack must make a DC 23 Will save. Failure means that the victim cowers in fear for 1d3 rounds. If a target is protected against fear by a dispellable effect (such as *heroes' feast* or *mind blank*), the banshee's touch attempts to dispel one such effect with *greater dispel magic* (CL 14th). Negative energy damage caused by a banshee's touch can only harm the living; it cannot heal undead. This is a mind-affecting fear effect. The save DC is Charisma-based.

Wail (Su) Once per minute, a banshee may wail as a full-round action. The wail lasts until the beginning of her next turn. All creatures within 40 feet of the banshee when she begins her wail, as well as all creatures that end their turn within that radius, must make a DC 23 Fortitude save. (This save is only required once per wail.) Creatures under the effects of a fear effect take a –4 penalty on this save. Creatures that make their save are sickened for 1d6 rounds. Those that fail take 140 points of damage (as if affected by a CL 14 *wail of the banshee*). If a wailing banshee is damaged during a wail, she must make a Will save (DC 15 + damage taken) to maintain the wail; otherwise it ends. This is a sonic death effect. Banshee wails are supernaturally powerful, and penetrate the effect of any spell of 3rd level or lower that creates silence. The save DC is Charisma-based.

A banshee is the enraged spirit of an elven woman who either betrayed those she loved or was herself betrayed. Maddened by grief, a banshee visits her vengeance on all living creatures—innocent or guilty—with her fearsome touch and deadly wails.

Illustration by Ben Wootten

BAT, MOBAT

This bat has a wingspan the length of two humans, over-sized ears, and a squat, upturned snout with rows of needle-like teeth.

MOBAT	CR 3
XP 800	

N Large magical beast
Init +2; **Senses** blindsense 120 ft., low-light vision; Perception +6

DEFENSE

AC 19, touch 13, flat-footed 13 (+2 Dex, +4 natural, –1 size)
hp 34 (4d10+12)
Fort +7, **Ref** +6, **Will** +2

OFFENSE

Speed 20 ft., fly 40 ft. (good)
Melee bite +6 (2d6+4)
Space 10 ft.; **Reach** 5 ft.
Special Attacks screech

STATISTICS

Str 17, **Dex** 15, **Con** 16, **Int** 6,
   Wis 13, **Cha** 6
Base Atk +4;
   CMB +8;
   CMD 26
Feats Flyby
   Attack, Skill
   Focus (Stealth)
Skills Fly +8, Perception
+6 (+10 when using
blindsense), Stealth +5; **Racial
Modifiers** +4 Perception when using blindsense
Languages Undercommon (cannot speak)

ECOLOGY

Environment temperate or warm forests, hills, or underground
Organization solitary or colony (2–8)
Treasure incidental

SPECIAL ABILITIES

Screech (Su) Once per day as a standard action, a mobat can produce an ear-splitting screech that stuns non-mobats in a 20-foot-radius burst. All creatures within the area must make a DC 15 Fortitude save or be staggered for 1d3 rounds. Other mobats and urdefhans (see page 276) are immune to this effect. This is a sonic mind-affecting effect. The save DC is Constitution-based.

Mobats are magical giant bats with wolfish grins and immense wingspans. Survivors of a lost era, they are rarely seen beyond the dark forests and deep caves they haunt. Although mobats are omnivores, they vastly prefer the flavor of fresh meat over that of other prey.

Mobats' fur varies in coloration, from deep auburn to almost black, and their skin is black. A mobat's wingspan is 15 feet across, and it weighs 250 pounds.

BAT, SKAVELING

This monstrously sized, undead bat has mottled, decayed flesh and eyes that smolder with an unholy green glow.

SKAVELING	CR 5
XP 1,600	

CE Large undead
Init +7; **Senses** blindsense 120 ft.; Perception +14

DEFENSE

AC 19, touch 13, flat-footed 15 (+3 Dex, +6 natural, –1 size)
hp 58 (9d8+18)
Fort +5, **Ref** +6, **Will** +8
Immune undead traits

OFFENSE

Speed 20 ft., fly 40 ft. (good)
Melee bite +10 (2d8+7 plus disease and paralysis)
Space 10 ft.; **Reach** 5 ft.
Special Attacks screech, paralysis (1d4+1 rounds, DC 16)

STATISTICS

Str 21, **Dex** 17, **Con** —, **Int** 8,
   Wis 15, **Cha** 14
Base Atk +6; **CMB** +12; **CMD** 26
Feats Dodge, Flyby Attack, Improved Initiative, Mobility, Skill Focus (Stealth)
Skills Fly +13, Perception +14 (+18 when using blindsense), Stealth +14; **Racial Modifiers** +4 Perception when using blindsense
Languages Undercommon

ECOLOGY

Environment any underground
Organization solitary or colony (2–8)
Treasure incidental

SPECIAL ABILITIES

Disease (Su) Ghoul Fever: Bite—injury; *save* Fort DC 16; *onset* 1 day; *frequency* 1/day; *effect* 1d3 Con and 1d3 Dex damage; *cure* 2 consecutive saves. The save DC is Charisma-based. A humanoid who dies of ghoul fever rises as a ghoul at the next midnight (*Pathfinder RPG Bestiary* 146).
Screech (Su) Once per day as a standard action, a skaveling can screech as a mobat, save that those who are affected are stunned for 1d3 rounds unless they make a DC 16 Fortitude save. The save DC is Charisma-based.

Known in some circles as ghoul bats, skavelings are the hideous result of necromantic manipulation by urdefhans, who create them from mobats specially raised on diets of fungus and humanoid flesh. Upon reaching maturity, urdefhans ritually slay the bats using necrotic poisons, then raise the corpses to serve as mounts and guardians.

Illustrations by Dean Spencer

BEE, GIANT

Striking yellow and black markings and a coat of bristling hairs cover this immense bee. Its stinger is the size of a dagger blade.

GIANT BEE	CR 1

XP 400

N Medium vermin

Init +2; **Senses** darkvision 60 ft.; Perception +1

DEFENSE

AC 13, touch 12, flat-footed 11 (+2 Dex, +1 natural)

hp 16 (3d8+3)

Fort +4, **Ref** +3, **Will** +2

Immune mind-affecting effects

Weaknesses vulnerable to smoke

OFFENSE

Speed 20 ft., fly 60 ft. (good)

Melee sting +2 (1d4 plus poison)

STATISTICS

Str 11, **Dex** 14, **Con** 13, **Int** —, **Wis** 12, **Cha** 9

Base Atk +2; **CMB** +2; **CMD** 14 (22 vs. trip)

Skills Fly +6

ECOLOGY

Environment temperate or warm plains

Organization solitary, group (2–5), or nest (6–19)

Treasure incidental

SPECIAL ABILITIES

Poison (Ex) Sting—injury; *save* Fort DC 12; *frequency* 1/round for 4 rounds; *effect* 1d2 Str; *cure* 1 save.

Vulnerable to Smoke (Ex) Smoke from particularly smoky fires or effects (such as that created by a *pyrotechnics* spell) causes a giant bee to become nauseated if it fails a DC 14 Fortitude save. This condition persists as long as the giant bee remains in the smoke, plus 1d4 rounds.

Like their smaller cousins, giant bees fill their ecological niche by playing matchmaker for a vast array of flowering plant life. As a giant bee feeds on plant nectars, clumps of pollen attach to the coarse hairs covering its body and legs.

Giant bees grow to approximately 5 feet in length, with a similar wingspan. These creatures weigh 60 pounds and live in their adult form for nearly 10 years. Giant bees' stingers are not barbed like those of their diminutive counterparts, so these creatures can sting foes repeatedly and do not die after one sting.

Giant Bumblebee (CR 2)

These bulky and aggressive giant bees have the advanced creature simple template. Their venom is deadly, and deals Constitution damage rather than Strength damage.

BEE, GIANT QUEEN

This giant bee is as large as a horse and unusually fat, with light brown stripes on her body.

GIANT QUEEN BEE	CR 5

XP 1,600

N Large vermin

Init +0; **Senses** darkvision 60 ft.; Perception +1

DEFENSE

AC 17, touch 9, flat-footed 17 (+8 natural, –1 size)

hp 59 (7d8+28)

Fort +9, **Ref** +2, **Will** +3

Immune mind-affecting effects

Weaknesses vulnerable to smoke

OFFENSE

Speed 20 ft., fly 60 ft. (good)

Melee sting +8 (1d8+6 plus poison)

Space 10 ft.; **Reach** 5 ft.

STATISTICS

Str 19, **Dex** 11, **Con** 18, **Int** —, **Wis** 12, **Cha** 13

Base Atk +5; **CMB** +10; **CMD** 20 (28 vs. trip)

Skills Fly +2

ECOLOGY

Environment temperate or warm plains

Organization solitary or colony (1 queen and 3–18 giant bees)

Treasure incidental (royal jelly)

SPECIAL ABILITIES

Poison (Ex) Sting—injury; *save* Fort DC 17; *frequency* 1/round for 4 rounds; *effect* 1d2 Con; *cure* 2 consecutive saves.

Bulbous and robust in comparison to others of the same species, giant queen bees are immense, fertile females, easily identified by their larger size and lighter stripes. They grow to 12 feet in length and weigh 140 pounds.

Royal Jelly

When a hive of bees needs a new queen to replace one that has died, they feed specially selected larvae royal jelly to trigger the larvae's transformation into new queens. The first queen to hatch then kills any other new queens.

Royal jelly has remarkable effects on other creatures if eaten. A pound of royal jelly provides enough nourishment for a full day, and grants a +4 resistance bonus on all saving throws against disease for the next 24 hours. If a creature sleeps enough to heal damage within 24 hours of eating at least a pound of royal jelly, it heals twice the hit points and ability damage as it otherwise would. A typical bee hive contains 2d6 pounds of royal jelly—a single pound sells for 100 gp.

Beetle, Goliath Stag

This massive beetle is the size of a small house. Its immense, horn-like mandibles clash with a hungry fervor.

GOLIATH STAG BEETLE	CR 8

XP 4,800
N Huge vermin
Init +0; **Senses** darkvision 60 ft.; Perception +0

DEFENSE

AC 21, touch 8, flat-footed 21 (+13 natural, −2 size)
hp 104 (11d8+55)
Fort +12, **Ref** +3, **Will** +3
Immune mind-affecting effects

OFFENSE

Speed 30 ft., fly 30 ft. (poor)
Melee bite +17 (3d8+16)
Space 15 ft.; **Reach** 10 ft.
Special Attacks trample (3d8+16, DC 26)

STATISTICS

Str 32, **Dex** 10, **Con** 21, **Int** —, **Wis** 10, **Cha** 4
Base Atk +8; **CMB** +21; **CMD** 31 (39 vs. trip)
Skills Fly −8

ECOLOGY

Environment warm forests or plains
Organization solitary, pair, or herd (3–8)
Treasure none

Making its home in tropical and subtropical forests across the globe, the goliath beetle is among the largest species of giant beetle. While its diminutive cousins are primarily herbivores, the goliath stag beetle is carnivorous, hunting herd animals, humanoids, and even giants with ease. They typically use their trample attack against creatures smaller than themselves, returning after this punishing assault to pick off anything that's still moving with swift and deadly bites.

A goliath stag beetle is 25 feet long and weighs 8,000 pounds.

Beetle, Slicer

This squat but nevertheless large beetle moves with a swift scuttling motion. Its mandibles appear to be remarkably sharp.

SLICER BEETLE	CR 4

XP 1,200
N Large vermin
Init +0; **Senses** darkvision 60 ft.; Perception +0

DEFENSE

AC 17, touch 9, flat-footed 17 (+8 natural, −1 size)
hp 39 (6d8+12)
Fort +7, **Ref** +2, **Will** +2
Immune mind-affecting effects

OFFENSE

Speed 40 ft., fly 20 ft. (poor)
Melee bite +8 (2d6+7/19–20)
Space 10 ft.; **Reach** 5 ft.
Special Attacks crippling bite

STATISTICS

Str 21, **Dex** 11, **Con** 15, **Int** —, **Wis** 10, **Cha** 6
Base Atk +4; **CMB** +10; **CMD** 20 (28 vs. trip)
Skills Fly −6
SQ compression

ECOLOGY

Environment temperate forests
Organization solitary or cluster (2–5)
Treasure none

SPECIAL ABILITIES

Crippling Bite (Ex) A slicer beetle's bite attack threatens a critical hit on a roll of 19–20. If a slicer beetle scores a critical hit on a target, its mandibles cut deep, resulting in a wound that causes 1d6 bleed and leaving its foe staggered for 1d3 rounds from the tremendous pain dealt.

The slicer beetle sports specialized mouthparts that scissor apart flesh for easier consumption. Each side of its horizontally closing mandibles fits into the other with barely a hair's breadth to spare. These creatures prefer to dwell in compact caves or warrens. A typical slicer beetle measures 10 feet long and weighs 800 pounds.

Illustration by Dean Spencer

BELKER

Dull, red eyes, grasping claws, and leathery wings give a demonic aspect to this creature's smoky form.

BELKER	CR 6

XP 2,400

NE Large outsider (air, elemental, evil)

Init +5; **Senses** darkvision 60 ft.; Perception +11

DEFENSE

AC 20, touch 14, flat-footed 15 (+5 Dex, +6 natural, −1 size)

hp 68 (8d10+24)

Fort +9, **Ref** +11, **Will** +2

DR 5/—

OFFENSE

Speed 30 ft., fly 50 ft. (perfect)

Melee bite +12 (1d6+2), 2 claws +12 (1d6+2), 2 wings +10 (1d6+1)

Space 10 ft.; **Reach** 10 ft.

Special Attacks smoke claws

STATISTICS

Str 14, **Dex** 21, **Con** 17, **Int** 6, **Wis** 11, **Cha** 10

Base Atk +8; **CMB** +11; **CMD** 26 (can't be tripped)

Feats Combat Reflexes, Flyby Attack, Multiattack, Weapon Finesse

Skills Acrobatics +16, Fly +22, Perception +11, Stealth +16;
    Racial Modifiers +4 Stealth

Languages Auran

SQ smoke form

ECOLOGY

Environment any (Plane of Air)

Organization solitary, pair, or clutch (3–4)

Treasure incidental

SPECIAL ABILITIES

Smoke Claws (Ex) A belker using its smoke form ability can enter a target's square as a standard action that does not provoke attacks of opportunity. The target must make a DC 17 Fortitude save or inhale part of the creature. Smoke inside the victim solidifies into a claw and attacks the target from within, dealing 3d4 points of damage per round as a swift action. If the target moves, the belker may automatically move with the target (this movement does not count toward the belker's movement and does not provoke attacks of opportunity against the belker). Each round, the target can attempt another DC 17 Fortitude to cough out the belker's smoke, which ends the smoke claws attack and forces the belker into an adjacent square. Creatures that do not need to breathe are immune to this attack. The save DC is Constitution-based.

Smoke Form (Su) A belker can switch from its normal form to one of pure smoke or back again a swift action. It can spend up to 20 rounds per day in smoke form. In smoke form, the belker acts as if under the effects of a *gaseous form* spell, except that it retains its natural fly speed of 50 feet (perfect).

Belkers are hateful elemental air creatures resembling fiends made of smoke. Xenophobic in the extreme, they see most non-elemental creatures as threats, and stalk and kill any such intruders in their territory. Among their elemental kin, they especially hate djinn and jann. They tolerate air mephits, dust mephits, steam mephits, air elementals, and fire elementals, but given the choice, prefer the company of their own kind.

Belkers create no permanent lairs, but do claim and defend large territories from other living things, particularly areas ravaged by frequent storms, volcanic eruptions, hot springs, or forest fires. Some sages believe the belkers worship these dangerous natural phenomena; others speculate the elementals somehow feed on the unusual air from these sites. Still other scholars theorize that the reclusive beasts require the energy from these phenomena to feed or reproduce.

Illustration by Mike Corriero

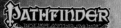

BLINDHEIM

The size of a short, stocky humanoid with webbed feet and claws, this frog-like creature has glowing white eyes.

BLINDHEIM	CR 2

XP 600

N Small magical beast

Init +2; **Senses** darkvision 60 ft., low-light vision; **Perception** +9

DEFENSE

AC 16, touch 14, flat-footed 13 (+2 Dex, +1 dodge, +2 natural, +1 size)

hp 22 (3d10+6)

Fort +5, **Ref** +5, **Will** +2

Immune blindness

OFFENSE

Speed 30 ft., climb 20 ft., swim 20 ft.

Melee bite +5 (1d4+1), 2 claws +5 (1d3+1)

Special Attacks blinding gaze

STATISTICS

Str 13, **Dex** 15, **Con** 15, **Int** 2, **Wis** 12, **Cha** 6

Base Atk +3; **CMB** +3; **CMD** 16

Feats Dodge, Skill Focus (Perception)

Skills Acrobatics +6 (+10 jumping), Perception +9, Swim +9; **Racial Modifiers** +4 Acrobatics when jumping

ECOLOGY

Environment any underground

Organization solitary, pair, or family (3–5)

Treasure incidental

SPECIAL ABILITIES

Blinding Gaze (Ex) A blindheim's eyes emit bright light to a range of 30 feet. Any creature within the area must make a DC 13 Fortitude save or be blinded for 1 hour. Blindheims can see normally in the light generated by their eyes, which illuminates a 30-foot spread with bright light. Creatures with light blindness or light sensitivity take the normal penalties within 30 feet of a blindheim that is using its blinding gaze. A blindheim can activate or suppress this ability as a free action. This save DC is Constitution-based.

Blindheims are grotesque, frog-like creatures that dwell beneath the surface, subsisting on meals of fungi, rodents, and other underground creatures. They live in the darkest, dampest regions of cavernous sprawls, particularly enjoying underground bogs, lakes, rivers, and swamps. Although not aquatic, blindheims are excellent swimmers. They prefer to latch onto branches or rock outcroppings, where they maintain the high ground while in pursuit of food. They use the light from their eyes to attract prey, but go dark when larger creatures approach. A blindheim uses its blinding gaze to disorient both prey and possible threats, then deactivates its gaze to scuttle away in the dark if the threat is too great. In very large caverns inhabited by blindheims, distant areas often flicker from brightly lit to absolutely dark as the creatures feed and flee. Though of animal-level intelligence, blindheims are cunning enough to coordinate their hunting tactics with others of their kind, using one creature to act as a lookout and make hit-and-run attacks with its gaze until its fellows can arrive to help finish off the prey.

Blindheims can convey simple information through gestures and flashes of their lights, and tend to be rather silent in combat, adding an eerie element to battles with them. They cannot be taught to perform humanoid-appropriate labors and thus make poor slaves, though the duergar and drow sometimes use them as bait or distractions when raiding. Other races have been known to train these creatures as mobile light sources when going on long underground expeditions.

Stout and thick-skinned, a blindheim is just under 4 feet in height and weighs 150 pounds. A blindheim gives birth to small litters of three or four young. Though gestation can last up to a full year, it only takes about 4 years for a blindheim to mature and become self-reliant, at which point the creatures generally form broods that stick together, only striking out on their own if their brethren have perished. Blindheims can live for up to 25 years.

Illustrations by Peter Lazarski

BLINK DOG

This sleek canine has a coarse, tawny coat, pointed ears, and pale eyes. A faint blue nimbus seems to dance upon its fur.

BLINK DOG CR 2

XP 600

LG Medium magical beast

Init +2; **Senses** darkvision 60 ft., low-light vision, scent;
Perception +7

DEFENSE

AC 14, touch 12, flat-footed 12 (+2 Dex, +2 natural)

hp 22 (3d10+6)

Fort +5, **Ref** +5, **Will** +4

OFFENSE

Speed 40 ft.

Melee bite +4 (1d6+1)

Spell-Like Abilities (CL 7th; concentration +7)
Constant—*blink*
At will—quickened *dimension door* (self only)

STATISTICS

Str 12, **Dex** 15, **Con** 14, **Int** 10, **Wis** 13, **Cha** 11

Base Atk +3; **CMB** +4; **CMD** 16 (20 vs. trip)

Feats Combat Reflexes, Iron Will

Skills Perception +7, Stealth +7, Survival +2 (+6 scent tracking)

Languages Sylvan

ECOLOGY

Environment temperate plains or forests

Organization solitary, pair, or pack (3–14)

Treasure incidental

Though they resemble sleek, long-eared canines, blink dogs are as smart as humans. As social creatures, blink dogs travel in large packs, roaming forests and plains, running off evil creatures, and hunting for phase spiders—one of their natural enemies. Despite their intelligence and friendly natures, blink dogs tend to avoid humanoids, keeping their packs either hidden or frequently on the move. This shyness doesn't keep the blink dogs from helping out when needed, however, and they have been known to come to the rescue of a prairie village in their territory. Packs are typically led by an older, experienced male or female, called an alpha.

Blink dogs are fiercely loyal, defending their own pack or creatures they befriend to the death, and maintaining oaths handed down from litter to litter. Honor is paramount to blink dogs, and different packs often have unique traditions (such as whether a pack's alpha is male or female, or an oath to always protect and aid a particular humanoid race like elves or halflings) in addition to those shared by most blink dogs. Blink dogs have a great interest in the stars and movements of celestial bodies. Through their myths and folklore, blink dogs have names for constellations, and through this zodiac they note the seasons, births under auspicious stars, and omens from unusual stellar conjunctions. Blink dog names often contain a reference to a specific constellation under which the dog was born.

Blink dogs stand nearly 3 feet at the shoulder and weigh upward of 180 pounds. They can live up to 75 years. They use their abilities to quickly surround prey, and make use of flanking to deal with especially dangerous opponents—particularly creatures like phase spiders.

Blink Dog Sages

A pack's alpha selects the wisest and most intelligent member of the pack to serve as its sage. This blink dog often has sorcerer levels (typically with the celestial or destined bloodline) and is charged with maintaining the long-running oral histories of the pack, which extend back for centuries and link the packs together. A blink dog sage also decides when a pup is old enough to join his first hunt, performs birth and burial rites, and counsels the alpha on the meaning of omens or upon tactical matters involving interactions with neighboring races and creatures. In some packs, the sage is the alpha's mate, while in others the sage is always a gray-muzzled elder hound beyond breeding age.

BODAK

The flesh of this emaciated creature appears charred or dried, and its empty eye sockets seep trails of smoke.

BODAK	CR 8

XP 4,800

CE Medium undead (extraplanar)

Init +6; **Senses** darkvision 60 ft.; Perception +14

DEFENSE

AC 21, touch 13, flat-footed 18 (+2 Dex, +1 dodge, +8 natural)

hp 85 (10d8+40)

Fort +6, **Ref** +5, **Will** +8

DR 10/cold iron; **Immune** electricity, undead traits; **Resist** acid 10, fire 10

Weaknesses vulnerability to sunlight

OFFENSE

Speed 20 ft.

Melee 2 slams +9 (1d8+1)

Special Attacks death gaze

STATISTICS

Str 13, **Dex** 15, **Con** —, **Int** 6, **Wis** 13, **Cha** 16

Base Atk +7; **CMB** +8; **CMD** 21

Feats Dodge, Improved Initiative, Mobility, Toughness, Weapon Focus (slam)

Skills Intimidate +11, Perception +14, Stealth +10

Languages Common

ECOLOGY

Environment any land (evil Outer Plane)

Organization solitary, pair, or gang (3–4)

Treasure none

SPECIAL ABILITIES

Death Gaze (Su) 1d4 negative levels, 30 feet; Fortitude DC 18 negates. The save DC is Charisma-based. A humanoid slain by a bodak's death gaze rises as a bodak 24 hours later. This is a death effect.

Vulnerability to Sunlight (Ex) Bodaks loathe sunlight, for its merest touch burns their impure flesh. Each round of exposure to direct sunlight deals 2d6 points of damage to a bodak.

When mortal humanoids find themselves exposed to profound, supernatural evil, a horrific, occult transformation can strip them of their souls and damn them to the tortured existence of a bodak. Changed into a twisted, misanthropic husk, a bodak wanders the endless tracts of evil-aligned planes, periodically stumbling into other realms by passing through portals or otherwise being conjured elsewhere. Possessing only fragmented memories of its former existence, the bodak is driven by profound emptiness, sorrowful longing, and vengeful hatred of all life.

A bodak's appearance is profoundly disturbing. Its flesh looks dried, taut, and desiccated, though it possesses a strange, otherworldly sheen. Its body is disproportionate and distinctly androgynous. Hairless and with only vague hints of facial structure, the bodak's eyes are deep set in their sockets and constantly weep foul-smelling smoky vapors. A planes-wise traveler who recognizes its shape knows to flee, for most travelers can outrun the relatively slow bodak.

Bodaks vehemently despise all living creatures and immediately seek to destroy any they encounter. A bodak retains the ability to speak one language it knew in life (typically Common), but it rarely engages in conversation, instead spitting out an incomprehensible stream of vile accusations, curses, and threats. On occasion, a bodak might wield weapons, but most rely primarily upon the effects of their deadly gaze.

Bodaks are rarely encountered outside of the Abyss. As they are slow-witted, powerful evil creatures such as liches and nabasu demons sometimes use bodaks as thralls, assassins, or guardians. Bodaks encountered on the Material Plane exude extreme malevolence when forced to confront the realization of their abhorrent transformations. So great is their desire to inflict their fate upon others that many attempt to drag off the bodies of their slain victims and guard them until they rise as undead.

A 20th-level spellcaster can use *create greater undead* to create a bodak, but only if the spell is cast while the spellcaster is located on one of the evil outer planes (traditionally the Abyss).

Illustration by Kelly Harris

BROWNIE

Knee-high to a human, this large-headed creature has an almost manically friendly look on its expressive face.

BROWNIE	CR 1	

XP 400

N Tiny fey

Init +8; **Senses** low-light vision; Perception +8

DEFENSE

AC 17, touch 17, flat-footed 12 (+4 Dex, +1 dodge, +2 size)

hp 4 (1d6+1)

Fort +1, **Ref** +6, **Will** +4; +2 vs. illusions

DR 5/cold iron; **SR** 12

OFFENSE

Speed 20 ft.

Melee short sword +6 (1d2–2/19–20)

Space 2–1/2 ft.; **Reach** 0 ft.

Spell-Like Abilities (CL 7th; concentration +10)

At will—*dancing lights, mending, prestidigitation*

1/day—*lesser confusion* (DC 14), *dimension door* (self only), *mirror image, ventriloquism* (DC 14)

STATISTICS

Str 7, **Dex** 18, **Con** 12, **Int** 14, **Wis** 15, **Cha** 17

Base Atk +0; **CMB** +2; **CMD** 11

Feats Dodge, Improved Initiative[B], Weapon Finesse[B]

Skills Acrobatics +8 (+4 jump), Bluff +7, Craft (any one) +6, Escape Artist +8, Handle Animal +4, Perception +8, Sense Motive +6, Stealth +16 (+20 in forest); **Racial Modifiers** +2 Perception, +4 Stealth in forests

Languages Common, Elven, Gnome, Sylvan

ECOLOGY

Environment temperate forests or plains

Organization solitary, gang (2–5), or band (7–12)

Treasure standard

Brownies make their homes in the trunks of hollow trees, small earthy burrows, and even under porches and within the crawlspaces of farmhouses. Often attired in clothes that appear to be made of plants or leaves, brownies wear belts lined with pouches and tools. Whatever language they choose to speak is often riddled with odd pronunciations and colloquialisms. Brownies stand barely 2 feet tall and weigh 20 pounds.

When facing danger, brownies rarely engage in combat, preferring instead to confound and confuse their attackers in order to buy enough time for escape. Content with honest toil and the love of their kin, brownies maintain a pacifist nature, only harassing creatures to run them off or punish them for an insult. Despite this nature, all brownies carry a blade. They refer to their swords with a hint of disgust, and jokingly call their blades the "final trick," using them only in the direst of consequences.

Honest to a fault, brownies take freely, but always repay their debt through work or leave something behind as an offering. They may eat an apple from a farmer's orchard, but will harvest the entire tree as repayment. A brownie might eat an entire pie left on a windowsill, only to straighten up the kitchen or wash the dishes. A brownie can share a home with a family for years and years while avoiding detection. A family that is aware of a brownie usually finds this a beneficial relationship and leaves dishes of milk, pieces of fruit, trinkets, and sometimes even wine as gifts. In exchange, the brownie keeps the home clean, mends clothes, repairs tools, and shoos away vermin and small predators. Bragging about having a brownie in the house is the best way to lose one. Brownies distrust foxes and fear wolves, and tend to avoid farms with dogs.

A 5th-level neutral spellcaster with the Improved Familiar feat can gain a brownie as a familiar.

Illustrations by Branko Bistrovic

49

BUNYIP

A disturbing combination of shark and seal, this brown-furred creature has a wide mouth filled with razor-sharp teeth.

BUNYIP	CR 3

XP 800

N Medium magical beast (aquatic)

Init +3; **Senses** darkvision 60 ft., low-light vision, keen scent 180 ft.; Perception +8

DEFENSE

AC 15, touch 13, flat-footed 12 (+3 Dex, +2 natural)

hp 32 (5d10+5)

Fort +5, **Ref** +7, **Will** +1

OFFENSE

Speed 10 ft., swim 50 ft.

Melee bite +7 (1d8+1/19–20 plus bleed)

Special Attacks bleed (1d6), blood frenzy, roar

STATISTICS

Str 13, **Dex** 16, **Con** 13, **Int** 2, **Wis** 11, **Cha** 7

Base Atk +5; **CMB** +6; **CMD** 19

Feats Improved Critical (bite)^B, Skill Focus (Perception), Skill Focus (Stealth), Weapon Focus (bite)

Skills Escape Artist +5, Perception +8, Stealth +10, Swim +9

SQ amphibious

ECOLOGY

Environment any aquatic

Organization solitary or pair

Treasure none

SPECIAL ABILITIES

Blood Rage (Ex) A bunyip's blood rage ability activates whenever it detects blood in the water using its keen scent, but otherwise functions as the universal monster rule of the same name.

Roar (Su) A bunyip's roar is supernaturally loud and horrifying. When a bunyip roars (a standard action the creature can perform at will), all hearing creatures with 4 or fewer HD within a 100-foot spread must succeed on a DC 13 Will save or become panicked for 2d4 rounds. Whether or not the save is successful, creatures in the area are immune to the roar of that bunyip for 24 hours. This is a sonic, mind-affecting fear effect. The save DC is Constitution-based.

The bunyip is a fierce and avid hunter, possessing a primal ruthlessness that seems almost evil in its rapacity. A bunyip typically inhabits large freshwater inlets or sheltered coastal sea caves where food is plentiful—the bunyip is equally at home in fresh or salt water. It prefers feeding on animals of Small size or larger, though it isn't averse to eating humanoids when presented the opportunity. Bunyips are quite territorial, and readily attack when intruders threaten their hunting grounds. Bunyips mate annually, during the late spring. During this period, bunyips become even more aggressive. After mating, couples split, with the female wandering off to find a place to birth a small litter of four to six pups. Females watch their pups for a few days, until they become independent enough for the mothers to move on.

Reports of bunyip sightings come from every end of the map. Though the accuracy of all such reports remains doubtful, enough reliable accounts exist to confirm their widespread adaptability. The species thrives in numerous ecological climes, from frigid polar fjords to idyllic tropical lagoons. The bunyip is not a deep-sea creature, and even avoids larger freshwater lakes, as it prefers to lurk near shorelines where its favorite food is more common.

While bunyips vary in appearance, all possess similar basic physical structures. The bunyip's head exhibits strong seal-like features, save for its shark-like jaws. Its upper torso is thick and muscular, with long, fin-like limbs. Some species even have a single, shark-like dorsal fin. The remaining portion of the body extends into a long tail. Those with fur usually only grow a short coat on the upper body in shades of pale gray, brown, or black.

Carnivorous Blob

Rolling and twitching like a massive wad of translucent ooze, this crimson blob reaches out amorphous pseudopods in all directions.

CARNIVOROUS BLOB CR 13

XP 25,600

N Colossal ooze

Init +0; **Senses** blindsight 60 ft., tremorsense 120 ft.; Perception –5

DEFENSE

AC 2, touch 2, flat-footed 2 (–8 size)

hp 184 (16d8+112)

Fort +12, **Ref** +5, **Will** +0

Defensive Abilities reactive strike, split (sonic or slashing, 32 hp); **DR** 10/–; **Immune** acid, ooze traits; **Resist** electricity 30, fire 30

Weaknesses vulnerable to cold

OFFENSE

Speed 20 ft., climb 20 ft., swim 20 ft.

Melee slam +17 (8d6+19 plus 1d4 Con drain and grab)

Space 30 ft.; **Reach** 30 ft.

Special Attacks absorb flesh, constrict (8d6+19 plus 1d4 Con drain)

STATISTICS

Str 36, **Dex** 11, **Con** 24, **Int** —, **Wis** 1, **Cha** 1

Base Atk +12; **CMB** +33 (+37 grapple); **CMD** 43 (can't be tripped)

Skills Climb +21, Swim +21

ECOLOGY

Environment any

Organization solitary

Treasure none

SPECIAL ABILITIES

Absorb Flesh (Ex) A carnivorous blob cannot eat plant matter or inorganic matter, but it devours living flesh with a voracious speed by dealing Constitution drain on creatures it slams or constricts. Whenever the blob deals Constitution drain in this manner, it heals 10 hit points for each point of Constitution it drains. Excess hit points above its normal maximum are gained as temporary hit points. As soon as a carnivorous blob has at least 50 temporary hit points, it loses those temporary hit points and splits as an immediate action.

Reactive Strike (Ex) Whenever a carnivorous blob takes damage, it reflexively lashes out with a slam attack. This ability effectively grants the carnivorous blob an attack of opportunity against any adjacent foe that deals it damage. These attacks of opportunity do not count

against the normal limit the creature can make in a round. Attacks that deal sonic or slashing damage do not trigger a reactive strike—rather, they cause the creature to split. Whenever a carnivorous blob takes cold damage, the creature cannot use its reactive strike ability until after it takes its next action in combat.

Vulnerable to Cold (Ex) A carnivorous blob takes half again as much damage (+50%) from cold attacks.

While sages debate whether the first carnivorous blobs were created by a mad wizard, formed in foul fleshwarping vats in some sinister city, or traveled to this world trapped in the core of a meteor, there is one thing they all agree on—none wish to get close enough to study the monstrosity.

Carnivorous blobs move like a typical ooze, rolling out blobs of its fleshy material in haphazard directions, and pulling its bulk across the ground, up walls, and even through the water. If a carnivorous blob goes for more than 24 hours without a source of food, it drops into a sort of hibernation, resembling nothing so much as a pool of gelatinous blood. The creature springs to life quickly and hungrily as soon as any living prey comes within range of its senses.

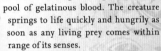

CATOBLEPAS

This ugly creature has a boar-like head with short antlers, a thick bullish body covered in spines, and cloven hooves on its stumpy legs.

CATOBLEPAS	CR 12	

XP 19,200

N Large magical beast

Init –1; **Senses** darkvision 60 ft., low-light vision; Perception +25

Aura stench (30 ft., DC 23, 10 rounds)

DEFENSE

AC 27, touch 8, flat-footed 27 (–1 Dex, +19 natural, –1 size)

hp 161 (14d10+84)

Fort +15, **Ref** +8, **Will** +8

SR 23

OFFENSE

Speed 40 ft., swim 20 ft.

Melee bite +18 (3d6+5), gore +18 (2d8+5/19–20), 2 hooves +16 (1d8+2)

Space 15 ft.; **Reach** 15 ft.

Special Attacks breath weapon (60-ft. cone, poison, Fortitude DC 23, usable every 1d4 rounds), trample (4d6+7, DC 22)

STATISTICS

Str 20, **Dex** 8, **Con** 22, **Int** 5, **Wis** 15, **Cha** 10

Base Atk +14; **CMB** +20; **CMD** 29 (33 vs. trip)

Feats Diehard, Endurance, Improved Critical (gore), Improved Iron Will, Iron Will, Multiattack, Skill Focus (Perception)

Skills Perception +25, Swim +13

Languages Aklo

ECOLOGY

Environment any swamps

Organization solitary, pair, or herd (3–6)

Treasure incidental

SPECIAL ABILITIES

Poison Breath (Ex) A catoblepas's horrid, stinking breath is 60-foot cone of poison gas. Breath—contact; *save* Fort DC 23; *frequency* 1/ round for 6 rounds; *effect* 1d6 Con damage; *cure* 3 consecutive saves. The save DC is Constitution-based.

The catoblepas is an aggressive beast at the best of times, willing to knock down trees, fences, even small houses to eat whatever it finds interesting, be that meal plant or animal or human being. Though it prefers swamps, the catoblepas has been known

to forage in plains and forests for short periods before returning to the buoyant support of water and mud. Few creatures linger near a catoblepas's feeding ground because of the monster's bad temper and poisonous breath, and only rot-loving predators such as oozes or exceptionally large otyughs have any interest in hunting them.

A catoblepas' primary motivation is hunting and exerting its dominance over lesser creatures in its territory. Easily detected by its foul odor, the creature tolerates the presence of wild animals, humanoid tribes, and even predators that it can bully as long as these things flee or act submissive when the poisonous brute lumbers into view. The catoblepas is known to engage in physical battles with other Large swamp creatures such as crocodiles or even froghemoths. Some humanoid tribes claim to know techniques to domesticate a catoblepas for use as a guard animal, but the monster's intractable nature and not insignificant intelligence almost certainly means magic is involved, as the creature has little need for alliances and can wipe out entire villages with its breath. Some have been known to use their breath underwater, creating a churning cloud of bubbles that kills fish in the area and starves out other creatures.

A catoblepas's sense of smell is blunted by its own ungodly stench, and it can't easily recognize rival odors such as skunk musk (though this provides the beast no immunity to odor-based effects from other creatures).

A catoblepas is 15 feet long and weighs 2,200 pounds.

Illustration by Peter Lazarski

CENTIPEDE, GIANT WHIPTAIL

An elephantine centipede scurries about, its double tail lashing angrily behind it.

GIANT WHIPTAIL CENTIPEDE CR 3

XP 800

N Huge vermin

Init +0; **Senses** darkvision 60 ft.; Perception +4

DEFENSE

AC 15, touch 8, flat-footed 14 (+7 natural, −2 size)

hp 38 (4d8+20)

Fort +9, **Ref** +1, **Will** +1

Immune mind-affecting effects

OFFENSE

Speed 40 ft., climb 40 ft.

Melee bite +8 (2d6+7 plus poison), tail slap +3 (1d3 nonlethal plus trip)

Space 15 ft.; **Reach** 15 ft. (20 ft. with tail slap)

STATISTICS

Str 25, **Dex** 11, **Con** 21, **Int** —, **Wis** 10, **Cha** 2

Base Atk +3; **CMB** +12; **CMD** 22 (can't be tripped)

Skills Climb +15, Perception +4, Stealth +0; **Racial Modifiers** +4 Perception, +8 Stealth

SQ compression

ECOLOGY

Environment temperate or warm forests or underground

Organization solitary, pair, or colony (3–6)

Treasure none

SPECIAL ABILITIES

Poison (Ex) Bite—injury; *save* Fort DC 17; *frequency* 1/round for 6 rounds; *effect* 1d4 Dex; *cure* 1 save. The save DC is Constitution-based.

Tail Slap (Ex) A giant whiptail centipede's tail slap deals nonlethal damage and gains no bonus from its Strength score on damage dealt.

Whiptail centipedes are carrion eaters, though corpses large enough to satiate them are a rarity. Corpses of Huge or larger creatures left to rot often attract whiptail centipedes, who viciously defend their bounty against any who would intrude upon their lairs.

CENTIPEDE, TITAN

A writhing, seemingly endless segmented monstrosity crawls forth, its great mandibles clacking as it spies prey.

TITAN CENTIPEDE CR 9

XP 6,400

N Colossal vermin

Init +0; **Senses** darkvision 60 ft.; Perception +4

DEFENSE

AC 21, touch 2, flat-footed 21 (+19 natural, −8 size)

hp 135 (10d8+90)

Fort +16, **Ref** +3, **Will** +3

Immune mind-affecting effects

OFFENSE

Speed 60 ft., climb 60 ft.

Melee bite +15 (4d6+24 plus poison)

Space 30 ft.; **Reach** 30 ft.

Special Attacks trample (6d6+24, DC 31)

STATISTICS

Str 43, **Dex** 11, **Con** 29, **Int** —, **Wis** 10, **Cha** 2

Base Atk +7; **CMB** +31; **CMD** 41 (can't be tripped)

Skills Climb +24, Perception +4, Stealth −8; **Racial Modifiers** +4 Perception, +8 Stealth

SQ compression

ECOLOGY

Environment temperate or warm forests or underground

Organization solitary, pair, or colony (3–6)

Treasure none

SPECIAL ABILITIES

Poison (Ex) Bite—injury; *save* Fort DC 24; *frequency* 1/round for 6 rounds; *effect* 1d6 Dex; *cure* 2 consecutive saves.

The largest of their kind, titan centipedes are thankfully also the rarest. They attack other living creatures fearlessly, and require constant sustenance to nourish their vast bulk. Humanoids are in most danger from titan centipedes when mounted rather than afoot—a good-sized horse makes a much more satisfying meal to the centipede than a few bites of human. Titan centipedes are solitary by nature and because of the demands of their appetite, though when food is plentiful, multiple centipedes sometimes lurk in the same area.

Illustration by KyuShik Shin

CHAOS BEAST

This thing is a horrid mass of barbed tentacles, glaring eyes, and gnashing teeth, twisting upon itself and reshaping into new forms.

CHAOS BEAST	CR 7

XP 3,200

CN Medium outsider (chaotic, extraplanar)

Init +6; **Senses** darkvision 60 ft.; Perception +13

DEFENSE

AC 20, touch 13, flat-footed 17 (+2 Dex, +1 dodge, +7 natural)

hp 85 (9d10+36)

Fort +9, **Ref** +8, **Will** +4

Defensive Abilities amorphous, resistant to transformation; **SR** 18

OFFENSE

Speed 20 ft.

Melee 4 claws +13 (1d6+3 plus corporeal instability)

STATISTICS

Str 17, **Dex** 15, **Con** 16, **Int** 10, **Wis** 12, **Cha** 11

Base Atk +9; **CMB** +12; **CMD** 25 (can't be tripped)

Feats Dodge, Improved Initiative, Mobility, Toughness, Weapon Focus (claw)

Skills Acrobatics +14 (+10 jump), Climb +15, Escape Artist +14, Perception +13, Stealth +14, Swim +15

ECOLOGY

Environment any

Organization solitary or invasion (2–5)

Treasure none

SPECIAL ABILITIES

Corporeal Instability (Su) Claw—contact (curse); *save* Fort DC 17; *effect* amorphous body and 1 Wisdom drain per round (see below); *cure* 3 consecutive saves. The save DC is Con-based.

A creature cursed with an amorphous body becomes a spongy, shapeless mass. Unless the victim manages to control the effect (see below), its shape constantly melts, flows, writhes, and boils. An affected creature is unable to hold or use any item. Clothing, armor, helmets, and rings become useless. Large items worn or carried—armor, backpacks, even shirts—hamper more than help, reducing the victim's Dexterity score by 4. Speed is reduced to 10 feet or one-quarter normal, whichever is less. The victim gains the amorphous quality, but cannot cast spells or use magic items, and it attacks blindly, unable to distinguish friend from foe (–4 penalty on attack rolls and a 50% miss chance, regardless of the attack roll).

A victim can temporarily regain its own shape by taking a standard action to attempt a DC 15 Will save (this check DC does not vary for a chaos beast with different Hit Dice or ability scores). A success reestablishes the creature's normal form for 1 minute. Spells that change the victim's shape (such as *alter self*, *beast shape*, *elemental body*, and *polymorph*) do not remove the curse, but hold the creature in a stable form (which might not be its own form, depending

on the spell) and prevent additional Wisdom drain for the duration of the spell; *shapechange* and *stoneskin* have a similar effect. The victim takes 1 point of Wisdom drain from mental shock every round that it ends its turn in an amorphous shape—upon being drained to 1 Wisdom, further Wisdom drain ceases and the amorphous body effect is permanent until removed via magic (no further number of saving throws can cure the condition at this time).

Resistant to Transformation (Ex) Transmutation effects, such as polymorphing or petrification, force a chaos beast into a new shape, but at the start of its next turn, it immediately returns to its normal form as a free action.

A chaos beast's form changes without any goal or purpose. Though at any particular second a chaos beast may appear to have dozens of limbs, whether claws, tentacles, stingers, and so on, the lightning-quick shifts of its body mean most of these are gone before it has a chance to use them, and its attacks are always treated as claws regardless of the creature's appearance.

CHARDA

Armored in dense, bony plates, this four-armed creature drools wretched strings of black bile from its fanged maw.

CHARDA	CR 7

XP 3,200

CN Small monstrous humanoid (aquatic)

Init +2; **Senses** darkvision 120 ft.; Perception +13

DEFENSE

AC 20, touch 13, flat-footed 18 (+2 Dex, +7 natural, +1 size)

hp 85 (9d10+36)

Fort +7, **Ref** +10, **Will** +7

Defensive Abilities ferocity; **Immune** cold, poison

OFFENSE

Speed 20 ft., swim 60 ft.

Melee bite +13 (1d6+3 plus 1d6 cold), 4 claws +14 (1d4+3)

Special Attacks black bile

STATISTICS

Str 16, **Dex** 15, **Con** 19, **Int** 11, **Wis** 12, **Cha** 8

Base Atk +9; **CMB** +11 (+19 bull rush and trip); **CMD** 23

Feats Combat Expertise[B], Improved Bull Rush, Improved Trip, Lightning Reflexes, Power Attack, Weapon Focus (claw)

Skills Intimidate +6, Knowledge (religion) +4, Perception +13, Stealth +18, Survival +10, Swim +18

Languages Aklo, Undercommon

SQ amphibious, cold vigor, overwhelming

ECOLOGY

Environment cold aquatic or underground

Organization solitary, pair, gang (3–5), or tribe (6–14)

Treasure standard

SPECIAL ABILITIES

Black Bile (Su) A charda's body seethes with freezing black bile. Its supernaturally cold, black bile is the source of the additional cold damage when a charda bites a creature. As a standard action, a charda can expel its full store of bile as a breath weapon that can take the form of a 60-foot line or a 30-foot cone. All creatures in this area take 8d6 points of cold damage (DC 18 Reflex half). A charda can use this breath weapon once every 1d4 rounds—while its black bile is recharging, it does not deal additional cold damage with its bite. The save DC is Constitution-based.

Cold Vigor (Ex) When a charda is in a cold environment, it becomes more animated and gains a +1 racial bonus on attack rolls and weapon damage rolls.

Overwhelming (Ex) A charda gains a +8 racial bonus on bull rush and trip attacks.

In the darkest depths of the earth, in strange frozen rivers and subterranean lakes of frigid black water dwell the mysterious and ferocious chardas. These xenophobic humanoids rarely venture far from their domains, settling in small tribes and building rocky huts underwater or muddy domes along the subterranean shore.

A typical charda stands just under 4 feet tall but weighs 250 pounds. Chardas reproduce by laying eggs in small clutches of two to four, which they bury among rocks offshore. Females fiercely protect their own clutches, but show no predisposition toward protecting the clutches of other chardas, even those within their tribe.

Devoutly religious, chardas prefer to worship gods of war or cold. They hunt in small packs composed of both males and females. Hunting and slaying help determine an individual's power within the group. Chardas often engage in infanticide and cannibalism. While they patrol their territories in groups, they fight individually with little strategy or structure. Chardas do not assist each other with their kills, as they perceive aid as a weakness and a dishonor to both themselves and their foes.

CHARYBDIS

An immense spiny monster, its back plated in chitin and its belly in thick folds of blubber, rises hungrily from the center of a whirlpool.

CHARYBDIS	CR 13

XP 25,600

CN Gargantuan aberration (aquatic)

Init +3; **Senses** blindsight 60 ft., darkvision 120 ft.; Perception +23

DEFENSE

AC 28, touch 5, flat-footed 28 (–1 Dex, +23 natural, –4 size)

hp 184 (16d8+112); fast healing 10

Fort +12, **Ref** +6, **Will** +14

Immune acid; **Resist** cold 20

OFFENSE

Speed 20 ft., swim 50 ft.

Melee bite +20 (2d8+12/19–20 plus grab), 2 claws +20 (2d6+12)

Space 20 ft.; **Reach** 20 ft.

Special Attacks fast swallow, rending claws, swallow whole (6d6 bludgeoning damage plus 6d6 acid damage, AC 21, hp 18), vortex

STATISTICS

Str 34, **Dex** 9, **Con** 25, **Int** 4, **Wis** 19, **Cha** 6

Base Atk +12; **CMB** +28 (+32 grapple); **CMD** 37 (can't be tripped)

Feats Awesome Blow, Improved Bull Rush, Improved Critical (bite), Improved Initiative, Improved Vital Strike, Lightning Reflexes, Power Attack, Vital Strike

Skills Perception +23, Swim +20

Languages Aquan

ECOLOGY

Environment any oceans

Organization solitary

Treasure standard

SPECIAL ABILITIES

Rending Claws (Ex) A charybdis's claws are particularly devastating when used against objects, and ignore the first 10 points of an object's hardness rating.

Vortex (Su) A charybdis can generate a whirlpool as a standard action at will. This ability functions identically to the whirlwind special attack (see the Universal Monster Rules in Appendix 3), but the whirlpool can only form underwater and cannot leave the water. It's a DC 25 Reflex save to avoid being caught by the charybdis's vortex. The vortex itself is 20 feet across and 120 feet deep, and deals 2d6+12 points of damage per round. The save DC is Constitution-based.

Sailors tell many tales of the creatures of the deep, from the terrible kraken to the beautiful mermaid. Yet few are stranger or more feared than the dread charybdis, for it exists to capture ships, crack them open like nuts, and feast on the doomed sailors within. So legendary are these violent attacks that many sailors have come to view the charybdis not as a species of aberrant life, but as the vengeful personification of an angry sea god.

In truth, the charybdis is not the sending of an angry deity, but in fact little more than a monstrous predator capable of churning even the calmest of seas into a whirling maelstrom. The charybdis uses this vortex ability not only to capture prey like sharks or small whales, but also to entrap ships on the ocean surface above. The monster's claws are particularly well suited to puncturing the hulls of ships, and most charybdises have learned that a single large merchant vessel contains enough sailors to make a perfectly sized meal. Often, a charybdis settles in along a well-known shipping route near the shoreline or amid an archipelago of islands where ships are forced along relatively narrow lanes between rocky isles—such locations allow the charybdis to lie in wait and increases the chance of its prey being unable to circumvent its vortex.

A charybdis is 60 feet long and weighs 26,000 pounds.

CHUPACABRA

This lizard-like creature stalks forward upon two muscular legs, a mane of spikes running down its scaly back.

CHUPACABRA	CR 3

XP 800

N Small magical beast

Init +7; **Senses** darkvision 60 ft., low-light vision; Perception +6

DEFENSE

AC 16, touch 14, flat-footed 13 (+3 Dex, +2 natural, +1 size)

hp 30 (4d10+8)

Fort +6, **Ref** +7, **Will** +3

OFFENSE

Speed 30 ft.

Melee bite +6 (1d4+1 plus grab), 2 claws +6 (1d3+1)

Special Attacks chupar, pounce

STATISTICS

Str 13, **Dex** 16, **Con** 14, **Int** 3, **Wis** 15, **Cha** 6

Base Atk +4; **CMB** +4 (+8 grapple); **CMD** 17

Feats Combat Reflexes, Improved Initiative

Skills Acrobatics +7 (+11 jumping), Perception +6, Stealth +16;
  Racial Modifiers +4 Acrobatics when jumping, +4 Stealth
  (+8 in undergrowth or rocky areas)

Languages Aklo (cannot speak)

ECOLOGY

Environment warm hills or plains

Organization solitary, pair, or gang (3–7)

Treasure none

SPECIAL ABILITIES

Chupar (Ex) A chupacabra that pins an opponent or maintains a pin can suck blood from that opponent as a free action once per round, dealing 1 point of Constitution damage. Upon successfully draining blood, the chupacabra is invigorated, gaining a significant boost in speed for 10 rounds similar to the *haste* spell. The invigorated chupacabra can still drain blood—and in so doing increase the length of its invigoration—but it gains no additional effects.

These notorious predators have an undeniable thirst for blood. Chupacabras prefer to prey upon the weak and slow, often watching potential prey from hiding for long periods before attacking. Spry and stealthy, they prefer to keep to areas of high grass and protective rock, their slightly reflective scales allowing them to blend in well with such surroundings.

With a preference for lone travelers and farm animals (particularly goats), chupacabras leave little evidence of their presence apart from the grisly blood-drained husks of their meals, often leading locals to believe a reckless vampire lives in the area.

A typical chupacabra measures nearly 5-1/2 feet from muzzle to tail tip and stands just under 4 feet tall. Slightly built and light of bone, most weigh close to a hundred pounds. They mate rarely and only during the hottest months, with the females each producing a single egg that hatches into a tiny, dehydrated creature. The mother typically leaves helpless prey in her cave so the hatchling can immediately feed.

Although chupacabras are typically solitary, in bountiful areas small gangs of the beasts can form. These groups work well together, becoming bold enough to attack larger groups of animals and more dangerous prey. Stories of chupacabras attacking travelers or laying siege to farmhouses typically stem from the hunting practices of such gangs.

It is not unusual for older chupacabras to grow to Medium size. These larger specimens tend to be leaders of chupacabra gangs, or, more commonly, loners capable of tormenting entire villages on their own.

Some chupacabras are mutants with large reptilian wings, and have been known to carry off goats and children. A flying chupacabra has a fly speed of 60 feet (average), which increases to 90 feet (average) when invigorated from drinking blood. A winged chupacabra is the same CR as the normal variety.

Illustration by Eric Lofgren

COCKROACH, GIANT

A dog-sized cockroach skitters forth, greedily clicking its filth-slicked mandibles.

GIANT COCKROACH	CR 1/2	

XP 200

N Small vermin

Init +1; **Senses** darkvision 60 ft., tremorsense 60 ft.; Perception +4

DEFENSE

AC 14, touch 12, flat-footed 13 (+1 Dex, +2 natural, +1 size)

hp 8 (1d8+4)

Fort +6, **Ref** +1, **Will** +0

Weaknesses light sensitivity

OFFENSE

Speed 30 ft., climb 30 ft., fly 40 ft. (poor)

Melee bite +1 (1d4)

STATISTICS

Str 11, **Dex** 12, **Con** 19, **Int** —, **Wis** 11, **Cha** 2

Base Atk +0; **CMB** –1; **CMD** 10

Feats Diehard[B], Endurance[B]

Skills Climb +8, Fly –1, Perception +4, Stealth +9; **Racial Modifiers** +4 Perception, +4 Stealth

SQ hold breath

ECOLOGY

Environment any land

Organization solitary or intrusion (2–20)

Treasure none

Species	CR	Size	HD
Giant hissing cockroach	1	Medium	2
Venomroach	3	Large	3
Spitting cockroach	6	Huge	6
Sawback cockroach	9	Gargantuan	8
Dragonroach	12	Colossal	10

Much like their smaller kin, giant cockroaches are extremely adaptive and exist in any place they can find a ready source of food. Giant cockroaches are not normally very violent, but readily attack if threatened or if food becomes scarce.

A number of species of giant cockroach exist, as summarized on the table above. Most of these variants have additional abilities, such as poison stings.

COCKROACH SWARM

Like a pestilent black tide, a ravenous horde of thousands of tiny, clacking cockroaches washes over everything in its path.

COCKROACH SWARM	CR 2	

XP 600

N Diminutive vermin (swarm)

Init +2; **Senses** darkvision 60 ft., tremorsense 30 ft.; Perception +4

DEFENSE

AC 16, touch 16, flat-footed 14 (+2 Dex, +4 size)

hp 26 (4d8+8)

Fort +6, **Ref** +3, **Will** +1

Defensive Abilities swarm traits; **Immune** weapon damage

Weaknesses light sensitivity, swarm traits

OFFENSE

Speed 20 ft., climb 20 ft., fly 30 ft. (poor)

Melee swarm (1d6)

Space 10 ft.; **Reach** 0 ft.

Special Attacks distraction (DC 14)

STATISTICS

Str 1, **Dex** 15, **Con** 14, **Int** —, **Wis** 10, **Cha** 2

Base Atk +3; **CMB** —; **CMD** —

Skills Climb +10, Fly +4, Perception +4, Stealth +14; **Racial Modifiers** +4 Perception

SQ hold breath

ECOLOGY

Environment any temperate, warm, or urban

Organization solitary, pair, or intrusion (3–20 swarms)

Treasure none

Swarms of flesh-eating cockroaches are extremely virulent pests. Normally carnivorous scavengers, these vermin quickly transform into aggressive hunters when amassed in great numbers, actively seeking out territory and food and gravitating to locations that readily provide both, such as dumps, graveyards, sewers, swamps, and other foul areas filled with rotting waste. Although a flesh-eating cockroach swarm prefers to feed on rot and carrion, these ravenous creatures do not balk at attacking living creatures as large as an elephant if given a chance.

Illustration by Kevin Yan

CRAWLING HAND

With a jolt, this severed hand springs to life, its fingers propelling it forth at great speed like a deformed spider.

CRAWLING HAND	CR 1/2	

XP 200

NE Diminutive undead

Init +0; **Senses** blindsense 30 ft., darkvision 60 ft.;
Perception +4

DEFENSE

AC 14, touch 14, flat-footed 14 (+4 size)

hp 9 (1d8+5)

Fort +2, **Ref** +0, **Will** +2

Immune undead traits

OFFENSE

Speed 40 ft., climb 40 ft.

Melee claw +5 (1d1+1 plus grab)

Space 1 ft.; **Reach** 0 ft.

Special Attack mark quarry, strangle

STATISTICS

Str 13, **Dex** 11, **Con** —, **Int** 2,
Wis 11, **Cha** 14

Base Atk +0; **CMB** −4 (+0
grapple); **CMD** 7

Feats Toughness

Skills Climb +9, Perception +4,
Stealth +12, Survival +4; **Racial
Modifiers** +4 Survival

Languages Common (can't speak)

ECOLOGY

Environment any land

Organization solitary or gang (2–5)

Treasure none

SPECIAL ABILITIES

Grab (Ex) A crawling hand can use its grab ability on a creature
of up to Medium size.

Some say the origins of the crawling hand lie in the experiments of demented necromancers contracted to construct tiny assassins. Other tales tell of gruesome prosthetics sparked to life by evil magic, which then developed primitive sentience and vengefully strangled their hosts. Regardless, the crawling hand is an efficient killing tool.

When not commanded to kill, the crawling hand remains still and can be handled and transported safely. Typically, owners carry them about in small, velvet-lined boxes. Crawling hands can also be placed as guardians and programmed with contingency commands, such as to hunt down and slay an individual who performs a specific task like violating a shrine, opening a warded door, or breaking the seal of a casket.

CRAWLING HAND, GIANT

A giant rotting hand rocks unsteadily, propped upon thick, stubby fingers. Its pale, necrotic flesh pulses and crawls with sickly boils.

GIANT CRAWLING HAND	CR 5	

XP 1,600

NE Medium undead

Init +2; **Senses** blindsense 30 ft., darkvision 60 ft.; Perception +7

DEFENSE

AC 19, touch 13, flat-footed 16 (+2 Dex,
+1 dodge, +6 natural)

hp 52 (7d8+21)

Fort +4, **Ref** +6, **Will** +6

Immune undead traits

OFFENSE

Speed 30 ft.

Melee claw +11 (1d6+7 plus grab)

Special Attacks mark quarry,
pus burst

STATISTICS

Str 21, **Dex** 15, **Con** —, **Int** 2,
Wis 13, **Cha** 14

Base Atk +5; **CMB** +10 (+14
grapple); **CMD** 23

Feats Dodge, Lightning
Reflexes, Toughness,
Weapon Focus (claw)

Skills Acrobatics +3,
Perception +7, Stealth +12;
Racial Modifiers +4 Stealth

Languages Common (can't speak)

ECOLOGY

Environment any land or underground

Organization solitary or gang (2–5)

Treasure none

SPECIAL ABILITIES

Mark Quarry (Su) A crawling hand is assigned a quarry by anointing the hand with a drop of the intended quarry's blood. If the hand has no current quarry, it automatically gains the next creature it damages as its quarry. Once attuned to a target, it becomes aware of the target's location as if under the effect of a continuous *locate creature* spell. The hand gains a +1 bonus on all attack rolls, damage rolls, and skill checks made to seek out and destroy the marked quarry. The mark quarry ability lasts until the quarry or the hand is slain.

Pus Burst (Su) When damaged by a piercing or slashing melee weapon, a spray of vile pus strikes the attacker unless the attacker makes a DC 15 Reflex save. Weapons that provide reach protect the attacker completely from a pus burst. Creatures struck by pus become nauseated for 1d3 rounds and take 2d6 points of negative energy damage. The save DC is Charisma-based.

CRYPT THING

Shreds of leathery flesh cling to this skeletal figure's body, while twin motes of fiery light glow deep in its eye sockets.

CRYPT THING	CR 5

XP 1,600

NE Medium undead

Init +6; **Senses** darkvision 60 ft., low-light vision; Perception +15

Aura fear (10 ft., frightened for 1d4 rounds, Will DC 16 negates)

DEFENSE

AC 19, touch 13, flat-footed 16 (+2 Dex, +1 dodge, +6 natural)

hp 52 (8d8+16)

Fort +4, **Ref** +6, **Will** +8

Defensive Abilities channel resistance +2; **DR** 10/bludgeoning or magic; **Immune** undead traits

OFFENSE

Speed 30 ft.

Melee 2 claws +10 (1d8+4)

Special Attacks teleporting burst

Spell-Like Abilities (CL 8th; concentration +10)
  3/day—quickened *dimension door*

STATISTICS

Str 19, **Dex** 14, **Con** —, **Int** 13, **Wis** 14, **Cha** 15

Base Atk +6; **CMB** +10; **CMD** 23

Feats Alertness, Dodge, Improved Initiative, Lightning Reflexes

Skills Bluff +6, Intimidate +13, Knowledge (arcana) +6, Knowledge (dungeoneering) +5, Knowledge (history) +3, Perception +15, Sense Motive +15, Stealth +9

Languages Common

ECOLOGY

Environment any underground

Organization solitary

Treasure standard

SPECIAL ABILITIES

Teleporting Burst (Su) Once per day, a crypt thing can teleport all creatures within 50 feet of it to randomly determined locations. The crypt thing can only affect creatures of which it is aware and to which it has line of sight. A successful DC 16 Will save negates this effect. An affected creature is teleported in a random direction (roll 1d8, with 1 indicating north and the other numbers indicating compass going clockwise) and a random distance (1d10 × 100 feet) away from the crypt thing; determine each creature's direction randomly. A teleported creature arrives in the closest open space to the determined destination, but must appear on a solid surface capable of supporting its weight. If there is no appropriate destination in that direction, the creature does not teleport at all. The save DC is Charisma-based.

Crypt things are undead creatures found guarding tombs, graves, and crypts. Necromancers and other spellcasters create them to guard such areas, and the crypt things never leave their appointed lairs, even to pursue enemies. Their warded area may be a single room or passage, an entire grave complex, or even a city-sized necropolis. Though naturally solitary, multiple crypt things may guard a common area, often in conjunction with constructs or other undead.

A crypt thing only initiates combat if it is attacked or if the object or crypt it is guarding is touched or entered. Until this condition is met, a crypt thing is content to remain motionless—it may even answer questions or otherwise interact with visitors if its master has directed it to do so. Rumors exist of variant crypt things that do not teleport their foes, but instead paralyze opponents and turn them invisible, leaving victims to helplessly watch their allies being torn apart by the angry guardian.

CREATION

A 15th-level spellcaster can create a crypt thing using *create undead*. The spell also requires the creator or an assistant to be able to cast *teleport*, *greater teleport*, or *word of recall* (or provide this magic from a scroll or other source).

CRYSMAL

An animated cluster of translucent crystals shaped disturbingly like a gemstone scorpion scuttles into an aggressive stance.

CRYSMAL	CR 3

XP 800

N Small outsider (earth, elemental)

Init +2; **Senses** darkvision 60 ft., crystal sense; Perception +11

DEFENSE

AC 17, touch 13, flat-footed 15 (+2 Dex, +4 natural, +1 size)

hp 26 (4d10+4)

Fort +7, **Ref** +8, **Will** +2

DR 5/bludgeoning; **Immune** cold, fire; **Resist** electricity 10

OFFENSE

Speed 30 ft., burrow 20 ft.

Melee sting +7 (2d6+3)

Special Attacks shard spike +7 (3d6, range increment 60 ft.)

Spell-Like Abilities (CL 4th; concentration +6)

At will—*detect magic, ghost sound* (DC 12), *mage hand, silent image* (DC 13)

3/day—*dimension door, sanctuary* (DC 13), *touch of idiocy* (DC 14)

STATISTICS

Str 15, **Dex** 14, **Con** 13, **Int** 6, **Wis** 13, **Cha** 14

Base Atk +4; **CMB** +5; **CMD** 17 (29 vs. trip)

Feats Great Fortitude[B], Lightning Reflexes, Skill Focus (Perception)

Skills Acrobatics +9, Climb +9, Perception +11, Stealth +13 (+15 in rocky areas); **Racial Modifiers** +2 Stealth in rocky areas

Languages Terran

ECOLOGY

Environment any underground (Plane of Earth)

Organization solitary or cluster (2–5)

Treasure standard (gems and magic gemstones only)

SPECIAL ABILITIES

Crystal Sense (Sp) Crysmals can sense the presence of any crystals or gems within 30 feet as if using the scent ability.

Shard Spike (Ex) Once per day, a crysmal can launch its tail spike as a ranged attack that shatters when it hits, dealing 3d6 points of piercing damage to the target and 1d4 points of piercing damage to all creatures in adjacent squares. The spike regrows in 24 hours, but until it does, its impaired sting does only 1d6+3 damage.

Scorpion-like crysmals originate in the deepest caverns of the Plane of Earth. On rare occasions, these strange creatures wind up on the Material Plane, usually in subterranean areas rich with natural gem and crystal formations. The crystalline planes of their bodies absorb and refract natural light, which some claim is the source of their supernatural powers.

Singular in purpose, a crysmal seeks only to reproduce. It does so by gathering stone crystals and gemstones, fashioning them into a Tiny facsimile of its own body, and jolting the new creature to life with a burst of the crysmal's own life energy. These newly created crysmals are known as shardlings (treat as a crysmal with the young creature simple template), and grow to adulthood after a few months of gorging on crystals and gemstones.

To make a single shardling, a crysmal requires 1,000 gp worth of crystals. Until it has enough material to reproduce, it stores these gems inside its body, and if slain, the gems are visible among the shards of the creature's corpse. Because of this reproductive need for gemstones, crysmals are relentless in their pursuit of the treasures, valuing them much as other living creatures value infants of their own race. Crysmals do not recognize that other creatures treat gems as wealth, and attempt to seize gems carried by others whenever the opportunity arises. A crysmal normally uses its spell-like abilities to befuddle opponents, grabbing at pouches with gems when the bearer is distracted, and normally only resorts to physical violence once all other tactics fail.

Illustration by Florian Stitz

DAEMON

Harbingers of ruin and embodiments of the worst ways to die, daemons epitomize painful death, the all-consuming hunger of evil, and the utter annihilation of life. While demons seek to pervert and destroy in endless unholy rampages, and devils vex and enslave in hopes of corrupting mortals, daemons seek only to consume mortal life itself. While some use brute force to despoil life or prey upon vulnerable souls, others wage campaigns of deceit to draw whole realms into ruin. With each life claimed and each atrocity meted out, daemons spread fear, mistrust, and despair, tarnishing the luster of existence and drawing the planes ever closer to their final, ultimate ruin.

Notorious for their hatred of the living, daemons are the things of dark dreams and fearful tales, as their ultimate ambitions include extinguishing every individual mortal life—and the more violent or terrible the end, the better. Their methods vary wildly, typically differentiated by daemonic breed. Many seek to infiltrate the mortal plane and sow death by their own taloned hands, while others manipulate agents (both mortal and immortal) as malevolent puppet masters, instigating calamities on massive scales from their grim realms. Such diversity of methods causes many planar scholars to misattribute the machinations of daemons to other types of fiends. These often deadly mistakes are further propagated by daemons' frequent dealings with and manipulation of other outsiders. Yet in all cases, despair, ruin, and death, spreading like contagion, typify the touch of daemonkind, though such symptoms often prove recognizable only after the hour is far too late.

Daemons flourish upon the plane of Abaddon, a bleak expanse of cold mists, fearful shapes, and hunted souls. Upon these wastes, the souls of evil mortals flee predation by the native fiends, and terror and the powers of the evil plane eventually transform the most ruthless into daemons themselves. Amid these scarred wastelands, poison swamps, and realms of endless night rise the foul domains of the tyrants of daemonkind, the Four Horsemen of the Apocalypse. Lords of devastation, these powerful and unique daemons desire slaughter, ruin, and death on a cosmic scale, and drive hordes of their lesser kin to spread terror and sorrow across the planes. Although the Horsemen share a singular goal, their tactics and ambitions vary widely.

Along with mastery over vast realms, the Horsemen are served by unimaginably enormous armies of their lesser brethren, but are obeyed most closely by retinues of daemons enslaved to their titles. These specific strains of daemonic servitors, known among daemonkind as deacons, serve whoever holds the title of Horseman.

Although these instruments of the archdaemons differ in strength and ability, their numbers provide their lords with legions capable of near-equal terrorization.

More so than among any other fiendish race, several breeds of daemons lust after souls. While other foul inhabitants of the planes seek the corruption and destruction of living essences, many daemons value possession and control over mortal animas, entrapping and hoarding souls—and in so doing disrupting the natural progression of life and perverting the quintessence of creation to serve their own terrible whims. While not all daemons possess the ability to steal a mortal being's soul and turn it to their use, the lowliest of daemonkind, the maniacal cacodaemons, endlessly seek life essences to consume and imprison. These base daemons enthusiastically serve their more powerful kin, eager for increased opportunities to doom mortal spirits. While cacodaemons place little value upon the souls they imprison, greater daemons eagerly gather them as trophies, fuel for terrible rites, or offerings to curry the favor of their lords. Several breeds of daemons also posses their own notorious abilities to capture mortal spirits or draw upon the power of souls, turning the forces of utter annihilation to their own sinister ends.

THE FOUR HORSEMEN

Four dread lords, infamous across all the planes, rule the disparate hordes of daemonkind. Risen from among the ranks of their terrible brethren to displace those fiendish tyrants before them, they are the archdaemons, the End Bringers, the Four Horsemen of the Apocalypse. In the blasphemous annals of fiendish lore, they are the prophesied architects of multiversal ruin, destined to stand triumphant over cadaverous cosmoses and infinities of silence before also giving way to absolute oblivion. Undisputed in his power among their kind, each Horseman rules a vast realm upon the bleak plains of Abaddon and a distinctive method of mortal ruin: pestilence, famine, war, or death from old age. Yet while each archdaemon commands measureless influence, daemons know nothing of loyalty and serve only those they cannot overcome. Thus, though the Horsemen stand peerless in their power and manipulations among daemonkind, they must ever defend their thrones from the machinations of ambitious underlings and the plots of other archdaemons.

Upon the poisonous expanses of Abaddon, lesser daemonic peers carve petty fiefdoms and posture as lords, but despite their world-spanning intrigues, all bow before the Horsemen—though most do so only grudgingly. Ancient myths also tell of a mysterious fifth Horseman, the Oinodaemon, though nearly all mention of such a creature has been scoured from the multiverse.

DAEMON, ASTRADAEMON

Vaguely humanoid in shape, this gaunt fiend has the face of a hideous fish and a body of lanky limbs and writhing tendrils.

ASTRADAEMON	CR 16

XP 76,800

NE Large outsider (daemon, evil, extraplanar)

Init +7; **Senses** darkvision 60 ft., *deathwatch, true seeing*; Perception +22

Aura soul siphon (10 ft.)

DEFENSE

AC 29, touch 17, flat-footed 21 (+7 Dex, +1 dodge, +12 natural, −1 size)

hp 212 (17d10+119)

Fort +12, **Ref** +17, **Will** +14

Defensive Abilities displacement; **DR** 10/good and silver; **Immune** acid, death effects, disease, poison; **Resist** cold 10, electricity 10, fire 10; **SR** 27

OFFENSE

Speed 90 ft., fly 90 ft. (good)

Melee bite +23 (2d6+5 plus energy drain and grab), 2 claws +23 (1d8+5 plus energy drain), tail slap +18 (1d12+2 plus energy drain)

Space 10 ft.; **Reach** 10 ft. (15 ft. with tail)

Special Attacks devour soul, energy drain (1 level, DC 25)

Spell-Like Abilities (CL 17th; concentration +24)

Constant—*deathwatch, displacement, true seeing*

At will—*enervation, fear* (DC21), *greater teleport* (self plus 50 lbs. of objects only), *vampiric touch*

3/day—*locate creature, plane shift* (DC 24)

1/day—*energy drain* (DC 24), *finger of death* (DC 24), summon (level 6, 1d3 derghodaemons 50%)

STATISTICS

Str 21, **Dex** 25, **Con** 24, **Int** 14, **Wis** 15, **Cha** 24

Base Atk +17; **CMB** +23; **CMD** 41

Feats Combat Reflexes, Dodge, Flyby Attack, Iron Will, Mobility, Nimble Moves, Power Attack, Spring Attack, Weapon Finesse

Skills Acrobatics +24 (+48 jump), Escape Artist +27, Fly +9, Intimidate +27, Knowledge (planes) +22, Perception +22, Sense Motive +22, Stealth +23, Survival +22

Languages Abyssal, Infernal; telepathy 100 ft.

ECOLOGY

Environment any (Abaddon or Astral Plane)

Organization solitary, pair, or pack (3–6)

Treasure standard

SPECIAL ABILITIES

Devour Soul (Su) As a standard action, an astradaemon that begins its turn with a grappled opponent can attempt to draw out and consume the soul of its victim, killing it instantly. This ability only works on living creatures, which may resist with a DC 25 Fortitude saving throw. The save is Constitution-based. For every 5 HD of the slain creature, the daemon gains a +1 profane bonus on attacks, saving throws, and checks for 24 hours. This ability does not consume all of the soul, and pieces of it still exist after the daemon completes its feast (enough to be able to resurrect the slain victim normally).

Soul Siphon (Su) If a Small or larger living creature dies within 10 feet of an astradaemon, the daemon gains 1d8 temporary hit points and a +2 bonus to Strength for 10 minutes. These bonuses stack with themselves. Incorporeal undead and living spirits traveling outside the body (such as a person using *astral projection* or *magic jar*) take 1d8 points of damage each round within the daemon's aura.

Believed to be creations of the Four Horsemen, astradaemons live out their existence in search of souls to harvest. These deadly creatures are ravening planar predators, openly hunting throughout the void for souls on which to feed. These voracious creatures are the personifications of death resulting from negative energy or level drain. Their vile touch drains life force from their enemies, and even perishing near them sates their thirst for life and souls.

DAEMON, CACODAEMON

An ever-gnashing maw, filled with row after row of mismatched teeth, dominates this frightful creature's orb-like body.

CACODAEMON	CR 2			

XP 600

NE Tiny outsider (daemon, evil, extraplanar)

Init +4; **Senses** darkvision 60 ft., *detect good*, *detect magic*; Perception +7

DEFENSE

AC 16, touch 12, flat-footed 16 (+4 natural, +2 size)

hp 19 (3d10+3); fast healing 2

Fort +2, **Ref** +5, **Will** +4

DR 5/good or silver; **Immune** acid, death effects, disease, poison; **Resist** cold 10, electricity 10, fire 10

OFFENSE

Speed 5 ft., fly 50 ft. (perfect)

Melee bite +6 (1d4+1 plus disease)

Space 2-1/2 ft.; **Reach** 0 ft.

Special Attacks soul lock

Spell-Like Abilities (CL 6th; concentration +7)

Constant—*detect good, detect magic*

At will—*invisibility* (self only)

3/day—*lesser confusion* (DC 12)

1/week—*commune* (CL 12th, six questions)

STATISTICS

Str 12, **Dex** 11, **Con** 13, **Int** 8, **Wis** 13, **Cha** 12

Base Atk +3; **CMB** +1; **CMD** 12

Feats Improved Initiative, Lightning Reflexes

Skills Bluff +7, Fly +18, Knowledge (planes) +5, Perception +7, Stealth +14

Languages Abyssal, Common, Infernal; telepathy 100 ft.

SQ change shape (2 of the following forms: lizard, octopus, Small scorpion, venomous snake, *polymorph*)

ECOLOGY

Environment any (Abaddon)

Organization solitary or swarm (2–10)

Treasure standard

SPECIAL ABILITIES

Disease (Su) *Cacodaemonia*: Bite—injury; *save* Fort DC 12; *onset* 1 day; *frequency* 1/day; *effect* 1d2 Wis damage, *cure* 2 consecutive saves. In addition to the normal effects of the disease, as long as a victim is infected, the cacodaemon can telepathically communicate with the creature over any distance (as long as they remain on the same plane).

Soul Lock (Su) Once per day as a full-round action, a cacodaemon can ingest the spirit of any sentient creature that has died within the last minute. This causes a soul gem to grow inside of the cacodaemon's gut, which it can regurgitate as a standard action. A soul gem is a fine-sized object with 1 hit point and hardness 2. Destroying a soul gem frees the soul within, though it does not return the deceased creature to life. This is a death effect. Any attempt to resurrect a body whose soul is trapped in a soul gem requires a DC 12 caster level check. Failure results in the spell having no effect, while success shatters the victim's soul gem and returns the creature to life as normal. If the soul gem rests in an unholy location, such as that created by the spell *unhallow*, the DC of this caster level check increases by +2. The caster level check DC is Charisma-based.

Any evil outsider can, as a standard action, ingest a soul gem. Doing so frees the soul within, but condemns it to one of the lower planes (though the soul can be returned to life as normal). The outsider gains fast healing 2 for a number of rounds equal to its Hit Dice.

The least of daemonkind, cacodaemons spawn from eddies of angry, violent, and demented souls amid the mists of Abaddon. Dim-witted but utterly evil, they endlessly seek to cause pain and indulge their hunger for mortal souls. Many more powerful fiends keep cacodaemons as pets, if only to be able to harvest the tiny creatures' soul gems. A 7th-level spellcaster can gain a cacodaemon as a familiar if she has the Improved Familiar feat.

Illustrations by Tyler Walpole

DAEMON, CEUSTODAEMON

This brown, shaggy-furred beast stands on slate grey hooves. Its head resembles that of a maniacal horned ape.

CEUSTODAEMON	CR 6

XP 2,400

NE Large outsider (daemon, evil, extraplanar)

Init +1; **Senses** darkvision 60 ft., *detect good, detect magic, see invisibility*; Perception +15

DEFENSE

AC 20, touch 10, flat-footed 19 (+1 Dex, +10 natural, −1 size)

hp 68 (8d10+24)

Fort +9, **Ref** +3, **Will** +8

DR 10/good or silver; **Immune** acid, death effects, disease, mind-affecting effects, paralysis, poison, polymorph effects, sleep effects; **Resist** cold 10, electricity 10, fire 10

OFFENSE

Speed 30 ft.

Melee bite +11 (2d6+4), 2 claws +11 (1d6+4)

Space 10 ft.; **Reach** 10 ft.

Special Attacks breath weapon (30-ft. cone; 6d6 fire damage; Reflex DC 17 for half; usable once every 1d4 rounds)

Spell-Like Abilities (CL 8th; concentration +10)

Constant—*detect good, detect magic, see invisibility*

At will—*dimension door*

3/day—*dispel magic, fly*

1/day—*hold monster* (DC 17), *slow* (DC 15)

STATISTICS

Str 18, **Dex** 13, **Con** 16, **Int** 11, **Wis** 14, **Cha** 15

Base Atk +8; **CMB** +13; **CMD** 24

Feats Alertness, Blind-Fight, Power Attack, Step Up

Skills Bluff +13, Intimidate +11, Knowledge (planes) +9, Perception +15, Sense Motive +15, Stealth +8, Survival +9

Languages Abyssal, Infernal; telepathy 100 ft.

SQ drawn to service

ECOLOGY

Environment any (Abaddon)

Organization solitary

Treasure none

SPECIAL ABILITIES

Drawn to Service (Su) When brought to another plane with a *planar binding* or *planar ally* spell (or any similar calling effect), ceustodaemons take a −5 penalty on the initial Will save and on their Charisma check to refuse service. Ceustodaemons also take a −5 penalty on saves against *binding*, *planar binding*, and other spells designed to bind a creature to a particular plane as long as the daemon is commanded to serve as a guardian for a single area or small complex.

Some claim the Four Horsemen created these creatures to serve as summoning fodder. Others believe that they form from neutral evil souls who commit suicide. Wherever the truth lies, ceustodaemons find themselves on the Material Plane more often than any other daemon, as they are easily pressured into service—many call these creatures "guardian daemons" as a result. Yet in the back of their wicked minds, ceustodaemons always think about escaping their bonds and ripping to shreds the ones who summoned them.

Greater and lesser versions of these creatures exist. These variants can be represented by applying either the young creature or advanced creature simple templates, along with the following adjustments.

Lesser Ceustodaemon: This Medium daemon looks like a horned frog with a wide, toothy mouth. Its breath weapon is a chilling cone of ice that deals cold damage.

Greater Ceustodaemon: This daemon resembles a gigantic humanoid bear with the talons of an eagle and curling ram horns sprouting from its head. Its breath weapon is a fan of sparks that deals electricity damage.

Daemon, Derghodaemon

A deadly and vicious bouquet of insectile claws sprouts from this horrid, three-legged, multi-eyed beast.

DERGHODAEMON   CR 12

XP 19,200

NE Large outsider (daemon, evil, extraplanar)

Init +5; **Senses** all-around vision, darkvision 60 ft., *detect magic, see invisibility*; Perception +28

Aura *feeblemind* (DC 20)

DEFENSE

AC 27, touch 14, flat-footed 22 (+5 Dex, +13 natural, −1 size)

hp 161 (14d10+84)

Fort +15, **Ref** +14, **Will** +7

DR 10/good; **Immune** acid, death effects, disease, poison; **Resist** cold 10, electricity 10, fire 10; **SR** 23

OFFENSE

Speed 40 ft.

Melee 5 claws +21 (1d6+8/19–20)

Space 10 ft.; **Reach** 10 ft.

Special Attacks rend (2 claws, 1d8+12 plus 2 Con damage)

Spell-like Abilities (CL 12th; concentration +15)

    Constant—*detect magic, see invisibility*

    At will—*greater teleport* (self plus 50 lbs. of objects only)

    3/day—*fear* (DC 17), quickened *summon swarm*

    1/day—*creeping doom, insect plague,* summon (level 4, 1 derghodaemon 30%)

STATISTICS

Str 27, **Dex** 20, **Con** 22, **Int** 7, **Wis** 17, **Cha** 16

Base Atk +14; **CMB** +23; **CMD** 38 (40 vs. trip)

Feats Cleave, Critical Focus, Improved Critical (claws), Power Attack, Quicken Spell-Like Ability (*summon swarm*), Sickening Critical, Vital Strike

Skills Intimidate +20, Perception +28, Sense Motive +20, Stealth +18; **Racial Modifiers** +4 Perception

Languages Abyssal, Draconic, Infernal; telepathy 100 ft.

SQ swarmwalking

ECOLOGY

Environment any (Abaddon)

Organization solitary or infestation (2–6)

Treasure standard

SPECIAL ABILITIES

Feeblemind Aura (Su) By grinding and clicking its mandibles and chitinous plates together (a free action), a derghodaemon can affect all creatures within 30 feet as if by a *feeblemind* spell. Daemons are immune to this effect, but all other creatures must make a DC 20 Will save to resist the effects. A creature that makes this save is immune to the effect for 24 hours. A creature that fails remains affected as long as the derghodaemon continues to maintain the aura and the subject remains within 30 feet of the derghodaemon. Once either condition ends, the victim of this effect can attempt a new DC 20 Will save once per minute to recover from the effect; otherwise, it can be cured by a *heal, limited wish, miracle,* or *wish* spell. A derghodaemon cannot use its spell-like abilities or rend attack in any round in which it uses its feeblemind aura. This is a sonic mind-affecting effect. The save DC is Charisma-based.

Swarmwalking (Su) A derghodaemon is immune to damage or distraction effects caused by swarms.

These brutal daemons personify death resulting from violent insanity, such as being murdered by a maniac or torn to shreds by a pack of rabid predators. These insectoid creatures roam the Outer Planes, scavenging battlefields and following the inevitable trail of violence in those hostile worlds. They hunt the weak and dying along the fringe of battles, feeding off their victims' suffering until they make their kill. Attacks from a derghodaemon often come from within a cloud of biting insects.

Brutish and low on intellect, derghodaemons find themselves serving as front-line fighters in fiendish armies. A derghodaemon stands 9 feet tall and weighs 800 pounds.

DAEMON, HYDRODAEMON

The skin on this frog-like fiend is clammy and its eyes look dead and milky; its wide face is split by a fanged maw.

HYDRODAEMON	CR 8

XP 4,800
NE Large outsider (aquatic, daemon, evil, extraplanar)
Init +2; **Senses** darkvision 60 ft., *detect magic*; Perception +15

DEFENSE

AC 20, touch 11, flat-footed 18 (+2 Dex, +9 natural, –1 size)
hp 95 (10d10+40)
Fort +11, **Ref** +9, **Will** +3
DR 10/cold iron or silver; **Immune** acid, death effects, disease, poison, waters of the River Styx; **Resist** cold 10, electricity 10, fire 10; **SR** 19

OFFENSE

Speed 30 ft., fly 40 ft. (average; see glide, below), swim 60 ft.
Melee bite +13 (1d8+4 plus grab), 2 claws +13 (1d6+4)
Ranged sleep spittle +11 (sleep)
Space 10 ft.; **Reach** 10 ft.
Special Attacks rake (2 claws +13, 1d6+4)
Spell-Like Abilities (CL 9th; concentration +11)
Constant—*detect magic, water walk*
At will—*acid arrow, deeper darkness*
3/day—*control water, greater teleport* (self plus 50 lbs. of objects only), *summon monster V* (Large water elemental only)
1/day—*desecrate, summon* (level 3, 1 hydrodaemon 50%)

STATISTICS

Str 18, **Dex** 15, **Con** 18, **Int** 9, **Wis** 11, **Cha** 14
Base Atk +10; **CMB** +15 (+9 grapple); **CMD** 27
Feats Cleave, Point-Blank Shot, Power Attack, Precise Shot, Skill Focus (Perception)
Skills Fly +0, Intimidate +14, Knowledge (planes) +10, Perception +15, Sense Motive +12, Stealth +10, Swim +21
Languages Abyssal, Infernal; telepathy 100 ft.
SQ amphibious, glide

ECOLOGY

Environment any (Abaddon)
Organization solitary, gang (2–5), or mob (6–12)
Treasure standard

SPECIAL ABILITIES

Glide (Ex) A hydrodaemon can launch itself into the air and glide along for 1 minute, gaining a fly speed of 40 feet with average maneuverability. While gliding, the hydrodaemon gains the pounce ability.

Sleep Spittle (Su) A hydrodaemon can spit at a single target within 20 feet, making a ranged touch attack as a standard action. A target hit by this spittle must succeed on a DC 19 Will save or fall asleep for 6 rounds. The save DC is Constitution-based.

While at first glance these creatures seem like enormous and foul boggards, their dangerous gait, dead eyes, and wicked claws give away their fiendish nature. In their home environment, hydrodaemons swim the sickening rivers and seas of Abaddon and the River Styx, ducking beneath the rivers of pus and bile only to leap out at enemies and rend their flesh with tooth and claw. It is said these are among the few creatures able to survive in the deadly waters of the River Styx. When called to the Material Plane, hydrodaemons serve powerful spellcasters, protecting domains dotted with pools, streams, and even sewer complexes. Associated with death by drowning, these fiends use a favored tactic to draw the most anguish from their victims. Hydrodaemons first attack with their inky black sleep spittle, hoping to render victims unconscious. With their opponents unable to fight back, hydrodaemons drag their enemies into the foul waters they call home and delight as the liquid fills their victims' gasping lungs. If unable to drown a victim, they finish the job with jaws and claws.

Hydrodaemons possess an awkward gait, springing back on their heels and leaping about like humanoid frogs. Even so, they move in an unpredictable manner, twisting their bodies with each hopping movement. Hydrodaemons can also unfurl flaps of skin that allow them to glide through the air. Hydrodaemons stand 10 feet tall and weigh upward of 3,000 pounds.

DAEMON, LEUKODAEMON

This human-shaped beast has a horse's skull for a head. It walks on cracked hooves and bears the rotting wings of a carrion bird.

LEUKODAEMON   CR 9

XP 6,400

NE Large outsider (daemon, evil, extraplanar)

Init +11; **Senses** darkvision 60 ft., *deathwatch*, *detect good*; Perception +22

Aura infectious aura (50 ft.)

DEFENSE

AC 23, touch 16, flat-footed 16 (+7 Dex, +7 natural, −1 size)

hp 115 (10d10+60)

Fort +9, **Ref** +14, **Will** +12

DR 10/good or silver; **Immune** acid, death effects, disease, poison; **Resist** cold 10, electricity 10, fire 10; **SR** 20

OFFENSE

Speed 30 ft., fly 60 ft. (average)

Melee bite +16 (1d8+7), 2 claws +16 (1d6+7)

Ranged +1 *composite longbow* +18/+13 (2d6+8/×3 plus contagion)

Space 10 ft.; **Reach** 10 ft.

Special Attacks breath of flies

Spell-Like Abilities (CL 10th; concentration +13)

Constant—*deathwatch*, *detect good*

At will—*contagion* (DC 17), *dispel magic*, *greater teleport* (self plus 50 lbs. of objects only)

1/day—*harm* (DC 19), *summon* (level 3, 1 leukodaemon only, 35%)

STATISTICS

Str 25, **Dex** 24, **Con** 23, **Int** 16, **Wis** 21, **Cha** 16

Base Atk +10; **CMB** +18; **CMD** 35

Feats Alertness, Hover, Improved Initiative, Point-Blank Shot, Weapon Focus (longbow)

Skills Fly +18, Heal +18, Intimidate +16, Knowledge (planes) +16, Perception +22, Sense Motive +22, Stealth +16, Survival +15, Use Magic Device +16

Languages Abyssal, Draconic, Infernal; telepathy 100 ft.

ECOLOGY

Environment any (Abaddon)

Organization solitary or wake (2–10)

Treasure standard (+1 *composite longbow*, other treasure)

SPECIAL ABILITIES

Breath of Flies (Su) Once per minute as a standard action, a leukodaemon can unleash a cloud of corpse-bloated, biting black flies in a 20-foot cone. Those caught in the cone take 8d6 points of slashing damage. A DC 21 Reflex save halves this damage. Those who take any damage are also sickened for 1 minute. In addition, the flies linger for 1d4+1 rounds, congealing into a buzzing 20-foot-square cloud centered on the cone's original point of origin. Any creature that ends its turn in this cloud must make a DC 21 Reflex save to avoid taking 4d6 points of damage and becoming sickened for 1 minute. This cloud of flies may be dispersed by any area effect that does damage or creates wind of at least strong wind force. All daemons are immune to this effect. The save DCs are Constitution-based.

Contagion (Su) Any arrow a leukodaemon fires from a bow is tainted with disease. If a creature is damaged by a leukodaemon's arrow, it must make a DC 19 Fortitude save or be affected as if by the spell *contagion*. A leukodaemon can manifest arrows at will and never runs out of ammunition.

Infectious Aura (Su) All creatures within 50 feet of a leukodaemon take a −4 penalty on Fortitude saves against disease effects.

Deacons of the Horseman of Pestilence, leukodaemons serve their lord in Abaddon as well as across the planes by spreading plagues and pandemics.

Leukodaemons stand upward of 14 feet tall but weigh just over 200 pounds. The skulls that serve as their heads can be replaced with any skulls, yet these creatures choose horse skulls to show their loyalty to the Horsemen. The creature's true head is merely a blistered knob between its shoulders.

DAEMON, MELADAEMON

This foul creature looks like an emaciated humanoid with the head of a jackal.

MELADAEMON CR 11

XP 12,800

NE Large outsider (daemon, evil, extraplanar)

Init +6; **Senses** darkvision 60 ft., *detect good, detect magic*; Perception +20

Aura consumptive aura (20 ft.)

DEFENSE

AC 25, touch 15, flat-footed 19 (+6 Dex, +10 natural, –1 size)

hp 147 (14d10+70)

Fort +11, **Ref** +15, **Will** +14

DR 10/good; **Immune** acid, critical hits, death effects, disease, poison, sneak attack; **Resist** cold 10, electricity 10, fire 10; **SR** 22

OFFENSE

Speed 30 ft., fly 60 ft. (average)

Melee bite +20 (2d8+6/19–20 plus disease), 2 claws +19 (2d6+6 plus hunger)

Space 10 ft.; **Reach** 10 ft.

Spell-Like Abilities (CL 11th; concentration +15)

Constant—*detect good, detect magic, see invisibility*

At will—*cause fear* (DC 15), *deeper darkness, greater teleport* (self plus 50 lbs. of objects only)

3/day—*blight* (DC 19), *diminish plants, quickened magic missile*

1/day—*horrid wilting* (DC 22), *waves of fatigue*

STATISTICS

Str 22, **Dex** 22, **Con** 21, **Int** 21, **Wis** 17, **Cha** 18

Base Atk +14; **CMB** +21; **CMD** 37

Feats Blind-Fight, Combat Reflexes, Great Fortitude, Improved Critical (bite), Iron Will, Quicken Spell-Like Ability (*magic missile*), Weapon Focus (bite)

Skills Bluff +21, Fly +17, Heal +11, Intimidate +21, Knowledge (planes) +22, Knowledge (religion) +22, Perception +20, Sense Motive +20, Spellcraft +22, Stealth +19, Survival +20, Use Magic Device +14

Languages Abyssal, Draconic, Infernal; telepathy 100 ft.

ECOLOGY

Environment any (Abaddon)

Organization solitary, pack (2–5), or cabal (6–12)

Treasure standard

SPECIAL ABILITIES

Consumptive Aura (Su) A meladaemon radiates an aura of hunger to a radius of 20 feet. Every round a creature begins its turn within this aura, it must succeed at a DC 22 Fortitude save or take 1d6 nonlethal damage and become fatigued from extreme hunger. Creatures that do not need to eat are immune to this effect. The save DC is Constitution-based.

Disease (Ex) *Daemonic wasting:* Bite—injury; *save* Fort DC 22; *onset* 1 day; *frequency* 1/day; *effect* 1d4 Con and 1d4 Cha damage; *cure* 2 consecutive saves. The save DC is Constitution-based.

Hunger (Su) A meladaemon's claw attack deals an additional 1d6 points of nonlethal damage as it causes sudden pangs of horrific hunger in its foe. Creatures that do not need to eat are immune to this effect.

As personifications of death from starvation and thirst, these withered fiends spend their time destroying resources and spreading hunger. Deacons of the Horseman of Famine, these creatures visit worlds throughout the planes, destroying acres of crops and slaughtering livestock in order to harvest souls for their honored master. Meladaemons delight in the slow death of starvation, going so far as to experiment with various bodily deficiencies and mortal weaknesses. Arrogant and utterly bound to their patron, meladaemons rarely work with others of their kind and never serve any of the other three Horsemen except in the rarest of circumstances.

Meladaemons stand approximately 12 feet tall and weigh 350 pounds.

Illustration by Tyler Walpole

DAEMON, OLETHRODAEMON

Crowned with a wicked array of twisted horns, this wide-mouthed, spherical behemoth stands on four stout legs.

OLETHRODAEMON	CR 20

XP 307,200
NE Gargantuan outsider (daemon, evil, extraplanar)
Init +12; **Senses** darkvision 60 ft., *true seeing*; Perception +31
Aura unholy aura

DEFENSE
AC 38, touch 18, flat-footed 30 (+4 deflection, +8 Dex, +20 natural, −4 size)
hp 370 (20d10+260)
Fort +29, **Ref** +18, **Will** +26
DR 10/good and silver; **Immune** acid, death effects, disease, poison; **Resist** cold 10, electricity 10, fire 10; **SR** 31

OFFENSE
Speed 40 ft., burrow 50 ft.
Melee 2 bites +28 (2d8+12/19–20 plus grab), 4 claws +28 (2d6+12 plus grab), gore +28 (2d8+12)
Space 20 ft.; **Reach** 20 ft.
Special Attacks drain soul, soul-drained breath, trample (2d8+18, DC 32)
Spell-Like Abilities (CL 20th; concentration +27)
Constant—*air walk, true seeing, unholy aura* (DC 25)
At will—*greater teleport* (self plus 50 lbs. objects only), *telekinesis, wall of fire, wall of ice*
3/day—quickened *disintegrate* (DC 23), *wall of force*
1/day—*blasphemy* (DC 24), summon (level 9, any 1 CR 19 or lower daemon, 100%), *wail of the banshee* (DC 26)

STATISTICS
Str 35, **Dex** 26, **Con** 37, **Int** 12, **Wis** 26, **Cha** 25
Base Atk +20; **CMB** +36 (+40 grapple); **CMD** 54 (58 vs. trip)
Feats Awesome Blow, Cleave, Great Cleave, Improved Bull Rush, Improved Critical (bite), Improved Initiative, Improved Sunder, Iron Will, Power Attack, Quicken Spell-Like Ability (*disintegrate*)
Skills Climb +35, Intimidate +30, Knowledge (planes) +24, Perception +31, Sense Motive +31, Stealth +19, Survival +31
Languages Abyssal, Infernal; telepathy 100 ft.
SQ adamantine claws

ECOLOGY
Environment any (Abaddon)
Organization solitary, pair, or apocalypse (3–5)
Treasure standard

SPECIAL ABILITIES
Adamantine Claws (Ex) Able to tear through stone, an olethrodaemon's claws are treated as though they were adamantine. This ability also allows an olethrodaemon to make use of its burrow speed through stone.
Drain Soul (Su) A creature grappled by an olethrodaemon's grab attack from its claws can be transferred to its mouth

as a move action requiring no combat maneuver check. As a standard action, an olethrodaemon that begins its turn with an opponent grappled in either of its mouths can swallow the opponent by succeeding on another grapple check. If successful, the creature is swallowed into one of the olethrodaemon's many stomachs. These stomachs grind their contents and drain the life force from living creatures. Every round a creature remains in an olethrodaemon's stomach, it takes 4d8+18 points of damage and gains 1d4 negative levels. The creature can attempt to cut its way out of the olethrodaemon's stomach, but it suffers the chance of just cutting into another stomach chamber. An olethrodaemon's stomach is AC 20 and has 40 hit points. Once a creature deals enough damage to allow escape, it has a 50% chance to end up in another stomach chamber instead of escaping. Due to the multiple stomach chambers, an olethrodaemon can house and drain up to four medium creatures at one time. This ability otherwise functions as the swallow whole special attack. It is a DC 33 Fortitude save to remove negative levels gained in this fashion. This save is Constitution-based.

Soul-Drained Breath (Su) An olethrodaemon can convert life energy it has consumed into a potent breath weapon. Up to three times per day, but no more often than once every 1d4 rounds, an olethrodaemon can expel a 120-foot line or a 60-foot cone of shrieking black smoke and wind from one of its mouths as a standard action. Any living creature in the area of this attack takes 20d10 points of damage from negative energy, or half on a successful DC 27 Reflex save. Undead creatures caught in this negative energy are healed for the same amount instead of damaged. The save DC for this effect is Charisma-based.

While some of the more powerful daemons are servitors to one of the Four Horsemen, olethrodaemons serve as juggernauts for all of the Four. These massive creatures are the embodiment of death and destruction—the very vessels of apocalypse that daemons wish to see wrought upon the multiverse. These nihilistic behemoths roam the gray expanses of Abaddon, feasting on the souls of evil mortals damned to their realm. When on the Material Plane, olethrodaemons act as agents of destruction, spreading ruin and devouring mortal souls as they plow through cities and countrysides, bent on devastation. It's rare for a mortal to be able to control such a potent force, but sometimes mad spellcasters utilize effects like *gate* to urge an olethrodaemon to visit a devastating holocaust upon an enemy region—the olethrodaemon generally does not hold a grudge against a mortal that asks such a service from it.

These immense creatures stand over 25 feet tall and weigh close to 12,000 pounds, their powerful, muscular bodies covered by durable plates and head thronged with dangerous, twisted horns. Olethrodaemons stand on four stout legs, and possess an equal number of arms, each ending in wickedly sharp claws able to tear through stone as easily as flesh. The creature's eyes, as well as its two mouths, glow like coals in a kiln. The creature feeds on souls and has multiple stomachs to digest mortal essences.

While not as intelligent or scheming as many other powerful daemons (or other fiends who match their power, for that matter), olethrodaemons remain dangerous foes. They do not generally wish to lead armies and gain power by control, but rather to revel in the evil purity of annihilation. Among olethrodaemons, the greatest desire is to be the one to devour the very last mortal soul. They angle and shove for this honor, often ceding a city or group of victims to a rival if they believe that, in so doing, they might gain the advantage of positioning to consume the final soul once the multiverse has been devoured.

OLETHRODAEMON PARAGONS

Just as powerful balors become lords and pit fiends clamor for positions as infernal dukes, olethrodaemons can achieve a unique level of power among their kin. These creatures are known as paragons, and gain this level of power by pledging their loyalty to one of the Four Horsemen as a chosen agent of apocalypse. These advanced olethrodaemons specialize in their patron's particular method of annihilation, their abilities evolving to suit the method of ruin. An olethrodaemon paragon generally has from 4 to 8 additional Hit Dice, and is usually a CR 22 to CR 24 creature.

Some planar scholars postulate that olethrodaemons are actually the creations of the Four Horsemen, and that the Four worked foul rites upon a fifth Horseman, with these interactions spawning olethrodaemons to serve their will and spread oblivion throughout the multiverse. The abilities of these chosen spawn warp to the tendencies of their daemonic lords.

Olethrodaemons serving the Horseman of Pestilence can infect their victims with a powerful disease by means of all their natural attacks. Creatures who succumb to this attack are affected as if by a maximized *contagion* spell, heightened to 9th level.

Olethrodaemons serving the Horseman of War can imbue their natural attacks with additional properties. As a free action, an olethrodaemon can apply any special weapon property equivalent to a +2 enhancement to its bite, claw, gore, or trample attacks for 1 round—most of these olethrodaemon paragons elect to grant their natural weapons the unholy enhancement.

Olethrodaemons serving the Horseman of Famine gain the consumptive aura ability of the meladaemon, but the nonlethal damage dealt increases to 6d6 and victims who succumb become exhausted rather than merely fatigued.

Olethrodaemons serving the Horseman of Death gain the ability to inflict a negative level on a foe each time they strike with a claw attack, or else gain the ability to cause those they damage to age rapidly and grow old and frail with hideous speed.

DAEMON, PISCODAEMON

This hideous cross between a lobster, an octopus, and a human threatens enemies with powerful claws and writhing tentacles.

PISCODAEMON	CR 10			

XP 9,600

NE Medium outsider (aquatic, daemon, evil, extraplanar)

Init +8; **Senses** darkvision 60 ft., *detect good, detect magic, see invisibility;* Perception +16

DEFENSE

AC 24, touch 14, flat-footed 20 (+4 Dex, +10 natural)

hp 137 (11d10+77)

Fort +14, **Ref** +7, **Will** +9

DR 10/good; **Immune** acid, death effects, disease, poison; **Resist** cold 10, electricity 10, fire 10; **SR** 21

OFFENSE

Speed 30 ft., swim 50 ft.

Melee 2 claws +18 (2d6+7/18–20/×3 plus grab and 1d6 bleed), tentacles +16 (1d10+3 plus poison)

Special Attacks constrict (2d6+10)

Spell-Like Abilities (CL 11th; concentration +14)

    Constant—*detect good, detect magic, see invisibility*

    At will—*dispel magic, greater teleport* (self plus 50 lbs. of objects only)

    3/day—*fly, stinking cloud* (DC 16)

    1/day—*summon* (level 4, 1d3 hydrodaemons 35%)

STATISTICS

Str 25, **Dex** 18, **Con** 24, **Int** 14, **Wis** 15, **Cha** 17

Base Atk +11; **CMB** +18 (+22 grapple); **CMD** 32

Feats Critical Focus, Improved Initiative, Multiattack, Power Attack, Sickening Critical, Vital Strike

Skills Escape Artist +18, Intimidate +17, Knowledge (planes) +16, Perception +16, Sense Motive +16, Stealth +18, Survival +16, Swim +29

Languages Abyssal, Draconic, Infernal; telepathy 100 ft.

SQ amphibious, augmented critical

ECOLOGY

Environment any (Abaddon)

Organization solitary, pair, or knot (3–5)

Treasure standard

SPECIAL ABILITIES

Augmented Critical (Ex) A piscodaemon's claws threaten a critical hit on an 18–20 and inflict ×3 damage on a successful critical hit.

Poison (Ex) Tentacles—injury; *save* Fort DC 22; *frequency* 1/round for 6 rounds; *effect* 1d2 Con plus staggered for 1 round; *cure* 2 consecutive saves.

These aquatic daemons roam the lower planes sowing misery and blight. They delight in drawn-out deaths, poisoning creatures or dismembering victims to watch them slowly bleed out. On their home plane of Abaddon, piscodaemons gravitate toward the same aquatic regions inhabited by hydrodaemons, and often the stronger among their ranks end up leading armies of hydrodaemons against their enemies. These creatures serve as sergeants in the hierarchy of Abaddon, and run their units with an excess of cruelty and violence.

Instead of preying on the weak, piscodaemons enjoy targeting strong, well-armored warriors, knowing the pain of their weakening poison rests poorly on shoulders accustomed to bearing heavy weights and delivering devastating blows.

Piscodaemons are 7 feet tall and weigh 400 pounds.

DAEMON, PURRODAEMON

Dozens of weapons pierce this massive monster's body. Red eyes glow with wickedness in its vulture-like head.

PURRODAEMON	CR 18	

XP 153,600

NE Large outsider (daemon, evil, extraplanar)

Init +10; **Senses** darkvision 60 ft., *true seeing*; Perception +26

Aura fear (15 ft., DC 24), *unholy aura*

DEFENSE

AC 35, touch 19, flat-footed 29 (+4 deflection, +6 Dex, +16 natural, −1 size)

hp 294 (19d10+190)

Fort +25, **Ref** +21, **Will** +14

DR 10/good and silver; **Immune** acid, death effects, disease, poison; **Resist** cold 10, electricity 10, fire 10; **SR** 29

OFFENSE

Speed 30 ft., fly 60 ft. (good)

Melee +2 *wounding* halberd 2d8+18/19–20/×3, bite +24 (1d8+5)

Space 10 ft.; **Reach** 10 ft.

Special Attacks weapon steep

Spell-Like Abilities (CL 18th; concentration +23)

Constant—*true seeing*, *unholy aura* (DC 23)

At will—*greater teleport* (self plus 50 lbs. of objects only)

3/day—*chain lightning* (DC 21), *cone of cold* (DC 20), *flame strike* (DC 20)

1/day—*summon* (level 5, 2 derghodaemons 50%)

STATISTICS

Str 32, **Dex** 23, **Con** 30, **Int** 17, **Wis** 18, **Cha** 21

Base Atk +19; **CMB** +31; **CMD** 51

Feats Combat Expertise, Combat Reflexes, Greater Vital Strike, Improved Critical[B] (halberd), Improved Initiative, Improved Sunder, Improved Vital Strike, Lunge, Power Attack, Quick Draw, Vital Strike, Weapon Focus[B] (halberd)

Skills Acrobatics +28, Bluff +21, Diplomacy +17, Fly +16, Intimidate +27, Knowledge (planes) +25, Perception +26, Sense Motive +26, Spellcraft +23, Stealth +24, Survival +17

Languages Abyssal, Draconic, Infernal; telepathy 100 ft.

ECOLOGY

Environment any (Abaddon)

Organization solitary, patrol (2–5), or unit (6–12)

Treasure standard

SPECIAL ABILITIES

Weapon Steep (Su) A purrodaemon can sheathe a weapon in its flesh as a swift action. This does no damage to the daemon. If a weapon remains sheathed in its body for at least 24 hours, the weapon absorbs some of its essence and gains magical enhancements. A purrodaemon can have up to a dozen weapons lodged in its body at a time, but only one can possess magical enhancements at a time. The total enhancements cannot exceed a +4 effective enhancement—most purrodaemons opt to create +2 *wounding* weapons in this manner. A weapon's enhancements vanish as soon as the purrodaemon dies or releases the weapon. A purrodaemon gains Weapon Focus and Improved Critical as bonus feats as long as it wields a weapon benefiting from its weapon steep ability.

Deacons of War, purrodaemons ravage the planes as generals of massive battles. They employ creative tactics and never launch an assault without carefully looking over the plans or surveying the battlefield themselves. A purrodaemon is 12 feet tall and weighs 1,300 pounds.

Illustration by Tyler Walpole

73

DAEMON, THANADAEMON

Rattling with each stride, this looming, horned, skeletal figure clutches a wicked staff. A seething glow burns in its eye sockets.

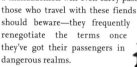

THANADAEMON	CR 13

XP 25,600

NE Medium outsider (daemon, evil, extraplanar)

Init +7; **Senses** darkvision 60 ft., *true seeing*; Perception +25

DEFENSE

AC 27, touch 14, flat-footed 23 (+3 Dex, +1 dodge, +13 natural)

hp 172 (15d10+90)

Fort +11, **Ref** +12, **Will** +14

DR 10/good; **Immune** acid, death effects, disease, poison; **Resist** cold 10, electricity 10, fire 10; **SR** 24

OFFENSE

Speed 30 ft.

Melee +2 *quarterstaff* +22/+17/+12 (1d6+9 plus energy drain) or 2 claws +20 (1d4+5 plus energy drain)

Special Attacks draining weapon, energy drain (1 level, DC 21), fear gaze, soul crush

Spell-Like Abilities (CL 15th; concentration +19)

Constant—*air walk, true seeing*

At will—*greater teleport* (self plus skiff and passengers only), *plane shift* (self plus skiff and passengers only, Astral, Ethereal, and evil-aligned planes only)

3/day—*animate dead, desecrate, enervation*

1/day—*summon* (level 4, 1d4 hydrodaemons 80% or 1 thanadaemon 35%)

STATISTICS

Str 21, **Dex** 16, **Con** 23, **Int** 17, **Wis** 17, **Cha** 18

Base Atk +15; **CMB** +20; **CMD** 34

Feats Alertness, Blind-Fight, Dodge, Improved Initiative, Iron Will, Lunge, Mobility, Power Attack

Skills Acrobatics +21, Bluff +22, Diplomacy +22, Intimidate +22, Knowledge (planes) +21, Knowledge (religion) +21, Perception +25, Sense Motive +25, Stealth +14, Survival +10

Languages Abyssal, Draconic, Infernal; telepathy 100 ft.

ECOLOGY

Environment any (Abaddon)

Organization solitary, pair, or council (3–11)

Treasure standard (+2 quarterstaff, other treasure)

SPECIAL ABILITIES

Draining Weapon (Su) A thanadaemon's energy drain attack functions through any melee weapon it wields.

Fear Gaze (Su) Cower in fear for 1d6 rounds, 30 feet, Will DC 21 negates. This is a mind-affecting fear effect. The save DC is Charisma-based.

Soul Crush (Su) A thanadaemon can crush a soul gem (see cacodaemon) as a standard action to gain fast healing 15 for 15 rounds (this is a standard action).

This action condemns the crushed soul to Abaddon—resurrecting this victim requires a DC 28 caster level check.

While all daemons represent death in some fashion, thanadaemons, the Deacons of Death, represent the inevitable death through old age. Thanadaemons effortlessly work eerie skiffs along every pus- and bile-choked river in Abaddon, including the legendary River Styx. For the right price (typically 50 pp or 2 gems worth at least 300 gp each), a thanadaemon will even carry passengers on its skiff, yet those who travel with these fiends should beware—they frequently renegotiate the terms once they've got their passengers in dangerous realms.

Dark Slayer

This small humanoid is clothed in tattered rags from head to foot. Only its sinister eyes and pale hands are visible.

DARK SLAYER	CR 3

XP 800

CE Small humanoid (dark folk)

Init +4; **Senses** *detect magic*, see in darkness; Perception +4

DEFENSE

AC 15, touch 15, flat-footed 11 (+4 Dex, +1 size)

hp 22 (4d8+4)

Fort +2, **Ref** +8, **Will** +1

Weaknesses light blindness

OFFENSE

Speed 30 ft.

Melee kukri +8 (1d3–1/18–20 plus black smear poison)

Special Attacks death throes, poison use, sneak attack +2d6, soul harvest

Spell-Like Abilities (CL 4th; concentration +6)

Constant—*detect magic*

At will—*bleed* (DC 12), *chill touch* (DC 13), *darkness*, *spectral hand*

3/day—*daze monster* (DC 14), *death knell* (DC 14), *inflict moderate wounds* (DC 14)

STATISTICS

Str 9, **Dex** 18, **Con** 12, **Int** 10, **Wis** 11, **Cha** 15

Base Atk +3; **CMB** +1; **CMD** 15

Feats Skill Focus (Use Magic Device), Weapon Finesse

Skills Climb +3, Perception +4, Spellcraft +7, Stealth +12, Use Magic Device +12;

Racial Modifiers +4 Climb, +4 Stealth, +4 Perception

Languages Dark Folk

SQ magical knack

ECOLOGY

Environment any underground

Organization solitary, gang (1 dark slayer and 2–5 dark stalkers), or clan (20–80 dark creepers plus 1 dark stalker or dark slayer per 20 dark creepers)

Treasure standard (kukri, black smear [2 doses] [see *Bestiary* 54], other gear)

SPECIAL ABILITIES

Death Throes (Su) When a dark slayer is slain, its body implodes violently into nothingness, leaving its gear in a heap on the ground. All creatures within a 10-foot burst take 1d8 points of sonic damage and must make a DC 13 Fortitude save or be deafened for 2d4 rounds. The save DC is Constitution-based.

Magical Knack (Ex) Spellcraft and Use Magic Device are always class skills for dark slayers.

Soul Harvest (Su) When a dark slayer damages a flat-footed foe or a foe it is flanking with a melee touch spell or spell-like ability that deals hit point damage, the spell does an additional 1d6 points of damage and the dark slayer gains an equal amount of temporary hit points. These temporary hit points last for a maximum of 1 hour.

Dark slayers are a relatively rare sub-race of the dark folk imbued with malign energies that grant them a suite of deadly spell-like abilities beyond those normally accessible to their kin. They are usually encountered leading small bands of dark creepers, and seethe with barely concealed envy of the dark stalkers, ever scheming to displace them and claim a dark folk tribe of their own. Dark stalkers direct the slayers for their own ends, grooming them for use against enemies, ever ready to sacrifice a slayer in battle for an advantage, however temporary.

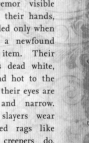

Unlike other dark folk, dark slayers embrace their evil impulses. Their pleasures extend more to murder and pain than to theft or mayhem. Dark slayers are obsessed with magical trinkets, coveting them above all else. Sadly, their obsessive need to fiddle and tinker often leaves their pretties broken or depleted.

Dark slayers stand just short of 4 feet tall and weigh 50 pounds. Most have a persistent tremor visible in their hands, stilled only when fondling a newfound magic item. Their skin is dead white, dry, and hot to the touch; their eyes are dark and narrow. Dark slayers wear salvaged rags like dark creepers do, but they discard the rags when they grow too tattered or foul-smelling.

Illustrations by Alberto Dal Lago

PATHFINDER
ROLEPLAYING GAME

DEATH WORM

This large worm's body is muscular and scaly, its mouth a nightmare of row upon row of triangular teeth.

DEATH WORM	CR 6

XP 2,400

N Large magical beast

Init +1; **Senses** darkvision 60 ft., low-light vision, tremorsense 60 ft.; Perception +11

DEFENSE

AC 19, touch 10, flat-footed 18 (+1 Dex, +9 natural, –1 size)

hp 68 (8d10+24)

Fort +9, **Ref** +7, **Will** +4

Defensive Abilities corrosive blood, venomous skin; **Immune** acid, electricity, poison

OFFENSE

Speed 20 ft., burrow 20 ft.

Melee bite +11 (2d8+6 plus poison)

Ranged electrical jolt +8 ranged touch (4d6 electricity)

Space 10 ft.; **Reach** 5 ft.

Special Attacks breath weapon (30-ft. line, 8d6 acid damage, Reflex DC 17 for half, usable every 1d4 rounds)

STATISTICS

Str 18, **Dex** 13, **Con** 16, **Int** 3, **Wis** 11, **Cha** 5

Base Atk +8; **CMB** +13; **CMD** 24

Feats Cleave, Improved Overrun, Iron Will, Power Attack

Skills Perception +11, Stealth –3 (+13 in deserts); **Racial Modifiers** +16 Stealth in deserts or rocky areas

Languages Terran

ECOLOGY

Environment warm deserts, plains, or hills

Organization solitary

Treasure none

SPECIAL ABILITIES

Corrosive Blood (Ex) A death worm's blood can corrode metal on contact. If a creature damages a death worm with a piercing or slashing weapon made of metal, the creature's blood deals 3d6 points of acid damage to the metal weapon (unlike most forms of energy damage, this damage is not halved when applied to a metal object, although it does still have to penetrate the metal's hardness). The weapon's wielder can halve the damage the weapon takes by making a successful DC 17 Reflex save. Creatures made of metal that deal slashing or piercing damage to a death worm with a natural attack take 3d6 points of acid damage (a DC 17 Reflex save

halves this damage). The corrosive elements of the blood fade 1 round after it leaves the worm's body or the worm dies. The save DC is Constitution-based.

Electrical Jolt (Su) A death worm can fire a jolt of electricity from its mouth as a standard action. The range increment for this ranged touch attack is 60 feet.

Poison (Ex) Bite—injury, or skin—contact; save Fort DC 17; *frequency* 1/round for 6 rounds; *effect* 1d2 Con damage; *cure* 2 saves.

Venomous Skin (Ex) A death worm's skin secretes a noxious, waxy substance. This venomous sheen poisons any creature that touches a death worm, either by making a successful attack with an unarmed strike or natural weapon or with a touch attack. A creature that grapples a death worm is also exposed to the creature's venomous skin.

The reclusive death worm is much feared in the deserts, badlands, and steppes in which it dwells, for it brings to a battle multiple harrowing ways of inflicting death upon its foes—acid, lightning, poison, and its ravenous jaws. The creatures are remarkably good at hiding amid the sands and rocks of their favored terrain, and devilishly efficient at selecting foes that they can easily kill. This combination makes stories of these creatures hard to confirm, and in most urban centers, common wisdom is that the tales of death worms are fabrications— attempts to impress city folk or hallucinations born of too much drink.

A death worm is 15 feet long and weighs 1,200 pounds— although rumors of much larger death worms persist.

DECAPUS

This swollen cephalopod has ten writhing tentacles and a hideously monstrous face with pale, milky eyes on its bulbous body.

DECAPUS	CR 4

XP 1,200
CE Medium aberration
Init +1; **Senses** darkvision 60 ft.; Perception +11

DEFENSE

AC 16, touch 11, flat-footed 15 (+1 Dex, +5 natural)
hp 45 (6d8+18)
Fort +4, **Ref** +3, **Will** +5

OFFENSE

Speed 10 ft., climb 30 ft.
Melee bite +7 (1d6+3), tentacles +8 (2d4+3 plus grab)
Space 5 ft.; **Reach** 5 ft.
Special Attacks constrict (2d4+4)
Spell-Like Abilities (CL 6th; concentration +7)
　At will—*minor image* (DC 13)

STATISTICS

Str 16, **Dex** 13, **Con** 15, **Int** 10, **Wis** 11, **Cha** 12
Base Atk +4; **CMB** +7 (+11 grapple); **CMD** 18 (can't be tripped)
Feats Skill Focus (Bluff), Toughness, Weapon Focus (tentacles)
Skills Acrobatics +7 (−1 jump), Bluff +7, Climb +16, Escape Artist +5, Intimidate +7, Perception +11, Spellcraft +6, Stealth +9; **Racial Modifiers** +4 Perception
Languages Aklo
SQ sound mimicry (voices), tentacles

ECOLOGY

Environment temperate forests or underground
Organization solitary or mated pair
Treasure standard

SPECIAL ABILITIES

Tentacles (Ex) A decapus's tentacles must all strike at a single target, but they do so as a primary attack.

Named for its resemblance to a 10-armed octopus, the strange decapus is one of many bizarre creatures that hail from the deepest caverns of the world. When they are encountered aboveground, their affinity for forests (they particularly enjoy clambering around in tangled canopies) suggests that their original source might be some strange, deep underground cavern wherein magical jungles grow.

The decapus is a fairly intelligent creature—an ambush predator that makes excellent use of its ability to weave magical visual illusions and to imitate the voices of other creatures it has heard speaking. Typical decapuses know only the Aklo tongue, but when they use their sound mimicry ability to imitate creatures speaking in other languages, they can typically form short (up to three words long) sentences even when imitating a language they don't actually know.

The decapus's physical structure most resembles that of a bloated octopus with 10 tentacles. It lacks bones and takes its shape from its rubbery, muscular flesh. Most have sickly, olive skin patched with scraggly tangles of hair, with darker blue or purple coloration around their faces and crimson or orange tips to their tentacles. These tentacles are covered with tiny suction cups and hooks, affording them great skill at climbing or clutching prey. On the ground, though, they are slow, plodding creatures that flop and wriggle relatively inefficiently. As a result, they prefer regions like forest canopies, narrow fissures, stalactite forests, or other regions where they can use their climb speed.

The decapus favors humanoid flesh over all other food; most are quite fond of gnome flesh in particular. This creature has an enormous appetite that often drives it to consume whatever food is available—the decapus is not above cannibalism when other food sources are scarce. For this reason, these monsters are largely solitary creatures, except when the urge to mate overwhelms their urge to feed. Females give birth to small litters of 2–4 live offspring. The females often need to defend them from the males, which, if left unsupervised, typically eat the newborn decapuses. The young mature rapidly, growing to full size after a mere 7 to 11 months, after which they depart to claim their own territories. Once a decapus reaches maturity, it can live to 100 years old—although their violent natures usually result in much shorter lifespans.

A typical decapus has a legspan of 8 feet and weighs 200 pounds.

DEMON, KALAVAKUS

This muscular, violet demon walks upon elephantine feet. Large, razor-sharp horns cover its body.

KALAVAKUS	CR 10

XP 9,600

CE Medium outsider (chaotic, demon, evil, extraplanar)

Init +1; **Senses** darkvision 60 ft.; Perception +24

DEFENSE

AC 25, touch 11, flat-footed 24 (+1 Dex, +14 natural)

hp 125 (10d10+70)

Fort +10, **Ref** +8, **Will** +10

DR 10/good; **Immune** electricity, poison; **Resist** acid 10, cold 10, fire 10; **SR** 21

OFFENSE

Speed 30 ft.

Melee bite +16 (1d6+6), 2 claws +16 (1d8+6), gore +16 (2d6+6)

Special Attacks enslave soul, horns, powerful charge (gore, 4d6+12)

Spell-Like Abilities (CL 12th; concentration +15)

At will—*command* (DC 14), *greater teleport* (self plus 50 lbs. of objects only), *telekinesis* (DC 18)

3/day—*air walk*, *dominate person* (DC 18), *haste*

1/day—*greater command* (DC 18), *summon* (level 4, 1 kalavakus 40%), *symbol of persuasion* (DC 19)

STATISTICS

Str 22, **Dex** 13, **Con** 24, **Int** 15, **Wis** 17, **Cha** 16

Base Atk +10; **CMB** +16 (+22 disarm); **CMD** 27

Feats Combat Expertise, Improved Bull Rush, Improved Disarm, Improved Trip, Power Attack

Skills Acrobatics +14, Climb +19, Intimidate +16, Knowledge (planes) +15, Perception +24, Sense Motive +16, Stealth +14, Use Magic Device +16; **Racial Modifiers** +8 Perception

Languages Abyssal, Celestial, Common, Draconic; telepathy 100 ft.

ECOLOGY

Environment any (the Abyss)

Organization solitary, pair, or slaver gang (3–6 kalavakuses plus 10–20 slaves)

Treasure standard

SPECIAL ABILITIES

Enslave Soul (Su) A kalavakus can attempt to enslave the soul of any mortal creature within 60 feet as a swift action. The kalavakus must have line of sight to the target. The target can resist this special attack with a DC 18 Will save, but is staggered for 1 round even if the save is successful. If the save is successful, the creature is immune to this ability for 24 hours. If the save is a failure, the target's soul is enslaved—this creature takes a –6 penalty on all attack rolls and saving throws against that kalavakus. If a creature with an enslaved soul is slain by that kalavakus, the soul immediately infuses the demon's body, affecting it with a *heal* spell (CL 12th). A kalavakus can have only one mortal soul enslaved at a time—if it enslaves a second soul, the first is released. This is a mind-affecting death effect. The save DC is Charisma-based.

Horns (Ex) The kalavakus's numerous horns can easily catch weapons and yank them away from opponents. The demon gains a +4 racial bonus on all disarm attempts as a result.

Known to some as "horned demons," the kalavakus demons are hulking, muscled beasts. They work as slavers on the Abyss, sometimes as harem keepers or captains of the guard for a more powerful demon, and at other times as mercenaries who sell their captured victims for profit to anyone with the funds to pay.

A kalavakus is 7 feet tall and weighs 450 pounds. They form from the souls of evil mortals who were slavers in their mortal lives.

DEMON, OMOX

This rancid-smelling mound of animated ooze has about its shifting countenance the hideous shape of a half-melted man.

OMOX	CR 12	

XP 19,200
CE Medium outsider (aquatic, chaotic, demon, evil, extraplanar)
Init +11; **Senses** darkvision 120 ft.; Perception +28

DEFENSE

AC 28, touch 18, flat-footed 20 (+7 Dex, +1 dodge, +10 natural)
hp 162 (13d10+91)
Fort +15, **Ref** +13, **Will** +12
DR 10/good; **Immune** acid, critical hits, disease, electricity, paralysis, poison, polymorph, sleep effects, stunning; **Resist** cold 10, fire 10; **SR** 23

OFFENSE

Speed 40 ft., climb 20 ft., swim 80 ft.
Melee 2 slams +21 (1d6+8 plus 3d6 acid and grab)
Ranged slime +20 (1d6 plus 3d6 acid and entangle)
Special Attacks smothering
Spell-Like Abilities (CL 12th; concentration +16)
At will—*create water, greater teleport* (self plus 50 lbs. of objects only), *liquid leap* (see below), *telekinesis* (DC 19)
3/day—*gaseous form, control water, poison* (DC 18), *stinking cloud* (DC 17)
1/day—*acid fog, summon* (level 4, 1 omox 30% or 1d4 babaus 60%)

STATISTICS

Str 26, **Dex** 25, **Con** 24, **Int** 15, **Wis** 19, **Cha** 18
Base Atk +13; **CMB** +21; **CMD** 39 (can't be tripped)
Feats Combat Reflexes, Dodge, Improved Initiative, Lightning Reflexes, Mobility, Spring Attack, Vital Strike
Skills Acrobatics +23 (+27 jump), Climb +32, Escape Artist +23, Knowledge (dungeoneering) +18, Knowledge (planes) +18, Perception +28, Sense Motive +20, Stealth +23 (+33 when submerged), Swim +32; **Racial Modifiers** +16 Escape Artist, +8 Perception, +10 Stealth when submerged
Languages Abyssal, Celestial, Draconic; telepathy 100 ft.
SQ amorphous, amphibious, compression

ECOLOGY

Environment any (the Abyss)
Organization solitary or clot (2–6)
Treasure standard

SPECIAL ABILITIES

Liquid Leap (Sp) As long as an omox is in contact with liquid, it can use *dimension door* as a swift action (CL 12th); its starting and ending points must be connected by a contiguous mass of liquid.
Slime (Su) An omox's nauseating body is composed of sticky, acidic slime. As an attack action, it can hurl a glob of slime (range increment 20 feet). Any creature that is struck by the glob must make a DC 23 Reflex

save or become entangled for 1d6 rounds. The save DC is Constitution-based.
Smothering (Ex) An omox can use its grab ability against a creature of any size. When it grabs a foe, it attempts to flow over and into the victim's mouth and nose to smother it. Each round the omox maintains its grapple, its victim cannot breathe or speak. See page 445 of the *Pathfinder RPG Core Rulebook* for rules on how long a victim can hold its breath and the consequences of suffocation.

Amorphous beings of living slime, these repulsive demons lurk in fetid pools and lakes of filth, eager to drown unwary passersby. When summoned to the Material Plane, omoxes typically guard places of sacred filth or waters watched over by cults of Jubilex, the demon lord with which these foul demons are most commonly associated.

A typical omox stands 7 feet tall and weighs 1,200 pounds. They form from the souls of those who destroyed beautiful things in life, or who befouled and desecrated objects of purity.

Demon, Shemhazian

This enormous, bestial demon combines the worst aspects of a bear, a mantis, a wolf, and a reptilian humanoid.

SHEMHAZIAN	CR 16

XP 76,800

CE Gargantuan outsider (chaotic, demon, evil, extraplanar)

Init +4; **Senses** darkvision 60 ft., *detect good*, scent, *true seeing*; Perception +36

DEFENSE

AC 31, touch 11, flat-footed 26 (+4 Dex, +1 dodge, +20 natural, −4 size)

hp 246 (17d10+153)

Fort +19, **Ref** +11, **Will** +18

DR 10/cold iron and good; **Immune** electricity, poison; **Resist** acid 10, cold 10, fire 10; **SR** 27

OFFENSE

Speed 40 ft., climb 20 ft., fly 60 ft. (good)

Melee bite +25 (2d6+12 plus 2d4 Strength drain), 2 claws +25 (2d6+12), 2 pincers +23 (1d12+6), tail slap +23 (2d6+6)

Space 20 ft.; **Reach** 20 ft. (30 ft. with tail slap)

Special Attacks paralyzing gaze, rend (2 claws, 2d6+18)

Spell-Like Abilities (CL 15th; concentration +18)

Constant—*detect good*, *fly*, *true seeing*

At will—*greater teleport* (self plus 50 lbs. of objects only), *invisibility*, *telekinesis* (DC 18)

3/day—*clairaudience/clairvoyance*, *mass inflict serious wounds* (DC 20), *prying eyes*

1/day—*blasphemy* (DC 20), summon (level 5, 1 shemhazian 30% or 1d4 vrocks 60%)

STATISTICS

Str 35, **Dex** 19, **Con** 29, **Int** 10, **Wis** 26, **Cha** 16

Base Atk +17; **CMB** +33; **CMD** 48

Feats Awesome Blow, Combat Reflexes, Dodge, Improved Bull Rush, Improved Vital Strike, Lightning Reflexes, Multiattack, Power Attack, Vital Strike

Skills Bluff +23, Climb +20, Fly +2, Heal +28, Intimidate +23, Knowledge (religion) +20, Perception +36, Sense Motive +28; **Racial Modifiers** +8 Perception

Languages Abyssal, Celestial, Draconic; telepathy 100 ft.

ECOLOGY

Environment any (the Abyss)

Organization solitary

Treasure standard

SPECIAL ABILITIES

Paralyzing Gaze (Su) Paralysis for 1 round, 30 feet, Fortitude DC 21 negates. Evil creatures are immune to this effect. The save DC is Charisma-based.

Strength Drain (Su) A shemhazian demon deals 2d4 points of Strength drain with each successful bite. A DC 27 Fortitude save reduces this amount to 1d4 points of Strength damage. The save DC is Constitution-based.

Although nearly all the horrors of the Abyss prey upon one another in an endless, eternal bloodbath, shemhazians are predators among predators. They are more intimidating and physically powerful than most demons, combining the features of numerous insectile and bestial hunters into one massive, deadly form. Although they don't require sustenance, shemhazians take perverse delight in mutilating and eating their victims.

A shemhazian stands 35 feet tall and weighs 12,000 pounds. They form from the sinful souls of torturers and those who enjoyed mutilating living victims to death.

Illustration by Imaginary Friends

DEMON, VROLIKAI

This black-skinned, bat-winged demon has four arms; a long, thin tail; and a leering, fanged face with dead, white eyes.

VROLIKAI	CR 19

XP 204,800
CE Large outsider (chaotic, demon, evil, extraplanar)
Init +10; **Senses** darkvision 120 ft., low-light vision, *true seeing*;
Perception +36

DEFENSE

AC 35, touch 16, flat-footed 28 (+6 Dex, +1 dodge, +19 natural,
–1 size)
hp 332 (19d10+228)
Fort +18, **Ref** +17, **Will** +17
DR 15/cold iron and good; **Immune** death effects, electricity,
poison; **Resist** acid 10, cold 10, fire 10; **SR** 30

OFFENSE

Speed 40 ft., fly 60 ft. (perfect)
Melee +1 black flame knife +29/+24/+19/+14 (1d6+11/19–20 plus
energy drain), 3 +1 black flame knives +29 (1d6+6/19–20 plus
energy drain), bite +23 (1d8+5), sting +23 (1d6+5 plus madness)
or bite +28 (1d8+10), 4 claws +28 (1d6+10), sting +28 (1d6+10
plus madness)
Space 10 ft.; **Reach** 10 ft.
Special Attacks black flame knives,
death-stealing gaze, multiweapon
mastery
Spell-Like Abilities (CL 19th; concentration +27)
Constant—*true seeing*
At will—*deeper darkness, enervation, greater
teleport* (self plus 50 lbs. of objects only),
telekinesis (DC 23)
3/day—quickened *enervation, regenerate, silence*
(DC 20), *vampiric touch*
1/day—*mass hold monster* (DC 27), *summon*
(level 6, 1 marilith 50% or 1d4 glabrezus
75%), *symbol of death* (DC 26)

STATISTICS

Str 30, **Dex** 23, **Con** 35, **Int** 22, **Wis** 23, **Cha** 26
Base Atk +19; **CMB** +30; **CMD** 47
Feats Cleave, Combat Expertise, Dodge, Flyby
Attack, Improved Initiative, Improved Vital
Strike, Mobility, Power Attack, Quicken
Spell-Like Ability (*enervation*), Vital Strike
Skills Acrobatics +25 (+29 jump), Bluff +30,
Fly +34, Intimidate +27, Knowledge
(arcana) +25, Knowledge (planes) +28,
Perception +36, Sense Motive +28, Spellcraft +25,
Stealth +24 (+32 in shadowy areas), Survival +25, Use
Magic Device +27; **Racial Modifiers** +8 Perception, +8
Stealth in shadowy areas
Languages Abyssal, Celestial, Draconic; telepathy 100 ft.

ECOLOGY

Environment any (the Abyss)
Organization solitary
Treasure double

SPECIAL ABILITIES

Black Flame Knives (Su) A vrolikai can manifest daggers made
of crystallized black flames in each of its four hands as a free
action. These weapons function as +1 *daggers* that bestow
one permanent negative level on a successful hit. A DC 27
Fortitude negates the negative level, although on a critical
hit, no save is allowed. The save DC is Charisma-based.

Death-Stealing Gaze (Su) 1 permanent negative level, 30 ft.,
Fort DC 27 negates. Creatures slain by these negative levels
become juju zombies (see page 291) under the vrolikai's
control. The save DC is Charisma-based.

Madness (Su) A creature stung by a vrolikai's tail must make
a DC 27 Will save to resist taking 1d6 points of Charisma
drain and becoming confused for 1d4 rounds. On a
successful save, the victim is instead staggered for 1d4
rounds as strange visions assault its mind. This is a mind-
affecting effect. The save DC is Charisma-based.

Multiweapon Mastery (Ex) A vrolikai never takes penalties on
its attack roll when fighting with multiple weapons.

A vrolikai is 14 feet tall but weighs only 500 pounds.
Unlike other demons, it does not form from a sinful
soul—it instead manifests from a nabasu demon
that returns to the Abyss after growing to maturity
on the Material Plane. Not all nabasus survive this
transformation, but those who do become powerful
indeed—vrolikai usually rule large regions of
unclaimed Abyssal land, and often serve as
assassins or ambassadors to demon lords in
need of an agent in a distant realm.

Illustration by Tyler Walpole

81

DENIZEN OF LENG

*Shrouded in tattered leather robes, this strange humanoid looks
more alien and horrific the more one studies its twitching visage.*

DENIZEN OF LENG	CR 8

XP 4,800

CE Medium outsider (chaotic, evil, extraplanar)

Init +4; **Senses** darkvision 60 ft.; Perception +16

DEFENSE

AC 21, touch 15, flat-footed 16 (+4 Dex, +1 dodge, +6 natural)

hp 95 (10d10+40); planar fast healing 5

Fort +11, **Ref** +11, **Will** +6

Defensive Abilities no breath, unusual anatomy; **Immune**
poison; **Resist** cold 30, electricity 30; **SR** 19

OFFENSE

Speed 40 ft.

Melee bite +14 (1d6+2 plus 1d6 Dexterity drain),
2 claws +14 (1d4+2)

Special Attacks sneak attack +5d6

Spell-Like Abilities (CL 10th;
concentration +15)

Constant—*tongues*

3/day—*detect thoughts* (DC 17),
hypnotic pattern (DC 17), *levitate,
minor image* (DC 17)

1/day—*locate object, plane shift*
(DC 20, self only)

STATISTICS

Str 14, **Dex** 18, **Con** 19, **Int** 18,
Wis 17, **Cha** 21

Base Atk +10; **CMB** +12; **CMD** 27

Feats Deceitful, Dodge, Mobility,
Persuasive, Weapon Finesse

Skills Bluff +22, Diplomacy +7, Disable
Device +14, Disguise +12 (+16
as humanoid), Intimidate +12,
Knowledge (any one) +17,
Perception +16, Profession
(sailor) +8, Sense Motive +16,
Sleight of Hand +17, Spellcraft +12,
Stealth +17, Use Magic Device +18;
Racial Modifiers +4 Disguise
when disguised as a
Medium humanoid

Languages Aklo; *tongues*

ECOLOGY

Environment any land

Organization solitary, gang
(2–5), or crew (6–15)

Treasure double (500
to 2,000 gp in rubies,
other treasure)

SPECIAL ABILITIES

Dexterity Drain (Su) The otherworldly teeth and tongues of
a denizen of Leng deal 1d6 points of Dexterity drain with a
bite. Constructs, elementals, and other creatures that do not
possess flesh are immune to this effect. A successful DC 19
Fortitude save reduces the Dexterity drain to 1 point. The
save DC is Constitution-based.

Planar Fast Healing (Su) A denizen of Leng maintains a
connection to Leng at all times, and when away from
Leng, it has fast healing 5. It loses this ability on Leng or in
areas where planar connections do not function. If killed,
a denizen's body dissolves into nothingness in 1d4 rounds,
leaving behind its equipment. A slain denizen reforms in
Leng, similar to a slain summoned creature; it can only be
permanently killed if its fast healing is negated.

Unusual Anatomy (Ex) A denizen's internal anatomy varies
from individual to individual, and has a 50% chance to treat
any critical hit or sneak attack against it as a normal hit.

These eerie denizens travel the universe from their
strange homeland of Leng, walking uncontested only
when they disguise themselves as humans by wearing
loose-fitting robes and wrappings about the
head and face. Under these disguises, they
have horned brows, clawed fingers,
mouths full of tentacles, and crooked
goatish legs with cloven hooves.
Many scholars have argued over where
the otherworldly realm of Leng lies—
some believe it can be found among
the Outer Planes, while others are
convinced it can only be reached
via a dimension of dreams. The
denizens of Leng can travel to
other planes freely, and often
do so in strange, black ships,
constantly seeking new breeds
of slaves or trading rubies for
unusual services or magical treasures.
At other times, their visits
are much more violent,
focusing on abducting
victims for use as slaves
or worse. On Leng, these
denizens have long fought
a war against that realm's
monstrous spiders, a war
that sometimes spills
over into other worlds.

A denizen of Leng
weighs 200 pounds
and stands roughly 5-1/2
feet tall.

Illustration by Kevin Yan

Destrachan

The hunched, reptilian beast lopes on two clawed feet, its eyeless head dominated by a huge circular maw filled with jagged teeth.

DESTRACHAN	CR 8

XP 4,800

NE Large aberration

Init +5; **Senses** blindsight 100 ft.; Perception +27

DEFENSE

AC 19, touch 11, flat-footed 17 (+1 Dex, +1 dodge, +8 natural, –1 size)

hp 90 (12d8+36)

Fort +9, **Ref** +7, **Will** +12

Defensive Abilities protection from sonics; **Immune** gaze attacks, visual effects, illusions, and attacks relying on sight; **Resist** sonic 30

OFFENSE

Speed 30 ft.

Melee bite +12 (2d6+4), 2 claws +12 (1d8+4)

Space 10 ft.; **Reach** 5 ft.

Special Attacks destructive harmonics

STATISTICS

Str 18, **Dex** 13, **Con** 16, **Int** 13, **Wis** 18, **Cha** 13

Base Atk +9; **CMB** +14; **CMD** 26

Feats Dodge, Great Fortitude, Improved Initiative, Lightning Reflexes, Mobility, Vital Strike

Skills Climb +19, Perception +27, Sense Motive +16, Stealth +12, Survival +19; **Racial Modifiers** +8 Perception (hearing only)

Languages Common (cannot speak)

ECOLOGY

Environment underground

Organization solitary, pair, or pack (3–5)

Treasure incidental

SPECIAL ABILITIES

Destructive Harmonics (Su)

A destrachan can project a blast of sonic energy in a cone up to 80 feet long or in a 30-foot-radius burst centered on itself as a standard action. It can adjust the harmonics of its sonic cry to generate one of two different effects on targets within the area of effect, but can only create one of these effects with each use of this ability. The save DCs are Constitution-based.

Destruction: All creatures within the area of effect of the destructive harmonics take 8d6 points of sonic damage—a DC 19 Reflex save halves this damage. If the destrachan wishes, this damage can instead deal nonlethal damage rather than sonic damage. Alternatively, the destrachan can target a single crystal, metal, stone, or wooden object within 80 feet with this attack—that object takes 8d6 points of damage. This damage is not halved when applied to the object's hit points, but is reduced by the object's hardness. A magical or attended object can attempt a DC 19 Reflex save to halve the damage.

Pain: Rather than deal damage, the destrachan can cause intense pain and overwhelming sound to affect all creatures within the area. Targets in the area must succeed on a DC 19 Fortitude save to avoid being stunned for 1 round and deafened for 1d6 rounds.

Protection from Sonics (Ex) A destrachan gains a +4 racial bonus on all saves against sonic attacks. It is immune to the effects of its own destructive harmonics. A destrachan whose sense of hearing is impaired is effectively blinded, treating all targets as if they had total concealment.

Despite its bestial appearance, the destrachan is in fact a creature of cunning and cruel intellect that enjoys inflicting pain and viciously toying with its prey. It has no eyes, and is completely blind, but possesses a pair of complex, tripartite ears it can adjust to different levels of sensitivity to sound, allowing the destrachan to hunt in absolute darkness as if it were able to see.

Destrachans are carnivores, preferring to stalk and kill live prey, although they also feast on carrion. This habit serves them well, since they often kill more than they can immediately consume. They often hunt in packs, using a complex series of clicks, shrieks, and whistles to communicate with each other. While destrachans cannot speak, they are capable of understanding spoken languages like the common tongue, and often take pleasure in their victims' cries and pleas for mercy.

Illustration by Damien Mammoliti

DEVIL, ACCUSER

This childlike blasphemy conjoins the features of a plump human infant and a gigantic, gore-fattened fly.

ACCUSER DEVIL (ZEBUB)   CR 3

XP 800

LE Small outsider (devil, evil, extraplanar, lawful)

Init +8; **Senses** darkvision 60 ft.; Perception +9

DEFENSE

AC 17, touch 15, flat-footed 13 (+4 Dex, +2 natural, +1 size)

hp 30 (4d10+8)

Fort +6, **Ref** +10, **Will** +3

DR 5/good or silver; **Immune** fire, poison; **Resist** acid 10, cold 10

OFFENSE

Speed 20 ft., fly 60 ft. (perfect)

Melee bite +5 (1d6 plus 1d6 acid and disease)

Spell-Like Abilities (CL 8th; concentration +9)

At will—*greater teleport* (self plus 50 lbs. of objects only), *invisibility* (self only)

3/day—*grease, summon swarm, whispering wind*

1/day—*summon* (level 3, 1 zebub or 1d4 lemures, 40%)

STATISTICS

Str 11, **Dex** 18, **Con** 14, **Int** 9, **Wis** 15, **Cha** 12

Base Atk +4; **CMB** +3; **CMD** 17

Feats Improved Initiative, Lightning Reflexes

Skills Bluff +8, Fly +21, Knowledge (planes) +6, Perception +9, Stealth +15

Languages Celestial, Draconic, Infernal; telepathy 100 ft.

SQ infernal eye

ECOLOGY

Environment any (Hell)

Organization solitary, pair, or swarm (3–28)

Treasure standard

SPECIAL ABILITIES

Disease (Ex) *Devil Chills:* Bite—injury; *save* Fort DC 14; *onset* 1d4 days; *frequency* 1 day; *effect* 1d4 Str damage; *cure* 3 consecutive saves.

Infernal Eye (Su) A zebub records all that it sees and may pass its visions on to another creature. By remaining in contact with a willing creature, it can replay up to 24 hours of witnessed events, or shorter incidents if it so chooses. It takes a zebub 1 round to replay 1 hour of recorded images, which the target receives in a flash of information, without sound or other sensory information. After relaying its findings, the zebub cannot replay its visions of those events again. A zebub cannot replay its visions for an unwilling creature or as an attack, no matter how horrific the events it might have witnessed.

Childlike souls tormented and scoured of innocence by the flames of Hell and then reshaped by the mad whims of the archdevil Baalzebul, accuser devils embody the foul, merciless, and pervasive corruptions of the infernal host. From the depths of the Pit they rise in buzzing, shrieking plagues unleashed to taint the land, despoil weak flesh, and reveal exploitable secrets. En masse they display little of the cunning or subtlety typical of devilkind, spreading ruin at the will of their fiendish masters. Alone, though, a zebub is a craven, deceitful thing, lurking in darkness and filth, endlessly spying and vying for the petty favors of greater evils.

Accuser devils are almost exclusively formed amid the cesspits of frozen Cocytus, the seventh layer of Hell. Within the Pit they serve countless infernal lords as messengers and spies, with droves being unleashed upon myriad mortal worlds with a mandate to seek out souls ripe for corruption or those whose sins might lead to greater damnations. Many zebubs overstep the freedoms of such vague missions, seeking to manipulate weak-willed or easily intimidated mortals into all manner of trivial evils, dispensing shrill orders in their buzzing, childlike voices. Despite the fact that many zebub plots end in the zebubs' own revelation and destruction, few diabolical lords allow the slaying of their spies to go unpunished.

The zebub's ability to grant other creatures visions of what it has witnessed makes it an unusually useful creature to many conjurers. Relatively easy to conjure with a spell like *lesser planar ally* or *lesser planar binding*, an accuser devil can be an invaluable spy. One simply orders the foul little devil to become invisible and then infiltrate an area where visual information is hidden, with orders to teleport back to its point of origin to grant visions of what it observed to its master. Those who make use of accuser devils in this manner should take care to watch their own actions or what they reveal, of course, for such a creature can just as easily be bribed or intimidated into revealing visions that some conjurers might not want being made public. It's common practice among conjurers to kill their accuser devils once they've completed their missions of infiltration and observation.

These lesser devils stand just over 2 feet tall and rarely weigh more than 25 pounds.

Illustration by Kekai Kotaki

DEVIL, BELIER

This amphisbaenic monstrosity has the body of a slug with a leech's mouth at one end and a knot of three human heads at the other.

BELIER DEVIL (BDELLAVRITRA) CR 16

XP 76,800

LE Large outsider (devil, evil, extraplanar, lawful)

Init +10; **Senses** darkvision 60 ft., see in darkness; Perception +28

DEFENSE

AC 33, touch 15, flat-footed 27 (+6 Dex, +18 natural, −1 size)

hp 212 (17d10+119)

Fort +17, **Ref** +11, **Will** +20

DR 10/good and silver; **Immune** fire, poison; **Resist** acid 10, cold 10; **SR** 28

OFFENSE

Speed 20 ft., fly 60 ft. (perfect)

Melee bite +23 (4d8+7), 3 tongues +23 (2d6+7/19–20 plus grab)

Space 10 ft.; **Reach** 10 ft. (20 ft. with tongues)

Special Attacks blood drain (1d4 Con damage), constrict (1d6+7), possession, strangle

Spell-Like Abilities (CL 17th; concentration +24)

At will—*acid arrow, greater dispel magic, greater teleport* (self plus 50 pounds of objects only), *persistent image* (DC 22)

3/day—*acid fog, dimensional anchor, dominate person* (DC 22), *greater scrying* (DC 24), *mass suggestion* (DC 23)

1/day—*blasphemy* (DC 24), *demand* (DC 25), *magic jar* (DC 22), *plane shift* (DC 22), *summon* (level 6, 3 barbed devils 45%), *waves of exhaustion*

STATISTICS

Str 24, **Dex** 23, **Con** 25, **Int** 25, **Wis** 26, **Cha** 24

Base Atk +17; **CMB** +25 (+29 grapple); **CMD** 41 (can't be tripped)

Feats Combat Expertise, Combat Reflexes, Greater Disarm, Greater Trip, Improved Critical (tongue), Improved Disarm, Improved Initiative, Improved Trip, Iron Will

Skills Appraise +24, Bluff +27, Diplomacy +27, Fly +32, Intimidate +24, Knowledge (arcana, local, nobility, and planes) +27, Perception +28, Sense Motive +28, Spellcraft +24, Stealth +22

Languages Celestial, Common, Draconic, Infernal; telepathy 100 ft.

ECOLOGY

Environment any (Hell)

Organization solitary

Treasure double

SPECIAL ABILITIES

Possession (Su) When a belier devil uses its *magic jar* spell-like ability, it can identify and pinpoint life forces accurately, allowing it to select its victims with ease. It does not require a receptacle to use *magic jar*. If it uses *magic jar* on a host while on the Material Plane, its own body becomes ethereal for the duration of the possession and the *magic jar* effect lasts until the effect is dispelled, the devil ends the effect, it is forced out of its host body, or it or its host body is slain.

Masterful possessors and foul manipulators, belier devils are among the most feared masterminds of Hell. Known as bdellavritras to devilkind, these worm-like fiends avoid physical confrontation. Instead, they target influential individuals for possession, using them to manipulate events by proxy. If their schemes are uncovered, the devils retaliate with all the power at their host bodies' disposal.

A bdellavritra's voice can emanate from its worm-like maw, from any of its human-like mouths, or from all four at once, as it desires. Each mouth has its own distinct voice, often pleasing to the human ear. Bdellavritras typically reach lengths of 16 feet from worm-mouth to human heads, and weigh 3,000 pounds.

Illustration by Kekai Kotaki

85

DEVIL, HANDMAIDEN

Twin tentacles stretch from the crown of this feminine fiend's head, while her lower body blooms in a gown of writhing tendrils.

HANDMAIDEN DEVIL (GYLOU) CR 14

XP 38,400

LE Medium outsider (devil, evil, extraplanar, lawful)

Init +11; **Senses** darkvision 60 ft., *true seeing*; Perception +23

DEFENSE

AC 31, touch 17, flat-footed 24 (+7 Dex, +14 natural)

hp 187 (15d10+105)

Fort +16, **Ref** +16, **Will** +10

DR 10/good; **Immune** fire, poison; **Resist** acid 10, cold 10; **SR** 25

OFFENSE

Speed 40 ft., fly 60 ft. (average)

Melee 2 claws +22 (2d8+7/19–20/x3), 2 tentacles +20 (1d6+3 plus grab)

Space 5 ft.; **Reach** 5 ft. (10 ft. with tentacle)

Special Attacks tentacle cage (4d8+10 bludgeoning, AC 17, 18 hp)

Spell-Like Abilities (CL 14th; concentration +19)

Constant—*spider climb, true seeing*

At will—*alter self, dispel good* (DC 20), *enthrall* (DC 17), *greater teleport* (self plus 1 entrapped creature and 50 lbs. of goods only), *persistent image* (DC 20)

3/day—*black tentacles, charm monster* (DC 19)

1/day—*summon* (level 5, 3 erinyes 65%)

STATISTICS

Str 24, **Dex** 25, **Con** 25, **Int** 22, **Wis** 21, **Cha** 20

Base Atk +15; **CMB** +22 (+26 grapple); **CMD** 39 (can't be tripped)

Feats Acrobatic Steps, Combat Expertise, Combat Reflexes, Improved Initiative, Improved Trip, Multiattack, Nimble Moves, Strike Back

Skills Acrobatics +25 (+29 jump), Bluff +23, Diplomacy +23, Disguise +23, Escape Artist +22, Fly +14, Knowledge (arcana) +21, Knowledge (planes) +24, Perception +23, Perform (sing) +23, Sense Motive +23, Spellcraft +21, Stealth +25

Languages Celestial, Common, Draconic, Infernal, telepathy 100 ft.

SQ agile grappler

ECOLOGY

Environment any (Hell)

Organization solitary, retinue (1 gylou and 2d4 erinyes), or cortege (1–4 gylous and 2d10 erinyes)

Treasure standard

SPECIAL ABILITIES

Agile Grappler (Ex) A gylou does not gain the grappled condition if she grapples a foe.

Tentacle Cage (Su) If a gylou successfully grapples a creature, she transfers that creature into her lower body's nest of cage-like tentacles. This works like swallow whole. The gylou's tentacles are AC 17 and have 18 hp for

the purpose of an entrapped creature cutting itself out. A gylou's tendrils heal quickly, allowing her to use this ability 1 round after a creature cuts itself free.

Known as handmaiden devils, Mothers of Pain, and Maids of Miscarriage, gylous attend to the whims and schemes of Hell's few female overlords. Like manipulative matrons amid decadent mortal courts, these deceivers hide their fathomless evil beneath illusions of beauty, graciousness, and tradition. Gylous particularly loathe children. It's said that the persistent cry of a babe can sometimes cause these fiends to abandon their illusions and viciously attack.

As greater devils, gylous can command many lesser devils, yet harbor an exclusive favoritism for erinyes. A gylou weighs 160 pounds and stands stiffly at 5-1/2 feet—though many wear their head-sprouting tentacles in tall, elaborate coiffures.

DEVIL, IMMOLATION

Ash and embers encrust the smoldering humanoid frame of this imperious, dragon-winged devil.

IMMOLATION DEVIL (PURAGAUS) CR 19

XP 204,800

LE Large outsider (devil, evil, extraplanar, lawful)

Init +8; **Senses** darkvision 60 ft., *true seeing*; Perception +27

DEFENSE

AC 36, touch 17, flat-footed 28 (+8 Dex, +19 natural, –1 size)

hp 315 (18d10+216); regeneration 5 (good weapons or good spells)

Fort +23, **Ref** +19, **Will** +14

DR 15/good and silver; **Immune** fire, poison; **Resist** acid 10, cold 10; **SR** 30

OFFENSE

Speed 30 ft., fly 80 ft. (good)

Melee bite +29 (2d6+12 plus burn), 2 claw +29 (1d8+12 plus burn), gore +29 (2d8+12 plus burn), 2 wings +27 (1d8+6)

Space 10 ft.; **Reach** 10 ft.

Special Attacks burn (2d6, DC 31), hellfire

Spell-Like Abilities (CL 17th; concentration +24)

Constant—*fire shield*, *true seeing*

At will—*fireball* (DC 20), *greater teleport* (self plus 50 lbs. of objects only), *persistent image* (DC 22), *wall of fire*

3/day—*dictum* (DC 24), *fire storm* (DC 25), *mass charm monster* (DC 25)

1/day—*summon* (level 9, any 2d4 devils of CR 10 or lower, 90%)

STATISTICS

Str 34, **Dex** 26, **Con** 35, **Int** 24, **Wis** 23, **Cha** 24

Base Atk +18; **CMB** +31; **CMD** 49

Feats Blind-Fight, Blinding Critical, Combat Expertise, Combat Reflexes, Critical Focus, Iron Will, Multiattack, Power Attack, Stand Still

Skills Bluff +28, Diplomacy +28, Disable Device +26, Fly +31, Intimidate +28, Knowledge (arcana, nobility) +25, Knowledge (engineering, planes) +28, Perception +27, Sense Motive +27, Spellcraft +28, Stealth +25

Languages Celestial, Common, Draconic, Infernal; telepathy 100 ft.

ECOLOGY

Environment any (Hell)

Organization solitary, pair, or council (3–6)

Treasure double

SPECIAL ABILITIES

Hellfire (Su) Any fire damage caused by an immolation devil's abilities and spells is half fire damage, half unholy damage.

Immolation devils are tyrant warlords and terrifying field generals among Hell's legions. While many other greater devils manipulate and corrupt subtly and from afar, puragaus surround themselves with lesser diabolical minions, lead interplanar incursions, hold infernal redoubts upon mortal worlds, or strike against any who would defy the will of Hell.

Immolation devils stand just over 10 feet tall, with wingspans nearing 20 feet, and weigh 900 pounds.

DEVILFISH

This purple, seven-armed octopoid monstrosity is the size of a horse, with hook-lined tentacles and cold, blue eyes.

DEVILFISH	CR 4

XP 1,200

NE Large magical beast (aquatic)

Init +3; **Senses** low-light vision, see in darkness; Perception +5

DEFENSE

AC 17, touch 12, flat-footed 14 (+3 Dex, +5 natural, −1 size)

hp 42 (5d10+15)

Fort +7, **Ref** +7, **Will** +2

Resist cold 10

OFFENSE

Speed 10 ft., swim 40 ft.; jet (240 ft.)

Melee tentacles +7 (3d6+4 plus grab)

Space 10 ft.; **Reach** 15 ft.

Special Attacks savage bite (+7 melee, 2d6+4/18–20 plus poison), unholy blood

STATISTICS

Str 17, **Dex** 17, **Con** 16, **Int** 3, **Wis** 12, **Cha** 8

Base Atk +5; **CMB** +9 (+13 grapple); **CMD** 22 (can't be tripped)

Feats Cleave, Combat Reflexes, Power Attack

Skills Escape Artist +5, Perception +5, Stealth +3, Swim +15

Languages Abyssal, Aquan, Common

SQ water dependency

ECOLOGY

Environment any aquatic

Organization solitary

Treasure none

SPECIAL ABILITIES

Poison (Ex) Savage bite—injury; *save* Fort DC 15; *frequency* 1/round for 6 rounds; *effect* 1d2 Str; *cure* 2 consecutive saves.

Savage Bite (Ex) A devilfish can attack with its savage bite whenever it makes a successful grapple check. This attack is in place of any other action made with a successful grapple check. The bite threatens a critical hit on a roll of 18–20, and injects the target with poison as well.

Unholy Blood (Su) A devilfish's blood is infused with fiendish magic. Once per day, as a swift action, a devilfish can emit a night-black cloud of this foul liquid, filling a 20-foot-radius cloud if underwater, or a 20-foot-radius burst on land. In water, the blood provides total concealment for everything but a devilfish (which can see through the blood with ease); on land the slippery blood coats the ground, making the area difficult terrain. The blood persists for 1 minute before fading. Anyone who enters a cloud of the blood in the water or who is within the area of a burst of blood on land must make a DC 15 Fortitude save or be nauseated for 1d4 rounds—this save need be made only once per cloud. The save DC is Constitution-based.

Water Dependency (Ex) A devilfish can survive out of the water for 1 hour, after which it becomes fatigued. After 2 hours, the devilfish becomes exhausted and begins to suffocate (*Pathfinder RPG Core Rulebook 445*).

Although the devilfish superficially resembles a seven-armed octopus, it is an altogether different creature. Possessing a rudimentary intellect, a devilfish can understand and even speak a few words and phrases in various languages, although when it speaks, it has a tendency to mix languages together, making it somewhat difficult to understand for anyone who doesn't speak all the languages known by the devilfish.

More than those of a mere animal, the devilfish's intelligence and several of its abilities are gifts from a fiendish legacy—most sages believe that the original devilfish were once outsiders from the Abyss, and that over the course of thousands of years they became true natives of the Material Plane's oceans. Rumors of far more intelligent devilfish dwelling in the deepest ocean trenches persist, although if these rumors are true, these deep-dwelling devilfish do not often come to the surface.

A devilfish is 10 feet long and weighs 500 pounds.

DHAMPIR

This unnaturally graceful man moves without a sound, his gaze just as piercing as the needle-sharp blade he effortlessly wields.

DHAMPIR	CR 1/2

XP 200

Dhampir fighter 1

CE Medium humanoid (dhampir)

Init +3; **Senses** darkvision 60 ft., low-light vision; Perception +1

DEFENSE

AC 17, touch 13, flat-footed 14 (+4 armor, +3 Dex)

hp 13 (1d10+3)

Fort +2, **Ref** +3, **Will** −1 (+2 vs. disease and mind-affecting effects)

Defensive Abilities negative energy affinity, resist level drain

Weakness light sensitivity

OFFENSE

Speed 30 ft.

Melee rapier +4 (1d6+1/18–20)

Spell-Like Abilities (CL 1st)

3/day—*detect undead*

STATISTICS

Str 13, **Dex** 17, **Con** 10, **Int** 10, **Wis** 8, **Cha** 16

Base Atk +1; **CMB** +2; **CMD** 15

Feats Toughness, Weapon Finesse

Skills Bluff +5, Intimidate +7, Perception +1, Ride +5, Survival +3; **Racial Modifiers** +2 Bluff, +2 Perception

Languages Common

ECOLOGY

Environment any land

Organization solitary, pair, or court (3–8 and 1 vampire)

Treasure NPC gear (chain shirt, rapier, other treasure)

SPECIAL ABILITIES

Resist Level Drain (Ex) A dhampir takes no penalties from energy draining effects, though he can still be killed if he accrues more negative levels then he has Hit Dice. After 24 hours, any negative levels a dhampir takes are removed without the need for an additional saving throw.

Cursed from birth, dhampirs result from the rare and unnatural union of vampires and humans. Although not driven to consume blood for survival as their undead progenitors are, dhampirs nonetheless know a lifelong desire for blood that nothing else can truly sate. Those who survive their early years face a life of fear and mistrust, their unnatural beauty and incredible reflexes marking them as scions of the night just as surely as their sensitivity to light. Although polluted by undeath, dhampirs do grow old and die, aging at a rate similar to elves.

DHAMPIR CHARACTERS

Dhampirs are defined by class levels—they don't possess racial Hit Dice. All dhampirs have the following racial traits.

+2 Dexterity, +2 Charisma, −2 Constitution: Dhampirs are fast and seductive, but closer to death than most mortals.

Senses: Low-light vision and darkvision 60 feet.

Manipulative: +2 racial bonus on Bluff and Perception.

Undead Resistance: Dhampirs gain a +2 racial bonus on saving throws against disease and mind-affecting effects.

Light Sensitivity, Negative Energy Affinity: See universal monster rules.

Spell-Like Ability: A dhampir can use *detect undead* three times per day as a spell-like ability. The caster level for this ability equals the dhampir's class level.

Resist Level Drain: See above.

Languages: Dhampirs begin play speaking Common. Those with high Intelligence can choose any language as a bonus language (except druidic and other secret languages).

Illustration by Kekai Kotaki

89

DINOSAUR, ALLOSAURUS

This bipedal dinosaur has a mouth filled with sharp teeth and short, powerful arms that end in sharp claws.

ALLOSAURUS   CR 7

XP 3,200

N Huge animal

Init +5; **Senses** low-light vision, scent; Perception +28

DEFENSE

AC 19, touch 9, flat-footed 18 (+1 Dex, +10 natural, –2 size)

hp 93 (11d8+44)

Fort +11, **Ref** +8, **Will** +7

OFFENSE

Speed 50 ft.

Melee bite +14 (2d6+8/19–20 plus grab), 2 claws +4 (1d8+8)

Space 15 ft.; **Reach** 15 ft.

Special Attacks pounce, rake (2 talons +14, 1d8+8)

STATISTICS

Str 26, **Dex** 13, **Con** 19, **Int** 2, **Wis** 15, **Cha** 10

Base Atk +8; **CMB** +18; **CMD** 29

Feats Alertness, Improved Critical (bite), Improved Initiative, Iron Will, Nimble Moves, Run

Skills Perception +30; **Racial Modifiers** +8 Perception

ECOLOGY

Environment temperate or warm forests or plains

Organization solitary, pair, or pack (3–6)

Treasure None

A huge, swift hunter, the allosaurus measures 30 feet in length and weighs 10,000 pounds.

DINOSAUR, COMPSOGNATHUS

This small reptile has a snake-like neck and head, a bird-like body with strong legs for running, and a whip-like tail.

COMPSOGNATHUS   CR 1/2

XP 200

N Tiny animal

Init +6; **Senses** low-light vision, scent; Perception +4

DEFENSE

AC 15, touch 14, flat-footed 13 (+2 Dex, +1 natural, +2 size)

hp 6 (1d8+2)

Fort +4, **Ref** +4, **Will** +0

OFFENSE

Speed 40 ft., swim 20 ft.

Melee bite +1 (1d3–1 plus poison)

Space 2-1/2 ft.; **Reach** 0 ft.

STATISTICS

Str 8, **Dex** 15, **Con** 14, **Int** 2, **Wis** 11, **Cha** 5

Base Atk +0; **CMB** +0; **CMD** 9

Feats Improved Initiative

Skills Perception +4, Swim +10

ECOLOGY

Environment temperate or warm forests or plains

Organization solitary, pair, or pack (5–20)

Treasure none

SPECIAL ABILITIES

Poison (Ex) Bite—injury; *save* Fort DC 12; *frequency* 1/round for 4 rounds; *effect* 1d2 Str; *cure* 1 save.

The compsognathus is a small dinosaur that moves in swift, darting motions. Its bite injects a venom that causes numbness and weakness, a trait that the animal uses to bring down larger prey. A compsognathus measures 3 feet long and weighs 15 pounds.

These dinosaurs can serve spellcasters as a familiar. A compsognathus familiar grants its master a +4 bonus on Initiative checks.

ALLOSAURUS COMPANIONS

Starting Statistics: Size Medium, **Speed** 40 ft.; **AC** +4 natural armor; **Attack** bite (1d6), 2 claws (1d4); **Ability Scores** Str 14, Dex 16, Con 10, Int 2, Wis 15, Cha 10; **Special Qualities** low-light vision, scent.

7th-Level Advancement: Size Large; **AC** +2 natural armor; **Attack** bite (1d8), 2 claws (1d6); **Ability Scores** Str +8, Dex –2, Con +4; **Special Qualities** grab, pounce.

Illustrations by Dean Spencer

DINOSAUR, PARASAUROLOPHUS

This thick-bodied dinosaur has a whip-like tail and a long neck, its head topped by the crest of a backward-curving horn.

PARASAUROLOPHUS	CR 4	

XP 1,200
N Huge animal
Init +2; **Senses** low-light vision, scent; Perception +13

DEFENSE
AC 17, touch 10, flat-footed 15 (+2 Dex, +7 natural, −1 size)
hp 45 (6d8+18)
Fort +8, **Ref** +7, **Will** +3

OFFENSE
Speed 30 ft.
Melee tail slap +8 (2d6+9)
Space 15 ft.; **Reach** 15 ft.
Special Attack trample (2d6+9; DC 19)

STATISTICS
Str 23, **Dex** 14, **Con** 17, **Int** 2, **Wis** 13, **Cha** 10
Base Atk +4; **CMB** +12; **CMD** 24 (28 vs. trip)
Feats Improved Bull Rush, Power Attack, Skill Focus (Perception)
Skills Perception +13

ECOLOGY
Environment warm forests or plains
Organization solitary, pair, or herd (3–12)
Treasure none

This herbivore is 30 feet long and weighs 10,500 pounds. It is notable for the long, curved crest atop its skull.

PARASAUROLOPHUS COMPANIONS

Starting Stats: Size Medium; **Speed** 30 ft.; **AC** +2 natural armor; **Attack** tail (1d6); **Ability Scores** Str 11, Dex 18, Con 9, Int 2, Wis 13, Cha 10; **SQ** low-light vision, scent.

  7th-level Advancement: Size Large; **AC** +2 natural armor; **Attack** tail (1d8); **Ability Scores** Str +8, Dex −2, Con +4; **SQ** trample (1d8).

TYLOSAURUS COMPANIONS

Starting Stats: Size Medium; **Speed** 20 ft., swim 50 ft.; **AC** +3 natural armor; **Attack** bite (1d6); **Ability Scores** Str 10, Dex 17, Con 10, Int 2, Wis 13, Cha 9; **SQ** low-light vision, scent.

  7th-level Adv.: Size Large; **AC** +2 natural armor; **Attack** bite (1d8); **Ability Scores** Str +8, Dex −2, Con +4; **SQ** grab.

DINOSAUR, TYLOSAURUS

Surging out of the water, this massive lizard is shaped like a giant fish with a powerful, toothed maw.

TYLOSAURUS	CR 8	

XP 4,800
N Gargantuan animal
Init +1; **Senses** low-light vision, darkvision 60 ft.; Perception +14

DEFENSE
AC 20, touch 8, flat-footed 18 (+1 Dex, +1 dodge, +12 natural, −4 size)
hp 105 (10d8+60)
Fort +15, **Ref** +8, **Will** +4

OFFENSE
Speed 20 ft., swim 50 ft.
Melee bite +15 (2d8+18 plus grab)
Space 15 ft.; **Reach** 15 ft.
Special Attacks swallow whole (2d6+12 bludgeoning, AC 16, hp 10)

STATISTICS
Str 34, **Dex** 13, **Con** 22, **Int** 2, **Wis** 13, **Cha** 9
Base Atk +7; **CMB** +23 (+27 grapple); **CMD** 35 (39 vs. trip)
Feats Cleave, Dodge, Great Fortitude, Mobility, Power Attack
Skills Perception +14, Swim +20

ECOLOGY
Environment warm aquatic
Organization solitary, pair, or school (3–6)
Treasure None

This predatory marine lizard swims with four flippered limbs and a powerful, fluke-like tail. Its extended snout is filled with sharp teeth, and it feeds on both aquatic and surface prey. They are known to attack ships, mistaking them for basking whales or other creatures. A tylosaurus grows up to 50 feet in length and weighs 30,000 pounds.

DRAGON, PRIMAL

Though chromatic and metallic dragons are the most widely known, other categories of true dragon exist. Presented on the following pages are the five primal dragons—powerful creatures that hail from the elemental planes and the Plane of Shadows.

AGE CATEGORIES

Many of a true dragon's abilities, attacks, and other statistics improve as a dragon grows older. These increases are divided into 12 age categories—as a dragon ages, its base statistics change as noted on the Dragon Age Categories table.

Age Category: This is the age category's name.

Age in Years: This is the dragon's actual age.

CR: This column modifies the dragon's base CR.

Size: This column shows the number of size categories to increase the dragon's base size by, depending on its age (from Tiny to Small, Small to Medium, and so on). A true dragon does not gain the standard increases to ability scores when it achieves a larger size—instead, true dragons gain ability score increases according to their age category, as indicated on the Dragon Ability Scores table.

Hit Dice: This shows how many additional Hit Dice a dragon gains over its base Hit Dice as it grows. Increases to Hit Dice grant extra hit points, feats, and skill ranks as well as increasing the dragon's base attack bonus and base save bonuses. Dragons have skill ranks equal to 6 + their Intelligence modifier per Hit Die. A dragon's increases to ability scores for gaining Hit Dice are included in the total ability score increases (see the Dragon Ability Scores table).

Natural Armor: This shows the amount the dragon's base natural armor bonus increases with each age category.

Breath Weapon: Each dragon has a breath weapon (see Combat) that deals a base amount of damage. This multiplier increases the number of dice of damage dealt by the dragon's breath weapon. For example, a mature adult dragon with a base breath weapon that deals 2d6 acid damage would deal 14d6 acid damage (due to the ×7 multiplier).

COMBAT

The Dragon Attacks and Speeds table lists the attacks a dragon can employ and the damage it deals (a dash indicates a dragon of that size does not possess that natural attack). Dragons gain other abilities described here when they reach a specific age category.

Fly Speed: A dragon's fly speed increases as indicated, according to its size.

Bite: This is a primary attack that deals the indicated damage plus 1-1/2 times the dragon's Strength bonus (even though it has more than one attack). A dragon's bite attack has reach as if the creature were one size category larger (+10 feet for Colossal dragons).

Claws: These primary attacks deal the indicated damage plus the dragon's Strength bonus.

Wings: The dragon can slam foes with its wings, even when flying. Wing attacks are secondary attacks that deal the indicated damage plus 1/2 the dragon's Strength bonus.

Tail Slap: The dragon can slap one foe each round with its tail. A tail slap is a secondary attack that deals the indicated damage plus 1-1/2 times the dragon's Strength bonus (this is an exception to the normal secondary attack rules).

Crush (Ex) A flying or jumping Huge or larger dragon can land on foes as a standard action, using its whole body to crush them. Crush attacks are effective only against opponents three or more size categories smaller than the dragon. A crush attack affects as many creatures as fit in the dragon's space. Creatures in the affected area must succeed on a Reflex save (DC equal to that of the dragon's breath weapon) or be pinned, automatically taking bludgeoning damage during the next round unless the dragon moves off them. If the dragon chooses to maintain the pin, it must succeed at a combat maneuver check as normal. Pinned foes take damage from the crush each round if they don't escape. A crush attack deals the indicated damage plus 1-1/2 times the dragon's Strength bonus.

Tail Sweep (Ex) This allows a Gargantuan or larger dragon to sweep with its tail as a standard action. The sweep affects a half-circle with a radius of 30 feet (or 40 feet for a Colossal dragon), extending from an intersection on the edge of the dragon's space in any direction. Creatures within the swept area are affected if they are four or more size categories smaller than the dragon. A tail sweep automatically deals the indicated damage plus 1-1/2 times the dragon's Strength bonus (round down). Affected creatures can attempt Reflex saves to take half damage (DC equal to that of the dragon's breath weapon).

Breath Weapon (Su) Using a breath weapon is a standard action. A dragon can use its breath weapon once every 1d4 rounds, even if it possesses more than one breath weapon. A breath weapon always starts at an intersection adjacent to the dragon and extends in a direction of the dragon's choice. Breath weapons come in two shapes, lines and cones, whose areas vary with the dragon's size. If a breath weapon deals damage, those caught in the area can attempt Reflex saves to take half damage. The save DC against a breath weapon is 10 + 1/2 dragon's HD + dragon's Con modifier. Saves against various breath weapons use the same DC; the type of saving throw is noted in the variety descriptions. A dragon can use its breath weapon when it is grappling or being grappled.

Additional Dragon Rules

Dragon Senses (Ex) Dragons have darkvision 120 feet and blindsense 60 feet. They see four times as well as a human in dim light and twice as well in normal light.

Dragon Age Categories

Age Category	Age in Years	CR	Size	Hit Dice	Natural Armor	Breath Weapon
1 Wyrmling	0–5	Base	Base	Base	Base	Base
2 Very young	6–15	Base + 2	Base + 1	Base + 2	Base + 3	Base × 2
3 Young	16–25	Base + 4	Base + 2	Base + 4	Base + 6	Base × 3
4 Juvenile	26–50	Base + 5	Base + 2	Base + 6	Base + 9	Base × 4
5 Young adult	51–100	Base + 7	Base + 3	Base + 8	Base + 12	Base × 5
6 Adult	101–200	Base + 8	Base + 3	Base + 10	Base + 15	Base × 6
7 Mature adult	201–400	Base + 9	Base + 3	Base + 12	Base + 18	Base × 7
8 Old	401–600	Base + 11	Base + 4	Base + 14	Base + 21	Base × 8
9 Very old	601–800	Base + 12	Base + 4	Base + 16	Base + 24	Base × 9
10 Ancient	801–1,000	Base + 13	Base + 4	Base + 18	Base + 27	Base × 10
11 Wyrm	1,001–1,200	Base + 14	Base + 4	Base + 20	Base + 30	Base × 11
12 Great wyrm	1,201+	Base + 16	Base + 5	Base + 22	Base + 33	Base × 12

Dragon Ability Scores

Age Category	Str	Dex	Con	Int	Wis	Cha
1 Wyrmling	Base	Base	Base	Base	Base	Base
2 Very young	Base + 4	Base − 2	Base + 2	Base + 2	Base + 2	Base + 2
3 Young	Base + 8	Base − 2	Base + 4	Base + 2	Base + 2	Base + 2
4 Juvenile	Base + 10	Base − 2	Base + 6	Base + 4	Base + 4	Base + 4
5 Young adult	Base + 12	Base − 4	Base + 6	Base + 4	Base + 4	Base + 4
6 Adult	Base + 14	Base − 4	Base + 8	Base + 6	Base + 6	Base + 6
7 Mature adult	Base + 16	Base − 4	Base + 8	Base + 6	Base + 6	Base + 6
8 Old	Base + 18	Base − 6	Base + 10	Base + 8	Base + 8	Base + 8
9 Very old	Base + 20	Base − 6	Base + 10	Base + 8	Base + 8	Base + 8
10 Ancient	Base + 22	Base − 6	Base + 12	Base + 10	Base + 10	Base + 10
11 Wyrm	Base + 24	Base − 8	Base + 12	Base + 10	Base + 10	Base + 10
12 Great wyrm	Base + 26	Base − 8	Base + 14	Base + 12	Base + 12	Base + 12

Dragon Attacks and Speeds

Size	Fly Speed (maneuverability)	1 Bite	2 Claws	2 Wings	1 Tail Slap	1 Crush	1 Tail Sweep	Breath Weapon Line	Cone
Tiny	100 ft. (average)	1d4	1d3	—	—	—	—	30 ft.	15 ft.
Small	150 ft. (average)	1d6	1d4	—	—	—	—	40 ft.	20 ft.
Medium	150 ft. (average)	1d8	1d6	1d4	—	—	—	60 ft.	30 ft.
Large	200 ft. (poor)	2d6	1d8	1d6	1d8	—	—	80 ft.	40 ft.
Huge	200 ft. (poor)	2d8	2d6	1d8	2d6	2d8	—	100 ft.	50 ft.
Gargantuan	250 ft. (clumsy)	4d6	2d8	2d6	2d8	4d6	2d6	120 ft.	60 ft.
Colossal	250 ft. (clumsy)	4d8	4d6	2d8	4d6	4d8	2d8	140 ft.	70 ft.

Frightful Presence (Ex) A dragon's frightful presence has a range equal to 30 feet × the dragon's age category, but otherwise functions as detailed in the universal monster rules in the appendix.

Spells: A dragon knows and casts arcane spells as a sorcerer of the level indicated in its specific description. Its caster level depends on its age, as shown for each type.

Spell-Like Abilities: A dragon's caster level for its spell-like abilities is equal to its total Hit Dice.

Damage Reduction: Dragons gain damage reduction as they age, as indicated on each dragon's specific entry.

Their natural weapons are treated as magic weapons for the purpose of overcoming damage reduction.

Immunities (Ex) Every dragon is immune to sleep effects and paralysis effects. In addition, a dragon is immune to one or more additional forms of attack or energy damage no matter what its age, as given in its specific description.

Spell Resistance (Ex) As dragons grow older, they become more resistant to spells and spell-like abilities, as indicated in the specific dragon descriptions. A dragon's SR is equal to 11 + its CR.

PRIMAL DRAGON, BRINE

A blue-green neck frill sweeps back from the head of this dragon, leading to a body of shiny scales and fin-like crests.

BRINE DRAGON

LN dragon (extraplanar, water)

BASE STATISTICS

CR 3; **Size** Tiny; **Hit Dice** 4d12

Speed 60 ft., swim 60 ft.

Natural Armor +3; **Breath Weapon** line, 2d6 acid

Str 16, **Dex** 15, **Con** 11, **Int** 13, **Wis** 10, **Cha** 11

ECOLOGY

Environment any aquatic (Plane of Water)

Organization solitary

Treasure triple

SPECIAL ABILITIES

Capsize (Ex) An old or older brine dragon can attempt to capsize a boat or ship by ramming it as a charge attack and making a CMB check. The DC of this check is 25 or the result of the boat captain's Profession (sailor) check, whichever is higher. For each size category larger the ship is than the brine dragon's size, the dragon takes a cumulative −10 penalty on the check.

Desiccating Bite (Su) An ancient brine dragon's bite causes weakness, dealing 1d2 points of Strength drain in addition to its normal damage. A great wyrm's bite deals 1d4 points of Strength drain. A Fortitude save (DC equals the dragon's breath weapon save DC) negates the Strength drain.

Painful Strikes (Su) A great wyrm brine dragon's natural attacks are so laden with salt and acidic crystals that every time it strikes a creature with one of these attacks, the target must make a Fortitude save (DC equals the dragon's breath weapon save DC) or be stunned for a round from the pain.

Spell-like Abilities (Sp) A brine dragon gains the following spell-like abilities, usable at will (unless indicated otherwise) at the listed age. Very young—*speak with animals* (fish only); Young—*obscuring mist*; Juvenile—*water breathing*; Adult—*control water*; Ancient—*horrid wilting* (3/day); Great wyrm—*tsunami** (3/day).

* This spell is from the *Pathfinder RPG Advanced Player's Guide.*

Age Category	Special Abilities	Caster Level
Wyrmling	Immunity to acid, water breathing	—
Very young	*Speak with animals* (fish only)	—
Young	*Obscuring mist*	1st
Juvenile	*Water breathing*	3rd
Young adult	DR 5/magic, spell resistance	5th
Adult	Frightful presence, *control water*	7th
Mature adult	DR 10/magic	9th
Old	Capsize	11th
Very old	DR 15/magic	13th
Ancient	Desiccating bite, *horrid wilting*	15th
Wyrm	DR 20/magic	17th
Great wyrm	Painful strikes, *tsunami**	19th

XP 3,200

LN Medium dragon (extraplanar, water)

Init +5; **Senses** dragon senses; Perception +12

DEFENSE

AC 20, touch 11, flat-footed 19 (+1 Dex, +9 natural)

hp 68 (8d12+16)

Fort +8, **Ref** +7, **Will** +7

Immune acid, paralysis, sleep

OFFENSE

Speed 60 ft., fly 150 ft. (average), swim 60 ft.

Melee bite +15 (1d8+10), 2 claws +15 (1d6+7), 2 wings +10 (1d4+3)

Special Attacks breath weapon (60-ft. line, 6d6 acid, DC 16)

Spell-Like Abilities (CL 8th; concentration +9)

At will—*obscuring mist*, *speak with animals* (fish only)

Spells Known (CL 1st; concentration +2)

1st (4/day)—*color spray* (DC 12), *touch of the sea**

0 (at will)—*detect magic*, *mage hand*, *open/close*, *prestidigitation*

STATISTICS

Str 24, **Dex** 13, **Con** 15, **Int** 15, **Wis** 12, **Cha** 13

Base Atk +8; **CMB** +15; **CMD** 26 (30 vs. trip)

Feats Hover, Improved Initiative, Power Attack, Skill Focus (Swim)

Skills Diplomacy +12, Fly +12, Heal +12, Knowledge (nature) +13, Perception +12, Sense Motive +12, Survival +12, Swim +29

Languages Aquan, Common, Draconic

SQ water breathing

XP 12,800

LN Large dragon (extraplanar, water)

Init +4; **Senses** dragon senses; Perception +20

Aura frightful presence (180 ft., DC 20)

DEFENSE

AC 27, touch 9, flat-footed 27 (+18 natural, −1 size)

hp 147 (14d12+56)

Fort +13, **Ref** +11, **Will** +12

DR 5/magic; **Immune** acid, paralysis, sleep; **SR** 22

OFFENSE

Speed 60 ft., fly 200 ft. (poor), swim 60 ft.

Melee bite +23 (2d6+15), 2 claws +23 (1d8+10), tail slap +18 (1d8+15), 2 wings +18 (1d6+5)

Space 10 ft.; **Reach** 5 ft. (10 ft. with bite)

Special Attacks breath weapon (80-ft. line, 12d6 acid, DC 21)

Spell-Like Abilities (CL 14th; concentration +17)

At will—*control water*, *obscuring mist*, *speak with animals* (fish only), *water breathing*

Spells Known (CL 7th; concentration +10)

3rd (5/day)—*aqueous orb** (DC 16), *sleet storm* (DC 16)

2nd (7/day)—*alter self*, *invisibility*, *slipstream**

1st (7/day)—*color spray* (DC 14), *feather fall*, *flare burst** (DC 14), *ray of enfeeblement* (DC 14), *touch of the sea**

0 (at will)—*detect magic*, *detect poison*, *mage hand*, *open/close*, *prestidigitation*, *read magic*, *resistance*

Illustration by Andrew Hou

STATISTICS

Str 30, **Dex** 11, **Con** 19, **Int** 19, **Wis** 16, **Cha** 17

Base Atk +14; **CMB** +25; **CMD** 35 (39 vs. trip)

Feats Hover, Improved Initiative, Improved Vital Strike, Lightning Reflexes, Power Attack, Skill Focus (Swim), Vital Strike

Skills Bluff +20, Diplomacy +20, Fly +11, Heal +20, Knowledge (arcana and nature) +21, Perception +20, Sense Motive +20, Survival +20, Swim +41

Languages Aquan, Common, Draconic, Elven, Halfling

SQ water breathing

ANCIENT BRINE DRAGON	CR 16

XP 76,800

LN Huge dragon (extraplanar, water)

Init +3; **Senses** dragon senses; Perception +30

Aura frightful presence (300 ft., DC 26)

DEFENSE

AC 37, touch 7, flat-footed 37 (–1 Dex, +30 natural, –2 size)

hp 275 (22d12+132)

Fort +19, **Ref** +14, **Will** +18

DR 15/magic; **Immune** acid, paralysis, sleep; **SR** 27

OFFENSE

Speed 60 ft., fly 200 ft. (poor), swim 60 ft.

Melee bite +34 (2d8+21 plus 1d2 Str), 2 claws +34 (2d6+14), tail slap +29 (2d6+21), 2 wings +29 (1d8+7)

Space 15 ft.; **Reach** 10 ft. (15 ft. with bite)

Special Attacks breath weapon (100-ft. line, 20d6 acid, DC 27), capsize, crush, desiccating bite

Spell-Like Abilities (CL 22nd; concentration +27)

At will—control water, obscuring mist, speak with animals (fish only), water breathing

3/day—horrid wilting (DC 23)

Spells Known (CL 15th; concentration +20)

7th (4/day)—control weather, mass fly*

6th (6/day)—fluid form*, true seeing, transformation

5th (7/day)—break enchantment, dismissal, teleport, wall of force

4th (7/day)—ball lightning* (DC 19), ice storm, greater invisibility, solid fog

3rd (7/day)—aqueous orb* (DC 18), deep slumber (DC 18), dispel magic, sleet storm (DC 18)

2nd (7/day)—alter self, detect thoughts (DC 17), invisibility, make whole, slipstream*

1st (8/day)—color spray (DC 16), feather fall, flare burst* (DC 16), ray of enfeeblement, touch of the sea*

0 (at will)—arcane mark, detect magic, detect poison, mage hand, message, open/close, prestidigitation, read magic, resistance

STATISTICS

Str 38, **Dex** 9, **Con** 23, **Int** 23, **Wis** 20, **Cha** 21

Base Atk +22; **CMB** +38; **CMD** 47 (51 vs. trip)

Feats Awesome Blow, Greater Vital Strike, Hover, Improved Bull Rush, Improved Initiative, Improved Vital Strike, Lightning Reflexes, Power Attack, Skill Focus (Swim), Vital Strike, Wingover

Skills Bluff +30, Diplomacy +30, Fly +16, Heal +30, Knowledge (arcana, geography, nature) +31, Perception +30, Sense Motive +30, Survival +30, Swim +53, Use Magic Device +30

Languages Aquan, Common, Draconic, Dwarven, Elven, Gnome, Halfling

SQ water breathing

Although not inherently evil, brine dragons have little patience for kindness and philanthropy. As they age, they grow more and more opinionated and obsessed with power—by adult age, a brine dragon counts itself a failure if it doesn't rule over a collection of "lesser beings" such as humans, merfolk, locathah, or even sahuagin.

95

Primal Dragon, Cloud

The blue-white scales of this four-horned dragon exude wisps of fog. The dragon's snout is short but filled with sharp teeth.

CLOUD DRAGON

CN dragon (air, extraplanar)

BASE STATISTICS

CR 5; **Size** Small; **Hit Dice** 6d12

Speed 40 ft., swim 40 ft.

Natural Armor +5; **Breath Weapon** cone, 2d8 electricity

Str 10, **Dex** 13, **Con** 13, **Int** 10, **Wis** 14, **Cha** 13

ECOLOGY

Environment any sky (Plane of Air)

Organization solitary

Treasure triple

SPECIAL ABILITIES

Cloud Form (Su) An adult or older cloud dragon can change itself into a cloudy vapor as a swift action for a number of rounds per day equal to its Hit Dice. This ability functions as *gaseous form* but the dragon's fly speed is unchanged.

Cloud Breath (Su) A great wyrm cloud dragon's breath weapon creates a cloud that persists in its cone shape for 1d4 rounds. Treat this cloud as a *fog cloud* that deals electricity damage equal to half the dragon's breath weapon damage to any creature that ends its turn still within the cloud (Reflex save halves the damage—DC equals the dragon's breath weapon save DC).

Mist Vision (Su) A cloud dragon can see through fog, clouds, and similar obscuring effects with perfect clarity.

Spell-Like Abilities (Sp) A cloud dragon gains the following spell-like abilities, usable at will (unless indicated otherwise) on reaching the listed age category. Very young—*obscuring mist*; Young—*fog cloud*; Adult—*solid fog*; Old—*cloudkill* (3/day); Ancient—*wind walk*; Great wyrm—*storm of vengeance* (1/day).

Thundering Bite (Su) An ancient or older cloud dragon's bite makes a thundering crash whenever it attacks, dealing an additional 2d6 points of sonic damage. A great wyrm's thundering bite deals an additional 4d6 sonic damage.

Age Category	Special Abilities	Caster Level
Wyrmling	Immune to electricity, mist vision	—
Very young	*Obscuring mist*	—
Young	*Fog cloud*	—
Juvenile	Frightful presence	1st
Young adult	DR 5/magic, spell resistance	3rd
Adult	Cloud form, *solid fog*	5th
Mature adult	DR 10/magic	7th
Old	*Cloudkill*	9th
Very old	DR 15/magic	11th
Ancient	Thundering bite, *wind walk*	13th
Wyrm	DR 20/magic	15th
Great wyrm	Cloud breath, *storm of vengeance*	17th

YOUNG CLOUD DRAGON — CR 9

XP 6,400

CN Large dragon (air, extraplanar)

Init +0; **Senses** dragon senses, mist vision; Perception +16

DEFENSE

AC 20, touch 9, flat-footed 20 (+11 natural, −1 size)

hp 95 (10d12+30)

Fort +10, **Ref** +7, **Will** +10

Immune electricity, paralysis, sleep

OFFENSE

Speed 40 ft., fly 200 ft. (poor), swim 40 ft.

Melee bite +13 (2d6+6), 2 claws +14 (1d8+4), 2 wings +11 (1d6+2), tail slap +11 (1d8+4)

Special Attacks breath weapon (40-ft. cone, 6d8 electricity, DC 18)

Spell-Like Abilities (CL 10th; concentration +12)

At will—*fog cloud, obscuring mist*

STATISTICS

Str 18, **Dex** 11, **Con** 17, **Int** 12, **Wis** 16, **Cha** 15

Base Atk +10; **CMB** +15; **CMD** 25 (29 vs. trip)

Feats Dazzling Display, Multiattack, Power Attack, Skill Focus (Diplomacy), Weapon Focus (claws)

Skills Appraise +14, Diplomacy +21, Fly +7, Intimidate +15, Knowledge (planes) +14, Perception +16, Stealth +9, Swim +12

Languages Auran, Draconic

ADULT CLOUD DRAGON — CR 13

XP 25,600

CN Huge dragon (air, extraplanar)

Init +3; **Senses** dragon senses, mist vision; Perception +24

Aura frightful presence (180 ft., DC 22)

DEFENSE

AC 29, touch 7, flat-footed 29 (−1 Dex, +22 natural, −2 size)

hp 184 (16d12+80)

Fort +15, **Ref** +9, **Will** +15

DR 5/magic; **Immune** electricity, paralysis, sleep; **SR** 24

OFFENSE

Speed 40 ft., fly 200 ft. (poor), swim 40 ft.

Melee bite +22 (2d8+10/19–20), 2 claws +22 (2d6+7), tail slap +19 (2d6+10), 2 wings +19 (1d8+3)

Space 15 ft.; **Reach** 10 ft. (15 ft. with bite)

Special Attacks breath weapon (50-ft. cone, 12d8 electricity, DC 23), crush

Spell-Like Abilities (CL 16th; concentration +20)

At will—*fog cloud, obscuring mist, solid fog*

Spells Known (CL 5th; concentration +9)

2nd (5/day)—*blur, see invisibility*

1st (7/day)—*charm person* (DC 15), *detect secret doors, shield, true strike*

0 (at will)—*dancing lights, detect poison, light, message, prestidigitation, read magic*

STATISTICS

Str 24, **Dex** 9, **Con** 21, **Int** 16, **Wis** 20, **Cha** 19

Base Atk +16; **CMB** +25; **CMD** 34 (38 vs. trip)

Feats Critical Focus, Improved Critical (bite), Improved
Initiative, Multiattack, Power Attack, Skill Focus
(Diplomacy), Weapon Focus (bite, claws)

Skills Appraise +22, Diplomacy +29, Fly +10, Intimidate +23,
Knowledge (planes) +22, Perception +24, Sense Motive +24,
Stealth +10, Survival +24, Swim +15

Languages Auran, Common, Draconic, Elven

SQ cloud form (16 rounds/day)

ANCIENT CLOUD DRAGON	CR 18

XP 153,600

CN Gargantuan dragon (air, extraplanar)

Init +2; **Senses** dragon senses, mist vision; Perception +34

Aura frightful presence (300 ft., DC 28)

DEFENSE

AC 36, touch 4, flat-footed 36 (–2 Dex, +32 natural, –4 size)

hp 324 (24d12+168)

Fort +21, **Ref** +12, **Will** +21

DR 15/magic; **Immune** electricity, paralysis, sleep; **SR** 29

OFFENSE

Speed 40 ft., fly 250 ft. (clumsy), swim 40 ft.

Melee bite +32 (4d6+16/19–20 plus
2d6 sonic), 2 claws +32 (2d8+11),
tail slap +29 (2d8+16), 2 wings
+29 (2d6+5)

Space 20 ft.; **Reach** 15 ft. (20 ft.
with bite)

Special Attacks breath
weapon (60-ft. cone,
20d8 electricity, DC 29),
crush, tail sweep

Spell-Like Abilities (CL
24th; concentration +30)
At will—*fog cloud,*
obscuring mist, solid
fog, wind walk
3/day—*cloudkill* (DC 21)

Spells Known (CL 13th;
concentration +19)
6th (5/day)—*chain lightning*
(DC 22), *greater dispel magic*
5th (7/day)—*cone of cold* (DC 21),
dismissal (DC 21), *teleport*
4th (7/day)—*elemental body I, ice storm,*
lesser geas (DC 20), *river of wind**
3rd (7/day)—*arcane sight, cloak of winds**,*
stinking cloud (DC 19), *suggestion* (DC 19)
2nd (8/day)—*eagle's splendor, glitterdust* (DC 18), *gust*
of wind, locate object, see invisibility
1st (8/day)—*alter winds**, charm person* (DC 17),
detect secret doors, erase, true strike
0 (at will)—*dancing lights, detect*
poison, light, mage

hand, message, prestidigitation, read magic, resistance,
touch of fatigue
* This spell is from the *Pathfinder RPG Advanced Player's Guide.*

STATISTICS

Str 32, **Dex** 7, **Con** 25, **Int** 20, **Wis** 24, **Cha** 23

Base Atk +24; **CMB** +39; **CMD** 47 (51 vs. trip)

Feats Critical Focus, Dazzling Display, Flyby Attack, Improved
Critical (bite), Improved Initiative, Multiattack, Power
Attack, Skill Focus (Diplomacy), Snatch, Staggering Critical,
Weapon Focus (bite, claws)

Skills Appraise +32, Diplomacy +39, Fly +11, Intimidate +33,
Knowledge (local) +32, Knowledge (planes) +32, Perception
+34, Sense Motive +34, Stealth +13, Survival +34, Swim +46

Languages Auran, Common, Draconic, Elven

SQ cloud form (24 rounds/day)

Cloud dragons stay out of the complicated political
schemes and obsessions of other dragons (especially the
chromatic dragons), preferring to live their lives freely
and as the whim to travel strikes them. Exploration and
viewing new lands from far above
are the cloud dragon's greatest joy,
rivaled only by speaking
with new creatures and
gaining exotic treasures
from them. They keep
lairs on high mountain
peaks, but are often away
on journeys of discovery,
returning home only when
they've claimed a new treasure
that needs to be placed in
safekeeping back home.

PRIMAL DRAGON, CRYSTAL

This brilliantly colored dragon has scales, teeth, and claws made of multicolored crystal, and its wings are sheets of flexible glass.

CRYSTAL DRAGON

CG dragon (earth, extraplanar)

BASE STATISTICS

CR 2; **Size** Tiny; **Hit Dice** 3d12

Speed 60 ft., burrow 30 ft., climb 30 ft.

Natural Armor +2; **Breath Weapon** cone, 2d4 sonic

Str 9, **Dex** 16, **Con** 13, **Int** 10, **Wis** 11, **Cha** 16

ECOLOGY

Environment any underground (Plane of Earth)

Organization solitary

Treasure triple

SPECIAL ABILITIES

Razor Sharp (Sp) All of a crystal dragon's natural attacks deal slashing damage.

Ray Reflection (Ex) An ancient crystal dragon's scales reflect ray spells back upon the ray's source if the ray fails to overcome the dragon's spell resistance.

Scintillating Aura (Su) A great wyrm crystal dragon radiates an aura of scintillating color from its jeweled scales to a radius of 60 feet. All within this area must make a Will save each round to avoid being stunned (if the victim has 15 or fewer Hit Dice) or confused (if the victim has more than 15 Hit Dice) for 1 round. The save DC is equal to the dragon's breath weapon save DC. This is a mind-affecting effect. The dragon can activate or suppress this aura as a free action.

Spell-Like Abilities (Sp) A crystal dragon gains the following spell-like abilities, usable at will (unless indicated otherwise) upon reaching the listed age category. Very young—*color spray*; Juvenile—*glitterdust*; Adult—*rainbow pattern*; Old—*stone to flesh* (3/day); Ancient—*prismatic spray* (3/day); Great wyrm—*imprisonment* (1/day).

Tremorsense (Ex) Crystal dragons do not gain tremorsense until juvenile age (30 ft.), improving at adult (60 ft.) and old (120 ft.).

Age Category	Special Abilities	Caster Level
Wyrmling	Immunity to sonic, razor sharp	—
Very young	*Color spray*	—
Young	Tremorsense	—
Juvenile	*Glitterdust*	—
Young adult	DR 5/magic, spell resistance	—
Adult	Frightful presence, *rainbow pattern*	1st
Mature adult	DR 10/magic	3rd
Old	*Stone to flesh*	5th
Very old	DR 15/magic	7th
Ancient	Ray reflection, *prismatic spray*	9th
Wyrm	DR 20/magic	11th
Great wyrm	*Imprisonment*, scintillating aura	13th

YOUNG CRYSTAL DRAGON — CR 6

XP 2,400

CG Medium dragon (earth, extraplanar)

Init +2; **Senses** dragon senses, tremorsense 30 ft.; Perception +11

DEFENSE

AC 20, touch 12, flat-footed 18 (+2 Dex, +8 natural)

hp 66 (7d12+21)

Fort +10, **Ref** +9, **Will** +6

Immune paralysis, sleep, sonic

OFFENSE

Speed 60 ft., burrow 30 ft., climb 30 ft., fly 150 ft. (average)

Melee bite +10 (1d8+4), 2 claws +10 (1d6+3), 2 wings +5 (1d4+1)

Space 5 ft.; **Reach** 5 ft. (10 ft. with bite)

Special Attacks breath weapon (30-ft. cone, 6d4 sonic, DC 16)

Spell-Like Abilities (CL 7th; concentration +11)

At will—*color spray* (DC 15)

STATISTICS

Str 17, **Dex** 14, **Con** 17, **Int** 12, **Wis** 13, **Cha** 18

Base Atk +7; **CMB** +10; **CMD** 22 (26 vs. trip)

Feats Deceitful, Great Fortitude, Lightning Reflexes, Power Attack

Skills Bluff +16, Climb +21, Disguise +6, Fly +12, Intimidate +14, Knowledge (dungeoneering) +11, Perception +11, Stealth +12

Languages Draconic, Undercommon

SQ razor sharp

ADULT CRYSTAL DRAGON — CR 10

XP 9,600

CG Large dragon (earth, extraplanar)

Init +1; **Senses** dragon senses, tremorsense 60 ft.; Perception +19

Aura frightful presence (180 ft., DC 22)

DEFENSE

AC 27, touch 10, flat-footed 26 (+1 Dex, +17 natural, −1 size)

hp 149 (13d12+65)

Fort +15, **Ref** +11, **Will** +11

DR 5/magic; **Immune** paralysis, sleep, sonic; **SR** 21

OFFENSE

Speed 60 ft., burrow 30 ft., climb 30 ft., fly 200 ft. (poor)

Melee bite +19 (2d6+9/19–20), 2 claws +18 (1d8+6), tail slap +16 (1d8+9), 2 wings +16 (1d6+3)

Space 10 ft.; **Reach** 5 ft. (10 ft. with bite)

Special Attacks breath weapon (40-ft. cone, 12d4 sonic, DC 21)

Spell-Like Abilities (CL 13th; concentration +18)

At will—*color spray* (DC 17), *glitterdust* (DC 18), *rainbow pattern* (DC 20)

Spells Known (CL 1st; concentration +7)

1st (5/day)—*shield, unseen servant*

0 (at will)—*acid splash, detect magic, ghost sound, read magic*

STATISTICS

Str 23, **Dex** 12, **Con** 21, **Int** 16, **Wis** 17, **Cha** 22

Base Atk +13; **CMB** +20; **CMD** 31 (35 vs. trip)

Feats Deceitful, Great Fortitude, Improved Critical (bite),

Lightning Reflexes, Multiattack, Power Attack, Weapon
Focus (bite)

Skills Bluff +26, Climb +30, Disguise +23, Fly +11, Intimidate
+22, Knowledge (dungeoneering) +19, Perception +19, Sense
Motive +19, Stealth +13

Languages Common, Draconic, Terran, Undercommon

SQ razor sharp

ANCIENT CRYSTAL DRAGON   CR 15

XP 51,200

CG Huge dragon (earth, extraplanar)

Init +4; **Senses** dragon senses, tremorsense 120 ft.;
Perception +29

Aura frightful presence (300 ft., DC 28)

DEFENSE

AC 37, touch 8, flat-footed 37 (+29 natural, −2 size)

hp 283 (21d12+147)

Fort +21, **Ref** +14, **Will** +17

Defensive Abilities ray reflection; **DR** 15/magic; **Immune**
paralysis, sleep, sonic; **SR** 26

OFFENSE

Speed 60 ft., burrow 30 ft., climb 30 ft., fly 200 ft. (poor)

Melee bite +30 (2d8+15/19–20), 2 claws +29 (2d6+10), tail slap
+27 (2d6+15), 2 wings +27 (1d8+5)

Space 10 ft.; **Reach** 5 ft. (10 ft.
with bite)

Special Attacks breath weapon
(50-ft. cone, DC 27, 20d4
sonic, DC 27),
crush

**Spell-Like
Abilities**
(CL 21st;
concentration +29)
At will—*color spray*
(DC 19), *glitterdust*
(DC 20), *rainbow pattern* (DC 22)
3/day—*prismatic spray* (DC 25),
stone to flesh (DC 24)

Spells Known (CL 9th;
concentration +17)
4th (6/day)—*dimension door,
phantasmal killer* (DC 22)
3rd (8/day)—*displacement, lightning
bolt* (DC 21), *major image* (DC 21)
2nd (8/day)—*blindness/deafness* (DC 20),
invisibility, minor image (DC 20),
mirror image
1st (8/day)—*alarm, feather fall,
magic aura, silent image*
(DC 19), *unseen
servant*

0 (at will)—*acid splash, detect magic, detect poison, ghost
sound, mage hand, message, read magic, touch of fatigue*

STATISTICS

Str 31, **Dex** 10, **Con** 25, **Int** 20, **Wis** 21, **Cha** 26

Base Atk +21; **CMB** +33; **CMD** 43 (47 vs. trip)

Feats Deceitful, Great Fortitude, Greater Vital Strike,
Improved Critical (bite), Improved Initiative, Improved Vital
Strike, Lightning Reflexes, Multiattack, Power Attack, Vital
Strike, Weapon Focus (bite)

Skills Bluff +36, Climb +42, Disguise +33, Fly +16, Intimidate
+32, Knowledge (dungeoneering, geography) +29, Perception
+29, Sense Motive +29, Stealth +16, Survival +29

Languages Common, Draconic, Dwarven, Elven, Terran,
Undercommon

SQ razor sharp

Crystal dragons are generally good-natured, though their
incredible vanity sometimes causes them to seem aloof
and cocky. Any perceived insult against its appearance is
all but assured to send a crystal dragon into a rage—which
is a problem, as most crystal dragons are prone to seeing
insults even where none are intended. Crystal dragons
prefer underground lairs, and often go for decades or
even centuries without emerging from their extensive
cavern lairs onto the surface world above.

Crystal dragons tend to be exacting and even obsessive-
compulsive, their personalities mirroring the precise and
ordered nature of the facets of their scales. A crystal
dragon's lair is a well-ordered place—these
dragons find the very idea of the
classic sprawl of a dragon's
hoard to be shameful.

99

PRIMAL DRAGON, MAGMA

Between this dragon's jet-black scales run glowing rivulets of lava, and veins aglow with heat shine in the membranes of its wings.

MAGMA DRAGON

CN dragon (extraplanar, fire)

BASE STATISTICS

CR 4; **Size** Tiny; **Hit Dice** 5d12
Speed 40 ft.
Natural Armor +4; **Breath Weapon** cone, 2d6 fire
Str 13, **Dex** 16, **Con** 13, **Int** 12, **Wis** 12, **Cha** 11

ECOLOGY

Environment any mountains or underground (Plane of Fire)
Organization solitary
Treasure triple

SPECIAL ABILITIES

Magma Tomb (Su) Once per day, a great wyrm magma dragon can spit lava onto a target within 120 feet, dealing damage normally for its breath weapon. This magma cools instantly—it does not continue doing damage at this point but does entrap the victim (see universal monster rules in appendix; DC equals the dragon's breath weapon save DC, 3d6 minutes, hardness 8, hp 45).

Magma Breath (Su) Three times per day, an ancient or older magma dragon can breathe a cone of lava instead of fire. The damage is unchanged, but the magma clings to those it damages, dealing half damage each round thereafter for 1d3 rounds. After this magma cools, it crumbles to dust.

Spell-Like Abilities (Sp) A magma dragon gains the following spell-like abilities, usable at will (unless indicated otherwise) on reaching the listed age category. Very young—*burning hands*; Juvenile—*scorching ray*; Adult—*wall of fire*; Old—*fire shield* (warm shield, constant); Ancient—*delayed blast fireball* (3/day); Great wyrm—*wall of lava*.

* This spell is from the *Pathfinder RPG Advanced Player's Guide*.

Superheated (Su) At young age and older, a magma dragon's bite attack deals additional fire damage equal to its age category.

Age Category	Special Abilities	Caster Level
Wyrmling	Immune to fire, vulnerable to cold	—
Very young	*Burning hands*	—
Young	Superheated	1st
Juvenile	*Scorching ray*	3rd
Young adult	DR 5/magic, spell resistance	5th
Adult	Frightful presence, *wall of fire*	7th
Mature adult	DR 10/magic	9th
Old	*Fire shield*	11th
Very old	DR 15/magic	13th
Ancient	Magma breath, *delayed blast fireball*	15th
Wyrm	DR 20/magic	17th
Great wyrm	Magma tomb, *wall of lava**	19th

YOUNG MAGMA DRAGON — CR 8

XP 4,800

CN Medium dragon (extraplanar, fire)
Init +6; **Senses** dragon senses; Perception +14

DEFENSE

AC 22, touch 12, flat-footed 20 (+2 Dex, +10 natural)
hp 85 (9d12+27)
Fort +11, **Ref** +8, **Will** +10
Immune fire, paralysis, sleep
Weaknesses vulnerable to cold

OFFENSE

Speed 40 ft., fly 150 ft. (average)
Melee bite +17 (1d8+12 plus 3 fire), 2 claws +17 (1d6+8), 2 wings +12 (1d4+4)
Special Attacks breath weapon (30-ft. cone, 6d6 fire, DC 17)
Spell-Like Abilities (CL 9th; concentration +10)
 At will—*burning hands* (DC 12)
Spells Known (CL 1st; concentration +2)
 1st (4/day)—*flare burst** (DC 12), *grease* (DC 12)
 0 (at will)—*bleed* (DC 11), *detect magic, open/close, spark**

STATISTICS

Str 21, **Dex** 14, **Con** 17, **Int** 14, **Wis** 14, **Cha** 13
Base Atk +9; **CMB** +14; **CMD** 26 (30 vs. trip)
Feats Great Fortitude, Improved Initiative, Iron Will, Power Attack, Vital Strike
Skills Acrobatics +11 (+15 jump), Climb +17, Fly +14, Intimidate +13, Perception +14, Sense Motive +14, Stealth +14, Swim +17
Languages Common, Draconic, Ignan
SQ superheated

ADULT MAGMA DRAGON — CR 12

XP 19,200

CN Large dragon (extraplanar, fire)
Init +5; **Senses** dragon senses; Perception +22
Aura frightful presence (180 ft., DC 20)

DEFENSE

AC 29, touch 10, flat-footed 28 (+1 Dex, +19 natural, –1 size)
hp 172 (15d12+75)
Fort +16, **Ref** +10, **Will** +15
DR 5/magic; **Immune** fire, paralysis, sleep; **SR** 23
Weaknesses vulnerable to cold

OFFENSE

Speed 40 ft., fly 200 ft. (poor)
Melee bite +22 (2d6+12/19–20 plus 6 fire), 2 claws +22 (1d8+8/19–20), tail slap +17 (1d8+12), 2 wings +17 (1d6+4)
Space 10 ft.; **Reach** 5 ft. (10 ft. with bite)
Special Attacks breath weapon (40-ft. cone, 12d6 fire, DC 22)
Spell-Like Abilities (CL 15th; concentration +18)
 At will—*burning hands* (DC 14), *scorching ray, wall of fire*
Spells Known (CL 7th; concentration +10)
 3rd (5/day)—*dispel magic, fireball* (DC 16)
 2nd (7/day)—*dust of twilight** (DC 15), *flaming sphere* (DC 15), *glitterdust* (DC 15), *pyrotechnics* (DC 15)

Illustration by Andrew Hou

1st (7/day)—*feather fall, flare burst** (DC 14), *grease* (DC 14),
shield, true strike

0 (at will)—*bleed* (DC 13), *detect magic, detect poison, open/
close, read magic, spark**, *touch of fatigue*

STATISTICS

Str 27, **Dex** 12, **Con** 21, **Int** 18, **Wis** 18, **Cha** 17

Base Atk +15; **CMB** +24; **CMD** 35 (39 vs. trip)

Feats Great Fortitude, Improved Critical (bite), Improved
Critical (claws), Improved Initiative, Improved Vital Strike,
Iron Will, Power Attack, Vital Strike

Skills Acrobatics +16 (+20 jump), Climb +26, Escape Artist +16,
Fly +13, Intimidate +21, Perception +22, Sense Motive +22,
Sleight of Hand +16, Stealth +15, Swim +26

Languages Common, Draconic, Dwarven, Elven, Ignan

SQ superheated

ANCIENT MAGMA DRAGON   CR 17

XP 102,400

CN Huge dragon (extraplanar, fire)

Init +4; **Senses** dragon senses; Perception +32

Aura frightful presence (300 ft., DC 26)

DEFENSE

AC 39, touch 8, flat-footed 39 (+31 natural, −2 size)

hp 310 (23d12+161)

Fort +22, **Ref** +13, **Will** +21

DR 15/magic; **Immune** fire, paralysis, sleep; **SR** 28

Weaknesses vulnerable to cold

OFFENSE

Speed 40 ft., fly 200 ft. (poor)

Melee bite +33 (2d8+18/19–20 plus 10 fire),
2 claws +33 (2d6+12/19–20), tail slap +31
(2d6+18), 2 wings +31 (1d8+6)

Space 15 ft.; **Reach** 10 ft. (15 ft. with bite)

Special Attacks breath weapon (50-ft. cone, DC 28, 20d6
fire plus special), crush, magma breath

Spell-Like Abilities (CL 23rd; concentration +28)

Constant—*fire shield* (warm)

At will—*burning hands* (DC 16), *scorching ray, wall of fire*

3/day—*delayed blast fireball* (DC 22)

Spells Known (CL 15th; concentration +20)

7th (4/day)—*greater polymorph, prismatic spray* (DC 22)

6th (6/day)—*chain lightning* (DC 21), *contagious
flame** (DC 21), *eyebite* (DC 21)

5th (7/day)—*hungry pit** (DC 20),
polymorph, teleport, wall of force

4th (7/day)—*acid pit** (DC 19),
confusion (DC 19),
*dimensional anchor,
fire shield*

3rd (7/day)—
*displacement, dispel
magic, fireball* (DC 18),
wind wall

2nd (7/day)—*darkness, dust of twilight**, *flaming sphere* (DC 17),
glitterdust (DC 17), *pyrotechnics* (DC 17)

1st (8/day)—*feather fall, flare burst** (DC 16), *grease* (DC 16),
shield, true strike

0 (at will)—*bleed* (DC 15), *detect magic, detect poison, ghost
sound, light, open/close, read magic, spark**, *touch of fatigue*

STATISTICS

Str 35, **Dex** 10, **Con** 25, **Int** 22, **Wis** 22, **Cha** 21

Base Atk +23; **CMB** +37; **CMD** 47 (51 vs. trip)

Feats Flyby Attack, Great Fortitude, Greater Vital Strike,
Improved Bull Rush, Improved Critical (bite), Improved
Critical (claws), Improved Initiative, Improved Vital Strike,
Iron Will, Multiattack, Power Attack, Vital Strike

Skills Acrobatics +23 (+27 jump), Climb +38, Escape Artist +23,
Fly +18, Intimidate +31, Knowledge (planes) +32, Perception
+32, Sense Motive +32, Sleight of Hand +23, Stealth +18,
Survival +32, Swim +38

Languages Common, Draconic, Dwarven, Elven, Gnome,
Halfling, Ignan

SQ superheated

Temperamental and prone to violent outbursts, magma
dragons are regarded by most other dragons as dangerously
insane—an assumption that, more often than not, proves
correct. One can rarely predict a magma dragon's state of
mind until it either attacks or attempts to
engage in conversation. For their part,
magma dragons can justify all
of their actions—they just
rarely feel the need to
do so.

PRIMAL DRAGON, UMBRAL

This sleek, dark dragon moves with a disturbing, serpentine grace, its eyes glowing as if lit from within by crimson embers.

UMBRAL DRAGON

CE dragon (extraplanar)

BASE STATISTICS

CR 6; **Size** Small; **Hit Dice** 7d12

Speed 40 ft.

Natural Armor +6; **Breath Weapon** cone, 2d8 negative energy

Str 13, **Dex** 14, **Con** 13, **Int** 14, **Wis** 15, **Cha** 14

ECOLOGY

Environment any

Organization solitary

Treasure triple

SPECIAL ABILITIES

Breath Weapon (Su) Although it deals negative energy damage, an umbral dragon's breath weapon does not heal undead creatures.

Create Shadows (Su) Any creature slain by an ancient or older umbral dragon rises as a shadow (if 8 HD or less) or greater shadow (if above 8 HD) under the umbral dragon's control 1d4 rounds later.

Energy Drain (Su) A great wyrm umbral dragon deals 1 negative level with each successful bite or claw attack (1 level, DC 32).

Ghost Bane (Su) A young or older umbral dragon's physical attacks deal damage to incorporeal creatures normally.

Umbral Scion (Ex) Umbral dragons have negative energy affinity and are immune to energy drain and death effects.

Shadow Breath (Su) Three times per day, an adult or older umbral dragon can breathe a cone of shadows. Creatures who fail a Fortitude save are blinded for 1d4 rounds and take 1 point of Str drain per age category possessed by the dragon. A successful save negates the blindness and reduces Str drain to 1d4 points.

Spell-Like Abilities (Sp) An umbral dragon gains the following spell-like abilities, usable at will (unless indicated otherwise) on reaching the listed age category. Young—*darkness*; Juvenile—*vampiric touch*; Adult—*shadow walk*; Old—*project image*; Ancient—*finger of death* (3/day), Great wyrm—*shades*.

Age Category	Special Abilities	Caster Level*
Wyrmling	Umbral scion, immune to cold	—
Very young	*Darkness*	—
Young	Ghost bane	1st
Juvenile	Frightful presence, *vampiric touch*	3rd
Young adult	DR 5/magic, spell resistance	5th
Adult	Shadow breath, *shadow walk*	7th
Mature adult	DR 10/magic	9th
Old	*Project image*	11th
Very old	DR 15/magic	13th
Ancient	Create shadows, *finger of death*	15th
Wyrm	DR 20/magic	17th
Great wyrm	Energy drain, *shades*	19th

* An umbral dragon can cast cleric spells as arcane spells.

YOUNG UMBRAL DRAGON — CR 10

XP 9,600

CE Large dragon (extraplanar)

Init +5; **Senses** dragon senses; Perception +17

DEFENSE

AC 22, touch 10, flat-footed 21 (+1 Dex, +12 natural, −1 size)

hp 104 (11d12+33)

Fort +10, **Ref** +8, **Will** +10

Immune cold, death effects, energy drain, paralysis, sleep

OFFENSE

Speed 40 ft., fly 200 ft. (poor)

Melee bite +15 (2d6+7/19–20), 2 claws +15 (1d8+5), 2 wings +13 (1d6+2), tail slap +13 (1d8+7)

Space 10 ft.; **Reach** 5 ft. (10 ft. with bite)

Special Attacks breath weapon (40-ft. cone, 6d8 neg. energy, DC 18)

Spell-Like Abilities (CL 11th; concentration +14)

At will—*darkness*

Spells Known (CL 1st; concentration +4)

1st (4/day)—*inflict light wounds* (DC 14), *shield*

0 (at will)—*bleed* (DC 13), *detect magic*, *detect poison*, *read magic*

STATISTICS

Str 21, **Dex** 12, **Con** 17, **Int** 16, **Wis** 17, **Cha** 16

Base Atk +11; **CMB** +17; **CMD** 28 (32 vs. trip)

Feats Hover, Improved Critical (bite), Improved Initiative, Multiattack, Power Attack, Vital Strike

Skills Bluff +17, Diplomacy +17, Fly +9, Knowledge (arcana, local, planes) +17, Perception +17, Sense Motive +17, Stealth +11

Languages Abyssal, Common, Draconic, Undercommon

SQ ghost bane, umbral scion

ADULT UMBRAL DRAGON — CR 14

XP 38,400

CE Huge dragon (extraplanar)

Init +4; **Senses** dragon senses; Perception +25

Aura frightful presence (180 ft., DC 23)

DEFENSE

AC 29, touch 8, flat-footed 29 (+21 natural, −2 size)

hp 195 (17d12+85)

Fort +15, **Ref** +10, **Will** +15

DR 5/magic; **Immune** cold, death effects, energy drain, paralysis, sleep; **SR** 25

OFFENSE

Speed 40 ft., fly 200 ft. (poor)

Melee bite +23 (2d8+12/19–20), 2 claws +23 (2d6+8), tail slap +21 (2d6+12), 2 wings +21 (1d8+4)

Space 15 ft.; **Reach** 10 ft. (15 ft. with bite)

Special Attacks breath weapon (50-ft. cone, DC 23, 12d8 negative energy, DC 23), crush, shadow breath (6 Str)

Spell-Like Abilities (CL 17th; concentration +22)

At will—*darkness*, *shadow walk*, *vampiric touch*

Spells Known (CL 7th; concentration +12)

3rd (5/day)—*dispel magic*, *inflict serious wounds* (DC 18)

2nd (7/day)—*command undead* (DC 17), *invisibility*, *web* (DC 17)

Illustration by Andrew Hou

1st (8/day)—*grease* (DC 16), *inflict light wounds* (DC 16),
magic missile, *reduce person* (DC 16), *shield*

0 (at will)—*bleed* (DC 15), *detect magic*, *detect poison*, *disrupt
undead* (DC 15), *mage hand*, *ray of frost*, *read magic*

STATISTICS

Str 27, **Dex** 10, **Con** 21, **Int** 20, **Wis** 21, **Cha** 20

Base Atk +17; **CMB** +27; **CMD** 37 (41 vs. trip)

Feats Hover, Imp. Critical (bite), Imp. Initiative, Imp. Vital Strike,
Multiattack, Power Attack, Skill Focus (Stealth), Snatch, Vital Strike

Skills Bluff +25, Diplomacy +25, Fly +16, Knowledge (arcana,
local, planes) +25, Perception +25, Sense Motive +25,
Spellcraft +25, Stealth + 18, Survival +25

Languages Abyssal, Common, Draconic, Undercommon, 2 more

SQ ghost bane, umbral scion

ANCIENT UMBRAL DRAGON   CR 19

XP 204,800

CE Gargantuan dragon (extraplanar)

Init +3; **Senses** dragon senses; Perception +35

Aura frightful presence (300 ft., DC 29)

DEFENSE

AC 38, touch 5, flat-footed 38 (–1 Dex, +33 natural, –4 size)

hp 337 (25d12+175)

Fort +21, **Ref** +13, **Will** +21

DR 15/magic; **Immune** death effects, energy drain, paralysis,
sleep; **SR** 30

OFFENSE

Speed 40 ft., fly 250 ft. (clumsy)

Melee bite +33 (4d6+18/19–20), 2 claws +33 (2d8+12), tail slap
+31 (2d8+18), 2 wings +31 (2d6+6)

Space 20 ft.; **Reach** 15 ft. (20 ft. with bite)

Special Attacks breath weapon (60-ft. cone, 20d8 neg. energy, DC
29), create shadows, crush, shadow breath (10 Str), tail sweep

Spell-Like Abilities (CL 25th; concentration +32)

At will—*darkness, project image, shadow walk, vampiric touch*

3/day—*finger of death* (DC 24)

Spells Known (CL 15th; concentration +22)

7th (5/day)—*destruction* (DC 24), *limited wish*

6th (7/day)—*harm* (DC 23), *mislead, veil* (DC 23)

5th (7/day)—*greater command* (DC 22), *slay living*
(DC 22), *teleport, unhallow*

4th (7/day)—*enervation, inflict critical wounds*
(DC 21), *phantasmal killer* (DC 21), *unholy
blight* (DC 21)

3rd (8/day)—*dispel magic, haste, inflict serious
wounds* (DC 20), *lightning bolt* (DC 20)

2nd (8/day)—*alter self, blur, command
undead* (DC 19), *invisibility, web* (DC 17)

1st (8/day)—*inflict light wounds* (DC 18),
grease (DC 18), *magic missile, reduce person*
(DC 18), *shield*

0 (at will)—*acid splash, bleed* (DC 17), *detect magic,
detect poison, disrupt undead* (DC 17), *ghost sound,*
mage hand, ray of frost, read magic

STATISTICS

Str 35, **Dex** 8, **Con** 25, **Int** 24, **Wis** 25, **Cha** 24

Base Atk +25; **CMB** +41; **CMD** 50 (54 vs. trip)

Feats Bleeding Critical, Critical Focus, Flyby Attack, Greater Vital
Strike, Hover, Imp. Critical (bite), Imp. Initiative, Imp. Vital Strike,
Multiattack, Power Attack, Skill Focus (Stealth), Snatch, Vital Strike

Skills Appraise +35, Bluff +35, Diplomacy +35, Fly +13,
Knowledge (arcana, local, planes, religion) +35, Perception +35,
Sense Motive +35, Spellcraft +35, Stealth +21, Survival +35

Languages Abyssal, Common, Draconic, Undercommon, 4 more

SQ ghost bane, umbral scion

Cruel and sadistic, umbral dragons prefer the taste of
undead flesh or ghostly ectoplasm, yet never turn down
opportunities to consume living flesh.

DRAGON HORSE

The glossy alabaster coat of this noble horse ripples with muscles, while its hooves shimmer with pale blue energy.

DRAGON HORSE	CR 9

XP 6,400

NG Large magical beast (air)

Init +7; **Senses** darkvision 120 ft., know alignment, low-light vision; Perception +17

DEFENSE

AC 23, touch 13, flat-footed 19 (+3 Dex, +1 dodge, +10 natural, −1 size)

hp 105 (10d10+50)

Fort +12, **Ref** +10, **Will** +9

OFFENSE

Speed 60 ft., fly 120 ft. (good)

Melee 2 hooves +16 (2d6+7 plus 1d6 electricity)

Special Attacks breath weapons, flying charge

Space 10 ft.; **Reach** 10 ft.

STATISTICS

Str 24, **Dex** 17, **Con** 21, **Int** 16, **Wis** 18, **Cha** 21

Base Atk +10; **CMB** +18; **CMD** 32 (36 vs. trip)

Feats Dodge, Flyby Attack, Improved Initiative, Iron Will, Mobility

Skills Fly +18, Knowledge (planes) +13, Perception +17, Sense Motive +14, Survival +14

Languages Auran, Common, Draconic; telepathy 100 ft.

SQ shift planes

ECOLOGY

Environment any

Organization solitary

Treasure none

SPECIAL ABILITIES

Breath Weapons (Su) As a standard action, a dragon horse can breathe out a 30-foot cone of mist. This mist either deals 10d6 points of cold damage (DC 20 Reflex half), creates a region of fog in the area that lasts for 1 minute (similar to that created by a *fog cloud* spell), or creates a blast of severe wind (see *Pathfinder RPG Core Rulebook* 439) in the area. The dragon horse may use this breath weapon once every 1d4 rounds. The save DC is Constitution-based.

Flying Charge (Ex) A dragon horse gains a +4 bonus on damage rolls if it charges while flying.

Know Alignment (Su) Dragon horses automatically know the alignment of any creature they can see.

Shift Planes (Su) A dragon horse can enter the Ethereal Plane, Astral Plane, Plane of Air, or Material Plane once per day as a standard action. This functions as *plane shift*, but the dragon horse can only bring up to two other willing creatures with it, and only if they are on its back.

Despite their name, dragon horses are not related to dragons. These noble creatures gain their name from their ability to fly through the air without wings and to create different effects with their misty breath.

Dragon horses are solitary creatures, spending most of their time up among the clouds and rarely setting hoof to solid ground. A mated pair of dragon horses remains together to raise its young, but otherwise individuals prefer to be on their own. They are fierce and reclusive, but peaceful and even playful under the right circumstances. Dragon horses sometimes offer aid and assistance to decent folk in need, taking care to use their ability to know alignment to avoid accidentally providing aid to evil creatures, whom they despise.

Dragon horse foals are highly prized as potential steeds, but as dragon horses are highly intelligent creatures, they cannot be trained as if they were animals. Instead, one who seeks a dragon horse mount must use diplomacy to secure the creature's aid.

Peaceful creatures by nature, dragon horses prefer to avoid combat by flying away. When they are forced to fight (often in response to an evil creature's mayhem), they attempt to deal nonlethal damage to all but evil-aligned foes, leaving any unconscious opponents unharmed. Those who have chosen evil ways may sometimes receive the same mercy, in the hope that it helps them see the light, but innately evil foes are dispatched as quickly and cleanly as possible.

DRAGONFLY, GIANT

This glittering blue dragonfly is about the size of a horse and is large enough to carry off small farm animals or people.

GIANT DRAGONFLY   **CR 4**

XP 1,200
N Medium vermin
Init +2; **Senses** darkvision 60 ft.; Perception +1

DEFENSE
AC 17, touch 12, flat-footed 15 (+2 Dex, +5 natural)
hp 45 (7d8+14)
Fort +7, **Ref** +4, **Will** +3
Immune mind-affecting effects

OFFENSE
Speed 20 ft., fly 80 ft. (perfect)
Melee bite +9 (2d8+6 plus grab)
Special Attack darting charge

STATISTICS
Str 19, **Dex** 15, **Con** 14, **Int** —, **Wis** 12, **Cha** 9
Base Atk +5; **CMB** +9 (+13 grappling, or +17 grappling on a charge); **CMD** 21 (29 vs. trip)
Feats Flyby Attack[B]
Skills Fly +10

ECOLOGY
Environment temperate or warm land
Organization solitary or flight (2–5)
Treasure incidental

SPECIAL ABILITIES
Darting Charge (Ex) A giant dragonfly is adept at swooping in to attack prey with a powerful bite and then, just as quickly, swooping back up out of reach. As a result, a giant dragonfly gains Flyby Attack as a bonus feat. In addition, if a giant dragonfly charges while flying, it receives a +4 bonus on CMB checks made to grapple foes.

Giant dragonflies are rare compared to other varieties of giant insects, and fortunately so, since they are voracious hunters of warm-blooded prey, including humanoids.

The creatures typically lair in overgrown or lightly wooded areas, using foliage as cover. When they spot potential prey out in the open, the dragonflies swoop to the attack, using their superior flight speed and maneuverability to run most prey to ground or carrying off smaller foes to eat them somewhere safe. Giant dragonflies feed on carrion when fresh prey is not available, and the scent of a fresh kill often attracts them.

Many swamp-dwelling cultures attach religious significance to brightly colored and ravenous giant dragonflies, particularly boggards. The frog-men attach particular significance to a giant dragonfly's color, and their priest-kings often refuse to eat anything but specific colors of giant dragonflies.

GIANT DRAGONFLY NYMPH   **CR 3**

XP 800
N Small vermin (aquatic)
Init +1; **Senses** darkvision 60 ft.; Perception +1

DEFENSE
AC 15, touch 12, flat-footed 14 (+1 Dex, +3 natural, +1 size)
hp 32 (5d8+10)
Fort +6, **Ref** +2, **Will** +2
Immune mind-affecting effects

OFFENSE
Speed 10 ft., swim 30 ft.
Melee bite +6 (2d6+3)
Space 5 ft.; **Reach** 5 ft. (10 ft. with bite)
Special Attacks extending jaw

STATISTICS
Str 15, **Dex** 13, **Con** 14, **Int** —, **Wis** 12, **Cha** 5
Base Atk +3; **CMB** +4; **CMD** 15 (23 vs. trip)
Skills Stealth +5 (+13 in shallow water) , Swim +10; **Racial Modifiers** +8 Stealth in shallow water

ECOLOGY
Environment temperate or warm water
Organization solitary, pair, or brood (3–8)
Treasure incidental

SPECIAL ABILITIES
Extending Jaw (Ex) A giant dragonfly nymph can extend its jaws with surprising speed. Not only does this extend the nymph's reach with its bite attack, but during the surprise round, a nymph gains a +4 bonus on attack rolls with its bite.

Giant dragonflies lay clutches of eggs in swampy terrain or areas of standing water. Their young, called nymphs, voraciously eat carrion and small prey, growing and maturing rapidly until they sprout fully functional wings and become adult dragonflies.

Illustration by Andrew Hou

DRAKE, FLAME

This ferocious creature looks like a red-and-yellow scaled dragon, but with only two legs.

FLAME DRAKE — CR 5

XP 1,600

CE Large dragon (fire)

Init +5; **Senses** darkvision 60 ft., low-light vision, scent; Perception +10

DEFENSE

AC 18, touch 10, flat-footed 17 (+1 Dex, +8 natural, –1 size)

hp 57 (6d12+18)

Fort +8, **Ref** +6, **Will** +6

Immune fire, paralysis, sleep

Weakness vulnerability to cold

OFFENSE

Speed 20 ft., fly 60 ft. (average)

Melee bite +10 (2d6+5 plus 1d6 fire), tail slap +5 (1d6+2)

Space 10 ft.; **Reach** 10 ft.

Special Attacks fireball breath

STATISTICS

Str 21, **Dex** 13, **Con** 16, **Int** 9, **Wis** 12, **Cha** 10

Base Atk +6; **CMB** +12; **CMD** 23

Feats Flyby Attack, Improved Initiative, Power Attack

Skills Fly +8, Intimidate +9, Perception +10, Stealth +6, Survival +10

Languages Draconic

SQ speed surge

ECOLOGY

Environment temperate mountains or hills

Organization solitary, pair, or rampage (3–12)

Treasure standard

SPECIAL ABILITIES

Fireball Breath (Su) A flame drake can, as a standard action, breathe a ball of flame that explodes like a *fireball*. This attack has a range of 180 feet and deals 5d6 points of fire damage (DC 16 Reflex half) to all creatures within a 20-foot-radius spread. Once a flame drake has used its fireball breath, it cannot do so again for 1d6 rounds. The save DC is Constitution-based.

Speed Surge (Ex) Three times per day as a swift action, a flame drake may draw on its draconic heritage for a boost of strength and speed to take an additional move action in that round.

Flame drakes are the degenerate cousins of red dragons, with all of the rage and temper of true red dragons but little of the reason and intelligence. Flame drakes are brutal bullies who terrorize the lands they inhabit. From those they can frighten, flame drakes exact harsh tribute, and they viciously attack any not so easily cowed.

Flame drakes gather in small hunting packs called "rampages," working together easily during raids but often falling prey to squabbling and infighting over the spoils. Males and females form their own packs divided by gender, coming together only during the annual mating season.

Flame drakes mate once a year. Males play no part in raising their offspring, and abandon their partners soon after mating. Females lay clutches of two or three eggs in secluded mountain nests, and raise their hatchlings for only 2 years before rejoining their packs and abandoning their offspring to their fates. Flame drakes mature in 5 years, and can live up to 150 years. They generally grow to 12 feet long and weigh 1,500 pounds.

DRAKE, FOREST

This green-scaled dragon has two powerful legs and a pair of long, leathery wings. A long spike adorns its thrashing tail.

FOREST DRAKE	CR 4

XP 1,200

LE Large dragon (earth)

Init +6; **Senses** darkvision 60 ft., low-light vision, scent; Perception +11

DEFENSE

AC 17, touch 11, flat-footed 15 (+2 Dex, +6 natural, −1 size)

hp 42 (5d12+10)

Fort +6, **Ref** +6, **Will** +4

Immune acid, paralysis, sleep

OFFENSE

Speed 30 ft., fly 60 ft. (average), swim 30 ft.

Melee bite +8 (1d8+4), tail slap +3 (1d8+2)

Space 10 ft.; **Reach** 10 ft.

Special Attacks acidic cloud

STATISTICS

Str 19, **Dex** 14, **Con** 14, **Int** 9, **Wis** 11, **Cha** 12

Base Atk +5; **CMB** +10; **CMD** 22

Feats Improved Initiative, Power Attack, Skill Focus (Perception)

Skills Fly +8, Intimidate +9, Perception +11, Stealth +6, Swim +20

Languages Draconic

SQ aquatic adaptation, speed surge

ECOLOGY

Environment any forests

Organization solitary, pair, or rampage (3–12)

Treasure standard

SPECIAL ABILITIES

Acidic Cloud (Su) A forest drake can, as a standard action, spit a ball of acid that bursts into a cloud on impact. This attack has a range of 60 feet and deals 4d6 points of acid damage (Reflex DC 14 half) to all creatures within the resulting 10-foot-radius spread. The cloud remains for 1d4 rounds once created, acting as a 10-foot-radius *obscuring mist* (it no longer causes damage), but a strong wind disperses it in a single round. Once a forest drake has used its acidic cloud breath, it cannot do so again for 1d6 rounds. The Reflex save is Constitution-based.

Aquatic Adaptation (Ex) A forest drake can breathe underwater indefinitely and can freely use its breath weapon and other abilities while underwater. The acidic cloud created by that attack dissipates after 1 round if used underwater.

Speed Surge (Ex) Three times per day as a swift action, a forest drake may draw on its draconic heritage for a boost of strength and speed to take an additional move action in that round.

Forest drakes are the degenerate cousins of green dragons, possessed of cruel cunning but little actual wit. Like most drakes, forest drakes are bullies, prowling deep forests in search of their favorite prey—elves and fey. Forest drakes eagerly attack communities of such forest creatures unless driven off with arrows or other shows of force.

Like many other drake types, forest drakes organize themselves in packs called "rampages," and keep communal lairs in secluded forest locations. Such packs are usually made up of siblings who break from the pack only during mating season. A forest drake pack has a distinct pecking order, with younger and newer members receiving the least desirable portions of pack kills and the fewest mating options.

Forest drakes mate once a year, but do little to raise their offspring. A female lays a clutch of four to eight eggs, but abandons her young as soon as they hatch. Forest drake hatchlings immediately band together in a pack.

While few survive so long, forest drakes can live up to 200 years. Forest drakes are typically about 10 feet long with equally long tails, and weigh around 1,000 pounds.

Illustration by Kevin Yan

DRAKE, FROST

This two-legged dragon has dull blue scales tinged with bright blue ice. A freezing mist issues from between its powerful jaws.

FROST DRAKE	CR 7

XP 3,200

CE Large dragon (cold)

Init +5; **Senses** darkvision 60 ft., low-light vision, scent, snow vision; Perception +10

DEFENSE

AC 20, touch 10, flat-footed 19 (+1 Dex, +10 natural, −1 size)

hp 84 (8d12+32)

Fort +10, **Ref** +7, **Will** +5

Immune cold, paralysis, sleep

Weaknesses vulnerability to fire

OFFENSE

Speed 20 ft., burrow 20 ft. (snow only), fly 60 ft. (average)

Melee bite +13 (2d6+6 plus 1d6 cold), tail slap +8 (1d8+3)

Space 10 ft.; **Reach** 10 ft.

Special Attacks freezing mist breath

STATISTICS

Str 22, **Dex** 13, **Con** 18, **Int** 8, **Wis** 9, **Cha** 13

Base Atk +8; **CMB** +15; **CMD** 26

Feats Flyby Attack, Improved Initiative, Power Attack, Vital Strike

Skills Climb +17, Fly +10, Intimidate +12, Perception +10, Stealth +8

Languages Draconic

SQ speed surge, icewalking

ECOLOGY

Environment cold mountains

Organization solitary, pair, or rampage (3–12)

Treasure standard

SPECIAL ABILITIES

Freezing Mist Breath (Su) A frost drake can, as a standard action, spit a ball of liquid that bursts into a cloud of freezing mist. This attack has a range of 60 feet and deals 7d6 points of cold damage (DC 18 Reflex half) to all creatures in a 20-foot-radius spread. The mist cakes all surfaces in the area with a sheet of slippery ice that turns the area into difficult terrain for 2d4 rounds, after which the ice cracks or melts enough to revert to the normal terrain features in the area. Once a frost drake has used its freezing mist breath, it cannot do so again for 1d6 rounds. The Reflex save is Constitution-based.

Icewalking (Ex) This ability works like *spider climb*, but the surfaces the drake climbs must be icy. It can move across icy surfaces without penalty and does not need to make Acrobatics checks to run or charge on ice.

Speed Surge (Ex) Three times per day as a swift action, a frost drake may draw on its draconic heritage for a boost of strength and speed to take an additional move action in that round.

Snow Vision (Ex) A frost drake can see perfectly well in snowy conditions, and does not take any penalties on Perception checks while in snow.

Degenerate cousins of white dragons, frost dragons are ferocious predators. They are larger than other drakes, reaching heights of up to 16 feet and weighing upward of 2,500 pounds. Their wide, clawed feet enable them to easily burrow through snow, though not through dirt or clay.

Young frost drakes form adolescent hunting packs divided along gender lines, but older frost drakes are usually encountered in mated pairs. Frost drakes mate for life, leaving their packs when they find a suitable mate. Mated pairs make a nest together, and the female lays a clutch of two to five eggs. Both parents care for their offspring when they hatch, and families usually form small packs until the young reach maturity at 5 years of age. At this point, the parents abandon their offspring, usually laying a new clutch of eggs in a new nest elsewhere, and leaving the fledgling drakes to find their own adolescent packs to join.

Illustrations by Craig J. Spearing

DRAKE, SEA

Not quite sea serpent or dragon, this vicious beast is covered with shiny blue-green scales. Its arms serve as both wings and flippers.

SEA DRAKE — CR 6

XP 2,400
NE Large dragon (aquatic)
Init +6; **Senses** darkvision 60 ft., low-light vision, scent;
    Perception +10

DEFENSE

AC 19, touch 11, flat-footed 17 (+2 Dex, +8 natural, −1 size)
hp 73 (7d12+28)
Fort +9, **Ref** +9, **Will** +5
Immune electricity, paralysis, sleep

OFFENSE

Speed 20 ft., fly 60 ft. (average), swim 60 ft.
Melee bite +12 (1d8+6 plus 1d6 electricity),
    tail slap +7 (1d8+3)
Space 10 ft.; **Reach** 10 ft.
Special Attacks ball lightning breath, capsize

STATISTICS

Str 23, **Dex** 15, **Con** 18, **Int** 8, **Wis** 10, **Cha** 9
Base Atk +7; **CMB** +14; **CMD** 26
Feats Improved Initiative, Lightning Reflexes,
    Power Attack, Skill Focus (Stealth)
Skills Fly +10, Intimidate +9, Perception +10,
    Stealth +11, Swim +24
Languages Draconic
SQ amphibious, speed surge

ECOLOGY

Environment any coastlines
Organization solitary, pair, or rampage (3–12)
Treasure standard

SPECIAL ABILITIES

Ball Lightning Breath (Su) A sea drake can, as a standard action, breathe a ball of electricity that strikes one target first, then arcs to other targets like *chain lightning*. This attack has a range of 100 feet, and deals 6d6 points of electricity damage (DC 17 Reflex half) to the primary target. After it strikes, the ball lightning can arc to a number of secondary targets equal to the sea drake's Hit Dice (usually 7) within 20 feet of the primary target. The secondary bolts each strike one target and deal as much damage as the primary bolt. Once a sea drake has used its ball lightning breath, it cannot do so again for 1d6 rounds. The Reflex save is Constitution-based.

Capsize (Ex) A sea drake can attempt to capsize a boat or ship of its size or smaller by ramming it as a charge attack and making a combat maneuver check. The DC of this check is 25 or the result of the boat captain's Profession (sailor) check, whichever is higher.

Speed Surge (Ex) Three times per day as a swift action, a sea drake may draw on its draconic heritage for a boost of strength and speed to take an additional move action in that round.

While obviously the product of draconic inbreeding, the heritage of sea drakes is less clear than that of other drakes. Among the strongest of the drakes, sea drakes still lack the mental acuity of their true dragon forebears, though they remain as brutally cunning as other drakes. Although amphibious, sea drakes spend the majority of their time in shallow coastal waters.

Sea drakes are up to 14 feet long from their noses to the tips of their powerful tails. They weigh 2,000 pounds.

The most solitary of all drakes, sea drakes prefer to hunt alone. Occasionally, however, they band together in packs to hunt larger prey. Such rampages can be a significant danger to coastal shipping.

DRAUGR

This barnacle-encrusted walking corpse looks like a zombie, but is dripping with water and gives off a nauseating stench.

DRAUGR	CR 2

XP 600

CE Medium undead (water)

Init +0; **Senses** darkvision 60 ft., Perception +6

DEFENSE

AC 14, touch 10, flat-footed 14 (+2 armor, +2 natural)

hp 19 (3d8+6)

Fort +2, **Ref** +1, **Will** +3

DR 5/bludgeoning or slashing; **Immune** undead traits;
Resist fire 10

OFFENSE

Speed 30 ft., swim 30 ft.

Melee greataxe +5 (1d12+4/×3 plus nausea) or
slam +5 (1d10+4 plus nausea)

STATISTICS

Str 17, **Dex** 10, **Con** —, **Int** 8, **Wis** 10, **Cha** 13

Base Atk +2; **CMB** +5; **CMD** 15

Feats Power Attack, Toughness

Skills Climb +9, Perception +6, Stealth +6,
Swim +11

Languages Common (cannot speak)

ECOLOGY

Environment any coastal

Organization solitary or crew (2–8)

Treasure standard (greataxe, leather armor,
other treasure)

SPECIAL ABILITIES

Nausea (Su) A creature that is damaged by a draugr
must make a DC 12 Fortitude save or be nauseated
for 1 round. The save DC is Charisma-based.

Draugr smell of decay and the sea, and
drip water wherever they go. These foul
beings are usually created when humanoid
creatures are lost at sea in regions haunted by
evil spirits or necromantic effects. The corpses
of these drowned sailors cling fiercely to
unlife, attacking any living creatures that
intrude upon them. Their attacks smear
rancid flesh, rotting seaweed, and swaths
of vermin on whatever they hit.

In the case of draugr who manifest
when an entire ship sinks, these
undead usually stay with the wreck
of their ship. Some draugr may
be found under the control of aquatic
necromancers, while others may wander
the seas as undead pirates aboard ghost ships.

DRAUGR CAPTAIN (CR 3)

Draugr captains have malevolent, burning red eyes. They
may be more richly dressed than other draugr, though
their clothes are always in a similar tattered condition.

A draugr captain is a draugr with the advanced simple
template. In addition to this, most draugr captains have
additional class levels, usually as barbarians, fighters, or
rogues. Draugr captains can also use *obscuring mist* as a
spell-like ability (CL 5th, concentration +8) three times
per day, and instead of causing nausea with a successful
hit, they bestow 1 negative level on a hit. A draugr captain
can even bestow a negative level via a weapon it wields,
but if it gains multiple attacks with a weapon, it can only
bestow 1 negative level per round in this manner.

DULLAHAN

Clad in ragged black robes and tarnished armor, this grim, headless rider is surrounded by an aura of menace.

DULLAHAN	CR 7

XP 3,200
LE Medium undead
Init +2; **Senses** blindsight 60 ft.; Perception +16
Aura frightful presence (30 ft., DC 19)

DEFENSE
AC 21, touch 11, flat-footed 20 (+10 armor, +1 Dex)
hp 85 (10d8+40); fast healing 5
Fort +7, **Ref** +5, **Will** +12
Defensive Abilities channel resistance +4; **Immune** undead traits; **SR** 18

OFFENSE
Speed 30 ft. (20 ft. in armor)
Melee +1 keen longsword +14/+9 (1d8+6/17–20 plus 1d6 cold)
Special Attacks chilling blade, death's calling, summon mount

STATISTICS
Str 20, **Dex** 14, **Con** —, **Int** 14, **Wis** 16, **Cha** 18
Base Atk +7; **CMB** +12; **CMD** 24
Feats Iron Will, Mounted Combat, Ride-By Attack, Trample, Weapon Focus (longsword)
Skills Handle Animal +14, Intimidate +17, Perception +16, Ride +7, Spellcraft +15, Stealth +10
Languages Common, Sylvan

ECOLOGY
Environment any
Organization solitary
Treasure double (+1 full plate, +1 longsword, other treasure)

SPECIAL ABILITIES
Chilling Blade (Su) A dullahan is proficient with all simple and martial slashing weapons. When it wields a slashing weapon, the blade inflicts +1d6 cold damage and gains the *keen* weapon property.

Death's Calling (Su) Once per day as a standard action, a dullahan may place death's calling on a target within 60 feet (DC 22 Fortitude negates). If the dullahan knows and speaks the target's name, the target takes a –2 penalty on the save. If the victim fails the save, he becomes staggered for 1d6 rounds. For the next 24 hours (or until the dullahan is slain), all critical hits against the victim automatically confirm. Finally, the victim automatically fails all Constitution checks to stabilize while dying. This is a mind-affecting curse effect.

The save DC is Charisma-based.

Summon Mount (Su) As a standard action, a dullahan can summon a war-trained heavy horse with the fiendish creature simple template. This horse remains until it is slain or the dullahan dismisses it. He can only have one such horse in his service at a time.

Terrifying reapers of souls, dullahans are created by powerful fiends from the souls of particularly cruel generals, watch-captains, or other military commanders. Sent back from the pits of Hell to sow terror and harvest new souls, dullahans return to the towns or villages they lived in as mortals. While their favored victims are evil men and women (or their living descendants) whose souls are destined for Hell, the dullahans have no qualms about adding innocents to their lists of victims.

Legends tell of powerful dullahans who can summon not just a single fiendish mount, but an entire carriage pulled by six powerful ebony horses. Known as a "Coach of the Silent," these powerful undead are CR 14 with 20 Hit Dice, the advanced creature simple template, and the ability to cast *trap the soul* on those who fail to resist their death's calling. These souls take seats in the coach, where they languish forever—or at least until the dullahan himself is slain.

Illustration by Eva Widermann

III

Dust Digger

A tremendous starfish-like creature emerges from the sand, its five long arms surrounding a circular toothy maw.

DUST DIGGER	CR 4

XP 1,200

N Large aberration

Init +4; **Senses** darkvision 60 ft., tremorsense 60 ft.; Perception +5

DEFENSE

AC 16, touch 9, flat-footed 16 (+7 natural, −1 size)

hp 42 (5d8+20)

Fort +5, **Ref** +1, **Will** +4

OFFENSE

Speed 10 ft., burrow 20 ft.

Melee bite +5 (1d8+3 plus grab), 5 tentacles +3 (1d4+1 plus grab)

Space 10 ft.; **Reach** 10 ft.

Special Attacks sinkhole, swallow whole (2d8+4 bludgeoning, AC 13, 4 hp)

STATISTICS

Str 17, **Dex** 11, **Con** 18, **Int** 2, **Wis** 11, **Cha** 10

Base Atk +3; **CMB** +7; **CMD** 17

Feats Improved Initiative, Multiattack, Skill Focus (Stealth)

Skills Perception +5, Stealth +5 (+13 in ambush);
Racial Modifiers +8 Stealth in ambush

ECOLOGY

Environment warm deserts

Organization solitary, pair, or colony (3–10)

Treasure none

SPECIAL ABILITIES

Sinkhole (Ex) A dust digger can burrow into sand, loose soil, or dirt to lie in ambush just under the surface. When it feels (via tremorsense) prey walk into a square it threatens, it can deflate its body as an immediate action, causing the sand and other loose soil above to shift and slide. All creatures who were standing in the dust digger's reach must make a DC 15 Reflex save or become entangled as long as they remain in the dust digger's reach. All creatures who were standing at least partially in the dust digger's actual space must make a DC 15 Reflex save or become entangled and fall prone—if such a creature makes this save, it immediately moves to the closest adjacent unoccupied square. If this results in more than a 5-foot move, the creature moves that distance and then falls prone. The save DC is Strength-based.

Dust diggers most resemble mammoth starfish, with thick sandy-colored exoskeletons covered with rough, burr-like spines. Its five arms are long and thin, and covered with hundreds of barbed, tubular cilia that the creature uses to move as well at grab and grapple prey. At the fleshy center of the creature's body gapes a circular maw lined with large sharp teeth.

As ambush predators, dust diggers spend the majority of their lives buried beneath the sand, waiting patiently for prey to stumble over their ambush site.

Dust diggers are asexual. They reproduce by budding, splitting off young three to four times over the course of their 10-year lives—smaller versions of themselves that must immediately move away from the parent to avoid being snatched up and eaten. Dust digger young are just over 4 feet across, and can move relatively quickly through sand (their burrow speed is 40 feet). Usually, a young dust digger travels at least a mile from its parent before it settles down to create its first ambush—the amount of life in the region it has chosen as its new lair often determines whether the new dust digger thrives or starves to death, for once it digs its first ambush, it rarely moves more than a few hundred feet away over the course of its life.

D'ZIRIAK

This four-armed creature looks like a cross between a human and a black and ochre termite. Its body and arms display glowing runes.

D'ZIRIAK CR 3

XP 800

N Medium outsider (extraplanar)

Init +2; **Senses** darkvision 120 ft., low-light vision; Perception +9

DEFENSE

AC 16, touch 12, flat-footed 14 (+2 Dex, +4 natural)

hp 26 (4d10+4)

Fort +2, **Ref** +6, **Will** +6

OFFENSE

Speed 30 ft.

Melee 2 claws +6 (1d6+1 plus grab)

Special Attacks dazzling burst

Spell-Like Abilities (CL 3rd;

concentration +6)

1/day—*plane shift* (self only, to Plane of

Shadow only)

STATISTICS

Str 13, **Dex** 15, **Con** 12, **Int** 13, **Wis** 14,

Cha 16

Base Atk +4; **CMB** +5 (+9 grapple);

CMD 17

Feats Combat Reflexes, Weapon

Focus (claw)

Skills Climb +8, Knowledge (arcana) +8,

Knowledge (planes) +8, Perception +9, Sense

Motive +9, Stealth +9, Survival +7, Use

Magic Device +8

Languages D'ziriak; telepathy 100 ft.

SQ glow

ECOLOGY

Environment any land (Plane of Shadow)

Organization solitary, pair, swarm (3–20), or

hive (21–100)

Treasure standard

SPECIAL ABILITIES

Dazzling Burst (Su) Once per day, a d'ziriak can
cause its body to flare with intense, colorful
light as a swift action. Non-d'ziriaks within a
20-foot radius must make a DC 13 Fortitude
save or be dazzled for 1 minute. After using
this ability, the d'ziriak's brilliant glow is
extinguished for 24 hours. This ability is
a light effect, and creatures that cannot
see are immune to it. The save DC is
Constitution-based.

Glow (Ex) The colorful runes that decorate
a d'ziriak's body create dim light in a 20-
foot radius from its body.

Natives of the Plane of Shadow, d'ziriaks are a mysterious race of human-sized insectoids. From their partially buried hive cities rise spires and steeples adorned with alchemical fire and illusory flame, dim beacons of sanctuary in the foreboding twilight. The d'ziriaks remain staunchly neutral in most affairs, and are typically happy to converse with travelers via their eerie telepathy (their own language of buzzes and chitters is an obscure one known by few outside their race), but their unknown, obscure goals lead most others to regard this race with caution.

The average d'ziriak is 7 feet tall and has four arms, two legs, a termite-like abdomen, and a mandibled visage somewhere between that of insect and human. Two of its arms are large and possess sharp claws, while the other two are relatively small and used for fine manipulations, not combat. Strangely for a race native to the realm of shadows, the d'ziriaks have a colorful collection of runic shapes, almost like glowing tattoos, upon their chitinous flesh. These runes help to denote what role in d'ziriak society each of these beings serves.

D'ziriaks rarely travel off the Plane of Shadow except on orders of their rulers, and prefer to live out their lives out in their hive cities. They remain open to trade and diplomacy with any brave enough to travel the Plane of Shadow, and are valued by many both on and off their plane for their artisans' ability to weave light into tangible art and create weapons of great quality and beauty.

Illustration by Jim Pavelec

113

ELEMENTAL, ICE

From the waist up, this icy creature's features are humanoid, but below its body is a snake-like, slithering tail.

ICE ELEMENTAL

Languages Aquan

ECOLOGY

Environment any land or water (Plane of Water)

Organization solitary, pair, or gang (3–8)

Treasure none

SPECIAL ABILITIES

Ice Glide (Su) A burrowing ice elemental can pass through nonmagical ice and snow as easily as a fish swims through water. Its burrowing leaves behind no tunnel or hole, nor does it create any ripple or other sign of its presence. A *control water* spell cast on an area containing a burrowing ice elemental flings the elemental back 30 feet, stunning the creature for 1 round unless it succeeds on a DC 15 Fortitude save.

Icewalking (Ex) This ability works like the *spider climb* spell, but the surfaces the elemental climbs must be icy. The elemental can move across icy surfaces without penalty and does not need to make Acrobatics checks to run or charge on ice.

Numbing Cold (Su) When an ice elemental deals cold damage to a creature, that creature must succeed on a Fortitude save or be staggered for 1 round. The save DC is listed in the elemental's stat block and is Constitution-based.

Snow Vision (Ex) An ice elemental can see perfectly well in snowy conditions and does not take any penalties on Perception checks while in snow.

SMALL ICE ELEMENTAL   CR 1

XP 400

N Small outsider (air, cold, elemental, extraplanar, water)

Init –1; **Senses** darkvision 60 ft., snow vision; Perception +5

DEFENSE

AC 16, touch 10, flat-footed 16 (–1 Dex, +6 natural, +1 size)

hp 13 (2d10+2)

Fort +4, **Ref** +2, **Will** +0

Immune cold, elemental traits

Weaknesses vulnerable to fire

OFFENSE

Speed 20 ft., burrow (ice and snow only) 20 ft., swim 60 ft.

Melee slam +4 (1d4+1 plus 1d3 cold)

Special Attacks numbing cold (DC 12)

STATISTICS

Str 12, **Dex** 8, **Con** 13, **Int** 4, **Wis** 11, **Cha** 11

Base Atk +2; **CMB** +2; **CMD** 11 (can't be tripped)

Feats Power Attack

Skills Knowledge (planes) +2, Perception +5, Stealth +8, Swim +9

SQ ice glide, icewalking

MEDIUM ICE ELEMENTAL   CR 3

XP 800

N Medium outsider (air, cold, elemental, extraplanar, water)

Init +0; **Senses** darkvision 60 ft., snow vision; Perception +7

DEFENSE

AC 16, touch 10, flat-footed 16 (+6 natural)

hp 30 (4d10+8)

Fort +6, **Ref** +4, **Will** +1

Immune cold, elemental traits

Weaknesses vulnerable to fire

OFFENSE

Speed 20 ft., burrow (ice and snow only) 20 ft., swim 60 ft.

Melee slam +7 (1d6+4 plus 1d4 cold)

Special Attacks numbing cold (DC 14)

STATISTICS

Str 16, **Dex** 10, **Con** 15, **Int** 4, **Wis** 11, **Cha** 11

Base Atk +4; **CMB** +7; **CMD** 17 (can't be tripped)

Feats Cleave, Power Attack

Skills Knowledge (planes) +4, Perception +7, Stealth +7, Swim +11

SQ ice glide, icewalking

LARGE ICE ELEMENTAL   CR 5

XP 1,600

N Large outsider (air, cold, elemental, extraplanar, water)

Init +5; **Senses** darkvision 60 ft., snow vision; Perception +11

DEFENSE

AC 17, touch 10, flat-footed 16 (+1 Dex, +7 natural, –1 size)

hp 68 (8d10+24)

Fort +9, **Ref** +7, **Will** +2

DR 5/—; **Immune** cold, elemental traits

Weaknesses vulnerable to fire

OFFENSE

Speed 20 ft., burrow (ice and snow only) 20 ft., swim 60 ft.

Melee 2 slams +12 (1d8+5 plus 1d6 cold)

Space 10 ft.; **Reach** 10 ft.

Special Attacks numbing cold (DC 17)

STATISTICS

Str 20, **Dex** 12, **Con** 17, **Int** 6, **Wis** 11, **Cha** 11

Base Atk +8; **CMB** +14; **CMD** 25 (can't be tripped)

Feats Cleave, Great Cleave, Improved Initiative, Power Attack

Skills Intimidate +11, Knowledge (planes) +9, Perception +11, Stealth +8, Swim +13

SQ ice glide, icewalking

HUGE ICE ELEMENTAL   CR 7

XP 3,200

N Huge outsider (air, cold, elemental, extraplanar, water)

Init +7; **Senses** darkvision 60 ft., snow vision; Perception +13

DEFENSE

AC 20, touch 12, flat-footed 16 (+3 Dex, +1 dodge, +8 natural, –2 size)

hp 95 (10d10+40)

Fort +11, **Ref** +10, **Will** +3

DR 5/—; **Immune** cold, elemental traits

Illustration by Alberto Dal Lago

Weaknesses vulnerable to fire

OFFENSE

Speed 20 ft., burrow (ice and snow only) 20 ft., swim 60 ft.

Melee 2 slams +15 (2d6+7 plus 1d8 cold)

Space 15 ft.; **Reach** 15 ft.

Special Attacks numbing cold (DC 19)

STATISTICS

Str 24, **Dex** 16, **Con** 19, **Int** 6, **Wis** 11, **Cha** 11

Base Atk +10; **CMB** +19; **CMD** 33 (can't be tripped)

Feats Cleave, Dodge, Great Cleave, Improved Initiative, Power Attack

Skills Intimidate +13, Knowledge (planes) +11, Perception +13, Stealth +8, Swim +15

SQ ice glide, icewalking

GREATER ICE ELEMENTAL   CR 9
XP 6,400

N Huge outsider (air, cold, elemental, extraplanar, water)

Init +8; **Senses** darkvision 60 ft., snow vision; Perception +16

DEFENSE

AC 23, touch 13, flat-footed 18 (+4 Dex, +1 dodge, +10 natural, –2 size)

hp 123 (13d10+52)

Fort +12, **Ref** +14, **Will** +4

DR 10/—; **Immune** cold, elemental traits

Weaknesses vulnerable to fire

OFFENSE

Speed 20 ft., burrow (ice and snow only) 20 ft., swim 60 ft.

Melee 2 slams +20 (2d8+9 plus 2d6 cold)

Space 15 ft.; **Reach** 15 ft.

Special Attacks numbing cold (DC 20)

STATISTICS

Str 28, **Dex** 18, **Con** 19, **Int** 8, **Wis** 11, **Cha** 11

Base Atk +13; **CMB** +24; **CMD** 39 (can't be tripped)

Feats Cleave, Combat Reflexes, Dodge, Improved Initiative, Lightning Reflexes, Power Attack, Vital Strike

Skills Escape Artist +20, Intimidate +16, Knowledge (planes) +15, Perception +16, Stealth +12, Swim +17

SQ ice glide, icewalking

ELDER ICE ELEMENTAL   CR 11
XP 12,800

N Huge outsider (air, cold, elemental, extraplanar, water)

Init +9; **Senses** darkvision 60 ft., snow vision; Perception +19

DEFENSE

AC 24, touch 14, flat-footed 18 (+5 Dex, +1 dodge, +10 natural, –2 size)

hp 152 (16d10+64)

Fort +14, **Ref** +17, **Will** +5

DR 10/—; **Immune** cold, elemental traits

Weaknesses vulnerable to fire

OFFENSE

Speed 20 ft., burrow (ice and snow only) 20 ft., swim 60 ft.

Melee 2 slams +24 (2d10+10/19–20 plus 2d8 cold)

Space 15 ft.; **Reach** 15 ft.

Special Attacks numbing cold (DC 22)

STATISTICS

Str 30, **Dex** 20, **Con** 19, **Int** 10, **Wis** 11, **Cha** 11

Base Atk +16; **CMB** +28; **CMD** 44 (can't be tripped)

Feats Cleave, Combat Reflexes, Dodge, Improved Critical (slam), Improved Initiative, Lightning Reflexes, Power Attack, Vital Strike

Skills Escape Artist +24, Intimidate +19, Knowledge (planes) +19, Perception +19, Stealth +16, Swim +37

SQ ice glide, icewalking

Ice elementals are creatures made of animated snow and ice. They form in especially cold parts of the Plane of Water and along its border with the Plane of Air, where giant icebergs careen off of world-high waterfalls into the open sky. Ice elementals vary in their exact appearance.

ELEMENTAL, LIGHTNING

This creature looks like a dark storm cloud, with sparks suggesting eyes and long sweeping arms charged with bolts of lightning.

LIGHTNING ELEMENTAL

Languages Auran

ECOLOGY

Environment any (Plane of Air)
Organization solitary, pair, or gang (3–8)
Treasure none

SPECIAL ABILITIES

Metal Mastery (Ex) A lightning elemental gains a +3 bonus on attack rolls if its opponent is wearing metal armor, is wielding a metal weapon, or is made of metal (such as an iron golem).

Spark Leap (Ex) A lightning elemental gains a +10 bonus on bull rush, disarm, overrun, and trip attacks when it charges a creature against whom its metal mastery ability applies.

SMALL LIGHTNING ELEMENTAL CR 1

XP 400
N Small outsider (air, elemental, extraplanar)
Init +6; **Senses** darkvision 60 ft.; Perception +5

DEFENSE

AC 14, touch 13, flat-footed 12 (+2 Dex, +1 natural, +1 size)
hp 11 (2d10)
Fort +3, **Ref** +5, **Will** +0
Immune electricity, elemental traits

OFFENSE

Speed fly 100 ft. (perfect)
Melee slam +5 (1d4 plus 1d3 electricity)
Special Attacks metal mastery, spark leap

STATISTICS

Str 10, **Dex** 15, **Con** 10, **Int** 4, **Wis** 11, **Cha** 11
Base Atk +2; **CMB** +1; **CMD** 13
Feats Improved Initiative, Weapon Finesse[B]
Skills Acrobatics +7, Escape Artist +6, Fly +12, Knowledge (planes) +1, Perception +5

MEDIUM LIGHTNING ELEMENTAL CR 3

XP 800
N Medium outsider (air, elemental, extraplanar)
Init +8; **Senses** darkvision 60 ft.; Perception +7

DEFENSE

AC 16, touch 15, flat-footed 11 (+4 Dex, +1 dodge, +1 natural)
hp 26 (4d10+4)
Fort +5, **Ref** +8, **Will** +1
Immune electricity, elemental traits

OFFENSE

Speed fly 100 ft. (perfect)
Melee slam +8 (1d6+3 plus 1d4 electricity)

Special Attacks metal mastery, spark leap

STATISTICS

Str 14, **Dex** 19, **Con** 12, **Int** 4, **Wis** 11, **Cha** 11
Base Atk +4; **CMB** +6; **CMD** 21
Feats Dodge, Improved Initiative, Weapon Finesse[B]
Skills Acrobatics +11, Escape Artist +9, Fly +12, Knowledge (planes) +2, Perception +7

LARGE LIGHTNING ELEMENTAL CR 5

XP 1,600
N Large outsider (air, elemental, extraplanar)
Init +10; **Senses** darkvision 60 ft.; Perception +11

DEFENSE

AC 18, touch 16, flat-footed 11 (+6 Dex, +1 dodge, +2 natural, −1 size)
hp 60 (8d10+16)
Fort +8, **Ref** +12, **Will** +2
DR 5/—; **Immune** electricity, elemental traits

OFFENSE

Speed fly 100 ft. (perfect)
Melee 2 slams +13 (1d8+3 plus 1d6 electricity)
Space 10 ft.; **Reach** 10 ft.
Special Attacks metal mastery, spark leap

STATISTICS

Str 16, **Dex** 23, **Con** 14, **Int** 6, **Wis** 11, **Cha** 11
Base Atk +8; **CMB** +12; **CMD** 29
Feats Dodge, Flyby Attack, Improved Initiative, Mobility, Weapon Finesse[B]
Skills Acrobatics +17, Escape Artist +17, Fly +12, Knowledge (planes) +9, Perception +11

HUGE LIGHTNING ELEMENTAL CR 7

XP 3,200
N Huge outsider (air, elemental, extraplanar)
Init +12; **Senses** darkvision 60 ft.; Perception +13

DEFENSE

AC 19, touch 17, flat-footed 10 (+8 Dex, +1 dodge, +2 natural, −2 size)
hp 85 (10d10+30)
Fort +10, **Ref** +15, **Will** +5
DR 5/—; **Immune** electricity, elemental traits

OFFENSE

Speed fly 100 ft. (perfect)
Melee 2 slams +16 (2d6+5 plus 1d8 electricity)
Space 15 ft.; **Reach** 15 ft.
Special Attacks metal mastery, spark leap

STATISTICS

Str 20, **Dex** 27, **Con** 16, **Int** 6, **Wis** 11, **Cha** 11
Base Atk +10; **CMB** +17; **CMD** 36
Feats Dodge, Flyby Attack, Improved Initiative, Iron Will, Mobility, Weapon Finesse[B]
Skills Acrobatics +21, Escape Artist +21, Fly +12, Knowledge (planes) +11, Perception +13

Illustration by Alberto Dal Lago

GREATER LIGHTNING ELEMENTAL — CR 9

XP 6,400

N Huge outsider (air, elemental, extraplanar)

Init +13; **Senses** darkvision 60 ft.; Perception +16

DEFENSE

AC 22, touch 18, flat-footed 12 (+9 Dex, +1 dodge, +4 natural, −2 size)

hp 110 (13d10+39)

Fort +11, **Ref** +17, **Will** +6

DR 10/—; **Immune** electricity, elemental traits

OFFENSE

Speed fly 100 ft. (perfect)

Melee 2 slams +20 (2d8+6 plus 2d6 electricity)

Space 15 ft.; **Reach** 15 ft.

Special Attacks metal mastery, spark leap

STATISTICS

Str 22, **Dex** 29, **Con** 16, **Int** 8, **Wis** 11, **Cha** 11

Base Atk +13; **CMB** +21; **CMD** 41

Feats Blind-Fight, Dodge, Flyby Attack, Improved Initiative, Iron Will, Mobility, Power Attack, Weapon Finesse[B]

Skills Acrobatics +25, Escape Artist +25, Fly +13, Intimidate +16, Knowledge (planes) +15, Perception +16

ELDER LIGHTNING ELEMENTAL — CR 11

XP 12,800

N Huge outsider (air, elemental, extraplanar)

Init +14; **Senses** darkvision 60 ft.; Perception +19

DEFENSE

AC 25, touch 19, flat-footed 14 (+10 Dex, +1 dodge, +6 natural, −2 size)

hp 136 (16d10+48)

Fort +13, **Ref** +20, **Will** +7

DR 10/—; **Immune** electricity, elemental traits

OFFENSE

Speed fly 100 ft. (perfect)

Melee 2 slams +24 (2d8+8 plus 2d8 electricity)

Space 15 ft.; **Reach** 15 ft.

Special Attacks metal mastery, spark leap

STATISTICS

Str 26, **Dex** 31, **Con** 16, **Int** 10, **Wis** 11, **Cha** 11

Base Atk +16; **CMB** +26; **CMD** 47

Feats Blind-Fight, Combat Reflexes, Dodge, Flyby Attack, Improved Initiative, Iron Will, Mobility, Power Attack, Weapon Finesse[B]

Skills Acrobatics +29, Escape Artist +29, Fly +14, Intimidate +19, Knowledge (planes) +19, Perception +19, Stealth +21

Though most think of the Plane of Air as a vast expanse of clear sky, that plane also holds the power of the storm, including monstrous hurricanes larger than entire worlds and thunderstorms whose peals and claps can shatter stone. Whether lightning elementals are the by-product of common air elementals spending too much time near these electrically charged storms or are merely calved off like forgotten flurries, they are aggressive and almost suicidal in their willingness to leap into battle. They particularly enjoy attacking creatures that are made of metal and creatures that wear metal armor or wield metal weapons.

Many lightning elementals have a roughly humanoid shape, but some prefer animalistic shapes (particularly birds and dragons), and a few appear to be nothing more than large disembodied heads made of dark clouds with flickering lightning tongues. Regardless of the shape a lightning elemental takes, the air around the creature hums and throbs with the promise of electrocution and the tangy stink of ozone.

Elemental, Magma

This rocky monster glows with an internal heat. Red light spills from its eyes and mouth, as well as fractures in its outer surface.

MAGMA ELEMENTAL

Languages Ignan

ECOLOGY

Environment any (Plane of Fire)

Organization solitary, pair, or gang (3–8)

Treasure none

SPECIAL ABILITIES

Burn (Ex) A magma elemental's burn DC includes a −2 racial penalty, as their fires don't burn quite as hot as true elemental flames.

Earth Glide (Ex) A burrowing magma elemental can pass through stone, dirt, lava, or almost any other sort of earth except metal as easily as a fish swims through water. Its burrowing leaves behind no tunnel or hole, nor does it create any ripple, though the area it passes through feels warm for 1 round afterward and often retains a strangely smooth texture, as if the stone had been polished. A *move earth* spell cast on an area containing a burrowing magma elemental flings the elemental back 30 feet, stunning the creature for 1 round unless it succeeds on a DC 15 Fortitude save.

Lava Puddle (Su) Once per day as a full-round action, a magma elemental can vomit forth a puddle of lava (*Pathfinder RPG Core Rulebook* 444) that fills its space to a depth of 2–3 inches and counts as difficult terrain. Any creature that moves through this puddle of lava takes 2d6 points of fire damage. This damage continues for 1d3 rounds after the creature leaves the lava pool, although then it only inflicts 1d6 points of fire damage per round. The lava puddle solidifies and is safe to touch after a number of rounds equal to the elemental's Hit Dice. At the GM's discretion, this puddle of lava could start secondary fires.

SMALL MAGMA ELEMENTAL   CR 1
XP 400
N Small outsider (earth, elemental, extraplanar, fire)

Init +3; **Senses** darkvision 60 ft.; Perception +5

DEFENSE

AC 15, touch 10, flat-footed 15 (−1 Dex, +5 natural, +1 size)

hp 11 (2d10)

Fort +3, **Ref** +2, **Will** +0

Immune fire, elemental traits

Weaknesses vulnerable to cold

OFFENSE

Speed 20 ft., burrow 20 ft.; earth glide

Melee slam +3 (1d3 plus burn)

Special Attacks burn (1d4, DC 9), lava puddle

STATISTICS

Str 10, **Dex** 8, **Con** 11, **Int** 4, **Wis** 11, **Cha** 11

Base Atk +2; **CMB** +1; **CMD** 10

Feats Improved Initiative

Skills Knowledge (dungeoneering) +2, Perception +5, Stealth +8

SQ earth glide

MEDIUM MAGMA ELEMENTAL   CR 3
XP 800
N Medium outsider (earth, elemental, extraplanar, fire)

Init +3; **Senses** darkvision 60 ft.; Perception +7

DEFENSE

AC 16, touch 9, flat-footed 16 (−1 Dex, +7 natural)

hp 30 (4d10+8)

Fort +6, **Ref** +3, **Will** +1

Immune fire, elemental traits

Weaknesses vulnerable to cold

OFFENSE

Speed 20 ft., burrow 20 ft.; earth glide

Melee slam +6 (1d6+3 plus burn)

Special Attacks burn (1d4, DC 12), lava puddle

STATISTICS

Str 14, **Dex** 8, **Con** 15, **Int** 4, **Wis** 11, **Cha** 11

Base Atk +4; **CMB** +6; **CMD** 15

Feats Improved Initiative, Power Attack

Skills Knowledge (dungeoneering) +4, Perception +7, Stealth +6

LARGE MAGMA ELEMENTAL   CR 5
XP 1,600
N Large outsider (earth, elemental, extraplanar, fire)

Init +3; **Senses** darkvision 60 ft.; Perception +11

DEFENSE

AC 16, touch 8, flat-footed 16 (−1 Dex, +8 natural, −1 size)

hp 60 (8d10+16)

Fort +8, **Ref** +5, **Will** +2

DR 5/—; **Immune** fire, elemental traits

Weaknesses vulnerable to cold

OFFENSE

Speed 20 ft., burrow 20 ft.; earth glide

Melee 2 slams +11 (1d8+4 plus burn)

Space 10 ft.; **Reach** 10 ft.

Special Attacks burn (1d6, DC 14), lava puddle

STATISTICS

Str 18, **Dex** 8, **Con** 15, **Int** 6, **Wis** 11, **Cha** 11

Base Atk +8; **CMB** +13; **CMD** 22

Feats Cleave, Improved Bull Rush, Improved Initiative, Power Attack

Skills Climb +15, Knowledge (dungeoneering) +9, Perception +11, Stealth +6

HUGE MAGMA ELEMENTAL   CR 7
XP 3,200
N Huge outsider (earth, elemental, extraplanar, fire)

Init +3; **Senses** darkvision 60 ft.; Perception +13

DEFENSE

AC 17, touch 7, flat-footed 17 (−1 Dex, +10 natural, −2 size)

hp 85 (10d10+30)

Fort +10, **Ref** +6, **Will** +3

DR 5/—; **Immune** fire, elemental traits

Weaknesses vulnerable to cold

Speed 20 ft., burrow 20 ft.; earth glide

Melee 2 slams +14 (2d6+6 plus burn)

Space 15 ft.; **Reach** 15 ft.

Special Attacks burn (1d8, DC 16), lava puddle

STATISTICS

Str 22, **Dex** 8, **Con** 17, **Int** 6, **Wis** 11, **Cha** 11

Base Atk +10; **CMB** +18; **CMD** 27

Feats Cleave, Greater Bull Rush, Improved Bull Rush, Improved Initiative, Power Attack

Skills Climb +19, Knowledge (dungeoneering) +11, Perception +13, Stealth +4

GREATER MAGMA ELEMENTAL   CR 9
XP 6,400

N Huge outsider (earth, elemental, extraplanar, fire)

Init +3; **Senses** darkvision 60 ft.; Perception +16

DEFENSE

AC 19, touch 7, flat-footed 19 (–1 Dex, +12 natural, –2 size)

hp 123 (13d10+52)

Fort +12, **Ref** +7, **Will** +4

DR 10/—; **Immune** fire, elemental traits

Weaknesses vulnerable to cold

OFFENSE

Speed 20 ft., burrow 20 ft.; earth glide

Melee 2 slams +18 (2d8+7 plus burn)

Space 15 ft.; **Reach** 15 ft.

Special Attacks burn (2d6, DC 18), lava puddle

STATISTICS

Str 24, **Dex** 8, **Con** 19, **Int** 8, **Wis** 11, **Cha** 11

Base Atk +13; **CMB** +22; **CMD** 31

Feats Cleave, Greater Bull Rush, Greater Overrun, Improved Bull Rush, Improved Initiative, Improved Overrun, Power Attack

Skills Climb +23, Intimidate +16, Knowledge (dungeoneering) +15, Perception +16, Stealth +7

ELDER MAGMA ELEMENTAL   CR 11
XP 12,800

N Huge outsider (earth, elemental, extraplanar, fire)

Init +3; **Senses** darkvision 60 ft.; Perception +19

DEFENSE

AC 25, touch 7, flat-footed 25 (–1 Dex, +18 natural, –2 size)

hp 152 (16d10+64)

Fort +14, **Ref** +9, **Will** +5

DR 10/—; **Immune** fire, elemental traits

Weaknesses vulnerable to cold

OFFENSE

Speed 20 ft., burrow 20 ft.; earth glide

Melee 2 slams +22 (3d6+8 plus burn)

Space 15 ft.; **Reach** 15 ft.

Special Attacks burn (3d6, DC 20), lava puddle

STATISTICS

Str 26, **Dex** 8, **Con** 19, **Int** 10, **Wis** 11, **Cha** 11

Base Atk +16; **CMB** +26; **CMD** 35

Feats Cleave, Greater Bull Rush, Greater Overrun, Improved Bull Rush, Improved Initiative, Improved Overrun, Power Attack, Vital Strike

Skills Climb +27, Intimidate +19, Knowledge (dungeoneering) +19, Knowledge (planes) +19, Perception +19, Stealth +10

In the border areas between the Plane of Earth and Plane of Fire, volcanoes and continent-sized lava flows are commonplace. Elementals in this area tend to have aspects of both planes, and the typical sort is the magma elemental, an earth elemental with a core of liquid fire. Magma elementals generally have a somewhat feral or bestial appearance.

ELEMENTAL, MUD

This animate pile of mud seems barely able to maintain the semblance of a humanoid form made of dripping sludge.

MUD ELEMENTAL

Languages Terran

ECOLOGY

Environment any land or water (Plane of Earth)
Organization solitary, pair, or gang (3–8)
Treasure none

SPECIAL ABILITIES

Earth Glide (Ex) A burrowing mud elemental can pass through dirt, gravel, or other loose or porous solid matter as easily as a fish swims through water. It cannot use this ability to pass through a solid barrier such as a stone or brick wall. Its burrowing leaves behind no tunnel or hole, nor does it create any ripple or other sign of its presence. A *move earth* spell cast on an area containing a burrowing mud elemental flings the elemental back 30 feet, stunning the creature for 1 round unless it succeeds on a DC 15 Fortitude save.

Entrap (Ex) The mud from an elemental's entrap ability can be washed away in 1d3 rounds of immersion in water.

SMALL MUD ELEMENTAL   CR 1

XP 400

N Small outsider (earth, elemental, extraplanar, water)
Init –1; **Senses** darkvision 60 ft., tremorsense 30 ft.; Perception +5

DEFENSE

AC 16, touch 10, flat-footed 16 (–1 Dex, +6 natural, +1 size)
hp 13 (2d10+2)
Fort +4, **Ref** +2, **Will** +0
Immune acid, elemental traits

OFFENSE

Speed 20 ft., burrow 10 ft., swim 30 ft.; earth glide
Melee slam +5 (1d4+3 plus entrap)
Special Attacks entrap (DC 12, 10 minutes, hardness 5, hp 5)

STATISTICS

Str 14, **Dex** 8, **Con** 13, **Int** 4, **Wis** 11, **Cha** 11
Base Atk +2; **CMB** +3; **CMD** 12
Feats Improved Bull Rush[B], Power Attack
Skills Climb +6, Escape Artist +3, Knowledge (planes) +1, Perception +5, Stealth +7, Swim +10

MEDIUM MUD ELEMENTAL   CR 3

XP 800

N Medium outsider (earth, elemental, extraplanar, water)
Init +0; **Senses** darkvision 60 ft., tremorsense 30 ft.; Perception +7

DEFENSE

AC 16, touch 10, flat-footed 16 (+6 natural)
hp 30 (4d10+8)
Fort +6, **Ref** +4, **Will** +1
Immune acid, elemental traits

OFFENSE

Speed 20 ft., burrow 10 ft., swim 30 ft.; earth glide
Melee slam +7 (1d6+4 plus entrap)
Special Attacks entrap (DC 14, 10 minutes, hardness 5, hp 5)

STATISTICS

Str 16, **Dex** 10, **Con** 15, **Int** 4, **Wis** 11, **Cha** 11
Base Atk +4; **CMB** +7; **CMD** 17
Feats Cleave, Improved Bull Rush[B], Power Attack
Skills Climb +8, Escape Artist +5, Knowledge (planes) +2, Perception +7, Stealth +5, Swim +11

LARGE MUD ELEMENTAL   CR 5

XP 1,600

N Large outsider (earth, elemental, extraplanar, water)
Init +1; **Senses** darkvision 60 ft., tremorsense 30 ft.; Perception +11

DEFENSE

AC 17, touch 10, flat-footed 16 (+1 Dex, +7 natural, –1 size)
hp 68 (8d10+24)
Fort +9, **Ref** +7, **Will** +2
DR 5/—; **Immune** acid, elemental traits

OFFENSE

Speed 20 ft., burrow 10 ft., swim 30 ft.; earth glide
Melee 2 slams +12 (1d8+5 plus entrap)
Space 10 ft.; **Reach** 10 ft.
Special Attacks entrap (DC 17, 10 minutes, hardness 5, hp 10)

STATISTICS

Str 20, **Dex** 12, **Con** 17, **Int** 4, **Wis** 11, **Cha** 11
Base Atk +8; **CMB** +14; **CMD** 25
Feats Cleave, Great Cleave, Greater Bull Rush, Improved Bull Rush[B], Power Attack
Skills Climb +12, Escape Artist +8, Knowledge (planes) +4, Perception +11, Stealth +4, Swim +13

HUGE MUD ELEMENTAL   CR 7

XP 3,200

N Huge outsider (earth, elemental, extraplanar, water)
Init +3; **Senses** darkvision 60 ft., tremorsense 30 ft.; Perception +13

DEFENSE

AC 20, touch 12, flat-footed 16 (+3 Dex, +1 dodge, +8 natural, –2 size)
hp 95 (10d10+40)
Fort +11, **Ref** +10, **Will** +3
DR 5/—; **Immune** acid, elemental traits

OFFENSE

Speed 20 ft., burrow 10 ft., swim 30 ft.; earth glide
Melee 2 slams +15 (2d6+7 plus entrap)
Space 15 ft.; **Reach** 15 ft.
Special Attacks entrap (DC 19, 10 minutes, hardness 5, hp 15)

STATISTICS

Str 24, **Dex** 16, **Con** 19, **Int** 6, **Wis** 11, **Cha** 11
Base Atk +10; **CMB** +19; **CMD** 33
Feats Cleave, Dodge, Great Cleave, Greater Bull Rush, Improved Bull Rush[B], Power Attack

Skills Climb +17, Escape Artist +13, Knowledge (planes) +7, Perception +13, Stealth +8, Swim +15

GREATER MUD ELEMENTAL   CR 9

XP 6,400

N Huge outsider (earth, elemental, extraplanar, water)

Init +4; **Senses** darkvision 60 ft., tremorsense 30 ft.; Perception +16

DEFENSE

AC 22, touch 13, flat-footed 17 (+4 Dex, +1 dodge, +9 natural, −2 size)

hp 123 (13d10+52)

Fort +12, **Ref** +14, **Will** +4

DR 10/—; **Immune** acid, elemental traits

OFFENSE

Speed 20 ft., burrow 10 ft., swim 30 ft.; earth glide

Melee 2 slams +20 (2d8+9 plus entrap)

Space 15 ft.; **Reach** 15 ft.

Special Attacks entrap (DC 20, 10 minutes, hardness 10, hp 15)

STATISTICS

Str 28, **Dex** 18, **Con** 19, **Int** 8, **Wis** 11, **Cha** 11

Base Atk +13; **CMB** +24; **CMD** 39

Feats Awesome Blow, Cleave, Dodge, Great Cleave, Greater Bull Rush, Improved Bull Rush[B], Lightning Reflexes, Power Attack

Skills Climb +25, Escape Artist +20, Knowledge (planes) +15, Perception +16, Stealth +12, Swim +17

ELDER MUD ELEMENTAL   CR 11

XP 12,800

N Huge outsider (earth, elemental, extraplanar, water)

Init +5; **Senses** darkvision 60 ft., tremorsense 30 ft.; Perception +19

DEFENSE

AC 23, touch 14, flat-footed 17 (+5 Dex, +1 dodge, +9 natural, −2 size)

hp 152 (16d10+64)

Fort +14, **Ref** +17, **Will** +5

DR 10/—; **Immune** acid, elemental traits

OFFENSE

Speed 20 ft., burrow 10 ft., swim 30 ft.; earth glide

Melee 2 slams +24 (2d10+10/19–20 plus entrap)

Space 15 ft.; **Reach** 15 ft.

Special Attacks entrap (DC 22, 10 minutes, hardness 10, hp 15)

STATISTICS

Str 30, **Dex** 20, **Con** 19, **Int** 10, **Wis** 11, **Cha** 11

Base Atk +16; **CMB** +28; **CMD** 44

Feats Awesome Blow, Cleave, Dodge, Great Cleave, Greater Bull Rush, Improved Bull Rush[B], Improved Critical (slams), Lightning Reflexes, Power Attack

Skills Climb +29, Escape Artist +24, Intimidate +19, Knowledge (planes) +19, Perception +19, Stealth +16, Swim +18

Where the Plane of Earth borders the Plane of Water, a mixing of the fundamental elements occurs—it is in this borderland that the mud elementals dwell. Scorned by earth and water elementals, mud elementals usually look like vaguely recognizable blobs of mud in the shape of a Material Plane creature, whether a humanoid, an animal, or even an immense insect. The exact density of their muddy bodies varies—some might be composed of silty water, while others are thick, like river clay. Large and powerful mud elementals tend to have worm-like, reptilian, or frog-like forms.

FACELESS STALKER

This hairless, leathery biped has a face dominated by grotesque and unsettling whorls and slits instead of actual features.

FACELESS STALKER (UGOTHOL) CR 4

XP 1,200

CE Medium aberration (shapechanger)

Init +7; **Senses** darkvision 60 ft.; Perception +2

DEFENSE

AC 17, touch 13, flat-footed 14 (+3 Dex, +4 natural)

hp 42 (5d8+20)

Fort +5, **Ref** +4, **Will** +6

DR 5/piercing or slashing

OFFENSE

Speed 30 ft.

Melee mwk longsword +8 (1d8+4/19–20), slam +2 (1d6+2 plus grab)

Space 5 ft.; **Reach** 10 ft.

Special Attacks blood drain (1 Constitution), sneak attack +2d6

Spell-Like Abilities (CL 5th; concentration +8)

Constant—*tongues*

STATISTICS

Str 18, **Dex** 17, **Con** 18, **Int** 13, **Wis** 15, **Cha** 16

Base Atk +3; **CMB** +7 (+11 grapple); **CMD** 20

Feats Combat Reflexes, Deceitful, Improved Initiative

Skills Bluff +10, Disguise +14 (+24 when using change shape), Escape Artist +19, Sleight of Hand +8, Stealth +11

Racial Modifier +4 Disguise, +8 Escape Artist

Languages Aquan, Common; *tongues*

SQ change shape (Medium humanoid, *alter self*), compression, faceless

ECOLOGY

Environment any swamps or underground

Organization solitary, pair, or gang (3–9)

Treasure standard (masterwork longsword, other treasure)

SPECIAL ABILITIES

Change Shape (Su) A faceless stalker can assume the form of a Medium humanoid at will but requires 10 uninterrupted minutes to alter its body. Performing this transformation is somewhat painful, but the faceless stalker can maintain its new form indefinitely once it has achieved

it. It can change back to its true form as a swift action and gains a +2 morale bonus on attack rolls, damage rolls, skill checks, and saving throws for 1 round after it does so. Faceless stalkers retain their own innate abilities when they assume their new form and do not gain any of those belonging to the creature they mimic. A faceless stalker gains a +10 bonus on Disguise checks when they are used in conjunction with this ability.

Faceless (Su) In its natural form, a faceless stalker has no discernible facial features. It gains a +4 bonus on saving throws made to resist attacks or effects that target the senses. This includes gaze attacks, odor-based attacks, sonic attacks and similar attacks. This bonus does not apply to illusions.

Ugothols (as faceless stalkers call themselves) are one of the many tools created and then discarded by the aboleths in their long war against the surface dwellers. Scorned by their former masters when the scheme for which they were designed unraveled, the faceless stalkers fled into swamps, marshes, or any other dark, wet places they could find—the closest they could come to the aquatic cities they once considered home.

Originally designed to serve as spies that could walk uncontested among the air-breathing races, faceless stalkers adopt new forms by reshaping their skin and contorting their rubbery bodies. This painful process takes approximately 10 uninterrupted minutes—an ugothol typically seeks a private place to do it, avoiding even others of its own kind. The sensation of returning to its true form is quite exhilarating and results in a momentary burst of euphoria.

Faceless stalkers cannot digest solid food even when in the form of a creature with a mouth. Instead, they subsist on liquids, including blood. In their natural forms, they have three hollow tongues which they use to penetrate and lap blood from their victims. Since they have no particular skill at grappling foes, most ugothols wait until a victim is helpless or asleep before attempting to drink its blood—although the best is when a victim is helpless but conscious during the process, so that the faceless stalker can "play with its food" by having grisly and cruel conversations with it.

FETCHLING

This gaunt man appears drained of color, like a person viewed at twilight or in a dark alley.

FETCHLING (KAYAL) CR 1/2

XP 200

Fetchling rogue 1

N Medium outsider (native)

Init +3; **Senses** darkvision 60 ft., low-light vision; Perception +3

DEFENSE

AC 17, touch 13, flat-footed 14 (+4 armor, +3 Dex)

hp 10 (1d8+2)

Fort +2, **Ref** +5, **Will** −1

Defensive Abilities shadow blending; **Resist** cold 5, electricity 5

OFFENSE

Speed 30 ft.

Melee dagger +3 (1d4+1/19–20)

Special Attacks sneak attack +1d6

Spell-Like Abilities (CL 1st; concentration +3)

1/day—*disguise self* (humanoid only)

STATISTICS

Str 13, **Dex** 17, **Con** 14, **Int** 8, **Wis** 8, **Cha** 14

Base Atk +0; **CMB** +1; **CMD** 14

Feats Weapon Finesse

Skills Appraise +3, Bluff +6, Diplomacy +6, Knowledge (local) +3, Knowledge (planes) +2, Perception +3, Sense Motive +3, Stealth +7; **Racial Modifiers** +2 Knowledge (planes), +7 Stealth

Languages Common

SQ trapfinding +1

ECOLOGY

Environment any (Plane of Shadow)

Organization solitary, pair, guild (3–12), or enclave (13–30 plus 1–4 2nd–4th level rogue spies, 1–4 2nd–4th level sorcerers, and 1 3rd–6th level fighter/rogue leader)

Treasure NPC gear (chain shirt, dagger, other treasure)

SPECIAL ABILITIES

Shadow Blending (Su) Attacks against a fetchling in dim light have a 50% miss chance instead of the normal 20% miss chance. This ability does not grant total concealment; it just increases the miss chance.

Fetchlings are descended from generations of humans trapped on the Plane of Shadow. Infused with the essence of that plane, they are more and less than human, and often serve as middlemen in planar trade and politics. Other than their yellow eyes, their flesh has no color—it is either stark white, midnight black, or a shade of gray. On the Material Plane, they conceal themselves with heavy clothing or dim light so they can work without prejudice. The name "fetchling" is a human word; their own name for their race is *kayal*, meaning "shadow people."

A fetchling stands 6 feet tall, but is generally lithe and wiry of frame, weighing only 150 pounds. Fetchlings live as long as half-elves.

FETCHLING CHARACTERS

Fetchlings are defined by their class levels—they do not possess racial HD. They have the following racial traits.

+2 Dexterity, +2 Charisma, –2 Wisdom: Fetchlings are quick and forceful, but often strange and easily distracted by errant thoughts.

Darkvision: Fetchlings see in the dark up to 60 feet.

Low-Light Vision: Fetchlings can see twice as far as humans in conditions of dim light.

Skilled: Fetchlings have a +2 racial bonus on Knowledge (planes) and Stealth checks.

Shadow Blending: See above.

Shadowy Resistance: Fetchlings have cold resistance 5 and electricity resistance 5.

Spell-Like Abilities (Sp): A fetchling can use *disguise self* once per day as a spell-like ability. It can assume the form of any humanoid creature using this spell-like ability. When a fetchling reaches 9th level in any combination of classes, it gains *shadow walk* (self only) as a spell-like ability usable once per day, and at 13th level, it gains *plane shift* (self only, to the Plane of Shadow or the Material Plane only) usable once per day. A fetchling's caster level is equal to its total Hit Dice.

Languages Fetchlings begin play speaking Common. A fetchling with a high Intelligence score can choose any of the following languages: Aklo, Aquan, Auran, Draconic, D'ziriak (understanding only, cannot speak), Ignan, Terran, and any regional human tongue.

Illustration by Damien Mammoliti

123

FLY, GIANT

Bristling with coarse hairs, this enormous fly's legs twitch just before it launches into the air on buzzing wings.

GIANT FLY	CR 1	

XP 400

N Medium vermin

Init +3; **Senses** darkvision 60 ft.; Perception +2

DEFENSE

AC 13, touch 13, flat-footed 10 (+3 Dex)

hp 15 (2d8+6)

Fort +6, **Ref** +3, **Will** –2

Immune disease, mind-affecting effects

OFFENSE

Speed 20 ft., climb 20 ft., fly 60 ft. (good)

Melee bite +2 (1d6+1 plus disease)

STATISTICS

Str 12, **Dex** 17, **Con** 16, **Int** —, **Wis** 7, **Cha** 2

Base Atk +1; **CMB** +2; **CMD** 15 (21 vs. trip)

Skills Climb +9, Fly +7, Perception +2; **Racial Modifiers** +4 Perception

ECOLOGY

Environment any temperate or tropical

Organization solitary, pair, or swarm (3–12)

Treasure none

SPECIAL ABILITIES

Disease (Ex) *Filth Fever*: Bite—injury; *save* Fortitude DC 14; *onset* 1d3 days; *frequency* 1/day; *effect* 1d3 Dex damage and 1d3 Con damage; *cure* 2 consecutive saves. Some flies might carry other diseases, at the GM's discretion. The save DC is Constitution-based.

Much like their tiny cousins, giant flies feed upon carrion. Wholly monstrous, these disgusting creatures have been known to sometimes attack still-living foes, particularly when they are hungry or living creatures disturb their meals. Some species of giant fly bear their larva live, ejecting piles of undulating giant maggots from their engorged abdomens rather than laying eggs in decaying corpses.

MAGGOT, GIANT

This enormous maggot has greasy, pale flesh and a dripping, circular mouth filled with tiny, sharp teeth.

GIANT MAGGOT	CR 1/2	

XP 200

N Medium vermin

Init –1; **Senses** darkvision 60 ft.; Perception –3

DEFENSE

AC 9, touch 9, flat-footed 9 (–1 Dex)

hp 7 (1d8+3)

Fort +5, **Ref** –1, **Will** –3

Immune disease, mind-affecting effects

OFFENSE

Speed 10 ft., burrow 5 ft.

Melee bite +0 (1d6)

Special Attacks regurgitate

STATISTICS

Str 10, **Dex** 8, **Con** 16, **Int** —, **Wis** 5, **Cha** 1

Base Atk +0; **CMB** +0; **CMD** 9 (can't be tripped)

ECOLOGY

Environment any temperate or tropical

Organization solitary or swarm (2–12)

Treasure none

SPECIAL ABILITIES

Regurgitate (Ex) Once per day, a giant maggot can empty its putrid stomach upon one creature within 5 feet. The target must make a DC 13 Fortitude save or be sickened for 1 minute (or until the target spends a full-round action with at least a gallon of water to wash off the filth). The save DC is Constitution-based.

Voracious scavengers, giant maggots feed constantly, gorging themselves on the dead in preparation for their transformation into giant flies. Their pallid, corpulent bodies are the size of human children, and their rasping teeth are capable of eating even the bones of a corpse. Giant maggots have no legs, and move with a disturbing undulation as they crawl over their meals. Giant maggots feed for 2 weeks (often moving from one corpse to another) before entering a pupal stage, after which they emerge as giant flies.

Illustration by Andrew Hou

FORLARREN

This humanoid creature has the legs of a bald goat, a completely hairless body, and a horned head with a sinister expression.

FORLARREN	CR 2

XP 600

NE Medium fey

Init +2; **Senses** low-light vision; Perception +11

DEFENSE

AC 15, touch 12, flat-footed 13 (+2 Dex, +3 natural)

hp 18 (4d6+4)

Fort +2, **Ref** +6, **Will** +5

DR 5/cold iron

Weaknesses remorse

OFFENSE

Speed 30 ft.

Melee 2 claws +4 (1d6+1)

Spell-Like Abilities (CL 4th; concentration +3)

3/day—*heat metal* (DC 11)

STATISTICS

Str 12, **Dex** 15, **Con** 12, **Int** 4, **Wis** 13, **Cha** 9

Base Atk +2; **CMB** +3; **CMD** 15

Feats Skill Focus (Perception), Weapon Finesse

Skills Acrobatics +9, Perception +11, Stealth +9

Languages Common, Sylvan

ECOLOGY

Environment temperate plains or forests

Organization solitary

Treasure standard

SPECIAL ABILITIES

Remorse (Ex) Whenever a forlarren kills a living creature, it must make a DC 15 Will save to avoid becoming overwhelmed with remorse. If it fails this save, the forlarren becomes nauseated for 1d6 rounds. This is a mind-affecting effect.

A nymph's charm and beauty are such that she can seduce nearly any creature that she sets her attentions on—and often, unfortunately, creatures she would rather not consort with. When a nymph catches the attention of a fiend and the fiend takes advantage of the creature, the resulting offspring is not always a half-fiend. Roughly one in 20 such incidents results instead in a strange creature known as a forlarren—a unique creature that possesses its own unusual abilities and qualities.

Few nymphs survive the ordeal of giving birth to a forlarren—those who do might attempt to raise their children in loving environments, but the evil that lurks in a forlarren's soul is powerful. In most cases where a nymph attempts to raise a forlarren child, it's only a matter of time before the forlarren grows resentful and its evil nature compels it to murder its mother.

Most forlarrens are female, and few are capable of conceiving children of their own. A forlarren grows to adulthood with astonishing speed, reaching full growth in only a year—even those who come into the world as orphans are capable of defending themselves and seeking out food. Yet despite the rapidity with which they reach maturity, few forlarrens survive to adulthood. Cast out from both sylvan and fiendish society, the typical forlarren is a lonely creature, cursed by its own existence. It detests itself and everything it sees, and soon becomes consumed by hatred of life itself. The forlarren vents its rage on good and evil alike, lashing out at anything that approaches it.

The forlarren attacks with its clawed hands, typically focusing on a single opponent at a time and attacking until it or its opponent is slain. Yet curiously, when a forlarren succeeds in killing an opponent, the kindly traits of its fey mother sometimes surface, and it shows profound remorse for its cruelty. With such a pendulum of erratic behavior, it is no wonder that forlarrens are all but incapable of forming lasting friendships—even with others of their own kind.

The majority of forlarrens inherit little in the way of the magical abilities possessed by their fey mothers, but they do gain a small measure of the powers of their fiendish fathers. In most cases, this manifests as the ability to use *heat metal* three times per day, but some forlarren instead gain a different spell-like ability chosen from the following list: *chill metal, flame blade, flaming sphere, gust of wind, summon swarm,* or *warp wood.*

A forlarren stands 6 feet tall and weighs about 160 pounds. In theory, these creatures can live for hundreds of years, but most perish through violence before they turn 10.

FROST WORM

This immense white worm has a single circular eye in the center of its head. Wisps of icy fog waft up from between its mandibles.

FROST WORM	CR 12

XP 19,200

N Huge magical beast (cold)

Init +7; **Senses** darkvision 60 ft., low-light vision; Perception +17

DEFENSE

AC 27, touch 11, flat-footed 24 (+3 Dex, +16 natural, –2 size)

hp 168 (16d10+80)

Fort +15, **Ref** +13, **Will** +10

Immune cold

Weaknesses vulnerable to fire

OFFENSE

Speed 30 ft., burrow 10 ft.

Melee bite +25 (4d10+15 plus 4d6 cold)

Space 15 ft.; **Reach** 10 ft.

Special Attacks breath weapon (60-ft. cone, 15d6 cold damage, Reflex DC 23 half, usable once per hour), death throes, trill

STATISTICS

Str 31, **Dex** 16, **Con** 21, **Int** 2, **Wis** 16, **Cha** 11

Base Atk +16; **CMB** +28; **CMD** 41 (can't be tripped)

Feats Cleave, Combat Reflexes, Improved Initiative, Iron Will, Power Attack, Skill Focus (Perception), Stand Still, Weapon Focus (bite)

Skills Perception +17, Stealth +6 (+14 in ice and snow); **Racial Modifiers** +8 Stealth in ice and snow

SQ cold

ECOLOGY

Environment cold plains or mountains

Organization solitary

Treasure incidental

SPECIAL ABILITIES

Cold (Su) A frost worm's body generates intense cold, allowing it to deal an additional 4d6 cold damage with its bite attack. Any creature that attacks a frost worm with an unarmed strike or a natural weapon takes 1d6 points of cold damage per successful hit. A creature that grapples or is grappled by a frost worm takes 4d6 points of cold damage per round the grapple is maintained.

Death Throes (Su) When killed, a frost worm explodes in a 100-foot-radius burst that deals 12d6 cold damage and 8d6 piercing damage (DC 23 Reflex half). The save DC is Constitution-based.

Trill (Su) As a full-round action, a frost worm can emit a strange trilling sound that affects all creatures within a 100-foot radius. Creatures must succeed on a DC 18 Will save or be fascinated for as long as the worm continues to trill (the frost worm can maintain this trill by concentrating). Once a creature has resisted or broken the effect, it cannot be affected again by that same frost worm's trill for 24 hours. This is a sonic mind-affecting effect. The save DC is Charisma-based.

With armor-crushing jaws, flesh that radiates cold, and a terrible keening cry capable of holding creatures fascinated, frost worms are apex predators of the frozen tundra and glaciers. In the frost worms' far-reaching hunting grounds, they fear only the remorhaz, for the heat generated by an enraged remorhaz causes intense pain to a frost worm.

This extreme aversion to heat, as well as its freezing touch and devastating breath weapon, stems from an unusual facet of frost worm physiology—veins that run with magically cold blood. This creature's ichor is clear, but infused with such sub-freezing temperatures that the monster's flesh can freeze water in the skin of creatures that touch it. When a frost worm dies, this magical energy dissipates, and both blood and muscle immediately freeze solid and then explode into a catastrophic barrage of icy shrapnel. As a result, even those predators that might legitimately prey upon the burrowing monstrosities tend to leave frost worms well enough alone.

An adult frost worm measures 35 feet long and weighs 8,000 pounds.

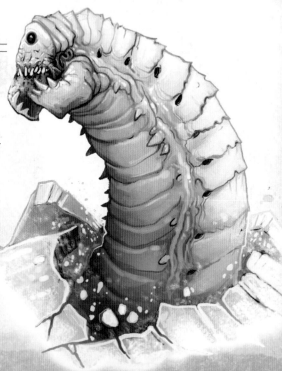

Illustration by Peter Lazarski

FUNGAL CRAWLER

This giant fanged cricket is caked in pungent fungal growths and topped with a mushroom-like cap.

FUNGAL CRAWLER — CR 3

XP 800

N Small aberration

Init +9; **Senses** darkvision 60 ft.; Perception +6

DEFENSE

AC 16, touch 16, flat-footed 11 (+5 Dex, +1 size)

hp 26 (4d8+8)

Fort +3, **Ref** +6, **Will** +5

Defensive Abilities plant defenses; **Immune** mind-affecting effects, paralysis, poison, polymorph effects, sleep, stunning

OFFENSE

Speed 20 ft., climb 40 ft.

Melee bite +6 (1d6+2 plus poison), 2 claws +6 (1d4+2)

Special Attacks leap

STATISTICS

Str 14, **Dex** 20, **Con** 15, **Int** 2, **Wis** 13, **Cha** 7

Base Atk +3; **CMB** +4; **CMD** 19 (27 vs. trip)

Feats Improved Initiative, Step Up

Skills Acrobatics +10 (+14 jumping), Climb +10, Perception +6; **Racial Modifiers** +14 on Acrobatics checks made to jump

ECOLOGY

Environment any underground

Organization solitary, pair, or swarm (3–12)

Treasure none

SPECIAL ABILITIES

Leap (Ex) A fungal crawler can perform a special kind of pounce attack by jumping into combat. When a fungal crawler charges, it can make a DC 20 Acrobatics check to jump into the air and land next to its enemies. If it makes the Acrobatics check, it can follow up with four claw attacks against foes in reach, but it cannot make a bite attack.

Plant Defenses (Ex) A fungal crawler is part plant and shares many of the immunities that plant creatures possess. A fungal crawler is immune to mind-affecting effects, paralysis, poison, polymorph, sleep, and stunning.

Poison (Ex) Bite—injury; *save* Fort DC 14; *frequency* 1/ round for 4 rounds; *effect* 1d2 Str and 1d2 Con; *cure* 1 save. The save DC is Constitution-based.

Fungal crawlers are a perverse fusion of animal and plant. Over thousands of years, they have prospered and spread beneath the world,

dominating the wildest depths of these underground regions. Like hyenas, fungal crawlers are top-tier scavengers. They are efficient hunters, but just as often feed on found carrion or take meals from other predators. When times are especially lean, fungal crawlers can even survive without food, subsisting on radiation and heat absorbed through the fungal flutes covering their pale, sickly bellies.

Thousands of breeds of fungal crawlers exist across the world, varying in appearance and habits, but all share a few common features. They invariably appear as monstrous crickets or locusts fused with fungal growths, often topped with mushroom-like caps. This hybridization makes them adept survivors, and infestations are notoriously difficult to clear out entirely. Their needle-like teeth cannot chew solid food, so most fungal crawlers rely on digestive enzymes injected through their bite to make their meals palatable. Average specimens grow to 30 pounds and 3 feet in length. They reproduce by releasing spores, which remain viable for decades until they contact organic matter and eventually develop into small, pale grubs.

Many subterranean civilizations tame fungal crawlers as guard animals, pets, or food. Though simple-minded, they are amicable enough to be trained when well-fed. Fungal crawlers hold no loyalties, though, and often flee or attack their keepers at the slightest provocation.

Thanks to the bizarre energies that suffuse their homes, fungal crawlers are incredibly diverse. They have adapted over millennia to fill every environment: flying variants fill subterranean rifts with the deafening drone of their wings, while aquatic breeds skim across the surfaces of underground lakes, and still others thrive in the fiery chambers and tunnels of volcanic networks.

Illustration by Kevin Yan

GAR

This long, lean fish has a muscular body and a head with long jaws filled with sharp teeth.

GAR	CR 1

XP 400

N Medium animal (aquatic)

Init +6; **Senses** low-light vision; Perception +6

DEFENSE

AC 12, touch 12, flat-footed 11 (+2 Dex, +1 natural)

hp 13 (2d8+4)

Fort +5, **Ref** +5, **Will** +1

OFFENSE

Speed swim 60 ft.

Melee bite +13 (1d6+3 plus grab)

STATISTICS

Str 14, **Dex** 14, **Con** 15, **Int** 1, **Wis** 13, **Cha** 2

Base Atk +1; **CMB** +3 (+7 grapple); **CMD** 15 (can't be tripped)

Feats Improved Initiative

Skills Perception +6, Swim +10

ECOLOGY

Environment temperate freshwater

Organization solitary, pair, or school (3–6)

Treasure none

Gars are predatory fish that live in deep lakes and rivers. Sleek and swift, they regard anything their own size or smaller as food. A typical gar is 7 feet long and weighs 200 pounds. One species known as the alligator gar can grow to lengths of 10 feet. An alligator gar is a gar with the advanced creature template.

GAR COMPANIONS

Starting Statistics: Size Medium; **Speed** swim 60 ft., **AC** +1 natural, **Attack** bite 1d6; **Ability Scores** Str 14, Dex 14, Con 15, Int 1, Wis 13, Cha 2; **Special Ability** grab.

7th-Level Advancement: Size Large; **AC** +3 natural, **Attack** bite 1d8, **Ability Scores** +8 Str, −2 Dex, +4 Con.

GAR, GIANT

This fish is enormous—a sleek predator with bony scales and a long set of toothy jaws.

GIANT GAR	CR 6

XP 2,400

N Huge animal (aquatic)

Init +4; **Senses** low-light vision; Perception +11

DEFENSE

AC 19, touch 8, flat-footed 19 (+11 natural, −2 size)

hp 73 (7d8+42)

Fort +11, **Ref** +7, **Will** +5

OFFENSE

Speed swim 60 ft.

Melee bite +13 (2d6+15 plus grab)

Space 15 ft.; **Reach** 15 ft.

Special Attacks swallow whole (2d6+10 bludgeoning damage, AC 15, hp 7)

STATISTICS

Str 30, **Dex** 10, **Con** 23, **Int** 1, **Wis** 13, **Cha** 2

Base Atk +5; **CMB** +17 (+21 grapple); **CMD** 27 (can't be tripped)

Feats Improved Initiative, Iron Will, Lightning Reflexes, Power Attack

Skills Perception +11, Swim +18

ECOLOGY

Environment temperate freshwater

Organization solitary, pair, or school (3–6)

Treasure none

Although typical gars are frightening enough, tales of enormous giant gars that lurk in the deepest rivers and lakes persist in many regions. These creatures are true monsters, often growing to lengths of 30 feet or more and capable of swallowing a horse and rider in a single gulp. Fortunately, giant gars are much rarer than their smaller kin.

Giant gars are often kept as pets and guard animals by aquatic creatures such as merrows, scrags (aquatic trolls), and the rare sea hags who dwell in freshwater dens.

GIANT, MARSH

Cold, black eyes stare out from the fish-like face of this hideous green-skinned, web-fingered, and obese giant.

MARSH GIANT	CR 8

XP 4,800

CE Large humanoid (giant)

Init +3; **Senses** low-light vision; Perception +11

DEFENSE

AC 21, touch 12, flat-footed 18 (+3 Dex, +9 natural, −1 size)

hp 102 (12d8+48)

Fort +12, **Ref** +7, **Will** +8

Defensive Abilities rock catching

OFFENSE

Speed 40 ft., swim 20 ft.

Melee gaff +16/+11 (2d6+12) or

2 slams +16 (1d6+8)

Ranged rock +12 (2d6+9)

Space 10 ft.; **Reach** 10 ft.

Special Attacks rock throwing (120 ft.)

Spell-Like Abilities (CL 12th; concentration +13)

3/day—*augury, bestow curse* (DC 15), *fog cloud*

STATISTICS

Str 27, **Dex** 17, **Con** 19, **Int** 8, **Wis** 15, **Cha** 12

Base Atk +9; **CMB** +18; **CMD** 31

Feats Combat Reflexes, Improved Iron Will, Improved Sunder, Iron Will, Power Attack, Vital Strike

Skills Perception +11, Stealth +5 (+13 in swamps), Swim +16;

Racial Modifiers +8 Stealth in swamps

Languages Boggard, Giant

ECOLOGY

Environment temperate marshes

Organization solitary, gang (2–6), or tribe (7–22, plus 20% noncombatants plus 1 cleric or witch leader of 4th–8th level, 1–3 barbarian or fighter champions of 2nd–5th level, 2–12 merrows, 10–20 boggards, and 6–12 giant frogs)

Treasure standard (gaff, other treasure)

Hideously ugly, marsh giants dwell in the most desolate of swamps—preferably those that share a sodden border with the sea. Marsh giants typically use a hooked club called a gaff (wielded in both hands) in combat—treat these weapons as flails, save that they do piercing damage.

Marsh giants are hateful thugs bound together by a common zealotry. Powerful opponents and beasts are the most prized of meals, though many marsh giants are also cannibals—they often attack fellow tribe members just to gorge on a particularly fearsome or delicious-looking relative.

Some marsh giants mingle with abominations from the deepest seas, creatures they believe are sent by their god. This has further contributed to their racial degradation, but the immediate offspring of these unholy unions are powerful. Deformed with tentacles, scales, and other aquatic traits, these marsh giants are known as "brineborn." They are advanced marsh giants with the aquatic subtype, a swim speed of 40 feet, the amphibious special quality, and the following additional spell-like abilities:

Constant—*speak with animals*; 3/day—*contagion* (DC 15), *confusion* (DC 15), *quench* (DC 14).

Illustration by Kieran Yanner

Giant, Rune

This giant's skin is black and pitted, like roughly cast iron, and etched with glowing red runes.

RUNE GIANT	CR 17

XP 102,400

LE Gargantuan humanoid (giant)

Init +0; **Senses** low-light vision; Perception +29

DEFENSE

AC 30, touch 6, flat-footed 30 (+9 armor, +15 natural, −4 size)

hp 270 (20d8+180)

Fort +15, **Ref** +6, **Will** +20

Immune cold, electricity, fire

OFFENSE

Speed 35 ft. (50 ft. without armor); *air walk*

Melee mwk longsword +27/+22/+17 (4d6+22/17–20) or

2 slams +26 (2d6+15)

Ranged mwk spear +12/+7/+2 (4d6+15/×3)

Space 20 ft.; **Reach** 20 ft.

Special Attacks command giants, runes, spark shower

Illustrations by Kieran Yanner

Spell-Like Abilities (CL 20th; concentration +24)

Constant—*air walk*

At will—*charm person* (DC 15), *suggestion* (DC 17)

3/day—*mass charm monster* (DC 22), *dominate person* (DC 19)

1/day—*demand* (DC 22), *true seeing*

STATISTICS

Str 41, **Dex** 11, **Con** 28, **Int** 14, **Wis** 23, **Cha** 18

Base Atk +15; **CMB** +34; **CMD** 44

Feats Awesome Blow, Critical Focus, Improved Bull Rush, Improved Critical (longsword), Improved Vital Strike, Iron Will, Power Attack, Quick Draw, Staggering Critical, Vital Strike

Skills Acrobatics +15 (+23 jump), Craft (any one) +25, Knowledge (history) +12, Knowledge (nobility) +12, Perception +29

Languages Common, Giant, Terran

ECOLOGY

Environment cold mountains

Organization solitary, pair, patrol (3–6), squad (7–12), or company (13–30 plus 2–4 fighters or rogues of 2nd–4th level, 1 oracle or sorcerer of 5th–8th level, 1 ranger or monk commander of 5th–6th level, 10–20 yetis, 1–4 cloud giants, 8–12 frost giants, 10–16 stone giants, 4–8 lamia matriarchs, and 1–2 adult blue dragons)

Treasure standard (masterwork full plate armor, masterwork longsword, 3 masterwork spears, other treasure)

SPECIAL ABILITIES

Command Giant (Su) A rune giant gains a +4 racial bonus on the save DC of charm or compulsion effects used against giants.

Runes (Ex) As a free action, whenever a rune giant uses its spark shower or spell-like abilities, it can cause the runes on its body to flash with light. All creatures within 10 feet of the giant must make a DC 24 Fortitude save or be blinded for 1 round. The saving throw is Charisma-based.

Spark Shower (Su) As a standard action, a rune giant can cause a shower of sparks to erupt out of one of the runes on its body. These sparks function as a breath weapon (30-ft. cone; 10d6 fire and 10d6 electricity damage; Reflex DC 29 half; usable once every 1d4 rounds). The save DC is Constitution-based.

Magically crafted and crossbred from taiga and fire giant slaves by ancient wizards, rune giants are anathema to their own kind. Given power to command and magically control other giants, the rune giants themselves served their even more powerful masters, and in so doing granted ancient empires armies of giants to command. In the eons since these ancient empires collapsed, rune giants have persisted as a race of their own, little more than bogeymen, horrors whispered of late at night by superstitious giants.

Rune giants' charcoal flesh is decorated by dozens of runes—manifestations of their eldritch powers. Rune giants are 40 feet tall and weigh 25,000 pounds.

GIANT, TAIGA

This muscular giant has dark gray skin and fiery red hair. Its lower jaw bears sharp fangs, and it wields a huge, primitive spear.

TAIGA GIANT	CR 12	

XP 19,200

CN Huge humanoid (giant)

Init +2; **Senses** low-light vision; Perception +13

DEFENSE

AC 26, touch 14, flat-footed 24 (+4 armor, +4 deflection, +2 Dex, +8 natural, –2 size)

hp 157 (15d8+90)

Fort +15, **Ref** +9, **Will** +10

Defensive Abilities rock catching; **Immune** enchantment and illusion spells

OFFENSE

Speed 30 ft. (40 ft. without armor)

Melee spear +19/+14/+9 (3d6+15/×3) or 2 slams +19 (1d8+10)

Ranged rock +12 (2d6+15) or spear +11 (3d6+10/×3)

Space 15 ft.; **Reach** 15 ft.

Special Attacks rock throwing (140 ft.)

STATISTICS

Str 31, **Dex** 14, **Con** 22, **Int** 12, **Wis** 17, **Cha** 15

Base Atk +11; **CMB** +23; **CMD** 39

Feats Alertness, Cleave, Endurance, Iron Will, Lightning Reflexes, Power Attack, Self-Sufficient, Shot on the Run[B], Vital Strike

Skills Climb +15, Knowledge (religion) +11, Perception +13, Stealth +6 (+12 in undergrowth), Survival +20; **Racial Modifiers** +6 Stealth in undergrowth

Languages Common, Giant

SQ spirit summoning

ECOLOGY

Environment cold mountains or forests

Organization solitary, warband (2–7), or tribe (20–50 plus 30% noncombatants, 1 druid or oracle of 3rd–5th level, 2–4 barbarian or ranger hunters of 3rd–5th level, 1 chieftain barbarian or fighter of 4th–7th level, 2–6 dire bears, 2–6 dire tigers, and 8–12 stone giants)

Treasure standard (hide armor, spear, other treasure)

SPECIAL ABILITIES

Spirit Summoning (Su) Once per day, a taiga giant may perform a 10-minute ritual to tap into the power and insight of his ancestral spirits. These spirits provide a +4 deflection bonus to AC, immunity to enchantment and illusion spells, and one of the following spell effects: *bless, endure elements, protection from evil, protection from good,* or *see invisibility.* The effects of a spirit summoning persist for 24 hours.

Taiga giants wander endlessly to keep from depleting the food supply of any one area. Aurochs and mammoths are their preferred inland prey, while whales, seals, and walruses provide food in coastal regions. These animals form the cornerstone of tribal survival, not just for the food they provide but because nearly all of a tribe's possessions, from their portable shelters to their weapons, are crafted from the bone, hides, and sinews of felled beasts. Little is wasted.

Taiga giants are also deeply spiritual, worshiping their ancestors. Every tribe member learns to call forth ancestor spirits at a young age. Taiga giants are ashamed of being the ancestors of rune giants as, like most giants, they both hate and fear rune giants as slavers and monsters.

A typical taiga giant stands 20 feet in height and weighs 10,000 pounds. Skin tones vary from dark to pale gray, with hair color ranging from dark brown to red.

GIANT, WOOD

Standing tall and graceful, this sharp-eared giant's skin is pale.
Its large brow gives it a somewhat primitive visage.

WOOD GIANT	CR 6

XP 2,400

CG Large humanoid (giant)

Init +5; **Senses** low-light vision; Perception +11

DEFENSE

AC 20, touch 14, flat-footed 15 (+2 armor, +5 Dex, +4 natural, –1 size)

hp 67 (9d8+27)

Fort +9, **Ref** +8, **Will** +7

Defensive Abilities rock catching

OFFENSE

Speed 40 ft.

Melee longsword +10/+5 (2d6+5/19–20) or

2 slams +10 (1d6+5)

Ranged mwk composite longbow +9/+9/+4 (2d6+5/×3)

Space 10 ft.; **Reach** 10 ft.

Spell-Like Abilities (CL 7th; concentration +8)

Constant—*pass without trace, speak with animals*

3/day—*charm animal* (DC 12), *quench, tree shape*

1/day—*enlarge person* (self only), *spike growth*

STATISTICS

Str 20, **Dex** 21, **Con** 17, **Int** 14, **Wis** 15, **Cha** 12

Base Atk +6; **CMB** +12; **CMD** 27

Feats Deadly Aim, Iron Will, Point-Blank Shot, Precise Shot, Rapid Shot

Skills Acrobatics +11 (+15 when jumping), Climb +14, Knowledge (nature) +8, Perception +11, Profession (farmer) +8, Stealth +7 (+11 in forests), Survival +8; **Racial Modifiers** +4 Stealth in forests

Languages Common, Giant, Sylvan; *speak with animals*

ECOLOGY

Environment temperate forests

Organization solitary, gang (2–4), hunting party (5–9, plus 1–4 dire wolves), or clan (10–40, plus 35% noncombatants, 1–3 druids or witches of 2nd–4th level, 1 ranger chieftain of 3rd–7th level, 4–10 dire wolves, and 2–8 giant eagles)

Treasure standard (leather armor, longsword, masterwork composite longbow with 20 arrows, other treasure)

Wood giants are the wardens of the deepest, wildest portions of the world's forests. Unlike many of their kin, wood giants are slow to anger, peaceful, and artistic, and display an infinite patience in their duty. A wood giant's role is to preserve and protect the wilderness—a role they believe that nature itself granted them, the proof of which manifests in their magical abilities tied to the natural world.

Wood giant culture is as complex as their forest homes. Much of a tribe's time is spent tending to a forest's health: planting new trees, clearing away dead brush, and hunting abominations that pervert the natural order. Individuals may even cultivate their forest homes into elaborate demesnes, mazes, or living temples. They are an isolated race, only rarely meeting to trade with other tribes or the occasional elven settlement. While primarily good-natured, wood giants are distrustful of outsiders and prone to great melancholies.

Small clans claim enormous tracts of wooded land, but rarely build permanent homes. Members may spread out over their entire region by day only to gather and bed down, exposed to the elements, after sundown. In harsh weather, tribes cluster close together in the densest thickets with their backs turned outward.

Wood giants stand 14 feet tall and weigh 1,200 pounds. They are vegetarians by choice, resorting to eating meat only when no other option is available.

GLOOMWING

This immense moth has huge purple wings marked with spiraling black patterns that seem to shift and writhe.

GLOOMWING	CR 4

XP 1,200

N Large outsider (extraplanar)

Init +3; **Senses** darkvision 60 ft.; Perception +8

DEFENSE

AC 19, touch 12, flat-footed 16 (+3 Dex, +7 natural, −1 size)

hp 37 (5d10+10)

Fort +3, **Ref** +7, **Will** +5

OFFENSE

Speed 10 ft., fly 40 ft. (good)

Melee bite +6 (1d8+2), 2 claws +6 (1d6+2)

Space 10 ft.; **Reach** 5 ft.

Special Attacks confusion, implant, pheromones

STATISTICS

Str 15, **Dex** 17, **Con** 15, **Int** 2, **Wis** 12, **Cha** 10

Base Atk +5; **CMB** +8; **CMD** 21

Feats Ability Focus (confusion), Flyby Attack, Hover

Skills Fly +5, Perception +9, Stealth +7 (+11 in dim light); **Racial Modifiers** +4 Stealth in dim light

ECOLOGY

Environment any (Plane of Shadow)

Organization solitary

Treasure none

SPECIAL ABILITIES

Confusion (Su) The eerie shifting of patterns on a gloomwing's wings is hypnotic—any creature within 30 feet that does not avert its gaze from the gloomwing must make a DC 14 Will save at the start of each turn or become confused for 1 round. This is a mind-affecting effect—gloomwings and tenebrous worms are immune to this effect. The save DC is Charisma-based.

Implant (Ex) A gloomwing can lay eggs inside a Small or larger helpless or dead creature as a full-round action that provokes attacks of opportunity. A creature implanted with gloomwing eggs must make a DC 14 Fortitude save each morning to avoid suffering 1d4 points of Constitution damage. Within 24 hours of a creature's death from this damage, 1d4 young tenebrous worms (see page 259) emerge from the corpse, devouring it completely in the process. The eggs can be destroyed via any effect that cures disease, but the eggs themselves are not treated as a disease for purposes of what creatures are immune to this effect. The save DC is Constitution-based.

Pheromones (Su) After the first round of combat, a gloomwing can emit a strange, musky scent in a 30-foot radius as a free action. All creatures within this area (save for other gloomwings or tenebrous worms) must make

a DC 14 Fortitude save each round to avoid becoming weakened by the pheromones. Once a creature fails a save against this effect, it takes a −4 penalty to its Strength score—this penalty lasts for as long as the battle continues and for 1 hour thereafter. *Lesser restoration* or any other effect capable of healing ability damage immediately removes this Strength penalty. The save DC is Constitution-based.

Gloomwings are strange, moth-like natives of the Plane of Shadow. Despite their appearance, they are not vermin and possess a crude but serviceable intelligence. While gloomwings can be conjured via spells like *lesser planar ally* or *lesser planar binding* to serve as guardians or even mounts, occasionally a gloomwing will slip through a tear in the fabric of the planes and make the journey to the Material Plane on its own. A gloomwing loose on the Material Plane is active for 2 to 3 hours at dawn and again for 2 to 3 hours at dusk, preferring to spend the remaining hours of the day hiding in abandoned buildings, caves, or deep canyons or foliage where the shadows are thickest. During its periods of activity, it flies through the sky on the hunt for creatures to attack and implant its eggs in—the gloomwing does not need to eat, leaving this urge to propagate its species as its primary drive.

For all the dangers a gloomwing presents, it is the creature's young that pose the gravest threat. These creatures are known as tenebrous worms (see page 260), and despite being the larval form of the adult gloomwing, are much more dangerous creatures. The fact that a gloomwing can lay several eggs a day if presented with enough living hosts makes them dangerous not for what they can inflict themselves, but for what they can spawn.

Illustration by Branko Bistrovic

133

GOLEM, ADAMANTINE

This huge construct of black metal is all spikes and armor, save for several forge-like stacks that burn atop its crown and back.

ADAMANTINE GOLEM	CR 19

XP 204,800

N Huge construct

Init –1; **Senses** darkvision 60 ft., low-light vision; Perception +0

DEFENSE

AC 33, touch 7, flat-footed 33 (–1 Dex, +26 natural, –2 size)

hp 205 (30d10+40); fast healing 10

Fort +10, **Ref** +9, **Will** +10

Defensive Abilities indestructible; DR 15/epic; **Immune** construct traits, magic

OFFENSE

Speed 30 ft.

Melee 2 slams +41 (6d10+13/19–20)

Space 15 ft.; **Reach** 15 ft.

Special Attacks destructive strike, trample (6d10+19, DC 38)

STATISTICS

Str 36, **Dex** 9, **Con** —, **Int** —, **Wis** 11, **Cha** 1

Base Atk +30; **CMB** +45; **CMD** 54

ECOLOGY

Environment any

Organization solitary or gang (2–4)

Treasure none

SPECIAL ABILITIES

Destructive Strike (Ex) An adamantine golem's slam attacks threaten a critical hit on a 19 or 20. In addition, whenever an adamantine golem scores a critical hit, it deals 6d10+13 points of damage to the target's armor or shield in addition to the normal damage, as if it had also made a successful sunder combat maneuver.

Indestructible (Ex) An adamantine golem is nearly impossible to destroy. Even if reduced below 0 hit points, its fast healing continues to restore hit points, though the golem is helpless unless above 0 hit points. It can only be permanently destroyed if reduced to negative hit points and then decapitated using an adamantine *vorpal* weapon—alternatively, *miracle* or *wish* can be used to slay it while it is at negative hit points.

Immunity to Magic (Ex) An adamantine golem is immune to any spell or spell-like ability that allows spell resistance, except as noted below.

- *Transmute metal to wood* slows an adamantine golem for 1d4 rounds, during which time its damage reduction is reduced to 15/adamantine (no save).

Made using one of the hardest and most precious substances, the adamantine golem is a deadly work of art. It can crush the life from foes that dare to get in its way and is nearly impossible to permanently destroy. The vast amount of adamantine required to build even one of these destructive golems is so significant that most worlds do not have enough resources, forcing the creator to travel to the Plane of Earth or remote Outer Planes simply to gather the raw materials needed to build the golem's body.

CONSTRUCTION

A adamantine golem's body is made of more than 4,000 pounds of adamantine, mithral, gold, platinum, and other metals worth a total of 100,000 gp.

ADAMANTINE GOLEM	

CL 20th; **Price** 600,000 gp

CONSTRUCTION

Requirements Craft Construct, *crushing fist, geas/quest, heal, stoneskin, wish,* creator must be caster level 20th; **Skill** Craft (sculpture) DC 35; **Cost** 350,000 gp

Illustrations by Damien Mammoliti

GOLEM, ALCHEMICAL

A rickety construction of glass tubing, metal, and wood convey the brain and two eyes afloat in this figure's glass skull.

This golem is a walking alchemical nightmare, capable of inflicting all manner of painful wounds on its foes. Its ability to follow orders is granted by the otherwise mindless humanoid brain that floats in its dome-like head, while its animating force is a curious combination of alchemy and elemental spirits bound into the fluids and metals of its body.

CONSTRUCTION

An alchemical golem's body is made of alchemical gear weighing 1,000 pounds and worth a total of 3,000 gp.

ALCHEMICAL GOLEM	CR 9	

XP 6,400

N Large construct

Init +4; **Senses** darkvision 60 ft., low-light vision; Perception +0

DEFENSE

AC 23, touch 13, flat-footed 19 (+4 Dex, +10 natural, −1 size)

hp 96 (12d10+30)

Fort +4, **Ref** +8, **Will** +4

DR 10/adamantine or bludgeoning; **Immune** construct traits, magic

OFFENSE

Speed 30 ft.

Melee 2 slams +19 (2d8+8 plus alchemy)

Ranged bomb +15 (8d6 energy damage)

Space 10 ft.; **Reach** 10 ft.

Special Attacks alchemy, bombs, splash

STATISTICS

Str 27, **Dex** 18, **Con** —, **Int** —, **Wis** 11, **Cha** 1

Base Atk +12; **CMB** +21; **CMD** 35

ECOLOGY

Environment any

Organization solitary or gang (2–4)

Treasure none

SPECIAL ABILITIES

Alchemy (Ex) When an alchemical golem strikes a foe, the attack has an additional random effect, chosen from the options below. The attack can either deal 1d6 points of acid, cold, electricity, or fire damage, or cause the target to become sickened (Fortitude DC 16 negates) or entangled (Reflex DC 16 negates) for 1d4 rounds. These save DCs are Constitution-based.

Bombs (Ex) As a standard action, an alchemical golem can throw a bomb as a ranged touch attack to a distance of 60 feet (no range increment). If the attack misses, treat it as a thrown splash weapon to determine where it lands. Anyone struck by an alchemical golem's bomb takes 8d6 points of acid, cold, electricity, or fire damage (determine type randomly). All creatures adjacent to the location where the bomb hits take 1d6 points of energy damage of the same type.

Immunity to Magic (Ex) An alchemical golem is immune to spells or spell-like abilities that allow spell resistance, save for spells with the sonic descriptor. *Shatter* damages an alchemical golem as if it were a crystalline creature.

Splash (Ex) Any strike on an alchemical golem with a non-reach melee weapon deals 1 point of acid, cold, electricity, or fire damage (determine type randomly) to the attacker. This amount increases to 1d6 points of damage if the attack is a critical hit.

ALCHEMICAL GOLEM	

CL 10th; **Price** 33,000 gp

CONSTRUCTION

Requirements Craft Construct, *geas/quest, gentle repose, major creation, resist energy, telekinesis,* creator must be caster level 10th; **Skill** Craft (alchemy) DC 20; **Cost** 18,000 gp

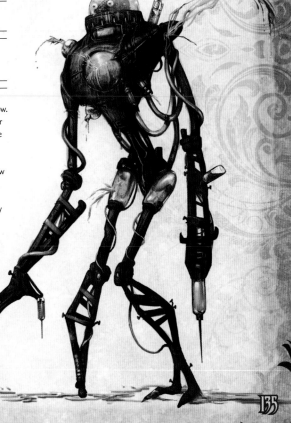

GOLEM, CARRION

A lurching mash-up of rotting flesh, jagged bone, and coarse hair, this humanoid monstrosity reeks of death and decay.

CARRION GOLEM	CR 4

XP 1,200

N Medium construct

Init +1; **Senses** blindsense 10 ft., darkvision 60 ft., low-light vision; Perception +0

Aura foul stench (DC 12, 1 round)

DEFENSE

AC 17, touch 11, flat-footed 16 (+1 Dex, +6 natural)

hp 42 (4d10+20)

Fort +1, **Ref** +2, **Will** +1

DR 5/bludgeoning or slashing; **Immune** construct traits, magic

OFFENSE

Speed 30 ft.

Melee 2 slams +7 (1d8+3 plus disease)

Special Attacks plague carrier

STATISTICS

Str 17, **Dex** 12, **Con** —, **Int** —, **Wis** 11, **Cha** 1

Base Atk +4; **CMB** +7; **CMD** 18

ECOLOGY

Environment any land

Organization solitary or gang (2–4)

Treasure none

SPECIAL ABILITIES

Foul Stench (Ex) This functions as the stench ability, but causes affected creatures to be nauseated rather than sickened.

Immune to Magic (Ex) A carrion golem is immune to any spell or spell-like ability that allows spell resistance. In addition, certain spells and effects function differently against the creature, as noted below.

- *Gentle repose* causes a carrion golem to become stiff and helpless for 1d4 rounds if it fails a Will save against the spell.
- *Animate dead* causes the various parts of the golem's body to shudder and tear, dealing 1d6 points of damage per caster level to the golem (no save).
- Any magical attack that deals cold or fire damage slows a carrion golem (as the *slow* spell) for 2d6 rounds (no save).
- Any magical attack that deals electricity damage hastes a carrion golem (as the *haste* spell) for 2d6 rounds.

Plague Carrier (Ex) When a carrion golem is created, its creator infects it with a specific disease. The carrion golem can then infect those it strikes with its slams with this disease—most carrion golems inflict filth fever. The save DC is Constitution-based and includes a +2 racial bonus.

Filth Fever: Slam—injury; *save* Fortitude DC 14; *onset* 1d3 days; *frequency* 1/day; *effect* 1d3 Dex damage and 1d3 Con damage; *cure* 2 consecutive saves.

Carrion golems are made from the partially decayed parts of numerous dead creatures—no two carrion golems are exactly alike in appearance. Most are created from the corpses of humanoid creatures that are then augmented here and there with parts taken from animals, resulting in a monster that stands 6 feet tall and weighs 120 pounds.

CONSTRUCTION

A carrion golem's body can be constructed using at least two Medium corpses and four smaller corpses. Special reagents worth 500 gp are also required.

CARRION GOLEM

CL 7th; **Price** 10,500 gp

CONSTRUCTION

Requirements Craft Construct, *animate dead, contagion, false life, gentle repose, lesser geas,* creator must be caster level 7th; **Skill** Craft (leather) or Heal DC 13; **Cost** 5,500 gp

GOLEM, CLOCKWORK

A vaguely humanoid shape made of metal lurches to life with the grinding whir and frantic ticking of hundreds of gears.

CLOCKWORK GOLEM	CR 12

XP 19,200

N Large construct

Init +1; **Senses** darkvision 60 ft., low-light vision; Perception +0

DEFENSE

AC 26, touch 10, flat-footed 25 (+1 Dex, +16 natural, −1 size)

hp 118 (16d10+30)

Fort +5, **Ref** +6, **Will** +5

DR 10/adamantine; **Immune** construct traits, magic

OFFENSE

Speed 30 ft.

Melee 2 slams +23 (2d10+8 plus grab)

Space 10 ft.; **Reach** 10 ft.

Special Attacks death burst, grind, wall of gears

STATISTICS

Str 27, **Dex** 12, **Con** —, **Int** —, **Wis** 11, **Cha** 1

Base Atk +16; **CMB** +25 (+29 grapple); **CMD** 36

ECOLOGY

Environment any

Organization solitary or gang (2–4)

Treasure none

SPECIAL ABILITIES

Death Burst (Ex) When a clockwork golem is reduced to 0 or fewer hit points, it explodes in a shower of razor-sharp gears and debris. All creatures within a 10-foot burst take 12d6 points of slashing damage—a DC 18 Reflex save results in half damage. The save DC is Constitution-based.

Grind (Ex) A clockwork golem deals an additional 2d10+12 points of slashing damage when it makes a successful grapple check as razor-sharp gears and blades emerge from its body to grind and slice its foe.

Immunity to Magic (Ex) A clockwork golem is immune to any spell or spell-like ability that allows spell resistance. In addition, certain spells and effects function differently against a clockwork golem, as noted below.

- A *grease* spell cast on the golem causes it to move quickly for 1d6 rounds, as if under the effects of *haste*.
- A *rusting grasp* spell deals damage to a clockwork golem normally, and makes the golem staggered for 1d6 rounds (no save).

Wall of Gears (Su) As a standard action, a clockwork golem can fold into a whirling wall of grinding gears measuring 10 feet by 10 feet or 5 feet by 20 feet. Anyone passing through the wall takes 15d6 points of slashing damage. If the wall appears in a creature's space, that creature can attempt a DC 18 Reflex save to leap to one side and avoid the damage entirely. The clockwork

golem can take no actions while in this form except to resume its normal form as a move action. A clockwork golem's AC and immunities remain the same while it is in this form.

Forged from thousands of gears, the clockwork golem is a precision creation. In combat, a clockwork golem is ruthlessly efficient, moving with swift conviction to grind and slice its foes to ribbons.

CONSTRUCTION

A clockwork golem's body is made up of hundreds of carefully crafted copper, iron, and silver gears, weighing almost 1,500 pounds, and worth a total of 10,000 gp.

CLOCKWORK GOLEM	

CL 15th; **Price** 120,000 gp

CONSTRUCTION

Requirements Craft Construct, *animate objects*, *blade barrier*, *geas/quest*, *grease*, *telekinesis*, creator must be caster level 15th; **Skill** Craft (clocks) or Craft (locks) DC 20; **Cost** 65,000 gp

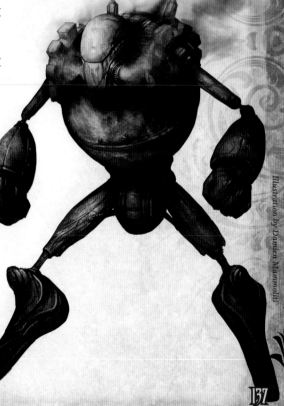

Illustration by Damien Mammoliti

137

GOLEM, GLASS

*This jagged construct of glass has a human's shape, save that one
arm ends in a jagged hammer and another in a spike of glass.*

GLASS GOLEM   CR 8

XP 4,800

N Large construct

Init −1; **Senses** darkvision 60 ft., low-light vision; Perception +0

DEFENSE

AC 21, touch 8, flat-footed 21 (−1 Dex, +13 natural, −1 size)

hp 96 (12d10+30)

Fort +4, **Ref** +3, **Will** +4

Defensive Abilities reflect spells; **DR** 5/adamantine; **Immune**
magic, construct traits

OFFENSE

Speed 30 ft.

Melee 2 slams +16 (2d8+5 plus bleed)

Space 10 ft.; **Reach** 10 ft.

Special Attacks bleed (1d8), dazzling brightness

STATISTICS

Str 20, **Dex** 9, **Con** —, **Int** —, **Wis** 11, **Cha** 1

Base Atk +12; **CMB** +18; **CMD** 27

ECOLOGY

Environment any land

Organization solitary or gang (2–5)

Treasure none

SPECIAL ABILITIES

Dazzling Brightness (Ex) A glass golem in an
area of bright
light dazzles
any creature
within 30 feet
that sees it
for 1 round
(Fortitude DC
16 negates). Once
a creature makes
its save against this
ability, it is immune to that
golem's brightness for 24 hours.
The DC is Constitution-based.

Immune to Magic (Ex) A glass golem
is immune to any spell or spell-like
ability that allows spell resistance. In
addition, certain spells and effects
function differently against a glass
golem, as noted below.

- A *shatter* spell damages a glass golem
as if it were a crystalline creature.
- A *keen edge* spell affects all of a
glass golem's slam attacks as if
they were slashing weapons.

- A magical attack that deals cold damage slows a glass
golem (as the *slow* spell) for 3 rounds (no saving throw).
- A magical attack that deals fire damage ends any slow
effect on the golem and heals 1 point of damage for
each 3 points of damage the attack would otherwise
deal. If the amount of healing would cause the golem to
exceed its full normal hit points, it gains any excess as
temporary hit points. A glass golem gets no saving throw
against fire effects.

Reflect Spells (Ex) As a free action once every 1d4 rounds,
a glass golem can align its internal structure to enhance
its resistance to magic for 1 round. During this time, the
golem reflects spells (even spells that function differently
against the golem as described in its immune to magic
ability) as if under the effect of a *spell turning* spell.

A glass golem is a sizable guardian constructed by a
powerful caster, usually in the shape of an armored
humanoid. They are more common
in desert lands where quartz-based
sand is readily available, or in
urban centers where glassblowing is
commonplace.

A typical glass golem is 10 feet tall
and weighs 2,500 pounds.

Stained Glass Golems (+0 CR):
Divine casters sometimes
build glass golems that
resemble the windowpanes
commonly found in temples.
Thin and agile, these colorful
beings often act as spies,
wielding powers of stealth that
their other counterparts do not
possess. A stained glass golem has
a +8 racial bonus on Stealth checks.

CONSTRUCTION

A glass golem's body is made from
2,500 pounds of glass mixed with special
salts and rare minerals worth 1,000 gp.

GLASS GOLEM

CL 10th; **Price** 33,000 gp (glass);
39,400 (stained glass)

CONSTRUCTION

Requirements Craft Construct,
*animate objects, flame strike, geas/
quest, spell turning,* creator must
be caster level 10th; **Skill** Craft
(sculptures) DC 17; **Cost** 17,000 gp
(glass golem); 20,200 gp (stained
glass golem)

Illustrations by Damien Mammoliti

GOLEM, MITHRAL

Made of polished silvery metal, this immense humanoid construct moves with shocking grace and speed.

MITHRAL GOLEM CR 16

XP 76,800

N Huge construct

Init +7; **Senses** darkvision 60 ft., low-light vision; Perception +0

DEFENSE

AC 32, touch 16, flat-footed 24 (+7 Dex, +1 dodge, +16 natural, –2 size)

hp 172 (24d10+40)

Fort +8, **Ref** +15, **Will** +8

DR 15/adamantine, evasion; **Immune** construct traits, magic

OFFENSE

Speed 50 ft.

Melee 2 slams +33 (4d10+11)

Space 15 ft.; **Reach** 15 ft.

Special Attacks fluid form, quickness

STATISTICS

Str 33, **Dex** 24, **Con** —, **Int** —, **Wis** 11, **Cha** 1

Base Atk +24; **CMB** +37; **CMD** 55

Feats Dodge^B, Mobility^B, Run^B, Spring Attack^B

ECOLOGY

Environment any

Organization solitary or gang (2–4)

Treasure none

SPECIAL ABILITIES

Fluid Form (Ex) A mithral golem's body can take on a form like liquid silver as a swift action. While in this form, the mithral golem's reach increases to 30 feet and its DR becomes 15/bludgeoning and adamantine. A mithral golem in this form can also move through any crack or hole in a wall or door, no matter how small, without impeding its movement. A mithral golem can maintain this form for up to 10 rounds per day, but these rounds do not need to be consecutive. Reverting to its normal form is a free action.

Immunity to Magic (Ex) A mithral golem is immune to any spell or spell-like ability that allows spell resistance. In addition, certain spells and effects function differently against a mithral golem, as noted below.

- A *slow* spell cast on the golem causes it to lose its quickness ability for 1d6 rounds.
- A *haste* spell heals the golem of 1d6 points of damage per level of the caster (maximum 10d6).
- Hitting a mithral golem in fluid form with any spell of 6th level or higher with the cold descriptor causes the golem to take 10d6 points of damage (no save) and lose the use of its fluid form ability for 24 hours.

Quickness (Ex) A mithral golem is incredibly quick. It can take an extra move action during its turn each round. This means it can move up to its speed and still make a full attack.

Created from a massive quantity of the purest mithral, this golem is a thing of shining beauty. Unlike most golems, mithral golems are extremely agile, capable of moving at great speed and striking swiftly.

CONSTRUCTION

A mithral golem's body is made of 3,000 pounds of mithral and other precious metals, worth a total of 50,000 gp.

MITHRAL GOLEM

CL 18th; **Price** 250,000 gp

CONSTRUCTION

Requirements Craft Construct, *animate objects, geas/quest, haste, polymorph any object, wish,* creator must be caster level 18th; **Skill** Craft (sculpture) DC 25; **Cost** 150,000 gp

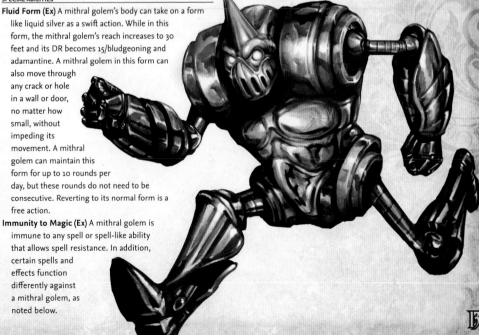

GRAY RENDER

This hulking beast has slick, gray, hairless skin. Its numerous yellow eyes and wide toothy maw are its only facial features.

GRAY RENDER	CR 8

XP 4,800

N Large magical beast

Init +1; **Senses** darkvision 60 ft., low-light vision, scent; Perception +13

DEFENSE

AC 21, touch 10, flat-footed 20 (+1 Dex, +11 natural, –1 size)

hp 100 (8d10+56)

Fort +13, **Ref** +7, **Will** +4

OFFENSE

Speed 30 ft.

Melee bite +14 (2d6+7), 2 claws +15 (1d8+7 plus grab)

Space 10 ft.; **Reach** 10 ft.

Special Attacks rend (2 claws, 1d8+10)

STATISTICS

Str 25, **Dex** 13, **Con** 24, **Int** 3, **Wis** 14, **Cha** 8

Base Atk +8; **CMB** +16 (+20 grapple); **CMD** 27

Feats Awesome Blow, Improved Bull Rush, Power Attack, Weapon Focus (claw)

Skills Perception +13, Survival +6; **Racial Modifiers** +4 Perception

SQ double damage against objects

Languages Giant

ECOLOGY

Environment temperate marshes

Organization solitary (plus bonded creatures if any)

Treasure incidental

SPECIAL ABILITIES

Double Damage Against Objects (Ex)

A gray render that makes a full attack against an object or structure deals double damage.

Standing over 9 feet tall and weighing in excess of 4,000 pounds, a gray render is a solitary and savage predator. Renders are gifted with immense strength, and some reports claim to have witnessed a gray render uprooting a fully grown tree and tearing it to splinters in order to catch prey hiding within. Gray renders actively avoid forming groups or communities with their own kind, and perhaps only tolerate the presence of other renders when it is time to mate. Some sages claim they are asexual, but it is more likely they are hermaphrodites able to self-fertilize, and reproduce only rarely.

Despite its solitary existence, a gray render often develops an affectionate bond with other creatures, typically a herd of herbivores or a small tribe of humanoids, but in some cases a solitary denizen of its swamp. The render acts as a guardian for this creature or creatures, never straying more than a mile away, running to protect them if they are attacked, and providing an offering of meat once each day, as might a domesticated cat. A gray render never harms its protected creatures, and retreats in confusion if they attack it. Most animal "pets" grow to accept its presence, and primitive humanoid "pets" often believe their guardian is a sign of favor from the gods. A render's bond may last from a few months to as long as 10 years, after which it wanders to a new territory and ignores its former favorites.

Renders are generally not malicious, and only attack if hungry or if they or their pets are threatened. A render protecting its pets fights to the death.

Gremlin

Well known for their mischievous natures, their nasty senses of humor, and their destructive habits, the fey creatures known as gremlins rightfully earn their reputations as cruel pranksters and sadistic saboteurs. Ranging in size from 3 feet in height down to barely over a foot tall, numerous types of gremlins stalk the world's dark and unseen reaches, tending to linger near thin spots in reality between the Material Plane and the realms of the fey. The smaller a gremlin is, the stronger its ties to the realm of the fey remain, and the stranger and more potent its powers.

Gremlins understand that they lack physical power, and thus are usually encountered in large groups that work together to defend each other and their lair. While all gremlins share certain traits in common, such as a resistance to damage from weapons save those made of cold iron, a cruel and sadistic sense of humor, the ability to use prestidigitation to enhance their mischievous plans, and their slight statures, the single trait that gremlins are most well known for is their ability to break, curse, and otherwise ruin the works of other creatures. Gremlins take great delight in ruining and breaking things, and while each gremlin race has a particular "specialty" (be it magical auras, complex machinery, coordinated tactics, or even luck itself), all gremlins are fascinated by complex devices and intricate social constructs. Nothing pleases a gremlin more than being involved in the collapse of something complex.

Although gremlins originally hailed from the mysterious realm of the fey, they have lived upon the Material Plane for countless generations. In that time, they have become natives of this realm, both in body and soul. Yet not all gremlins have managed to retain their strange powers to disrupt and destroy—the most unfortunate gremlins are not even commonly known as gremlins at all. These bizarre creatures are known as mites. While they retain the gremlin ability to use a few spell-like abilities, mites represent to their fellow gremlins the ultimate shame and horror—a fall into pathetic self-loathing and pitiful cowardice. As a result, gremlins grow particularly sadistic and violent when presented with an opportunity to torment a tribe of mites, abandoning their more subtle methods of disrupting communities and machinery in favor of all-out war, invading mite homes and lairs with tiny knives in hand and murder on their minds. Only mite tribes that have managed to ally themselves with particularly dangerous vermin generally have any chance at all to withstand an invasion of this sort, and most tribes quickly surrender to the gremlins. In some cases, the wholesale act of surrender can cool the gremlins' rage, and the attackers simply take steps to subjugate and enslave the tribe of mites, using them from that point on as a slave class to serve their whims, but in other cases not even the mite tribe's complete surrender can save them.

Against larger creatures, particularly humanoids (whom gremlins particularly love to torment and vex), gremlins adopt a much more subtle approach. Gremlins know that they lack the physical strength to withstand a fight against even the weakest humanoid societies, and thus keep to the shadows when moving through cities and villages. Gremlins seek out regions within urban areas where the "big folk" don't bother to visit often—places like sewers, dumps, graveyards, and abandoned buildings make for perfect gremlin lairs. Once a gremlin tribe establishes itself in the shadows of a humanoid society, it begins its work. Operating in pairs or even alone, the gremlins move out into the society, seeking ways to undo anything that can be undone. If a gremlin can arrange it, it prefers to leave an object, relationship, or situation in such a condition that it may seem stable and undamaged to the casual observer, but falls apart or fails spectacularly the next time it is used or encountered. A gremlin often waits in hiding nearby so it can observe the calamitous results of its mayhem, but takes pains to be well out of reach when such a disaster occurs. Gremlins know that it's not good to be in arm's reach of an angry humanoid once it realizes it's been visited by a gremlin.

In areas where gremlin activity is well established, many societies have developed unique and clever ways to both protect themselves from gremlin-related mayhem and root out the little monsters from their lairs. One common method of dealing with gremlins is to use objects known as gremlin bells. Crafted from bronze, brass, or other semiprecious metals and measuring no more than an inch tall, gremlin bells are hung from delicate chains or silken cords over door frames and windows, or affixed to precious objects. The belief is that the presence of a gremlin bell sickens the creatures and even renders their supernatural and spell-like abilities useless. Strangely enough, many gremlins believe this as well, and even when the gremlin bells aren't magic, gremlins won't risk tinkering with most objects that seem to be warded in such a manner.

Other communities take a much more active path in ridding themselves of gremlins, training small animals like cats, dogs, falcons, or even weasels to seek out and attack gremlins on sight. Tiny trained animals can pursue gremlins into their cramped warrens with ease and, when their claws are fitted with cleverly constructed cold iron spikes, can inflict significant damage on a tribe of these creatures. Many gremlin tribes have learned from such tactics, however, and utilize trained (or not) animals in their own lairs for protection.

GREMLIN, JINKIN

Grimacing like a maniac, this lean little bat-eared horror displays a mouth full of needle-like teeth and glowing, orange eyes.

JINKIN	CR 1

XP 400

CE Tiny fey

Init +4; **Senses** darkvision 120 ft., low-light vision; Perception +6

DEFENSE

AC 18, touch 17, flat-footed 13 (+4 Dex, +1 dodge, +1 natural, +2 size)

hp 6 (1d6+3)

Fort +0, **Ref** +6, **Will** +4

DR 5/cold iron; **SR** 12

OFFENSE

Speed 40 ft.

Melee short sword +6 (1d3–4/19–20), bite +1 (1d2–4)

Space 2-1/2 ft.; **Reach** 0 ft.

Special Attacks sneak attack +1d6, tinker

Spell-Like Abilities (CL 1st; concentration +3)

At will—*prestidigitation*

1/hour—*dimension door* (self plus 5 lbs. only)

STATISTICS

Str 3, **Dex** 19, **Con** 11, **Int** 14, **Wis** 14, **Cha** 15

Base Atk +0; **CMB** +2; **CMD** 9

Feats Dodge, Toughness^B, Weapon Finesse^B

Skills Bluff +6, Craft (traps) +10, Disable Device +9, Escape Artist +8, Perception +6, Sleight of Hand +8, Stealth +16, Use Magic Device +6; **Racial Modifiers** +4 Craft (traps), +4 Disable Device

Languages Undercommon

ECOLOGY

Environment any underground or urban

Organization solitary, pair, mob (3–12), or infestation (13–20 with 1–3 sorcerers of 1st–3rd level, 1 rogue leader of 2nd–4th level, 2–8 trained stirges, 2–5 trained darkmantles, and 1–2 trained dire bats)

Treasure standard (short sword, other treasure)

SPECIAL ABILITIES

Tinker (Sp) A group of six jinkins working together over the course of an hour can create an effect identical to *bestow curse* on any living creature. This effect functions at CL 6th and has a range of 60 ft., and the target creature must be either willing or helpless (but still gets a saving throw to resist). The save is DC 14 + the Charisma modifier of the jinkin with the highest Charisma score (DC 16 for most groups of jinkins). Alternatively, the group of jinkins can attempt to infuse a magic item with a curse. The nature of this curse is determined randomly; half of these curses make the magic item unreliable (each time the item is used, there is a 20% chance it does not function), while the other half give the item a random requirement (see page 537 of the *Pathfinder RPG Core Rulebook*). A jinkin can take part in a tinkering only once per day, and may only tinker with a creature or object that isn't already cursed. Once a tinkering curse is in place, it is permanent until removed via an effect like *remove curse*. All jinkin tinkerings function as a curse created by a 6th-level caster.

Sneaky and sadistic, jinkins are hideous gremlins that inhabit the dark places underground. Well acclimated to the shadows, they hide in cramped quarters and attack larger creatures when they're strategically positioned. Jinkins commonly work with or near larger or more powerful creatures; these larger creatures provide cover for the jinkins' trickery. They use *dimension door* to exit any battle that goes badly, taking any stolen goods with them.

Jinkins delight in leading larger creatures into dangerous caves or pits, usually by lunging out of the shadows to make a single sneak attack against a creature and then running away, taking care while "fleeing" to remain visible to their target so that they can lure the victim into a trap.

Jinkins also hold dangerous grudges, and one might follow a creature that supposedly slighted it for weeks, looking for an opportunity to take revenge. This revenge can take many forms, from leading horses astray to contaminating food supplies to directing larger monsters toward the begrudged creature.

One of the most direct and unwelcome revenges of the jinkins is the destruction or cursing of magical items. Many times they'll observe camped enemies from a distance and either steal an item to tinker with it or just use their tinkering magic at a distance to annoy the item's owner. Once a jinkin has worked its sabotage on a stolen item, the jinkin either grows bored with the item or may attempt to return it to its owner. Jinkin lairs are often cluttered with stolen items that bear curses the jinkins themselves have forgotten all about.

Dwarves in particular hate jinkins, with numerous tales in their folklore telling of tragedy at the hands of the gremlins. The loathing is largely mutual.

The average jinkin stands almost 2 feet tall and weighs about 13 pounds.

GREMLIN, NUGLUB

This hideous, hunchbacked creature has three glowing blue eyes.
Oily hair grows from its head and back, covering it like a cloak.

NUGLUB	CR 2

XP 600

CE Small fey

Init +4; **Senses** darkvision 120 ft., low-light vision;
Perception +9

DEFENSE

AC 18, touch 15, flat-footed 14 (+4 Dex, +3 natural, +1 size)

hp 19 (3d6+9)

Fort +3, **Ref** +7, **Will** +2

DR 5/cold iron; **SR** 13

OFFENSE

Speed 30 ft., climb 20 ft.

Melee bite +3 (1d4+1 plus grab), 2 claws +4 (1d3+1 plus trip)

Spell-Like Abilities (CL 3rd; concentration +4)

At will—*prestidigitation*

1/hour—*heat metal* (DC 13), *shocking grasp*, *snare*

STATISTICS

Str 13, **Dex** 18, **Con** 15, **Int** 8, **Wis** 9, **Cha** 12

Base Atk +1; **CMB** +1 (+5 grapple and trip); **CMD** 15

Feats Step Up, Toughness[B], Weapon Focus (claw)

Skills Acrobatics +10, Climb +9, Craft (traps) +9, Intimidate +8,
Perception +9, Stealth +14; **Racial Modifiers** +4 Craft (traps),
+4 Intimidate, +4 Perception

Languages Undercommon

SQ kneecapper

ECOLOGY

Environment any underground or urban

Organization solitary, pair, or mob (3–6)

Treasure standard

SPECIAL ABILITIES

Kneecapper (Ex) A nuglub has a +4 racial bonus on combat
maneuver checks to trip an opponent.

Nuglub gremlins are deranged; they enjoy combat with
a manic glee that other gremlins reserve for destroying
devices or creating complex traps. Indeed,
they spend long hours sharpening their
claws, filing their teeth, and looking
for the perfect ledge from which to leap
into the fray. If combat doesn't come to
them, they seek it out, entering villages
and killing innocents by night. Their idea of a good time
is murder so silent that the victim never wakes up, so the
family members find the remains the next morning and
accuse one another of the atrocity.

Nuglubs jealously attack armored foes, as the
gremlins' hunchbacked forms make it difficult to wear
armor made for other humanoids. A group may use
its *heat metal* and *shocking grasp* abilities to weaken an
opponent before mobbing it and trying to knock the
foe prone. As soon as an enemy falls to the ground, all
nuglubs descend on that target in a frenzy of bloodlust,
grappling and biting, holding on like perverse leeches
until nothing remains.

Though less technically inclined than some of their
kin, nuglubs like using traps. Unlike most gremlins, who
prefer to sabotage existing machines, nuglubs delight in
the stealthy construction of traps in areas their victims
consider familiar, rigging these painful and often deadly
surprises on front doors, around the floor of beds, or
near cribs in nurseries.

Nuglubs are the brutes of gremlin-kind. Groups of
nuglubs remain small, as they tend to quarrel with each
other and cannibalize those on the wrong side of an
angry argument. Lone nuglubs often work with other
gremlins, as they like proving they're the strongest,
and aren't likely to kill and eat their smaller allies
(though those slain by other enemies are fair game for
a little snacking).

Nuglubs typically stand 2-1/2 feet tall and weigh
approximately 25 pounds.

Illustration by Damien Mammoliti

GREMLIN, PUGWAMPI

As if the world's most revolting lapdog had somehow learned to walk on its back legs, this sickly creature slinks forward carefully.

PUGWAMPI   CR 1/2

XP 200

NE Tiny fey

Init +5; **Senses** darkvision 120 ft., low-light vision; Perception +6

Aura unluck (20 ft.)

DEFENSE

AC 13, touch 13, flat-footed 12 (+1 Dex, +2 size)

hp 6 (1d6+3)

Fort +0, **Ref** +3, **Will** +4

DR 2/cold iron; **SR** 7

OFFENSE

Speed 30 ft.

Melee dagger +3 (1d2–4/19–20)

Ranged shortbow +3 (1d3–4/×3)

Space 2-1/2 ft.; **Reach** 0 ft.

Spell-Like Abilities (CL 1st; concentration –1)

At will—*prestidigitation*, *speak with animals*

1/day—*shatter* (DC 10)

STATISTICS

Str 3, **Dex** 13, **Con** 11, **Int** 10, **Wis** 14, **Cha** 6

Base Atk +0; **CMB** –1; **CMD** 5

Feats Improved Initiative, Toughness[B], Weapon Finesse[B]

Skills Bluff +2, Craft (traps) +4, Disable Device +2, Perception +6 (+2 Listening), Ride +2, Stealth +17; **Racial Modifiers** +4 Stealth, –4 Perception when listening

Languages Gnoll, Undercommon

ECOLOGY

Environment warm hills

Organization solitary, pair, mob (3–12), or infestation (13–20 with 1–3 druids of 1st–3rd level, 1 fighter leader of 2nd–4th level, 2–8 trained stirges, and 2–5 trained baboons)

Treasure standard (dagger, shortbow with 20 arrows, other treasure)

SPECIAL ABILITIES

Unluck Aura (Su) A pugwampi radiates an aura of unluck to a radius of 20 feet. Any creature in this area must roll two d20s whenever a situation calls for a d20 roll (such as an attack roll, a skill check, or a saving throw) and must use the lower of the two results generated. This is a mind-affecting effect that does not work on animals, other gremlins, or gnolls. Any character who gains any sort of luck bonus (such as that granted by a *luckstone* or *divine favor*) is immune to the pugwampi unluck aura.

Mean, dog-faced, and cowardly, pugwampis are loved by no one—not even other gremlins. These gremlins take disproportionate amounts of enjoyment from the accidents and missteps of other creatures, often going to great lengths to manufacture the perfect deadfalls or stumbling blocks. They then wait nearby, both to laugh at the inevitable mishaps and to make sure their personal unluckiness is passed off on their victims.

Pugwampis live in caves or ruined buildings, occasionally venturing forth to find victims upon which to inflict their sick senses of humor. Their "jokes" tend to involve spikes and excrement, or sometimes pits full of spiders or campsites that flood with swamp water. Certainly only the pugwampis consider their jokes funny. As all pugwampis are somewhat deaf, when not trying to be stealthy, they tend to scream and yell loudly so they can hear themselves and each other.

At some point in the distant past, pugwampis became enamored of gnolls, seeing in the beast-men a kindred form and thus aspiring to the height and deadly prowess of the savage warriors, whom they honor as gods. Gnolls, for their part, hate pugwampis even more than other creatures, mostly because of the gremlins' weakness and sickening fawning, though they sometimes keep the gremlins around just to torment them.

144

GREMLIN, VEXGIT

With a head like an angry crustacean, this fierce little insectoid creature clacks and rattles with a tiny but solid-looking hammer.

VEXGIT	CR 1

XP 400

LE Tiny fey

Init +1; **Senses** darkvision 120 ft., low-light vision; Perception +5

DEFENSE

AC 15, touch 13, flat-footed 14 (+1 Dex, +2 natural, +2 size)

hp 8 (1d6+5)

Fort +2, **Ref** +3, **Will** +3

DR 5/cold iron; **SR** 12

OFFENSE

Speed 20 ft., climb 20 ft.

Melee warhammer +0 (1d4–2/×3), bite –2 (1d3–2)

Space 2-1/2 ft.; **Reach** 0 ft.

Special Attacks speedy sabotage, wrecking crew

Spell-Like Abilities (CL 1st; concentration +1)

At will—*prestidigitation*

1/hour—*rusting grasp, snare*

STATISTICS

Str 6, **Dex** 13, **Con** 14, **Int** 12, **Wis** 13, **Cha** 11

Base Atk +0; **CMB** –1; **CMD** 7

Feats Skill Focus (Disable Device), Toughness[B], Weapon Finesse[B]

Skills Appraise +2, Climb +13, Craft (traps) +5, Disable Device +9, Knowledge (engineering) +2, Perception +5, Stealth +13 (+17 in metal or stony areas, +9 when moving); **Racial Modifiers** +4 Disable Device, +4 Stealth in metal or stony areas, –4 Stealth when moving

Languages Undercommon

ECOLOGY

Environment any underground or urban

Organization solitary, pair, mob (3–12), or infestation (13–20 with 1–3 sorcerers of 1st–3rd level, 1 rogue leader of 2nd–4th level, 2–14 trained dire rats, 2–5 trained venomous snakes, and 1–3 rat swarms)

Treasure standard (warhammer, other treasure)

SPECIAL ABILITIES

Speedy Sabotage (Su) Vexgits are adept at disassembling machinery, reducing even complex devices to trash with shocking speed. When using the Disable Device skill, these gremlins treat all devices as being one category simpler for the purposes of determining how long it takes to use the skill. Thus, difficult devices count as tricky, tricky devices count as simple, and simple devices can be dismantled as a free action.

Wrecking Crew (Su) A group of up to six vexgits can work together to dismantle a device. This ability functions like the aid another action, but a single vexgit can receive help from up to five other vexgits, granting it up to a +10 bonus on its Disable Device check.

Maniacally destructive little brutes, vexgits delight in scrapping and sabotaging the works of larger races. The larger and more complicated the target, the better. While one of these spiteful gremlins might delight in trapping someone behind a door with a jammed lock, loosening the wheels on a carriage, or sneakily removing all the nails from a small boat, it's when groups of vexgits get together that they're truly dangerous. In such instances, the portcullis of a vexgit-infested gatehouse turns into a deadly weapon, while a clock tower becomes an avalanche of gears waiting to topple. Engineers warn apprentices of masterful constructions destroyed by these unruly gremlins, with many blaming their greatest failures on such tiny saboteurs.

Like most gremlins, vexgits prefer to live underground, but cities and the devices they find there fascinate them, often drawing mobs of the dangerous fey to sewer tunnels and abandoned warehouses.

Vexgits stand 1-1/2 feet tall and weigh approximately 16 pounds.

GRICK

This pallid, slimy, worm-like creature is the size of a human, its mouth a sickening tangle of tentacles and hooked jaws.

GRICK	CR 3

XP 800

N Medium aberration

Init +2; **Senses** darkvision 60 ft., scent; Perception +12

DEFENSE

AC 15, touch 12, flat-footed 13 (+2 Dex, +3 natural)

hp 27 (5d8+5)

Fort +2, **Ref** +3, **Will** +6

DR 10/magic

OFFENSE

Speed 30 ft., climb 20 ft.

Melee bite +4 (1d4+1), 4 tentacles −1 (1d4)

STATISTICS

Str 12, **Dex** 14, **Con** 13, **Int** 3, **Wis** 14, **Cha** 5

Base Atk +3; **CMB** +4; **CMD** 16 (can't be tripped)

Feats Combat Reflexes, Skill Focus (Perception), Stand Still

Skills Climb +9, Perception +12, Stealth +6 (+14 in rocky terrain); **Racial Modifiers** +8 Stealth in rocky terrain

Languages Aklo (cannot speak)

ECOLOGY

Environment any underground

Organization solitary or cluster (2–5)

Treasure incidental

The worm-like grick is a terror of the caverns and tunnels in which it dwells, lying in wait near heavily traveled underground passages or subterranean cities for the chance to reach forth from the darkness and take its prey. Those laid low by a grick are rarely consumed on the spot. Instead, fresh food is hauled back to the grick's lair in a tight burrow or high on a cavern ledge, where it is consumed in small bites at the grick's leisure.

The origins of the grick are not known. Even though the grick has a rudimentary intelligence, it does not have any society to speak of, and most are encountered alone. On those occasions when unfortunate travelers meet multiple specimens, groups of gricks do not appear to communicate or work together; each instead attacks individual targets and retreats with its prize as soon as it manages to bring down an opponent. Capable predators, gricks also have a strangely weapon-resistant hide that makes them especially dangerous. Many novice adventurers have fallen to grick attacks merely because they were unable to damage the creature with their nonmagical weapons. Those that are familiar with gricks (especially dwarves, morlocks, and troglodytes) know the best strategy for dealing with them is to fall back and wait for more powerful or magical reinforcements.

Gricks rely on their dark coloration and ability to climb walls to keep them out of sight until they're ready to spring an ambush. On occasions when food is scarce in a given region, gricks have been known to travel to the surface and roam the wilderness in search of prey, but these sojourns are almost always out of necessity, and end as soon as the gricks find entrances to new subterranean lairs. They prefer darkness and the comfort of a ceiling overhead, avoiding the open sky and going to great lengths to keep the cover of trees, low clouds, or buildings between them and the empty gulf overhead.

JUNGLE GRICKS

These surface-adapted varieties of the underground grick are shades of green and lurk in the undergrowth of jungles or climb low-hanging branches to drop on unsuspecting prey. Their racial bonus on Stealth checks applies in forested terrain instead of rocky terrain. Jungle gricks are heartier creatures than their underground-dwelling kin—all jungle gricks possess the advanced creature simple template and gain Toughness as a bonus feat.

GRIG

Perched on the prickly legs of a cricket, this tiny creature has gossamer wings and the upper body of an elven woman.

GRIG	CR 1

XP 400
NG Tiny fey
Init +4; **Senses** low-light vision; Perception +5

DEFENSE

AC 17, touch 17, flat-footed 12 (+4 Dex, +1 dodge, +2 size)
hp 4 (1d6+1)
Fort +1, **Ref** +6, **Will** +3
DR 5/cold iron; **SR** 16

OFFENSE

Speed 30 ft., fly 40 ft. (average)
Melee short sword –1 (1d3–3/19–20)
Ranged longbow +6 (1d4–3/×3)
Space 2-1/2 ft.; **Reach** 0 ft.
Special Attacks fiddle
Spell-Like Abilities (CL 9th; concentration +11)
  3/day—*disguise self*, *entangle* (DC 13), *invisibility* (self only), *pyrotechnics* (DC 14)

STATISTICS

Str 5, **Dex** 18, **Con** 13, **Int** 10, **Wis** 13, **Cha** 14
Base Atk +0; **CMB** +2; **CMD** 10 (16 vs. trip)
Feats Dodge
Skills Acrobatics +8 (+12 when jumping), Escape Artist +8, Fly +12, Perception +5, Perform (string) +6, Stealth +16; **Racial Modifiers** +4 Acrobatics when jumping
Languages Common, Sylvan

ECOLOGY

Environment temperate forests
Organization solitary, gang (2–5), or band (6–11)
Treasure NPC gear (short sword, longbow with 20 arrows, other treasure)

SPECIAL ABILITIES

Fiddle (Su) Grigs are capable of rubbing their legs together like a cricket to create a surprisingly pleasant sound not unlike that of a tiny fiddle. As a standard action, a grig can create a catchy tune that compels any creature within a 20-foot spread to dance and caper. A creature can resist this compulsion by making a DC 12 Will save. Creatures that fail are compelled to dance and shuffle their feet, and are effectively staggered as long as the grig continues to fiddle. A grig can maintain this effect for up to 10 rounds per day by concentrating. Once a creature makes the save against a grig's fiddle, it is immune to further fiddle effects from that grig for 24 hours. This is a sonic mind-affecting effect. The save DC is Charisma-based.

Grigs are tiny fey with the upper bodies of elf-like sprites and cricket bodies below. Their humanoid features vary wildly in individual appearance, but they usually wear their brown, silver, or green hair long and uncombed. In most cases, grigs' skin bears gold or green stripes or markings, and their legs are brightly colored. They prefer to eschew clothes entirely, wearing clothing only when such apparel has desirable magical effects. Grigs stand 1-1/2 feet tall, and weigh just under 10 pounds.

Grigs make their homes in thick woods alongside rolling hills, often near bodies of water. In every grig community may be found a clearing where the group observes the moon during its many lunar holidays.

Despite their tiny size, grigs are eager to confront evil and vanquish ugliness—as a result, grigs often find themselves in trouble. They rarely attack directly, instead preferring the element of surprise. In combat, grigs maintain their distance and either depend on their spell-like abilities or fire their longbows from afar. Grigs use their movement to their advantage, frequently jumping about their enemies or flying beyond their reach.

Gigs excel at music, and can create lively ditties simply by sawing their legs against their bodies. Grig music often stirs people to dance, even when the grigs don't enhance their music with supernatural compulsions. In addition to loving music, grigs enjoy the visual arts, especially paintings and sketches, and they often decorate their homes with bright colors and delightful images.

Illustration by Anna Christenson

GRINDYLOW

With a large head and numerous teeth, this unsightly creature resembles a goblin from the waist up and a greasy octopus below.

GRINDYLOW	CR 1/2

XP 200

CE Small aberration (aquatic)

Init +2; **Senses** darkvision 60 ft.; Perception +4

DEFENSE

AC 15, touch 13, flat-footed 13 (+2 Dex, +2 natural, +1 size)

hp 5 (1d8+1)

Fort +1, **Ref** +2, **Will** +2

OFFENSE

Speed 15 ft., swim 30 ft., jet 200 ft.

Melee spear +2 (1d6+1/×3), bite −2 (1d3)

Ranged spear +3 (1d6+1/×3)

Special Attack tangling tentacles

STATISTICS

Str 12, **Dex** 14, **Con** 13, **Int** 9, **Wis** 10, **Cha** 9

Base Atk +0; **CMB** +0; **CMD** 12 (18 vs. trip)

Feats Weapon Finesse

Skills Perception +4, Stealth +14, Swim +13; **Racial Modifiers** +4 Stealth

Languages Aquan

SQ amphibious

ECOLOGY

Environment any water

Organization solitary, pair, gang (3–9), warband (10–16 with 1–2 octopus minions), or tribe (17–40 plus 1 ranger sergeant of 1st–3rd level per 20 members, 1 cleric or barbarian leader of 4th–8th level, 2–8 octopus pets, and 1–2 devilfish guardians)

Treasure NPC gear (spear, other treasure)

SPECIAL ABILITIES

Tangling Tentacles (Ex) Although a grindylow can't attack to cause damage with its six tentacles, these wriggling legs constantly writhe and reach out to tug at and trip adjacent foes. During the grindylow's turn, it can make a single trip attack against any adjacent foe as a swift action. It gains a +4 racial bonus on trip attacks made with its tangling tentacles, and if it fails to trip a foe, that creature can't attempt to trip the grindylow in retaliation.

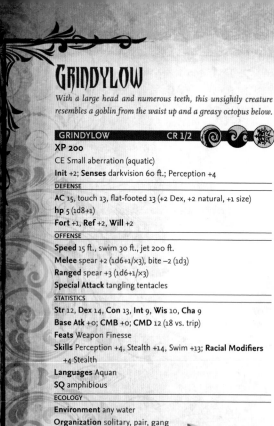

About 4 feet long from head to tentacle tip, grindylows appear to be half-goblin and half-octopus, the split occurring at the waist. Grindylows are violent, ravenous creatures that use their spears to hunt or just to poke at things that scream and cry.

While grindylows resemble goblins, they are not humanoid creatures. Nonetheless, these aquatic monsters are just as wicked as the most sadistic of goblins, and take immense pleasure in others' misfortunes and the spread of mayhem. Thanks to this twisted desire, grindylows have a nasty reputation among both other intelligent water-dwelling creatures and most land-dwelling beings.

Grindylows eat whatever they can kill, giving them a rather wide selection of meals. High or low, no one is safe from the brutish assaults; tribes of merfolk have been overwhelmed by bands of grindylows, as have galleons full of experienced sailors. While obvious predators such as giant eels or sharks evoke great fear from grindylows, no enemies are more hated than the squid, be it common or giant. None are sure where this disdain stems from, but it is speculated that a squid is to an octopus for a grindylow what a dog is to a goblin dog for goblins. Incredibly fond of their similarly designed kin, grindylows believe octopuses to be the epitome of beauty, with squids being regarded as hideous freaks in comparison. There is no greater insult to a grindylow than being called a squid.

While grindylows can take class levels to gain power, certain grindylows are freakish throwbacks to a primal age—these grindylows never cease growing, and in time can become massive beasts of Huge size. Unlike the typical grindylow, these giants can attack with all six of their tentacles and constrict with great effect. Giant grindylows are fortunately quite rare.

GRIPPLI

Its slick skin a mottled pattern of bright colors, this agile, frog-like humanoid carries a bow and wears leather armor.

GRIPPLI	CR 1/2

XP 200

Grippli ranger 1

N Small humanoid (grippli)

Init +3; **Senses** darkvision 60 ft.; Perception +5

DEFENSE

AC 16, touch 14, flat-footed 13 (+2 armor, +3 Dex, +1 size)

hp 12 (1d10+2)

Fort +3, **Ref** +5, **Will** +1

OFFENSE

Speed 30 ft., climb 20 ft.

Melee short sword +3 (1d4+1/19–20)

Ranged dart +5 (1d3+1) or

net +5 (special)

Special Attacks favored enemy (vermin +2)

STATISTICS

Str 12, **Dex** 17, **Con** 13, **Int** 12, **Wis** 12, **Cha** 8

Base Atk +1; **CMB** +1; **CMD** 14

Feats Self-Sufficient

Skills Acrobatics +4, Climb +13, Handle Animal +3, Heal +7, Perception +5, Stealth +11 (+15 in forests or marshes), Survival +7; **Racial Modifiers** +4 Stealth in forests or marshes

Languages Common, Grippli

SQ swamp stride, track, wild empathy

ECOLOGY

Environment warm forests or marshes

Organization solitary, gang (2–5), pack (6–11), or tribe (21–30 plus 1 cleric leader of 3rd level)

Treasure NPC gear (leather armor, 4 darts, net, short sword, other treasure)

SPECIAL ABILITIES

Swamp Stride (Ex) A grippli can move through difficult terrain at its normal speed while within a swamp. Magically altered terrain affects a grippli normally.

These small, intelligent, humanoid tree frogs live in primitive societies deep in the forests and marshes of the world. They hunt giant insects and eat fruits and flowers from their tree homes. They often barter with more advanced creatures for metal and gemstone ornaments.

Grippli hatchlings develop into adults in less than a year. Unless they meet a savage end from a forest threat, they can live 60 years, their skin graying and losing its luster as they age. A grippli stands just over 2 feet in height and weighs 30 pounds.

GRIPPLI CHARACTERS

Gripplis are defined by their class levels—they do not possess racial Hit Dice. They have the following racial traits.

+2 Dexterity, +2 Wisdom, –2 Strength: Gripplis are nimble and alert, but spindly.

Small: Gripplis are Small sized.

Fast Speed: Gripplis have a base speed of 30 feet and a base climb speed of 20 feet.

Darkvision: Gripplis can see in the dark up to 60 feet.

Camouflage: +4 Stealth in marshes or forested areas.

Swamp Stride: See above.

Weapon Familiarity: Gripplis are proficient with nets.

Languages: Gripplis speak Common and Grippli. Gripplis with high Int scores can choose from the following: Boggard, Draconic, Elven, Gnome, Goblin, Sylvan.

Illustration by Florian Stitz

GRYPH

This hawk-sized avian looks much like a six-legged stork. Its feathers are unkempt and greasy, and its beak is razor-sharp.

GRYPH	CR 1

XP 400

NE Small magical beast

Init +2; **Senses** darkvision 60 ft., low-light vision; Perception +5

DEFENSE

AC 13, touch 13, flat-footed 11 (+2 Dex, +1 size)

hp 15 (2d10+4)

Fort +5, **Ref** +5, **Will** +1

OFFENSE

Speed 30 ft., fly 50 ft. (good)

Melee bite +5 (1d6/×3), claw +5 (grab)

Special Attacks implant eggs

STATISTICS

Str 11, **Dex** 15, **Con** 14, **Int** 2, **Wis** 12, **Cha** 7

Base Atk +2; **CMB** +1 (+5 start grapple, +9 maintain grapple); **CMD** 13 (21 vs. trip)

Feats Weapon Finesse

Skills Fly +8, Perception +5, Stealth +10

ECOLOGY

Environment temperate forests or underground

Organization solitary, flock (2–8), or throng (9–20)

Treasure incidental

SPECIAL ABILITIES

Grab (Ex) A gryph can use its grab attack on a creature of up to Medium size. It has a +4 racial bonus on grapple checks to maintain a grapple (in addition to the +4 from the grab ability).

Implant Eggs (Ex) Once per day, a gryph can implant eggs into a helpless target or a target it is grappling. As a full-round action, the gryph extends an ovipositor from its abdomen and penetrates the victim's flesh by making a successful sting attack (+5 melee). On a hit, the ovipositor deals 1 point of damage and implants 1d4 eggs in the victim. The eggs draw nutrients from the target's flesh, and give the target the sickened condition. The eggs grow swiftly, hatching in a mere 1d4 minutes into ravenous gryph chicks that immediately burrow out of the victim's body. This deals 2 points of Constitution damage per gryph chick, after which the hatchlings immediately take wing and fly away (if needed, use game statistics for a bat familiar to represent a hatchling). Removing implanted eggs requires a DC 20 Heal check (a full-round action); each attempt deals 1 hit point of damage. Although immunity to disease offers no special protection against gryph egg implantation, *remove disease*, *heal*, or similar effects automatically destroy any implanted gryph eggs.

Gryphs are bird-like creatures usually found underground, but they also favor dark and tangled forests. Gryphs normally survive on carrion and small animals, but take on larger game when driven by hunger or if they feel threatened. Most disturbing is their means of reproduction. Gryphs are hermaphroditic and mate frequently, such that their egg pouches are rarely empty. When they encounter a suitable host—a warm-blooded creature of size Small or larger, ideally alone—the gryphs swoop down, latch on to the target, and implant their eggs directly into its flesh. As long as the target is conscious, the flock continues its assault, though if the target flees the area, the gryphs return to their nest. The eggs quicken swiftly once implanted, and gryph chicks hatch forth mere minutes later in a bloody birth that is often fatal to the host.

Gryphs have a strange affinity for vermin, often lairing in close proximity to one or more insect swarms or vermin of Medium size or smaller. The insects avoid the gryphs instinctively, feeding off the remains of the flock's meals and on creatures too small for the gryphs to bother with.

Most gryphs have six legs, but some have four or even eight. Individual flocks are always made up of gryphs with the same number of limbs. A gryph is 3 feet tall and weighs 45 pounds.

Illustration by Tyler Walpole

GUG

This towering menace has a horrible, vertically aligned mouth and arms that split at the elbows into twin clawed hands.

GUG	CR 10

XP 9,600

CE Large aberration

Init +1; **Senses** darkvision 60 ft.; Perception +27

DEFENSE

AC 24, touch 10, flat-footed 23 (+1 Dex, +14 natural, −1 size)

hp 127 (15d8+60)

Fort +9, **Ref** +6, **Will** +12

Immune disease, poison

OFFENSE

Speed 40 ft., climb 20 ft.

Melee bite +17 (1d8+7), 4 claws +17 (1d6+7)

Space 10 ft.; **Reach** 15 ft.

Special Attacks rend (2 claws, 1d6+10)

STATISTICS

Str 25, **Dex** 12, **Con** 18, **Int** 11, **Wis** 16, **Cha** 11

Base Atk +11; **CMB** +19; **CMD** 30

Feats Awesome Blow, Blind-Fight, Combat Reflexes, Greater Bull Rush, Improved Bull Rush, Lunge, Power Attack, Skill Focus (Perception)

Skills Climb +15, Escape Artist +13, Knowledge (dungeoneering) +10, Perception +27, Stealth +15, Survival +21; **Racial Modifiers** +4 Escape Artist

Languages Undercommon

SQ compression

ECOLOGY

Environment any underground

Organization solitary, pair, or camp (3–10)

Treasure standard

Gugs are inhuman monstrosities that dwell in the deep places of the world. Whether they were banished to the dark lands by ancient gods or the light-loving races they terrorized, or perhaps were brought to the deep realms by dark powers from some even more inhuman nightmare realm, is unknown, but gugs are loathed by other races for their carnal rites of slaughter.

Gugs are 16 feet tall and weigh nearly 2,000 pounds, but they move with an eerie, unnatural gait as though their limbs contained far too many joints. They can contort and distend their limbs for greater reach or to wriggle easily through impossibly small passages. Gugs may cling for long hours to cave walls or just within dark side-caverns, lying in wait for prey to stumble too close. Their senses are keen, however, and their joy in the bloody hunt is considerable and gugs who catch the scent of blood may stalk their prey for long days, even venturing at times beyond their caves to dare the bright lands of the surface in search of tasty meat to drag back for their horrific sacrifices.

Gugs are savage fighters when driven by a strong leader, but on their own may flee if brought to fewer than half their hit points, carrying off fresh meat for later feasting if they are able. They can subsist on fungi, slimes, and molds as well as carrion and even undead flesh—particularly that of ghouls.

Some bloodthirsty gugs gain awful powers as gifts from their alien patrons. These monsters are known as savants. They have a Charisma of 18 and can use *invisibility, spike stones, transmute rock to mud,* and *unholy blight* once per day each as spell-like abilities (CL 10th, concentration +14). Some become actual clerics or oracles of their mad gods—strange powers of darkness, insanity, and blood. Gug savants add +1 to their CR.

Illustration by Andrew Hou

HANGMAN TREE

This sinister tree looms above a field strewn with bones. Numerous leafy vines, their tips looped into nooses, hang from its branches.

HANGMAN TREE	CR 7

XP 3,200

NE Huge plant

Init +3; **Senses** blindsight 60 ft.; Perception +11

DEFENSE

AC 20, touch 7, flat-footed 20 (−1 Dex, +13 natural, −2 size)

hp 84 (8d8+48)

Fort +12, **Ref** +3, **Will** +5

Immune plant traits; **SR** 18

Weaknesses vulnerable to electricity

OFFENSE

Speed 10 ft.

Melee 3 vines +11 (1d6+7 plus grab and pull)

Space 15 ft.; **Reach** 15 ft.

Special Attacks constrict (1d6+7), hallucinatory spores, pull (vine, 5 feet), strangle, swallow whole (2d6+7 bludgeoning damage, AC 16, 8 hp), vines

STATISTICS

Str 25, **Dex** 8, **Con** 23, **Int** 7, **Wis** 12, **Cha** 10

Base Atk +6; **CMB** +15 (+19 grapple); **CMD** 24

Feats Improved Initiative, Iron Will, Lightning Reflexes, Skill Focus (Perception)

Skills Perception +11, Stealth −2

Languages Sylvan

ECOLOGY

Environment temperate forests

Organization solitary or pair

Treasure standard

SPECIAL ABILITIES

Hallucinatory Spores (Ex) Once per day as a standard action, a hangman tree can release a cloud of spores in a 50-foot-radius spread. Creatures in the area must make a DC 20 Will save or believe the hangman tree to be a perfectly ordinary tree— or at worst, a treant or some other friendly tree-like creature. An affected creature becomes passive for 2d6 minutes and refuses to attack the hangman tree during this time. An affected creature can attempt a new Will save each round that the tree attacks an ally—if a hallucinating creature is attacked by the tree, it gains a +4 bonus on its Will save to see through the hallucination. This is a mind-affecting compulsion effect. The save DC is Constitution-based.

Vines (Ex) A hangman tree's vines are primary attacks that deal bludgeoning damage. When a hangman tree grapples a foe with its vines, the tree does not gain the grappled condition. A hangman tree that uses swallow whole transfers a pinned creature from a vine to inside its trunk.

The hangman tree prefers to lie in wait near remote forest tracks and game trails, waiting for victims to wander by. These carnivorous plants are incredibly patient, and can wait for months in a single location for food to approach. When prey does draw near, the tree's vines lash like striking snakes. The tree often uses its pull ability to hoist grappled foes 10 to 15 feet in the air so that they are out of reach of allies while they slowly strangle. The tree generally only swallows one foe whole at a time, letting its other captured victims dangle and ripen until it is ready to feed on them.

A hangman tree is 30 feet tall and weighs 12,000 pounds.

HELLCAT

This eerie beast appears to be the animated skeleton of a huge fanged cat, its bones glowing with fire and seething with smoke.

HELLCAT	CR 7

XP 3,200

LE Large outsider (evil, extraplanar, lawful)

Init +9; **Senses** darkvision 60 ft., scent; Perception +18

DEFENSE

AC 21, touch 15, flat-footed 15 (+5 Dex, +1 dodge, +6 natural, –1 size)

hp 85 (9d10+36)

Fort +10, **Ref** +13, **Will** +5

Defensive Abilities invisible in light; **DR** 5/good; **Resist** fire 10;
   SR 18

OFFENSE

Speed 40 ft.

Melee bite +13 (1d8+5), 2 claws +13 (1d6+5/19–20 plus grab)

Space 10 ft.; **Reach** 5 ft.

Special Attacks pounce, rake (2 claws +13, 1d6+5/19–20)

STATISTICS

Str 21, **Dex** 21, **Con** 19, **Int** 10, **Wis** 14, **Cha** 10

Base Atk +9; **CMB** +15 (+19 grapple); **CMD** 31 (35 vs. trip)

Feats Combat Reflexes, Dodge, Improved Initiative, Lightning
   Reflexes, Mobility

Skills Acrobatics +17 (+21 jump), Climb +17, Perception +18,
   Stealth +17, Survival +14, Swim +17; **Racial Modifiers** +4
   Perception, +4 Stealth

Languages Infernal (can't speak); telepathy 100 ft.

ECOLOGY

Environment any land (Hell)

Organization solitary, pair, or pack (3–8)

Treasure standard

SPECIAL ABILITIES

Invisible in Light (Su) In bright light, a hellcat has natural
   invisibility. In normal light, a hellcat has partial
   concealment (20% miss chance). In dim light, it has no
   concealment. In darkness, a hellcat's flickering glow
   limits it to partial concealment, unless the darkness
   is magical in nature.

The hellcat is a devious predator native to the fiery pits of Hell. While the hellcat is not a devil itself, it often acts as a guardian or mount for devils. Some might assume that hellcats serve devils as pets, but since hellcats are as intelligent as humans, they take offense to the idea that they might be anyone's pet.

On its own, a hellcat prefers to spend its time hunting and stalking prey. While the hellcat, as an outsider, need not eat to survive, it does enjoy eating for pleasure, often leaving significant portions of its kills behind for others to find. A hellcat that enters into an alliance with a devil is often used as a sort of hunter as a result. Human mortals can use spells like *planar ally* or *planar binding* to conjure hellcats for similar purposes. Those who do so are well advised to treat the hellcat with respect, for should any master prove too haughty with his hellcat or treat it as a dumb animal, the hellcat nurtures a lasting grudge. In such instances, the hellcat goes to great lengths to plan and coordinate revenge on the spellcaster, hoping to satisfy its own pride and to provide a lesson and example to all those who would deal with their kind.

Though incapable of speech themselves, hellcats understand the Infernal tongue of their home plane, and can communicate by telepathy with any creature capable of speech. Hellcats are quick to retreat if they are clearly overmatched or up against foes they cannot reach, but they never forget prey that escapes them, and will often track potential victims and try to lead allies (including other hellcats) to them in order to make coordinated attacks or ambushes.

The hellcat is only clearly visible in dim light, at these times appearing as a skeletal dire tiger with hellish flames burning and flickering along the surface of its bones. Despite this eerie appearance, the hellcat is neither undead nor an elemental creature. The "fires" are actually its blood coursing through transparent flesh. In bright light, the hellcat's entire body fades away into obscurity, while in darkness its glowing blood is muted. Hellcats are as large as tigers, measuring 9 feet long and weighing 900 pounds.

153

HERD ANIMAL, CAMEL

This somewhat irritated-looking, one-humped camel has been outfitted with a bridle and saddle.

CAMEL	CR 1

XP 400

N Large animal

Init +3; **Senses** low-light vision, scent; Perception +5

DEFENSE

AC 13, touch 12, flat-footed 10 (+3 Dex, +1 natural, −1 size)

hp 13 (2d8+4)

Fort +5, **Ref** +6, **Will** +0

OFFENSE

Speed 50 ft.

Melee bite +4 (1d4+6)

Special Attack spit (+3 ranged touch)

STATISTICS

Str 18, **Dex** 16, **Con** 14, **Int** 2, **Wis** 11, **Cha** 4

Base Atk +1; **CMB** +6; **CMD** 19 (23 vs. trip)

Feats Endurance

Skills Perception +5

ECOLOGY

Environment warm deserts

Organization solitary

Treasure none

SPECIAL ABILITIES

Spit (Ex) Once per hour, a camel can regurgitate the contents of its stomach, spitting the foul material at a single target within 10 feet. The target must make a DC 13 Fortitude save or be sickened for 1d4 rounds. The save DC is Constitution-based.

Camels are large, desert-dwelling herd animals noted for their stamina and ill tempers. A typical camel stands about 6 feet at the shoulder and 7 feet at the hump.

HERD ANIMAL, RAM

A formidable pair of heavy horns curls from the forehead of this sturdy, brown-and-white-furred ram.

RAM	CR 1

XP 400

N Medium animal

Init +2; **Senses** low-light vision, scent; Perception +6

DEFENSE

AC 13, touch 12, flat-footed 11 (+2 Dex, +1 natural)

hp 11 (2d8+2)

Fort +4, **Ref** +5, **Will** +2

OFFENSE

Speed 40 ft.

Melee gore +3 (1d4+3)

Special Attacks powerful charge (gore, 1d8+3)

STATISTICS

Str 14, **Dex** 15, **Con** 13, **Int** 2, **Wis** 14, **Cha** 7

Base Atk +1; **CMB** +3; **CMD** 15 (19 vs. trip)

Feats Improved Bull Rush[B], Skill Focus (Acrobatics)

Skills Acrobatics +13 (+17 jump), Perception +6; **Racial Modifiers** +4 Acrobatics

ECOLOGY

Environment temperate mountains

Organization solitary, pair, or herd (3–30)

Treasure none

Rams are mountain-dwelling herd animals noted for their prominent horns.

A typical ram stands about 3 feet tall, is 5 feet long, and weighs about 300 pounds. You can create stats for smaller, similar animals (such as goats) by applying the young creature template to a ram.

RAM COMPANIONS

Starting Statistics: Size Small; **Speed** 40 ft.; **AC** +1 natural; **Attack** gore (1d3); **Ability Scores** Str 10, Dex 17, Con 11, Int 2, Wis 14, Cha 7; **Special Qualities** low-light vision, scent.

4th-Level Advancement: Size Medium; **Attack** gore (1d4); **Ability Scores** Str +4, Dex −2, Con +2; **Special Attacks** powerful charge (1d8); **Bonus Feat** Improved Bull Rush.

Illustration by Eric Belisle

Hippocampus

This creature has the foreparts of a horse and the hindquarters of a fish. Its forelegs end in splayed fins rather than hooves.

HIPPOCAMPUS	CR 1

XP 400

N Large magical beast (aquatic)

Init –1; **Senses** darkvision 60 ft., low-light vision, scent; Perception +6

DEFENSE

AC 12, touch 8, flat-footed 12 (–1 Dex, +4 natural, –1 size)

hp 15 (2d10+4)

Fort +5, **Ref** +2, **Will** +1

OFFENSE

Speed 5 ft., swim 60 ft.

Melee bite +4 (1d4+3), tail slap –1 (1d4+1)

Space 10 ft.; **Reach** 5 ft.

STATISTICS

Str 16, **Dex** 9, **Con** 15, **Int** 2, **Wis** 12, **Cha** 11

Base Atk +2; **CMB** +6; **CMD** 15

Feats Endurance

Skills Perception +6, Swim +11

SQ water dependency

ECOLOGY

Environment any water

Organization solitary, pair, or school (3–16)

Treasure none

SPECIAL ABILITIES

Water Dependency (Ex) A hippocampus can survive out of the water for 1 minute per point of Constitution. Beyond this limit, a hippocampus runs the risk of suffocation, as if it were drowning.

A hippocampus's scales vary in color from ivory to deep green to cerulean blue with shades of silver. Aquatic races such as merfolk and locathahs often train hippocampi as steeds or as draft animals used to pull cunningly designed underwater carriages. In the wild, hippocampi prefer to dwell in relatively shallow waters where their favorite food (seaweed and kelp) is more plentiful and larger predators are less common. These creatures often travel in large schools, analogous to free-roaming herds of wild horses on the surface world.

The hippocampus is relatively easily trained—the amount of work and cost it requires is equivalent to what it takes to train a horse. As armor impacts the creature's swim speed, those who train hippocampi for war rarely bother to put

barding on these creatures—when they do, they generally opt for the lightest armor, such as padded or leather barding. Mounted combat on a hippocampus is similar to fighting while riding a horse, although the hippocampus is a clumsy creature on land and cannot move at all out of the water if it has a rider weighing it down. Although a hippocampus has only two front legs, determine its carrying capacity as if it were a quadruped. Thus, a light load for a hippocampus is up to 228 pounds. Medium loads are up to 459 pounds, and heavy loads up to 690 pounds.

A number of variant species of hippocampus exist, although the majority of these species differ from the creature presented here only in color and feat choice. Common feats other than Endurance for alternative hippocampus species are Great Fortitude, Improved Initiative, Iron Will, Lightning Reflexes, Skill Focus (Swim), and Toughness. A few species of hippocampus are heartier and tougher all around—these creatures are generally those found in colder waters and are known as polar hippocampi. A polar hippocampus has the advanced creature simple template. Most impressive of all are hippocampi that dwell in the deeper seas. These creatures, known as giant hippocampi, are much larger— to generate stats for a giant hippocampus, advance the standard hippocampus to Huge size and increase its Hit Dice to 10. A giant hippocampus is CR 8.

Illustration by Andrew Hou

HIPPOGRIFF

This large, brown, horse-like creature has a hawk's wings, talons, and hooked beak.

HIPPOGRIFF	CR 2

XP 600

N Large magical beast

Init +2; **Senses** darkvision 60 ft., low-light vision, scent; Perception +9

DEFENSE

AC 14, touch 12, flat-footed 11 (+2 Dex, +1 dodge, +2 natural, −1 size)

hp 22 (3d10+6)

Fort +5, **Ref** +5, **Will** +2

OFFENSE

Speed 40 ft., fly 100 ft. (average)

Melee bite +4 (1d6+2), 2 claws +4 (1d4+2)

Space 10 ft.; **Reach** 5 ft.

STATISTICS

Str 15, **Dex** 15, **Con** 14, **Int** 2, **Wis** 12, **Cha** 9

Base Atk +3; **CMB** +6; **CMD** 19

Feats Dodge, Wingover

Skills Fly +5, Perception +9; **Racial Modifiers** +4 Perception

ECOLOGY

Environment temperate hills or plains

Organization solitary, pair, or flight (7–12)

Treasure none

Illustration by Florian Stitz

The hippogriff bears the wings, forelegs, and head of a great raptor bird and the tail and body of a magnificent horse. As horses are a preferred meal for griffons, sages claim some flesh-warping wizard with an ironic sense of humor long ago created this unfortunate fusion of horse and hawk as a joke.

A hippogriff's feathers bear coloration similar to those of a hawk or an eagle; however, some breeders have managed to produce specimens with stark white or coal black feathers. A hippogriff's torso and hind end are most often bay, chestnut, or gray, with some coats bearing pinto or even palomino coloration. Hippogriffs measure 11 feet long and weigh upward of 1,500 pounds.

Territorial, hippogriffs fiercely protect the lands under their domain. Hippogriffs must also watch the skies for other predators, as they are a preferred meal of griffons, wyverns, and young dragons. Hippogriffs nest in sweeping grasslands, rugged hills, and flowing prairies. Exceptionally hardy hippogriffs make their home nestled into niches on canyon walls, from which they comb the rocky deserts for coyotes, deer, and the occasional humanoid. Hippogriffs prefer mammalian prey, yet they graze after every meal of flesh to aid their digestion. Their dietary habits can be dangerous to both ranchers and their livestock, so ranching communities often set bounties on them. Victims of these hunts are often taxidermied, and preserved hippogriffs frequently decorate frontier taverns and remote outposts.

Far easier to train than griffons, yet easily as intelligent as horses, hippogriffs are trained as mounts by some elite companies of mounted soldiers, patrolling the skies and swooping down on unsuspecting enemies. Although they are magical beasts, if captured young, hippogriffs can be trained using Handle Animal as if they were animals. An adult hippogriff is more difficult to train, and attempts to do so follow the normal rules for training magical beasts using the skill. A hippogriff saddle must be specially crafted so as to not impact the movement of the creature's wings—these saddles are always exotic saddles.

Hippogriffs lay eggs rather than birthing live young— as a general rule, a hippogriff nest only contains one egg at a time. A hippogriff's egg is worth 200 gp, but a healthy young hippogriff is worth 500 gp. A fully trained hippogriff mount can command prices of up to 5,000 gp or more. A hippogriff can carry 198 pounds as a light load, 399 pounds as a medium load, and 600 pounds as a heavy load.

HIPPOPOTAMUS

This lumbering bull hippopotamus lunges out of the water and yawns wide, displaying an impressive set of tusk-like teeth.

HIPPOPOTAMUS	CR 5

XP 1,600

N Large animal

Init +4; **Senses** low-light vision, scent; Perception +8

DEFENSE

AC 17, touch 9, flat-footed 17 (+8 natural, −1 size)

hp 59 (7d8+28)

Fort +8 (+10 vs. nonmagical disease), **Ref** +5, **Will** +3

Defensive Abilities sweat

OFFENSE

Speed 40 ft.

Melee bite +8 (2d8+6)

Space 10 ft.; **Reach** 5 ft.

Special Attacks capsize, trample (1d8+6, DC 17)

STATISTICS

Str 19, **Dex** 10, **Con** 16, **Int** 2, **Wis** 13, **Cha** 5

Base Atk +5; **CMB** +10; **CMD** 20 (24 vs. trip)

Feats Endurance, Imp. Initiative, Power Attack, Skill Focus (Perception)

Skills Perception +8, Stealth +1 (+11 underwater), Swim +11;

 Racial Modifiers +10 Stealth underwater

SQ hold breath

ECOLOGY

Environment warm rivers

Organization solitary, pair, or bloat (3–20)

Treasure none

SPECIAL ABILITIES

Capsize (Ex) A hippopotamus can overturn a boat of its size or smaller by ramming it as a charge attack and making a CMB check. The DC of this check is 25 or the result of the boat captain's Profession (sailor) check, whichever is higher.

Sweat (Ex) A hippo's reddish sweat protects it from nonlethal damage from hot environments, and grants it a +2 racial bonus on saving throws against nonmagical disease.

The ill-tempered "river horse" has a well-earned reputation for hostility, despite the fact that it is a herbivore.

HIPPO COMPANIONS

Starting Statistics: Size Medium; **Speed** 40 ft.; **AC** +6 natural armor; **Attack** bite (1d8); **Ability Scores** Str 11, Dex 12, Con 12, Int 2, Wis 13, Cha 5; **Special Qualities** low-light vision, scent, sweat.

 7th-Level Advancement: Size Large; **AC** +2 nat. arm.; **Attack** bite (2d8); **Ability Scores** Str +8, **Dex** −2, **Con** +4; **Special Ability** trample.

HIPPOPOTAMUS, BEHEMOTH

This immense behemoth of a hippo is larger than an elephant. Its teeth are like scimitars, and it moves with an indomitable gait.

BEHEMOTH HIPPOPOTAMUS	CR 10

XP 9,600

N Huge animal

Init +3; **Senses** low-light vision; Perception +12

DEFENSE

AC 23, touch 7, flat-footed 23 (−1 Dex, +16 natural, −2 size)

hp 133 (14d8+70)

Fort +14 (+16 vs. nonmagical disease), **Ref** +8, **Will** +7

Defensive Abilities sweat

OFFENSE

Speed 50 ft.

Melee bite +17 (4d8+13/19–20 plus grab)

Space 15 ft.; **Reach** 15 ft.

Special Attacks capsize, trample (2d6+13, DC 26)

STATISTICS

Str 29, **Dex** 8, **Con** 20, **Int** 2, **Wis** 13, **Cha** 5

Base Atk +10; **CMB** +21 (+25 grapple); **CMD** 30 (34 vs. trip)

Feats Diehard, Endurance, Improved Critical (bite), Improved Initiative, Iron Will, Power Attack, Skill Focus (Perception)

Skills Perception +12, Stealth +2 (+12 underwater), Swim +13;

 Racial Modifiers +10 Stealth underwater

SQ hold breath

ECOLOGY

Environment warm rivers

Organization solitary or bloat (2–8)

Treasure none

The behemoth hippopotamus is a true monster. Standing taller than an elephant, this animal has few enemies in the natural world—even dinosaurs and dire crocodiles avoid fights with them. Making them even more dangerous is the fact that they are practically carnivores—while not above eating plant matter, they devour carrion or foolish creatures that come too close.

Illustration by Jorge Maese

HOUND OF TINDALOS

This gaunt, long-limbed quadruped has huge, soulless eyes and a toothy maw. The lean creature moves with a predatory grace.

HOUND OF TINDALOS	CR 7

XP 3,200

NE Medium outsider (evil, extraplanar)

Init +9; **Senses** darkvision 120 ft.; Perception +18

DEFENSE

AC 20, touch 15, flat-footed 15 (+5 Dex, +5 natural)

hp 85 (10d10+30)

Fort +10, **Ref** +12, **Will** +8

DR 10/magic; **Immune** mind-affecting effects, poison

OFFENSE

Speed 40 ft.

Melee bite +15 (2d6+3), 2 claws +15 (1d8+3)

Special Attacks ripping gaze

Spell-Like Abilities (CL 10th; concentration +13)

Constant—*air walk*

At will—*fog cloud, invisibility, locate creature*

3/day—*dimensional anchor, discern location, greater scrying* (DC 20), *haste, slow* (DC 16)

STATISTICS

Str 17, **Dex** 21, **Con** 16, **Int** 16, **Wis** 21, **Cha** 16

Base Atk +10; **CMB** +13; **CMD** 28 (32 vs. trip)

Feats Blind-Fight, Combat Reflexes, Improved Initiative, Vital Strike, Weapon Finesse

Skills Acrobatics +18 (+22 jump), Intimidate +16, Knowledge (arcana) +16, Knowledge (geography) +13, Knowledge (planes) +16, Perception +18, Sense Motive +18, Stealth +18, Survival +18

Languages Aklo

SQ angled entry, otherworldly mind

ECOLOGY

Environment any

Organization solitary or pack (2–12)

Treasure none

SPECIAL ABILITIES

Angled Entry (Su) Hounds of Tindalos move through the dimensions in ways other creatures cannot comprehend. They may use *greater teleport* (self only) once per round as a swift action and *plane shift* (self only) 3/day as a standard action (caster level 10th). A hound of Tindalos can use these powers anywhere, but its destination point must be adjacent to a fixed angle or corner in the physical environment, such as a wall, floor, or ceiling (as determined by the GM); temporary angles created by cloth, flesh, or small items are not sufficient. It cannot use these abilities to enter curved architecture or open outdoor environments.

Otherworldly Mind (Ex) Any non-outsider attempting to read the thoughts of a hound of Tindalos or communicate with it telepathically takes 5d6 points of nonlethal damage and must make a DC 18 Will save or become confused for 2d4 rounds. This is a mind-affecting effect. The save DC is Charisma-based.

Ripping Gaze (Su) 5d6 slashing damage, 30 feet, Fortitude DC 18 negates. A creature that succeeds on its save is immune to that hound's gaze for 24 hours. Damage caused by a ripping gaze can be defeated by damage reduction, but it bypasses DR/magic and slashing. The save DC is Charisma-based.

Hounds of Tindalos are otherworldly predators from beyond the bounds of known reality, usually appearing only when summoned by reckless spellcasters. Little is known about their nature outside of blood-spattered notes and deranged writings of the nearly insane survivors of their attacks. Although possessed of great cunning and cruel intellect, the hounds show no evidence of understanding or communicating with mortals. They enter the physical world on their own in pursuit of those who have trodden too much the netherways beyond time and reality—time travelers (be it physical travel or simply divinatory glimpses forward or backward in time) and creatures that teleport without regard to how this movement impacts subtle magical currents in the multiverse particularly draw their interest.

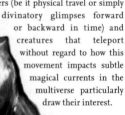

HOWLER

This vile predator has a hide as thick and tough as leather.
Wicked ebony quills run from its head, tail, and back.

HOWLER	CR 3	

XP 800

CE Large outsider (chaotic, evil, extraplanar)

Init +6; **Senses** darkvision 60 ft.; Perception +13

DEFENSE

AC 15, touch 11, flat-footed 13 (+2 Dex, +4 natural, –1 size)

hp 37 (5d10+10)

Fort +6, **Ref** +6, **Will** +3

Defensive Abilities quill defense

OFFENSE

Speed 60 ft.

Melee bite +8 (1d8+4), quills +3 (1d4+2 plus pain)

Space 10 ft.; **Reach** 5 ft.

Special Attacks howl

STATISTICS

Str 18, **Dex** 15, **Con** 15, **Int** 6, **Wis** 14, **Cha** 11

Base Atk +5; **CMB** +10; **CMD** 22

Feats Combat Reflexes, Improved Initiative, Skill Focus (Perception)

Skills Acrobatics +10 (+22 jump), Climb +12, Perception +13, Stealth +6

Languages Abyssal (cannot speak)

ECOLOGY

Environment any land (Abyss)

Organization solitary or pack (2–4)

Treasure incidental

SPECIAL ABILITIES

Howl (Su) A howler's constant howling is a grating, exhausting baying that can drive listeners insane. All beings other than outsiders within 120 feet of a howling howler must succeed on a DC 12 Will save or become cursed by the creature's howl. Once a creature becomes cursed in this way, she takes no additional penalty for being exposed to additional howlers' howls until the current howler curse is lifted. This is a sonic mind-affecting effect. The save DC is Charisma-based.

Howler Howl: Curse—howl; *save* Will DC 12 negates; *frequency* 1/hour; *effect* 1 Wis damage; *cure* 1 save.

Pain (Ex) Whenever a creature takes damage from a howler's quill attack or its quill defense, that creature must make a successful DC 14 Reflex save or one quill breaks off in its flesh, causing the target to become sickened until all embedded quills are removed. Removing one quill requires a DC 15 Heal check made as a full-round action. For every 5 by which the check is exceeded, one additional quill can be removed. On a failed check, a quill is still removed, but the process deals 1d4+1 points of damage to the victim. The save DC is Dexterity-based.

Quill Defense (Ex) Any creature that strikes a howler with a non-reach melee weapon, unarmed strike, or natural weapon takes 1d4+1 points of piercing damage from the howler's quills and suffers from the howler's pain attack.

The howler is a native to the Abyss, an Outer Plane where madness is the norm and cruelty is expected and often rewarded. The howler prowls these Abyssal realms, serving the role of a hungry predator like a lion or tiger, save for the fact that the typical howler is much more intelligent than a big cat. Worse, howlers have little interest in eating their prey—they need not feed to live, but rather enjoy the process of stalking, mauling, and killing living creatures. In a way, the act of inflicting intense pain and madness upon mortal life is what fills a howler's life instead of the desire to feed.

The howler's mane of razor-sharp quills makes it a poor choice of mount for most creatures, but it serves quite well as a guardian or sentinel—especially for outsiders, who may not enjoy the creature's constant howling, but aren't adversely affected by the supernatural sounds. When a howler sees prey, the tenor of its howls changes— howlers cannot speak, but they can use their howls to communicate quite a bit of information if required. They understand the Abyssal tongue, and when serving demons as guardians, their howls can not only alert their masters to the presence of intruders, but also to their number, appearance, and weaknesses.

A howler is about the size of a tiger—12 feet from snout to tail and weighing 6,000 pounds. They are normally pale in color, with darker quills and milky eyes.

Illustration by Tyler Walpole

159

IFRIT

This muscular, fiery-skinned man has flaming hair and spotted horns upon his brow.

IFRIT	CR 1/2

XP 200

Ifrit sorcerer 1

N Medium outsider (native)

Init +3; **Senses** darkvision 60 ft.; Perception −2

DEFENSE

AC 13, touch 13, flat-footed 10 (+3 Dex)

hp 8 (1d6+2)

Fort +1, **Ref** +3, **Will** +0

Resist fire 5

OFFENSE

Speed 30 ft.

Melee scimitar +0 (1d6/18–20)

Illustration by Florian Stitz

Bloodline Spell-Like Abilities (CL 1st; concentration +4)

6/day—elemental ray (1d6 fire)

Ifrit Spell-Like Abilities (CL 1st; concentration +4)

1/day—burning hands (DC 14)

Sorcerer Spells Known (CL 1st; concentration +4)

1st (4/day)—burning hands (DC 15), mage armor

0 (at will)—acid splash, detect magic, flare (DC 14), prestidigitation

Bloodline elemental (fire)

STATISTICS

Str 10, **Dex** 16, **Con** 12, **Int** 13, **Wis** 6, **Cha** 17

Base Atk +0; **CMB** +0; **CMD** 13

Feats Eschew Materials[B], Martial Weapon Proficiency (scimitar)

Skills Bluff +7, Knowledge (arcana) +5, Spellcraft +5

Languages Common, Gnome, Ignan

SQ bloodline arcana, fire affinity

ECOLOGY

Environment any land

Organization solitary, pair, or gang (3–5)

Treasure NPC gear (scimitar, other treasure)

SPECIAL ABILITIES

Fire Affinity (Ex) Ifrit sorcerers with the elemental (fire) bloodline treat their Charisma score as 2 points higher for all sorcerer spells and class abilities. Ifrit spellcasters with the Fire domain use their domain powers and spells at +1 caster level.

Ifrits are humans whose ancestry includes beings of elemental fire, such as efreet. Ifrits have pointed ears, red or mottled horns on the brow, and hair that flickers and waves as if it were aflame.

All ifrits are at some level pyromaniacs. Adoring fire in all its forms, they tend to be passionate and quick to action, with a predilection for striking first in any conflict—a trait which keeps them alive but doesn't make them a lot of friends. Ifrits generally seek out the company of either less-powerful minions who can be browbeaten into following orders, or calm, cool individuals who can balance the ifrits out.

IFRIT CHARACTERS

Ifrits are defined by class levels—they do not possess racial Hit Dice. Ifrits have the following racial traits.

+2 Dexterity, +2 Charisma, −2 Wisdom: Ifrits are passionate and quick, but also impetuous and destructive.

Darkvision: Ifrits can see in the dark up to 60 feet.

Spell-Like Ability: Burning hands 1/day (caster level equals the ifrit's total Hit Dice).

Energy Resistance: Ifrits have fire resistance 5.

Fire Affinity: See above.

Languages: Ifrits begin play speaking Common and Ignan. Ifrits with high Intelligence scores can choose any of the following bonus languages: Aquan, Auran, Dwarven, Elven, Gnome, Halfling, and Terran.

Inevitable

Originally invented and forged in the Outer Planes by the axiomites (see page 36), inevitables are living machines whose sole purpose is to seek out and destroy agents of chaos wherever they can.

During the height of the first war between law and chaos, while the Outer Planes were still forming from the raw chaos of the primal reality, inevitables were constructed by the axiomites as an unflinching army—soldiers powerful and devoted enough to march on the madness-inducing hordes of proteans who sought to unmake reality and return it all to the primal chaos they so adored. While this war has long since cooled to a simmer, and the reality of the Outer Planes is now not so easily threatened by the entropic influence of the proteans and their home plane, the defense of the axiomites' home plane remains the inevitables' primary goal. Despite the proteans' subsequent adaptation and study of how best to make themselves more resistant to the inevitables' attacks, these constructed soldiers remain imposingly effective.

Today, many inevitables—almost all of those encountered on the Material Plane—pursue a new aspect of their original mission: tracking down those who flagrantly flout the forces of law and redeeming them or, more often, eliminating the threat they present to the ordered nature of the multiverse. Matched on the side of chaos by the manipulative imentesh proteans, new inevitables awake to find themselves locked in a proxy war, knowing that losing the Material Plane to chaos would place their masters in a dangerous position.

Genderless, incorruptible, and caring nothing for power or personal advancement, inevitables are cunning and valiant shock troops in the service of law. Though they regularly interact with their creator race on their home plane, they have no society of their own, and are almost always encountered singly on other planes, each more than capable of pursuing its own mission. These individual crusades range from enforcing important or high-profile contracts and laws to forcibly correcting those mortals who would seek to cheat death. How they deal with the guilty varies according to the transgression: sometimes this means a simple *geas* or *mark of justice* to ensure that the target works to right his wrongs or never again strays from the path of law, but just as often an offense worthy of an inevitable's attention is severe enough that only immediate execution will suffice. Such decisions are not always popular—for the kindly priest who transcends mortality and the freedom fighter who battles the evil-yet-rightful king are every bit as guilty as grave-robbing necromancers and demon-worshipers—but the inevitables are always just, and few dare stand in the way of their judgment. Those inevitables who have completed a given mission often wander through whatever society they find themselves in, seeking other lawbreakers worthy of their ministrations. Brave souls with a worthy cause are always welcome to approach an inevitable and present their case, but should be wary of invoking the help of such powerful, single-minded beings—for an inevitable may not see the situation the same way they do, and though all inevitables do their best to preserve innocent life, they're not above sacrificing a few allies or innocents in an effort to bring down a greater villain.

Physically, inevitables often have humanoid forms or aspects, but their bodies appear somewhere between clockwork constructs and fine statues in the greatest classical tradition. Constructed of stone, adamantine, and even more precious materials, each inevitable is brought to sentience in the axiomites' forges already programmed with the details of its first target. Though they know that all beings outside of the lawful planes harbor chaos in their hearts, inevitables also understand that such conflicted creatures may yet be forces for law as much as for chaos, and thus overlook all but the most flagrant offenses. The most commonly recognized types of inevitables are as follows.

Arbiters: Scouts and diplomats, often assigned to wizards as familiars in the hopes of directing such individuals to the cause of law.

Kolyaruts: Cloaked and stealthy humanoid warriors who track and punish those who break contracts.

Lhaksharuts: Juggernauts who search for permanent breaches and links between planes and invasions from one dimension to another.

Maruts: Towering beings of stone, steel, and storm who bring a fitting end to those mortals who try to cheat death in attempts to live forever.

Zelekhuts: Winged, centaur-like constructs who track down those who flee just and legal punishment, returning them to their rightful judges or carrying out the sentence themselves.

PRIMAL INEVITABLES

While the lhaksharuts are generally thought of as the most powerful caste of inevitable, there exist others of even greater skill and strength—these are known as the primal inevitables. These goliaths were among the first weapons of war forged by the axiomites to fight the protean menace—the methods to create more have long been lost to the axiomites, and those few primals who remain alive to this day have become legendary. None have been encountered in living memory, but the possibility of a primal's emergence is enough to give the proteans second thoughts when ideas of invading the inevitables' home plane arise.

Inevitable, Arbiter

A sphere of bronze and copper set with a single eye, this winged creature has two clawed hands, one of which clutches a knife.

ARBITER	CR 2

XP 600

LN Tiny outsider (extraplanar, inevitable, lawful)

Init +3; **Senses** darkvision 60 ft., *detect chaos*, low-light vision; Perception +5

DEFENSE

AC 16, touch 15, flat-footed 13 (+3 Dex, +1 natural, +2 size)

hp 15 (2d10+4); regeneration 2 (chaotic)

Fort +5, **Ref** +3, **Will** +3

Defensive Abilities constant vigilance, constructed; **SR** 13

OFFENSE

Speed 20 ft., fly 50 ft. (average)

Melee short sword +7 (1d3/19–20)

Space 2-1/2 ft.; **Reach** 0 ft.

Special Attacks electrical burst

Spell-Like Abilities (CL 2nd; concentration +4)

Constant—*detect chaos*

3/day—*command* (DC 13), *make whole*, *protection from chaos*

1/week—*commune* (CL 12th, 6 questions)

STATISTICS

Str 11, **Dex** 16, **Con** 14, **Int** 11, **Wis** 11, **Cha** 14

Base Atk +2; **CMB** +3; **CMD** 13

Feats Flyby Attack, Weapon Finesse[B]

Skills Diplomacy +7, Fly +12, Knowledge (planes) +5, Perception +5, Sense Motive +5, Stealth +16

Languages truespeech

SQ locate inevitable

ECOLOGY

Environment any

Organization solitary, pair, or flock (3–14)

Treasure none

SPECIAL ABILITIES

Constant Vigilance (Su) An arbiter gains a +4 bonus to recognize and disbelieve illusions created by creatures with the chaotic subtype or possessing the chaotic descriptor.

Electrical Burst (Ex) An arbiter can release electrical energy from its body in a 10-foot-radius burst that deals 3d6 electricity damage (DC 13 Reflex half). Immediately following such a burst, the arbiter becomes stunned for 24 hours. The save DC is Constitution-based.

Locate Inevitable (Su) An arbiter can always sense the direction of the nearest non-arbiter inevitable on the plane, the better to help it report back to its superiors. It cannot sense the range to this inevitable.

Stealthy, observant, and frequently persuasive, arbiter inevitables are the scouts and diplomats of the inevitable race. Found throughout the multiverse in courts and on battlefields, arbiters keep a close eye on the forces of chaos and do their best to keep the lawful from straying, while simultaneously winning over the hearts and minds of those who might yet be saved. Though their assorted abilities make them extremely useful, arbiters see themselves less as servants than as advisers and counselors, preferring to ride around on their summoners' shoulders and help guide their "partners" on the path of law. They detest being summoned by chaotic individuals, and when teamed with such a creature, they aren't above using Diplomacy to try to influence the summoner's friends or refusing to undertake actions that seem contrary to their programming.

An arbiter who comes across evidence of a significant insurgence of chaos upon a given plane does everything in its power to rally its allies against the dangerous instability, and in situations that are clearly beyond its ability to handle, it may refuse to continue onward until the group agrees to help it reach the nearest greater inevitable and make a full report, or else may travel to Utopia itself and present its urgent information in person.

Arbiters typically bear the shapes of tiny clockwork spheres with shiny metal wings. Generally peaceful unless combating true creatures of chaos, arbiters prefer to cast *protection from chaos* on their allies and use *command* to make opponents drop their weapons and run. Their most powerful weapon, the ability to release their internal energy as a deadly burst, is reserved for dire need and battles of the utmost service to law, as the resulting period of darkness while they're powered down is the only thing that seems to truly scare the tiny automatons.

An arbiter inevitable can serve a spellcaster as a familiar. Such a spellcaster must be lawful neutral, must be at least caster level 7th, and must have the Improved Familiar feat. Arbiter inevitables measure 1 foot in diameter but are surprisingly heavy, weighing 60 pounds. Their ability to fly on metal wings is as much a supernatural ability as a physical one.

INEVITABLE, KOLYARUT

Beneath its cloak, this man-shaped creature appears to be part statue and part metallic machine.

KOLYARUT	CR 12

XP 19,200
LN Medium outsider (extraplanar, inevitable, lawful)
Init +8; **Senses** darkvision 60 ft., low-light vision; Perception +22

DEFENSE

AC 26, touch 14, flat-footed 22 (+4 Dex, +12 natural)
hp 158 (12d10+92); regeneration 5 (chaotic)
Fort +14, **Ref** +10, **Will** +11
Defensive Abilities constructed; **DR** 10/chaotic; **SR** 23

OFFENSE

Speed 30 ft.
Melee +2 *bastard sword* +20/+15/+10 (1d10+8/19–20), slam +13 (2d6+3) or
2 slams +18 (2d6+6)
Spell-Like Abilities (CL 12th; concentration +15)
At will—*discern lies* (DC 17), *disguise self*, *enervation*, *fear* (DC 17), *hold person* (DC 16), *invisibility* (self only), *locate creature*, *suggestion* (DC 16), *vampiric touch*
3/day—*hold monster* (DC 18), *mark of justice*, quickened *suggestion* (DC 16)
1/week—*geas/quest*

STATISTICS

Str 22, **Dex** 19, **Con** 23, **Int** 10, **Wis** 17, **Cha** 16
Base Atk +12; **CMB** +18; **CMD** 32
Feats Alertness, Combat Casting, Combat Reflexes, Improved Initiative, Lightning Reflexes, Quicken Spell-Like Ability (*suggestion*)
Skills Diplomacy +22, Disguise +22, Knowledge (planes) +15, Perception +22, Sense Motive +22, Survival +18; **Racial Modifiers** +4 Diplomacy, +4 Disguise
Languages truespeech

ECOLOGY

Environment any
Organization solitary, pair, or inquisition (3–6)
Treasure standard (+2 *bastard sword*, other treasure)

Kolyaruts are enforcers of bargains, traveling to the very edges of the planes in order to punish oathbreakers and see that contracts are kept. They care little for the terms of the agreements in question, only that promises are fulfilled, debts are paid, and balance is maintained.

Least conspicuous of the inevitables, even in their natural form, kolyaruts are the size of tall humans, though they weigh far more because of their composition.

Capable of using both *invisibility* and *disguise self* to pass completely unnoticed through humanoid lands, kolyaruts most frequently appear as cloaked warriors bearing finely crafted bastard swords, allowing others to chalk up any metallic noises to the clanking of hidden armor until the moment when they pull back their hoods and let their quarries look upon their mechanical faces, understanding only too late the nature of the mysterious strangers.

Perhaps because their missions can be the murkiest and most open to interpretation, kolyaruts are by far the most talkative of the inevitables, naturally possessing a courtly grace and an encyclopedic knowledge of social customs, which they use both to assist them in gathering information on their targets and in issuing challenges (or executing dignified sentences) on the battlefield. Though naturally as solitary as their kindred, kolyaruts are occasionally content to let members of other races tag along and assist them in achieving shared goals, though they have little problem abandoning or even exploiting these "comrades" if it brings them closer to fulfilling their mission.

Illustration by Tyler Walpole

INEVITABLE, LHAKSHARUT

This six-armed creature appears to be made of stone. Its lower torso is a collection of whirring rings of metal.

LHAKSHARUT	CR 20

XP 307,200

LN Huge outsider (extraplanar, inevitable, lawful)

Init +5; **Senses** darkvision 60 ft., *detect chaos, detect magic*, low-light vision, *true seeing*; Perception +34

Aura *shield of law* (DC 23)

DEFENSE

AC 36, touch 18, flat-footed 35 (+4 deflection, +1 Dex, +5 insight, +18 natural, −2 size)

hp 337 (22d10+216); regeneration 10 (chaotic)

Fort +25, **Ref** +12, **Will** +22

Defensive Abilities constructed; **DR** 15/chaotic; **Immune** energy spells; **SR** 31

OFFENSE

Speed fly 60 ft. (perfect)

Melee *+2 wounding spear* +32/+27/+22/+17 (3d6+17/×3 plus 1 bleed), *+2 wounding longsword* +32 (3d6+12/19–20 plus 1 bleed), *+2 wounding morningstar* +32 (3d6+12 plus 1 bleed) or 4 slams +30 (2d8+10)

Ranged 2 energy bolts +21 (10d6 energy)

Space 15 ft.; **Reach** 15 ft.

Special Attacks cunning reflexes, multiweapon mastery, wounding weapons

Spell-Like Abilities (CL 22th; concentration +27)

Constant—*detect chaos, detect magic, shield of law* (DC 23), *true seeing*

At will—*dispel magic, greater teleport* (self plus 50 lbs. of objects only), *sending*

3/day—*dictum* (DC 22), *dimensional anchor* (DC 19), *dimensional lock* (DC 23), *disintegrate* (DC 21), *dismissal* (DC 20), *greater scrying* (DC 22), *plane shift* (DC 20), *wall of force*

1/day—*imprisonment* (DC 24)

STATISTICS

Str 31, **Dex** 13, **Con** 26, **Int** 14, **Wis** 21, **Cha** 20

Base Atk +22; **CMB** +34; **CMD** 50 (can't be tripped)

Feats Blind-Fight, Combat Expertise, Combat Reflexes, Greater Bull Rush, Greater Vital Strike, Improved Bull Rush, Improved Disarm, Improved Initiative, Improved Vital Strike, Power Attack, Vital Strike

Skills Fly +30, Intimidate +30, Knowledge (arcana) +24, Knowledge (geography) +24, Knowledge (planes) +27, Perception +34, Sense Motive +30, Spellcraft +24; **Racial Modifiers** +4 Perception

Languages truespeech

SQ perfect prediction

ECOLOGY

Environment any

Organization solitary

Treasure double (*+2 longsword, +2 spear, +2 morningstar*, other treasure)

SPECIAL ABILITIES

Cunning Reflexes (Ex) A lhaksharut uses its Wisdom modifier, rather than its Dexterity modifier, to determine how many additional attacks of opportunity it gains with the Combat Reflexes feat. For most lhaksharut inevitables, this benefit equates to 5 additional attacks of opportunity per round.

Energy Bolt (Su) A lhaksharut can fire bolts of elemental energy from two of its six arms—it never wields weapons in these hands. These attacks have a range increment of 100 feet and deal 10d6 energy damage of the inevitable's choice (acid, cold, electricity, or fire, chosen for each bolt as it is thrown). It can throw two bolts of energy as a standard action, and cannot attack with these hands when it makes weapon or slam attacks with its other limbs.

Immunity to Energy Spells (Ex) A lhaksharut is immune to any spell or spell-like ability with the acid, cold, electricity, fire, or sonic descriptor that allows spell resistance.

Multiweapon Mastery (Ex) A lhaksharut never takes penalties on its attack rolls when fighting with multiple weapons.

Perfect Prediction (Su) A lhaksharut gains an insight bonus to AC equal to its Wisdom bonus.

Wounding Weapons (Su) Any weapon wielded by a lhaksharut gains the *wounding* weapon quality as long as it remains in the creature's grasp.

A typical lhaksharut is a six-armed construct that appears to be made of a mix of metals and stone. Where a human would have legs, it instead possesses a complex orb of spinning rings similar in shape to an orrery—it is this whirling machine that grants the lhaksharut the ability to fly. Though a lhaksharut has huge, metal wings, they serve as little more than stabilizers when it's in flight. Four of the construct's arms end in functional hands that it normally uses to carry a mix of weapons. The lhaksharut's lower two arms hold large, flaming metal spheres in their hands—it uses these spheres to generate elemental bolts of energy that it can hurl great distances to damage foes.

Lhaksharuts are tasked with maintaining the separation between different planes of reality, especially the elemental planes. They do not concern themselves with petty trespasses by visitors from one plane to another, nor even the occasional creation of a pocket plane or hijacking of a chunk of one reality to serve as a base within another. What does trouble a lhaksharut is anything that represents a permanent link between planes, or an effort by the denizens of one plane to invade and conquer another. They often find themselves in conflict with the machinations of powerful outsiders who seek to create beachheads on other planes to serve as launching pads for massive incursions.

When possible, a lhaksharut enforces the separation of planes through the simple expedient of smashing any device that creates a dangerous breach, or killing any creature that seems determined to mix or blend realities. The inevitable does not care why such infractions occur, and is often deaf to any excuse suggesting even a temporary linking of planes is a good idea. However, while singled-mined, a lhaksharut is not mindless or incapable of reason. They are emotionless, but can be negotiated with if a problem cannot be solved by smashing and killing violators.

Rarely, a lhaksharut can even be convinced that maintaining a planar link is important enough to let the gate stand, if only temporarily. In such cases, the lhaksharut always volunteers to guard the portal until the time comes to shut it down. These arrangements must include a detailed explanation on how a desired course of action will directly lead to meeting the lhaksharut's goal. Only when facing the most overwhelmingly powerful foe does a lhaksharut agree to assist in a task not related to its primary function, and then only to win allies to help it achieve success in an area where the lhaksharut has already met with failure. Even if convinced to undertake such an alliance, a lhaksharut is likely to insist its mission be accomplished first. A creature of pure order, a lhaksharut is incapable of defaulting on a promise made in good faith, but it is aware that not all creatures are so bound. If for some reason the needs of its allies must be put first, a lhaksharut insists on guarantees that its allies will meet their commitments to it once they have what they want.

In combat, a lhaksharut uses its speed and mobility to get close to targets. A lhaksharut sees groups as imperfect machines, and knows that the best way to overcome them is to disrupt their smooth functioning. While creatures able to directly harm the inevitable are dealt with if necessary, it much prefers to first eliminate healers, scouts, and shield-bearers before tackling powerful fighters or spellcasters. A lhaksharut cannot be taunted or baited into changing its course of action—it is completely emotionless and only cares about the efficiency of its battle plan. It also fights without care for its own survival, trusting that either its regeneration will restore it to life, or a new inevitable will be created to replace it.

When unaware of a threat to the sanctity of the division of the planes, and not threatened, a lhaksharut can be a surprisingly good conversationalist. They are as likely to be found floating through a void as maintaining any kind of stronghold. Lhaksharuts are aware that the domains they wish to patrol are too vast to be directly viewed with any efficiency. Some lhaksharuts thus forge networks of informants who can patrol the many planes, and send word to the inevitable to alert it of any apparent breaches. The constructs have no other need for the treasure that they gather from transgressors, and sometimes even pay for tips that might lead to a planar infraction. Anyone who might prove to be a valuable informant is treated with respect, and may even be able to gain insights into the planes from the lhaksharut's vast knowledge on the subject, as long as questions never wander into the dangerous territory of combining two planes.

INEVITABLE, MARUT

This humanoid is mostly hidden behind plates of elaborate golden armor, the spaces in between revealing flesh of black stone.

MARUT	CR 15

XP 51,200

LN Large outsider (extraplanar, inevitable, lawful)

Init +3; **Senses** darkvision 60 ft., low-light vision, *true seeing*; Perception +26

DEFENSE

AC 30, touch 13, flat-footed 26 (+3 Dex, +1 dodge, +17 natural, –1 size)

hp 214 (16d10+126); regeneration 10 (chaotic)

Fort +16, **Ref** +8, **Will** +13

Defensive Abilities constructed; **DR** 15/chaotic; **SR** 26

OFFENSE

Speed 30 ft.

Melee 2 slams +27 (2d6+12 plus 3d6 electricity or sonic and blindness or deafness)

Space 10 ft.; **Reach** 10 ft.

Special Attacks fists of lightning and thunder

Spell-Like Abilities (CL 16th; concentration +23)

  Constant—*air walk, true seeing*

  At will—*dimension door, fear* (DC 21), *greater command* (DC 22), *greater dispel magic, mass inflict light wounds* (DC 22), *locate creature*

  1/day—*chain lightning* (DC 23), *circle of death* (DC 23), *mark of justice, wall of force*

  1/week—*earthquake* (DC 25), *geas/quest, plane shift* (DC 22)

STATISTICS

Str 35, **Dex** 16, **Con** 23, **Int** 12, **Wis** 17, **Cha** 24

Base Atk +16; **CMB** +29; **CMD** 43

Feats Ability Focus (fists of lightning and thunder), Awesome Blow, Combat Casting, Dodge, Improved Bull Rush, Improved Vital Strike, Power Attack, Vital Strike

Skills Diplomacy +26, Intimidate +26, Knowledge (planes) +20, Knowledge (religion) +20, Perception +26, Sense Motive +22, Survival +22; **Racial Modifiers** +4 Perception

Languages truespeech

ECOLOGY

Environment any

Organization solitary, pair, or patrol (3–5)

Treasure none

SPECIAL ABILITIES

Fists of Lightning and Thunder (Su) A marut's fists strike with the power of a thunderstorm. For any given slam attack, a marut can choose whether that attack uses lightning or thunder. A lightning attack deals an additional 3d6 points of electricity damage, and the resulting flash blinds the target for 2d6 rounds (Fortitude DC 26 negates the blindness). A thunder attack deals an additional 3d6 points of sonic damage, and the resulting thunderclap deafens the target for 2d6 rounds (Fortitude DC 26 negates the deafness). The save DCs are Constitution-based.

Behemoths of onyx and golden armor, maruts shake the ground when they walk, each thunderous step ringing a death knell for those they've come to take. Rarely seeming to hurry, a marut's onslaught is deliberate, purposeful, and relentless. Its quarry may impede it or flee, running for decades or centuries, but from the initial meeting onward, the target must always look over its shoulder with the knowledge that, like death itself, the marut is ever at its heels, slowly but surely approaching, bringing balance through inevitable oblivion.

Maruts primarily target those mortal souls who have artificially extended their lifespans beyond what is feasible for their race, such as liches and other powerful magic users. Extraordinary but natural means of cheating death are sometimes also punished, such as the magistrate who murders an entire starving town to save himself, or those who foresee their own deaths via divination magic and are therefore able to avoid them.

Although they are capable of speaking eloquently in any language, and frequently gather vast amounts of information from those who are intimidated by their mere presence, maruts rarely engage in conversation or strategic alliances with mortals. Even on the battlefield, the juggernauts prefer to remain silent, knowing that their targets are already aware of their own transgressions and that all mortals secretly harbor dreams of immortality.

INEVITABLE, ZELEKHUT

This creature looks like a mechanical centaur. Golden, clockwork wings sprout from its back, and its arms end in barbed chains.

ZELEKHUT	CR 9

XP 6,400

LN Large outsider (extraplanar, inevitable, lawful)

Init +9; **Senses** darkvision 60 ft., low-light vision, *true seeing*; Perception +20

DEFENSE

AC 24, touch 15, flat-footed 18 (+5 Dex, +1 dodge, +9 natural, −1 size)

hp 115 (10d10+60); regeneration 5 (chaotic)

Fort +10, **Ref** +8, **Will** +10

Defensive Abilities constructed; **DR** 10/chaotic; **SR** 20

OFFENSE

Speed 50 ft., fly 60 ft. (average)

Melee 2 chains +17 (2d6+7 plus 1d6 electricity and trip)

Space 10 ft.; **Reach** 10 ft.

Spell-Like Abilities (CL 10th; concentration +13)

Constant—*true seeing*

At will—*clairaudience/clairvoyance, dimensional anchor, dispel magic, fear* (DC 17), *hold person* (DC 16), *locate creature*

3/day—*hold monster* (DC 18), *mark of justice*

1/week—*lesser geas* (DC 17)

STATISTICS

Str 25, **Dex** 20, **Con** 16, **Int** 10, **Wis** 17, **Cha** 17

Base Atk +10; **CMB** +18; **CMD** 34 (38 vs. trip)

Feats Dodge, Improved Initiative, Mobility, Weapon Focus (chain), Vital Strike

Skills Acrobatics +18 (+26 jump), Diplomacy +16, Fly +16, Perception +20, Sense Motive +20, Survival +16; **Racial Modifiers** +4 Perception, +4 Sense Motive

Languages truespeech

SQ chains

ECOLOGY

Environment any land (lawful plane)

Organization solitary

Treasure none

SPECIAL ABILITIES

Chains (Ex) A zelekhut's arms end in long lengths of barbed metal. These chains deal slashing damage and 1d6 points of electricity damage with each hit.

Zelekhuts are bounty hunters and executioners all rolled into one. They seek out those beings who continually evade justice—either through active flight, or through power and station—and bring law and justice to the multiverse's most notorious fugitives and criminals.

Ironically, while zelekhuts are implacable and unrelenting in their duty, they have little interest in passing judgment of their own, a fact that often confuses other races. Rather, a zelekhut is content to enforce the laws of any given society, and while it might hunt a condemned serial killer or notorious thief across half a dozen planes, it will not shift a single hoof to capture a corrupt ruler whose offenses are 10 times worse, so long as the atrocities are within her technical rights as ruler. All zelekhuts understand that laws can and must differ from place to place, and it is not the zelekhut's job to moralize, merely to track down those who seek to flee their punishment.

JABBERWOCK

This dragon has a long neck and terrible claws. The beast shrieks and babbles, thrashing its tail and wings in a violent manner.

JABBERWOCK	CR 23

XP 819,200
CE Huge dragon (air, fire)
Init +5; **Senses** blindsight 120 ft., darkvision 120 ft., low-light vision, scent, *true seeing*; Perception +38
Aura frightful presence (120 ft., DC 31)

DEFENSE

AC 40, touch 14, flat-footed 34 (+5 Dex, +1 dodge, +26 natural, –2 size)
hp 455 (26d12+286); fast healing 15
Fort +26, **Ref** +20, **Will** +24
DR 15/*vorpal*; **Immune** fire, paralysis, sleep; **Resist** acid 30, electricity 30, sonic 30; **SR** 31
Weaknesses fear of *vorpal* weapons, vulnerable to cold

OFFENSE

Speed 40 ft., fly 80 ft. (poor)
Melee bite +37 (4d8+19/19–20/×3), 2 claws +37 (3d6+13/19–20 plus grab), tail slap +32 (2d8+19), 2 wings +32 (1d8+6)
Ranged 2 eye rays +29 touch (15d6 fire/19–20 plus burn)
Space 15 ft.; **Reach** 15 ft.
Special Attacks burble, burn (6d6, DC 34), eye rays, whiffling

STATISTICS

Str 37, **Dex** 20, **Con** 33, **Int** 12, **Wis** 29, **Cha** 26
Base Atk +26; **CMB** +41 (+45 grapple); **CMD** 57
Feats Awesome Blow, Bleeding Critical, Critical Focus, Dodge, Flyby Attack, Improved Bull Rush, Improved Critical (bite, claws, eye rays), Mobility, Power Attack, Spring Attack, Vital Strike
Skills Acrobatics +31 (+35 jump), Escape Artist +31, Fly +26, Intimidate +37, Knowledge (nature) +30, Perception +38, Sense Motive +38
Languages Aklo, Common, Draconic, Gnome, Sylvan
SQ planar acclimation

ECOLOGY

Environment any forests
Organization solitary
Treasure triple

SPECIAL ABILITIES

Burble (Su) A jabberwock can burble once every 1d4 rounds as a standard action. This blast of strange noises and shouted nonsense in the various languages known to the jabberwock (and invariably some languages it doesn't know) affects all creatures within a 60-foot-radius spread—these creatures must make a DC 31 Will save or become confused for 1d4 rounds. Alternatively, the jabberwock can focus its burble attack to create a 60-foot line of sonic energy that deals 20d6 points of sonic damage (DC 31 Reflex save for half). The confusion effect is mind-affecting; both are sonic effects. The save DC is Charisma-based.

Damage Reduction (Ex) A jabberwock's damage reduction can be bypassed only by weapons that possess the *vorpal* weapon enhancement.

Eye Rays (Su) The jabberwock can project beams of fire from its eyes as a ranged touch attack as a standard action, with a range increment of 60 feet. It projects two beams, and can target different creatures with these beams if it wishes as long as both targets are within 30 feet of each other. A creature that takes damage from an eye beam suffers burn.

Fear of Vorpal Weapons (Ex) A jabberwock knows that a *vorpal* weapon can kill it swiftly. As soon as it takes damage from a *vorpal* weapon, a jabberwock becomes shaken for 1 round. If it is hit by a critical threat from a *vorpal* weapon, whether or not the critical hit is confirmed, the jabberwock is staggered for 1 round.

Planar Acclimation (Ex) A jabberwock is always considered to be on its home plane, regardless of what plane it finds itself upon. It never gains the extraplanar subtype.

Whiffling (Ex) A jabberwock's wings and violent motions create a significant amount of wind whenever it makes a full attack action. These winds surround the monster to a radius of 30 feet, and are treated as severe winds—ranged attacks take a –4 penalty when targeting a jabberwock while it is whiffling, and Medium creatures must make a DC 10 Strength check to approach the creature. Small or smaller creatures in this area that fail a DC 15 Strength check are blown away. See page 439 of the *Pathfinder RPG Core Rulebook* for further details on the effects of severe winds.

The jabberwock is a true creature of legend—a subject of poetry, song, and myth in many cultures. It is known to be a devastating creature in combat whose arrival presages times of ruin and violence; these stories also tell of the creature's fear of the tools some say were created in ancient times for the sole purpose of defeating them—*vorpal* weapons. A jabberwock is 35 feet tall and weighs 8,000 pounds.

The jabberwock is not a creature of the Material Plane, but one from the primal world of the fey. It comes from a region of reality where life is more robust, where emotions are more potent, and where dreams and nightmares can come alive. Even in such incredible realms, though, the jabberwock is a creature to be feared. It belongs to a category of powerful creatures whose shapes and types run the gamut of possibility—a group known collectively as the "Tane." Of the Tane, the jabberwock is said to be the most powerful, but the others in this grouping are far from helpless. Said to have been created as goliaths of war and madness, dreamt and stitched into being by the strange gods of this primeval reality, the Tane are as mysterious as they are powerful. Two other creatures of

Illustration by Eric Belisle

the Tane are presented in this book—the sard and the thrasfyr. None of the Tane are lower than CR 16 in power and all possess the planar acclimation special quality, but beyond that, they generally share no specific abilities or characteristics save for their common source in the primal world.

When a jabberwock comes to the Material Plane, it does so to spread destruction and ruin. Typically, the monster seeks out a remote forest lair at least a day's flight from civilization, then emerges from this den once a week to seek out a new place to destroy. It has no true interest in amassing treasure, but often gathers objects of obvious value to bring back to its den in order to encourage heroes to seek it out—to a jabberwock, it makes no difference whether it seeks out things to destroy or lets those things come to it.

Jabberwocks age, eat, drink, and sleep like any living creature, but they do not reproduce in the classic sense of the word. The creation of a new jabberwock—or of any of the Tane, in fact—is regulated by the strange and unknowable godlike entities that dwell in the primeval world. These fey lords create new jabberwocks as they are needed—sometimes varying the exact particulars (see Variant Jabberwocks, below), but always creating a fully formed adult creature. No young jabberwock has ever been encountered as a result.

The strange vulnerability a jabberwock possesses against *vorpal* weapons has long been a matter of intrigue and speculation among scholars. Most believe that, once upon a time, only one jabberwock existed, a creature of such great power that nothing could hurt it. Nothing, that is, save for a legendary sword forged for a mortal hero by a now-forgotten artisan or god. So epic was this battle that it created strange echoes throughout reality, and as a result, these echoes, in the form of the *vorpal* swords and jabberwocks known today, can be found on many worlds.

VARIANT JABBERWOCKS

The notion of a "lesser" jabberwock is something of a misnomer, for even these creatures are powerful foes. A lesser jabberwock is generally a CR 20 version of the typical jabberwock—you can achieve a creature of this power by lowering the typical jabberwock's Hit Dice by 3 and by reducing its ability scores by 4 points each. Alternatively, you can apply the young creature simple template, but bear in mind that such a monster isn't technically any younger than a typical jabberwock.

As creatures from the primal world of the fey, some jabberwocks are as varied as the strange terrains and realms in that primal world, as if these environs have more to do with their manifestation than most scholars suspect. Generally, these changes simply alter the type of damage a jabberwock's eye beams deal and the types of energy it is immune to. A jabberwock from a primeval glacial world would possess eye beams that deal cold damage, while a jabberwock from a storm-lashed world would deal electricity damage with its eye beams. If the nature of a jabberwock's eye beams change, its burn ability changes to match, and it replaces its immunity to fire with immunity to the new energy type (while gaining resist fire 30 in place of the lost immunity to fire).

JELLYFISH, GIANT

The bell of this enormous amber jellyfish is as large as a carriage. A sinister bloom of tentacles dangles and writhes below.

GIANT JELLYFISH	CR 7

XP 3,200

N Large vermin (aquatic)

Init +2; **Senses** darkvision 60 ft.; Perception +0

DEFENSE

AC 11, touch 11, flat-footed 9 (+2 Dex, –1 size)

hp 94 (9d8+54)

Fort +12, **Ref** +5, **Will** +3

Defensive Abilities amorphous; **DR** 10/ piercing or slashing; **Immune** mind-affecting effects

OFFENSE

Speed swim 20 ft.

Melee 4 tentacles +9 (1d6+4 plus poison)

Space 10 ft.; **Reach** 15 ft.

STATISTICS

Str 18, **Dex** 15, **Con** 22, **Int** —, **Wis** 11, **Cha** 1

Base Atk +6; **CMB** +11; **CMD** 23 (can't be tripped)

Skills Swim +12

SQ compression

ECOLOGY

Environment any oceans

Organization solitary, pack (2–5), or bloom (6–12)

Treasure None

SPECIAL ABILITIES

Poison (Ex) Tentacles—injury; *save* Fort DC 17; *frequency* 1/round for 6 rounds; *effect* 1d4 Con; *cure* 2 consecutive saves. The save DC is Constitution based.

Unlike its smaller cousins, the giant jellyfish is an active predator that seeks out prey. Capable of slithering through narrow cracks, a giant jellyfish is a horrifying beast to encounter lurking in the hold of a flooded or sunken ship. Other species of these vermin exist, as summarized on the following table—these variants often have different types of poison or other abilities like translucency or constriction.

Species	CR	Size	HD
Death's head jellyfish	1	Small	2
Crimson jellyfish	4	Medium	5
Sapphire jellyfish	11	Huge	12
Vampire jellyfish	14	Gargantuan	16
Whaler jellyfish	17	Colossal	20

JELLYFISH SWARM

All but invisible in the water, this foul swarm of fist-sized jellyfish wriggles and writhes, a virtual wall of stinging tentacles.

JELLYFISH SWARM	CR 6

XP 2,400

N Diminutive vermin (aquatic, swarm)

Init +1; **Senses** darkvision 60 ft.; Perception +0

DEFENSE

AC 15, touch 15, flat-footed 14 (+1 Dex, +4 size)

hp 54 (12d8)

Fort +8, **Ref** +5, **Will** +4

Immune swarm traits, weapon damage

OFFENSE

Speed swim 20 ft.

Melee swarm (3d6 plus poison)

Space 10 ft.; **Reach** 0 ft.

Special Attacks distraction (DC 16)

STATISTICS

Str 1, **Dex** 13, **Con** 10, **Int** —, **Wis** 10, **Cha** 2

Base Atk +9; **CMB** —; **CMD** —

Skills Swim +9, Stealth +29; **Racial Modifiers** Stealth +16

ECOLOGY

Environment any aquatic

Organization solitary or bloom (2–8)

Treasure none

SPECIAL ABILITIES

Poison (Ex) Swarm—injury; *save* Fort DC 16; *frequency* 1/round for 6 rounds; *effect* 1d4 Dex; *cure* 2 consecutive saves.

Jellyfish often cluster together during springtime or when environmental conditions such as an increase in ocean temperature favor it. When conditions are right, jellyfish shift from being a nuisance to being a menace, if accidentally so, for a jellyfish swarm, unlike more aggressive monstrous kin like the giant jellyfish, comprises not aggressive hunters but rather opportunistic strikers. They do not generally move to attack nearby prey, but their nearly translucent coloration makes it horrifically easy for a creature to swim into a swarm unawares. Once a jellyfish swarm deals damage to a creature, the swarm pursues it for several rounds before giving up the chase. Many aquatic races use jellyfish swarms as defensive guardians, trusting a swarm's lack of interest in moving to keep it stationary for long periods of time.

JYOTI

This phoenix-like humanoid is surrounded by a halo of radiant energy. Its spear is tipped with a carved crystal blade.

JYOTI	CR 9

XP 6,400

N Medium outsider (extraplanar)

Init +5; **Senses** darkvision 60 ft., low-light vision; Perception +20

DEFENSE

AC 24, touch 16, flat-footed 18 (+4 armor, +5 Dex, +1 dodge, +4 natural)

hp 104 (11d10+44); fast healing 10

Fort +11, **Ref** +8, **Will** +11; +2 vs. divine

Defensive Abilities divine aversion, positive energy affinity; **Immune** death attacks, disease, energy drain, poison; **Resist** acid 10, cold 10, electricity 10, fire 10, sonic 10; **SR** 20

OFFENSE

Speed 30 ft., fly 90 ft. (good)

Melee +1 *ghost touch* spear +14/+9/+4 (1d8+4/×3 plus 1d6 fire), bite +8 (1d6+1 plus 1d6 fire)

Ranged ray +16 ranged touch (by spell)

Special Attacks breath weapon (60-ft. cone, 11d6 fire, Reflex DC 19 half, usable once every 1d4 rounds), positive energy

Spell-Like Abilities (CL 11th; concentration +13)

Constant—*mage armor*

3/day—*aid, cure serious wounds, daylight, dimension door, lesser restoration, searing light*

1/day—*breath of life, disrupting weapon*

STATISTICS

Str 14, **Dex** 20, **Con** 19, **Int** 12, **Wis** 15, **Cha** 15

Base Atk +11; **CMB** +13; **CMD** 29

Feats Combat Casting, Dodge, Flyby Attack, Iron Will, Mobility, Wind Stance

Skills Fly +9, Heal +16, Intimidate +16, Knowledge (planes) +19, Knowledge (religion) +19, Perception +20, Sense Motive +16, Stealth +19; **Racial Modifiers** +4 Knowledge (planes), +4 Knowledge (religion), +4 Perception

Languages Aquan, Auran, Common, Ignan, Terran

ECOLOGY

Environment any (Positive Energy Plane)

Organization solitary, pair, or flight (3–8)

Treasure double (+1 *ghost touch* spear, other treasure)

SPECIAL ABILITIES

Breath Weapon (Su) A jyoti's breath weapon is a focused burst of searing fire infused with positive energy. Undead in the area take 11d8 damage rather than 11d6.

Divine Aversion (Su) Jyoti dislike deities and are never divine spellcasters. Jyoti gain a +2 racial bonus on saves against divine magical effects.

Positive Energy (Su) A jyoti's natural weapons and any weapons it wields strike as if they were *ghost touch* weapons. In addition, any weapon (natural or manufactured) a jyoti uses deals +1d6 fire damage on a hit.

Positive Energy Affinity (Ex) A jyoti can exist comfortably on the Positive Energy Plane, and does not benefit (or suffer) from that plane's overwhelming infusions of life-giving energies. Whenever a jyoti is subjected to a magical healing effect, that effect functions at its full potential, as if enhanced by Maximize Spell.

Enigmatic and swift to anger, the avian race known as the jyoti are xenophobic natives of the Positive Energy Plane. Though some believe the jyoti are inherently good because their home plane is the source of all life, these beliefs are quite in error, for the jyoti react to all other races with wary suspicion at best, and usually assume the worst and attack before they can themselves be attacked. They guard their crystalline cities from all intrusion, especially by creatures from other planes and servants of the gods. They have been known to hold dangerous artifacts in their vaults on behalf of desperate visitors, though in the case of holy or unholy artifacts, the jyoti are more likely to destroy the artifacts as soon as possible.

Jyoti loathe natives of the Shadow Plane and the Negative Energy Plane in particular, though there is an element of pity in their actions toward undead. They never discuss the sceaduinar, and even hearing that name inflames jyoti into immediate anger. Those who dare argue on the sceaduinar's behalf are immediately attacked.

Illustration by Mike Corriero

KELPIE

*This hideous humanoid creature has slimy, transparent skin;
webbed, humanoid hands; and a snaggletoothed, horse-like face.*

KELPIE	CR 4

XP 1,200

NE Medium fey (aquatic, shapechanger)

Init +7; **Senses** low-light vision; Perception +13

DEFENSE

AC 17, touch 13, flat-footed 14 (+3 Dex, +4 natural)

hp 38 (7d6+14)

Fort +4, **Ref** +8, **Will** +6

Resist fire 10

OFFENSE

Speed 40 ft., swim 40 ft.

Melee 2 slams +6 (1d6+2 plus grab)

Special Attacks captivating lure

STATISTICS

Str 15, **Dex** 16, **Con** 15, **Int** 8, **Wis** 12, **Cha** 17

Base Atk +3; **CMB** +5 (+9 grapple); **CMD** 18

Feats Alertness, Deceitful, Improved Initiative, Weapon Finesse

Skills Bluff +15, Disguise +15, Perception +13, Sense Motive +13,
Stealth +13, Swim +10

Languages Aquan, Common, Sylvan; telepathy (1 mile,
previously touched creatures only)

SQ amphibious, change shape (hippocampus or horse, *beast
shape IV*; Small or Medium humanoid, *alter self*)

ECOLOGY

Environment any water

Organization solitary or shoal (2–5)

Treasure standard

SPECIAL ABILITIES

Captivating Lure (Su) Once per day, a kelpie can use a
powerful mental attack to lure in a single creature within
60 feet. The target must make a DC 16 Will saving throw
or become captivated by the kelpie, thinking it is a
desirable woman in mortal danger or (if in hippocampus
or horse form) a valuable steed. A victim under the effects
of the captivating lure moves toward the kelpie using the
most direct means available. If the path leads it into a
dangerous area such as through fire or off a cliff, that
creature receives a second saving throw to end the
effect before moving into peril; the victim does not
consider water a dangerous area, and will enter the
water even if it cannot swim or breathe. A captivated
creature can take no actions other than to move toward
the kelpie and defend itself, even if it is drowning. A
victim within 5 feet of the kelpie simply stands and offers
no resistance to its attacks. This effect continues as long
as the kelpie is alive and the victim is within 1 mile of the
kelpie. This is a mind-affecting charm effect. The save DC
is Charisma-based.

A kelpie is a deadly shapechanging predator that, in
its natural form, appears as a hideous combination
of emaciated horse and sickly humanoid, with slimy,
transparent skin and long, stringy hair. Its face is long
and equine, with a mouth filled with jagged teeth.
Few, however, ever see a kelpie in its true form, for
kelpies almost always encounter other creatures while
in disguise as a humanoid, horse, or hippocampus,
reverting to their true form only after their targets have
drowned so that they can feast on their victims, leaving
behind only the heart and liver (as both of these organs
are distasteful to most kelpies).

Kelpies can be found in saltwater and freshwater
environments, including fens, rivers, swamps, and
underground pools and lakes. Communities living
near kelpie lairs believe that folk who die on the water
or are killed by a kelpie become kelpies themselves.
Kelpies may serve as steeds for aquatic fey or other water
monsters while in their hippocampus forms, sometimes
without their riders ever knowing the truth of the steed's
sinister nature.

A typical kelpie is 6 feet tall and weighs 170 pounds.

KORRED

This knobby-kneed, stunted humanoid, has a particularly thick beard and wild mane of hair, hiding most of its body from view.

KORRED	CR 4

XP 1,200

CN Small fey

Init +3; **Senses** low-light vision; Perception +14

DEFENSE

AC 17, touch 15, flat-footed 13 (+3 Dex, +1 dodge, +2 natural, +1 size)

hp 33 (6d6+12)

Fort +4, **Ref** +8, **Will** +7

DR 5/cold iron; **SR** 15

OFFENSE

Speed 30 ft.

Melee club +8 (1d4+6)

Ranged rock +8 (1d6+4)

Special Attacks animated hair, stunning laugh, rock throwing (100 ft.)

Spell-Like Abilities (CL 6th; concentration +7)

At will—*animate rope, shatter* (DC 13), *stone shape*

1/day—*stone tell*

STATISTICS

Str 19, **Dex** 17, **Con** 14, **Int** 12, **Wis** 14, **Cha** 13

Base Atk +3; **CMB** +6; **CMD** 20

Feats Dodge, Mobility, Skill Focus (Perception)

Skills Acrobatics +12, Bluff +10, Craft (rope) +10, Craft (sculpture) +10, Perception +14, Perform (dance) +10, Stealth +16

Languages Common, Sylvan

SQ stone stride

ECOLOGY

Environment temperate forests

Organization solitary, pair, or gang (3–6)

Treasure standard (club, rope, shears, other treasure)

SPECIAL ABILITIES

Animated Hair (Su) A korred's hair is constantly writhing and twitching. As a free action, a korred can cause its long hair to reach out and interfere with adjacent creatures— tugging at clothes and weapons, tangling feet and arms, tickling, and generally making a nuisance of itself. The korred can select which adjacent targets are affected by its animated hair. These targets must make a successful DC 16 Reflex save each round to avoid becoming entangled for 1 round. The save DC is Dexterity-based.

Stone Stride (Su) This ability works like *tree stride*, except it requires loose boulders at least as large as the korred, and only has a range of 30 feet. The korred can use this ability once per round as a standard action.

Stunning Laugh (Su) Three times per day as a standard action, a korred can unleash a strange laugh that stuns all creatures within a 30-foot burst for 1d2 rounds (Fortitude DC 14 negates). This is a sonic, mind-affecting effect. Fey are immune to this ability. The save DC is Charisma-based.

Korreds are an ancient fey race who like forested areas with nice, rocky ground. They resemble small, wild-haired humanoids with wild, knotted hair. Korreds especially like to dance in ancient stone circles within forest glades, often led by satyrs with panpipes. They are a shy race and do not take kindly to outsiders discovering them, even by accident. They almost always attack non-korreds who stumble into their territory, seeking to kill them or at least drive them off.

Korred clothing normally consists of a simple leather apron, jerkin, or kilt, leaving their legs uncovered and their feet bare. Their clothes usually have a large pocket or pouch to hold their belongings. A korred's hair and beard grow quickly, sometimes an inch a day, and the korred trims its hair when the locks become too unruly, saving the trimmings in its pocket so it can weave them into ropes for its *animate rope* spell-like ability.

Illustration by Eva Widermann

KRENSHAR

This earless, panther-like beast snarls as the skin of its face twitches, then peels back to reveal the bone and flesh beneath.

KRENSHAR	CR 1	

XP 400

N Medium magical beast

Init +6; **Senses** darkvision 60 ft., low-light vision, scent; Perception +5

DEFENSE

AC 15, touch 12, flat-footed 13 (+2 Dex, +3 natural)

hp 13 (2d10+2)

Fort +4, **Ref** +5, **Will** +1

OFFENSE

Speed 40 ft.

Melee bite +2 (1d6), 2 claws +2 (1d4)

Special Attacks skullface

STATISTICS

Str 11, **Dex** 14, **Con** 13, **Int** 6, **Wis** 12, **Cha** 13

Base Atk +2; **CMB** +2; **CMD** 14 (18 vs. trip)

Feats Improved Initiative

Skills Intimidate +1 (+5 to demoralize), Perception +5, Stealth +10; **Racial Modifiers** +4 Intimidate to demoralize, +4 Stealth

Languages Sylvan (can't speak)

ECOLOGY

Environment temperate forests or plains

Organization solitary, pair, or pride (6–10)

Treasure none

SPECIAL ABILITIES

Skullface (Su) As a standard action, a krenshar can pull the skin back from its face, revealing the musculature and bony structures of its skull. This counts as using Intimidate to demoralize an opponent, and is an extraordinary ability. The krenshar can emit a loud screech while peeling back its skin, causing potent fear in a single creature within 100 feet that can see the krenshar. The targeted creature must make a DC 12 Will save or become frightened (if the target has 6 or fewer Hit Dice) or shaken (if the target has more than 6 Hit Dice) for 1d4 rounds. A creature that successfully saves cannot be affected again by the same krenshar's skullface ability for 24 hours. This is a sonic, mind-affecting fear effect. The save DC is Charisma-based.

The krenshar is a strange creature that resembles a large but earless hunting cat, save that it can retract the fur and skin on its face to reveal the glistening skull and musculature underneath. Combined with its strange, keening wail, this horrifying display is enough to paralyze prey and send formidable opponents running.

Krenshar's retractable skin allows it to dine on carrion with a lower risk of picking up disease-carrying vermin, much like a vulture's bare head and neck. When the creature finishes eating, restoring the facial skin to its normal position scrapes off gore and clinging bugs. The ability to retract their skin is demonstrated in other contexts as well—male krenshars bare their skulls at rivals as a challenge over mates, females use this ability to ward off undesired suitors, and hunting adults use it to scare prey into ambushes.

Though krenshars generally prefer to stalk herd animals like deer or cattle, they have no qualms about taking on humanoids when food is scarce. They average 4 to 5 feet in length and weigh approximately 175 pounds.

Scholars have long debated the confusing nature of krenshar intelligence. While clearly more intelligent than mere animals, the creatures seem to lack all but the most rudimentary language of snarls and yowls, and aside from the scare tactics that make them notorious, tend to behave much like mundane cats or wolves, even going so far as to occasionally be befriended by rangers or druids. Those who deny krenshars' intelligence, however, need only look into their strange violet eyes or observe the ease with which they manipulate and outmaneuver their prey to realize their folly—an error few make twice.

Illustration by Peter Lazarski

LAMIA MATRIARCH

This creature looks like a beautiful human woman from the waist up, but below is the body and tail of an immense snake.

LAMIA MATRIARCH	CR 8

XP 4,800

CE Large monstrous humanoid (shapechanger)

Init +4; **Senses** darkvision 60 ft., low-light vision; Perception +3

DEFENSE

AC 21, touch 13, flat-footed 17 (+4 Dex, +8 natural, –1 size)

hp 102 (12d10+36)

Fort +7, **Ref** +12, **Will** +11

Immune mind-affecting effects; **SR** 19

OFFENSE

Speed 40 ft., climb 40 ft., swim 40 ft.

Melee +1 *scimitars* +14/+14/+9/+9/+4 (1d6+6/15–20 plus 1 Wisdom drain on first hit each round) or touch +16 (1d4 Wisdom drain)

Space 10 ft.; **Reach** 5 ft.

Special Attacks Wisdom drain

Spell-Like Abilities (CL 12th; concentration +17)

At will—*charm monster* (DC 19), *ventriloquism* (DC 16)

3/day—*deep slumber* (DC 18), *dream*, *major image* (DC 18), *mirror image*, *suggestion* (DC 18)

Spells Known (CL 6th; concentration +11)

3rd (4/day)—*haste*

2nd (6/day)—*death knell* (DC 17), *invisibility*

1st (8/day)—*cure light wounds*, *divine favor*, *mage armor*, *magic missile*

0 (at will)—*dancing lights*, *daze* (DC 15), *detect magic*, *ghost sound* (DC 15), *mage hand*, *mending*, *prestidigitation*

STATISTICS

Str 20, **Dex** 19, **Con** 17,

Int 16, **Wis** 16, **Cha** 21

Base Atk +12; **CMB** +18;

CMD 32 (can't be tripped)

Feats Double Slice, Extend Spell, Improved Critical (scimitar), Improved Two-Weapon Fighting, Two-Weapon Fighting, Weapon Focus (scimitar)

Skills Acrobatics +8 (+12 jump), Bluff +21, Climb +13, Diplomacy +11, Disguise +11, Intimidate +20, Knowledge (any one) +15, Knowledge (arcana) +15, Spellcraft +15, Swim +13, Use Magic Device +21; **Racial Modifiers** + 4 Acrobatics, +4 Bluff, +4 Use Magic Device

Languages Abyssal, Common, Draconic

SQ change shape (fixed Medium humanoid form, *alter self*), undersized weapons

ECOLOGY

Environment any land

Organization solitary, pair, or cult (3–6)

Treasure double (two +1 *scimitars*, other treasure)

SPECIAL ABILITIES

Spells A lamia matriarch casts spells as a 6th-level sorcerer, and can cast spells from the cleric list as well as those normally available to a sorcerer. Cleric spells are considered arcane spells for a lamia matriarch.

Wisdom Drain (Su) A lamia matriarch drains 1d4 points of Wisdom each time she hits with her melee touch attack. The first time each round that she strikes a foe with a melee weapon, she also drains 1 point of Wisdom. A DC 21 Will save negates the Wisdom drain. Unlike with other kinds of ability drain attacks, a lamia matriarch does not heal damage when she uses her Wisdom drain. The save DC is Charisma-based.

The queens of a race consumed by bitterness and predatory instinct, lamia matriarchs mastermind all manner of foul plots in hopes of breaking the bestial curse that afflicts their race. They move with shocking ease from silken-tongued temptresses to dervishes, striking with all the deadly precision of vipers. Quick to covet, enslave, and overindulge, lamia matriarchs luxuriate in gory feasts, violent trysts, and bloody entertainments, reveling until their playthings are broken or until they tire and move on.

175

LENG SPIDER

This immense purple spider has a legspan of nearly forty feet and a hideously bloated body, yet still moves with fluid grace.

LENG SPIDER	CR 14

XP 38,400

CE Huge magical beast (extraplanar)

Init +13; **Senses** *arcane sight*, darkvision 60 ft., low-light vision, tremorsense 60 ft.; Perception +21

DEFENSE

AC 29, touch 17, flat-footed 20 (+9 Dex, +12 natural, −2 size)

hp 202 (15d10+120); fast healing 10

Fort +17, **Ref** +18, **Will** +10

Immune cold, confusion and insanity effects, poison, sonic; **SR** 25

OFFENSE

Speed 40 ft., climb 40 ft.

Melee mwk flail +22/+17/+12 (3d6+8), bite +16 (2d6+4 plus poison)

Ranged mwk bolas +23 (1d8+8)

Space 15 ft.; **Reach** 15 ft.

Special Attacks web (+24 ranged, DC 25, 15 hp), web weaponry

Spell-Like Abilities (CL 15th; concentration +21)

Constant—*arcane sight, freedom of movement, tongues*

At will—*dispel magic, fabricate* (webs only)

3/day—*air walk, invisibility, major image* (DC 19)

1/day—*charm monster* (DC 20), *insanity* (DC 23), *mirage arcana* (DC 21), *veil* (DC 22)

STATISTICS

Str 26, **Dex** 29, **Con** 26, **Int** 21, **Wis** 17, **Cha** 22

Base Atk +15; **CMB** +25; **CMD** 44 (54 vs. trip)

Feats Combat Expertise, Combat Reflexes, Improved Initiative, Improved Trip, Iron Will, Point-Blank Shot, Precise Shot, Vital Strike

Skills Acrobatics +27 (+31 jump), Climb +34, Craft (traps) +20, Knowledge (any one) +20, Perception +21, Spellcraft +20, Use Magic Device +21

Languages Aklo; *tongues*

ECOLOGY

Environment any

Organization solitary, pair, or cult (3–6)

Treasure double

SPECIAL ABILITIES

Poison (Su) Bite—injury; *save* Fort DC 25; *frequency* 1/round for 6 rounds; *effect* 1d4 Con plus confusion for 1 round; *cure* 2 consecutive saves. A Leng spider's venom causes flesh to blister and rot away and the mind to experience vivid and horrific hallucinations—these visions cause the poisoned creature to react in an unpredictable manner, as if confused. The hallucination element of this poison is mind-affecting. The save DC is Constitution-based.

Web Weaponry (Ex) A Leng spider is talented at using its webs to construct masterwork weapons. This technique of weapon creation allows the spider to effectively create a flail or bolas by attaching a heavy object such as a rock or chunk of metal to a cord of webbing. The spider attaches one end of this webbing to a leg and can then wield the weighted cord as a masterwork flail or a masterwork bolas. It can only wield one such weapon at a time—it must use its other legs to walk. If a Leng spider drops or loses a web weapon, it can create a new one as a full-round action, provided it has access to heavy-weight objects of the correct size (such as loose rocks or skulls).

The spiders of Leng have long warred with that realm's more humanoid denizens, yet this does not make the spiders allies of sane life. These spiders see themselves as deserving of true positions of power, and the only creatures they suffer to live apart from their kin are their magically controlled slaves. Fortunately, the spiders have no intrinsic way to travel to the Material Plane, and must use portals or other methods to visit this world. Artistic trap builders, Leng spiders construct lairs of dangerous and haunting beauty made of webs and other materials found nearby.

A Leng spider's body is 18 feet long and weighs 6,000 pounds. Most leng spiders possess only 7 legs, but some possess 9, 11, or only 5—they never possess an even number.

LEPRECHAUN

This small humanoid has pointed ears, green eyes, and a wicked grin. He carries a bottle in one hand and a club in the other.

LEPRECHAUN	CR 2

XP 600
CN Small fey
Init +7; **Senses** low-light vision; Perception +17

DEFENSE

AC 14, touch 14, flat-footed 11 (+3 Dex, +1 size)
hp 18 (4d6+4)
Fort +2, **Ref** +7, **Will** +6
DR 5/cold iron; **SR** 13

OFFENSE

Speed 40 ft.
Melee +1 club +7 (1d8–1)
Spell-Like Abilities (CL 4th; concentration +7)
 Constant—*shillelagh*
 At will—*dancing lights, ghost sound* (DC 13), *invisibility* (self only), *mage hand, major image* (visual and auditory elements only, DC 16), *prestidigitation, ventriloquism* (DC 14)
 3/day—*color spray* (DC 14), *fabricate* (1 cubic foot of material only)
 1/day—*major creation*

STATISTICS

Str 7, **Dex** 16, **Con** 13, **Int** 14, **Wis** 15, **Cha** 16
Base Atk +2; **CMB** –1; **CMD** 12
Feats Improved Initiative, Weapon Finesse
Skills Bluff +10, Escape Artist +10, Knowledge (nature) +9, Perception +17, Perform (comedy) +8, Perform (dance) +8, Sense Motive +9, Sleight of Hand +14, Stealth +14; **Racial Modifiers** +8 Perception, +4 Sleight of Hand
Languages Common, Elven, Halfling, Sylvan
SQ leprechaun magic

ECOLOGY

Environment temperate forests
Organization solitary, pair, band (3–6), or family (7–10)
Treasure standard (club, other treasure)

SPECIAL ABILITIES

Leprechaun Magic (Sp) When a leprechaun uses any of its spell-like abilities to deceive, trick, or humiliate a creature (at the GM's discretion), the spell-like ability resolves at caster level 8th rather than 4th. If a leprechaun uses its spell-like abilities in this manner, it has a bonus of +11 on concentration checks.

Leprechauns are small, fun-loving tricksters. They are most commonly found in forests and share the close connection with nature that is possessed by most fey creatures. Leprechauns love playing tricks on unknowing passersby—almost as much as they love a fine bottle of wine and a plateful of hot food in their bellies. They often steal something of worth from adventurers just to provoke a chase. Using their ability to disappear at will to its full potential, they wait until their victims appear to be about to give up the chase before reappearing once more to let the chase resume. They are not greedy creatures, and eventually drop what they've stolen, slipping away while their angry pursuers claim the lost property. The exception is gold—leprechauns love gold and often hoard it in secret, hidden places. It is rumored that a person who finds a gold coin in the forest and returns it to the leprechaun that dropped it will be granted a *wish* as a reward. Unfortunately, these rumors are false—likely perpetuated by the leprechauns themselves in order to trick others into bringing them gold.

Leprechauns prefer not to kill other creatures unless the ones attacking them are malicious or known enemies of the forest or fey. They often use their powers to befuddle and annoy evil folk, tricking creatures such as goblins and orcs into thinking a forest is haunted.

Illustration by Eva Widermann

LEUCROTTA

This freakish beast has the head of a badger, the hooves of a stag, and a wide mouth with sharp ridges of bone instead of teeth.

LEUCROTTA	CR 5

XP 1,600

CE Large magical beast

Init +5; **Senses** darkvision 60 ft., low-light vision, scent; Perception +2

DEFENSE

AC 18, touch 10, flat-footed 17 (+1 Dex, +8 natural, –1 size)

hp 57 (6d10+24)

Fort +9, **Ref** +6, **Will** +4

Immune disease, poison

OFFENSE

Speed 60 ft., climb 30 ft.

Melee bite +10 (2d6+7/19–20), 2 hooves +5 (1d6+2)

Space 10 ft.; **Reach** 5 ft.

Special Attacks lure, powerful bite

STATISTICS

Str 21, **Dex** 12, **Con** 18, **Int** 11, **Wis** 14, **Cha** 17

Base Atk +6; **CMB** +12; **CMD** 23 (27 vs. trip)

Feats Improved Initiative, Skill Focus (Bluff), Skill Focus (Stealth)

Skills Bluff +12, Climb +13, Stealth +9

Languages Common

SQ sound mimicry (voices)

ECOLOGY

Environment temperate or tropical forests or hills

Organization solitary, pair, or pack (3–12)

Treasure standard

SPECIAL ABILITIES

Lure (Su) At any point that a leucrotta's targets are unaware of it (for example, if the leucrotta is hiding or concealed in darkness), the leucrotta can call out to the targets, who must be in line of sight and within 60 feet. When the leucrotta calls out, the targets must make a DC 16 Will save or fall under the effects of a *suggestion* to approach the sound of the leucrotta's voice. This effect functions identically to a *mass suggestion* spell with a caster level equal to the leucrotta's Hit Dice. A creature that saves cannot be affected again by the same leucrotta's lure for 24 hours. The lure is a language-dependant effect, and if the leucrotta uses the victim's name during the lure, the victim takes a –4 penalty on its saving throw. This is a sonic mind-affecting charm effect. The save DC is Charisma-based.

Powerful Bite (Ex) A leucrotta's bite attack always applies 1-1/2 times its Strength modifier on damage rolls and threatens a critical hit on a roll of 19–20. When a leucrotta bites an object, its bite treats the object as having a hardness of 5 less than the object's actual hardness rating.

Reputed to be descended from hyenas and a demon lord, these creatures are intelligent and cruel, using their astounding vocal mimicry to lure foolish and unsuspecting creatures to where the pack can torment them at its leisure before finally devouring them.

Five feet tall at the shoulder, its tawny fur often coated with dried and clotted filth, the leucrotta is a powerful beast weighing over 800 pounds. The sharp bone ridges that line its oversized jaws instead of teeth are incredibly durable and, combined with massive jaw muscles, allow its bite to shear through bone and even steel. Leucrottas consume their prey gear and all; they vomit up what they cannot digest and pick through the debris in search of valuable items that might help them lure in prey.

Leucrottas sometimes lead packs of gnolls, or even of their bestial cousins the crocottas (see below). They refuse to let themselves be used as beasts of burden, but sometimes allow favored gnoll companions to ride them into battle as steeds. The leucrotta in a gnoll pack generally thinks of itself as the leader of that group, and treats any established gnoll chieftain poorly in an attempt to goad that gnoll into attacking it. Those leucrottas that succeed in slaying a gnoll leader typically find it much easier to assume the role of tribal leader.

CROCOTTA

These degenerate offshoots of leucrottas have animal-level intelligence, but sense a kinship with leucrottas and obey them instinctively. Treat a crocotta as an advanced dire hyena with Improved Critical (bite) as a bonus feat.

A crocotta looks similar to a leucrotta, save that it has shorter back legs, giving it a hunched, more hyena-like appearance. Leucrottas view crocottas with disdain and even shame, but it's not unusual to find these large hyena-like beasts in close proximity to a leucrotta pack. Crocottas are popular attractions in traveling carnivals, where unscrupulous con artists bill them as cursed humanoids or animals.

Illustration by Ben Wootten

178

LOCATHAH

This lean humanoid bears crested fins on its head and back, and has the wide-eyed and wide-lipped face of a fish.

LOCATHAH	CR 1/2

XP 200

N Medium humanoid (aquatic)

Init +1; **Senses** low-light vision; Perception +3

DEFENSE

AC 13, touch 11, flat-footed 12 (+1 Dex, +2 natural)

hp 9 (2d8)

Fort +3, **Ref** +1, **Will** +1

OFFENSE

Speed 10 ft., swim 60 ft.

Melee longspear +2 (1d8/×3)

Ranged light crossbow +2 (1d8/19–20)

STATISTICS

Str 10, **Dex** 12, **Con** 10, **Int** 13, **Wis** 13, **Cha** 11

Base Atk +1; **CMB** +1; **CMD** 12

Feats Weapon Focus (longspear)

Skills Craft (any one) +6, Perception +3, Survival +6, Swim +8

Languages Aquan

SQ amphibious

ECOLOGY

Environment temperate or warm aquatic

Organization solitary, band (2–10), or tribe (11–30 plus 2 fighter sergeants of 1st–3rd level and 1 cleric leader of 3rd–6th level)

Treasure standard (longspear, light crossbow and 10 bolts, other treasure)

Simple aquatic creatures shunned by landwalkers and undersea folk alike, locathahs live in tight-knit communities scattered throughout the world's seas, lakes. and waterways. Locathahs possess scaly ochre skin tinged with green and yellow. Ridged, rust-colored skin covers their chests and stomachs, and a mottled wash of green, brown, and orange colors their fins like aging kelp. Locathahs exude a strong fishy odor when above water that, in addition to their already unnerving appearance, repulses most land-dwellers. Despite this animosity, locathahs go to great lengths to befriend surface folk, offering safe passage through the waters, pointing out dangerous reefs, and hinting at sunken treasures in return for durable ceramics and metal tools and weapons, as well as tubers, which they view as a delicacy.

These creatures dislike combat and flee when disarmed or outnumbered. Locathahs hold community in the highest regard, never leaving a friend behind and often going to great lengths to retrieve a fallen companion. Among their own kind and races friendly toward them, locathahs are social creatures who live a very human-like, albeit simple, lifestyle. Locathahs work in stone, coral, and bone to produce the crude implements they use. Some take coral work to obsessive levels, with certain clans taking generations to grow their preferred medium in its desired form before carving it. They feed on crustaceans, undersea plants, and shellfish, and rarely on large fish that are caught during ritualized hunts.

Locathah matriarchs serve their undersea tribes not only as chieftains, but also as the primary egg layers of the community. Each adult member of the tribe is responsible for raising a single young locathah as his or her own. Locathahs tame moray eels, keeping them near their lairs as humans keep dogs. Some locathah soldiers and hunting groups use giant moray eels as mounts, chasing down their quarry and attacking with narrow-tipped spears. More powerful aquatic races use locathahs as slaves, abducting breeding matriarchs to produce a constant wave of new workers.

Locathahs stand roughly as tall as humans, yet their fins jut out, giving them an imposing stature. Lean and strong, locathahs weigh roughly 160 pounds.

Illustration by Eva Widermann

LURKER IN LIGHT

This large-eyed humanoid looks like a glowing, emaciated elven child save for its small, transparent wings.

LURKER IN LIGHT	CR 5

XP 1,600

NE Small fey (extraplanar)

Init +8; **Senses** low-light vision; Perception +16

DEFENSE

AC 18, touch 15, flat-footed 14 (+4 Dex, +3 natural, +1 size)

hp 44 (8d6+16)

Fort +4, **Ref** +10, **Will** +9

Defensive Abilities blend with light; **Immune** blindness DR 5/cold iron

OFFENSE

Speed 30 ft., fly 30 ft. (average)

Melee 2 claws +9 (1d3+1) or dagger +9 (1d3+1/19–20 plus poison)

Special Attacks sneak attack +3d6

Spell-Like Abilities (CL 8th; concentration +11)

At will—*dancing lights, flare* (DC 13), *ghost sound* (DC 13), *light, mage hand*

3/day—*daylight, blindness/deafness* (DC 16)

STATISTICS

Str 13, **Dex** 18, **Con** 15, **Int** 14, **Wis** 16, **Cha** 17

Base Atk +4; **CMB** +4; **CMD** 18

Feats Alertness, Flyby Attack, Improved Initiative, Weapon Finesse

Skills Acrobatics +15, Escape Artist +15, Fly +17, Knowledge (arcana) +10, Knowledge (planes) +10, Perception +16, Stealth +19, Survival +11

Languages Aklo, Common, Sylvan

SQ daylight door, poison use, ritual gate

ECOLOGY

Environment any land (extraplanar)

Organization solitary, pair, or gang (3–8)

Treasure standard (dagger, other treasure)

SPECIAL ABILITIES

Blend With Light (Su) In areas of bright light, lurkers are invisible. As with *greater invisibility*, they may attack and still remain invisible. In shadowy illumination, a lurker loses this invisibility, though like all creatures in shadows, they have concealment unless the viewer has darkvision. If the lurker is flying, its fluttering wings partially negate this effect, giving it only partial concealment (20%) rather than total concealment.

Daylight Door (Sp) Once per day, a lurker can use *dimension door*, transporting only itself and up to 50 pounds of material. The start and end points of the teleport must be in areas of bright light; if the destination lacks sufficient light, the teleport fails but does not expend the ability for the day.

Illustration by Sarah Stone

Poison (Ex) Lurkers typically coat their daggers with shadow essence poison.

Shadow essence poison: Injury; *save* Fortitude DC 17; *frequency* 1/round for 6 rounds; *initial effect* 1 Str drain; *secondary effect* 1d3 Str damage; *cure* 1 save.

Ritual Gate (Su) By sacrificing one or more humanoid victims, a lurker or group of lurkers can create a *gate* to the Material Plane, one of the Elemental Planes, or the realm of the fey, either to return home or to conjure allies. Creating a *gate* for travel requires the sacrifice of five victims; the *gate* created remains open for 1 minute. Creating a *gate* to bring allies to the Material Plane requires one sacrifice for every HD of the creature intended to pass through the *gate* (so five sacrifices can bring a lurker or a Medium air elemental, eight can bring a Large earth elemental, and so on). The sacrifices do not need to be simultaneous; as long all sacrifices occur at some point during the hour-long ritual, the magic continues to build until it reaches the required total.

Malicious and alien fey, lurkers in light venture to the Material Plane to perpetrate strangely targeted mischief, stealing and killing according to a logic or system of justice only they understand. Gnomes in particular seem to incur these unexplained attacks, leading some to believe that lurkers may be agents of ancient and vengeful forces. Creatures of the light, lurkers are visible only in dim illumination, with anything brighter than a flickering torch making them completely invisible, even as they savage their enemies—a prospect terrifying to those civilized races that equate light with safety.

A lurker in light turns conventional wisdom on its head, for they detest darkness and the creatures that dwell in it, yet they themselves are sadistic and evil. They particularly hate darkmantles, dwarves, and creatures from the Plane of Shadow, and given the time, they enjoy torturing such creatures to death if they can capture them alive.

If killed, a lurker in light disintegrates over the course of several minutes into 2d6 pounds of dust that radiates faint evocation magic and glows for 1d6 days with a cold light equal to that provided by a candle. This dust damages shadows as if it were holy water, with a pound of dust equal to one flask of holy water.

A lurker in light is 3 feet tall, but weighs only 20 pounds.

LYCANTHROPE, WEREBEAR

This humanoid is covered in shaggy fur and carries a heavy axe in one of his clawed hands.

WEREBEAR (HUMAN FORM) CR 4

XP 1,200

Human natural werebear ranger 4

LG Medium humanoid (human, shapechanger)

Init +2; **Senses** low-light vision, scent; Perception +8

DEFENSE

AC 16, touch 12, flat-footed 14 (+4 armor, +2 Dex)

hp 34 (4d10+8)

Fort +5, **Ref** +6, **Will** +2

OFFENSE

Speed 30 ft.

Melee mwk battleaxe +9 (1d8+4/×3)

Ranged mwk throwing axe +7 (1d6+3)

Special Attacks favored enemy (orcs +2)

Ranger Spells Prepared (CL 1st; concentration +2)

1st—*detect poison*

STATISTICS

Str 16, **Dex** 14, **Con** 13, **Int** 12, **Wis** 12, **Cha** 8

Base Atk +4; **CMB** +7; **CMD** 19

Feats Endurance, Point-Blank Shot, Power Attack, Run, Weapon Focus (battleaxe)

Skills Climb +8, Handle Animal +6, Heal +8, Knowledge (nature) +8, Perception +8, Stealth +7, Survival +8, Swim +8

Languages Common, Sylvan

SQ change shape (human, hybrid, and grizzly bear; *polymorph*), favored terrain (forest +2), hunter's bond (companions), lycanthropic empathy (bears and dire bears), track +2

ECOLOGY

Environment any forests

Organization solitary, pair, family (3–6), or troupe (3–6 plus 1–4 black or grizzly bears)

Treasure NPC gear (chain shirt, masterwork battleaxe, 2 masterwork throwing axes, other treasure)

WEREBEAR (HYBRID FORM)

XP 1,200

Human natural werebear ranger 4

LG Large humanoid (human, shapechanger)

Init +2; **Senses** low-light vision, scent; Perception +8

DEFENSE

AC 23, touch 11, flat-footed 21 (+4 armor, +2 Dex, +8 natural, −1 size)

hp 46 (4d10+20)

Fort +6, **Ref** +6, **Will** +2

DR 10/silver

OFFENSE

Speed 30 ft.

Melee mwk battleaxe +10 (2d6+5/×3), bite +3 (1d8+2 plus curse of lycanthropy), claw +3 (1d6+2 plus grab)

Ranged mwk throwing axe +7 (1d6+5)

Space 10 ft.; **Reach** 10 ft.

Special Attacks favored enemy (orcs +2)

Ranger Spells Prepared (CL 1st; concentration +2)

1st—*detect poison*

STATISTICS

Str 21, **Dex** 14, **Con** 19, **Int** 12, **Wis** 12, **Cha** 8

Base Atk +4; **CMB** +10 (+14 grapple); **CMD** 22

Feats Endurance, Point-Blank Shot, Power Attack, Run, Weapon Focus (battleaxe)

Skills Climb +10, Handle Animal +6, Heal +8, Knowledge (nature) +8, Perception +8, Stealth +3, Survival +8, Swim +10

Languages Common

SQ change shape (human, hybrid, and bear; *polymorph*), favored terrain (forest +2), hunter's bond (companions), lycanthropic empathy (bears and dire bears), track +2

In their humanoid forms, werebears tend to be muscular and broad-shouldered, with stark facial features and dark eyes. Their hair is usually red, brown, or black, and they look like they are used to a lifetime of hard work. Though by far the most benign of common lycanthropes, werebears are shunned by most normal folk, who fear and mistrust their animal transformations. Most live as recluses in forested areas or in small family units among their own kind. They avoid confrontations with strangers but do not hesitate to drive evil humanoids out of their territory.

Some werebears are angry and violent, because of either temperament or a lifetime of harassment from others, and these mean ones aren't afraid to put an axe in a trespasser's face or eat someone who pushes them too far. Cool-headed werebears don't like to speak of these individuals with strangers.

Illustration by Concept Art House

LYCANTHROPE, WEREBOAR

This potbellied creature has the body of a man and the head of a crazed boar. Large tusks jut from his upper jaw.

WEREBOAR (HUMAN FORM) CR 2

XP 600

Human natural wereboar barbarian 2

CN Medium humanoid (human, shapechanger)

Init +1; **Senses** low-light vision, scent; Perception +7

DEFENSE

AC 12, touch 9, flat-footed 11 (+3 armor, +1 Dex, –2 rage)

hp 31 (2d12+13)

Fort +7, **Ref** +1, **Will** +4

Defensive Abilities uncanny dodge

OFFENSE

Speed 40 ft.

Melee dagger +6 (1d4+4/19–20), bite +1 (1d4+4)

Ranged dagger +4 (1d4+4/19–20)

Special Attacks rage (8 rounds/day), rage powers (animal fury)

STATISTICS

Str 19, **Dex** 13, **Con** 18,
Int 10, **Wis** 14, **Cha** 8

Base Atk +2; **CMB** +6;
CMD 17

Feats Power Attack,
Toughness

Skills Handle Animal +4,
Intimidate +4, Knowledge
(nature) +5, Perception +7,
Profession (farmer) +4

Languages Common

SQ change shape
(human, hybrid, and
boar; *polymorph*),
fast movement,
lycanthropic empathy
(boars and dire boars)

ECOLOGY

Environment any forests or plains

Organization solitary, pair,
brood (3–8), or troupe (3–8
plus 1–4 boars)

Treasure NPC gear (studded leather
armor, 2 daggers, other treasure)

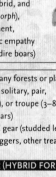

WEREBOAR (HYBRID FORM)

XP 600

Human natural wereboar barbarian 2

CN Medium humanoid (human,
shapechanger)

Init +1; **Senses** low-light vision,
scent; Perception +7

DEFENSE

AC 14, touch 9, flat-footed 13 (+3 armor, +1 Dex, +2 natural, –2 rage)

hp 30 (2d12+17)

Fort +8, **Ref** +1, **Will** +4

Defensive Abilities ferocity, uncanny dodge; **DR** 10/silver

OFFENSE

Speed 40 ft.

Melee dagger +8 (1d4+6/19–20), bite +3 (1d4+3 plus curse of lycanthropy), gore +3 (1d8+3)

Ranged dagger +3 (1d4+3/19–20)

Special Attacks rage (8 rounds/day), rage powers (animal fury)

STATISTICS

Str 23, **Dex** 13, **Con** 23, **Int** 10, **Wis** 14, **Cha** 8

Base Atk +2; **CMB** +8; **CMD** 19

Feats Power Attack, Toughness

Skills Handle Animal +4, Intimidate +4, Knowledge (nature) +5, Perception +7, Profession (farmer) +4

Languages Common

SQ lycanthropic empathy (boars and dire boars), fast movement, change shape (human, hybrid, and boar; *polymorph*)

In their humanoid forms, wereboars tend to be stout with upturned noses, bristly hair, and a noticeable overbite. They usually have red, brown, or black hair, though a few are golden blond, pale blond, or even bald. Chin whiskers are common, but males often can't grow full beards. Because they can be stubborn and aggressive when riled up, wereboars usually live in their own communities rather than mixing with non-lycanthropes; a wereboar's farm or ranch doesn't look out of the ordinary. Wereboars tend to have large families with many children.

Many wereboars are known to have especially bad tempers, rivaling those of murderous werewolves, and even other lycanthropes tend to avoid them. This suits the wereboars fine, especially as some weretigers and werewolves have been known hunt young wereboars.

Note that the statistics presented here for wereboars assume that the creatures are in their barbarian rage—if the creatures are encountered at another time, simply adjust their statistics accordingly.

Illustration by Scott Purdy

LYCANTHROPE, WERETIGER

This humanoid tiger has striped fur and a muscular, lanky frame. Its feline face has sharp fangs and slitted eyes.

WERETIGER (HUMAN FORM) CR 4

XP 1,200

Human natural weretiger rogue 4

NE Medium humanoid (human, shapechanger)

Init +7; **Senses** low-light vision, scent; Perception +10

DEFENSE

AC 16, touch 13, flat-footed 13 (+3 armor, +3 Dex)

hp 29 (4d8+8)

Fort +2, **Ref** +7, **Will** +4

Defensive Abilities evasion, trap sense +1, uncanny dodge

OFFENSE

Speed 30 ft.

Melee mwk short sword +5 (1d6+1/19–20)

Ranged mwk dagger +6 (1d4+1/19–20)

Special Attacks sneak attack +2d6

STATISTICS

Str 13, **Dex** 16, **Con** 12, **Int** 10, **Wis** 16, **Cha** 8

Base Atk +3; **CMB** +4; **CMD** 17

Feats Improved Initiative, Power Attack, Skill Focus (Stealth)

Skills Acrobatics +9, Climb +7, Handle Animal +3, Intimidate +6, Perception +10, Sense Motive +10, Stealth +12, Survival +7, Swim +7

Languages Common

SQ change shape (human, hybrid, and tiger; *polymorph*), lycanthropic empathy (tigers and dire tigers), rogue talents (bleeding attack +2, fast stealth), trapfinding +2

ECOLOGY

Environment any plains or swamps

Organization solitary or pair

Treasure NPC gear (studded leather, masterwork short sword, 2 masterwork daggers, other treasure)

WERETIGER (HYBRID FORM)

XP 1,200

Human natural weretiger rogue 4

NE Large humanoid (human, shapechanger)

Init +7; **Senses** low-light vision, scent; Perception +10

DEFENSE

AC 20, touch 12, flat-footed 17 (+3 armor, +3 Dex, +5 natural, −1 size)

hp 37 (4d8+16)

Fort +4, **Ref** +7, **Will** +4

Defensive Abilities evasion, trap sense +1, uncanny dodge

DR 10/silver

OFFENSE

Speed 30 ft.

Melee bite +8 (2d6+6 plus grab and curse of lycanthropy), 2 claws +8 (1d8+6 plus grab)

Ranged mwk dagger +6 (1d6+6/19–20)

Special Attacks pounce, rake (2 claws +8, 1d8+6), sneak attack +2d6

STATISTICS

Str 23, **Dex** 16, **Con** 17, **Int** 10, **Wis** 16, **Cha** 8

Base Atk +3; **CMB** +10 (+14 grapple); **CMD** 23

Feats Improved Initiative, Power Attack, Skill Focus (Stealth)

Skills Acrobatics +9, Climb +12, Handle Animal +3, Intimidate +6, Perception +10, Sense Motive +10, Stealth +8, Survival +7, Swim +2

Languages Common

SQ change shape (human, hybrid, and tiger; *polymorph*), lycanthropic empathy (tigers and dire tigers), rogue talents (bleeding attack +2, fast stealth), trapfinding +2

Weretigers in humanoid form have large eyes, long noses, and sharp cheekbones. Most have brown or red hair, though a few have white, black, or even blue-gray. Their movements appear careful yet casual, and a person observing one could easily assume he's watching a skilled pickpocket, graceful dancer, or sultry courtesan.

Weretigers tend to be solitary creatures, only spending time with others of their kind when they feel the urge to breed. Evil weretigers enjoy the thrill of hunting intelligent prey.

Illustration by Mariusz Gandzel

183

Magma Ooze

This seething mass of bubbling molten rock churns and moves of its own hungry accord.

MAGMA OOZE	CR 7

XP 3,200

N Large ooze (fire)

Init –5; **Senses** blindsight 60 ft.; Perception –5

DEFENSE

AC 4, touch 4, flat-footed 4 (–5 Dex, –1 size)

hp 85 (9d8+45)

Fort +8, **Ref** –2, **Will** –2

Defensive Abilities split (cold and slashing, 8 hp); **Immune** fire, ooze traits

Weaknesses vulnerability to cold, vulnerability to water

OFFENSE

Speed 10 ft., climb 10 ft.

Melee slam +14 (2d6+13 plus burn and grab)

Space 10 ft.; **Reach** 5 ft.

Special Attacks burn (2d6, DC 19), constrict (2d6+13 plus burn)

STATISTICS

Str 28, **Dex** 1, **Con** 21, **Int** —, **Wis** 1, **Cha** 1

Base Atk +6; **CMB** +16 (+20 grapple); **CMD** 21 (can't be tripped)

Skills Climb +17

SQ lava body

ECOLOGY

Environment any volcano or underground

Organization solitary

Treasure none

SPECIAL ABILITIES

Lava Body (Ex) The magma ooze is formed of molten rock. Whenever a creature strikes a magma ooze with a weapon, that weapon takes 4d6 points of fire damage unless the attacker makes a DC 19 Fortitude save. Damage caused to weapons in this manner is not halved, but hardness does help prevent some of the damage dealt. The save DC is Constitution-based.

Vulnerability to Water (Ex) A significant amount of water, such as that created by a *create water* spell, the contents of a large bucket, or a blow from a water elemental, that strikes a magma ooze forces the creature to make a DC 20 Fortitude save to avoid being staggered for 2d4 rounds. A magma ooze that is immersed in water must make a DC 20 Fortitude save each round (this DC increases by +1 each subsequent round) or become petrified, reverting once the water is gone.

Magma oozes are living pools of molten rock. They roam the borders of the Plane of Earth and Plane of Fire, and on the Material Plane they sometimes arise spontaneously from strange magic, usually in the vicinity of volcanoes. Magma oozes avoid water, and if forced into enough of it, they become encased in a cooled stony shell, unharmed but immobilized, waiting indefinitely until the water retreats.

A typical magma ooze grows to 10 feet across and is about 6 inches thick.

VARIANT MAGMA OOZES

Differing types of molten stone and the nature of the magic that created them can influence what types of magma ooze form.

Brimstone: Influenced by fiendish energy, brimstone magma oozes stink of evil, and the patterns of cooled stone and hot lava on their surfaces resemble tortured or demonic faces. They have the fiendish creature simple template.

Crystalline: Formed from rock densely laced with rare minerals, crystalline magma oozes have hot gases trapped within their bodies. Striking a crystalline magma ooze with a non-reach melee weapon causes this gas to erupt, dealing 1d6 points of fire damage to the attacking creature.

Poisonous: Whether from toxic metals or magical contamination, these oozes are deadly poison in addition to mobile burning death. A poisonous ooze is +1 CR.

Magma Ooze Poison: Slam—injury; *save* Fort DC 19; *frequency* 1/round for 6 rounds; *effect* 1d2 Con; *cure* 2 consecutive saves.

Illustration by Adam Vehige

Mandragora

This filthy creature resembles a small, wide-mouthed fat child made from leaves, vines, tree bark, dirt, and pallid tubers.

MANDRAGORA	CR 4

XP 1,200

CE Small plant

Init +4; **Senses** low-light vision; Perception +9

DEFENSE

AC 17, touch 15, flat-footed 13 (+4 Dex, +2 natural, +1 size)

hp 37 (5d8+15)

Fort +7, **Ref** +7, **Will** +2

Immune plant traits; **Resist** acid 5, cold 5, electricity 10

Weaknesses vulnerable to supernatural darkness

OFFENSE

Speed 40 ft., burrow 10 ft., climb 40 ft.

Melee bite +8 (1d6+2 plus grab), 2 slam +8 (1d4+2 plus poison)

Space 5 ft.; **Reach** 5 ft. (10 ft. with slam)

Special Attacks blood drain (1d2 Constitution), shriek

STATISTICS

Str 15, **Dex** 18, **Con** 17, **Int** 8, **Wis** 13, **Cha** 10

Base Atk +3; **CMB** +4 (+8 grapple); **CMD** 18

Feats Lightning Reflexes, Skill Focus (Perception), Weapon Finesse

Skills Climb +10, Perception +9, Stealth +14 (+22 in vegetation); **Racial Modifiers** +8 Stealth in vegetation

Languages Abyssal, Common

ECOLOGY

Environment cold or temperate forests

Organization solitary, pair, or grove (3–12)

Treasure standard

SPECIAL ABILITIES

Poison (Ex) Slam—injury; *save* Fort DC 15; *frequency* 1/round for 4 rounds; *effect* confusion and fatigue; *cure* no saves but "act normally" result on the confusion behavior table ends the effect.

Shriek (Su) Once per day as a standard action, a mandragora can give voice to an unsettling shriek. All creatures within a 30-foot spread of a shrieking mandragora must make a DC 15 Will save or become nauseated for 1d4 rounds. This is a sonic, mind-affecting ability. The save DC is Constitution-based.

Vulnerable to Supernatural Darkness (Ex) In areas of supernatural darkness (such as those created by *deeper darkness*, but not by *darkness*), a mandragora is slowed, as the *slow* spell.

A mandragora rises spontaneously from a mandrake root that has drawn nutrition from the corpse or ichor of a demon.

A typical mandragora stands at just over 3 feet tall and only weighs 30 pounds. However, its size hides the creature's fantastic strength and brutality. When a mandragora attacks, its fingers grow into whipping, thorny vines nearly 10 feet long, with which it makes its slam attacks.

A mandragora rarely strays far from its lair amid tangled roots or vines, but when it encounters any other creature, it attacks regardless of the odds. However, a mandragora can usually recognize druids and does not attack them or their animal companions unless they attack it first. It has no qualms about attacking a druid's allies.

When mandragora poison is mixed with its thick, gooey, sap-like blood and 1,000 gp worth of alchemical reagents, the resulting fluid can be used as a focus for the *scrying* spell. The fluid only lasts for the duration of the spell's casting time and resulting effects but the subject of the spell takes a –4 penalty on the save to resist it.

A mandrake root that is growing on or near a demon's corpse or ichor has a 2% chance of awakening as a mandragora within a day of first absorbing the tainted material. A creature that wants to create a mandragora can do so with alchemy; the process requires a day of work, a mandrake root, several pints of ichor or the body of a demon of CR 6 or above, and a successful DC 25 Craft (alchemy) check. The newly created mandragora is hostile, even to its creator.

Illustration by Ben Wootten

MEGAFAUNA, ARSINOITHERIUM

This creature is much like a rhino, some six feet tall and ten feet long, with a pair of massive, knife-like horns curving up from its nose.

ARSINOITHERIUM CR 7

XP 3,200
N Large animal
Init +0; **Senses** low-light vision, scent; Perception +13

DEFENSE

AC 20, touch 9, flat-footed 20 (+11 natural, −1 size)
hp 85 (9d8+45)
Fort +13, **Ref** +6, **Will** +4

OFFENSE

Speed 30 ft.
Melee gore +14 (4d8+13)
Space 10 ft.; **Reach** 5 ft.
Special Attacks powerful charge (4d8+13), trample (2d8+13, DC 23)

STATISTICS

Str 28, **Dex** 10, **Con** 21, **Int** 2, **Wis** 13, **Cha** 3
Base Atk +6; **CMB** +16; **CMD** 26 (30 vs. trip)
Feats Diehard, Endurance, Great Fortitude, Improved Overrun, Power Attack
Skills Perception +13

ECOLOGY

Environment temperate plains
Organization solitary, pair, or herd (3–12)
Treasure none

The arsinoitherium is a herbivore, but it displays a fierce and threatening behavior when it perceives danger: bellowing, stamping, and tossing its head. Threats that do not recede from such warnings are met with a fierce bellow and a charge.

ARSINOITHERIUM COMPANIONS

Starting Statistics: Size Medium; **Speed** 30 ft.; AC +4 natural; **Attack** gore (1d8); **Ability Scores** Str 14, Dex 12, Con 15, Int 2, Wis 13, Cha 3; **Special Qualities** low-light vision, scent.

7th-Level Adv.: Size Large; AC +2 natural; **Attack** gore (2d8); **Ability Scores** Str +8, Dex −2, Con +4; **Special Qualities** powerful charge (2d8), trample.

MEGAFAUNA, GLYPTODON

This armored creature has a bony, turtle-like shell from which protrude short limbs, a blunt head, and a short spiky tail.

GLYPTODON CR 6

XP 2,400
N Large animal
Init +0; **Senses** low-light vision, scent; Perception +16

DEFENSE

AC 21, touch 9, flat-footed 21 (+12 natural, −1 size)
hp 67 (9d8+27)
Fort +11, **Ref** +6, **Will** +4

OFFENSE

Speed 20 ft.
Melee 2 claws +12 (1d10+7)
Space 10 ft.; **Reach** 5 ft.

STATISTICS

Str 25, **Dex** 10, **Con** 17, **Int** 2, **Wis** 13, **Cha** 6
Base Atk +6; **CMB** +14; **CMD** 24 (28 vs. trip)
Feats Endurance, Great Fortitude, Improved Bull Rush, Power Attack, Skill Focus (Perception)
Skills Perception +16

ECOLOGY

Environment temperate plains
Organization solitary or pair
Treasure none

The glyptodon is often hunted for the value of its outer armor, made up of bony plates in turn composed of many smaller, knobby "scales." The creature is quite capable of defending itself with swipes from its deadly claws, as its ill-tempered nature often urges it to do.

GLYPTODON COMPANIONS

Starting Statistics: Size Medium; **Speed** 20 ft.; **AC** +5 natural armor; **Attack** 2 claws (1d8); **Ability Scores** Str 13, Dex 12, Con 13, Int 2, Wis 13, Cha 6; **Special Qualities** low-light vision, scent.

7th-Level Advancement: Size Large; **AC** +2 natural armor; **Attack** 2 claws (1d10); **Ability Scores** Str +8, Dex −2, Con +4.

MEGAFAUNA, MEGALOCEROS

The massive and majestic elk stands fully the height of a human at its shoulder, and its antlers stretch over ten feet across.

MEGALOCEROS	CR 4

XP 1,200

N Large animal

Init +2; **Senses** low-light vision, scent; Perception +9

DEFENSE

AC 16, touch 11, flat-footed 14 (+2 Dex, +5 natural, −1 size)

hp 34 (4d8+16)

Fort +8, **Ref** +8, **Will** +3

OFFENSE

Speed 50 ft.

Melee gore +7 (2d6+5), 2 hooves +2 (1d4+2)

Space 10 ft.; **Reach** 5 ft.

Special Attacks powerful charge (4d6+7)

STATISTICS

Str 20, **Dex** 15, **Con** 18, **Int** 2, **Wis** 15, **Cha** 5

Base Atk +3; **CMB** +9; **CMD** 21 (25 vs. trip)

Feats Endurance, Lightning Reflexes, Run[B]

Skills Perception +9

ECOLOGY

Environment cold or temperate forest and plains

Organization solitary, pair, or herd (3–50)

Treasure none

The megaloceros is a powerful and enormous elk, also known as a "great elk" or "king stag." It stands about 6 feet tall at the shoulder and has antlers spanning up to 12 feet. It weighs 1,400 pounds.

MEGALOCEROS COMPANIONS

Starting Statistics: Size Medium; **Speed** 50 ft.; **AC** +3 natural armor, **Attack** gore (1d8); **Ability Scores** Str 12, Dex 17, Con 14, Int 2, Wis 15, Cha 5; **Special Abilities** low-light vision, scent.

7th-Level Adv.: Size Large; **AC** +2 natural armor; **Attack** gore (2d6), 2 hooves (1d4); **Ability Scores** Str +8, Dex −2, Con +4; **Special Qualities** powerful charge (2d6).

MEGAFAUNA, MEGATHERIUM

The great sloth, standing on its hind legs, can reach the treetops with its agile tongue to grab at foliage.

MEGATHERIUM	CR 5

XP 1,600

N Huge animal

Init +0; **Senses** low-light vision, scent; Perception +14

DEFENSE

AC 18, touch 8, flat-footed 18 (+10 natural, −2 size)

hp 59 (7d8+28)

Fort +9, **Ref** +5, **Will** +3

OFFENSE

Speed 30 ft., climb 10 ft.

Melee 2 claws +10 (1d8+7 plus trip)

Space 15 ft.; **Reach** 10 ft.

Special Attacks rend (2 claws, 1d8+10)

STATISTICS

Str 25, **Dex** 10, **Con** 19, **Int** 2, **Wis** 13, **Cha** 6

Base Atk +5; **CMB** +14; **CMD** 24 (28 vs. trip)

Feats Awesome Blow, Improved Bull Rush, Power Attack, Skill Focus (Perception)

Skills Climb +15, Perception +14

ECOLOGY

Environment temperate or warm forest

Organization solitary or pair

Treasure none

The megatherium is a massive sloth weighing 10,000 pounds. It can balance on its hind legs and tail, allowing it to reach up to 20 feet high.

MEGATHERIUM COMPANIONS

Starting Statistics: Size Medium; **Speed** 40 ft., climb 10 ft.; **AC** +5 natural armor, **Attack** 2 claws (1d4); **Ability Scores** Str 9, Dex 14, Con 11, Int 2, Wis 13, Cha 6; **Special Qualities** low-light vision, scent.

7th-Level Adv.: Size Large; **AC** +2 natural armor; **Attack** 2 claws (1d6), **Ability Scores** Str +8, Dex −2, Con +4; **Special Qualities** rend (2 claws, 1d8).

187

MERCANE

The tall, blue-skinned humanoid is clad in loose, flowing robes. Its alien face has too many eyes and its hands have too few fingers.

MERCANE	CR 5

XP 1,600

LN Large outsider (extraplanar)

Init +2; **Senses** darkvision 60 ft.; Perception +12

DEFENSE

AC 16, touch 12, flat-footed 13 (+2 Dex, +1 dodge, +4 natural, −1 size)

hp 51 (6d10+18)

Fort +8, **Ref** +4, **Will** +8

SR 20

OFFENSE

Speed 30 ft.

Melee mwk Large falchion +8/+3 (2d6+3/18–20)

Space 10 ft.; **Reach** 10 ft.

Spell-Like Abilities (CL 9th; concentration +11)

3/day—*dimension door, invisibility* (self only)

1/day—*plane shift* (DC 17)

STATISTICS

Str 15, **Dex** 14, **Con** 16, **Int** 20, **Wis** 17, **Cha** 15

Base Atk +6; **CMB** +9; **CMD** 22

Feats Combat Casting, Combat Expertise, Dodge

Skills Appraise +14, Bluff +11, Diplomacy +8, Intimidate +8, Knowledge (arcana) +14, Knowledge (planes) +14, Perception +12, Profession (merchant) +9, Sense Motive +12, Sleight of Hand +11, Spellcraft +14

Languages Abyssal, Celestial, Common, Draconic, Infernal; telepathy 100 ft.

SQ *secret chest*

ECOLOGY

Environment any land or underground

Organization solitary or company (1–4 and 3–12 bodyguards of various races)

Treasure double (masterwork Large falchion, other treasure)

SPECIAL ABILITIES

Secret Chest (Sp) A mercane can retrieve or hide an extradimensional storage chest, as the *secret chest* spell

(caster level 5th). The mercane does not need an expensive replica chest to use this ability; any chest will do. It can only use this ability on one chest at a time.

Mysterious merchants of all things magical, mercanes are relatively weak and noncombative for creatures of their size. They prefer to bargain and haggle rather than to fight, but because they wander the planes seeking and trading magical goods, they typically travel with an entourage of hired bodyguards. Mercanes are capable of defending themselves, and often carry masterwork Large falchions. Yet these weapons are primarily for show, as mercanes prefer to let their bodyguards deal with violent opponents. If a situation turns ugly, mercanes typically use their magical abilities to flee, abandoning their hirelings if necessary.

Mercanes are known throughout the planes as traders in magical items. Each has a *secret chest* filled with wares stashed away, ready to be pulled out when it's time to haggle and close a deal (or to bribe a potential obstacle). Mercanes are therefore not easily robbed, and they only surrender the contents of a *secret chest* when they have no other choice. Mercanes have no interest in mundane goods, no matter how fine or rare. Only magical objects earn their attention and their coin. They're known for driving hard, but fair, bargains, and for hiring adventurers from time to time to recover certain goods of interest for a fair price. Although they are not particularly brave, they hold contracts sacrosanct and keep their agreements.

Rumors and legends abound as to the origins of the mercanes and their reasons for seeking out and buying magical items. Their home plane is unknown, and they have wandered between the worlds for as long as any can recall. Stories claim the mercanes feed on the magic items they acquire, or even need them in order to reproduce. There are also tales of a war in a far corner of the planes, with the mercanes serving the roles of arms merchants, aggressors, or defenders, depending on who tells the story.

Mercanes are 10 feet tall and weigh 500 pounds.

MERROW

This giant has pale green, scaled skin and large, webbed hands and feet. On either side of its neck are slotted gills.

MERROW, FRESHWATER   CR 3

XP 800

NE Large humanoid (aquatic, giant)

Init +4; **Senses** low-light vision; Perception +5

DEFENSE

AC 17, touch 13, flat-footed 13 (+4 Dex, +4 natural, −1 size)

hp 30 (4d8+12)

Fort +7, **Ref** +5, **Will** +3

OFFENSE

Speed 40 ft., swim 40 ft.

Melee 2 claws +6 (1d6+4 plus grab)

Ranged javelin +6 (1d8+4)

Space 10 ft.; **Reach** 10 ft.

STATISTICS

Str 19, **Dex** 18, **Con** 17, **Int** 6, **Wis** 10, **Cha** 7

Base Atk +3; **CMB** +8 (+12 grapple); **CMD** 22

Feats Iron Will, Power Attack

Skills Perception +5, Stealth +2 (+6 in water), Swim +12; **Racial Modifiers** +4 Stealth in water

Languages Giant

SQ amphibious

ECOLOGY

Environment temperate lakes or rivers

Organization solitary, pair, gang (3–4), or family (5–16)

Treasure standard (2 javelins, other treasure)

MERROW, SALTWATER   CR 6

XP 2,400

NE Huge humanoid (aquatic, giant)

Init +3; **Senses** low-light vision; Perception +7

DEFENSE

AC 19, touch 11, flat-footed 16 (+3 Dex, +8 natural, −2 size)

hp 80 (7d8+49)

Fort +11, **Ref** +5, **Will** +4

OFFENSE

Speed 40 ft., swim 40 ft.

Melee 2 claws +11 (1d8+7 plus grab)

Ranged javelin +6 (2d6+7)

Space 15 ft.; **Reach** 15 ft.

STATISTICS

Str 25, **Dex** 16, **Con** 23, **Int** 6, **Wis** 10, **Cha** 7

Base Atk +5; **CMB** +14 (+18 grapple); **CMD** 27

Feats Iron Will, Power Attack, Vital Strike, Weapon Focus (claw)

Skills Perception +7, Stealth −2 (+2 in water), Swim +15; **Racial Modifiers** +4 Stealth in water

Languages Giant

SQ amphibious

ECOLOGY

Environment temperate oceans

Organization solitary, pair, gang (3–4), or family (5–16)

Treasure standard (2 javelins, other treasure)

Merrows are best described as the aquatic cousins of ogres. Although their green, scaled skin and webbed hands and feet make them appear different, merrows are just as cruel, savage, and wicked as their ogre relatives.

The saltwater variety grows much larger than the freshwater variety, but the behavior and society of the two types are otherwise similar.

Merrows are known for pillaging small fishing villages and towns under cover of night. Similar to ogres, merrows have a strong sense of family and typically hunt in gangs, preferring to grab a couple of villagers and head back into the water rather than sticking around and dealing with armed resistance. Merrows have a stronger sense of unity than ogres do, and rarely will the leader of a tribe be challenged. When they have chosen a village or town to plunder, they attack as a gang and share the spoils.

A freshwater merrow is 12 feet tall and weighs 500 pounds. Saltwater merrows easily reach 20 feet tall and 4,000 pounds, and have been known to hunt whales. The two species do not often come in contact, but when they do, feuding and conflict are swift to develop.

MIHSTU

A miasmal form roils as barbed tentacles emerge from the central mass, coalescing into razor-sharp talons and claws.

MIHSTU	CR 8

XP 4,800

NE Medium outsider (air, elemental, extraplanar)

Init +10; **Senses** darkvision 60 ft.; Perception +13

DEFENSE

AC 22, touch 17, flat-footed 15 (+6 Dex, +1 dodge, +5 natural)

hp 92 (8d10+48)

Fort +12, **Ref** +12, **Will** +4

Defensive Abilities wind defense; DR 10/magic; **Immune** electricity, elemental traits; SR 19

Weaknesses susceptible to cold

OFFENSE

Speed 20 ft., fly 20 ft. (good)

Melee 4 tentacles +14 (1d4+1 plus grab)

Special Attacks deadly embrace

STATISTICS

Str 12, **Dex** 23, **Con** 23, **Int** 14, **Wis** 14, **Cha** 13

Base Atk +8; **CMB** +9 (+13 grapple); **CMD** 26 (can't be tripped)

Feats Dodge, Improved Initiative, Mobility, Weapon Finesse

Skills Acrobatics +17, Bluff +12, Escape Artist +17, Fly +21, Knowledge (planes) +13, Perception +13, Sense Motive +13, Stealth +17

Languages Auran

SQ gaseous

ECOLOGY

Environment any (Plane of Air)

Organization solitary

Treasure standard

SPECIAL ABILITIES

Gaseous (Ex) A mihstu can pass through small holes, even cracks, without reducing its speed.

Deadly Embrace (Ex) A mihstu that pins an opponent completely surrounds that creature and deals 1d2 Constitution damage every round as it siphons away blood, tears, and other vital fluids. Maintaining a pin is a free action for a mihstu and it does not gain the grappled condition (allowing it to attack other creatures with its tentacles).

Susceptible to Cold (Ex) Magical cold stuns a mihstu rather than damaging it. If the creature fails its save against a magical cold effect, it is stunned for 1 round and then staggered for an additional 1d4 rounds.

Wind Defense (Ex) The churning winds of a mihstu's body automatically deflect nonmagical projectiles (such as arrows, bolts, and sling stones). All other ranged weapons (including magical projectiles and thrown weapons) have a 20% miss chance. Weapons of significant size, such as giant-thrown boulders, siege engine projectiles, and other massive ranged weapons are not affected by this ability.

The deadly mihstus hail from the Plane of Air. When they come to the Material Plane, they prefer to inhabit dank dungeon corridors, abandoned ruins, and the forgotten corridors of lost civilizations. Scholars dispute what drives the ambitions of these creatures, or even what they seek on the Material Plane, but all agree that they are deadly combatants and merciless hunters. Their semi-solid bodies appear to be composed of a strange, white smoke, and they can shape their vaporous bodies at will to seep through small cracks and openings in pursuit of prey. When attacking, they coalesce the tips of their misty tentacles into wickedly barbed talons, slashing at opponents with these razor-sharp appendages. Mihstus rely on their insubstantial nature to close with opponents quickly, engulfing the nearest threat while continuing to attack any who seek to deprive them of their chosen victim. When a mihstu manages to embrace a foe with its body, it drains away the creature's vital fluids at an alarming rate. These fluids churn in the creature's body for a few rounds before spattering against nearby walls or on the floor—the mihstu seems to gain no nourishment from these fluids, so this attack may be nothing more than a favorite method of cruelty.

Mihstus are immortal unless slain by violence, and if properly bargained with, these deadly outsiders can actually be intriguing sources of information. Mihstus are normally interested in little more than stalking and consuming prey, and as a result only tend to provide reliable information or cooperate when supplied with intriguing victims to pursue and destroy. Nefarious creatures such as rakshasas and evil cloud giants often utilize mihstus as trackers and assassins, or sometimes employ them as guards in the forgotten corridors of their lairs.

Mongrelman

Ivory tusks, insect chitin, matted fur, scaly flesh, and more combine to form a hideous humanoid shape.

MONGRELMAN	CR 1

XP 400

LN Medium monstrous humanoid

Init +1; **Senses** darkvision 60 ft., low-light vision; Perception +6

DEFENSE

AC 13, touch 11, flat-footed 12 (+1 Dex, +2 natural)

hp 15 (2d10+4)

Fort +2, **Ref** +4, **Will** +4

OFFENSE

Speed 30 ft.

Melee club +4 (1d6+3) or

slam +4 (1d4+3)

STATISTICS

Str 14, **Dex** 13, **Con** 15, **Int** 10, **Wis** 12, **Cha** 7

Base Atk +2; **CMB** +4; **CMD** 15

Feats Skill Focus (Stealth)

Skills Climb +6, Perception +6, Sleight of Hand +7,
Stealth +13, Survival +5; **Racial Modifiers** +4 Sleight
of Hand, +4 Stealth

Languages Common, Undercommon

SQ sound mimicry (voices)

ECOLOGY

Environment any ruins or underground

Organization solitary, pair, gang (3–6),
band (7–12), or tribe (21–30 plus
30% noncombatants, 2–4 rogues
of 1st–3rd level, 1–2 oracles
or witches of 2nd–4th level, 1
fighter or ranger chieftain of
3rd–6th level, 4–6 dire bats, and 3–20 dire rats)

Treasure standard (club, other treasure)

These creatures pride themselves on their survival skills, for the bowels of the earth are no place for weaklings. Other foul and intelligent races who claim dominion in the underworld take mongrelmen as slaves (particularly morlocks), finding this deformed race's docile nature and hardworking attitude makes them extremely useful as tools of labor. In this role, mongrelmen still fall back on their pride of survival, slow to rebel and patiently waiting for the overthrow of their masters.

Mongrelmen dwelling on the surface sometimes live amid the hustle and bustle of cities, sequestering themselves in ghettos and sewers to avoid notice. Urban mongrelmen may rely on begging and pickpocketing to get by, but most form rural communities near trading routes.

Despite their varied physical forms, most mongrelmen average 5–6 feet tall and weigh between 150 and 250 pounds on average. A tragically short lifespan limits the creatures' population growth—mongrelmen rarely live past 35 years.

Despite their monstrous appearances, mongrelmen are generally hardworking and peaceful creatures. A mongrelman can produce offspring with any humanoid, mixing bloodlines in strange ways to create hardier crossbreeds. No two mongrelmen look the same. One may have a face that is half hobgoblin, half lizardfolk, with one human-like foot and one cloven hoof, while his sister may have elven ears, a dwarven beard, orc tusks, and clawed hands. Each mongrelman usually has characteristics from at least a half-dozen different races. This strange mixture enforces mongrelmen's place in the edges of the world, for they are shunned by all who fear their twisted appearance. Mistaken as enemies by all, mongrelmen prefer to be left alone.

Most mongrelmen live deep below the surface of the world in hidden caves far from civilization.

MOONFLOWER

A twisted trunk clustered with bulbous blossoms holds up a gaping mouth ready to swallow a victim whole.

MOONFLOWER	CR 8

XP 4,800

N Huge plant

Init +4; **Senses** darkvision 60 ft., low-light vision; Perception +9

DEFENSE

AC 21, touch 8, flat-footed 21 (+13 natural, –2 size)

hp 104 (11d8+55); fast healing 5

Fort +12, **Ref** +3, **Will** +4

DR 10/slashing; **Immune** electricity, plant traits; **Resist** cold 10

Weaknesses vulnerable to fire

OFFENSE

Speed 20 ft.

Melee bite +15 (2d6+9 plus grab), 2 tentacles +13 (1d8+4)

Space 15 ft.; **Reach** 15 ft.

Special Attacks light pulse, pod prison

STATISTICS

Str 28, **Dex** 10, **Con** 21, **Int** 5, **Wis** 12, **Cha** 17

Base Atk +8; **CMB** +19 (+23 grapple);

  CMD 29 (can't be tripped)

Feats Blind-Fight, Improved Initiative, Improved Sunder, Multiattack, Power Attack, Skill Focus (Stealth)

Skills Perception +9, Stealth +4 (+20 in thick vegetation); **Racial Modifiers** +16 Stealth in thick vegetation

Languages telepathy (1 mile, other moonflowers only)

SQ pod spawn

ECOLOGY

Environment any land

Organization solitary or cluster (2–8)

Treasure standard

SPECIAL ABILITIES

Light Pulse (Su) As a standard action, a moonflower can release a pulse of bright light. All creatures within a 50-foot burst that can see the moonflower must make a DC 20 Fortitude save or be blinded for 1d4 rounds. Moonflowers are immune to this ability. The save DC is Constitution-based.

Pod Prison (Ex) This works like the swallow whole ability, except the moonflower can only use it once every 1d4 rounds, and the swallowed creature is immediately wrapped in a tight digestive cocoon and expelled into an adjacent square, where it takes damage every round (2d6 bludgeoning and 2d6 acid, AC 15, 25 hp). The cocooned target cannot use Escape Artist to get out of the cocoon. Other creatures can aid the target by attacking the cocoon with piercing or slashing weapons, but the creature within takes half the damage from any attack against the cocoon. Once the cocoon is destroyed, it deflates and decays. Each creature swallowed by a moonflower is encased in its own cocoon.

Pod Spawn (Ex) Should a moonflower's pod prison kill and digest a Small or larger creature, the pod transforms into an adult moonflower with full hit points after 1d4 hours. The newly formed moonflower has its own consciousness, but some aspect of its trunk or blossoms resembles the creature that died within. The dead creature's equipment remains inside the new moonflower and can be retrieved by killing it.

A fully grown moonflower easily stands 20 feet tall, its massive trunk frequently 4 feet or more in diameter. The roots extend away from the base and into the soil, making the plant seem well anchored, but the roots themselves possess an agility that belies the great size of the plant and allows the moonflower to uproot itself and move with surprising speed. The tendrils of the plant are independently prehensile and writhe around the large flytrap-like "head" that crowns the stem.

Moonflowers have never been known to communicate with other creatures, even with druids and others who regularly converse with plants. The plants do possess some manner of strange telepathy, though, and are in constant communication with their nearby brethren. Those who manage to intrude upon the creatures' alien thoughts face an assault of horrible visions of terrifying jungles filled with ancient, sentient, and malign plants.

MOSQUITO, GIANT

A bloated, red belly dangles beneath the furiously beating wings of this massive mosquito.

GIANT MOSQUITO	CR 6

XP 2,400

N Medium vermin

Init +7; **Senses** darkvision 60 ft., scent; Perception +9

DEFENSE

AC 19, touch 17, flat-footed 12 (+7 Dex, +2 natural)

hp 60 (8d8+24)

Fort +9, **Ref** +9, **Will** +3

Immune mind-affecting effects

OFFENSE

Speed 20 ft., fly 60 ft. (good)

Melee bite +10 (1d8+6 plus bleed, disease, and grab)

Special Attacks bleed (2d4), blood drain (1d2 Constitution)

STATISTICS

Str 18, **Dex** 25, **Con** 17, **Int** —, **Wis** 13, **Cha** 6

Base Atk +6; **CMB** +10 (+14 grapple); **CMD** 27 (35 vs. trip)

Skills Fly +11, Perception +9; **Racial Modifiers** Perception+8

ECOLOGY

Environment temperate or tropical swamps

Organization solitary, pair, or swarm (3–12)

Treasure none

SPECIAL ABILITIES

Disease (Ex) *Malaria*: Bite—injury; *save* Fortitude DC 17; *onset* 1d3 days; *frequency* 1 day; *effect* 1d3 Con damage and 1d3 Wis Damage; *cure* 2 consecutive saves. The save DC is Constitution-based.

Horrifically enlarged versions of the common mosquito, giant mosquitoes bring death on swift wings. A single specimen can drain the blood from a human adult with shocking speed, while swarms of fist-sized mosquitoes can lay waste to herds of livestock or entire villages. In the wild, giant mosquitoes prey upon megafauna like dinosaurs and other huge creatures.

Giant mosquitoes grow to 6 feet in length, and weigh up to 150 pounds. Variant species of giant mosquitoes exist, although not in the great diversity seen in many other giant vermin. The most common variant is the smaller goblin mosquito (a giant mosquito with the young creature template), but stories of Large jungle mosquitoes (giant mosquitoes with the advanced and giant simple templates) are not unheard of.

MOSQUITO SWARM

The droning and spastic movements of this cloud of hungry mosquitoes promise a painful ordeal.

MOSQUITO SWARM	CR 3

XP 800

N Diminutive vermin (swarm)

Init +1; **Senses** darkvision 60 ft.; Perception +9

DEFENSE

AC 15, touch 15, flat-footed 14 (+1 Dex, +4 size)

hp 31 (7d8)

Fort +5, **Ref** +3, **Will** +3

Defensive Abilities swarm traits; **Immune** mind-affecting effects, weapon damage

OFFENSE

Speed 5 ft., fly 40 ft. (good)

Melee swarm (2d6 plus disease and bleed)

Space 10 ft.; **Reach** 5 ft.

Special Attacks bleed (1d6), disease (malaria, DC 13), distraction (DC 13)

STATISTICS

Str 1, **Dex** 13, **Con** 10, **Int** —, **Wis** 12, **Cha** 9

Base Atk +5; **CMB** —; **CMD** —

Skills Fly +11, Perception +9; **Racial Modifiers** Perception +8

ECOLOGY

Environment tropical swamps

Organization solitary, pair, fury (3–6 swarms), or scourge (7–12 swarms)

Treasure none

Illustration by Eric Belisle

MOTHMAN

A shroud of dark wings cloaks this thin, humanoid shape. Two monstrous red eyes glare malevolently from its narrow face.

MOTHMAN	CR 6

XP 2,400

CN Medium monstrous humanoid

Init +8; **Senses** darkvision 60 ft.; Perception +16

DEFENSE

AC 20, touch 14, flat-footed 16 (+4 Dex, +6 natural)

hp 76 (9d10+27)

Fort +6, **Ref** +10, **Will** +10

SR 17

OFFENSE

Speed 30 ft., fly 60 ft. (good)

Melee 2 claw +13 (1d6+1)

Special Attacks mind-warping gaze

Spell-Like Abilities (CL 12th;

   concentration +16)

   Constant—*blur*

   At will—*detect thoughts* (DC

      16), *ghost sound* (DC 14),

      misdirection (DC 16)

   3/day—*greater invisibility*, *major*

      image (DC 17), *modify memory*

      (DC 18), *nightmare* (DC 19),

      phantasmal killer (DC 18), *shadow*

      walk (DC 20), *suggestion* (DC 17)

   1/day—*agent of fate*, *false vision*, *mind*

      fog (DC 19), *mislead* (DC 20), *project*

      image (DC 21)

STATISTICS

Str 12, **Dex** 19, **Con** 16, **Int** 17, **Wis** 19, **Cha** 18

Base Atk +9; **CMB** +13; **CMD** 24

Feats Agile Maneuvers, Blind-Fight, Flyby Attack,

   Improved Initiative, Weapon Finesse

Skills Fly +20, Knowledge (any two) +12,

   Perception +16, Sense Motive +13,

   Spellcraft +12, Stealth +16

Languages Common, Sylvan, Undercommon

   (can't speak); telepathy 100 ft.

ECOLOGY

Environment any land

Organization solitary

Treasure standard

SPECIAL ABILITIES

Agent of Fate (Sp) A mothman may recreate the

   effects of any spell of 5th level or lower once

   per day as a spell-like ability, but only if doing

   so steers the flow of fate in its proper course.

   What the proper flow of fate entails is determined

   by the GM. Typical uses of this ability include

casting *major image* to coax someone to a portentous location, casting *raise dead* to return someone with an important fate to life, or using *rusting grasp* to weaken a structure and cause some necessary calamity.

Mind-Warping Gaze (Su) Fear, 30 feet, Will DC 18 negates. A creature that fails a save against this attack becomes shaken for 1d6 rounds. A creature currently suffering from a fear effect that fails this save instead takes 1d4 points of Wisdom damage. This is a mind-affecting fear effect. The save DC is Charisma-based.

Little is known of these strange creatures, save that when they appear, calamity follows. Mothmen see themselves as agents of fate, exhibiting extraordinary powers to guide the hands of destiny. More often than not, citizens encounter a mothman and never recall the meeting, yet fall right into the creature's obscure plans. Mothmen stand almost 7 feet tall and weigh 100 pounds.

Illustration by Tyler Walpole

Mu Spore

Tentacles and eyes cover this floating, fungoid monster, and its vast mouth opens like a toothy cavern.

MU SPORE	CR 21

XP 409,600

CN Colossal plant

Init +3; **Senses** blindsight 240 ft., low-light vision; Perception +43

DEFENSE

AC 37, touch 1, flat-footed 37 (−1 Dex, +36 natural, −8 size)

hp 418 (31d8+279); fast healing 10

Fort +26, **Ref** +11, **Will** +19

Defensive Abilities grasping tendrils; **DR** 10/epic; **Immune** plant traits; **Resist** acid 30

OFFENSE

Speed 40 ft., fly 30 ft. (perfect)

Melee bite +32 (6d6+16/19–20 plus grab), 4 tentacles +27 (3d8+8/19–20 plus grab)

Space 30 ft.; **Reach** 30 ft. (60 ft. with tentacle)

Special Attacks spore cough, constrict (3d8+16), swallow whole (20d8 acid, AC 28, 41 hp)

STATISTICS

Str 42, **Dex** 9, **Con** 29, **Int** 18, **Wis** 28, **Cha** 29

Base Atk +23; **CMB** +47 (+51 grapple); **CMD** 56 (can't be tripped)

Feats Awesome Blow, Critical Focus, Greater Bull Rush, Greater Vital Strike, Improved Bull Rush, Improved Critical (bite), Improved Critical (tentacles), Improved Initiative, Improved Lightning Reflexes, Improved Vital Strike, Lightning Reflexes, Power Attack, Staggering Critical, Vital Strike, Weapon Focus (bite), Weapon Focus (tentacles)

Skills Fly +33, Knowledge (dungeoneering, geography, nature) +35, Perception +43, Sense Motive +40

Languages Aklo, Common, Terran, Undercommon

ECOLOGY

Environment any

Organization solitary or pair

Treasure standard

SPECIAL ABILITIES

Grasping Tendrils (Ex) Sticky, arm-length tendrils cover a mu spore. A mu spore can use these tendrils to attempt a grab as an immediate action when an adjacent creature hits it with a melee attack. As it is only using the tendrils (instead of conducting the grapple normally), it takes a −20 penalty to its CMB to make and maintain the grapple (+31 CMB with tendrils). The mu spore does not gain the grappled condition while grappling a creature with its tendrils.

Spore Cough (Su) Once every 1d4 rounds as a standard action, a mu spore can release a cloud of burrowing spores in a 100-foot cone. The burrowing spores deal 20d8 points of damage to all creatures and wooden structures in the area, or half damage to any creatures that make a DC 34 Reflex save. Plants and plant creatures are immune to this damage. The save DC is Constitution-based.

A mu spore is a thankfully rare plant of vast power and strange intellect. The smallest of mu spores (such as the one presented here) are never less than a hundred feet long from tentacle tip to tentacle tip, and weigh a minimum of 200,000 pounds. Yet despite their vast bulk, mu spores are capable of flying with an uncommon grace, venting jets of foul-smelling spores to guide their flight through the air.

Mu spores dwell in vast caverns, but sometimes drift up to the surface through immense pits or tunnels—they have no fear of sunlight, but prefer nocturnal habits. Mu spores are more than just ravenous eaters of nations—they possess uncommon intellects, and if peaceful contact can be made, their knowledge can be quite valuable. Even more valuable, to many debased alchemists, are the strange secretions and spores they emit, for these rare materials can be brewed into the strangest of drugs and elixirs.

Illustration by Mike Corriero

NECROPHIDIUS

The soft scrape of bone reveals the long, sinuous skeleton of a large snake, its head a humanoid skull with a snake's jaws.

NECROPHIDIUS	CR 3

XP 800

N Medium construct

Init +3; **Senses** darkvision 60 ft., low-light vision; Perception +0

DEFENSE

AC 15, touch 13, flat-footed 12 (+3 Dex, +2 natural)

hp 36 (3d10+20)

Fort +1, **Ref** +4, **Will** +1

DR 5/bludgeoning; **Immune** construct traits

OFFENSE

Speed 30 ft.

Melee bite +6 (1d8+4 plus paralysis)

Special Attacks dance of death

STATISTICS

Str 16, **Dex** 17, **Con** —, **Int** —, **Wis** 11, **Cha** 1

Base Atk +3; **CMB** +6; **CMD** 19 (can't be tripped)

Skills Stealth +15; **Racial Modifiers** +12 Stealth

ECOLOGY

Environment any

Organization solitary or coil (2–6)

Treasure none

SPECIAL ABILITIES

Dance of Death (Ex) A necrophidius can entrance opponents by swaying back and forth as a full-round action. All creatures within 30 feet who can see the necrophidius when it uses its dance of death must succeed on a DC 15 Will save or be dazed for 2d4 rounds. This is a mind-affecting effect. The save DC is Constitution-based and includes a +4 racial bonus.

Paralysis (Su) Any living creature that is bitten by a necrophidius must succeed on a DC 13 Fortitude save or be paralyzed for 1d4 rounds. The save DC is Constitution-based and includes a +2 racial bonus.

Despite its sinister appearance, the snake-like necrophidius is not an undead creature. Rather, it is a magical construct built from the skeleton of a giant snake and then mounted with the skull of a humanoid creature. Fangs are cemented into the jaws of the skull, after which the entire creation can be brought to life by a series of obscure and expensive rituals—these rituals are traditionally well guarded by those who discover them.

As a mindless construct that requires neither food nor sleep, a necrophidius makes an excellent guardian, and its innate stealth allows it to slip up on the unwary undetected. In certain areas, the necrophidius is commonly employed as an assassin, able to disable its quarries with its dance of death or paralyzing bite before disposing of them in a gruesome manner—as long as the assassination doesn't require any particular intelligence to carry out. Particularly macabre creators might even construct the creature from the skull of a friend or loved one of the intended victim in order to magnify the horror of the assassination, leaving much of the flesh on the skull so the victim can recognize its source. This flesh rots eventually—only freshly crafted necrophidiuses have this grisly feature (although regular applications of *gentle repose* spells can keep such a morbid decoration fresh for a much longer period of time).

Although a necrophidius is mindless, it can follow the simple commands of its creator. These can include commands to lie dormant until some specific condition is met or to follow and kill an indicated target to the exclusion of all other activities.

A typical necrophidius is 10 feet long and weighs 200 pounds.

CONSTRUCTION

A necrophidius's body consists of a human skull and the skeletal remains of a constrictor snake, all treated with rare oils and powders worth 1,000 gp.

NECROPHIDIUS

CL 10th; **Price** 7,500 gp

CONSTRUCTION

Requirements Craft Construct, *cat's grace*, *daze monster*, *geas/quest*, *ghoul touch*, creator must be caster level 7th; **Skill** Craft (sculpture) or Heal DC 15; **Cost** 4,250 gp

Illustration by Eric Belisle

NEH-THALGGU

This crab-like nightmare has a lamprey mouth, twitching eyes on its legs, and several blisters along its back that hold human brains.

NEH-THALGGU	CR 8

XP 4,800
CE Large aberration
Init +7; **Senses** darkvision 60 ft.; Perception +17

DEFENSE

AC 21, touch 19, flat-footed 18 (+3 Dex, +2 natural, +7 insight, –1 size)
hp 105 (10d8+60)
Fort +9, **Ref** +6, **Will** +11
DR 10/magic; **Immune** confusion effects; **SR** 19

OFFENSE

Speed 10 ft., fly 40 ft. (perfect)
Melee bite +13 (1d8+7 plus poison), 2 claws +13 (1d6+7)
Space 10 ft.; **Reach** 5 ft.
Special Attacks rend (2 claws, 2d6+7)
Sorcerer Spells Known (CL 7th; concentration +17)
  3rd (5/day)—*lightning bolt* (DC16), *hold person* (DC 16)
  2nd (7/day)—*acid arrow, alter self, invisibility*
  1st (7/day)—*grease* (DC 14), *magic missile, ray of enfeeblement* (DC 14), *shield, unseen servant*
  0 (at will)—*acid splash, dancing lights, detect magic, mage hand, open/close, prestidigitation, read magic*

STATISTICS

Str 24, **Dex** 16, **Con** 23, **Int** 19, **Wis** 18, **Cha** 17
Base Atk +7; **CMB** +15; **CMD** 35 (can't be tripped)
Feats Arcane Strike, Extend Spell, Combat Reflexes, Eschew Materials[B], Improved Initiative, Power Attack
Skills Fly +15, Knowledge (arcana, dungeoneering, and planes) +23, Perception +17, Sense Motive +17, Spellcraft +17, Stealth +12, Use Magic Device +16
Languages Abyssal, Aklo, Common, Draconic, Protean, Undercommon; telepathy (100 feet)
SQ brain collection, strange knowledge

ECOLOGY

Environment any
Organization solitary
Treasure double

SPECIAL ABILITIES

Brain Collection (Ex) A neh-thalggu can store up to seven humanoid brains and use them to enhance its knowledge and power. Each stored brain grants a neh-thalggu a cumulative +1 insight bonus to AC, concentration checks, and Knowledge checks. A neh-thalggu can extract a brain from a helpless opponent with a coup de grace attack, or as a standard action from a body that has been dead for no more than 1 minute. A neh-thalggu that has fewer than seven brains gains one negative level for each missing brain. These negative levels can never become permanent, but they can only be removed by replacing one of its collected brains. The stats presented here assume a monster with a full collection.

Poison (Ex) Bite—injury; *save* Fort DC 21; *frequency* 1/round for 6 rounds; *effect* 1d2 Strength damage and staggered for 1 round; *cure* 2 consecutive saves. The save DC is Constitution-based.

Spells A neh-thalggu casts spells as a 7th-level sorcerer. For each negative level it takes from missing brains, its caster level is reduced by 1. A neh-thalggu with no collected brains cannot cast any of its spells.

Strange Knowledge (Ex) All knowledge skill are class skills for neh-thalggus.

Known also as brain collectors, the alien neh-thalggus hail from distant worlds, traveling the gulfs of space on immense living ships that swiftly decay when they land upon a new world, leaving behind a deadly cargo of hungry monsters. Neh-thalggus are carnivores, but they do not digest humanoid brains they eat—rather, these brains lodge in one of several bulbous blisters on the creature's back and help to increase its intellect.

Some speculate that neh-thalggus encountered in this reality may merely be juveniles of their kind, perhaps exiled from their home worlds by greater kin until they can prove their worth on other worlds. Their brain collections may be a morbid form of currency in their home realm, or the thoughts in these brains may merely be fuel for a dark apotheosis into an even more sinister mature form.

Illustration by Jim Pavelec

NEREID

This beautiful woman has pearlescent skin and long, dark hair. Her nudity is barely hidden by a diaphanous, wet shawl.

NEREID	CR 10

XP 9,600

CN Medium fey (water)

Init +9; **Senses** low-light vision; Perception +21

Aura beguiling aura (30 ft., DC 23)

DEFENSE

AC 25, touch 25, flat-footed 15 (+5 deflection, +9 Dex, +1 dodge)

hp 126 (12d6+84)

Fort +11, **Ref** +17, **Will** +14

Defensive Abilities transparency; **DR** 10/cold iron; **Immune** cold, poison; **SR** 21

Weaknesses shawl

OFFENSE

Speed 30 ft., swim 60 ft.

Melee touch +10 (poison)

Ranged spray +15 touch (poison)

Special Attacks drowning kiss

Spell-Like Abilities (CL 12th; concentration +17)

At will—*control water, suggestion* (DC 18; only against creatures that are currently fascinated by her beguiling aura)

1/day—*summon monster VI* (water elementals only)

STATISTICS

Str 11, **Dex** 29, **Con** 24, **Int** 14, **Wis** 22, **Cha** 21

Base Atk +6; **CMB** +15; **CMD** 37

Feats Ability Focus (beguiling aura), Agile Maneuvers, Defensive Combat Training, Dodge, Mobility, Weapon Finesse

Skills Bluff +20, Escape Artist +24, Knowledge (nature) +17, Perception +21, Perform (sing) +20, Sense Motive +21, Stealth +24, Swim +23

Languages Aquan, Common, Sylvan

SQ change shape (Medium water elemental, *elemental body II*), unearthly grace

ECOLOGY

Environment any aquatic

Organization solitary or troupe (1 nereid plus 1 giant squid, 1 giant octopus, 1 giant moray eel, or an orca)

Treasure standard

SPECIAL ABILITIES

Beguiling Aura (Su) Any creature sexually attracted to women runs the risk of being beguiled by a nereid if it looks upon her beauty from a distance of 30 feet or less. If the creature fails a DC 23 Will save, it is immediately fascinated. A nereid may use her *suggestion* spell-like ability at will against creatures that are fascinated by her beguiling aura. This is a mind-affecting compulsion effect. The save DC is Charisma-based.

Drowning Kiss (Su) A nereid can flood the lungs of a willing, helpless, or fascinated creature by touching it (traditionally by kissing the creature on the lips). If the target cannot breathe water, it cannot hold its breath and immediately begins to drown. On its turn, the target can attempt a DC 23 Fortitude save to cough up this water; otherwise it falls unconscious at 0 hp. On the next round, the target must save again or drop to –1 hit points and be dying; on the third round it must save again or die (see page 445 of the *Pathfinder RPG Core Rulebook*). The save DC is Constitution-based.

Poison (Ex) Touch or spray (range 30 ft.)—contact; *save* Fort DC 23; *frequency* 1/round for 6 rounds; *effect* 1d2 Con plus blindness; *cure* 2 consecutive saves.

Shawl (Ex) A nereid's shawl (hardness 2, hp 6) contains a portion of her life force. If the shawl is ever destroyed, the nereid takes 1d6 points of Constitution drain per hour until she dies. A nereid can craft a new shawl from water by making a DC 25 Will save, but each attempt takes 1d4 hours to complete. Attempts to destroy or steal a nereid's shawl require the sunder or disarm attempts.

Transparency (Su) When underwater, a nereid's body becomes transparent, effectively rendering her invisible. She can become visible or transparent at will as a free action.

Unearthly Grace (Su) A nereid adds her Charisma bonus as a deflection bonus to her Armor Class and CMD if she wears no armor.

Nereids are capricious and often dangerous aquatic fey that appear as strikingly beautiful women, often seen bathing unclothed in the water. Many sailors have met their doom following a nereid, for though a nereid's beauty is otherworldly, her watery kiss is death. Others seek out nereids, for if one can secure control over the creature's shawl, the cloth can be used to force the nereid's compliance. A nereid forced to obey in this manner immediately attempts to slay her master as soon as she can secure her shawl's safety.

NIGHTSHADE

The malevolent nightshades are a mysterious form of necrotic abominations composed of equal parts darkness and ineffable evil. They are living wells of hatred and death, their mere presence sapping the light, heat, and life from all around them, leaving nothing but the heavy, hanging pallor of an open grave in their passing. To nightshades, life is a corruption and a blight. Creation must be purged of this disruption, so that all existence can be welcomed into the sweet embrace of darkness and death. To this end, nightshades seek nothing less than the annihilation of all that is, that was, and that will be.

Nightshades call to themselves legions of undead and shadow-spirits—those who hate the burning sun and the sweet spark of life as much as they themselves do. They rarely ally with living beings who share their vision of extinguishing the sun and exterminating all who stand before them, though such alliances do, at times, occur. Adapting the forms of their kind to pursue the cause of death in every environment and situation, upon the land, in the sky and the sea, and even in the deep places of the world beneath, nightshades marshal their unliving armies. Yet for all their singleness of purpose, they are no mindless beasts. They are clever and patient planners, willing to grant favors to allies or minions as long as they prove themselves useful, and equally willing to turn on them and destroy them the moment their usefulness has been exhausted, rendering their tortured and murdered spirits into deathless slaves.

Nightshades originate in the deepest voids at the planar juncture of the Plane of Shadow and the Negative Energy Plane, where reality itself ends. Here lies a vast adumbral gulf where the weight of infinite existence compresses the null-stuff of unlife and the tenebrous webs of shadow-reality into matte, crystalline plates and shards of condensed entropy. Many fiends seeking the power of ultimate destruction have sought this place, hoping to harness its power for their own ends, but the majority discover the power of distilled entropy is far greater than they bargained for. Their petty designs are washed away as they become one with the nothing, with first their minds and then their bodies being remade, forged no longer of living flesh but of the lifeless, deathless matter of pure darkness incarnate. Recast into one of a handful of perfected entropic forms (some whisper, forged by a dark being long imprisoned at the uttermost end of reality), these immortal fiendish spirits still burn with the freezing fire of insensate evil, but are now distilled and refined through the turning of ages to serve entropy alone. To say that nightshades form from the necrotic flesh and transformed souls of powerful fiends is technically correct, but the transformation that these foolish paragons of evil undergo is even more hideous than such words might suggest.

While the majority of nightshades are the product of such fiendish arrogance, this is by no means the only source for these powerful undead creatures. Many nightshades commit themselves to the harvesting of immortal souls of every race and loyalty, casting their broken and shattered bodies into the negative voidspace, where the residue of their divine essence slowly precipitates and congeals in the nighted gulf. Whatever their origin, in this heart of darkness all souls embrace destruction. When a critical mass of immortal soul energy is reached, a new nightshade is spawned. The souls of mortals lost to the negative plane are drawn up and reborn as undead long before becoming co-opted within the gulf; mortal spirits are the servants of the nightshades, but only the essence of immortality can provide the spiritual fuel to ignite the fire of their unlife.

The most common nightshades are the nightwalkers, long-striding giant fiends often found at the head of undead armies. They are the generals of the nightshade army, the commanders of legions and the organizers of the deaths of worlds.

Yet in places the nightwalkers cannot easily reach, the vast gulfs of the sea and the soaring heights of the clouds above, other nightshades rule. Above flop the immense bat-like nightwings, deadly in their own right yet content to serve at the behest of their stronger cousins. When these monstrosities come to the Material Plane, they swoop down in the dawn to take shelter in abandoned necropolises or vast crypts, emerging at dusk to prey upon nations.

As above, so do the realms below quake from the passage of nightshades. Here, immense nightcrawlers slither and creep. These umbral worms do not often venture forth from the deep, forgotten caverns they dwell in, but when they do, entire kingdoms die as their nighted coils writhe and work their inevitable way through the population.

But for all of the nightmare potential posed by these undead paragons, they all pale in comparison to the mightiest nightshades of all—the shark-like nightwave. This monstrosity prowls the lightless depths of ocean trenches, gathering the souls of the countless drowned dead or preying upon deep aquatic races. Yet those who cleave to the shallows or ply the surface of the seas are not safe from the ravenous nightwaves either, for in the darkest night, these undead monsters rise up to harvest souls from ships and shore as well.

Yet even the dreaded nightwaves are not enough to fill the nightmares of great heroes. Rumors of more powerful nightshades are whispered fearfully in certain circles—creatures of such immense power that their mere existence can drain entire planets of life in a matter of weeks. If such monstrosities truly exist, then all life may be but a fleeting spark in the dark folds of a forever-doomed future.

NIGHTSHADE, NIGHTCRAWLER

This immense worm is covered with plates of dead-black, chitinous armor. Its toothy maw yawns like a cave.

NIGHTCRAWLER	CR 18

XP 153,600

CE Gargantuan undead (extraplanar, nightshade)

Init +4; **Senses** darksense, darkvision 120 ft., detect magic, low-light vision, tremorsense 120 ft.; Perception +33

Aura desecrating aura (30 ft.)

DEFENSE

AC 33, touch 6, flat-footed 33 (+27 natural, –4 size)

hp 312 (25d8+200)

Fort +16, **Ref** +10, **Will** +23

DR 15/good and silver; **Immune** cold, undead traits; **SR** 29

Weaknesses light aversion

OFFENSE

Speed 30 ft., burrow 60 ft.

Melee bite +32 (4d10+18/19–20 plus 4d6 cold and grab), sting +32 (4d6+18/19–20 plus 4d6 cold and poison)

Space 20 ft.; **Reach** 20 ft.

Special Attacks channel negative energy (9d6, DC 31, 9/day), energy drain (1 level, DC 28), swallow whole (4d10+22 bludgeoning plus energy drain, AC 23, 31 hp)

Spell-Like Abilities (CL 18th; concentration +24)

Constant—*air walk, detect magic, magic fang*

At will—*contagion* (DC 20), *deeper darkness, greater dispel magic, invisibility, unholy blight* (DC 20)

3/day—quickened *cone of cold* (DC 21), *confusion* (DC 20), *haste, hold monster* (DC 21)

1/day—*finger of death* (DC 23), *mass hold monster* (DC 25), *plane shift* (DC 23), summon (level 8, 6 greater shadows)

STATISTICS

Str 41, **Dex** 10, **Con** —, **Int** 20, **Wis** 21, **Cha** 23

Base Atk +18; **CMB** +37 (+41 grapple); **CMD** 47 (can't be tripped)

Feats Combat Expertise, Command Undead, Critical Focus, Greater Vital Strike, Improved Critical (bite), Improved Critical (sting), Improved Initiative, Improved Vital Strike, Iron Will, Power Attack, Quicken Spell-Like Ability (*cone of cold*), Staggering Critical, Vital Strike

Skills Intimidate +34, Knowledge (arcana) +33, Knowledge (planes) +30, Knowledge (religion) +33, Perception +33, Sense Motive +33, Spellcraft +33,

Stealth +16 (+24 in darkness), Swim +40; **Racial Modifiers** +8 Stealth in dim light and darkness

Languages Abyssal, Common, Infernal; telepathy 100 ft.

ECOLOGY

Environment any (Negative Energy Plane)

Organization solitary or pair

Treasure standard

SPECIAL ABILITIES

Energy Drain (Su) A creature that has been swallowed whole by a nightcrawler gains 1 negative level each round.

Poison (Su) Sting—injury; *save* Fort DC 28; *frequency* 1/round for 6 rounds; *effect* 1d4 Constitution drain and 1 negative level; *cure* 3 consecutive saves. The save DC is Charisma-based.

Although the nightcrawler might appear to be little more than an immense and frightening vermin, with its centipede-like body and numerous glowing eyes, it is actually incredibly intelligent. When not cleansing the deep caverns of life, the nightcrawler spends its time plotting how best to carry out its own private stages of the overall nightshade plan to expunge life from all worlds, conferring with its undead minions and, when necessary, observing living creatures from afar while invisible to learn about hidden enclaves that its depredations might otherwise have missed.

It would be one thing if the nightcrawlers remained in the deep caverns, for these regions are rife with foul life the world is better off without. Yet unfortunately for those who dwell upon the surface, nightcrawlers often crawl up through the tunnels to bring their devastation to the night above. Although they always retreat underground before the first tentative rays of dawn color the eastern skies, they can spread an incredible amount of ruin in the span of a few short hours each night.

A nightcrawler is 60 feet long and weighs 10,000 pounds.

Illustrations by Jorge Maese

NIGHTSHADE, NIGHTWALKER

This towering, night-black giant has demonic features, including a huge pair of ram-like horns. Its arms end in massive blades.

NIGHTWALKER	CR 16

XP 76,800

CE Huge undead (extraplanar, nightshade)

Init +2; **Senses** darksense, darkvision 60 ft., *detect magic*, low-light vision; Perception +29

Aura desecrating aura (30 ft.)

DEFENSE

AC 31, touch 10, flat-footed 29 (+2 Dex, +21 natural, −2 size)

hp 241 (21d8+147)

Fort +14, **Ref** +11, **Will** +19

DR 15/good and silver; **Immune** cold, undead traits; **SR** 27

Weaknesses light aversion

OFFENSE

Speed 40 ft.

Melee 2 claws +28 (3d6+15/19–20 plus 4d6 cold)

Space 15 ft.; **Reach** 15 ft.

Special Attacks channel energy (8d6, DC 29, 8/day), fear gaze, swift sundering

Spell-Like Abilities (CL 16th; concentration +21)

Constant—*air walk, detect magic, magic fang*

At will—*contagion* (DC 19), *deeper darkness, greater dispel magic, unholy blight* (DC 19)

3/day—*confusion* (DC 19), *haste, hold monster* (DC 20), *invisibility,* quickened *unholy blight* (DC 19)

1/day—*cone of cold* (DC 20), *finger of death* (DC 22), *plane shift* (DC 22), *summon* (level 7, 4 greater shadows)

STATISTICS

Str 35, **Dex** 14, **Con** —, **Int** 20, **Wis** 21, **Cha** 21

Base Atk +15; **CMB** +29; **CMD** 41

Feats Combat Expertise, Command Undead, Greater Sunder, Greater Vital Strike, Improved Critical (claws), Improved Disarm, Improved Sunder, Improved Vital Strike, Power Attack, Quicken Spell-Like Ability (*unholy blight*), Vital Strike

Skills Intimidate +29, Knowledge (arcana) +29, Knowledge (planes) +26, Knowledge (religion) +29, Perception +29, Sense Motive +29, Spellcraft +29, Stealth +18 (+26 in darkness), Swim +33; **Racial Modifiers** +8 Stealth in dim light and darkness

Languages Abyssal, Common, Infernal; telepathy 100 ft.

ECOLOGY

Environment any (Negative Energy Plane)

Organization solitary, pair, or gang (3–4)

Treasure standard

SPECIAL ABILITIES

Fear Gaze (Su) Cower in fear for 1 round, 30 feet, Will DC 25 negates. This is a mind-affecting fear effect. The save DC is Charisma-based.

Swift Sundering (Su) A nightwalker can make a sunder attempt as a swift action with one of its claws.

The most commonly encountered nightshade is the giant-like nightwalker. This powerful foe leads armies of undead against the living, but unlike most mortal generals the nightwalker is not content to stand back and observe the battles from safety. The undead creature is ever eager to put its tactics and plans to the test itself, and takes part in battles in every possible occurrence save for those that the creature has determined are self-destructive. This is not to say that the nightwalker never sacrifices its troops to gain a tactical advantage—just that these attacks are the only ones the monster feels no urge to participate in directly.

Nightwalkers enjoy inflicting despair before death, particularly by destroying valued objects or murdering loved ones before delivering the final blow to a foe.

A nightwalker is 20 feet tall and weighs 5,000 pounds.

NIGHTSHADE, NIGHTWAVE

Immense almost beyond belief, this sleek, midnight-black shark rises from the sea like an unholy island heaved up from below.

NIGHTWAVE	CR 20

XP 307,200

CE Colossal undead (aquatic, extraplanar, nightshade)

Init +7; **Senses** darksense, darkvision 120 ft., *detect magic*, low-light vision; Perception +37

Aura blackest depths (60 ft.), desecrating aura (30 ft.)

DEFENSE

AC 36, touch 5, flat-footed 33 (+3 Dex, +31 natural, −8 size)

hp 391 (29d8+261)

Fort +18, **Ref** +16, **Will** +25

DR 15/good and silver; **Immune** cold, undead traits; **SR** 29

Weaknesses light aversion

OFFENSE

Speed fly 60 ft. (good), swim 60 ft.

Melee bite +35 (5d10+22/19–20 plus 4d6 cold, energy drain, and grab), tail slap +30 (4d8+12/19–20 plus 4d6 cold)

Space 30 ft.; **Reach** 30 ft.

Special Attacks channel energy (10d6, DC 33, 10/day), energy drain (2 levels, DC 31), swallow whole (5d10+28 bludgeoning plus energy drain, AC 25, 39 hp)

Spell-Like Abilities (CL 20th; concentration +27)

Constant—*detect magic, magic fang, see invisibility*

At will—*confusion* (DC 21), *contagion* (DC 21), *deeper darkness, greater dispel magic, invisibility, unholy blight* (DC 21)

3/day—quickened *cone of cold* (DC 22), *finger of death* (DC 24), *haste, hold monster* (DC 22)

1/day—*mass hold monster* (DC 26), *plane shift* (DC 24), summon (level 9, 1 nightwing), *wail of the banshee* (DC 26)

STATISTICS

Str 49, **Dex** 16, **Con** —, **Int** 22, **Wis** 21, **Cha** 25

Base Atk +21; **CMB** +48 (+52 grapple); **CMD** 61 (can't be tripped)

Feats Combat Reflexes, Command Undead, Critical Focus, Greater Vital Strike, Improved Bull Rush, Improved Critical (bite, tail slap), Improved Initiative, Improved Vital Strike, Iron Will, Lightning Reflexes, Power Attack, Quicken Spell-Like Ability (*cone of cold*), Staggering Critical, Vital Strike

Skills Fly +31, Intimidate +39, Knowledge (arcana) +38, Knowledge (planes) +35, Knowledge (religion) +38, Perception +37, Sense Motive +37, Spellcraft +38, Stealth +19 (+27 in darkness), Swim +59; **Racial Modifiers** +8 Stealth in dim light and darkness

Languages Abyssal, Common, Infernal; telepathy 100 ft.

ECOLOGY

Environment any (Negative Energy Plane)

Organization solitary

Treasure standard

SPECIAL ABILITIES

Blackest Depths (Su) The waters in which a nightwave swims become as chill, dark, and heavy as those in the ocean's deepest reaches. All waters within 60 feet are completely dark (as *deeper darkness*), and creatures within this radius take 6d6 points of damage (half cold, half bludgeoning) at the end of their turn each round if they remain in the area at this time. A DC 31 Fortitude save negates the crushing damage. Incorporeal creatures and creatures with the aquatic or water subtypes native to deep waters do not take this damage, and *freedom of movement* protects completely against the damage. Any magical light effect within this radius at the beginning of the nightwave's turn is dispelled (treat as *greater dispel magic*). This effect does not extend out of the water. The save DC is Charisma-based.

Energy Drain (Su) A creature that has been swallowed whole by a nightwave gains 2 negative levels each round.

The most powerful of the known types of nightshade is the ravenous nightwave, an unholy personification of the remorseless gluttony of death given the form of a shark the size of the largest whales. Although the nightwave is most at home in the ocean's deeps, it has no need to breathe, and its constant *fly* spell-like ability allows it to bring ruin above the waves as the need presents itself.

A nightwave is 100 feet long and weighs 200 tons.

Illustrations by Jorge Maese

NIGHTSHADE, NIGHTWING

This enormous, bat-like creature is shaped from utter darkness, its eyes tiny red stars in the blackest night.

NIGHTWING — CR 14

XP 38,400

CE Huge undead (extraplanar, nightshade)

Init +8; **Senses** darksense, darkvision 60 ft., detect magic, low-light vision; **Perception** +25

Aura desecrating aura (30 ft.)

DEFENSE

AC 29, touch 12, flat-footed 25 (+4 Dex, +17 natural, −2 size)

hp 195 (17d8+119)

Fort +12, **Ref** +11, **Will** +17

DR 15/good and silver; **Immune** cold, undead traits; **SR** 25

Weaknesses light aversion

OFFENSE

Speed 30 ft., fly 60 ft. (good)

Melee bite +23 (4d10+18/19–20 plus 4d6 cold and magic drain)

Space 15 ft.; **Reach** 15 ft.

Special Attacks channel energy (7d6, DC 28, 8/day)

Spell-Like Abilities (CL 14th; concentration +19)

Constant—*detect magic, magic fang*

At will—*contagion* (DC 19), *deeper darkness, unholy blight* (DC 19)

3/day—*confusion* (DC 19), *greater dispel magic, haste, hold monster* (DC 20), *invisibility*

1/day—*cone of cold* (DC 20), *finger of death* (DC 22), *plane shift* (DC 22), *summon* (level 6, 2 greater shadows)

STATISTICS

Str 31, **Dex** 18, **Con** —, **Int** 18, **Wis** 21, **Cha** 21

Base Atk +12; **CMB** +24; **CMD** 38

Feats Cleave, Combat Reflexes, Command Undead, Great Cleave, Improved Critical (bite), Improved Initiative, Improved Sunder, Power Attack, Snatch

Skills Fly +24, Knowledge (arcana) +24, Knowledge (religion) +24, Perception +25, Sense Motive +25, Spellcraft +24, Stealth +16 (+24 in darkness), Swim +27; **Racial Modifiers** +8 Stealth in dim light and darkness

Languages Abyssal, Common, Infernal; telepathy 100 ft.

ECOLOGY

Environment any (Negative Energy Plane)

Organization solitary, pair, or flight (3–6)

Treasure standard

SPECIAL ABILITIES

Magic Drain (Su) The bite of a nightwing drains magical power and energy. When a nightwing bites a foe, the victim must make a DC 23 Will save or one spell effect currently affecting him immediately ends—determine which spell is drained randomly if the target is under the effects of more than one spell. The nightwing heals damage equal to twice the level of the spell drained—hit points in excess of its maximum are instead gained as temporary hit points that last for 1 hour. If a nightwing attempts to sunder a magic item with its bite, its magic-draining bite renders the item nonmagical for 1d4 rounds (if the item is a permanent magic item), drains 1d8 charges (if the item has charges), or renders it permanently nonmagical (if the item is a one-use item). The item (or its wielder, if the item is attended) can resist this effect with a DC 23 Will save. Damage dealt to an item is applied after the effects of magic drain are applied. The save DC is Charisma-based.

The least of the known types of nightshade, the nightwing is nevertheless a deadly foe. Nightwings often serve more powerful nightshades as aerial support. These nightshades are also the most likely to be found serving a non-undead master—nightwings are often used by powerful mortals as guardians or sentinels. Despite this, nightwings still hope to someday slay any master they serve. They enter servitude primarily as a method of aiding a destructive or murderous mortal in their task of mass murder; once this task is over, or if at any point the nightwing believes its master is slacking in its murderous duties, the nightwing is swift to turn on its one-time ally.

A nightwing found on the Material Plane not in the employ of a more powerful master is typically encountered in rugged terrain where there are numerous locations that can provide shelter when the sun rises. The monsters prefer caves and abandoned buildings for this purpose.

A nightwing's body is 20 feet long, but its wingspan is 80 feet. It weighs 4,500 pounds.

OGREKIN

Its body twisted and deformed, this lumbering giant has tiny eyes and a mouth of jagged teeth presented in a furious roar.

OGREKIN (HALF-OGRE)	CR 2	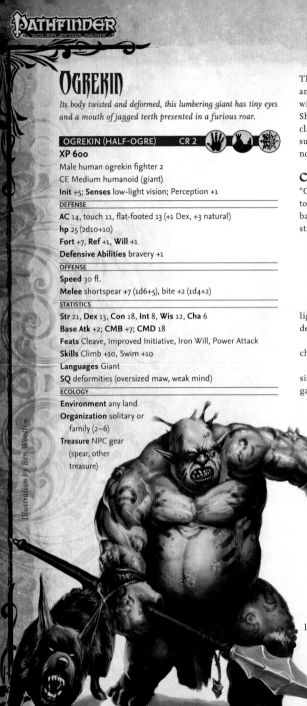

XP 600

Male human ogrekin fighter 2

CE Medium humanoid (giant)

Init +5; **Senses** low-light vision; Perception +1

DEFENSE

AC 14, touch 11, flat-footed 13 (+1 Dex, +3 natural)

hp 25 (2d10+10)

Fort +7, **Ref** +1, **Will** +1

Defensive Abilities bravery +1

OFFENSE

Speed 30 ft.

Melee shortspear +7 (1d6+5), bite +2 (1d4+2)

STATISTICS

Str 21, **Dex** 13, **Con** 18, **Int** 8, **Wis** 12, **Cha** 6

Base Atk +2; **CMB** +7; **CMD** 18

Feats Cleave, Improved Initiative, Iron Will, Power Attack

Skills Climb +10, Swim +10

Languages Giant

SQ deformities (oversized maw, weak mind)

ECOLOGY

Environment any land

Organization solitary or family (2–6)

Treasure NPC gear (spear, other treasure)

Illustration by Ben Wootten

The result of an unfortunate union between an ogre and a humanoid, the ogrekin (or half-ogre) is cursed with horrific malformations due to its tragic ancestry. Shunned by both parents, ogrekin tend to form unstable clans of their own, often resorting to inbreeding to sustain the collective. While good-natured ogrekin are not entirely unheard of, they are far and few between.

CREATING AN OGREKIN

"Ogrekin" is an inherited template that can be added to any Medium humanoid (referred to hereafter as the base creature). An ogrekin retains all the base creature's statistics and special abilities except as noted here.

CR: Same as base creature +1 (minimum 2).

Alignment: Usually evil.

Type: The creature's subtype changes to giant.

Armor Class: Natural armor improves by +3.

Ability Scores: Str +6, Con +4, Int –2, Cha –2.

Special Qualities and Defenses: An ogrekin gains low-light vision. In addition, ogrekin receive two random deformities—one beneficial and one disadvantageous.

Beneficial Deformities: The ogrekin gains one of these, chosen randomly.

1: *Oversized Limb*: The ogrekin can wield weapons one size category larger than normal without any penalty and gains a +2 bonus to its Strength.

2: *Oversized Maw*: The ogrekin gains a bite attack (1d4).

5: *Quick Metabolism*: The ogrekin gains a +2 racial bonus on Fortitude saves.

4: *Thick Skin*: Improve natural armor bonus by +2.

5: *Vestigial Limb*: Vestigial third arm (can't be used to use items) grants a +4 racial bonus on grapple checks.

6: *Vestigial Twin*: A malformed twin's head juts out from the ogrekin, providing the ogrekin with all-around vision.

Disadvantageous Deformities: The ogrekin gains one of these, chosen randomly.

1: *Deformed Hand*: One hand can't wield weapons; –2 penalty on attack rolls with two-handed weapons.

2: *Fragile*: The ogrekin is particularly frail and gaunt. It loses its +4 racial bonus to Con.

3: *Light Sensitive*: The ogrekin gains light sensitivity.

4: *Obese*: The ogrekin takes a –2 penalty to Dexterity (minimum score of 1).

5: *Stunted Legs*: The ogrekin's base speed is reduced by 10 feet (minimum base speed of 5 feet).

6: *Weak Mind*: The ogrekin's head is huge and misshapen. It gains a –2 penalty on Will saving throws.

OREAD

This large warrior appears heavy and solid, with chiseled, angular features that make her look almost like a statue brought to life.

OREAD	CR 1/2

XP 200
Oread fighter 1
N Medium outsider (native)
Init +2; **Senses** darkvision 60 ft.; Perception +2

DEFENSE

AC 14, touch 12, flat-footed 12 (+2 armor, +2 Dex)
hp 12 (1d10+2)
Fort +4, **Ref** +2, **Will** +4
Resist acid 5

OFFENSE

Speed 20 ft.
Melee longsword +3 (1d8+3/19–20)
Ranged composite longbow +4 (1d8+2/×3)
Spell-Like Abilities (CL 1st; concentration +0)
  1/day—*magic stone*

STATISTICS

Str 15, **Dex** 15, **Con** 14, **Int** 8, **Wis** 14, **Cha** 8
Base Atk +1; **CMB** +3; **CMD** 15
Feats Iron Will, Weapon Focus (longbow)
Skills Intimidate +4
Languages Common, Terran
SQ elemental affinity

ECOLOGY

Environment any land
Organization solitary, pair, or team (3–5)
Treasure NPC Gear (leather armor, longsword, composite longbow with 20 arrows, other treasure)

SPECIAL ABILITIES

Earth Affinity (Ex) Oread sorcerers with the Elemental (earth) bloodline treat their Charisma score as 2 points higher for all sorcerer spells and class abilities. Oread clerics with the Earth domain cast their domain powers and spells at +1 caster level.

Oreads are humans whose ancestry includes the touch of an elemental being of earth somewhere along its line, often that of a shaitan genie. Oreads are strong and solidly built, and prefer wearing earth tones that match the coloration of their flesh and hair—shades of gray, brown, black, or white. In rare cases, oreads' stone-like traits are so strong as to leave no question as to their nature, with growths like rocky outcroppings protruding from their skin or hair like crystalline spikes.

Oreads tend to be stoic and contemplative, slow to anger but terrible when roused. Outside of combat, they tend to be quiet, dependable, and protective of their friends.

OREAD CHARACTERS

Oreads are defined by class levels—they do not possess racial Hit Dice. Oreads have the following racial traits.

+2 Strength, +2 Wisdom, –2 Charisma: Oreads are strong, solid, stable, and stoic.

Darkvision: Oreads can see in the dark up to 60 feet.

Spell-Like Ability: *Magic stone* 1/day (caster level equals the oread's total Hit Dice).

Energy Resistance: Oreads have acid resistance 5.

Earth Affinity: See above.

Languages: Oreads begin play speaking Common and Terran. Oreads with high Intelligence scores can choose any of the following bonus languages: Aquan, Auran, Dwarven, Elven, Gnome, Halfling, Ignan, and Undercommon.

Illustration by Kekai Kotaki

PECH

This pale yellow humanoid has blank, bulging white eyes and gangly arms and legs. It clutches a pickaxe in its knobby hands.

PECH	CR 3

XP 800

N Small fey (earth)

Init +1; **Senses** darkvision 60 ft., low-light vision; Perception +10

DEFENSE

AC 16, touch 12, flat-footed 15 (+1 Dex, +4 natural, +1 size)

hp 27 (6d6+6)

Fort +5, **Ref** +6, **Will** +6

DR 5/cold iron; **Immune** petrification; **SR** 14

Weaknesses light blindness

OFFENSE

Speed 20 ft.

Melee mwk heavy pick +9 (1d4+6/×4)

Special Attacks earth mastery, pech magic, stone knowledge

Spell-Like Abilities (CL 10th; concentration +11)

3/day—*stone shape, stone tell*

STATISTICS

Str 19, **Dex** 12, **Con** 13, **Int** 12, **Wis** 13, **Cha** 12

Base Atk +3; **CMB** +6; **CMD** 17

Feats Cleave, Great Fortitude, Power Attack

Skills Climb +13, Craft (stonemasonry) +14, Knowledge (dungeoneering) +10, Knowledge (engineering) +10, Perception +10, Profession (miner) +14, Stealth +14; **Racial Modifiers** +4 Craft (stonemasonry), +4 Profession (miner)

Languages Terran, Undercommon

ECOLOGY

Environment any underground (Plane of Earth)

Organization solitary, pair, gang (3–4), pack (5–10), or tribe (11–40 plus 50% noncombatants, 1–4 fighters of 2nd–4th level, and 1–2 druids of 2nd–4th level)

Treasure standard (masterwork heavy pick, other treasure)

SPECIAL ABILITIES

Earth Mastery (Ex) A pech gains a +1 bonus on attack and damage rolls if both it and its foes are touching the ground. If an opponent is airborne or waterborne, the pech takes a –4 penalty on attack and damage rolls. These modifiers are not precalculated into the statistics here.

Pech Magic (Sp) Four pechs working together can cast *wall of stone* once per day. Eight pechs working together can cast *stone to flesh* (DC 17) once per day. These spell-like abilities function at CL 10th. Each pech must use a full-round action to take part in the casting. The save DCs are modified by the highest Charisma modifier in the group.

Stone Knowledge (Ex) A pech's knowledge of earth and stone grants a +1 racial bonus on attack and damage rolls and the benefits of the Improved Critical feat against creatures and objects made of stone or earth or with the earth subtype. Knowledge (dungeoneering), Knowledge (engineering) and Profession (miner) are always class skills for a pech.

Untold ages ago, the pechs served forgotten masters in the deepest caverns of the world. In time, their masters moved on, leaving the pechs bereft of guidance. Some sought refuge in seemingly safer tunnels nearer the surface. The unspeakable horrors they encountered there transformed them into derros over the course of several generations. Those pechs that stayed close to their ancestral caverns survive to this day, though in such small numbers and in such isolation that few of the surface world know of their existence. Pechs are skilled miners and stonemasons, and are at times employed or enslaved as such by other subterranean races. They have learned to hide the entrances to their lairs most carefully, blending their narrow entranceways into the living rock such that they can only be seen from exactly the right angle. When interlopers do find a pech's lair, they are met with open arms, friendly advice, and a firm insistence that the pech is to be left alone.

The typical pech stands only 3-1/2 feet tall, but its dense flesh gives it a weight of 100 pounds.

PERYTON

This creature has a stag's body, a hawk's wings and talons, and the head of a slavering wolf with a rack of sharp antlers on its brow.

PERYTON	CR 4

XP 1,200

CE Medium magical beast

Init +7; **Senses** darkvision 60 ft., low-light vision; Perception +10

DEFENSE

AC 17, touch 13, flat-footed 14 (+3 Dex, +4 natural)

hp 42 (5d10+15)

Fort +7, **Ref** +7, **Will** +3

DR 5/magic

OFFENSE

Speed 30 ft., fly 60 ft. (good)

Melee gore +9 (1d6+3/18–20), 2 hooves +3 (1d4+1)

Special Attacks horrific critical, shadow mark

STATISTICS

Str 17, **Dex** 16, **Con** 17, **Int** 11, **Wis** 14, **Cha** 12

Base Atk +5; **CMB** +8; **CMD** 21 (25 vs. trip)

Feats Flyby Attack, Improved Initiative, Weapon Focus (gore)

Skills Fly +12, Perception +10, Stealth +9

Languages Common

ECOLOGY

Environment any

Organization solitary, pair, or flock (3–9)

Treasure standard

SPECIAL ABILITIES

Horrific Critical (Ex) A peryton's gore attack threatens a critical hit on an 18–20. If a peryton kills a humanoid foe with a critical hit, it can tear out the victim's heart with its wolf-like teeth as a free action. Any creature that witnesses this savage event must make a DC 13 Fortitude save or be shaken for 1 round. This is a mind-affecting fear effect. The save DC is Charisma-based.

Shadow Mark (Su) As a free action, a peryton can make a ranged touch attack by flying over a humanoid target—the maximum range of this attack is 300 feet. If the peryton hits, its shadow transforms to match the shadow of the creature struck. Once a peryton has established this link, it gains a +2 morale bonus on attack rolls and damage rolls made against that target, and every time the peryton hits that target with an attack, the creature must make a DC 13 Will save or become frightened for 1 round. This is a mind-affecting fear effect. The save DC is Charisma-based.

Savage creatures of nightmare, perytons combine the features of stags, wolves, and great birds of prey. Though vicious beasts, perytons possess all the intelligence of a human.

Perytons hunt any creature weaker than themselves, but prefer humanoid prey, as they particularly relish the taste of such creatures' still-beating hearts.

Perytons loathe all other creatures, even their own kind, and adult male perytons often attack one another on sight. However, strong females sometimes lead small family flocks composed of the alpha female, two or three weaker females, and up to six fledglings. The flock drives off males when they come of age, but females are allowed to join the pack when they mature, provided they swear allegiance to the alpha female. Unpaired males frequently attack such flocks in the hope of making off with a mate; failing that, they approach more peacefully, with offers of warm humanoid hearts (or even still-living victims) to attract females.

Perytons mate once per year. The mating ritual is short, brutal, and in the end often fatal for the male. Afterward, the female lays a single, foot-tall black egg, which hatches 7 months later.

A peryton is 4 feet in length with a wingspan of 11 feet. It weighs 250 pounds.

Illustration by Eric Lofgren

PETITIONER

Something seems strange and disturbingly familiar about this wispy, ghostly humanoid shape.

PETITIONER	CR 1

XP 400

Human petitioner

Any alignment Medium outsider (extraplanar)

Init +0; **Senses** darkvision 60 ft., Perception +5

DEFENSE

AC 10, touch 10, flat-footed 10

hp 16 (2d10+5)

Fort +4, **Ref** +3, **Will** +0

Immune mind-affecting effects

OFFENSE

Speed 30 ft.

Melee slam +2 (1d4)

STATISTICS

Str 11, **Dex** 10, **Con** 13, **Int** 10, **Wis** 11, **Cha** 10

Base Atk +2; **CMB** +2; **CMD** 12

Feats Toughness

Skills Craft (any two) +5, Knowledge (planes) +5, Perception +5, Sense Motive +5, Stealth +5

Languages Common

SQ petitioner traits

ECOLOGY

Environment any (Outer Planes)

Organization solitary, pair, group (3–12), or army (13 or more)

Treasure none

SPECIAL ABILITIES

Petitioner Traits A petitioner has additional abilities and features depending upon its home plane. Its alignment matches the alignment of its home plane.

Petitioners are the souls of mortals brought to the Outer Planes after death in order to experience their ultimate punishment, reward, or fate. A petitioner retains fragments of its memories from life, and its appearance depends not only upon the shape it held in life but also upon the nature of the Outer Plane to which it has come. The stat block detailed above presents a typical petitioner formed from the soul of an average human—it does not include any of the plane-specific abilities or features a petitioner gains, and should be modified as appropriate depending on the plane to which the petitioner is assigned.

Creatures who die, become petitioners, and then return to life retain no memories of the time they spent as petitioners in the afterlife. A petitioner who dies is gone forever—its "life force" has either returned to the Positive Energy Plane or, in some cases, provided the energy to trigger the creation of another outsider. Petitioners who please a deity or another powerful outsider can be granted rewards—the most common such reward manifests as a transformation into a different outsider, such as an archon, azata, demon, or devil, depending upon the petitioner's alignment. In rare cases, a creature can retain its personality from life all the way through its existence as a petitioner and into its third "life" as an outsider, although such events are rare indeed.

CREATING A PETITIONER

"Petitioner" is an acquired template that can be added to any creature whose soul migrates to one of the Outer Planes following its death (henceforth referred to as the base creature). The petitioner uses all of the base creature's statistics and abilities except as noted below.

CR: A petitioner's CR is 1. In some cases, at the GM's discretion, particularly large or unusual petitioners with higher than normal ability scores may begin with a higher CR; compare the petitioner's statistics to the values on Table 1–1 on page 293 to help determine an unusual petitioner's starting CR.

Alignment: A petitioner's alignment is identical to that of its home plane.

Size and Type: The creature's type changes to outsider. It loses all subtypes. Its size does not change.

Senses: Petitioners lose any unusual senses they had, but gain darkvision 60 feet.

Armor Class: The petitioner loses all racial bonuses to its Armor Class.

Hit Dice: Petitioners lose all racial and class-based Hit Dice and gain 2d10 racial Hit Dice as outsiders.

Saves: Petitioners have good Fortitude and Reflex saves; a petitioner's base saves are Fort +3, Ref +3, Will +0.

Defensive Abilities: Petitioners lose all the defensive abilities of the base creature. Petitioners are immune to mind-affecting effects.

Attacks: The creature's BAB is +2, subject to modification for size and Strength. It loses all natural attacks and gains a slam attack as appropriate for a creature of its size.

Special Attacks: Petitioners lose all special attacks.

Abilities: Same as the base creature.

Feats: Petitioners lose all feats. As a 2 HD outsider, a petitioner gains one feat—typically Toughness.

Skills: Petitioners lose all skill ranks they possessed as mortals. As a 2 HD outsider, a petitioner has 12 skill ranks it can spend on skills (with a maximum of 2 ranks in any one skill), and gains bonus skill ranks as appropriate for its Intelligence. Unlike most outsiders, petitioners do not gain an additional 4 class skills beyond those available to all outsiders.

Special Qualities: Petitioners lose all special qualities, along with all abilities granted by class levels (including increases on saving throws and to HD and BAB).

PETITIONER TRAITS

A petitioner gains additional traits based on its home plane.

Abaddon (Neutral Evil): The "hunted" have bodies that are identical to what they had in life—these petitioners are doomed to be stalked and eventually consumed by the daemons that lust for souls. A hunted that survives long enough eventually warps and twists into a daemon. The hunted gain DR 5/— and fast healing 1 so that they provide a slightly more robust hunt for their daemonic predators.

Abyss (Chaotic Evil): "Larvae" are perhaps the most hideous of petitioners—they appear as pallid, maggot-like creatures with heads similar to those they possessed in life. Larvae that feed long enough on Abyssal filth eventually transform into demons. They have cold, electricity, and fire resistance 10, and instead of a slam attack gain a bite attack as appropriate for their size.

Elysium (Chaotic Good): The "chosen" have idealized versions of their mortal bodies. In time, after experiencing the pleasures Elysium has to offer, the chosen become azatas. The chosen gain resistance to cold and fire 10 and a +2 bonus to Charisma.

Heaven (Lawful Good): The "elect" appear similar to their mortal forms, save that they possess a golden halo and feathered wings. After spending enough time aiding heavenly tasks, the elect become archons. They gain a fly speed equal to their base speed (average mobility).

Hell (Lawful Evil): The "damned" retain their mortal forms, but are heavily scarred by various tortures. Those who endure the torments of Hell long enough may eventually be approved for transformation into devils. The damned gain immunity to fire (but not immunity to the pain caused by fire—whenever one of the damned takes fire damage, it must make a DC 15 Fortitude save to resist being stunned by the pain for 1d4 rounds).

Limbo (Chaotic Neutral): The "shapeless" retain their basic forms, but these forms constantly waver and shimmer, as if they were ghosts in peril of dissolving away. After wallowing in the chaos of Limbo for long enough, they can transform into proteans. The shapeless have the incorporeal subtype, an incorporeal touch attack, and all advantages granted by that defensive ability.

Nirvana (Neutral Good): The "cleansed" take on the forms of animals that closely approximate their personalities. Upon achieving true enlightenment, they transform into agathions. The cleansed gain cold and sonic resistance 10 and a +2 bonus to Wisdom.

Purgatory (Neutral): The "dead" appear as animated skeletons but are not undead—in time, they can earn the right to become aeons. They gain DR 10/bludgeoning and immunity to cold.

Utopia (Lawful Neutral): The "remade" retain the same body shape but have milky white skin covered in dense black script, as if some strange scribe had used them for parchment. Upon deciphering the riddles posed by these complex lines of script, one of the remade can enter an axiomite forge to be transformed into an inevitable. The remade are immune to hostile transmutation effects and gain a +2 bonus to Intelligence.

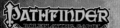
PHYCOMID

This tangle of purple-capped mushrooms growing out of a nasty green sludge shudders and writhes, wafting tendrils of smoke.

PHYCOMID	CR 4

XP 1,200

N Small plant

Init +0; **Senses** tremorsense 30 ft.; Perception +0

DEFENSE

AC 17, touch 11, flat-footed 17 (+6 natural, +1 size)

hp 39 (6d8+12)

Fort +7, **Ref** +2, **Will** +2

Immune acid, plant traits

OFFENSE

Speed 10 ft.

Ranged acid pellet +5 touch (2d6 acid plus spores)

STATISTICS

Str 5, **Dex** 10, **Con** 15, **Int** —, **Wis** 11, **Cha** 1

Base Atk +4; **CMB** +0; **CMD** 10 (can't be tripped)

ECOLOGY

Environment any underground

Organization solitary or infestation (2–8)

Treasure incidental

SPECIAL ABILITIES

Acid Pellet (Ex) A phycomid attacks by firing a glob of acid from one of its several mushroom-like stalks. This attack has a range increment of 10 feet. A phycomid can fire up to six acid pellets per minute—during rounds in which the fungus has no acid pellets, it has no method of attacking at all and must wait until its acid stores replenish in 4 rounds before continuing a battle.

Spores (Ex) Any creature that takes damage from a phycomid's acid pellet (or consumes even a small portion of the fungus) becomes exposed to the fungus's spores. These spores grow quickly in living creatures. This affliction is a disease effect, although its course runs much faster than most diseases and is more poison-like in its speed, and like a poison, the spores "burn out" after a short period. A creature that is slain by a phycomid spore infestation bursts open in 1d4 rounds as a fully grown new phycomid emerges.

Phycomid Spores: Disease—injury or ingested; *save* Fort DC 15; *frequency* 1/round for 6 rounds; *effect* 1d2 Con damage; *cure* 1 save. The save DC is Constitution-based.

Typically found in damp dungeons, refuse heaps, and forgotten, filthy chambers, phycomids are dangerous fungoid creatures that grow in small, steaming patches among decomposing organic matter. The phycomid's main body is a mass of green-brown mold that can slither and move when necessary to seek out new carrion to feed upon. Numerous mushrooms sprout from the main body—vile green stalks topped with purple or red caps that seem to steam with rank-smelling smoke. This smoke is in fact vapor escaping from the numerous globs of acid the plant produces as a method of both self-defense and reproduction.

This acidic substance is expelled from the phycomid whenever it senses movement nearby, and seasoned adventurers can often trick a phycomid into giving away its true nature by simulating movement within range of the fungus. Less fortunate encounters are typically marked by large infestations of phycomids growing among a scattered collection of dead bodies.

Because of the filthy environment in which this fungus thrives, goblins are one of the few races that have learned to coexist with phycomids. Not content to simply give the fungi a wide berth, these foolish goblins actually harvest the phycomids, prodding them into positions in their warrens where they can serve as guards and sentinels, utilizing long poles they call "slime sticks" or placing delicious-smelling carrion to attract the fungus to a desired position. Although phycomids are deadly to eat, many goblin tribes view those who eat a phycomid mushroom and survive as great heroes. Needless to say, most goblin lairs that attempt to utilize phycomids as guardians eventually become nothing more than phycomid lairs—a goblin tribe's luck can only hold up for so long, after all.

Illustration by Adam Vehige

POLTERGEIST

A ghostly, skeletal figure rises up amid a whirling cyclone of tools, plates, utensils, and other loose objects.

POLTERGEIST	CR 2

XP 600

LE Medium undead (incorporeal)

Init +1; **Senses** darkvision 60 ft.; Perception +9

DEFENSE

AC 12, touch 12, flat-footed 11
 (+1 deflection, +1 Dex)

hp 16 (3d8+3)

Fort +2, **Ref** +2, **Will** +4

Defensive Abilities incorporeal, natural invisibility, rejuvenation; **Immune** undead traits

OFFENSE

Speed fly 20 ft. (perfect)

Special Attacks frightener, telekinesis

STATISTICS

Str —, **Dex** 13, **Con** —, **Int** 5, **Wis** 12, **Cha** 12

Base Atk +2; **CMB** +3; **CMD** 14

Feats Ability Focus (fear), Alertness

Skills Fly +9, Perception +9, Sense Motive +3

Languages Common

SQ site bound

ECOLOGY

Environment any

Organization solitary or haunting (2–7)

Treasure incidental

SPECIAL ABILITIES

Frightener (Su) Once per minute as a standard action, a poltergeist can temporarily drop its natural invisibility, revealing itself to be a skeletal, ghost-like humanoid. All creatures within 30 feet when a poltergeist uses this ability must make a DC 14 Will save to avoid becoming frightened for 1d4 rounds. The poltergeist then resumes its invisibility at the end of its turn as a free action. A creature that successfully saves is immune to the fear effect of that poltergeist for 24 hours. If the poltergeist's natural invisibility is negated via other methods, it cannot use this ability. Likewise, those that can see invisible creatures are immune to this special attack. This is a mind-affecting fear effect. The save DC is Charisma-based.

Rejuvenation (Su) When a poltergeist is destroyed, it only remains destroyed for 2d4 days. After this time, the undead spirit reforms where it was destroyed, fully healed. The only way to permanently destroy a poltergeist is to determine the reason for its existence and set right whatever prevents it from resting in peace. The exact means varies with each spirit and may require a good deal of research, and should be created specifically for each different poltergeist or group of poltergeists by the GM.

Site Bound (Ex) A poltergeist cannot travel more than 120 feet from the point at which it was created or formed.

Telekinesis (Su) A poltergeist has no method of attacking apart from telekinesis. This ability functions as the spell *telekinesis*, with a CL equal to the poltergeist's Hit Dice (CL 3rd for most poltergeists). A typical poltergeist has a ranged attack roll of +3 when using telekinesis to hurl objects or creatures, and can use the ability on objects or creatures of up to 75 pounds. If a poltergeist attempts to hurl a creature with this ability, that creature can resist the effect with a successful DC 12 Will save. The save DC is Charisma-based.

A poltergeist is an angry spirit that forms from the soul of a creature that, for whatever reason, becomes unable to leave the site of its death. Sometimes, this might be due to an unfinished task—other times, it might be due to a powerful necromantic effect. Desecrating a grave site by building a structure over the body below is the most common method of accidentally creating a poltergeist. The poltergeist experiences great trauma over its condition; this trauma twists its psyche to evil and fosters an overall hatred of the living expressed in outbursts of rage. A poltergeist is bound to a specific place, usually a building, room, or recognizable area (a section of a cemetery, a stretch of lonely road, and so on). This place typically corresponds to its place of death or the resting place of its mortal remains.

Illustration by Branko Bistrovic

PRIMATE, BABOON

A hairy, stout animal with opposable thumbs, this creature has a pronounced muzzle and bright red buttocks.

BABOON	CR 1/2

XP 200

N Small animal

Init +2; **Senses** low-light vision; Perception +1

DEFENSE

AC 13, touch 13, flat-footed 11 (+2 Dex, +1 size)

hp 5 (1d8+1)

Fort +3, **Ref** +4, **Will** +1

OFFENSE

Speed 30 ft.

Melee bite +3 (1d4+1)

STATISTICS

Str 12, **Dex** 15, **Con** 12, **Int** 2, **Wis** 12, **Cha** 5

Base Atk +0; **CMB** +0; **CMD** 12

Feats Weapon Finesse

Skills Acrobatics +10, Climb +5; **Racial Modifiers** +4 Acrobatics, +4 Climb

ECOLOGY

Environment warm forests or plains

Organization solitary, pair, or mission (3–6)

Treasure none

Baboons are known for their aggressive nature and distinctive build, including a canine-like maw filled with sharp teeth, strong jaw muscles, a short tail, and prominent calluses on their brightly colored and protruding buttocks. Though they are primarily vegetarians, baboons are known to eat fish, insects, shellfish, and other small creatures. Ferociously territorial, baboons are quick to rise and defend their homes from any sort of intruders.

A baboon is 3 feet tall and weighs 70 pounds.

BABOON COMPANIONS

Starting Statistics: Size: Small; **Speed:** 30 ft.; **Attack** bite (1d4); **Ability Scores:** Str 12, Dex 15, Con 12, Int 2, Wis 12, Cha 5; **Special Qualities:** low-light vision.

4th-Level Advancement: Ability Scores Str +2, Con +2.

PRIMATE, MONKEY SWARM

Screeches and bestial calls precede this pack of monkeys, each primate propelling itself forward on calloused knuckles.

MONKEY SWARM	CR 2

XP 600

N Tiny animal (swarm)

Init +7; **Senses** low-light vision; Perception +5

DEFENSE

AC 15, touch 15, flat-footed 12 (+3 Dex, +2 size)

hp 22 (3d8+9)

Fort +6, **Ref** +8, **Will** +2

Defensive Abilities half damage from weapons, swarm traits

OFFENSE

Speed 30 ft., climb 20 ft.

Melee swarm (2d6 plus distraction)

Space 10 ft.; **Reach** 0 ft.

Special Attacks distraction (DC 14)

STATISTICS

Str 7, **Dex** 16, **Con** 17, **Int** 2, **Wis** 12, **Cha** 11

Base Atk +2; **CMB** —; **CMD** —

Feats Improved Initiative, Lightning Reflexes

Skills Acrobatics +11, Climb +10, Perception +5; **Racial Modifiers** +4 Acrobatics

SQ coordinated swarm

ECOLOGY

Environment warm forests

Organization solitary, pair, mission (3–6 swarms), or tribe (7–12 swarms plus 1–4 gorillas)

Treasure none

SPECIAL ABILITIES

Coordinated Swarm (Ex) A monkey swarm coordinates its attacks more than a typical swarm, and deals swarm damage one step higher than a swarm of its HD would normally cause.

Monkeys sometimes travel in huge colonies of hundreds of individuals. In such quantities, these primates can become quite dangerous, capable of overwhelming many foes by their sheer numbers.

Unlike most swarms, monkey swarms work well together. A swarm of monkeys does not possess a true hive mind, but it is capable of working in tandem with other swarms to make basic tactical decisions in combat.

Illustration by Peter Lazarski

Protean

Beings of pure chaos, the serpentine proteans slither through the anarchic improbabilities of Limbo, remaking reality according to their whims. According to their own history, they were already here when the first gods pulled forth the other planes from raw chaos—and they have been battling against the indignity ever since. Hereditary and ideological enemies of Axis, Heaven, and Hell, and especially of the residents of those planes, all proteans see it as their sacred duty to return the bland, static expanses of mundane reality to the beautiful incongruities of Limbo, for the planes' own good and for the greater glory of their mysterious god, a dualistic deity which may be a living aspect of Limbo itself. They are Limbo's living, breathing immune system, rooting out infections of mundanity and replacing them with beautiful entropy.

Primeval in shape and philosophy, proteans are the race that most perfectly embodies the twin aspects of creation and destruction (although certain aeons might contest this claim). Even their language is mutable, evolving so quickly that few outsiders can understand it without magical aid. Ecological study is nearly impossible, as reproduction can take a wide variety of forms, from sexual union to fission to spontaneous generation. Despite their deceptively similar natural appearances, the two things that truly unify the protean race are slavish devotion to their strange god and a fervent desire for the dissolution of reality as we know it.

Proteans are organized into several sub-races or castes, each with its own individual abilities and roles. Other proteans than the four presented here doubtless exist, but they do not interact with other races nearly to the extent that these four types do.

Voidworms: Disowned by greater proteans, who find these tiny beings shameful, voidworms nevertheless retain all the characteristics of true proteans, and are frequently found swimming through Limbo in vast schools or serving as spellcasters' familiars.

Naunets: Possessing little in the way of culture, the powerful naunets are the most bestial of the true proteans, representing the lowest recognized caste. Naunets are the shock troops of the protean race, and patrol the borderlands between Limbo and other planes, seeking out lawful incursions and making daring, savage raids into the realms of their enemies.

Imenteshes: These cunning proteans seek to subvert the forces of order from within their own systems, whispering information and insinuations where they can do the most damage. Endlessly creative, they adore reforming the landscapes of Limbo to suit their fancies, but enjoy warping the vistas and creatures of other planes even more.

Keketars: Priest-kings and voices of Limbo itself, keketars rule their fellows in the name of their bizarre god. Though their forms are extremely mutable, keketars can always be recognized thanks to eyes that glow amber or violet and floating crowns of swirling and changing symbols that often appear above their heads. Organized into cabals called choruses, keketars seek only to understand and follow the will of entropy.

PROTEAN LORDS

While the keketars are the highest caste of the protean race, there exist a few scattered individuals who put even the mightiest chorus to shame. Equal in power to demon lords or empyreal lords, the beings known as protean lords are an enigma, far older than other proteans and perhaps spawned in a previous iteration of the multiverse or somewhere beyond the depths of Limbo. Disdaining direct leadership, protean lords act according to their own desires, occasionally appearing to advise their lesser kin or keep an inscrutable eye on entities whose powers rival their own.

WARPWAVES

Many proteans, particularly the imenteshes, have the ability to create and manipulate ripples in reality known as warpwaves. Yet even a protean can't predict what effects a warpwave might have. When a creature is affected by a warpwave, roll 1d20 and consult the table below to see what effect the entropic energies have.

d20	Warpwave Effect
1	Target takes 2 Strength damage.
2	Target takes 2 Dexterity damage.
3	Target takes 2 Constitution damage.
4	Target takes 2 Intelligence damage.
5	Target takes 2 Wisdom damage.
6	Target takes 2 Charisma damage.
7	Target gains 1 negative level.
8	Target is blinded or deafened for 1d4 rounds.
9	Target is confused for 1d4 rounds.
10	Target is entangled by filaments of energy for 1d4 rounds.
11	Target becomes fatigued (or exhausted if already fatigued).
12	Target becomes nauseated for 1d4 rounds.
13	Target is stunned for 1d4 rounds.
14	Target is sickened for 1d4 rounds.
15	Target is staggered for 1d4 rounds.
16	Target gains 4d6 temporary hit points.
17	Target is affected by a *heal* spell (CL = protean's CR).
18	Target is turned to stone.
19	Target is affected by *baleful polymorph* (CL = protean's CR).
20	Portions of target's body burst with energy of a random type (choose between acid, cold, electricity, or fire), dealing 4d6 points of damage of the appropriate type to the target.

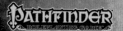

Protean, Imentesh

This serpentine creature has the lower body of a snake, a humanoid torso, and a bird-like head and claws.

IMENTESH	CR 10

XP 9,600

CN Large outsider (chaotic, extraplanar, protean, shapechanger)

Init +7; **Senses** blindsense 30 ft., darkvision 60 ft.; Perception +20

DEFENSE

AC 25, touch 12, flat-footed 22 (+3 Dex, +13 natural, −1 size)

hp 123 (13d10+52); fast healing 5

Fort +12, **Ref** +7, **Will** +14

Defensive Abilities amorphous anatomy, freedom of movement; **DR** 10/lawful; **Immune** acid, polymorph; **Resist** electricity 10, sonic 10; **SR** 21

OFFENSE

Speed 30 ft., fly 30 ft. (perfect), swim 30 ft.

Melee bite +19 (2d6+7), 2 claws +19 (1d8+7), tail +17 (1d8+3 plus grab)

Space 10 ft.; **Reach** 10 ft.

Special Attacks constrict (1d8+7), inflict warpwave, sneak attack +4d6

Spell-Like Abilities (CL 10th; concentration +15)

Constant—*detect law, tongues*

At will—*dimension door* (self plus 50 lbs. of objects only), *make whole, major creation, shatter* (DC 17), *shrink item*

3/day—*chaos hammer* (DC 19), *dispel magic, slow* (DC 18)

1/day—*break enchantment, dispel law* (DC 20), *haste, polymorph any object* (DC 23)

STATISTICS

Str 24, **Dex** 17, **Con** 18, **Int** 23, **Wis** 18, **Cha** 21

Base Atk +13; **CMB** +21 (+25 grapple); **CMD** 34 (can't be tripped)

Feats Combat Expertise, Combat Reflexes, Improved Feint, Improved Initiative, Iron Will, Multiattack, Persuasive

Skills Acrobatics +19, Bluff +21, Diplomacy +25, Disable Device +16, Fly +9, Intimidate +25, Knowledge (arcana) +22, Knowledge (planes) +22, Knowledge (any two) +19, Perception +20, Sense Motive +20, Stealth +15, Swim +15

Languages Abyssal, Protean; *tongues*

SQ change shape (*greater polymorph*)

ECOLOGY

Environment any (Limbo)

Organization solitary, pair, or envoy (3–10)

Treasure standard

SPECIAL ABILITIES

Inflict Warpwave (Su) As a standard action, an imentesh can inflict a warpwave upon any corporeal creature within 100 feet. The target can resist the warpwave's effects with a DC 20 Fortitude save. If the imentesh wishes, it can use this ability as a swift action, but if it does so, it is affected by the warpwave as well unless it resists the effects with its own Fortitude save. See page 213 for a list of possible effects caused by a warpwave. The save DC is Constitution-based.

Missionaries of chaos and heralds of reality's eventual unraveling, imenteshes are the proteans most likely to be encountered outside of Limbo. Despite their sometimes loquacious and courtly manner, imenteshes' entropic agenda is ever at the front of their minds, and this inherent madness is evident in the soft, telepathic susurrus that constantly surrounds them, threatening to warp the minds of the weak-willed.

An imentesh is 15 feet long and weighs 1,200 pounds.

Illustration by Jorge Maese

PROTEAN, KEKETAR

Colors dance over this serpentine creature's scales. A strange crown of energy glows above the thing's reptilian head.

KEKETAR		CR 17	

XP 102,400

CN Large outsider (chaotic, extraplanar, protean, shapechanger)

Init +5; **Senses** blindsense 60 ft., darkvision 60 ft.; Perception +33

Aura spatial riptide (30 ft.)

DEFENSE

AC 32, touch 14, flat-footed 27 (+5 Dex, +18 natural, −1 size)

hp 287 (23d10+161); fast healing 10

Fort +22, **Ref** +14, **Will** +22

Defensive Abilities amorphous anatomy, freedom of movement; **DR** 15/lawful; **Immune** acid, polymorph; **Resist** electricity 10, sonic 10; **SR** 28

OFFENSE

Speed 40 ft., fly 40 ft. (perfect), swim 40 ft.

Melee bite +31 (4d8+9 plus warpwave), 2 claws +31 (2d6+9 plus warpwave), tail slap +29 (2d8+4 plus grab)

Space 10 ft.; **Reach** 10 ft.

Special Attacks constrict (1d8+9), reshape reality

Spell-Like Abilities (CL 17th; concentration +24)

Constant—*detect law, tongues*

At will—*chaos hammer* (DC 21), *greater dispel magic, greater teleport* (self plus 50 lbs. of objects only), *major creation, move earth, shatter* (DC 19)

3/day—quickened *confusion* (DC 21), *dispel law* (DC 22), empowered *chaos hammer* (DC 21), *polymorph any object* (DC 25)

1/day—*disintegrate* (DC 23), *prismatic spray* (DC 24), *prismatic sphere* (DC 26), reshape reality

STATISTICS

Str 29, **Dex** 21, **Con** 24, **Int** 20, **Wis** 25, **Cha** 24

Base Atk +23; **CMB** +33 (+35 bull rush, +37 grapple); **CMD** 48 (can't be tripped)

Feats Combat Expertise, Combat Reflexes, Empower Spell-like Ability (*chaos hammer*), Great Fortitude, Improved Bull Rush, Improved Vital Strike, Iron Will, Lightning Reflexes, Multiattack, Power Attack, Quicken Spell-like Ability (*confusion*), Vital Strike

Skills Acrobatics +31, Bluff +33, Diplomacy +33, Fly +11, Intimidate +33, Knowledge (any two) +28, Knowledge (arcana, planes) +31, Perception +33, Stealth +27, Swim +40

Languages Abyssal, Protean; telepathy 100 ft.

SQ change shape (*greater polymorph*)

ECOLOGY

Environment any (Limbo)

Organization solitary or chorus (2–4)

Treasure standard

SPECIAL ABILITIES

Reshape Reality (Sp) This ability functions as the spell *mirage arcana* heightened to a 9th-level spell, except the changes created are quasi-real, like those created by *shadow conjuration*. A creature that interacts with reshaped reality may make a DC 26 Will save to see through the semi-real illusion. Terrain can provide concealment, and against foes who do not make the Will save to see through the facade, reshaped reality can provide cover. For disbelievers, quasi-real objects and terrain have only 20% normal hardness and hit points, and break DCs are 10 lower than normal. Dangerous terrain cannot exceed 5d6 points of damage per round (1d6 per round against disbelievers). This ability cannot damage existing structures, nor does it function in areas where planar travel is prohibited.

Spatial Riptide (Su) Any non-protean teleporting into or out of the protean's aura must make a DC 28 Fortitude save or enter a state of suspended animation (identical to *temporal stasis*) for 1d3 rounds; success means the creature is merely nauseated for 1 round. The save DC is Constitution-based.

Warpwave (Su) A creature struck by a keketar's claw or bite must make a DC 28 Fortitude save or be affected by a warpwave. The save DC is Constitution-based.

Priests and prophets, keketars are the leaders of their race, guiding proteans in their sacred mission to return all existence to primal chaos.

Illustration by Sarah Stone

Protean, Naunet

Tentacles tipped with snapping jaws emerge from this serpentine creature's back, complementing the vicious maw in its reptilian face.

NAUNET	CR 7

XP 3,200

CN Large outsider (chaotic, extraplanar, protean, shapechanger)

Init +7; **Senses** blindsense 30 ft., darkvision 60 ft., *detect law*; Perception +15

DEFENSE

AC 20, touch 12, flat-footed 17 (+3 Dex, +8 natural, –1 size)

hp 94 (9d10+45)

Fort +11, **Ref** +11, **Will** +6

Defensive Abilities amorphous anatomy, freedom of movement; **DR** 5/lawful; **Immune** acid, polymorph; **Resist** electricity 10, sonic 10; **SR** 18

OFFENSE

Speed 30 ft., fly 30 ft. (perfect), swim 30 ft.

Melee bite +14 (1d8+5), tail slap +11 (1d6+2 plus grab), 2 tentacles +11 (1d6+2 plus confusion)

Space 10 ft.; **Reach** 10 ft.

Special Attacks adaptive strike, coalesce chaos, constrict (1d6+5)

Spell-Like Abilities (CL 7th; concentration +9)

Constant—*detect law*

At will—*acid arrow, fog cloud, dimension door* (self plus 50 lbs. of objects only), *shatter* (DC 14)

1/day—*chaos hammer* (DC 16)

STATISTICS

Str 20, **Dex** 17, **Con** 20, **Int** 11, **Wis** 16, **Cha** 15

Base Atk +9; **CMB** +15; **CMD** 28

Feats Combat Reflexes, Improved Initiative, Lightning Reflexes, Multiattack, Weapon Focus (bite)

Skills Acrobatics +15, Fly +9, Intimidate +14, Perception +15, Stealth +11, Survival +15, Swim +25

Languages Abyssal, Protean

SQ change shape (*polymorph*)

ECOLOGY

Environment any (Limbo)

Organization solitary, pair, or cacophony (3–12)

Treasure none

SPECIAL ABILITIES

Adaptive Strike (Su) A naunet's natural weapons count as magical and chaotic for the purposes of overcoming damage reduction. As a free action once per round, a naunet may infuse all of its natural attacks with adamantine, silver, or cold iron, thereby allowing it to overcome damage reduction of those types as well.

Coalesce Chaos (Su) Once per day as a standard action, three or more naunets working together can create a roiling cloud of multicolored chaos matter. This effect is identical to *solid fog* (CL 12th) and lasts for 2d6 rounds. If six or more naunets are present, the coalesced chaos instead functions as *acid fog* (CL 12th).

Confusion (Su) A creature struck by a naunet's tentacle attack is infused with raw chaos, and must make a DC 19 Will save or be confused for 1 round. Rounds of confusion dealt in this manner stack. A creature with a chaotic component to its alignment gains a +4 bonus on saves against this effect, and creatures with the chaotic subtype are immune. This is a mind-affecting effect. The save DC is Constitution-based.

Far more bestial than their kin, naunets are the lowest caste of the true proteans, the shock troops of their race and roving marauders in the cause of chaos. Primarily found in the shifting borderlands between Limbo and other planes, naunets are driven half-insane by the stability and stasis of such areas, and frequently rampage through the edges of other planes, tearing up the very fabric of reality itself and returning vast swaths of land to the beautiful, formless potentiality of their home. A naunet is 12 feet long and weighs 900 pounds.

Illustrations by Jorge Maese

PROTEAN, VOIDWORM

This tiny, iridescent serpent slithers through empty space, the air around it distorting as if from heat.

VOIDWORM — CR 2

XP 600

CN Tiny outsider (chaotic, extraplanar, protean, shapechanger)

Init +3; **Senses** blindsense 30 ft., darkvision 30 ft., *detect law*; Perception +8

DEFENSE

AC 15, touch 15, flat-footed 12
(+3 Dex, +2 size)

hp 16 (3d10); fast healing 2

Fort +1, **Ref** +6, **Will** +2

Defensive Abilities amorphous anatomy, freedom of movement; **Immune** acid; **Resist** electricity 10, sonic 10

OFFENSE

Speed 20 ft., fly 50 ft. (perfect)

Melee bite +8 (1d3–2), tail slap +3 (1d3–2 plus confusion)

Space 2-1/2 ft.; **Reach** 0 ft.

Spell-Like Abilities (CL 6th; concentration +7)

Constant—*detect law*

At will—*dancing lights, ghost sound* (DC 11), *prestidigitation*

3/day—*blur* (self only), *obscuring mist*

1/week—*commune* (CL 12th, 6 questions)

STATISTICS

Str 7, **Dex** 17, **Con** 10, **Int** 8, **Wis** 8, **Cha** 13

Base Atk +3; **CMB** +4; **CMD** 12 (can't be tripped)

Feats Skill Focus (Perception), Weapon Finesse

Skills Acrobatics +9 (+5 jump), Bluff +7, Escape Artist +7, Fly +19, Knowledge (arcana) +5, Perception +8, Stealth +15

Languages Common, Protean

SQ change shape (2 forms, both of which must be Tiny animals; *beast shape II*)

ECOLOGY

Environment any (Limbo)

Organization solitary, pair, or school (3–18)

Treasure none

SPECIAL ABILITIES

Confusion (Su) A creature struck by a voidworm's tail slap must make a DC 12 Will save or become confused for 1 round. This is a mind-affecting effect. The save DC is Charisma-based.

Debate rages as to whether or not the strange and capricious creatures called voidworms are actually proteans at all. To the wizards and sorcerers who summon them as familiars, the answer seems obvious— these tiny dwellers of Limbo have all the requisite racial traits of proteans, down to their serpentine shapes. Yet the established protean castes find such claims outright insulting, claiming instead that it is such acts of conjuration that call voidworms forth from the raw stuff of Limbo, giving them shape and life according to the spellcasters' expectations, and that these lesser beings are but pale reflections of their formidable kin. Voidworms themselves have little to say on the matter—creatures of the moment, and sparing little thought for the constantly mutable concept of "reality," voidworms only barely grasp cause and effect, and the past has no more substance or significance for them than a dream. In order to gain a voidworm as a familiar, a spellcaster must be chaotic neutral, be caster level 7th, and have the Improved Familiar feat.

Regardless of their actual origins, voidworms maintain a thriving ecology in the chaos of Limbo, forming together into darting, flashing schools that are often hunted for sport by naunets and other predators of chaos. Mortal wizards, however, most commonly encounter voidworms as summoned familiars. These tiny, serpentine creatures are particularly valued by illusionists, evokers, and other magical practitioners who deal with distorting or molding reality, though the familiars' bizarre logic and miniscule attention spans sometimes make them more trouble than they're worth. Still, their confusing attack and remarkable hardiness have saved more than one wizard on the battlefield, and their strange thought processes can sometimes offer unique insights in the laboratory. When traveling in more mundane lands, wizards often order voidworm familiars to use their change shape ability to disguise themselves as ordinary pets or animal familiars, though these disguises tend to slip when the voidworm grows curious or playful.

A voidworm is only 2 feet long and weighs a mere 2 pounds. No two voidworms are exactly alike in their coloration or markings. Their two feathery wings generally take on brighter colors than the rest of their bodies, and in the case of voidworms conjured as familiars, these "wings" are the same color as their masters' eyes.

217

QLIPPOTH

Before the Abyss was taught how to process and transform larvae into demons—indeed, before larvae even existed or the idea of mortal life had been conceived—it was rife with foul life. These creatures exist still, yet in drastically reduced numbers and often only in the deepest pits of the plane. Known as the qlippoth (the singular and plural are identical), these fiends may well be the oldest form of life in the Great Beyond—certainly, they were already in existence before the proteans discovered them. Some believe that the qlippoth come from an unknowable realm on what might be described as the "outside shell" of the Outer Sphere, but if the qlippoth are to be taken as indicative of what order of existence rules in such a realm, it is a good thing indeed that this outer realm is so impossibly distant.

The qlippoth do not possess in their forms anything approximating the human shape except by cosmic fluke or sinister mockery. In their twitching, squirming visages, the mad might make comparisons to life's most primeval shapes—spiders and cephalopods, insects and worms, and even baser forms of life. What this might imply about these lower forms of life has disturbed philosophers for ages, and is not a train of thought that many enjoy lingering upon.

Since the rise of mortal sin, the rule of the Abyss has passed from the qlippoth to the much more fecund demons. When the Abyss first "learned" how to transform mortal souls into demons, the resulting explosion of demonic life culminated in a violent and destructive war with the then-rulers of the Abyss—the qlippoth. For unguessed millennia this war raged across the countless layers of the Abyss. The qlippoth had the advantage of knowing their ancient realm and, as a general rule, were individually more powerful than most demons, but the demons had numbers on their side. And as the demons continued to win battle after battle, new powers among their kind rose—balors, balor lords, nascent demon lords, and eventually demon lords themselves. Over time, the qlippoth were hunted nearly to extinction on the upper layers of the Abyss, and were forced to retreat deep into that realm's darkest and most remote realms, to places even the demons feared to tread.

Here, the qlippoth have festered and lurked for ages. None can say how many qlippoth survived that ancient war, for none can know how deep the Abyss goes. The qlippoth dwell in these darkest pits, periodically emerging to do battle against their hated demonic foes, yet their wrath is not limited to the demonic host. The qlippoth know that daemons played a role in "teaching" the Abyss how to birth demonic life, and their war with the denizens of Abaddon is one fueled more by a driving

need to punish than any need for survival. Yet as the eons have worn on, the qlippoth have come to realize that the true enemy is not a fiendish race—it is mortal life itself. For as long as mortal life continues to sin and die, the Abyss can continue to birth demons into its pits and rifts. The destruction of sin, by changing the way mortals live, would halt demonic growth, yet the qlippoth have no concept of how this goal might be achieved—to the qlippoth, only the murder of all mortality can suffice.

As a result, all qlippoth possess within their minds a burning hatred of mortal life, particularly humanoids, whom they know to be the primary seeds of sin. When a qlippoth is conjured to the Material Plane, it seeks any way to escape control in order to maul and destroy humans—they have a particular hatred of children and pregnant women, and if given a choice between harming someone already dying or close to death and someone with a full life ahead of them, they always choose to attack the latter, save for the rare case where the death of an elder or a dying loved one might result in a chain reaction of death among the young.

When called via spells like *planar ally* that require opposed Charisma checks or similar mechanics in order for the conjuring spellcaster to secure the outsider's aid, evil humanoids take a –6 penalty when interacting with qlippoth due to the sin in their souls. The promise of a task that would afford the qlippoth the opportunity to kill many humanoids, or a sacrifice of a pregnant woman or a child, can sometimes offset this penalty. When a qlippoth shakes off the shackles of a conjuration, it attempts to remain on the Material Plane as long as possible, and during that time tries to murder as many mortals as it can, doing its part to deprive the Abyss of possible future sinful souls to build demons from.

QLIPPOTH LORDS

That the qlippoth have among their kind paragons akin to demon lords is indisputable, yet these powers rarely, if ever, emerge from the deepest realms of the Abyss to interact with the rest of the multiverse. They are only rarely worshiped on the Material Plane, but such cults, where they exist, are singularly destructive and ruinous.

Yet the power granted by mortal worship can have a curious effect on a qlippoth—it can, in a way, infect it with the sins of its worshipers. Qlippoth who become so infected are either murdered by their kin or forced to flee to the upper realms of the Abyss, where they complete their transformation and, instead of remaining qlippoth lords, become demon lords. One can know the nature of a demon lord that began life as a qlippoth most easily by its shape—those demon lords, such as ichthyic Dagon or foul and festering Jubilex, bear little or no sign of a humanoid frame.

QLIPPOTH, AUGNAGAR

This enormous, spider-like creature has three clawed tails and eight legs connected by leathery webs of flesh.

AUGNAGAR **CR 14**

XP 38,400

CE Huge outsider (chaotic, evil, extraplanar, qlippoth)

Init +3; **Senses** blindsight 30 ft., darkvision 60 ft., scent, *true seeing*; Perception +22

DEFENSE

AC 29, touch 7, flat-footed 29 (–1 Dex, +22 natural, –2 size)

hp 203 (14d10+126)

Fort +18, **Ref** +10, **Will** +9

DR 10/lawful; **Immune** cold, poison, mind-affecting effects; **Resist** acid 10, electricity 10, fire 10

OFFENSE

Speed 50 ft., climb 50 ft., fly 50 ft. (average)

Melee bite +23 (2d6+11 plus 1d8 bleed and rotting curse), 3 claws +23 (1d8+11 plus 1d8 bleed)

Space 15 ft.; **Reach** 15 ft. (30 ft. with claws)

Special Attacks bleed, horrific appearance (DC 21)

Spell-Like Abilities (CL 14th; concentration +18)

　Constant—*true seeing*

　3/day—*dimension door, protection from law*

　1/day—*waves of exhaustion*

STATISTICS

Str 32, **Dex** 9, **Con** 28, **Int** 5, **Wis** 20, **Cha** 19

Base Atk +14; **CMB** +27; **CMD** 36 (44 vs. trip)

Feats Flyby Attack, Hover, Improved Initiative, Improved Vital Strike, Lightning Reflexes, Power Attack, Vital Strike

Skills Climb +19, Fly +12, Perception +22, Stealth +24; **Racial Modifiers** +16 Stealth

Languages Abyssal; telepathy 100 ft.

ECOLOGY

Environment any (Abyss)

Organization solitary

Treasure standard

SPECIAL ABILITIES

Horrific Appearance (Su) Creatures that succumb to an augnagar's horrific appearance are driven momentarily insane. This results in 2 points of Charisma damage and leaves the victim confused for 1d3 rounds.

Rotting Curse (Su): Bite—injury; *Save* Fort DC 26; *Frequency* 1/day; *Effect* 1d6 Con drain plus constant stench. A creature that suffers the rotting curse imparted by an augnagar's bite displays hideous, festering wounds that exude a horrific stench. This functions as the stench universal monster rule (see page 302), save that it affects all creatures except those that are immune to poison. The victim of this curse receives no saving throw to avoid becoming sickened by the stench, but other creatures can attempt a DC 26 Fortitude save to negate this condition—those who fail remain sickened as long as they remain within 30 feet of the cursed victim. The horrific stench also imparts a –8 penalty on all Stealth checks made by the cursed victim. The save DC is Constitution-based.

The immense augnagar is relatively slow-witted. As an outsider, it does not need to eat to survive, yet it remains ravenous and feeds on anything it can overpower. The augnagar prefers the taste of well-rotted flesh—particularly rotted demon flesh—and the horrific curse its bite imparts flavors its meals perfectly. Yet the augnagar's favorite feast is of a much more cannibalistic type. These creatures find the flesh of their own kind to be the greatest delicacy. When an augnagar feeds upon enough of its own kind, it grows enormously bloated such that it can no longer fly, at which point it uses its clawed tails to tear its body apart in a frenzy of self-destruction. From this storm of torn fat and shredded viscera emerges a fully grown thulgant qlippoth—a creature similar in shape to an augnagar, yet much more intelligent and even more dangerous.

An augnagar has a wingspan of 30 feet and weighs 6,000 pounds.

QLIPPOTH, CHERNOBUE

This slippery, writhing mass of tentacles and stalked mouths has one huge hideous eye and a fanged maw for a belly.

CHERNOBUE	CR 12	

XP 19,200

CE Large outsider (chaotic, evil, extraplanar, qlippoth)

Init +4; **Senses** darkvision 60 ft., scent; Perception +18

Aura misfortune (30 ft.)

DEFENSE

AC 27, touch 13, flat-footed 23 (+4 Dex, +14 natural, –1 size)

hp 150 (12d10+84)

Fort +15, **Ref** +10, **Will** +11

DR 10/lawful; **Immune** cold, poison, mind-affecting effects; **Resist** acid 10, electricity 10, fire 10; **SR** 23

Weaknesses light vulnerability

OFFENSE

Speed 40 ft.

Melee 2 slams +19 (1d6+8/19–20 plus 1 Con damage), bite +19 (2d6+8 plus poison), 2 tentacles +14 (1d6+4)

Space 10 ft.; **Reach** 5 ft. (10 ft. with slams and tentacles)

Special Attacks horrific appearance (DC 20)

Spell-Like Abilities (CL 12th; concentration +16)

Constant—*air walk, arcane sight*

At will—*chaos hammer* (DC 18), *darkness*

3/day—*confusion* (DC 18), quickened *darkness, dispel magic, protection from law*

1/day—*plane shift* (DC 21)

STATISTICS

Str 26, **Dex** 18, **Con** 24, **Int** 13, **Wis** 17, **Cha** 19

Base Atk +12; **CMB** +21; **CMD** 35 (39 vs. trip)

Feats Blind-Fight, Improved Critical (slam), Lightning Reflexes, Power Attack, Quicken Spell-Like Ability (*darkness*), Vital Strike

Skills Acrobatics +19 (+23 jump), Escape Artist +19, Intimidate +19, Knowledge (planes) +16, Perception +18, Sense Motive +18, Stealth +15

Languages Abyssal; telepathy 100 ft.

ECOLOGY

Environment any (the Abyss)

Organization solitary, pair, or gang (3–6)

Treasure standard

SPECIAL ABILITIES

Aura of Misfortune (Su) A chernobue radiates an aura of evil malaise to a radius of 30 feet. All lawful or good creatures in this area take a –1 penalty on attack rolls and weapon damage rolls. Lawful good creatures take a –3 penalty and upon first entering the aura must make a DC 20 Fortitude save or be sickened for as long as they remain in the area. This ability is Charisma-based.

Horrific Appearance (Su) Creatures that succumb to a chernobue's horrific appearance become paralyzed with disgust for 2d6 rounds; a paralyzed creature gets a new save each round to recover from the effect, provided he is no longer aware of the chernobue or within 30 feet of it.

Light Vulnerability (Ex) A chernobue within an area of bright light takes 1 point of Constitution damage per minute it remains in the area.

Poison (Su) Bite—injury; *save* Fort DC 23; *frequency* 1/round for 6 rounds; *effect* 1d2 Con drain; *cure* 1 save. The thick, orange poison injected by a chernobue is semi-alive. As soon as the poisoned victim is cured of the poison (by making a save, being targeted with an effect like *neutralize poison*, or enduring the full duration of the poison), the orange fluid bursts from the victim's body, causing 1d6 Charisma damage and rendering the victim unconscious for 2d6 rounds unless he makes a final DC 23 Fortitude save. The save DC is Constitution-based.

The chernobue is a living manifestation of the vile fecundity of the Abyss—a monstrous, alien pregnancy made flesh. By infecting creatures with the Abyssal taint they carry, they spread pain and misfortune wherever they flop and writhe—and with their *plane shift* ability, they are ready to spread their filth throughout the multiverse. A chernobue is 13 feet long and weighs 500 pounds.

QLIPPOTH, CYTHNIGOT

This six-legged horror has a spider's face and a fibrous stalk growing out of its back—a stalk ending in a snapping mouth.

CYTHNIGOT	CR 2

XP 600

CE Tiny outsider (chaotic, evil, extraplanar, qlippoth)

Init +1; **Senses** darkvision 60 ft., detect law, detect magic; Perception +5

DEFENSE

AC 14, touch 13, flat-footed 13 (+1 Dex, +1 natural, +2 size)

hp 16 (3d10)

Fort +1, **Ref** +6, **Will** +2

DR 5/cold iron or lawful; **Immune** cold, poison, mind-affecting effects; **Resist** acid 10, electricity 10, fire 10

OFFENSE

Speed 40 ft., fly 60 ft. (good)

Melee bite +6 (1d6+1 plus spores)

Space 2-1/2 ft.; **Reach** 0 ft.

Special Attacks horrific appearance (10 feet, DC 9)

Spell-Like Abilities (CL 6th, concentration +4)

Constant—*detect law, detect magic, fly*

1/day—*soften earth and stone, warp wood*

1/week—*commune* (six questions)

STATISTICS

Str 12, **Dex** 12, **Con** 11, **Int** 11, **Wis** 8, **Cha** 7

Base Atk +3; **CMB** +2; **CMD** 13 (21 vs. trip)

Feats Lightning Reflexes, Weapon Finesse

Skills Acrobatics +7 (+11 jump), Fly +15, Knowledge (nature) +6, Knowledge (planes) +6, Perception +5, Stealth +15

Languages Abyssal; telepathy (touch)

ECOLOGY

Environment any (Abyss)

Organization solitary or bloom (2–12)

Treasure standard

SPECIAL ABILITIES

Horrific Appearance (Su) Creatures that succumb to a cythnigot's horrific appearance become sickened for 1 round—a cythnigot's horrific appearance only functions to a range of 10 feet. Once a creature makes a saving throw against a particular cythnigot's horrific appearance, that creature is immune to the horrific appearance of all cythnigots for 24 hours. A spellcaster that has a cythnigot as a familiar is immune to the horrific appearance of all cythnigots, and also gains a +4 bonus on saving throws made against any qlippoth's horrific appearance.

Spores (Su) Any creature bitten by a cythnigot must make a DC 11 Fortitude save or become infested by the creature's otherworldly spores. These spores cause twitching spikes and hideous pallid growths of hair-like fibers to erupt from the bite wound and to writhe and wrap around the target's limbs. A creature suffering from these spores is entangled, and can attempt a new DC 11 Fortitude save in later rounds as a standard action to rip the tendrils free and escape the entangled condition. The effects of multiple cythnigot bites on a creature do not stack. Plant creatures take a –4 penalty on saves against this effect. This is a disease effect. The save DC is Constitution-based.

The cythnigot is a foul fungal parasite that grows and thrives within the corpses of small animals. The fungus transforms the host corpse in hideous ways, adding legs or rearranging features—a rat might gain an extra pair of legs and an insectoid visage, while a cat could lose all its legs and fur and gain a snake-like body. The only thing that all cythnigots have in common is a long stalk of fungal material that extends up from the creature's body, ending in a surprisingly strong set of fanged jaws. A cythnigot without a host body appears as little more than a foul-smelling puffball the size of a human's fist.

Chaotic evil spellcasters of caster level 7th who have the Improved Familiar feat can gain a cythnigot as a familiar—to do so, the spellcaster must already have a Tiny animal as a familiar. Infusing this familiar with the spores results in a cythnigot that is a loyal, if rather disgusting, minion of the spellcaster. A cythnigot is about 20 inches long and weighs 10 pounds.

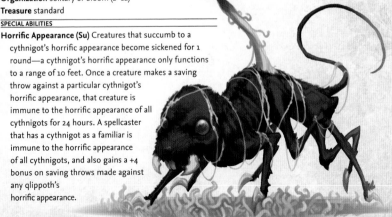

PATHFINDER

QLIPPOTH, IATHAVOS

This immense creature has four bat-like wings and a spherical body. Red eyes peer from all sides, and two huge claws dangle below.

IATHAVOS	CR 20	

XP 307,200

CE Colossal outsider (chaotic, evil, extraplanar, qlippoth)

Init −1; **Senses** all-around vision, darkvision 60 ft., low-light vision; Perception +37

Aura *cloak of chaos* (DC 26), stench (DC 32, 10 rounds)

DEFENSE

AC 37, touch 7, flat-footed 37 (+4 deflection, −1 Dex, +2 insight, +30 natural, −8 size)

hp 372 (24d10+240); fast healing 15

Fort +28, **Ref** +15, **Will** +28

Defensive Abilities ichor, never surprised or flat-footed; **DR** 15/cold iron and lawful; **Immune** cold, poison, mind-affecting effects; **Resist** acid 30, electricity 10, fire 10; **SR** 31

OFFENSE

Speed 20 ft., fly 50 ft. (perfect)

Melee 2 claws +31 (4d6+15/19–20 plus grab), 4 wings +26 (2d8+7)

Space 30 ft.; **Reach** 30 ft.

Special Attacks abyssal transformation, entropic beams, horrific appearance (DC 30)

Spell-Like Abilities (CL 20th; concentration +28)

Constant—*cloak of chaos* (DC 26), *foresight, freedom of movement, true seeing*

At will—*dimension door, dispel law, greater dispel magic, magic missile, plane shift* (DC 25), *wind walk, word of recall*

3/day—*black tentacles, dimensional lock, horrid wilting* (DC 26), *insanity* (DC 25), *word of chaos* (DC 25)

1/day—quickened *heal, imprisonment* (DC 27)

STATISTICS

Str 40, **Dex** 8, **Con** 31, **Int** 29, **Wis** 30, **Cha** 27

Base Atk +24; **CMB** +47 (+51 grapple); **CMD** 62 (can't be tripped)

Feats Awesome Blow, Critical Focus, Greater Vital Strike, Improved Bull Rush, Improved Critical (claw), Improved Vital Strike, Lightning Reflexes, Power Attack, Quicken Spell-Like Ability (*heal*), Spell Penetration, Staggering Critical, Vital Strike

Skills Bluff +35, Escape Artist +23, Fly +26, Intimidate +35, Knowledge (arcana) +36, Knowledge (dungeoneering) +33, Knowledge (geography) +33, Knowledge (history) +33, Knowledge (planes) +36, Knowledge (religion) +33, Perception +37, Sense Motive +37, Spellcraft +36, Stealth +10, Use Magic Device +35

Languages Abyssal; telepathy 300 ft.

ECOLOGY

Environment any (Abyss)

Organization solitary

Treasure double

SPECIAL ABILITIES

Abyssal Transformation (Su) If an iathavos establishes a hold on a creature of Large or smaller size, it can place that creature deep within the bristly folds of its flesh. Treat this as an engulf attack (see page 296), except that at the start of the iathavos's turn, an engulfed creature must make a DC 30 Fortitude save or be transformed into a nyogoth qlippoth that immediately squirms out of the iathavos's body to serve its new master. Creatures transformed into nyogoths are not controlled by the iathavos, but function and behave as if they were typical members of that species—they retain no memories or abilities they may have possessed in their previous lives. Items held or worn by the unfortunate victim remain lodged within the folds of the iathavos's body and can only be retrieved if the iathavos is helpless or dead. A creature transformed into a nyogoth in this manner can be restored to its true shape via *break enchantment, miracle,* or *wish*. Otherwise, slaying the nyogoth allows the poor soul to be restored to life via *reincarnation, resurrection,* or *true resurrection*. The save DC is Charisma-based.

Entropic Beams (Su) As a standard action once every minute, an iathavos can fire beams of entropic energy from its 10 eyes. Each of these beams of energy can be directed at a single target within 300 feet of the iathavos, but no more than one beam may be directed at any one creature. Beams that are not directed at a creature are wasted. The qlippoth must make a +15 ranged touch attack to hit with each beam. Each beam has the same effect as a CL 20th *disintegrate* (40d6 damage, DC 32 Fortitude partial for 5d6 damage), except a creature killed by this damage explodes in a 5-foot burst of energy, flesh, shadow, and smoke instead of turning into dust. Any creature in this burst must make a DC 32 Will save or be staggered for 1 round. The save DCs are Constitution-based.

Horrific Appearance (Su) Creatures that succumb to the iathavos's horrific appearance are affected by a *feeblemind* effect and permanently blinded.

Ichor (Su) As long as the iathavos has taken any hit point damage, thick and stringy ropes of black ichor weep from the fissures and folds in its bristly hide. This ichor extrudes from the creature's body in a writhing nimbus of filaments at a rate of 5 feet per round, to a maximum range equal to its reach (30 feet). At the start the iathavos's turn, all creatures in reach of these strands of ichor must make a DC 32 Reflex save or become entangled. At the start the iathavos's turn, all creatures entangled by the ichor take 4d6 points of acid damage. If the qlippoth ends its turn with no hit point damage, the ichor melts away into harmless mist, releasing all entangled creatures. The save DC is Constitution-based.

Stench (Su) The iathavos's stench ability is supernaturally disgusting—creatures that succumb to this ability are nauseated, while those that save are still sickened.

222

The most terrible of the qlippoth, with the exception of the qlippoth lords, is doubtless the immense iathavos. Believed by many to be a singular entity, a unique qlippoth so abhorrent that even the Abyss cannot bear to allow more than one to exist at any one time, the iathavos is often encountered attended by numerous nyogoth qlippoth that squirm over its body or under its bulk, feeding upon the wastes and fragments left behind by its shuddersome passing. These nyogoths are invariably other creatures that the iathavos has absorbed and remade—they represent one of the most heinous fates that could await would-be explorers of the deepest Abyssal rifts.

The iathavos crusades against the demonic scourge, but the monster does not limit its attentions to seeking out and destroying demons in preparation for the return of the Abyss to qlippoth rule. Indeed, the iathavos has the ability to shift among the various planes of the multiverse, and often travels to Material Plane worlds to systematically scour realms clean of mortal life, thus ensuring that these worlds can no longer provide the raw materials—sinful mortal souls—the Abyss relies upon to create new demons. Worlds visited by the iathavos are notable for the widespread devastation and the unusually large populations of nyogoths that remain behind to consume every last speck of decay the iathavos leaves behind.

The iathavos can be called via the most powerful spells, such as *gate*, but its immunity to mind-affecting effects and its vast size ensure that only the most desperate or most insane ever attempt such a self-destructive act. In all known cases, the deliberate conjuration of the iathavos to another world has done little more than draw the attention of the powerful creature to that world, so that even if it is banished back to the Abyss before it can cause too much devastation, the iathavos remembers the visit. It often returns under its own power at a later date to pursue its own goals on the newly discovered world. Only if the iathavos is presented with defenders that prevent it from achieving its destructive ruin does it flee back to the Abyss via *plane shift*— in such cases, the qlippoth often waits for centuries or even millennia before returning to that world, for there are always easier realms to destroy.

The iathavos is a powerful and horrifying monster made all the more devastating by its incredible intellect. The creature takes care to plan its major assaults on demonic enclaves or mortal cities, even though it is powerful enough that few creatures in the multiverse can give it pause.

When the iathavos is slain, the multiverse typically has only a relatively short time before the Abyss births a replacement monstrosity for the defeated qlippoth. This newly born iathavos is an entirely new creature—it does not share the memories of the previous incarnation, nor does it possess any advanced hit dice or class levels the previous monster may have gained, yet its appetite and hatred for demonic life and the sins that create such life remain constant and unending.

To call such an iathavos a "newborn" is somewhat misleading. Although technically a freshly created creature, newborn iathavoses do not undergo a "childhood." They form fully grown, as presented here. Yet with each new incarnation of the qlippoth monstrosity, changes can occur. A new iathavos might have slightly different spell-like abilities, for example, or the nature of its horrific appearance might change from that presented here. As an iathavos continues to hunt and destroy, it grows more powerful—an advanced iathavos typically gains more racial Hit Dice as a result. An iathavos that gains power by taking class levels is not unheard of, but it is quite rare— most who do take levels in sorcerer.

QLIPPOTH, NYOGOTH

This appears to be a mass of floating intestines tangled around a fanged mouth—the tips of its coils also end in toothy maws.

NYOGOTH	CR 10

XP 9,600

CE Medium outsider (chaotic, evil, extraplanar, qlippoth)

Init +5; **Senses** darkvision 60 ft.; Perception +17

DEFENSE

AC 24, touch 15, flat-footed 19 (+5 Dex, +9 natural)

hp 125 (10d10+70)

Fort +14, **Ref** +12, **Will** +7

Defensive Abilities acid spray; **DR** 10/lawful; **Immune** acid, cold, poison, mind-affecting effects; **Resist** electricity 10, fire 10

OFFENSE

Speed 5 ft., fly 30 ft. (good)

Melee 4 bites +15 (1d6+3/19–20 plus 1d4 acid), bite +15 (2d6+3/19–20 plus 1d4 acid)

Special Attacks horrific appearance (DC 18)

Spell-Like Abilities (CL 10th; concentration +13)

    At will—*acid arrow*

    7/day—*fear* (DC 17), *protection from law*

    1/day—*acid fog, dimension door*

STATISTICS

Str 16, **Dex** 21, **Con** 24, **Int** 9, **Wis** 19, **Cha** 16

Base Atk +10; **CMB** +13; **CMD** 28 (can't be tripped)

Feats Combat Reflexes, Improved Critical (bite), Power Attack, Vital Strike, Weapon Finesse

Skills Fly +22, Intimidate +16, Knowledge (planes) +12, Perception +17, Stealth +18

Languages Abyssal; telepathy 100 ft.

SQ flight

ECOLOGY

Environment any (the Abyss)

Organization solitary or brood (2–8)

Treasure standard

SPECIAL ABILITIES

Acid Spray (Su) A nyogoth's body is full of highly corrosive digestive fluid. Every time a nyogoth is damaged by a piercing or slashing weapon, all creatures adjacent to the nyogoth take 1d6 points of acid damage (2d6 acid damage if the attack is a critical hit).

Horrific Appearance (Su) Creatures that succumb to a nyogoth's horrific appearance become nauseated for 1d8 rounds.

The nyogoth's role on the Abyss is that of a scavenger. Essentially mobile clumps of buoyant intestines, these writhing creatures squirt through the air in convulsive movements like an octopus gliding through water, and are constantly on the search for anything smaller than one of their many mouths (either the relatively small ones that pinch and gasp at the tips of their intestinal limbs or the larger gaping one at their cores). They can subsist on the waste and filth left behind by other denizens of the Abyss, but particularly enjoy feeding on still-living creatures.

Despite their seemingly lowly role in Abyssal ecosystems, the nyogoths are far from stupid beasts. Most are nearly as intelligent as the average human, and are capable of solving relatively complex problems when it comes to securing the next meal. As outsiders, nyogoths do not need to eat to survive, yet this does not exempt them from hunger—a nyogoth that goes for longer than 12 hours without a meal becomes increasingly violent and erratic. Such a "starving" nyogoth typically fights to the death when the prospect of food is available, and may even resort to self-cannibalism, drinking its own spurting digestive juices from its wounds in a nauseating display.

A typical nyogoth is 5 feet in diameter and weighs 260 pounds, although they are known to grow much larger.

Illustrations by Andrew Hou

QLIPPOTH, SHOGGTI

This pale creature has four suckered arms that end in pincers. A gnashing maw gapes in its head between two staring eyes.

SHOGGTI CR 7

XP 3,200
CE Large outsider (chaotic, evil, extraplanar, qlippoth)
Init +7; **Senses** darkvision 60 ft.; Perception +18

DEFENSE

AC 21, touch 12, flat-footed 18 (+3 Dex, +9 natural, −1 size)
hp 80 (7d10+42)
Fort +11, **Ref** +5, **Will** +9
Defensive Abilities uncanny dodge; **DR** 10/cold iron or lawful; **Immune** cold, poison, mind-affecting effects; **Resist** acid 10, electricity 10, fire 10

OFFENSE

Speed 30 ft.
Melee bite +12 (1d8+6), 4 tentacles +8 (1d4+3 plus grab)
Space 10 ft.; **Reach** 10 ft.
Special Attacks braincloud, horrific appearance (DC 15), constrict (1d4+6)
Spell-Like Abilities (CL 7th; concentration +9)
   Constant—*tongues*
   At will—*command* (DC 13)
   3/day—*charm person* (DC 13), *protection from law*
   1/day—*charm monster* (DC 16), *dimension door*

STATISTICS

Str 22, **Dex** 16, **Con** 23, **Int** 12, **Wis** 19, **Cha** 15
Base Atk +7; **CMB** +14 (+18 grapple); **CMD** 27 (31 vs. trip)
Feats Combat Reflexes, Improved Initiative, Skill Focus (Use Magic Device), Weapon Focus (tentacles)
Skills Escape Artist +13, Intimidate +16, Knowledge (planes) +11, Perception +18, Sense Motive +14, Stealth +9, Use Magic Device +19; **Racial Modifiers** +4 Intimidate, +4 Perception, +4 Use Magic Device
Languages Abyssal; telepathy 100 ft.

ECOLOGY

Environment any (the Abyss)
Organization solitary, pair, or slaver band (3–10 plus 6–12 slaves of various races)
Treasure standard

SPECIAL ABILITIES

Braincloud (Su) Once per round, in place of a melee attack with a tentacle, a shoggti can make a melee touch attack with the pincer on the end of that tentacle. If it hits, the target takes 1d4 points of Wisdom damage. Shoggti use this ability to mentally debilitate their victims so they can more easily use their charm spell-like abilities against them.
Horrific Appearance (Su) Creatures that succumb to

a shoggti's horrific appearance become fascinated by the creature's hypnotically wriggling tentacles and the strange, shimmering colors in its eyes. This effect persists for 1d6 rounds (but can be ended by the normal methods of defeating the fascinated condition).

The shoggti are masters of mind manipulation, capable of seizing control of the thoughts of others and charming them into docile allies. They invade other realms in slaver bands, seeking out creatures to capture alive and return to the Abyss as charmed slaves—the fates of these poor souls is unknown, but likely has something to do with the qlippoth drive to reclaim the Abyss as their own.

Although a shoggti lacks proper hands, it is capable of performing incredibly dextrous manipulations with the pincers at the tips of its tentacles. It cannot wield weapons in these pincers, but it can utilize magic items like wands, rods, staves, and the like. Shoggti are fond of wands in particular, particularly those that create mind-affecting effects that are easy to inflict on victims of their braincloud ability.

A shoggti's body is an egg-shaped mass about 8 feet long—its tentacles are about 8 feet long as well. The whole creature weighs 900 pounds.

QLIPPOTH, THULGANT

This monster has ten spidery legs, a head writhing with dripping tentacles above a clutch of red eyes, and three whipping stingers.

THULGANT	CR 18

XP 153,600

CE Large outsider (chaotic, evil, extraplanar, qlippoth)

Init +12; **Senses** darkvision 60 ft., *true seeing*; Perception +31

Aura cloak of chaos (DC 25)

DEFENSE

AC 33, touch 25, flat-footed 21 (+4 deflection, +12 Dex, +8 natural, −1 size)

hp 290 (20d10+180); fast healing 10

Fort +25, **Ref** +30, **Will** +18

Defensive Abilities *displacement*, evasion, *freedom of movement*; **DR** 15/cold iron and lawful; **Immune** acid, cold, poison, mind-affecting effects; **Resist** electricity 10, fire 10; **SR** 25 vs. lawful spells and creatures

OFFENSE

Speed 40 ft., climb 40 ft., fly 60 ft. (good)

Melee 3 stings +27 (1d6+8/19–20 plus ability drain), 5 tentacles +22 (1d6+4 plus 2d6 acid)

Space 10 ft.; **Reach** 10 ft.

Special Attacks horrific appearance (DC 27), savage stingers

Spell-Like Abilities (CL 18th; concentration +25)

Constant—*cloak of chaos* (DC 25), *displacement*, *freedom of movement*, *true seeing*

At will—*dimension door*, *greater dispel magic*, *telekinesis* (DC 22)

3/day—quickened *dimension door*, *flesh to stone* (DC 23), *word of chaos* (DC 24)

1/day—*binding* (DC 25), *plane shift* (DC 24), *telekinetic sphere* (DC 25), *temporal stasis* (DC 25)

STATISTICS

Str 26, **Dex** 34, **Con** 29, **Int** 24, **Wis** 27, **Cha** 25

Base Atk +20; **CMB** +29; **CMD** 55 (71 vs. trip)

Feats Combat Expertise, Combat Reflexes, Critical Focus, Greater Vital Strike, Improved Critical (sting), Improved Vital Strike, Lightning Reflexes, Quicken Spell-Like Ability (*dimension door*), Staggering Critical, Vital Strike

Skills Acrobatics +35 (+39 jump), Bluff +30, Climb +36, Fly +33, Intimidate +27, Knowledge (arcana) +27, Knowledge (history) +30, Knowledge (planes) +30, Perception +31, Sense Motive +31, Spellcraft +27, Stealth +31, Use Magic Device +30

Languages Abyssal; telepathy 100 ft.

SQ demon hunter

ECOLOGY

Environment any (Abyss)

Organization solitary, pair, or patrol (3–4)

Treasure double

SPECIAL ABILITIES

Ability Drain (Su) A thulgant's stingers each drain a different ability score on a hit. One stinger drains 1d4 points of Strength, another drains 1d4 points of Dexterity, and the third drains 1d4 points of Charisma. Any sting's drain is negated by a DC 29 Fortitude save. The save DC is Constitution-based.

Demon Hunter (Ex) A thulgant gains a +10 racial bonus on caster level checks to penetrate the spell resistance of any demon. Its attacks are treated as cold iron and good against demons.

Horrific Appearance (Su) Creatures that succumb to a thulgant's horrific appearance are stunned for 1d4 rounds and take 1d6 points of Wisdom damage.

Savage Stingers (Ex) If a thulgant hits a single target with all three stings in the same round, it tears through the victim's body, dealing an extra 3d6+12 points of damage and draining an additional 2 ability points from all six of the victim's ability scores. A single DC 29 Fortitude save negates all of this additional ability drain. The save DC is Constitution-based.

The dreaded thulgant is among the most dangerous of the qlippoth, for it supports an array of deadly and painful physical attacks with a wide range of potent magical powers. Born from the cannibalistic orgies of augnagar qlippoth, each thulgant exists for one purpose only—the eradication of all demons from the Abyss.

Yet thulgants do not spend all of their lives hunting and destroying demons. They rule horrific hives deep in the Abyss populated by all manner of hideous minions, many of which are bound into servitude via *binding* spells. These qlippoth are fond of decorating their lairs with petrified or enstasised victims of great power—the more powerful the victims, the greater the prestige held by the thulgant.

Illustration by Andrew Hou

QUICKLING

This creature resembles a short and slight elf wearing drab clothes and a wicked grin. In a blink, the thing darts from sight.

QUICKLING	CR 3

XP 800

CE Small fey

Init +7; **Senses** low-light vision; Perception +9

DEFENSE

AC 20, touch 19, flat-footed 12 (+7 Dex, +1 dodge, +1 natural, +1 size)

hp 18 (4d6+4)

Fort +2, **Ref** +11, **Will** +6

Defensive Abilities evasion, natural invisibility, supernatural speed, uncanny dodge; **DR** 5/cold iron

Weaknesses slow susceptibility

OFFENSE

Speed 120 ft.

Melee short sword +10 (1d4–1/19–20)

Special Attacks sneak attack +1d6

Spell-Like Abilities (CL 6th; concentration +8)

1/day—*dancing lights, flare* (DC 12), *levitate, shatter* (DC 14), *ventriloquism* (DC 13)

STATISTICS

Str 8, **Dex** 24, **Con** 13, **Int** 15, **Wis** 15, **Cha** 14

Base Atk +2; **CMB** +0; **CMD** 18

Feats Dodge, Mobility[B], Spring Attack[B], Weapon Finesse

Skills Acrobatics +14 (+50 jump), Bluff +9, Craft (any one) +9, Escape Artist +14, Perception +9, Spellcraft +6, Stealth +18, Survival +4, Use Magic Device +7

Languages Aklo, Common, Sylvan

SQ poison use

ECOLOGY

Environment temperate forests

Organization solitary, gang (2–5), or band (4–11 plus one advanced leader)

Treasure NPC gear (blue whinnis poison [4 doses], Small short sword, other treasure)

SPECIAL ABILITIES

Natural Invisibility (Su) A quickling is invisible when motionless. It loses this invisibility and remains visible for 1 round in any round in which it takes an action other than a free action.

Supernatural Speed (Su) A quickling moves with incredible speed. Save for when it remains motionless (at which point it is invisible), the quickling's shape blurs and shimmers with this speed, granting it concealment (20% miss chance). In addition, this ability grants the quickling evasion and uncanny dodge (as the rogue abilities of the same names).

Slow Susceptibility (Ex) A quickling that succumbs to a *slow* effect loses its supernatural speed ability and is sickened as

long as the effect persists. This sickened condition persists for 1 round after the *slow* effect ends.

Few creatures can match the speed of a quickling. These malicious fey creatures delight in striking with blinding speed and accuracy, often killing their victims without ever fully revealing themselves; the victim simply spurts blood and falls over dead, with no witnesses to the quickling's deed. Though related to brownies and grigs, quicklings share none of their kin's generosity or merriment, choosing instead to live a life of cruelty and viciousness. Quicklings pride themselves on insults and brutality, and frequently stalk and harass their quarry until the victim gives up the chase. While quicklings are naturally invisible when motionless, they rarely contain themselves, and bob and twitch while standing and talking to other creatures. Quicklings hate every other race of creature, particularly elves, gnomes, and other kinds of fey. They barely tolerate their own kind, and rarely work together for longer than a few weeks.

Quicklings stand just over 2-1/2 feet tall and weigh 15 pounds.

Illustration by Eric Belisle

QUICKWOOD

Were it not for the image of a sinister face peeking out from its dark gray bark, this would look like any other ragged oak tree.

QUICKWOOD	CR 8

XP 4,800

N Huge plant

Init +3; **Senses** darkvision 120 ft., low-light vision, oaksight; Perception +21

Aura fear aura (variable distance, DC 20)

DEFENSE

AC 19, touch 7, flat-footed 19 (−1 Dex, +12 natural, −2 size)

hp 95 (10d8+50)

Fort +12, **Ref** +2, **Will** +5

Defensive Abilities spell absorption; **Immune** electricity, fire, plant traits; **SR** 19 (see spell absorption)

OFFENSE

Speed 10 ft.

Melee bite +14 (2d6+9), 3 roots +12 (1d6+4 plus pull)

Space 5 ft.; **Reach** 15 ft. (60 ft. with root)

Special Attacks pull (root, 10 ft.)

STATISTICS

Str 29, **Dex** 8, **Con** 21, **Int** 12, **Wis** 15, **Cha** 12

Base Atk +7; **CMB** +18; **CMD** 27 (can't be tripped)

Feats Improved Initiative, Lunge, Multiattack, Power Attack, Skill Focus (Perception)

Skills Knowledge (nature) +11, Perception +21, Stealth +4 (+8 in forests); **Racial Modifiers** +4 Stealth in forests

Languages Common, Sylvan

ECOLOGY

Environment temperate forests

Organization solitary

Treasure standard

SPECIAL ABILITIES

Fear Aura (Su) A quickwood with stored magical energy can activate its fear aura as a standard action. The aura has a radius of 10 feet per spell level of the effect and lasts for 1 round (Will DC 20 negates). Creatures that fail their saving throws become panicked for 1 minute. The DC is Charisma-based and includes a +4 racial bonus.

Oaksight (Su) A quickwood may observe the area surrounding any oak tree within 360 feet as if using *clairaudience/clairvoyance*. It can use this ability on any number of oak trees in the area. Although the quickwood does not need line of sight to establish this link, if it does have line of sight to even a single oak tree, it cannot be flanked.

Roots (Ex) A quickwood has dozens of long roots, but can only attack with up to three of them in any given round. If the quickwood uses its pull ability to pull a target within reach of its bite attack, it can immediately make a free bite attack with a +4 bonus on its attack roll against that target.

Spell Absorption (Su) If a quickwood's spell resistance protects it from a magical effect, the creature absorbs that magical energy into its body. It can release this energy to activate its fear aura ability. While the plant is storing a spell, its SR decreases by 5. It can only store one spell at a time.

These carnivorous plants prize human and elven flesh, but eat anything they manage to catch. Quickwoods typically explore an area, taking note of any oak trees, and then root themselves and wait for prey to wander by. They use their oaksight ability to maintain constant surveillance of their hunting grounds and send their roots out to drag likely prey back to them.

RAST

This bulbous creature consists of many tangled legs, a bulging body of puffed flesh, and a mouth filled with sharp fangs.

RAST	CR 5

XP 1,600

N Medium outsider (extraplanar, fire)

Init +5; **Senses** darkvision 60 ft.; Perception +10

DEFENSE

AC 18, touch 11, flat-footed 17 (+1 Dex, +7 natural)

hp 51 (6d10+18)

Fort +8, **Ref** +6, **Will** +3

Immune fire

Weaknesses vulnerability to cold

OFFENSE

Speed 5 ft., fly 60 ft. (good)

Melee bite +8 (1d6+2 plus grab), 4 claws +9 (1d4+2)

Special Attacks blood drain (1d2 Constitution), paralyzing gaze

STATISTICS

Str 14, **Dex** 12, **Con** 17, **Int** 3, **Wis** 13, **Cha** 12

Base Atk +6; **CMB** +8 (+12 grapple); **CMD** 19 (can't be tripped)

Feats Flyby Attack, Improved Initiative, Weapon Focus (claw)

Skills Fly +5, Perception +10, Stealth +10

Languages Ignan (cannot speak)

ECOLOGY

Environment any (Plane of Fire)

Organization solitary, pair, cluster (3–6), or pack (7–15)

Treasure none

SPECIAL ABILITIES

Paralyzing Gaze (Su) Paralyzed for 1d6 rounds, 30 feet, Fortitude (DC 14) negates. The save DC is Charisma-based.

them above mere animals, and use this innate cunning to aid in their hunts. As prey is scarce in the barren, ashy deserts of the Plane of Fire where they make their home, rasts prefer to hunt in packs, swarming through the skies like schools of fish, their movements precise and coordinated despite their thrashing limbs. When they come across a likely target, they descend en masse, paralyzing those foes susceptible to their gaze and then abandoning them temporarily to focus on any opponents that remain mobile and dangerous, slashing with their claws and latching on with thick-lipped mouths to suck their victims' blood and viscera. Though each rast has roughly a dozen limbs, it can only control up to four at any given time, leaving the others to dangle uselessly.

Hailing from the barren wastes of the Plane of Fire, the rast is as dangerous as it is bizarre. Its body is a single tumorous sack that bulges with hidden organs and veins and bears no sensory apparatus beyond two miniscule eyes almost lost in the folds and wattles of its flesh. Instead, its defining feature is a mouth of flesh-ripping teeth and a wriggling mass of tangled legs. The exact number of legs on a particular rast is seemingly a random trait. Strangely, these tangled limbs do not support the creature, but rather hang twitching and waving beneath it as the rast floats through the air with an easy grace, only reaching out to manipulate objects or—more often—to slash at its prey.

Though rasts do not appear to have any spoken language, they display a degree of intelligence that places

Rasts make their homes in small ashen burrows, no more than holes scooped out by the thrashing of their claws, and bear their squirming young live. An adult rast is the size of a human and weighs 200 pounds. Rasts tend to be red, yellow, or purple, with darker coloration on their legs and heads, the better to blend in with the fiery plains of their homeland. Though most other intelligent species on the Plane of Fire are powerful enough (or wise enough) to avoid direct conflict with a rast pack, a cluster that stumbles through a portal to the Material Plane (or perhaps more tragically, is summoned to the Material Plane by a foolish spellcaster) can prove disastrous for the local ecosystem, consuming everything in its path with seemingly no limit to its repulsive hunger.

Illustration by Jim Pavelec

RAVENER

This immense skeletal dragon rears up to its full, towering height, bones glowing and shimmering with vile green energy.

RED WYRM RAVENER	CR 22	

XP 614,400

CE Gargantuan undead (fire)

Init +3; **Senses** blindsense 120 ft., darkvision 240 ft., smoke vision; Perception +45

Aura cowering fear, fire, frightful presence (330 ft., DC 31)

DEFENSE

AC 45, touch 9, flat-footed 45 (+4 deflection, –1 Dex, +36 natural, –4 size)

hp 337 (27d8+216)

Fort +23, **Ref** +14, **Will** +23

Defensive Abilities channel resistance +4, soul ward (27 hp); **DR** 20/good; **Immune** fire, undead traits; **SR** 33

Weaknesses vulnerability to cold

OFFENSE

Speed 40 ft., fly 250 ft. (clumsy)

Melee bite +40 (4d6+24/17–20), 2 claws +40 (2d8+16/19–20), tail slap +38 (2d8+24/19–20), 2 wings +38 (2d6+8/19–20)

Space 20 ft.; **Reach** 15 ft. (20 ft. with bite)

Special Attacks breath weapon (60-ft. cone, DC 31, 22d10 fire and 2 negative levels), crush, manipulate flames, melt stone, soul consumption, soul magic, tail sweep

Spell-Like Abilities (CL 27th, concentration +35)

At will—*detect magic, find the path, pyrotechnics* (DC 20), *suggestion* (DC 21), *wall of fire*

Sorcerer Spells Known (CL 20th, concentration +28)

9th—*energy drain, time stop, wish*

8th—*dimensional lock, horrid wilting* (DC 26), *maze*

7th—*forcecage* (DC 25), *greater teleport, spell turning*

6th—*chain lightning* (DC 24), *greater dispel magic, true seeing*

5th—*cone of cold* (DC 23), *dominate person* (DC 23), *feeblemind* (DC 23), *wall of force*

4th—*charm monster* (DC 22), *confusion* (DC 22), *greater invisibility, solid fog*

3rd—*displacement, haste, slow* (DC 21), *vampiric touch*

2nd—*detect thoughts* (DC 20), *false life, mirror image, see invisibility, web* (DC 20)

1st—*mage armor, magic missile, ray of enfeeblement* (DC 19), *shield, true strike*

0—*arcane mark, detect magic, mage hand, mending, message, prestidigitation, ray of frost, read magic, touch of fatigue*

STATISTICS

Str 45, **Dex** 8, **Con** —, **Int** 24, **Wis** 25, **Cha** 26

Base Atk +27; **CMB** +48; **CMD** 57 (61 vs. trip)

Feats Cleave, Critical Focus, Greater Vital Strike, Improved Critical (bite), Improved Initiative, Improved Iron Will, Improved Vital Strike, Iron Will, Multiattack, Power Attack, Quicken Spell, Staggering Critical, Stunning Critical, Vital Strike

Skills Appraise +37, Bluff +37, Diplomacy +37, Fly +13, Intimidate +45, Knowledge (arcana) +37, Knowledge (history) +37, Knowledge (religion) +34, Perception +45, Sense Motive +37, Spellcraft +37, Stealth +25

Languages Abyssal, Aklo, Common, Draconic, Elven, Giant, Infernal

ECOLOGY

Environment warm mountains

Organization solitary

Treasure triple

Most evil dragons spend their lifetimes coveting and amassing wealth, but when the end draws near, some come to realize that all the wealth in the world cannot forestall death. Faced with this truth, most dragons vent their frustration on the countryside, ravaging the world before their passing. Yet some seek a greater solution to the problem and decide instead to linger on, hoarding life as they once hoarded gold. These foul wyrms attract the attention of dark powers, and through the blackest of necromantic rituals are transformed into undead dragons known as raveners.

Although its body quickly rots away, a ravener does not care for the needs of the flesh. It seeks only to consume life, be it from wild animals, would-be dragonslayers, or even other dragons. A ravener is often on the move, changing lairs frequently as its territories become devoid of life.

The ravener presented here is built from a red dragon wyrm. See page 98 of the *Pathfinder RPG Bestiary* for rules on this monster's fire aura, manipulate flames, melt stone, and smoke vision abilities.

CREATING A RAVENER

"Ravener" is an acquired template that can be added to any evil true dragon of an age category of ancient or older (referred to hereafter as the base creature). A ravener retains all the base creature's statistics and special abilities except as noted here.

CR: Same as the base creature +2.

Alignment: Any evil.

Type: The creature's type changes to undead. Do not recalculate BAB, saves, or skill ranks. It keeps any subtypes possessed by the base creature.

Senses: A ravener's darkvision increases to 240 feet, and its blindsense increases to 120 feet.

Armor Class: A ravener gains a deflection bonus to its AC equal to half its Charisma bonus (minimum +1).

Hit Dice: Change all of the base creature's racial Hit Dice to d8s. All Hit Dice derived from class levels remain unchanged. As an undead, a ravener uses its Charisma to determine bonus hit points instead of its Constitution.

Saving Throws: As undead, a ravener uses its Charisma modifier on Fortitude saves (instead of Constitution).

Illustration by Florian Stitz

Defensive Abilities: A ravener gains channel resistance +4 and all of the immunities derived from undead traits. Its damage reduction changes from DR/magic to DR/good. A ravener also gains the following ability.

Soul Ward (Su): An intangible field of siphoned soul energy protects a ravener from destruction. This ward has a maximum number of hit points equal to twice the ravener's Hit Dice, but starts at half this amount. Whenever a ravener would be reduced below 1 hit point, all damage in excess of that which would reduce it to 1 hit point is instead dealt to its soul ward. If this damage reduces the soul ward to fewer than 0 hit points, the ravener is destroyed.

Attacks: A ravener retains all of the natural attacks of the base creature, but each of these attacks threatens a critical hit on a 19 or 20. Feats like Improved Critical can increase this range further. If the ravener scores a critical hit with a natural weapon, the target gains 1 negative level. The DC to remove this negative level is equal to 10 + 1/2 the ravener's Hit Dice + the ravener's Charisma modifier. Whenever a creature gains a negative level in this way, the ravener adds 5 points to its soul ward.

Special Attacks: A ravener retains all of the special attacks of the base creature and gains the following special attacks as described below. All save DCs are equal to 10 + 1/2 the ravener's HD + the ravener's Charisma modifier.

Breath Weapon (Su): A ravener keeps the breath weapon of the base creature— the save DC for this breath weapon is now Charisma-based. In addition, a ravener's breath weapon bestows 2 negative levels on all creatures in the area. A successful Reflex save halves the damage and reduces the energy drain to 1 negative level. The save DC to remove these negative levels is equal to the ravener's breath weapon DC. The ravener adds 1 hit point to its soul ward ability for each negative level bestowed in this way.

Cowering Fear (Su): Any creature shaken by the ravener's frightful presence is cowering instead of shaken for the first round of the effect, and shaken for the rest of the duration. Any creature that is panicked by its frightful presence is instead cowering for the duration.

Soul Consumption (Su): When a living creature within 30 feet of a ravener dies, that creature's soul is torn from its body and pulled into the ravener's maw if the dying creature fails a Will save (DC equals the save DC of the ravener's breath weapon). This adds a number of hit points to the ravener's soul ward equal to the dead creature's Hit Dice. Creatures that have their souls consumed in this way can only be brought back to life through *miracle, true resurrection*, or *wish*.

Soul Magic (Sp): A ravener retains the base creature's spellcasting capability, adding three levels to the base creature's caster level. This increases the number of spells known by the ravener, but the ravener loses all spell slots. Instead, whenever a ravener wishes to cast any one of its spells known, it consumes a number of hit points from its soul ward equal to the spell slot level necessary to cast the spell (including increased levels for metamagic feats and so on). If the soul ward has insufficient hit points, the ravener cannot cast that spell. Casting a spell that reduces its soul ward to exactly 0 hit points does not harm the ravener (though most are not comfortable without this buffer of soul-energy and try to replenish it quickly).

Abilities: Str +4, Int +4, Wis +4, Cha +6. Being undead, a ravener has no Constitution score.

Skills: A ravener has a +8 racial bonus on Intimidate, Perception, and Stealth checks. The ravener's class skills are otherwise the same as those of the base creature.

RAY, MANTA

Gliding gracefully through the water on wing-like fins, this large ray scoops up tiny morsels in its wide mouth.

MANTA RAY	CR 1

XP 400

N Large animal (aquatic)

Init +1; **Senses** blindsense 30 ft., low-light vision; Perception +6

DEFENSE

AC 13, touch 10, flat-footed 12 (+1 Dex, +3 natural, −1 size)

hp 19 (3d8+6)

Fort +5, **Ref** +4, **Will** +2

OFFENSE

Speed swim 60 ft.

Melee tail slap +4 (1d6+4)

Space 10 ft.; **Reach** 10 ft.

STATISTICS

Str 16, **Dex** 13, **Con** 15, **Int** 1, **Wis** 13, **Cha** 2

Base Atk +2; **CMB** +6; **CMD** 17

Feats Improved Bull Rush, Power Attack

Skills Perception +6, Swim +15

ECOLOGY

Environment warm oceans

Organization solitary, pair, or flight (3–12)

Treasure none

MANTA RAY COMPANION

Starting Statistics: Size Medium; **Speed** swim 60 ft.; **AC** +1 natural; **Attack** tail slap (1d4); **Ability Scores** Str 8, Dex 15, Con 11, Int 1, Wis 13, Cha 2; **Special Qualities** low-light vision.

 4th-Level Advancement: Size: Large; **AC** +2 natural armor; **Attack** tail slap (1d6); **Ability Scores** Str +8, Dex −2, Con +4; **Special Qualities** blindsense 30 ft.

Illustration by Adam Vihiga

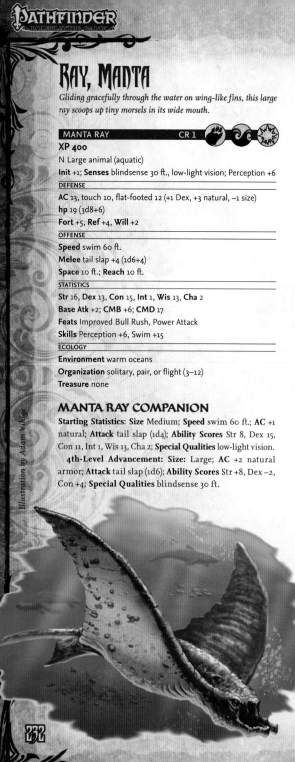

RAY, STINGRAY

A long tail fitted with a barbed stinger trails from this flat, triangular fish's body.

STINGRAY	CR 1/2

XP 200

N Medium animal (aquatic)

Init +1; **Senses** blindsense 30 ft., low-light vision; Perception +8

DEFENSE

AC 12, touch 11, flat-footed 11 (+1 Dex, +1 natural)

hp 13 (2d8+4)

Fort +5, **Ref** +4, **Will** +1

OFFENSE

Speed swim 40 ft.

Melee sting +1 (1d4 plus poison)

STATISTICS

Str 10, **Dex** 13, **Con** 15, **Int** 1, **Wis** 13, **Cha** 2

Base Atk +1; **CMB** +1; **CMD** 12

Feats Skill Focus (Perception)

Skills Perception +8, Stealth +5 (+13 in sand or mud), Swim +8; **Racial Modifier** +8 Stealth in sand or mud

ECOLOGY

Environment warm oceans

Organization solitary, pair, or flight (3–12)

Treasure none

SPECIAL ABILITIES

Poison (Ex) Sting—injury; *save* Fort DC 13; *frequency* 1/round for 4 rounds; *effect* 1d2 Dex and 1 Con; *cure* 1 save. The save DC is Constitution-based.

Often found buried in mud, sand, or sea grass, this normally passive creature raises its tail above its body like a scorpion when cornered or injured. Its stinger is a barbed spine with two grooves allowing the toxin to enter the wound. While often found in bays and estuaries, some breeds of stingray can make their home in rivers far upstream from salt water. Stingrays, like their larger manta ray cousins, use a form of electrolocation to find prey in the silt-laden waters.

 The stingray presented here is a relatively large member of the species; for smaller stingrays, apply the young creature template.

STINGRAY COMPANION

Starting Statistics: Size Small; **Speed** swim 40 ft.; **Attack** sting (1d3 plus poison); **Ability Scores** Str 6, Dex 15, Con 13, Int 1, Wis 13, Cha 2; **Special Qualities** low-light vision.

 4th-Level Advancement: Size Medium; **AC** +1 natural armor; **Attack** sting (1d4 plus poison); **Ability Scores** Str +4, Dex −2, Con +2; **Special Qualities** blindsense 30 ft.

REDCAP

Like some miniscule, wicked old man, this snarling little humanoid wears metal boots and a blood-red pointed cap.

REDCAP	CR 6

XP 2,400

NE Small fey

Init +8; **Senses** low-light vision; Perception +12

DEFENSE

AC 20, touch 15, flat-footed 16 (+2 armor, +4 Dex, +3 natural, +1 size)

hp 60 (8d6+32); fast healing 3

Fort +6, **Ref** +10, **Will** +7

DR 10/cold iron

Weaknesses irreligious

OFFENSE

Speed 60 ft.

Melee Medium scythe +10 (2d4+10/×4), kick +4 (1d4+6)

STATISTICS

Str 18, **Dex** 19, **Con** 18, **Int** 16, **Wis** 13, **Cha** 15

Base Atk +4; **CMB** +7; **CMD** 21

Feats Cleave, Improved Initiative, Power Attack, Weapon Focus (scythe)

Skills Acrobatics +15 (+27 jump), Bluff +13, Climb +15, Escape Artist +15, Intimidate +10, Knowledge (nature) +14, Perception +12, Sense Motive +12, Stealth +19

Languages Aklo, Common, Giant, Sylvan

SQ boot stomp, heavy weapons, red cap

ECOLOGY

Environment temperate forests, mountains, or underground

Organization solitary, pair, or gang (3–12)

Treasure NPC gear (leather armor, Medium scythe, other treasure)

SPECIAL ABILITIES

Boot Stomp (Ex) A redcap wears heavy iron boots with spiked soles that it uses to deadly effect in combat. These boots give the redcap a kick attack that it can make as a secondary attack, either as part of a full-attack action or as part of its movement just as if it had the Spring Attack feat.

Heavy Weapons (Ex) A redcap can wield weapons sized for Medium creatures without penalty.

Irreligious (Ex) Bitter and blasphemous, redcaps cannot stand the symbols of good-aligned religions. If a foe spends a standard action presenting such a holy symbol, any redcap who can see the creature must make a DC 15 Will save or become frightened for 1 minute and attempt to flee. A redcap who successfully saves is shaken for 1 minute.

Red Cap (Su) A redcap wears a tiny, shapeless woolen hat, dyed over and over with the blood of its victims. While wearing this cap, a redcap gains a +4 bonus on damage rolls (included in the above totals) and fast healing 3. These benefits are lost if the cap is removed or destroyed. Caps are not transferable, even between redcaps. A redcap can create a new cap to replace a lost cap with 10 minutes of work, although until the redcap takes a standard action to dip the cap in the blood of a foe the redcap helped to kill, the cap does not grant its bonuses.

Redcaps embody both capriciousness and sadism. These stumpy, misanthropic fey freaks exist seemingly to indulge in blissful bloodletting and self-indulgent slaughter. Like prune-faced, angry old men, they mollycoddle their own inefficiencies and miseries in gore. Redcaps are most widely recognized for their long woolen caps, which they drench in the blood of their victims. Rumors and fairy stories abound concerning rituals and the cultural significance of their blood-soaked caps, though the practice likely evolved as an easy way for the brutish runts to create both fear and spectacle. Redcaps typically stand only 3 feet tall, with twisted frames, pointed ears, and long white beards. They dress in soiled leather armor and wear oversized, iron-shod boots that make a distinctive clanging when they run.

Illustration by Christopher Burdett

REEFCLAW

Blood-red spines run the length of this frightening creature, which resembles a lobster in the front and an eel in the back.

REEFCLAW	CR 1

XP 400

CN Small aberration (aquatic)

Init +5; **Senses** darkvision 60 ft., low-light vision; Perception +6

DEFENSE

AC 14, touch 12, flat-footed 13 (+1 Dex, +2 natural, +1 size)

hp 13 (2d8+4)

Fort +2, **Ref** +1, **Will** +4

Defensive Abilities ferocity; **Resist** cold 5

OFFENSE

Speed 5 ft., swim 40 ft.

Melee 2 claws +2 (1d4 plus grab and poison)

Special Attacks death frenzy, constrict (1d4)

STATISTICS

Str 10, **Dex** 13, **Con** 14, **Int** 5, **Wis** 12, **Cha** 13

Base Atk +1; **CMB** +0 (+8 grapple); **CMD** 11 (can't be tripped)

Feats Improved Initiative

Skills Perception +6, Swim +8

Languages Common (can't speak)

SQ amphibious

ECOLOGY

Environment any water (coastal)

Organization solitary, school (2–5), or harem (6–11)

Treasure none

SPECIAL ABILITIES

Death Frenzy (Su) When a reefclaw is killed, its body spasms horrifically. Immediately upon dying, the reefclaw makes a full attack against a creature it threatens. If more than one creature is within reach, roll randomly for each attack to determine the target (which may be another reefclaw).

Grab (Ex) A reefclaw can use its grab ability on a target of any size. Reefclaws have a +8 racial bonus on grapple checks; this bonus replaces the normal +4 bonus a creature with grab receives.

Poison (Ex) Claw—injury; *save* Fort DC 13; *frequency* 1/round for 4 rounds; *effect* 1d2 Str; *cure* 1 save. The save DC is Constitution-based.

Reefclaws are vicious predators. They possess greater intelligence than animals, but rely mainly on their strength and instincts to survive. They hunt fish, giant crabs, dolphins, and even land-dwelling creatures that come within a hundred paces of the water.

In populated areas, reefclaws prey on beachcombers, divers, and fishermen, sometimes abandoning their usual solitary nature and coordinating attacks with other reefclaws. The creatures must be wary, however, because in some regions, these abominations find their way to the dinner plate. Brave fishermen troll bays and coastlines infested with reefclaws, baiting the creatures with fresh meat and then harvesting their powerful claws with axes.

Reefclaws cannot speak, but the creatures understand the languages used by humanoids near their hunting grounds. They use this knowledge in order to avoid fishermen and coordinate attacks. Reefclaws keep no treasure, instead savoring the taste of flesh and crunch of bone and shell as much as a miser covets his gold.

A typical reefclaw reaches approximately 3-1/2 feet long at adulthood and weighs 70 pounds. Females gather to breed once every 2 to 3 years, engaging in a predatory hunt for a male and leaving him shredded to pieces.

Revenant

This shambling corpse is twisted and mutilated. Fingers of sharpened bone reach out with malevolent intent.

REVENANT	CR 6

XP 2,400

LE Medium undead

Init +7; **Senses** darkvision 60 ft., sense murderer; Perception +13

DEFENSE

AC 19, touch 13, flat-footed 16 (+3 Dex, +6 natural)

hp 76 (9d8+36)

Fort +7, **Ref** +6, **Will** +7

DR 5/slashing; **Immune** cold, undead traits; **SR** 17

Weaknesses self-loathing

OFFENSE

Speed 30 ft.

Melee 2 claws +14 (1d8+7 plus grab)

Special Attacks baleful shriek, constrict (1d6+7)

STATISTICS

Str 24, **Dex** 17, **Con** —, **Int** 7, **Wis** 12, **Cha** 19

Base Atk +6; **CMB** +13 (+17 grapple); **CMD** 26

Feats Cleave, Improved Initiative, Power Attack, Step Up, Weapon Focus (claw)

Skills Intimidate +16, Perception +13

Languages Common

SQ reason to hate

ECOLOGY

Environment any land

Organization solitary

Treasure standard

SPECIAL ABILITIES

Baleful Shriek (Su) Once every 1d4 rounds, a revenant can shriek as a standard action. All creatures within a 60-foot spread must make a DC 18 Will save or cower in fear for 1d4 rounds. This is a mind-affecting fear effect. The save DC is Charisma-based.

Reason to Hate (Su) A revenant's existence is fueled by its hatred for its murderer. As long as the murderer exists, the revenant exists. If the murderer dies, the revenant is immediately slain. A murderer who becomes undead does not trigger a revenant's destruction. When a revenant encounters its murderer, it gains the benefits of a *haste* spell (CL 20th) that lasts as long as its murderer remains in sight. Against its murderer, the revenant also gains a +4 profane bonus on attack rolls, weapon damage rolls, grapple checks, and saving throws.

Self-Loathing (Ex) When confronted with its reflection or any object that was important to it in life, a revenant must make a DC 20 Will save to avoid becoming overwhelmed with self-pity. This condition renders the revenant helpless, and lasts until the revenant is attacked or sees its murderer. If a revenant resists becoming overwhelmed, the revenant becomes obsessed with the source that triggered the saving throw and does everything it can to destroy it, reacting to the trigger as if the trigger were its murderer and gaining bonuses from its reason to hate ability.

Sense Murderer (Su) A revenant knows the direction but not the distance to its murderer—this sense can be blocked by any effect that blocks scrying. Against its murderer, a revenant has *true seeing* and *discern lies* in effect at all times (CL 20th); these abilities cannot be dispelled.

Fueled by hatred and a need for vengeance, a revenant rises from the grave to hunt and kill its murderer. Devoid of any compassion, emotion, or logic, a revenant has but one purpose, and cannot rest until it has found vengeance.

Illustration by John Gravato

SANDMAN

A whirling cloud of fine desert sand piles up upon itself, forming into the shape of a humanoid figure.

SANDMAN	CR 3	

XP 800

NE Medium outsider (earth, elemental, extraplanar)

Init +5; **Senses** darkvision 60 ft., tremorsense 30 ft.; Perception +7

Aura sleep (20 ft., DC 14)

DEFENSE

AC 15, touch 11, flat-footed 14 (+1 Dex, +4 natural)

hp 30 (4d10+8)

Fort +6, **Ref** +5, **Will** +3

Defensive Abilities amorphous; **DR** 10/bludgeoning; **Immune** elemental traits

OFFENSE

Speed 30 ft., burrow 30 ft.

Melee slam +6 (1d6+3 plus sleep)

STATISTICS

Str 14, **Dex** 13, **Con** 15, **Int** 10, **Wis** 11, **Cha** 10

Base Atk +4; **CMB** +6; **CMD** 17

Feats Improved Initiative, Iron Will

Skills Acrobatics +8, Climb +9, Knowledge (planes) +7, Perception +7, Sense Motive +7, Stealth +8 (+12 in sand); **Racial Modifiers** +4 Stealth in sand

Languages Terran

SQ compression, sand form

ECOLOGY

Environment any land (Plane of Earth)

Organization solitary, gang (2–4), or shoal (5–10)

Treasure none

SPECIAL ABILITIES

Sand Form (Su) As a standard action, a sandman can cause its humanoid form to collapse into a pile of animated sand. In this form, treat the sandman as if it were a Small earth elemental made out of sand. The sandman retains its compression and sleep aura abilities when in sand form, but loses its sleep attack and its damage reduction, as its sandy body in this form is much more compact and easier to scatter with solid weapon blows.

Sleep (Su) A creature struck by a sandman's slam attack must succeed on a DC 14 Will save or immediately fall asleep, as if affected by a *sleep* spell (caster level 8th). There is no limit to the number of Hit Dice a sandman can affect with this ability. The save DC is Constitution-based.

Sleep Aura (Su) A sandman radiates a 20-foot-radius spread that puts creatures to sleep. Any creature in the area must succeed on a DC 14 Will save or fall asleep, as if affected by a *sleep* spell (caster level 8th). There is no limit to the number of Hit Dice a sandman can affect with this ability. A creature that successfully saves is immune to that sandman's sleep aura for 24 hours. The save DC is Constitution-based.

Stealthy and unpredictable, the sandman is a terror to all travelers in the desert, whether they be traders, messengers, or adventurers. When at rest, sandmen resemble ordinary piles of sand, blending in perfectly with barren surroundings or ancient tombs. They rely on their soporific powers in most situations, putting their enemies to sleep and killing their unconscious opponents or dragging them back to their summoner.

Although they themselves are elementals, sandmen don't typically associate with other elementals, seeing their unquestioning obedience as weak. Sandmen pride themselves as free thinkers, and when given a task by a summoner, often interpret the task as they see fit. Because of their arrogance, usually only the most confident or most desperate mages bother with sandmen. It is not uncommon for sandmen to voluntarily stay on the Material Plane, fiendishly playing with its inhabitants as they wreak silent havoc.

A sandman takes the form of a rough humanoid about 6 feet tall. Its shape is never quite certain, and its animate muscles constantly shift and flex as it pummels its targets. Sandmen can manipulate their bodies in many ways, but prefer to keep their legs and feet in the form of dusty clouds of sand, so as to easily maneuver about in their preferred environments. Some of these creatures pride themselves on their ability to control their shapes. Just as a mortal artist might sculpt incredible works of art from stone with a chisel, so do these artist sandmen sculpt their own bodies into works of art. Some enjoy using this ability to reshape their appearance to mimic that of their conjurer or their enemies, allowing them an additional level of theatrics by either assuming a beautiful form or by allowing their form to melt away in a hideous manner. Given the combination of their quick imaginations and their natural penchant for cruelty, most sandmen tend to opt for the latter method of tormenting their foes.

Illustration by Jim Pavelec

SARD

This wriggling and leafless tree moves on spidery legs. Flickering motes of blood-red lightning dance in the cracks of its bark.

SARD	CR 19

XP 204,800
CE Colossal plant
Init +8; **Senses** blindsight 30 ft., darkvision 60 ft., low-light vision, tremorsense 30 ft.; Perception +32

DEFENSE

AC 34, touch 10, flat-footed 26 (+8 Dex, +24 natural, –8 size)
hp 333 (23d8+230); fast healing 10
Fort +23, **Ref** +17, **Will** +13
Defensive Abilities death throes, electrical jolt; **DR** 15/cold iron and slashing; **Immune** electricity, plant traits; **Resist** cold 30, fire 30; **SR** 30
Weaknesses vulnerable to sonic

OFFENSE

Speed 50 ft., climb 30 ft.
Melee 2 slams +25 (4d10+16/19–20 plus 4d6 electricity)
Ranged 4 thorns +17 (2d8+16 plus poison)
Space 30 ft.; **Reach** 30 ft.
Spell-Like Abilities (CL 20th; concentration +27)
At will—*control weather, lightning bolt* (DC 20), *tree shape* (Colossal tree), *transport via plants*
3/day—*chain lightning* (DC 23), quickened *lightning bolt* (DC 20)
1/day—*storm of vengeance* (DC 26), *whirlwind* (DC 25)

STATISTICS

Str 42, **Dex** 27, **Con** 30, **Int** 9, **Wis** 22, **Cha** 25
Base Atk +17; **CMB** +41; **CMD** 59 (67 vs. trip)
Feats Awesome Blow, Improved Bull Rush, Improved Critical (slam), Improved Lightning Reflexes, Improved Precise Shot, Improved Sunder, Lightning Reflexes, Point-Blank Shot, Power Attack, Precise Shot, Quicken Spell-Like Ability (*lightning bolt*), Vital Strike

Skills Climb +24, Perception +32
Languages Aklo, Sylvan
SQ planar acclimation

ECOLOGY

Environment any forests
Organization solitary
Treasure triple

SPECIAL ABILITIES

Death Throes (Su) When a sard dies, its remains explode with a blast of lightning into razor-sharp splinters of wood. All creatures within 30 feet of a sard when it explodes in this manner take 12d6 points of electricity damage and 12d6 points of piercing damage. A DC 31 Reflex save halves this damage. The save DC is Constitution-based.

Electrical Jolt (Su) Every time a creature strikes a sard with a metal melee weapon, arcs of electricity deal 1d10 points of damage to the attacker.

Planar Acclimation (Ex) A sard is always considered to be on its home plane, regardless of what plane it finds itself upon. It never gains the extraplanar subtype.

Poison (Ex) Thorn—injury; *save* Fort DC 31; *frequency* 1/round for 6 rounds; *effect* 1d2 Dex and 4d6 electricity; *cure* 2 consecutive saves.

Thorns (Ex) A sard's thorns have a range of 180 ft. with no range increment.

The sard is an ancient elm, oak, or pine tree that has been infused with lightning and raw life by one of the strange gods of the fey realm. One of the legendary beasts known as the Tane, a sard has "sap" that consists of red lightning—all of the sard's electrical attacks manifest with this same eerie-colored energy.

A sard can pass for an old dead tree—especially when the creature uses its *tree shape* spell-like ability. Yet despite its enormous size and ungainly shape, the sard is in fact a swift and agile monster. It can move with unsettling grace and speed, crawling across the ground on long spidery roots like an immense insect. It attacks either with a single slam of its immense trunk or by launching volleys of foot-long thorns that inject the creature's poisonous, electrified sap.

Sards are nearly as intelligent as most humans, but few actually use this intelligence for productive purposes—the first sards were created as a form of living siege engine, and they quite enjoy this destructive role, often seeking out fortresses or even towns to systematically destroy.

Illustration by Kieran Yanner

237

Scarecrow

It suddenly becomes clear that this is no ordinary pumpkin-headed scarecrow when its eyes glow and it comes to jerky life.

SCARECROW	CR 4

XP 1,200

N Medium construct

Init +0; **Senses** darkvision 60 ft., low-light vision; Perception +0

DEFENSE

AC 16, touch 10, flat-footed 16 (+6 natural)

hp 47 (5d10+20)

Fort +1, **Ref** +1, **Will** +1

Immune cold, construct traits

Weaknesses vulnerability to fire

OFFENSE

Speed 20 ft.

Melee 2 slams +8 (1d8+3 plus fear)

Special Attacks fascinating gaze

STATISTICS

Str 16, **Dex** 10, **Con** —, **Int** —,

Wis 11, **Cha** 14

Base Atk +5; **CMB** +8; **CMD** 18

SQ freeze

ECOLOGY

Environment any land

Organization solitary, pair, or

gang (3–6)

Treasure none

SPECIAL ABILITIES

Fascinating Gaze (Su) Target is fascinated, 30 feet, Will DC 14 negates. Fascination lasts as long as the scarecrow remains within 300 feet of the fascinated creature. The approach or animation of the scarecrow does not count as an obvious threat to the victim of this particular fascination effect (although the scarecrow's attack does count as an obvious threat and ends the fascination immediately). This is a mind-affecting effect. The save DC is Charisma-based.

Fear (Su) A scarecrow's touch infuses its target with overwhelming waves of fear. If the victim fails a DC 14 Will save, she cowers and can take no actions other than attempting a new DC 14 Will save at the end of the following round

(and each round thereafter) to end this fear. A successful first save leaves the victim shaken for 1 round. This is a mind-affecting fear effect. The save DC is Charisma-based.

Animated scarecrows look just like mundane scarecrows until they come to life, at which point their eyes and mouths glow with fiery light. Scarecrows are usually created as guardians to warn away trespassers. Each scarecrow is unique, but most stand 5 to 6 feet tall and are made of wood, cloth, and rope. Their stuffing of dried grass or straw makes them vulnerable to fire.

A scarecrow cannot speak, and the only sound it makes is the creaking of its wooden frame and the rustling of its straw stuffing when it moves.

In combat, a scarecrow uses its fascinating gaze, then chooses the largest foe to pummel with its slams. Although unintelligent, the scarecrow does not ignore other enemies, using its fear touch to cow them until the scarecrow kills its first target. A scarecrow usually does not pursue fleeing foes unless specifically commanded to do so by its creator.

CONSTRUCTION

Scarecrows are constructed of a variety of materials, but usually include a frame of wood bound by rope or twine, covered in cloth or ragged garments, then stuffed with grass or straw. Some have simple heads made from bags stuffed with straw, with two holes cut for eyes, while others have more elaborate pumpkin or gourd heads carved with grotesque faces. Once the basic body has been constructed, unguents and special powders worth 500 gp are also required.

SCARECROW	

CL 6th; **Price** 15,500 gp

CONSTRUCTION

Requirements Craft Construct, *command*, *fear*, *geas/quest*, *hypnotic pattern*, creator must be caster level 6th; **Skill** Craft (carpentry), Craft (sculptures), or Profession (farmer) DC 12; **Cost** 8,000 gp

Illustration by Mariusz Gandzel

SCEADUINAR

This gargoyle-like creature has long spiky legs and a bat-like head—its body seems to be made of living, dark purple crystal.

SCEADUINAR CR 7

XP 3,200

NE Medium outsider (extraplanar)

Init +5; **Senses** darkvision 120 ft., lifesense, low-light vision; Perception +17

DEFENSE

AC 20, touch 16, flat-footed 14 (+5 Dex, +1 dodge, +4 natural)

hp 85 (9d10+36)

Fort +10, **Ref** +11, **Will** +5

Defensive Abilities entropic flesh, negative energy affinity, void child; **DR** 10/adamantine or good; **Immune** cold, death effects, disease, energy drain, poison; **Resist** acid 10, electricity 10, sonic 10; **SR** 18

OFFENSE

Speed 40 ft., fly 90 ft. (good)

Melee bite +14 (1d6+3 plus 1d6 negative energy and energy drain), 2 wings +9 (1d6+1 plus 1d6 negative energy)

Special Attacks energy drain (1 level, DC 17), entropic touch

Spell-Like Abilities (CL 9th; concentration +12)

Constant—*entropic shield, hide from undead* (DC 14)

At will—*bleed* (DC 13), *dimension door* (self only), *dispel magic*

3/day—*death knell* (DC 15), *deeper darkness, enervation, inflict serious wounds* (DC 16), *silence*

1/day—*antilife shell, greater teleport* (self plus 50 lbs. of objects only), *harm* (DC 19), *slay living* (DC 18)

STATISTICS

Str 17, **Dex** 20, **Con** 18, **Int** 13, **Wis** 14, **Cha** 17

Base Atk +9; **CMB** +12; **CMD** 28

Feats Dodge, Mobility, Skill Focus (Perception), Step Up, Weapon Finesse

Skills Escape Artist +17, Fly +9, Intimidate +15, Knowledge (nature) +13, Knowledge (planes) +17, Perception +17, Sense Motive +14, Stealth +25; **Racial Modifiers** +4 Knowledge (planes), +8 Stealth

Languages Aklo, Common

ECOLOGY

Environment any (Negative Energy Plane)

Organization solitary or death squad (2–11)

Treasure standard

SPECIAL ABILITIES

Entropic Flesh (Ex) Any creature that hits a sceaduinar with a melee attack takes 1d6 points of negative energy damage. Attacking with a weapon that provides reach allows a creature to avoid taking this damage.

Entropic Touch (Ex) A sceaduinar's natural attacks can strike incorporeal creatures as if they were *ghost touch* weapons. All of a sceaduinar's natural attacks deal +1d6 points of negative energy damage to the target. This energy does not heal creatures healed by *inflict* spells.

Void Child (Ex) Sceaduinars are immune to effects that target souls (such as *trap the soul*) or require knowledge of a creature's identity (such as *scrying*). When one is slain, it cannot be restored to life by magic save by a *miracle* or *wish*, or by divine intervention.

Sceaduinars are strange creatures born of pure entropy, the antithesis of creation and life. In the cold heart of the Negative Energy Plane, the un-substance of that realm coalesces into snowflake-like crystals, and it is from these strange formations that sceaduinars arise, breaking free from their jagged "eggs" fully grown. They hate the living and the undead with equal passion, perhaps out of jealousy for those who have a spark of life (even if that spark is provided by a corruption of life in the form of undeath), though they usually ignore creatures from the Outer Sphere. They believe their positive energy counterparts, the jyoti, long ago stole their ability to create, breaking the parallel between the two energy planes and forcing these void-dwellers into an unwanted role of pure destruction.

In a way, their hatred parallels that of another native of the Negative Energy Plane—the nightshade. Yet despite their similar goals, the sceaduinars see nightshades as just another corruption of life worthy of destruction—even though very few sceaduinars are powerful enough to directly oppose one of these deadly undead. Sceaduinars are quite intelligent, yet they have no real society to speak of. When they gather together, it is always to form a larger band to strike against a particularly dangerous foe.

Illustration by Kieran Yanner

SCORPION, BLACK

This towering scorpion's carapace is as black as coal, and its claws are each as long as a man's body.

BLACK SCORPION	CR 15	

XP 51,200

N Colossal vermin

Init +0; **Senses** darkvision 60 ft., tremorsense 60 ft.; Perception +4

DEFENSE

AC 30, touch 2, flat-footed 30 (+28 natural, –8 size)

hp 228 (24d8+120)

Fort +19, **Ref** +8, **Will** +8

Immune mind-affecting effects

OFFENSE

Speed 60 ft.

Melee 2 claws +23 (2d8+13 plus grab), sting +23 (2d6+13 plus poison)

Space 30 ft.; **Reach** 30 ft.

Special Attacks constrict (2d8+19), poison, rapid stinging

STATISTICS

Str 36, **Dex** 10, **Con** 20, **Int** —, **Wis** 10, **Cha** 2

Base Atk +18; **CMB** +39 (+43 grapple); **CMD** 49 (61 vs. trip)

Skills Climb +17, Perception +4, Stealth –12; **Racial Modifiers** +4 Climb, +4 Perception, +4 Stealth

ECOLOGY

Environment warm deserts

Organization solitary

Treasure none

SPECIAL ABILITIES

Poison (Ex) Sting—injury; *save* Fort DC 27; *frequency* 1/round for 6 rounds; *effect* 1d4 Str, 1d4 Dex, and 1d4 Con; *cure* 3 saves.

Rapid Stinging (Ex) A black scorpion's stinger strikes with astounding speed; it can make one additional attack in a round with its sting as a swift action.

The immense black scorpion is one of the largest desert predators. Capable of stinging with blinding speed, this creature is constantly on the hunt.

SCORPION, CAVE

This man-sized, bulky scorpion has thick, unyielding armor that makes it almost seem to be made of stone.

CAVE SCORPION	CR 1	

XP 400

N Medium vermin

Init +0; **Senses** darkvision 60 ft., tremorsense 60 ft.; Perception +4

DEFENSE

AC 12, touch 10, flat-footed 12 (+2 natural)

hp 16 (3d8+3)

Fort +4, **Ref** +1, **Will** +1

Immune mind-affecting effects

OFFENSE

Speed 60 ft., climb 40 ft.

Melee 2 claws +2 (1d4), sting +2 (1d4 plus poison)

Special Attacks rend (2 claws, 2d4)

STATISTICS

Str 11, **Dex** 10, **Con** 13, **Int** —, **Wis** 10, **Cha** 2

Base Atk +2; **CMB** +2 (+43 grapple); **CMD** 12 (24 vs. trip)

Skills Climb +8, Perception +4, Stealth +0 (+12 in caves); **Racial Modifiers** +4 Perception, +12 Stealth in caves

ECOLOGY

Environment any underground

Organization solitary, pair, or swarm (3–12)

Treasure none

SPECIAL ABILITIES

Poison (Ex) Sting—injury; *save* Fort DC 27; *frequency* 1/round for 4 rounds; *effect* 1d2 Str; *cure* 1 save.

The squat cave scorpion is quite well suited for life in caves. With its bulky armor, a cave scorpion at rest looks like a pile of stones. The cave scorpion's favorite food is dwarven meat, and when a cave scorpion finds a working dwarven mine, it can quickly become a major inconvenience. Dwarven societies often post hefty bounties on cave scorpion stingers.

Illustrations by Eric Belisle

SCYLLA

*This horrifying creature has the upper body of a beautiful woman,
but a lower body of snapping wolf heads and writhing tentacles.*

SCYLLA	CR 16

XP 76,800

CE Huge aberration (aquatic)

Init +11; **Senses** all-around vision, blindsight 30 ft., darkvision
60 ft., low-light vision, *see invisibility*; Perception +29

Aura frightful presence (30 ft., DC 26),

DEFENSE

AC 30, touch 20, flat-footed 18 (+11 Dex, +1 dodge, +10 natural,
−2 size)

hp 250 (20d8+160); fast healing 10

Fort +14, **Ref** +17, **Will** +18

Defensive Abilities *freedom of movement*, improved evasion;
DR 10/cold iron and lawful; **Immune** cold, charm effects,
confusion and insanity effects; **Resist** acid 20, fire 20; **SR** 27

OFFENSE

Speed 30 ft., swim 50 ft.

Melee 4 bites +25 (1d8+8/19–20 plus bleed), 4 tentacles +23
(1d6+4 plus grab)

Space 15 ft.; **Reach** 15 ft.

Special Attacks bleed (1d6), constrict (1d6+8)

Spell-Like Abilities (CL 16th; concentration +22)

Constant—*freedom of movement,
nondetection, see invisibility*

At will—*acid arrow, control water, fog cloud,
greater dispel magic, major image* (DC 19)

3/day—*black tentacles, charm monster* (DC 20),
insanity (DC 23), *mirage arcana* (DC 21), *solid fog*

1/day—*control weather, power word stun, project
image* (DC 23), *summon* (level 8, 1 charybdis)

STATISTICS

Str 27, **Dex** 32, **Con** 27, **Int** 20, **Wis** 23, **Cha** 22

Base Atk +15; **CMB** +25 (+29 grapple); **CMD** 47 (can't
be tripped)

Feats Combat Reflexes, Dodge, Improved Critical (bite),
Mobility, Multiattack, Power Attack, Vital
Strike, Weapon Finesse, Weapon Focus (bite),
Weapon Focus (tentacles)

Skills Acrobatics +34, Bluff +26, Intimidate
+29, Knowledge (nature) +25, Perception
+29, Sense Motive +26, Stealth +26,
Swim +39, Use Magic Device +26

Languages Abyssal, Aquan, Common

SQ amphibious, change shape (1 humanoid
form, *alter self*), undersized weapons

ECOLOGY

Environment any water

Organization solitary

Treasure triple

The scylla is one of the more nightmarish aberrations
to blight the mortal world. Conflicting tales of her
origins abound, from demonic flesh-crafting and arcane
experiments to a divine curse handed down by a vengeful
deity. The most popular stories cast the first scylla as
the monstrous spawn of a union between a mortal and a
god. Whatever the case, scyllas are fortunately quite rare,
enough so that many consider them nothing more than
tall tales told by sailors deep in their cups.

Scyllas dwell along major shipping lanes, often near
coastlines, where they use their spell-like abilities to
lure entire ships to their doom. The hideous monsters
are intelligent creatures, though half-mad with hunger
and self-loathing. They normally do not use weapons,
but when they do, they prefer to fight with light weapons
wielded by their human-sized upper arms. However, they
much prefer to keep their hands free to utilize magic
items like wands, staves, and other powerful devices.

Illustration by Tyler Walpole

SERPENTFOLK

This serpentine humanoid has bright scaly skin, a long sinuous tail, and a fanged serpent's head.

SERPENTFOLK	CR 4

XP 1,200

NE Medium monstrous humanoid

Init +9; **Senses** darkvision 60 ft., scent; Perception +10

DEFENSE

AC 18, touch 15, flat-footed 13 (+5 Dex, +3 natural)

hp 42 (5d10+15)

Fort +6, **Ref** +9, **Will** +6

Immune mind-affecting effects, paralysis, poison; **SR** 15

OFFENSE

Speed 30 ft.

Melee mwk dagger +11 (1d4–1/19–20), bite +5 (1d6–1 plus poison)

Spell-Like Abilities (CL 4th; concentration +7)

At will—*disguise self* (humanoid form only, DC 14), *ventriloquism*

1/day—*blur, mirror image, suggestion* (DC 16)

STATISTICS

Str 8, **Dex** 21, **Con** 17, **Int** 18, **Wis** 15, **Cha** 16

Base Atk +5; **CMB** +4; **CMD** 19

Feats Great Fortitude, Improved Initiative, Weapon Finesse

Skills Acrobatics +10, Disguise +8, Escape Artist +18, Knowledge (arcana) +9, Perception +10, Sense Motive +7, Spellcraft +9, Use Magic Device +12; **Racial Modifiers** +4 Use Magic Device, +8 Escape Artist

Languages Aklo, Common, Draconic, Undercommon; telepathy 100 ft.

ECOLOGY

Environment any land (usually jungles or underground)

Organization solitary, pair, or cult (3–12)

Treasure NPC gear (masterwork dagger, other treasure)

SPECIAL ABILITIES

Poison (Ex) Bite—injury; *save* Fort DC 15; *frequency* 1/round for 6 rounds; *effect* 1d2 Str; *cure* 2 saves. The save DC is Constitution-based.

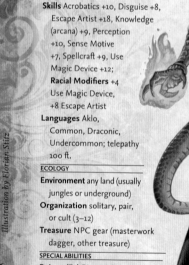

Illustration by Florian Stitz

To the serpentfolk, the pursuit of knowledge and magic is the highest goal. Their legends speak of how humanity rose to power only through the theft of serpent magic, a legend that may form the basis of the hatred toward humanity most serpentfolk harbor. They view themselves as the undisputed masters of magic, be it arcane or divine. Yet despite this, the majority of serpentfolk today are degenerates who have devolved to the point of primeval savagery and have lost much of their magical legacy—more civilized serpentfolk generally regard these degenerates with shame and disdain.

Serpentfolk are 6 feet tall and weigh 120 pounds. Degenerates are only 5 feet tall but weigh 200 pounds. All serpentfolk are quite long-lived, and generally live to the age of 500.

ADVANCED SERPENTFOLK

When a serpentfolk gains class levels, several of its abilities increase as well, as detailed below.

- Spell Resistance equals total Hit Dice + 10.
- Poison bite save DC equals 10 + Con modifier + 1/2 total Hit Dice.
- When it is 4th level in any class combination, it gains two spell-like abilities usable once per day each: *dominate person* and *major image*. When it reaches 9th level in any combination, it gains two more usable once per day each: *mass suggestion* and *teleport*.
- A serpentfolk's racial ability score modifiers are as follows: Str –2, Dex +10, Con +6, Int +8, Wis +4, Cha +6.

DEGENERATE SERPENTFOLK

Degenerate serpentfolk possess the same statistics as normal serpentfolk, save for the following adjustments.

- They have no spell-like abilities.
- They lose the +4 racial bonus on Use Magic Device checks, but gain a +4 racial bonus on Perception checks.
- Their natural armor bonus increases from +3 to +7.
- They have the following ability score modifiers: Str +10, Dex +2, Con +8, Int –6 (minimum 3), Wis +2, Cha –4. A typical degenerate serpentfolk's ability scores are Str 20, Dex 13, Con 19, Int 4, Wis 13, Cha 6.

SEUGATHI

This worm-like monster has a hideous face of eyes and hooked jaws. It wields a wand and a sword in its twin tentacle tails.

SEUGATHI	CR 6

XP 2,400

CE Large aberration

Init +9; **Senses** darkvision 120 ft., *detect thoughts*, tremorsense 30 ft.; Perception +15

Aura madness (30 ft.)

DEFENSE

AC 19, touch 14, flat-footed 14 (+4 armor, +5 Dex, +1 natural, –1 size)

hp 67 (9d8+27); fast healing 5

Fort +6, **Ref** +8, **Will** +9

DR 10/slashing or piercing; **Immune** mind-affecting effects, poison; **SR** 17

OFFENSE

Speed 30 ft.

Melee mwk short sword +11/+6 (1d8+3/19–20), bite +5 (1d8+1 plus poison)

Space 10 ft.; **Reach** 10 ft.

Special Attacks confusion command

Spell-Like Abilities (CL 6th; concentration +10)

Constant—*mage armor*

At will—*detect thoughts* (DC 16), *levitate*

3/day—*confusion* (DC 18), *dispel magic*, *suggestion* (DC 17)

1/day—*mind fog* (DC 19), *phantasmal killer* (DC 18)

STATISTICS

Str 16, **Dex** 20, **Con** 17, **Int** 14, **Wis** 17, **Cha** 19

Base Atk +6; **CMB** +10; **CMD** 25 (can't be tripped)

Feats Ability Focus (aura of madness), Combat Casting, Combat Reflexes, Improved Initiative, Weapon Finesse

Skills Escape Artist +17, Knowledge (religion) +14, Perception +15, Sense Motive +12, Stealth +13, Use Magic Device +16

Languages Aklo, Undercommon; telepathy 100 ft.

SQ item use

ECOLOGY

Environment any underground

Organization single, pair, or expedition (3–8)

Treasure double (masterwork short sword, *wand of magic missile* [CL 5th, 1d20+30 charges])

SPECIAL ABILITIES

Aura of Madness (Su) Any sane being within 30 feet of a conscious seugathi must make a DC 20 Will save each round or become confused for 1 round. A creature that fails 5 saves in a row becomes permanently insane, as per the *insanity* spell. A seugathi can suppress or activate this aura as a free action. This is a mind-affecting effect. The save DC is Charisma-based.

Confusion Command (Su) As an immediate action, a seugathi can issue a telepathic command to a confused creature within 30 feet. This allows the seugathi to pick a result from the confusion behavior table, rather than the confused creature rolling randomly for its actions that round.

Item Use (Ex) A seugathi can utilize spell trigger devices as if it were a spellcaster of the appropriate class. As a free action by touch, it can identify all spell trigger properties an item has. Use Magic Device is a class skill for seugathis.

Poison (Ex) Bite—injury; *save* Fort DC 17; *frequency* 1/round for 6 rounds; *effect* 1d2 Wis and deafness; *cure* 2 consecutive saves. Deafness persists as long as the ability damage caused by the poison lasts. The save DC is Constitution-based.

Seugathi are spawned by the hundreds by a single neothelid that has performed rituals to impregnate itself. As part of the strange process of being spawned in such rituals, the seugathi assimilates an extensive list of missions from its parent—once the seugathi completes these missions, it perishes. No single seugathi knows the purpose of these commands, but they trust that their neothelid masters have a reason for sending them on these diverse and usually cruel missions. A seugathi is 14 feet long and weighs 650 pounds.

Illustration by Peter Lazarski

Shantak

Larger than an elephant, this scaly, bird-like creature has a vaguely horse-like head and vast, slime-encrusted wings.

SHANTAK	CR 8

XP 4,800

CE Huge magical beast

Init +3; **Senses** darkvision 60 ft., low-light vision; Perception +3

DEFENSE

AC 21, touch 11, flat-footed 18 (+3 Dex, +10 natural, –2 size)

hp 104 (11d10+44)

Fort +11, **Ref** +10, **Will** +6

Defensive Abilities slippery; **Immune** cold, disease

OFFENSE

Speed 20 ft., fly 80 ft. (average)

Melee bite +17 (2d6+8), 2 talons +17 (1d8+8 plus grab)

Space 15 ft.; **Reach** 15 ft.

STATISTICS

Str 26, **Dex** 17, **Con** 19, **Int** 8, **Wis** 17, **Cha** 10

Base Atk +11; **CMB** +21 (+25 grapple); **CMD** 34 (42 vs. grapple)

Feats Awesome Blow, Flyby Attack, Hover, Improved Bull Rush, Power Attack, Wingover

Skills Escape Artist +11, Fly +13; **Racial Modifiers** +8 Escape Artist

Languages Aklo

SQ no breath, share defenses, starflight

ECOLOGY

Environment cold mountains

Organization solitary, pair, or flock (3–12)

Treasure none

SPECIAL ABILITIES

Share Defenses (Su) As a free action, a shantak can extend its no breath ability and cold immunity to a single creature touching it. It can withdraw this protection as a free action.

Slippery (Ex) A shantak's scales seep slippery slime. This grants the creature a +8 bonus on all Escape Artist checks and to its CMD against grapples, and imparts a –5 penalty on all Ride checks made by creatures attempting to ride a shantak.

Starflight (Su) A shantak can survive in the void of outer space. It flies through space at an incredible speed. Although exact travel times vary, a trip within a single solar system should take 3d20 hours, while a trip beyond should take 3d20 days (or more, at the GM's discretion)— provided the shantak knows the way to its destination.

Shantaks speak in a shrill voice that sounds like glass grinding against stone. They are intelligent creatures and cannot be trained as mounts—a would-be shantak rider must use diplomacy or magic to secure a shantak's cooperation as a mount, and even then, shantaks have a tendency to deliberately strand riders in dangerous areas.

Many shantaks have a strange and irrational fear of certain creatures, such as the faceless nightgaunts said to dwell in certain remote mountains, or specific types of harpies or gargoyles in more civilized regions. A shantak avoids confrontations with these types of creatures if possible.

A shantak's ability to travel the gulfs of space ensures that these scaly, bird-like creatures can be found on numerous worlds. Yet despite this unique ability, shantaks are generally quite reluctant to seek out new worlds unless faced with no other option, for a shantak knows well that an attempt to fly to an unknown world could easily result in being lost forever in the gulfs of space.

Illustration by Scott Purdy

SHINING CHILD

Surrounded by a nimbus of near-blinding light, this strange creature looks something like an emaciated child with clawed hands.

SHINING CHILD CR 12

XP 19,200

CE Medium outsider (evil, extraplanar)

Init +7; **Senses** darkvision 120 ft.; Perception +25

Aura blinding light (60 feet)

DEFENSE

AC 28, touch 21, flat-footed 24 (+7 deflection, +3 Dex, +1 dodge, +7 natural)

hp 152 (16d10+64)

Fort +14, **Ref** +10, **Will** +10

Immune blindness, fire, poison; **Resist** cold 10, sonic 10

OFFENSE

Speed 30 ft., fly 50 ft. (perfect)

Melee 2 touches +19 (4d10 fire plus burning touch)

Ranged searing ray +19 touch (10d6 fire)

Spell-Like Abilities (CL 12th; concentration +19)

At will—*greater teleport* (self plus 50 lbs. of objects only), *light, major image* (DC 20)

3/day—*greater dispel magic, mirage arcana* (DC 20), *rainbow pattern* (DC 22), *spell turning, sunbeam, wall of force*

1/day—*scintillating pattern* (DC 25), *screen* (DC 25), *symbol of insanity* (DC 25)

STATISTICS

Str 10, **Dex** 17, **Con** 18, **Int** 15, **Wis** 11, **Cha** 24

Base Atk +16; **CMB** +16; **CMD** 37

Feats Ability Focus (blinding light), Dodge, Improved Initiative, Lightning Reflexes, Mobility, Skill Focus (Perception), Spring Attack, Weapon Finesse

Skills Bluff +26, Diplomacy +23, Fly +11, Intimidate +26, Knowledge (arcana) +21, Knowledge (planes) +21, Perception +25, Spellcraft +21, Use Magic Device +26

Languages telepathy 120 ft.

SQ radiant armor

ECOLOGY

Environment any land (extraplanar)

Organization solitary, visitation (2–9), or incursion (11–20)

Treasure none

SPECIAL ABILITIES

Blinding Light (Ex) A shining child can radiate a 60-foot-radius aura of blinding light as a free action. Creatures within the affected area must succeed on a DC 25 Fortitude save or be permanently blinded. A creature that successfully saves cannot be affected again by the same shining child's aura for 24 hours. The save is Constitution-based.

Burning Touch (Su) A shining child corrupts the positive energy within a living creature into an unnatural burning light. For the next 5 rounds after a successful touch attack by a shining child, the target takes 2d6 points of fire damage. The burning light can be "extinguished" by casting *darkness* or *deeper darkness* on the target, or by entering an area of natural darkness (not counting the light from the burning target).

Radiant Armor (Su) The light that surrounds a shining child grants a deflection bonus to its AC equal to its Charisma bonus. The bonus is negated as long as the shining child is in the area of effect of a spell with the darkness descriptor that is at least 3rd level.

Searing Ray (Su) A shining child's primary attack is a ray of searing light. This attack has a range of 120 feet. The ray deals double damage to undead creatures.

Creatures of burning light and strange geometry, shining children are a terror to behold. Beyond the flares of energy that constantly burst from their forms (particularly in beam-like gouts from their eyes and mouths), the creatures are vaguely humanoid, with strange hands that each bear four fingers. Occasionally summoned by powerful wizards in search of rare arcane knowledge, the shining children (who disdain individual names) communicate via telepathy, a psychic roar like metal tearing that sometimes resolves into strained and raspy words. Though they harbor many secrets, their greatest secret may be their own origin. Numerous theories abound—that the shining children are beings from another dimension, avatars of a dying star grown sentient, or creatures of light battling living darkness at the edge of reality. A shining child stands just over 4-1/2 feet tall and weighs 85 pounds.

Illustration by Eric Belisle

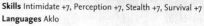

Sinspawn

This hairless humanoid lurches on back-bent, dog-like legs, its hideous mouth flanked by tiny arms with three-fingered hands.

SINSPAWN	CR 2

XP 600

NE Medium aberration

Init +5; **Senses** darkvision 60 ft., sin-scent; Perception +7

DEFENSE

AC 14, touch 12, flat-footed 12 (+1 Dex, +1 dodge, +2 natural)

hp 19 (3d8+6)

Fort +3, **Ref** +2, **Will** +4

Immune mind-affecting effects; **SR** 13

OFFENSE

Speed 40 ft.

Melee ranseur +3 (2d4+1/×3), bite –2 (1d6 plus sinful bite) or bite +3 (1d6+1 plus sinful bite), 2 claws +3 (1d4+1)

STATISTICS

Str 13, **Dex** 13, **Con** 14, **Int** 10, **Wis** 13, **Cha** 12

Base Atk +2; **CMB** +3; **CMD** 15

Feats Dodge, Improved Initiative

Skills Intimidate +7, Perception +7, Stealth +7, Survival +7

Languages Aklo

SQ martial proficiency

ECOLOGY

Environment any ruins

Organization solitary, pair, or cult (3–8)

Treasure standard (ranseur, other treasure)

SPECIAL ABILITIES

Martial Proficiency (Ex) Sinspawn are proficient in all simple and martial weapons, armor, and shields (except tower shields).

Sin-Scent (Su) Sinspawn have scent against creatures whose nature reflects the sinspawn's sin. For example, wrathful sinspawn can scent creatures using rage effects. The GM should adjudicate what creatures a particular sinspawn can scent.

Sinful Bite (Su) A creature bitten by a sinspawn is overwhelmed with sinful thoughts (DC 12 Will save negates). These emotions are so powerful that the target becomes sickened for 1d6 minutes. An affected target that is bitten a second time is staggered for 1 round if it fails its saving throw. *Calm emotions*, *remove curse*, or *break enchantment* negates the effects of sinful bite. The save DC is Charisma-based. This is a mind-affecting effect

Sinspawn are corrupted products of magic used by spellcasters in a past era as shock troops for their armies. Literally the embodiment of a sin made flesh, they are sentient abominations of distilled ectoplasm imprinted with the soul-image of slain creatures that possessed an abundance of a particular sin.

SEVEN TYPES OF SINSPAWN

The above stats represent a wrathspawn, the most common type of this creature. Each type possesses unique ability modifiers, which are listed after their name.

Envyspawn (+2 Str, –2 Cha): Short and thin, envyspawn often become rangers.

Gluttonspawn (+2 Con, –2 Dex): Obese yet hardy and strong, gluttonspawn often become fighters.

Greedspawn (+2 Dex, –2 Wis): Towering over 7 feet in height, greedspawn have gold-tinged veins and often become rogues.

Lustspawn (+4 Cha, –2 Con, –2 Wis): With perfectly formed bodies sitting in grotesque counterpoint to their monstrous faces and claws, lustspawn often become sorcerers.

Pridespawn (+4 Int, –2 Wis, –2 Cha): Unique among sinspawn for their long manes of hair, pridespawn are near-skeletal in their gauntness. They often become wizards.

Slothspawn (+2 Wis, –2 Dex): Thick rolls of excess skin drape a slothspawn's hunched frame. They often become clerics.

Wrathspawn: These sinspawn use the statistics given above. They often become barbarians.

Illustrations by Andrew Hou

SIREN

This creature has the body of a hawk and the head of a beautiful woman with long, shining hair.

SIREN	CR 5

XP 1,600
CN Medium magical beast
Init +3; **Senses** darkvision 60 ft., low-light vision; Perception +15

DEFENSE

AC 18, touch 14, flat-footed 14 (+3 Dex, +1 dodge, +4 natural)
hp 52 (8d10+8)
Fort +7, **Ref** +11, **Will** +6
Immune mind-affecting effects

OFFENSE

Speed 30 ft., fly 60 ft. (good)
Melee 2 talons +11 (1d6)
Special Attacks bardic performance, siren's song, sneak attack +2d6
Spell-Like Abilities (CL 7th; concentration +12)
   3/day—*cause fear* (DC 16), *charm person* (DC 16), *deep slumber* (DC 18), *shout* (DC 19)

STATISTICS

Str 10, **Dex** 17, **Con** 12, **Int** 14, **Wis** 19, **Cha** 21
Base Atk +8; **CMB** +8; **CMD** 22
Feats Dodge, Flyby Attack, Lightning Reflexes, Weapon Finesse
Skills Fly +7, Knowledge (history) +10, Perception +15, Perform (sing) +13, Stealth +14
Languages Auran, Common

ECOLOGY

Environment temperate or warm hills
Organization solitary or flight (2–7)
Treasure standard

SPECIAL ABILITIES

Bardic Performance (Su) A siren may use bardic performance as a 4th-level bard (9 rounds/day), and can use countersong, distraction, fascinate, inspire competence, and inspire courage. Levels in the bard class stack with this ability.

Siren Song (Su) When a siren sings, all non-sirens within a 300-foot spread must succeed on a DC 19 Will save or become enthralled (see below). The effect depends on the type of song the siren chooses, and continues for as long as the siren sings and for 1 round thereafter. A creature that successfully saves cannot be affected again by any of that siren's songs for 1 hour. These are sonic, mind-affecting effects. The save DC is Charisma-based. Enthralled creatures behave in one of the following four ways, which the siren chooses when she begins singing.

- *Captivation:* This functions exactly like a harpy's captivating song (*Pathfinder RPG Bestiary 172*).
- *Fascination:* Affected creatures are fascinated.
- *Obsession:* An obsessed victim becomes defensive of the siren and does all he can to prevent harm from coming

to her, going so far as attacking his allies in her defense. The victim is not controlled by the siren, but views her as a cherished ally. This is a charm effect.

- *Slumber:* The victim immediately falls asleep, rendering the creature helpless. While the siren is singing, no noise will wake the sleeping creature, though slapping or wounding him does. The creature continues sleeping for 1d4 minutes after the siren stops singing, but can be awakened by loud noises or any other normal method.

These bizarre beings have the bodies of hawks, owls, or eagles, but the heads of beautiful human women. Their faces typically reflect the human ethnicity dominant in the area in which they lair, and they almost always bear a vibrant and youthful countenance.

All sirens are female and long-lived. The oldest known sirens haunt their territories for nearly a millennium, although most only live for a few hundred years. Sirens require male humanoids to mate, and several times per decade either capture or rescue bold or comely sailors who enter their territories. Stories abound of sirens dying—either through heartache or suicide—when sailors they attempted to lure overcame their compelling powers and escaped their grasps. Sirens always live near the sea, where their powerful voices can carry over the waves and attract the attention of unwary sailors who trespass near their isles.

A typical siren has a wing span of 8 feet, and weighs 120 pounds.

SKULK

This smooth-skinned, hairless humanoid has penetrating eyes and skin that shifts and changes to mimic his surroundings.

SKULK	CR 1

XP 400

CE Medium humanoid (skulk)

Init +6; **Senses** low-light vision; Perception +5

DEFENSE

AC 12, touch 12, flat-footed 10 (+2 Dex)

hp 16 (3d8+3)

Fort +2, **Ref** +5, **Will** +3

OFFENSE

Speed 30 ft.

Melee short sword +2 (1d6/19–20)

Ranged dagger +4 (1d4/19–20)

Special Attacks sneak attack +1d6

STATISTICS

Str 11, **Dex** 14, **Con** 13, **Int** 10, **Wis** 14, **Cha** 7

Base Atk +2; **CMB** +2; **CMD** 14

Feats Improved Initiative, Skill Focus (Stealth)

Skills Perception +5, Stealth +16; **Racial Modifiers** +8 Stealth

Languages Common, Undercommon

SQ camouflaged step, chameleon skin

ECOLOGY

Environment any land or underground

Organization solitary, pair, band (3–8), or tribe (9–16)

Treasure standard (short sword, 2 daggers, other treasure)

SPECIAL ABILITIES

Camouflaged Step (Ex) Skulks can pass through forest and subterranean settings almost without a trace. Add +10 to the DC to track a skulk in these environments.

Chameleon Skin (Ex) A skulk's racial bonus to Stealth comes from his ability to change the color of his skin to match his surroundings, even complex or regular patterns like bricks and mortar. A skulk loses this conditional bonus if he is wearing armor, or if he wears any clothing that covers more than one-quarter of his body, as skulks can only change their own flesh, not things they carry. A skulk normally conceals small items behind his body; by putting his back to a wall and changing his front half, he can hide the item because observers don't have line of sight to the item.

Skulks are a race of cowardly and lazy humanoids that live on the fringes of society, stealing what they need and doing what they must—even committing casual murder—to survive. Their unabashed cowardice is perhaps their most widely known trait, but skulks don't see themselves as particularly craven. Instead, they view their dishonorable behaviors as the most expedient method of survival. They hate most other humanoids, viewing them as lazy and foolish, and think nothing of sneaking into a home, killing all the residents, and burglarizing what they can carry off without getting caught.

Skulks travel in small groups, rarely forming tribes of more than 16, for in larger groups bickering quickly leads to violent infighting. Murder between skulks is not uncommon, but they understand safety in numbers, and most frown upon treason within a group that is already relatively small, punishing traitors with a quick death. When possible, they set up camps in discreet spots near other settlements, commonly inhabiting sewers, caves, or forests—though their unsavory, murderous tactics often force them to relocate before local law enforcement, quickly alerted to their presence once the remains of a family of victims are discovered, finds them.

Skulks are roughly the same size as a human, averaging 6 feet tall, though they are significantly more gangly and nimble, and commonly weigh only 140 pounds. Skinny arms and legs help them sneak around obstacles and squeeze into narrow spaces. Skulks can live up to 50 years, though most die from violence long before that. Although skulks have racial Hit Dice, they generally advance in power by taking class levels. Rogue is a favorite choice among skulks, for their natural abilities at stealth and sneak attacks fit well with this choice, but they also excel in the roles of clerics, fighters and rangers who specialize in ranged weapons, and rarely as wizards (particularly illusionists).

Illustration by Jim Pavelec

SLIME MOLD

What at first seemed to be a carpet of fungi and mushrooms suddenly stirs to life, surging forward with a reek of decay.

SLIME MOLD	CR 2	

XP 600

N Large ooze

Init −1; **Senses** Perception −5

DEFENSE

AC 8, touch 8, flat-footed 8 (−1 Dex, −1 size)

hp 28 (3d8+15)

Fort +6, **Ref** +0, **Will** −4

Immune ooze traits; **Resist** fire 10

OFFENSE

Speed 20 ft.

Melee slam +4 (1d6+4 plus disease)

Space 10 ft.; **Reach** 10 ft.

Special Attacks engulf (DC 14, 1d6+4 bludgeoning plus disease)

STATISTICS

Str 16, **Dex** 8, **Con** 21, **Int** —, **Wis** 1, **Cha** 1

Base Atk +2; **CMB** +6; **CMD** 15 (can't be tripped)

SQ freeze

ECOLOGY

Environment temperate forests

Organization single or infestation (2–5)

Treasure none

SPECIAL ABILITIES

Disease (Ex) *Fungal rot*: Slam—contact; *save* Fortitude DC 16; *onset* 1 day; *frequency* 1/day; *effect* 1d2 Str damage and 1 Con damage and fatigue; *cure* 1 save. Any creature that touches a slime mold with an unarmed strike or a natural attack is also exposed to this foul disease. The save DC is Constitution-based.

Slime molds are revolting oozes that wallow in rot and decay. A perfect example of symbiosis, each slime mold is covered in a thick garden of fungi, mildew, and toadstools, which helps it blend in with the surroundings. As ambush hunters, they can lie silently in wait for days at a time, surging into frenzied movement as soon as prey comes within reach. Most commonly encountered in deep forests, variations have adapted to life in caverns and sewers as well. They lack any ability to digest

food, and rely entirely on their symbiotic fungal gardens to break down any organic matter they find into easily absorbed compost and decay. The molds and mushrooms that coat the ooze in turn receive ample food supplies, and over countless generations, many have developed into deadly variations of the forest or cave fungi from which they evolved. This fungal breakdown is in many ways akin to a disease—known as fungal rot, it can kill if allowed to progress for long. Those who succumb to fungal rot become tired and listless. Eventually, paralysis sets in and the victim's flesh begins to blacken and decay, running from the body in liquid streams that the slime mold can easily absorb. In a somewhat nauseating turnabout, certain creatures find the unusual fungus that grows upon a slime mold to be quite tasty, and these creatures actively hunt slime molds to devour their gardens—although they take care to avoid actual contact with the mold itself unless they happen to be immune to disease.

Slime molds are ovoid in shape, growing up to 12 feet in length and weighing more than 600 pounds. Their substance is normally a sickly greenish-brown, with the coloration varying depending on their environment and how recently they've fed. They instinctually keep their coating of fungus and other vegetable detritus exposed above them, granting the slime mold a distinctive, undulating gait rather than the fluid movement of most oozes.

To reproduce, slime molds split off small patches of their bodies whenever they encounter thick beds of fungi or mold. Over several months, these tiny blobs acclimate to the rot and absorb each another, until a single slime mold (with the young creature simple template) sprouts its own garden and begins hunting live prey.

Illustration by Adam Vehige

SLITHERING TRACKER

A long, moist streak along the dark stone suddenly undulates like a serpent and then rises up to attack.

SLITHERING TRACKER	CR 4

XP 1,200

N Small ooze

Init +4; **Senses** blindsense 60 ft.; Perception +7

DEFENSE

AC 15, touch 15, flat-footed 11 (+4 Dex, +1 size)

hp 42 (4d8+24)

Fort +7, **Ref** +5, **Will** +1

Immune mind-affecting effects, ooze traits

OFFENSE

Speed 10 ft., climb 10 ft.

Melee 2 slams +7 (1d6+3 plus grab and paralysis)

Special Attacks blood drain (1d2 Constitution), grab (Colossal)

STATISTICS

Str 16, **Dex** 18, **Con** 23, **Int** 11, **Wis** 10, **Cha** 1

Base Atk +3; **CMB** +5 (+9 grapple); **CMD** 19 (can't be tripped)

Feats Skill Focus (Perception), Skill Focus (Stealth)

Skills Climb +11, Perception +7, Stealth +20; **Racial Modifiers** +8 Stealth

Languages Undercommon (cannot speak)

SQ transparent

ECOLOGY

Environment any ruins or underground

Organization solitary or pair

Treasure incidental

SPECIAL ABILITIES

Paralysis (Ex) Any creature that is hit by a slithering tracker's slam attack comes into contact with the anesthetizing slime it secretes. The opponent must succeed on a DC 18 Fortitude save or be paralyzed—at the end of each round thereafter, the paralyzed victim can attempt a new Fortitude save to recover from this paralysis. When a victim recovers from a slithering tracker's paralysis, the victim is staggered for 1d6 rounds. This DC is Constitution-based.

Transparent (Ex) Because of its lack of coloration, a slithering tracker is difficult to discern from its surroundings in most environments. The slithering tracker gains a +8 racial bonus on Stealth checks as a result, and can move at full speed without taking a penalty on Stealth checks. A creature that fails to notice a slithering tracker and walks into it automatically takes

damage as if struck by the slithering tracker's slam attack and is immediately subject to a grab attempt and paralysis by the ooze.

An alien inhabitant of the dark underworld, the slithering tracker is a glistening creature of transparent ooze, typically about 3 inches thick and at least 3 feet in diameter. When still, it looks like a wet patch of stone or a patch of condensation on a wall. Comparatively slow moving, the slithering tracker relies on its transparency and knack for ambushing to surprise prey.

Once a slithering tracker has paralyzed a living creature, it flows over an exposed patch of flesh, grabbing on and draining blood from the victim. A slithering tracker can drain a human-sized creature of its blood with shocking swiftness, leaving only a desiccated carcass behind. A slithering tracker can go some time between meals, but never turns down easy prey. The larger a slithering tracker grows, the more voracious its appetite becomes, until, after a particularly large feeding, the creature splits into two smaller slithering trackers that eventually go their separate ways in search of feeding territory.

Slithering trackers are not harmed by bright light, but still prefer to avoid areas of intense illumination or natural sunlight, and so only venture aboveground at night. They prefer the cool, damp environment of their native caves and tunnels.

Although intelligent and cunning, slithering trackers are entirely alien creatures. They do not possess any language of their own, although they can usually understand the dominant language of the region they dwell in—usually Undercommon. Some underworld inhabitants do manage to forge alliances with slithering trackers, or at least exist with them in symbiosis by providing the creatures with easy and regular prey, but as one can never truly know a slithering tracker's desires or motivations, such alliances are dangerous to rely upon.

SLURK

This disgusting beast looks like a slime-covered toad, but with two walrus-like tusks jutting from its upper jaw.

SLURK	CR 2

XP 600

N Medium magical beast

Init +6; **Senses** darkvision 60 ft.; Perception +0

DEFENSE

AC 15, touch 12, flat-footed 13 (+2 Dex, +3 natural)

hp 17 (2d10+6)

Fort +6, **Ref** +5, **Will** +0

OFFENSE

Speed 30 ft., climb 30 ft.

Melee bite +4 (2d6+3)

Ranged slime squirt +4 ranged touch

Special Attacks belly grease, slime

STATISTICS

Str 15, **Dex** 14, **Con** 17, **Int** 3, **Wis** 10, **Cha** 10

Base Atk +2; **CMB** +4; **CMD** 16 (20 vs. bull rush, grapple, overrun, and trip)

Feats Improved Bull Rush^B, Improved Initiative, Improved Overrun^B

Skills Acrobatics +16, Climb +14, Escape Artist +6; **Racial Modifiers** +10 Acrobatics, +4 Escape Artist

Languages Boggard (can't speak)

SQ hunker

ECOLOGY

Environment temperate swamps or underground

Organization solitary, pair, or pack (3–8)

Treasure none

SPECIAL ABILITIES

Belly Grease (Ex) The slurk exudes a slippery grease from its belly that grants it a +4 bonus on Escape Artist skill checks and to its CMD versus grapples. Once per minute, a slurk may wallow on a solid surface as a full-round action to coat the floor in a 5-foot radius with this grease. The smear created turns that area of floor into difficult terrain for 10 minutes, after which the grease dries to a nasty crust.

Hunker (Ex) The slurk gains a +4 bonus to its CMD to avoid bull rush or overrun attempts.

Slime (Ex) A slurk's back is crusted with thick, dry slime and dozens of nodules. As a standard action at will, a slurk can squirt a jet of this slime from one of these nodules as a ranged touch attack against any target within 30 feet. The slime quickly hardens to the texture of cold tar, entangling the foe. Anyone the slurk successfully bull rushes or overruns is automatically squirted with back slime. The hardened slime can be removed as a full-round action with a DC 15 Strength check. The slurk's back slime grants a creature riding it a +8 bonus on Ride checks made to stay in the saddle, but a −8 penalty on Ride checks to dismount.

Slurks are frog-like creatures, the descendants of the failed result of a dwarven attempt to domesticate and breed subterranean frogs as food and labor animals. Though the dwarves failed to create suitable livestock, the sticky frog-beasts are often befriended by other underground races.

Slurks are carnivores and have a formidable bite, thanks to their massive tusks. Their true strength, however, lies in their foul-smelling and unnatural secretions. The mucus exuded from the slurk's back is incredibly sticky and quickly hardens into a powerful resin, a quality the creature turns to its advantage by squirting it at intruders and then waiting for it to harden before closing for the kill. At the same time, the liquid excreted by glands on a slurk's stomach is incredible slippery, allowing the slurk to keep from being immobilized by its own back slime and also making it extremely hard to grapple or maneuver without its consent. Combined with slurks' natural ability to climb walls and hang from ceilings with ease, these abilities make the foul-smelling creatures extremely desirable to kobolds, who domesticate and train the frog-beasts as powerful mounts and guardians.

Illustration by Eric Deschamps

Snake, Emperor Cobra

This massive green cobra rears its head upward aggressively, its brightly colored, scaly hood flaring in an unmistakable warning.

EMPEROR COBRA	CR 5	

XP 1,600

N Large animal

Init +6; **Senses** low-light vision, scent; Perception +13

DEFENSE

AC 18, touch 11, flat-footed 16 (+2 Dex, +7 natural, −1 size)

hp 51 (6d8+24)

Fort +9, **Ref** +7, **Will** +5

OFFENSE

Speed 30 ft., climb 30 ft., swim 30 ft.

Melee bite +10 (2d6+9 plus poison)

Space 10 ft.; **Reach** 10 ft.

STATISTICS

Str 22, **Dex** 15, **Con** 18, **Int** 1, **Wis** 17, **Cha** 2

Base Atk +4; **CMB** +11; **CMD** 23 (can't be tripped)

Feats Improved Initiative, Skill Focus (Stealth), Weapon Focus (bite)

Skills Acrobatics +10, Climb +14, Perception +13, Stealth +11, Swim +14; **Racial Modifiers** Acrobatics +8, +4 Perception, +4 Stealth

ECOLOGY

Environment temperate or warm swamps

Organization solitary, pair, or nest (3–8)

Treasure none

SPECIAL ABILITIES

Poison (Ex) Bite—injury; *save* Fort DC 17; *frequency* 1/round for 6 rounds; *effect* 1d3 Con; *cure* 2 consecutive saves.

Infamous among travelers for its deadly poisonous bite, the emperor cobra is a foul-tempered snake typically encountered in bogs. The snake's scales are generally a dark green, with a pale green or even ivory underbelly. Its eyes are bright red and lack the distinctive serpentine slit most snake eyes possess. Emperor cobras are often trained to serve as guardians in temples. They are 16 feet long and weigh 200 pounds.

Snake, Giant Anaconda

An enormous coil of muscle and scales, this giant snake flicks its arm-length tongue in the air as it scans the area for prey.

GIANT ANACONDA	CR 10	

XP 9,600

N Gargantuan animal

Init +6; **Senses** low-light vision, scent; Perception +22

DEFENSE

AC 25, touch 9, flat-footed 22 (+2 Dex, +1 dodge, +16 natural, −4 size)

hp 126 (12d8+72)

Fort +14, **Ref** +10, **Will** +5

OFFENSE

Speed 20 ft., climb 20 ft., swim 20 ft.

Melee bite +19 (4d6+19/19–20 plus grab)

Space 20 ft.; **Reach** 20 ft.

Special Attacks constrict (4d6+19)

STATISTICS

Str 36, **Dex** 14, **Con** 23, **Int** 1, **Wis** 13, **Cha** 2

Base Atk +9; **CMB** +26 (+30 grapple); **CMD** 39 (can't be tripped)

Feats Dodge, Improved Critical (bite), Improved Initiative, Power Attack, Skill Focus (Perception), Weapon Focus (bite)

Skills Climb +21, Perception +22, Swim +21

ECOLOGY

Environment warm swamps

Organization solitary or pair

Treasure none

Of the multitude of slithering predators that infest jungles, forests, and swamps, few inspire such terror as the giant anaconda. Incredibly strong, fearless hunters, these creatures are capable of taking down and eating elephants, dinosaurs, and giants. Their olive green and black mottled scales afford them exceptional camouflage in the murky waters they call home. A giant anaconda can grow to a length of 60 feet.

SOLIFUGID, GIANT

This tan-colored creature looks like a ten-legged spider. Oversized jaws grind together slowly beneath beady eyes.

GIANT SOLIFUGID	CR 1

XP 400
N Small vermin
Init +2; **Senses** darkvision 60 ft.; Perception +4

DEFENSE

AC 14, touch 13, flat-footed 12 (+2 Dex, +1 natural, +1 size)
hp 13 (2d8+4)
Fort +5, **Ref** +2, **Will** +0
Immune mind-affecting effects

OFFENSE

Speed 50 ft., climb 30 ft.
Melee bite +3 (1d6+1), 2 claws +3 (1d3+1)
Special Attacks rend (2 claws, 1d3+1)

STATISTICS

Str 12, **Dex** 15, **Con** 15, **Int** —, **Wis** 11, **Cha** 2
Base Atk +1; **CMB** +1; **CMD** 13 (25 vs. trip)
Skills Climb +9, Perception +4, Stealth +10; **Racial Modifiers** +4 Perception, +4 Stealth

ECOLOGY

Environment warm deserts
Organization solitary, pair, or colony (3–6)
Treasure none

SOLIFUGID, ALBINO CAVE

This spider-like creature's front legs end in immense, grasping claws. Its mouth sports a pair of huge vertical mandibles.

ALBINO CAVE SOLIFUGID	CR 4

XP 1,200
N Medium vermin
Init +1; **Senses** darkvision 60 ft.; Perception +4

DEFENSE

AC 17, touch 11, flat-footed 16 (+1 Dex, +6 natural)
hp 45 (6d8+18)
Fort +8, **Ref** +3, **Will** +2
Immune mind-affecting effects

OFFENSE

Speed 50 ft., climb 30 ft.
Melee bite +7 (1d8+3), 2 claws +7 (1d4+3)
Special Attacks pounce, rend (2 claws, 1d6+4)

STATISTICS

Str 16, **Dex** 13, **Con** 17, **Int** —, **Wis** 11, **Cha** 2
Base Atk +4; **CMB** +7; **CMD** 18 (26 vs. trip)
Skills Climb +11, Perception +4, Stealth +5; **Racial Modifiers** +4 Perception, +4 Stealth

ECOLOGY

Environment any underground
Organization solitary, pair, or colony (3–6)
Treasure none

Solifugids are sometimes called "camel spiders," "wind scorpions," or "sun spiders," despite the fact that they are neither spiders nor scorpions but rather their own unique species. They have large pedipalps near their heads, used to grab and hold prey while they feed with their twin sets of vertically aligned mandibles. When hunting in groups, they prefer to attack targets already grappled by other solifugids. The various species of enormous solifugids generally have eight legs, although the front two appendages are large enough that they can easily be mistaken for an additional pair of legs. Some species, like the albino cave solifugid, have fewer legs, but all solifugids are aggressive vermin.

The following table lists the most common variants beyond the two presented above. Many of these species have additional unique abilities, such as the razormouth's ability to cause hideous, bleeding wounds in those it attacks.

Species	CR	Size	HD
Dog-eating solifugid	1/2	Tiny	1
Yellow terror solifugid	8	Large	10
Razormouth solifugid	11	Huge	13
Banshee solifugid	15	Gargantuan	16
Duneshaker solifugid	18	Colossal	20

The six-legged albino cave solifugid is well known for its aggressive hunting patterns. It has a legspan of 5 feet, and weighs 100 pounds.

SOUL EATER

Two elongated and deathly pallid arms protrude from this creature's smoky body as it slithers silently through the air.

SOUL EATER	CR 7

XP 3,200

NE Medium outsider (evil, extraplanar)

Init +10; **Senses** darkvision 60 ft., all-around vision; Perception +14

DEFENSE

AC 21, touch 17, flat-footed 14 (+6 Dex, +1 dodge, +4 natural)

hp 82 (11d10+22)

Fort +5, **Ref** +13, **Will** +7

DR 10/magic; **Immune** critical hits, paralysis, poison, sleep, stunning

OFFENSE

Speed 30 ft., fly 100 ft. (perfect)

Melee 2 claws +18
(1d6+1/19–20 plus 1d6
Wisdom damage)

Special Attacks
find target,
soul drain

STATISTICS

Str 13, **Dex** 22,
Con 14, **Int** 12,
Wis 11, **Cha** 11

Base Atk +11;
CMB +12; **CMD** 29
(can't be tripped)

Feats Dodge, Flyby Attack,
Improved Critical (claw), Improved
Initiative, Weapon Finesse, Weapon
Focus (claw)

Skills Acrobatics +20 (+8 jump), Escape Artist +20,
Fly +28, Intimidate +14, Knowledge (planes) +15,
Perception +14, Stealth +20 (+28 darkness or smoke)

Languages Abyssal, Infernal

SQ caster link

ECOLOGY

Environment any Outer Plane (Abaddon)

Organization solitary

Treasure none

SPECIAL ABILITIES

Caster Link (Ex) When a soul eater is summoned, it creates a mental link between itself and its conjurer. If the soul eater's assigned target (see find target ability) dies before the soul eater can drain its soul, or if the soul eater is defeated by its target (but not slain), it returns to its conjurer at full speed and attacks her. While the soul eater and the conjurer are on the same plane (regardless of plane-traveling interruptions), it can use its find target ability to locate its conjurer.

Find Target (Su) When a soul eater's conjurer orders it to find a creature, it can do so unerringly, as though guided by a *locate creature* spell that has no maximum range and is not blocked by running water. The conjurer must have seen the desired target and must speak the target's name.

Soul Drain (Su) If the Wisdom damage from a soul eater's claw attacks equals or exceeds an opponent's actual Wisdom score, rendering the victim helpless, the soul eater can devour that creature's soul as a standard action that provokes an attack of opportunity. This attack kills the victim. The dead victim can resist having her soul eaten by making a (DC 17) Fortitude save; success means she is still dead, but can be restored to life normally. If she fails this save, her soul is consumed by the soul eater. A victim slain in this manner cannot be returned to life with *clone*, *raise dead*, or *reincarnation*. She can be restored to life via *resurrection*, *true resurrection*, *miracle*, or *wish*, but only if the caster can succeed on a DC 30 caster level check. If the soul eater is killed within 120 feet of its victim's corpse, and the victim has been dead for no longer than 1 minute, the victim's soul returns to her body and restores her to life, leaving her unconscious and at –1 hit point. This is a death effect. The save DC is Constitution-based.

Wisdom Damage (Su) A creature hit by a soul eater's claw must succeed on a DC 17 Fortitude save or take 1d6 points of Wisdom damage. The save DC is Constitution-based.

Summoned forth from the inky swamps of Abaddon, a soul eater is an extraplanar entity devoid of emotion or reason and possessing a hunger that may only be sated by devouring the souls of the living. The very nature of a soul eater makes it an ideal and terrifyingly efficient tool of death, and it is for this reason they are often conjured by vile spellcasters pursuing morbid agendas. Even when not seeing to the heinous commands of a sinister magic user, the soul eater prowls and hunts, constantly seeking living souls upon which to gorge itself.

SOULBOUND DOLL

This doll's glass eyes glisten with unmistakable curiosity as it comes to life with a fluid grace.

SOULBOUND DOLL	CR 2

XP 600

N (but see below) Tiny construct

Init +6; **Senses** darkvision 60 ft., low-light vision; Perception +3

DEFENSE

AC 15, touch 14, flat-footed 13 (+2 Dex, +1 natural, +2 size)

hp 19 (3d10+3)

Fort +1, **Ref** +3, **Will** +1

DR 2/magic; **Immune** construct traits

Weaknesses susceptible to mind-affecting effects

OFFENSE

Speed 20 ft.

Melee dagger +3 (1d2–2/19–20)

Space 2-1/2 ft.; **Reach** 0 ft.

Spell-Like Abilities (CL 3rd, concentration +2)

3/day—*light*, *mage hand*, *open/close*, *prestidigitation*

1/day—*levitate*, one additional ability dependent on alignment

STATISTICS

Str 7, **Dex** 14, **Con** —, **Int** 11, **Wis** 10, **Cha** 9

Base Atk +3; **CMB** +3; **CMD** 11

Feats Improved Initiative, Toughness

Skills Perception +3, Stealth +13

Languages Common

SQ alignment variation, soul focus

ECOLOGY

Environment any

Organization solitary, pair, or family (3–12)

Treasure standard

SPECIAL ABILITIES

Alignment Variation (Ex) Soulbound dolls are at least partially neutral in alignment, although they can also be chaotic, evil, good, or lawful. They have an alignment-dependent spell-like ability usable once per day as listed below.

- *Chaotic Neutral: rage*
- *Lawful Neutral: suggestion* (DC 12)
- *Neutral: deep slumber* (DC 12)
- *Neutral Evil: inflict serious wounds* (DC 12)
- *Neutral Good: heroism*

Susceptible to Mind-Affecting Effects (Ex) The weakened conviction of a soulbound doll's soul makes it susceptible to mind-affecting effects, despite the fact that it is a construct.

Soul Focus (Su) The soul bound to the doll lives within a focus integrated into the doll or its apparel, typically one of the doll's eyes or a gem embedded into its neck or chest. As long as this soul focus remains intact, it can be used to animate another doll, using the same cost as creating a new construct. Once bound into the soul focus, the soul continues to learn, and so if later it is put into a new doll body, the soul retains its personality and memories from its previous body or bodies. A soul focus has hardness 8, 12 hit points, and a break DC of 20.

These small, sentient dolls contain a fragment of another creature's soul. The binding process strips most of the individuality from the soul, making any soulbound doll an almost blank slate. Despite this process, fragments of the original creature's personality remain.

Soulbound dolls can serve as companions, surrogate children, servants, guards, and sentries, as desired by their creators. Creators of soulbound dolls typically take care to take soul fragments from people whose personality traits the crafters wish to see in their dolls.

CONSTRUCTION

A soulbound doll's body is made from wood, stone, or porcelain, with one exquisite item worth at least 300 gp to serve as the soul focus. Creation requires a soul fragment from a deceased creature that must die at some point during the creation of the doll—as a result, most soulbound dolls are created by evil spellcasters. Other spellcasters can create soulbound dolls, but if the donor soul is unwilling, they may have alignment repercussions. An unwilling soul can resist the procedure with a DC 20 Will save. Stripping a soul fragment from the dead does not prevent the rest of the soul from continuing on to the afterlife, nor does it prevent the body from later being resurrected or raised from the dead.

Illustration by Concept Art House

SOULBOUND DOLL

CL 7th; **Price** 4,300 gp

CONSTRUCTION

Requirements Craft Construct, *false life*, *lesser geas*, *magic jar*, *minor creation*, soul of a living creature who dies or is slain during the creation process; Skill Craft (sculptures);

Cost 2,300 gp.

SPIDER, GIANT BLACK WIDOW

This long-legged spider has a huge, glossy black abdomen, marked on the underside with the shape of a crimson hourglass.

GIANT BLACK WIDOW SPIDER CR 3

XP 800

N Large vermin

Init +2; **Senses** darkvision 60 ft., tremorsense 60 ft.; Perception +4

DEFENSE

AC 15, touch 11, flat-footed 13 (+2 Dex, +4 natural, −1 size)

hp 37 (5d8+15)

Fort +7, **Ref** +3, **Will** +1

Immune mind-affecting effects

OFFENSE

Speed 30 ft., climb 30 ft.

Melee bite +6 (1d8+6 plus poison)

Space 10 ft.; **Reach** 5 ft.

Special Attacks web (+4 ranged, DC 19, 5 hp)

STATISTICS

Str 19, **Dex** 15, **Con** 16, **Int** —, **Wis** 10, **Cha** 2

Base Atk +3; **CMB** +8; **CMD** 20 (32 vs. trip)

Skills Climb +20, Perception +4; **Racial Modifiers** +8 Climb, +4 Perception, +4 Stealth (+8 webs)

SQ strong webs

ECOLOGY

Environment any land

Organization solitary, pair, or colony (3–8)

Treasure incidental

SPECIAL ABILITIES

Poison (Ex) Bite—injury; *save* Fort DC 17; *frequency* 1/round for 6 rounds; *effect* 1d3 Con and staggered; *cure* 2 saves. Save DC is Con-based with a +2 racial bonus.

Strong Webs (Ex) A black widow's webs gain a +4 bonus to the DC to break or escape.

Females of this species are larger than males. Males are identical to the typical giant spider (*Pathfinder RPG Bestiary* 258).

SPIDER, GIANT TARANTULA

A massive tarantula covered in bristly hairs strides forward with deliberate steps, its eight eyes scanning for prey.

GIANT TARANTULA CR 8

XP 4,800

N Gargantuan vermin

Init +1; **Senses** darkvision 60 ft., tremorsense 60 ft.; Perception +4

DEFENSE

AC 21, touch 7, flat-footed 20 (+1 Dex, +14 natural, −4 size)

hp 115 (10d8+70)

Fort +14, **Ref** +4, **Will** +3

Defensive Abilities barbed hairs; **Immune** mind-affecting effects

OFFENSE

Speed 30 ft., climb 30 ft.

Melee bite +15 (3d6+18 plus poison)

Ranged barbed hairs +4 touch (nausea)

Space 20 ft.; **Reach** 20 ft.

STATISTICS

Str 35, **Dex** 13, **Con** 24, **Int** —, **Wis** 10, **Cha** 2

Base Atk +7; **CMB** +23; **CMD** 34 (46 vs. trip)

Skills Climb +28, Perception +4, Stealth −7 (−3 in webs); **Racial Modifiers** +8 Climb, +4 Perception, +4 Stealth (+8 in webs)

ECOLOGY

Environment any forests

Organization solitary, pair, or colony (3–8)

Treasure incidental

SPECIAL ABILITIES

Barbed Hairs (Ex) A tarantula can throw barbed hairs from its back at a creature as a ranged touch attack (range increment 20 feet). A creature struck by these hairs must make a DC 22 Fort save or be nauseated for 1d6 rounds. A creature that attacks a giant tarantula with a non-reach melee weapon must make a DC 22 Reflex save to avoid being struck by these hairs. The save DC is Con-based.

Poison (Ex) Bite—injury; *save* Fort DC 24; *frequency* 1/round for 6 rounds; *effect* 1d6 Str; *cure* 2 consecutive saves. Save DC is Con-based with a +2 racial bonus.

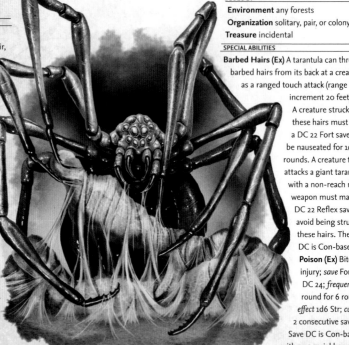

Illustration by Dean Spencer

SPRIGGAN

Flecks of saliva drip from the corners of this filthy and ill-smelling humanoid, and his large pointed ears twitch at every sound.

SPRIGGAN — CR 3

XP 800

CE Small humanoid (gnome)

Init +4; **Senses** low-light vision; Perception +7

DEFENSE

AC 17, touch 15, flat-footed 13 (+2 armor, +4 Dex, +1 size)

hp 22 (4d8+4)

Fort +5, **Ref** +5, **Will** +1

OFFENSE

Speed 20 ft.

Melee mwk morningstar +5 (1d6–1)

Ranged light crossbow +8 (1d6/19–20)

Special Attacks sneak attack +2d6

Spell-Like Abilities (CL 4th; concentration +4)

At will—*flare* (DC 10), *scare* (DC 12), *shatter* (DC 12)

STATISTICS

Str 9, **Dex** 19, **Con** 12, **Int** 10, **Wis** 10, **Cha** 9

Base Atk +3; **CMB** +1; **CMD** 15

Feats Combat Reflexes, Weapon Focus (morningstar)

Skills Climb +1, Disable Device +11, Perception +7, Sleight of Hand +11, Stealth +15; **Racial Modifiers** +2 Climb, +2 Disable Device, +2 Perception, +2 Sleight of Hand, +2 Stealth

Languages Aklo, Gnome

SQ size alteration, spriggan magic, spriggan skills

ECOLOGY

Environment any hills or forests

Organization solitary, pair, or mob (3–12)

Treasure NPC Gear (leather armor, masterwork morningstar, light crossbow with 10 bolts, other treasure)

SPECIAL ABILITIES

Size Alteration (Su) At will as a standard action, a spriggan can change his size between Small and Large. Weapons, armor, and other objects on the spriggan's person grow proportionally when he changes size (objects revert to normal size 1 round after a spriggan releases them). When a spriggan becomes Large, his speed increases to 30 feet, he gains +12 Strength, –2 Dexterity, and +6 Constitution, and he takes a –2 size penalty to his AC. While Large, a spriggan cannot use his sneak attack or his racial spell-like abilities (although if he possesses either from class levels or templates, he retains their use in both sizes).

Spriggan Magic (Ex) A spriggan gains a +1 racial bonus on concentration checks and to save DCs for all of its racial spell-like abilities.

Spriggan Skills (Ex) Climb, Disable Device, Perception, Sleight of Hand, and Stealth are class skills for spriggans.

SPRIGGAN (LARGE SIZE) — CR 3

XP 800

CE Large humanoid (gnome)

Init +3; **Senses** low-light vision; Perception +7

DEFENSE

AC 14, touch 12, flat-footed 11 (+2 armor, +3 Dex, –1 size)

hp 34 (4d8+16)

Fort +8, **Ref** +4, **Will** +1

OFFENSE

Speed 30 ft.

Melee mwk morningstar +9 (2d6 +5)

Ranged light crossbow +5 (2d6/19–20)

Space 10 ft.; **Reach** 10 ft.

STATISTICS

Str 21, **Dex** 17, **Con** 18, **Int** 10, **Wis** 10, **Cha** 9

Base Atk +3; **CMB** +9; **CMD** 22

Skills Climb +7, Disable Device +10, Perception +7, Sleight of Hand +10, Stealth +6

When the gnomes first traveled to the mortal realm from the distant land of the fey, some found the Material Plane so strange and terrifying that they lost their sense of joy. Seeing only the threats of the new world but none of its wonders, they grimly resolved to survive no matter the cost. Their innate magic responded to this twisted goal by reshaping them in mind and body over the course of many generations, transforming them into the creatures known as spriggans. Love, happiness, and beauty have no meaning for these poor souls, so they lead lives of violence and malice. The best they can manage in place of positive emotions is a muted satisfaction when they make another suffer.

Spriggans resemble ugly gnomes with an alien, feral appearance. Many are gaunt and haggard. When magically enlarged, they look the same except much more hale and muscular.

Illustration by Tyler Walpole

257

SYLPH

This pale, waifish woman, her hair waving in a nonexistent breeze, looks as if she might fade away into mist entirely at any minute.

SYLPH	CR 1/2	

XP 200

Sylph rogue 1

N Medium outsider (native)

Init +3; **Senses** darkvision 60 ft.; Perception +6

DEFENSE

AC 16, touch 14, flat-footed 12 (+2 armor, +3 Dex, +1 dodge)

hp 9 (1d8+1)

Fort +0, **Ref** +5, **Will** +2

Resist electricity 5

OFFENSE

Speed 30 ft.

Melee dagger −1 (1d4−1/19–20)

Ranged dagger +3 (1d4−1/19–20)

Special Attacks sneak attack +1d6

Spell-Like Abilities (CL 1st; concentration +1)

1/day—*feather fall*

STATISTICS

Str 8, **Dex** 17, **Con** 10, **Int** 15, **Wis** 14, **Cha** 10

Base Atk +0; **CMB** −1; **CMD** 13

Feats Dodge

Skills Acrobatics +7, Appraise +6, Bluff +4, Climb +3, Diplomacy +4, Knowledge (local) +6, Perception +6, Sleight of Hand +7, Stealth +7, Use Magic Device +4

Languages Auran, Common, Elven, Halfling

SQ air affinity, trapfinding +1

ECOLOGY

Environment any land

Organization solitary, pair, or gang (3–6)

Treasure NPC gear (leather armor, two daggers, other treasure)

SPECIAL ABILITIES

Air Affinity (Ex) Sylph sorcerers with the elemental (air) bloodline treat their Charisma score as 2 points higher for all sorcerer spells and class abilities. Sylph clerics with the Air domain cast their domain powers and spells at +1 caster level.

Sylphs are humans whose family trees include elemental beings of air, such as djinn. They tend to be pale and thin to the point of appearing delicate, though their skinny bodies are more resilient than they look. While many can pass unnoticed through crowds of humans, sylphs display their heritage in subtle ways, and those who study them carefully sometimes notice that breezes seem to follow a sylph wherever she goes, even inside rooms with no windows. When consumed by fits of anger or passion, these tendencies become more apparent, as winds surround the sylph and tousle her hair or knock small items from shelves. Many sylphs have complex markings on their pale flesh that resemble tiny swirling designs like blue and gray tattoos, and the most exotic of their kind have hair that twists and coils almost as if it were made of living mist.

As people, sylphs tend to be shy and reclusive, blending into crowds or skillfully avoiding those they don't desire to meet. Yet while they often prefer to manipulate situations and avoid conflict themselves, most sylphs remain intensely curious about other people, and often go to great lengths to spy or eavesdrop on those who spark their interest (a hobby frequently referred to as "listening to the wind"). This combined love of subterfuge and ability to slip away from any compromising situation makes sylphs perfectly suited to lives as rogues, thieves, and spies, and beneath the average sylph's veneer of shy waifishness lies a mind that's capable and calculating, constantly sizing up the competition and analyzing the most effective exits from any given room.

SYLPH CHARACTERS

Sylphs are defined by class levels—they do not possess racial Hit Dice. Sylphs have the following racial traits.

+2 Dexterity, +2 Intelligence, −2 Constitution: Sylphs are quick and insightful, but slight and delicate.

Darkvision: Sylphs can see in the dark up to 60 feet.

Sylph Magic: *Feather fall* 1/day (caster level equals the sylph's Hit Dice).

Energy Resistance: Sylphs have electricity resistance 5.

Air Affinity: See above.

Languages: Sylphs begin play speaking Common and Auran. Sylphs with high Intelligence scores can choose any of the following bonus languages: Aquan, Dwarven, Elven, Gnome, Halfling, Ignan, and Terran.

Illustration by Jorge Maese

Tendriculos

This plant's thick trunk is capped by a crown of wide leaves, whipping vines, mushrooms, and a ravenous purple maw.

TENDRICULOS	CR 6	

XP 2,400

N Huge plant

Init +3; **Senses** low-light vision; Perception +7

DEFENSE

AC 19, touch 7, flat-footed 19 (–1 Dex, +12 natural, –2 size)

hp 76 (9d8+36); regeneration 10 (bludgeoning or fire)

Fort +10, **Ref** +4, **Will** +4

Immune acid, plant traits

OFFENSE

Speed 20 ft.

Melee bite +11 (2d6+7 plus grab), 2 tentacles +6 (1d6+3 plus grab)

Space 15 ft.; **Reach** 15 ft.

Special Attacks paralysis (3d6 rounds, DC 18), swallow whole (2d6 acid damage plus paralysis, AC 15, 7 hp)

STATISTICS

Str 24, **Dex** 9, **Con** 18, **Int** 3, **Wis** 8, **Cha** 3

Base Atk +6; **CMB** +15 (+19 grapple); **CMD** 24 (can't be tripped)

Feats Improved Initiative, Iron Will, Lightning Reflexes, Power Attack, Skill Focus (Stealth)

Skills Perception +7, Stealth +1 (+9 in undergrowth); **Racial Modifiers** +8 Stealth in undergrowth

Languages Sylvan (cannot speak)

ECOLOGY

Environment temperate or warm forests

Organization solitary, pair, or grove (3–6)

Treasure standard

A tendriculos is a creature brought into being through a corruption of nature, often where foul magic has seeped into the environs for many years, or where the boundaries between the Material Plane and the mysterious realm of the fey have worn thin. Tales and myths speak of arcane manipulation from other planes, while others speak of a tendriculos as being the manifestation of an angered spirit of nature.

A voracious carnivore, the tendriculos is an active hunter when it needs to be but it prefers to rely on ambush tactics, choosing well-traveled areas in the forest where it can lie in wait in the undergrowth. The creature is quick to swallow any prey it happens to catch in its vines, relying upon the acid-filled reservoir in its trunk to finish off prey that may still have a bit of fight left in it. This acid not only consumes organic

material with shocking ease, but also contains a powerful paralytic enzyme that further reduces a creature's chance of escape once it's been gulped down by the plant.

Although incapable of speech itself, the tendriculos generally understands a handful of words in a single language (usually Sylvan). While they tend to see all smaller creatures as nothing more than food, tales exist of certain creatures, particularly fey or druids, having secured a sort of alliance with local tendriculoses. In such cases, the tendriculos is more than willing to serve its ally as a guardian, so long as the ally is diligent at providing the plant with a regular supply of food.

The fact that a tendriculos displays a curious mix of plant, fungal, and even animal traits (in the form of its almost fleshy, toothed maw) has long intrigued sages. That the creature is a plant is firmly established, yet it lays egg-like spheres when the need to reproduce strikes. These "eggs" are in fact massive, puffball-like fungi filled with spores—when jostled, the cloud of spores that is released can carry for miles, ensuring that a single tendriculos can seed a huge territory.

A tendriculos is 20 feet tall and weighs 3,500 pounds.

Illustration by Eric Belisle

TENEBROUS WORM

This pallid beast clatters upon dozens of small legs. Writhing bristles twitch on its back, and its shadow seems strangely mobile.

TENEBROUS WORM	CR 8

XP 4,800

N Medium outsider (extraplanar)

Init +7; **Senses** darkvision 60 ft.; Perception +14

DEFENSE

AC 21, touch 13, flat-footed 18 (+3 Dex, +8 natural)

hp 105 (10d10+50)

Fort +14, **Ref** +6, **Will** +8

Defensive Abilities bristles; **Immune** acid

OFFENSE

Speed 20 ft.

Melee bite +14 (2d6+4 plus 6d6 acid)

Special Attacks poison

STATISTICS

Str 17, **Dex** 16, **Con** 20, **Int** 2, **Wis** 13, **Cha** 7

Base Atk +10; **CMB** +13; **CMD** 26 (can't be tripped)

Feats Critical Focus, Great Fortitude, Improved Initiative, Iron Will, Weapon Focus (bite)

Skills Perception +14 Stealth +16

ECOLOGY

Environment any land (Plane of Shadow)

Organization solitary, pair, or swarm (3–6)

Treasure none

SPECIAL ABILITIES

Acid (Su) The acid of a tenebrous worm's bite affects only organic matter—as it dissolves creatures, it converts their flesh to shadow that swiftly fades away, leaving raw, jagged wounds behind. In dim light, acid damage dealt by a tenebrous worm's bite increases to 8d6 points of damage, while in darkness or bright light, the acid damage is reduced to 4d6.

Bristles (Su) Long bristles of shadowstuff extend from between the tenebrous worm's armor plates. These bristles react swiftly to attacks, stabbing at any creature that attempts to harm the worm. Each time a creature attacks a tenebrous worm, it must make a DC 18 Reflex save to avoid being punctured by several bristles. Each time a creature is punctured by these bristles, it takes 1d4 points of piercing damage and is exposed to the tenebrous worm's poison. A creature that grapples a tenebrous worm is automatically hurt by these bristles. The save DC to avoid the bristles is Dexterity-based.

Poison (Su) Bristles—injury; *save* Fort DC 20, *frequency* 1/round for 6 rounds, *effect* paralysis for 1d4 rounds plus 1d2 Con (the duration of the paralysis is cumulative with each failed save), *cure* 2 consecutive saves. The save DC is Constitution-based.

The caterpillar-like tenebrous worm is a voracious predator that hungers for mortal flesh. The tenebrous worm is the larval stage of the gloomwing (see page 133)—but in a strange reversal, these younger creatures are more dangerous than the adults they grow into. A native of the Plane of Shadow, a tenebrous worm hatches from the body of an unfortunate creature that has been implanted with an egg by a gloomwing. The tenebrous worm is fully grown upon hatching, and immediately begins to scour its environs for flesh to consume.

Although the tenebrous worm tends to be relatively pale-colored, its internal organs seethe and roil with shadowy energies and dark fluids. As the creature feeds, these shadowy innards begin to grow out of its body, forming strange bristle-like filaments of semisolid shadowstuff not only capable of piercing the flesh of those who would attack the worm, but also possessing a deadly paralytic poison. Additional shadowy fluids constantly seep from the worm's mandibles—when it bites prey, these fluids melt flesh into shadows that the creature can then consume. When a tenebrous worm feeds on enough of this shadowy flesh, the creature seeks out a secluded, shady area (typically just within a cave entrance or in a ruined building) and spins a shadowy cocoon around itself. A tenebrous worm's cocoon exudes the effects of a *darkness* spell (CL 8th), muting the surrounding light. After a period of several days, the cocoon tears open and a fully grown gloomwing emerges, ready to seek a host for its eggs.

TENTAMORT

This dark blue creature has a conical body covered in angry red eyes and numerous tentacles, two of which are longer than the rest.

TENTAMORT	CR 4

XP 1,200

N Medium aberration

Init +5; **Senses** all-around vision, blindsense 30 ft., darkvision 60 ft.; Perception +11

DEFENSE

AC 17, touch 11, flat-footed 16
(+1 Dex, +6 natural)

hp 39 (6d8+12)

Fort +4,

Ref +5,

Will +7

OFFENSE

Speed 20 ft., climb 20 ft.

Melee sting +6 (1d6+2 plus poison), tentacle +2 (1d6+1 plus grab)

Space 5 ft.; **Reach** 10 ft.

Special Attacks constrict (1d6+1)

STATISTICS

Str 15, **Dex** 13, **Con** 14, **Int** 1, **Wis** 14, **Cha** 6

Base Atk +4; **CMB** +6 (+10 grapple); **CMD** 17
(can't be tripped)

Feats Improved Initiative, Lightning Reflexes, Weapon Focus (tentacle)

Skills Climb +10, Perception +11

ECOLOGY

Environment any marshes or underground

Organization solitary, pair, or brood (3–6)

Treasure incidental

SPECIAL ABILITIES

Poison (Ex) Sting—injury; *save* Fort DC 15; *frequency* 2 rounds; *effect* 1d4 Con plus nausea; *cure* 1 save.

Tentamorts are eerie ambush predators, preferring to let prey come to them rather than seeking food out, and relying on their excellent senses to warn them of approaching meals. A tentamort possesses several tentacles, most of which are used for locomotion but two of which have evolved for singular purposes in securing food. One of these longer tentacles is covered with tiny, sticky nodules and is capable of constricting prey, while the other ends in a long, thin stinger. The tentamort's method of attack is to grab its prey with its constricting tentacle and sting the grappled target with the other. Tentamort poison is particularly horrific, as it swiftly liquefies the creature's internal organs into a rancid slurry the monster can then drink with the same stinger, siphoning out the

fluid with foul sucking sounds. Larger creatures often require multiple stings (and multiple failed saving throws against the venom) before they can be fully absorbed by a tentamort. Tentamorts are almost mindless, possessing just enough intellect to make crude animal judgments about peril and food. Once a tentamort has grabbed prey, it tends to focus entirely on that creature, ignoring attacks upon it from other sources as long as its current victim remains a source of nutrition. After a tentamort finishes consuming a creature, all that typically remains are the bones and skin.

A well-fed tentamort uses the hollow corpse of its meal as a sort of incubator for its eggs, injecting the body with a caviar-like mass of black eggs that mature in the rotting carcass for several weeks until a dozen or so hand-sized tentamorts hatch and crawl out of their host's orifices. Depending upon the availability of other prey, anywhere from one to six of these may survive, feeding on rats and Tiny vermin, until they eventually grow to adulthood. Tentamort young look like dark blue starfish with a single red eye in the center—they do not possess their longer, specialized tentacles until they mature. A young tentamort often attaches itself to a larger predator, clinging to it much the same way a remora clings to a shark, dropping off to feed innocuously on its host's kills while the creature sleeps.

Some tentamorts grow much larger than their human-sized kin. Known as greater tentamorts, these ogre-sized creatures have at least 10 Hit Dice and are Large sized. Their two specialized tentacles grow to 20 feet long, providing the creature with greater reach than a Large monster normally possesses. Greater tentamorts are never found in groups, for these creatures can only achieve such monstrous size through cannibalism, as if there were some key nutrient in another tentamort's body that allows them to exceed their typical physical limitations. Some of these creatures have mutations giving them two tentacles and two stingers. Yet the most disturbing quality possessed by these monsters is their unexpected intellect—greater tentamorts are often as intelligent as humans, or more so. They cannot speak, but possess an eerie form of telepathy that works only upon creatures they are in physical contact with—a feature they often use to "chat" with their food as they eat.

THOQQUA

This creature's thick, serpentine body is protected by dense, horny plates. A visible haze of heat rises from its red-hot scales.

THOQQUA	CR 2

XP 600

N Medium outsider (earth, elemental, extraplanar, fire)
Init +1; **Senses** darkvision 60 ft., tremorsense 60 ft.; Perception +10
Aura molten body

DEFENSE

AC 15, touch 11, flat-footed 14 (+1 Dex, +4 natural)
hp 22 (3d10+6)
Fort +5, **Ref** +4, **Will** +2
Immune fire, elemental traits
Weaknesses vulnerable to cold

OFFENSE

Speed 30 ft., burrow 20 ft.
Melee slam +4 (1d6+1 plus burn)
Special Attacks burn (1d6, DC 13)

STATISTICS

Str 13, **Dex** 13, **Con** 15, **Int** 6, **Wis** 12, **Cha** 10
Base Atk +3; **CMB** +4; **CMD** 15 (can't be tripped)
Feats Nimble Moves, Skill Focus (Perception)
Skills Acrobatics +7, Perception +10, Stealth +7, Survival +7
Languages Ignan (cannot speak)

ECOLOGY

Environment any land (Plane of Fire)
Organization solitary or pair
Treasure none

SPECIAL ABILITIES

Molten Body (Su) A thoqqua's body is hot

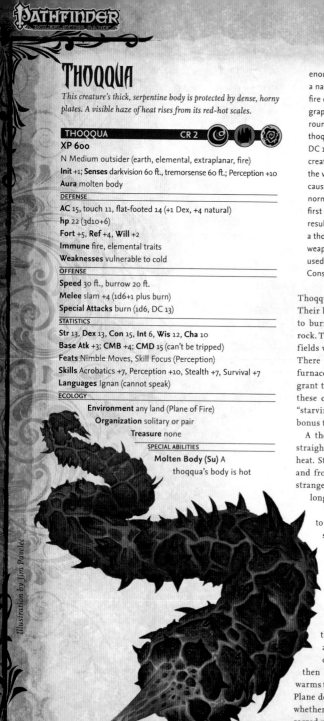

enough to melt stone. Anyone striking a thoqqua with a natural weapon or unarmed strike takes 1d6 points of fire damage. A creature that grapples a thoqqua or is grappled by one takes 3d6 points of fire damage each round the grapple persists. A creature that strikes a thoqqua with a manufactured weapon can attempt a DC 13 Reflex save to pull the weapon away from the creature's molten body quickly enough to avoid having the weapon take 1d6 points of fire damage—damage caused to a weapon in this manner is not halved as is normal for damage caused to items, and ignores the first 5 points of hardness possessed by the item. As a result, most metal weapons can generally safely strike a thoqqua without taking much damage, but wooden weapons have a significant chance of burning away if used against one of these creatures. The save DC is Constitution-based.

Thoqquas are cantankerous creatures of fire and slag. Their bodies generate incredible heat that allows them to burrow or melt through most surfaces, even solid rock. Thoqquas are native to the vast ash deserts and lava fields where the Plane of Fire abuts the Plane of Earth. There they consume ore and minerals, which their furnace-like bodies then smelt into armor plates that grant the creatures their natural armor—as outsiders, these creatures have no need to eat to survive, but a "starving" thoqqua generally has a lower natural armor bonus than a healthy one.

A thoqqua's frontmost body segment tapers into a straight, horn-like beak that glows with a blistering heat. Steam and smoke constantly hiss from its joints, and from a distance a thoqqua can be mistaken for a strange metallic construct. Adult thoqquas are 5 feet long and weigh 200 pounds.

Their fiery tempers make thoqquas dangerous to approach—they attack without thinking when startled or frustrated. If a thoqqua does not immediately chase away humanoids within its territory, then it gradually comes to view that settlement as property, and even guards it.

Mephits seem to understand the thoqqua thought process, and occasionally broker deals with the simple-minded worms. The mephits say that the mountain-sized ancestors of modern thoqquas were servants of the elemental lords, and dug the first volcanoes in the young worlds of the Material Plane. These progenitor worms then retired to the worlds' cores, where their heat warms the planets even today. Thoqquas on the Material Plane do indeed congregate around volcanoes—though whether this is to protect a mineral-rich food site or a sacred place is unknown.

THRASFYR

Neither quite bear nor bull nor serpent, this immense, six-legged
creature is bound in chains and covered with scintillating red scales.

THRASFYR	CR 17

XP 102,400

CE Huge magical beast (fire)

Init +5; **Senses** darkvision 120 ft., low-light vision, *see invisibility*; Perception +28

DEFENSE

AC 32, touch 9, flat-footed 31 (+1 Dex, +23 natural, –2 size)

hp 279 (18d10+180); regeneration 15 (acid or cold)

Fort +21, **Ref** +14, **Will** +15

DR 15/cold iron and slashing; **Immune** fire, sonic; **Resist** electricity 30; **SR** 28

Weaknesses vulnerable to cold

OFFENSE

Speed 50 ft., climb 50 ft.

Melee 2 bites +26 (2d6+10), 4 claws +26 (1d8+10), gore +26 (2d6+10)

Space 15 ft.; **Reach** 15 ft.

Special Attacks breath weapon (80-foot cone, 20d8 fire damage, Reflex DC 29 half, usable once every 1d4 rounds), entangling chains, powerful charge (gore, 4d8+24)

Spell-Like Abilities (CL 18th; concentration +23)

Constant—*air walk, see invisibility*

1/day—*greater teleport* (self plus 50 lbs. of objects only, and only to a master's side)

STATISTICS

Str 30, **Dex** 13, **Con** 31, **Int** 5, **Wis** 24, **Cha** 20

Base Atk +18; **CMB** +30; **CMD** 41 (49 vs. trip)

Feats Critical Focus, Greater Vital Strike, Improved Initiative, Improved Vital Strike, Iron Will, Lightning Reflexes, Power Attack, Staggering Critical, Vital Strike

Skills Climb +18, Perception +28

Languages Aklo, Sylvan

SQ master's bond, planar acclimation

ECOLOGY

Environment any

Organization solitary

Treasure double

SPECIAL ABILITIES

Entangling Chains (Su) A thrasfyr can control the six chains that hang from its body as if they were its own limbs. As a standard action, it can cause these chains to snake outward to a radius of 30 feet. All creatures in this area take 10d6 points of slashing damage and become entangled—a DC 20 Reflex save halves the damage and negates the entangled condition. An entangled creature can escape with a DC 20 Reflex save or a DC 30 Escape Artist check made as a full-round action. The chains can also be sundered (hardness 10, hp 20, Break DC 28). The thrasfyr creates these chains from its own body—destroyed chains regrow in 24 hours. The save DC is Dexterity-based.

Master's Bond (Su) A thrasfyr can form a bond with a willing creature by touching that creature. This allows the thrasfyr to communicate telepathically with the bonded creature with no range restriction (provided the thrasfyr and its master are on the same plane). Both thrasfyr and master can sense the other's condition as if both were under the effect of a *status* spell. A thrasfyr can maintain a bond with only one master at a time.

Planar Acclimation (Ex) A thrasfyr is always considered to be on its home plane, regardless of what plane it finds itself upon. It never gains the extraplanar subtype.

The legendary thrasfyr is one of the Tane—a group of powerful monsters created by godlike beings from the primal world of the fey. A thrasfyr prefers to dwell in rugged hilly regions, where it spends most of its time slumbering and dreaming—it is said that all thrasfyrs dream of themselves as graceful and beautiful fey, for legends say that the first thrasfyrs were created from such creatures as a form of punishment.

Illustration by Kieran Yanner

THUNDERBIRD

This enormous bird has feathers the color of a stormy sky, a resemblance enhanced by the lightning that dances over its body.

THUNDERBIRD	CR 11

XP 12,800

N Gargantuan magical beast

Init +7; **Senses** darkvision 60 ft., low-light vision, stormsight; Perception +20

Aura storm aura (100 ft.)

DEFENSE

AC 25, touch 10, flat-footed 21 (+3 Dex, +1 dodge, +15 natural, −4 size)

hp 147 (14d10+70)

Fort +14, **Ref** +12, **Will** +9

Immune electricity, sonic

OFFENSE

Speed 30 ft., fly 120 ft. (good)

Melee 2 claws +18 (2d6+8/19–20 plus grab), bite +18 (2d8+8/19–20)

Ranged thunderbolt +13 ranged touch (6d6 electricity and 6d6 sonic)

Space 20 ft.; **Reach** 20 ft.

Spell-Like Abilities (CL 11th; concentration +12)

At will—*control weather*

STATISTICS

Str 26, **Dex** 17, **Con** 21, **Int** 12, **Wis** 16, **Cha** 13

Base Atk +14; **CMB** +26 (+30 grapple); **CMD** 40

Feats Critical Focus, Dodge, Improved Critical (bite), Improved Critical (claw), Improved Initiative, Iron Will, Power Attack

Skills Acrobatics +13, Fly +11, Perception +20, Perform (sing) +8, Sense Motive +10

Languages Auran

ECOLOGY

Environment any hills or mountains

Organization solitary

Treasure none

SPECIAL ABILITIES

Thunderbolt (Su) A thunderbird can fire a ray of thunder and lightning from its outspread wings as a standard action. This attack has a range of 200 feet with no range increment, and requires a ranged touch attack to hit. A creature critically hit by a thunderbolt is stunned and deafened for 1 round if it fails a DC 22 Fortitude save. The save DC is Constitution-based.

Storm Aura (Su) A thunderbird is surrounded by a 100-foot-radius spread of severe winds that blow out from the center, dissipating swiftly at the limit of the aura's range. In this area, ranged weapons (but not siege weapons) take a −4 penalty on attack rolls, Fly checks are made at a −4 penalty, and exposed flames are extinguished. Small creatures must make a DC 10 Strength check (if on the ground) or a DC 20 Fly check to move toward the thunderbird, while Tiny or smaller creatures can be knocked backward (1d4 × 10 feet if they are on the ground and fail a DC 15 Strength check, or 2d6 × 10 feet if they are flying and fail a DC 25 Fly check). Creatures on the ground that are pushed back take 1d4 points of nonlethal damage per 10 feet, and flying creatures that are pushed back take 2d6 points of nonlethal damage regardless of the distance they are pushed. In addition, once every 1d4 rounds, a bolt of lightning strikes a random creature (other than the thunderbird) within the area of its storm aura. This bolt of lightning deals 12d6 points of electricity damage (DC 22 Reflex halves). The save DC for the lightning bolt is Constitution-based, while those for resisting the wind effects are fixed.

Stormsight (Ex) A thunderbird ignores all vision penalties and concealment from weather effects, including those created by *fog cloud*, *obscuring mist*, and similar spells.

Thunderbirds bring the storm on their wings. In times of drought, they are welcomed with joy and celebration. In other times, they are placated with gifts in hopes that they might leave quickly before flooding begins. When angered, thunderbirds can call down hurricanes and lay waste to entire villages, so in regions where these birds dwell, many villages maintain extensive rituals designed to appease and honor the local thunderbirds.

Thunderbirds nest near the base of waterfalls, where the constant thrum of crashing water prepares the hatchlings for a life at the heart of a storm. Once the chicks have hatched, their parents carry the offspring to nests at the top of mountains, where the young are struck by their first bolts of lightning and learn the mysteries of the storm.

Tick, Giant

This dog-sized tick has a grotesquely bulbous body and a thin head equipped with hooked mandibles.

GIANT TICK	CR 1

XP 400

N Small vermin

Init +0; **Senses** darkvision 60 ft., scent; Perception +0

DEFENSE

AC 16, touch 11, flat-footed 16 (+5 natural, +1 size)

hp 13 (2d8+4)

Fort +5, **Ref** +0, **Will** +0

Immune mind-affecting effects

OFFENSE

Speed 20 ft., climb 20 ft.

Melee bite +2 (1d4 plus grab, attach, and disease)

Special Attacks blood drain (1 Constitution)

STATISTICS

Str 11, **Dex** 10, **Con** 15, **Int** —, **Wis** 11, **Cha** 2

Base Atk +1; **CMB** +0 (+8 grapple); **CMD** 10 (22 vs. trip)

Skills Climb +8, Stealth +8; **Racial Modifiers** +4 Stealth

ECOLOGY

Environment temperate forests

Organization solitary, pair, cluster (3–6), or nest (7–12)

Treasure none

SPECIAL ABILITIES

Grab (Ex) A giant tick can grab targets of any size, and has a +8 racial bonus on grapple checks rather than the normal +4 bonus most creatures with grab possess.

Disease (Ex) Red ache: Bite—injury; *save* Fort DC 13; *onset* 1d3 days; *frequency* 1/day; *effect* 1d6 Str damage; *cure* 2 consecutive saves. The DC is Constitution-based.

In areas where large creatures like megafauna or dinosaurs dwell, the giant tick behaves much like its smaller kin—it lies in wait in the undergrowth, and when a suitable host passes by, it drops onto the body to feed. In other areas, these vermin are much more aggressive, and actively hunt smaller prey like dogs, livestock, or even humanoids. A giant tick drains blood quickly, but once it has caused 6 points of Constitution damage, it drops off, sated, to crawl away to digest. A giant tick is 3 feet long and weighs 50 pounds.

Tick Swarm

The rasping legs of this hideous, shining carpet of fist-sized ticks rattle ominously as the swarm skitters forward.

TICK SWARM	CR 9

XP 6,400

N Fine vermin (swarm)

Init +2; **Senses** darkvision 60 ft., scent; Perception +0

DEFENSE

AC 23, touch 20, flat-footed 21 (+2 Dex, +3 natural, +8 size)

hp 120 (16d8+48)

Fort +13, **Ref** +7, **Will** +5

Defensive Abilities swarm traits

Immune mind-affecting effects, weapon damage

OFFENSE

Speed 30 ft., climb 30 ft.

Melee swarm (4d6 plus disease, distraction, and blood drain)

Special Attacks blood drain (1d4 Con), cling, distraction (DC 21)

STATISTICS

Str 1, **Dex** 14, **Con** 16, **Int** —, **Wis** 11, **Cha** 1

Base Atk +12; **CMB** —; **CMD** —

Skills Climb +10; **Racial Modifiers** uses Dex on Climb checks

ECOLOGY

Environment temperate forests

Organization solitary, pair, or colony (3–6)

Treasure none

SPECIAL ABILITIES

Cling (Ex) If a creature leaves a tick swarm's square, the swarm takes 1d6 points of damage to reflect the loss of its numbers as several ticks cling to the victim. A creature with ticks clinging to it takes swarm damage at the end of its turn each round. As a full round action, the creature can remove the ticks with a DC 20 Reflex save. At least 10 points of damage from any area effect destroys all clinging ticks. The save DC is Dexterity-based.

Disease (Ex) Bubonic Plague: Bite—injury; *save* Fort DC 21; *onset* 1 day; *frequency* 1/day; *effect* 1d4 Con damage, 1 Cha damage, fatigue; *cure* 2 consecutive saves. The DC is Con-based.

Tick swarms are merciless blights, able to quickly reduce the larger animal life of a region they infest to blood-drained, diseased husks.

Illustration by Dean Spencer

TITAN, ELYSIAN

This titanic humanoid wears gilt-edged armor of ancient make and carries an immense hammer made of gleaming metal.

TITAN, ELYSIAN	CR 21	

XP 409,600

CG Colossal outsider (chaotic, extraplanar, good)

Init +7; **Senses** darkvision 120 ft., *true seeing*; Perception +33

DEFENSE

AC 37, touch 5, flat-footed 34 (+9 armor, +3 Dex, +23 natural, −8 size)

hp 409 (21d10+294); regeneration 15 (evil)

Fort +21, **Ref** +15, **Will** +21; +8 resistance vs. mind-affecting

DR 15/evil; **Immune** aging, death effects, disease; **SR** 32

OFFENSE

Speed 60 ft. (40 ft. in armor)

Melee maul of the titans +33/+28/+23/+18 (6d8+28/17–20) or 2 slams +30 (2d8+17)

Space 30 ft.; **Reach** 30 ft.

Special Attacks trample (2d8+25, DC 37)

Spell-Like Abilities (CL 20th; concentration +27)

Constant—*air walk, mind blank, true seeing*

At will—*bestow curse* (DC 21), *break enchantment, divination, greater dispel magic, sending*

3/day—*greater scrying* (DC 24), *heal, mass suggestion* (DC 23)

1/day—*freedom, greater planar ally, meteor swarm* (DC 26)

STATISTICS

Str 45, **Dex** 16, **Con** 39, **Int** 21, **Wis** 28, **Cha** 24

Base Atk +21; **CMB** +46; **CMD** 59

Feats Awesome Blow, Critical Focus, Greater Sunder, Greater Vital Strike, Improved Bull Rush, Improved Initiative, Improved Sunder, Improved Vital Strike, Power Attack, Staggering Critical, Vital Strike

Skills Bluff +31, Craft (any) +29, Diplomacy +31, Intimidate +31, Knowledge (engineering) +26, Knowledge (planes) +29, Perception +33, Perform (any) +28, Sense Motive +33, Spellcraft +29, Use Magic Device +31

Languages Abyssal, Celestial, Common; telepathy 300 ft.

SQ change shape (any humanoid; *alter self*)

ECOLOGY

Environment any land (Elysium)

Organization solitary, pair, or crusade (3–6)

Treasure standard (+3 *breastplate, maul of the titans*, other treasure)

A race that was old when the world was young, titans are very near to the divine. This nearness inspired bitterness in the hearts of the mightiest titans, and when they grew jealous of the adulation the gods received from mortals, they began a crusade to destroy mortal life. As this war began, the Elysian titans turned against their kin and, by sacrificing some of their power to the gods, convinced the deities to banish their arrogant kin to the Abyss.

Lone Elysian titans often wander the planes, seeking enlightenment or exploring ancient places of power. Others still have the crusading impulse of the ancient war and can be found manipulating events from behind the scenes, training aspiring heroes, counseling kings, marshaling armies to overthrow tyranny, and inspiring mortals to become legends. A titan does not age—unless slain by violence, a titan is immortal.

One in every dozen Elysian titans is a prophet—a titan who manifests the goodwill of the gods and possesses the spellcasting power of a 20th-level cleric. These titans do not gain access to domains or any other cleric class abilities. They are CR 22 creatures.

Elysian titans are 70 feet tall and weigh 20 tons.

TITAN, THANATOTIC

This titanic, armored figure wields an immense axe. Its hands end in claws, and its voice thunders with ruinous power.

TITAN, THANATOTIC	CR 22

XP 614,400

CE Colossal outsider (chaotic, evil, extraplanar)

Init +4; **Senses** darkvision 120 ft., *true seeing*; Perception +31

DEFENSE

AC 38, touch 2, flat-footed 38 (+12 armor, +24 natural, −8 size)

hp 471 (23d10+345)

Fort +22, **Ref** +15, **Will** +20; +8 resistance vs. mind-affecting

DR 15/lawful and epic; **Immune** aging, death effects, disease; **SR** 33

OFFENSE

Speed 60 ft. (40 ft. in armor)

Melee +3 *unholy battleaxe* +37/+32/+27/+22 (6d6+22/19–20/×3), claw +29 (2d8+9) or

2 claws +34 (2d8+19)

Ranged rock +16/+11/+6/+1 (4d6+28)

Space 30 ft.; **Reach** 30 ft.

Special Attacks godslayer, rock-throwing (100 ft.), trample (2d8+28, DC 40)

Spell-Like Abilities (CL 20th; concentration +27)

Constant—*air walk, mind blank, spell turning, true seeing*

At will—*bestow curse* (DC 21), *break enchantment, divination, greater dispel magic, sending*

3/day—*disintegrate* (DC 23), *greater scrying* (DC 24), *heal, mass suggestion* (DC 23)

1/day—*greater planar ally, imprisonment* (DC 26), *meteor swarm* (DC 26), *true resurrection*

STATISTICS

Str 49, **Dex** 10, **Con** 41, **Int** 27, **Wis** 20, **Cha** 24

Base Atk +23; **CMB** +50; **CMD** 60

Feats Awesome Blow, Bleeding Critical, Critical Focus, Greater Vital Strike, Improved Bull Rush, Improved Critical (battleaxe), Improved Initiative, Improved Vital Strike, Iron Will, Lightning Reflexes, Power Attack, Vital Strike

Skills Bluff +33, Craft (any one) +34, Diplomacy +30, Intimidate +30, Knowledge (arcana, history, and planes) +34, Knowledge (religion) +31, Perception +31, Perform (any one) +30 , Sense Motive +31, Spellcraft +34, Stealth +5, Use Magic Device +33

Languages Abyssal, Celestial, Common; telepathy 300 ft.

SQ change shape (any humanoid, *alter self*)

ECOLOGY

Environment any (Abyss)

Organization solitary, pair, or war band (3–6)

Treasure standard (+3 *full plate*, +3 *unholy battleaxe*, other treasure)

SPECIAL ABILITIES

Godslayer (Su) When a thanatotic titan damages a creature capable of casting divine spells, that creature must make a DC 28 Will save or be unable to cast any divine spells for 1d4 rounds and be shaken. If the save is successful, the creature struck is merely shaken for 1 round. A thanatotic titan's attacks are treated as epic and evil for the purposes of overcoming damage reduction. The save DC is Charisma-based.

Some believe that the titans were the first children of the gods—if this myth is true, then the fact that they waged war upon the gods becomes even more tragic. After they were betrayed to the gods by their own kin, the Thanatotic titans were banished into the Abyss. Today, they seethe with jealousy that their Elysian kin are allowed to wander the planes at will, while they can leave their Abyssal realm only by stealth. Now, these powerful outsiders spend much of their time brooding, fighting among themselves, and waging war for control of Abyssal realms against the legions of various demon lords.

Thanatotic titans see themselves as the true icons worthy of worship. Some work to found personal cults among mortals, while others simply wage unending crusades against the minions of the gods.

TOAD, GIANT

Stubby warts dot the skin of this horse-sized brown toad. Its throat bulges and ripples as though about to croak.

GIANT TOAD	CR 2

XP 600
N Large animal
Init +1; **Senses** low-light vision, scent; Perception +8

DEFENSE
AC 14, touch 10, flat-footed 13 (+1 Dex, +4 natural, −1 size)
hp 22 (3d8+9)
Fort +6, **Ref** +6, **Will** +0
Defensive Abilities poison skin

OFFENSE
Speed 30 ft., swim 15 ft.
Melee bite +5 (1d6+6 plus grab)
Space 10 ft.; **Reach** 10 ft.
Special Attacks swallow whole (1d4 bludgeoning, AC 12, 2 hp)

STATISTICS
Str 19, **Dex** 13, **Con** 16, **Int** 1, **Wis** 8, **Cha** 6
Base Atk +2; **CMB** +7 (+11 grapple); **CMD** 18 (22 vs. trip)
Feats Lightning Reflexes, Skill Focus (Perception)
Skills Acrobatics +5 (+9 jump), Perception +8, Stealth +5, Swim +12;
   Racial Modifiers +4 Acrobatics (+8 jump), +4 Stealth

ECOLOGY
Environment temperate forests, plains, or swamps
Organization solitary, pair, or knot (3–12)
Treasure none

SPECIAL ABILITIES
Poison Skin (Ex) A creature that strikes a giant toad with an unarmed strike or natural weapon exposes itself to the toad's poisonous skin.
   Skin—contact; *save* Fort DC 14; *frequency* 1/round for 4 rounds; *effect* 1d2 Wisdom damage; *cure* 1 save.

Most giant toads live in dryer areas after maturing, returning to the water only to mate and give birth.
   Giant toad companions are identical to giant frog companions (*Pathfinder RPG Bestiary* 135), save that they lack the frog's tongue and pull abilities. Instead, they gain the poison skin ability at 4th level.

TOAD, GLACIER

This improbably large toad has pale blue flesh and a body covered with jagged, icy growths.

GLACIER TOAD	CR 6

XP 2,400
N Large magical beast (cold)
Init +1; **Senses** low-light vision, scent; Perception +11
Aura bitter cold (20 ft.)

DEFENSE
AC 19, touch 10, flat-footed 18 (+1 Dex, +9 natural, −1 size)
hp 73 (7d10+35)
Fort +10, **Ref** +8, **Will** +3
Immune cold
Weaknesses vulnerable to fire

OFFENSE
Speed 30 ft., swim 15 ft.
Melee bite +13 (2d6+9 plus 1d6 cold and grab)
Space 10 ft.; **Reach** 10 ft.
Special Attacks swallow whole (1d4 bludgeoning and 1d6 cold, AC 14, 7 hp)

STATISTICS
Str 23, **Dex** 13, **Con** 20, **Int** 5, **Wis** 12, **Cha** 6
Base Atk +7; **CMB** +14 (+18 grapple); **CMD** 25 (29 vs. trip)
Feats Lightning Reflexes, Power Attack, Skill Focus (Perception), Weapon Focus (bite)
Skills Acrobatics +9 (+13 jumping), Perception +11, Stealth +6 (+14 in snow), Swim +14; **Racial Modifiers** +4 Acrobatics, (+8 jumping), +4 Stealth (+12 in snow)
Languages Aklo

ECOLOGY
Environment cold hills or glaciers
Organization solitary, pair, or knot (3–12)
Treasure standard

SPECIAL ABILITIES
Bitter Cold (Su) All creatures within 20 feet of a glacier toad take 1d6 points of cold damage each round on the toad's turn.

Glacier toads are strange, magical cousins of the more common giant toads. None can say for certain whether they were bred, or evolved from exposure to elemental energies. Glacier toads have no practical use for most treasure, but have a fondness for shiny objects like gems and glowing items.

TOTENMASKE

This spindly, skeletal humanoid has moldy green flesh, long talons for hands, and a head that seems to be mostly mouth.

TOTENMASKE	CR 7

XP 3,200

NE Medium undead (shapechanger)

Init +10; **Senses** darkvision 60 ft.; Perception +15

DEFENSE

AC 20, touch 16, flat-footed 14 (+6 Dex, +4 natural)

hp 85 (10d8+40)

Fort +7, **Ref** +9, **Will** +9

Immune undead traits; **Resist** cold 20

OFFENSE

Speed 50 ft.

Melee bite +13 (1d8+4 plus 1d4 Cha drain), 2 claws +13 (1d6+4)

Special Attacks fleshdrink, shape flesh

STATISTICS

Str 18, **Dex** 23, **Con** —, **Int** 16, **Wis** 15, **Cha** 19

Base Atk +7; **CMB** +11; **CMD** 27

Feats Ability Focus (Charisma drain), Combat Expertise, Combat Reflexes, Improved Initiative, Weapon Finesse

Skills Acrobatics +16 (+24 jump), Bluff +14, Diplomacy +14, Disguise +17, Perception +15, Sense Motive +15, Stealth +19

Languages Abyssal, Celestial, Common, Infernal

SQ change shape (the previous humanoid it successfully used its fleshdrink ability on; *alter self*)

ECOLOGY

Environment any land or underground

Organization solitary or pair

Treasure standard

SPECIAL ABILITIES

Charisma Drain (Su) A totenmaske can eat the hopes and dreams of a creature it bites, dealing 1d4 points of Charisma drain unless the victim makes a DC 21 Will save. The save DC is Charisma-based.

Fleshdrink (Su) If a totenmaske hits a single creature with both claw attacks, the hollow claws drain away some of the target's flesh, dealing 1d6 points of Constitution damage and making the victim sickened for 1d4 rounds. A successful DC 19 Fortitude save negates the Constitution damage and reduces the sickened condition duration to 1 round. The save DC is Charisma-based.

Shape Flesh (Su) By spending 1 minute in contact with a helpless creature, a totenmaske can reshape the target's face, causing flesh to cover vital features. The target may attempt a DC 19 Fortitude save to resist. Changes are permanent, but can be reversed with *heal*, *restoration*, or *regeneration*, or by surgically opening the sealed flesh with a DC 15 Heal check that takes 1d3 rounds and deals 1d4 points of damage even if the check is not successful. A totenmaske can use this ability on one of four different features per use: ears (target becomes deaf), eyes (target becomes blind), mouth (target cannot speak or eat), or nose (target cannot smell). Multiple uses can have increasingly serious effects (such as sealing the mouth and nose, which causes suffocation). The save DC is Charisma-based.

Consumed by the same lusts and excesses that led them in life, the souls of some sinners rise as totenmaskes, drinking the flesh and memories of living creatures and even stepping into their lives to once more pursue their base desires. Incapable of resuming their sinful pursuits in their natural form, totenmaskes often keep their victims alive for as long as possible, renewing their stolen identities regularly in order to continue indulging in pleasures of the flesh.

A totenmaske can be created from the corpse of a sinful mortal by a cleric of at least 18th level using the *create greater undead* spell.

A totenmaske is 6 feet tall and weighs 140 pounds.

Illustration by John Gravato

269

Triton

This scaly, finned humanoid has an athletic build and blue-green coloration. Its legs end in wide flippers rather than feet.

TRITON	CR 2

XP 600

NG Medium outsider (native, water)

Init +0; **Senses** darkvision 60 ft., low-light vision; Perception +7

DEFENSE

AC 14, touch 10, flat-footed 14 (+4 natural)

hp 19 (3d10+3)

Fort +4, **Ref** +1, **Will** +4

OFFENSE

Speed 5 ft., swim 40 ft.

Melee mwk trident +5 (1d8+1)

Ranged heavy crossbow +3 (1d10/19–20)

Spell-Like Abilities (CL 7th; concentration +7)

1/day—*summon nature's ally II* (Small water elemental or 1d3 dolphins only)

STATISTICS

Str 12, **Dex** 10, **Con** 12, **Int** 13, **Wis** 13, **Cha** 11

Base Atk +3; **CMB** +4; **CMD** 14

Feats Mounted Combat, Ride-By Attack

Skills Craft (any one) +7, Diplomacy +6, Perception +7, Ride +6, Sense Motive +7, Stealth +6, Survival +7, Swim +9

Languages Aquan, Common

ECOLOGY

Environment any oceans

Organization solitary, company (2–5), squad (6–11), or band (12–21 plus 2–16 dolphins)

Treasure standard (masterwork trident, heavy crossbow with 10 bolts, other treasure)

These aquatic outsiders resemble merfolk, except where a merman has a single fish tail, a triton has two scaly, finned legs. They are the watchers of the sea, often using dolphins or other aquatic creatures as mounts, and maintaining a vigil against the evil races below the waves. Originally hailing from the Plane of Water, long ago the triton race migrated to the oceans of the Material Plane, and they are now fully adapted to life there. Their split legs allow them to hobble about slowly on land, but they rarely do so, preferring their natural environment and the greater mobility their forms afford there.

Tritons make their homes on the sea floor, growing coral reefs and sculpting stones into gentle arcs to create living spaces that are beautiful and natural-looking. Many of these sites lie near great thermal vents, providing not only heat but also rich minerals and nutrients for the fish and other creatures tritons eat. Tritons can breathe air or water, but prefer water. While their cities are designed for water-breathers, they usually feature one or two airtight buildings set aside to hold air for landwalking visitors. Triton settlements can be found anywhere from arctic to tropical waters, but most are in temperate locations. They generally avoid the deepest reaches of the ocean, for it is here that creatures like aboleths and krakens rule—creatures that the tritons have long waged war against.

Tritons maintain relationships with other good undersea creatures, but mostly keep to themselves. They aid others in fights against their enemies (primarily krakens and aboleths, but also lesser evils like sahuagin or skum). They typically form strong squadrons of aquatic cavalry trained in coordinated attacks when they go to war. Tritons tend to distrust outsiders, and usually avoid land-dwellers. They sometimes provide aid to air-breathers, even though they often see them as trespassers under the sea; when they do help landwalkers, their price for this is high. Nevertheless, when they witness a landwalker do battle against and vanquish a great evil such as an aboleth, they are quick to cast aside their prejudices and accept the great hero into their societies with open and welcoming arms.

Tritons have silvery skin, hued in tones of aqua blue and kelp green. Older tritons often have barnacles, corals, and seashells crusting the back, chest, and shoulders, worn almost like jewelry as a mark of status among their kind. They have white, blue, or green hair. Tritons' eyes shine blue like sunlight upon a clear sea. A typical triton stands 6 feet in height and weighs 180 pounds. While most exceptional tritons advance by taking class levels (typically as druids, oracles, or rangers), a rare few tritons advance by increasing in size. These Large tritons are great heroes among their kind and have 8 racial Hit Dice or more.

Illustration by Mike Corriero

270

TROLL, ICE

This large creature has light blue-green skin and cold, piercing eyes. Dressed in rough furs, its tusked jaw juts forth in a long underbite.

ICE TROLL	CR 4

XP 1,200

CE Large humanoid (cold, giant)

Init +4; **Senses** darkvision 60 ft., low-light vision; Perception +9

DEFENSE

AC 17, touch 13, flat-footed 13 (+4 Dex, +4 natural, −1 size)

hp 45 (6d8+18); regeneration 5 (acid or fire)

Fort +8, **Ref** +8, **Will** +2

Immune cold

Weaknesses vulnerable to fire

OFFENSE

Speed 30 ft.

Melee battleaxe +7 (2d6+4), bite +2 (1d6+2), claw +2 (1d4+2) or bite +7 (1d6+4), 2 claws +7 (1d4+4)

Space 10 ft.; **Reach** 10 ft.

Special Attacks rend (2 claws, 1d6+6)

STATISTICS

Str 19, **Dex** 18, **Con** 16, **Int** 9, **Wis** 10, **Cha** 7

Base Atk +4; **CMB** +9; **CMD** 23

Feats Intimidating Prowess, Lightning Reflexes, Skill Focus (Perception)

Skills Intimidate +7, Perception +9, Survival +4

Languages Giant

ECOLOGY

Environment cold mountains or underground

Organization solitary or band (3–6)

Treasure standard

Ice trolls are somewhat smaller than normal trolls, but they possess greater intelligence and cunning and are just as voraciously hungry. They display the typical hunched posture of trolls, combined with long arms tipped with sharp claws and the distinctive troll underbite. Like normal trolls, ice trolls possess amazing regenerative powers that enable them to recover from almost any wound. Unlike most trolls, ice trolls often use weapons in battle, but in the heat of combat, they often cast aside weapons in favor of their rending claws. An ice troll stands about 10 feet tall and weighs up to 900 pounds.

Because of their greater intellects, ice trolls sometimes

work as mercenaries, and often serve as soldiers in monstrous armies. They frequently ally with frost giants, and may even be found among northern barbarian tribes, as long as they are well fed and well paid.

Ice trolls enjoy the taste of human flesh, and those not working with humans frequently set traps near civilized areas to catch their favorite prey. They will also raid isolated settlements for food, often bringing captured humans back to their icy lairs, where the unfortunate victims are caged and fattened up before finally being devoured by the voracious trolls.

In combat, ice trolls are more cautious than normal trolls. They do not normally rush headlong into battle, instead focusing on weaker foes or those bearing fire. They do not hesitate to attack opponents armed with fire, but work together to defeat such enemies before they can bring their dangerous weapons to bear.

Ice troll society is more patriarchal than normal troll society, and while males may form gangs to hunt or raid, most ice trolls live in small family groups comprised of a male, a female, and their offspring.

Illustration by Florian Stitz

TROLL, ROCK

This bulky creature has beady eyes, and rocky skin studded with small crystals. Its jutting underbite holds large, crystalline teeth.

ROCK TROLL	CR 6

XP 2,400

CE Large humanoid (earth, giant)

Init +1; **Senses** darkvision 60 ft., low-light vision, scent; Perception +6

DEFENSE

AC 19, touch 10, flat-footed 18 (+1 Dex, +9 natural, −1 size)

hp 80 (7d8+49); regeneration 5 (acid or sonic)

Fort +12, **Ref** +3, **Will** +3

Weaknesses sunlight petrification

OFFENSE

Speed 30 ft.

Melee bite +11 (1d8+7), 2 claw +12 (1d6+7)

Space 10 ft.; **Reach** 10 ft.

Special Attacks rend (2 claws, 1d6+9)

STATISTICS

Str 25, **Dex** 12, **Con** 24, **Int** 5, **Wis** 9, **Cha** 6

Base Atk +5; **CMB** +13; **CMD** 24

Feats Intimidating Prowess, Iron Will, Power Attack, Weapon Focus (claw)

Skills Climb +11, Intimidate +10, Perception +6

Languages Giant

ECOLOGY

Environment any underground

Organization solitary or gang (2–5)

Treasure standard

SPECIAL ABILITIES

Sunlight Petrification (Ex) A rock troll that is exposed to natural sunlight is staggered and must make a DC 20 Fortitude save each round to resist permanently turning to stone. A *stone to flesh* spell (or similar effect) restores a petrified rock troll, but if it remains exposed to sunlight, it must immediately start making new Fortitude saves to avoid petrification. Spells like *sunray* or *sunburst* that create powerful natural sunlight cannot petrify a rock troll, but the troll is staggered for 1d4 rounds after being exposed to such an effect.

Rock trolls are relatives of normal trolls and ice trolls, but make their lairs far beneath the earth in underground caverns. They rarely venture forth from their subterranean lairs, for they have a weakness unknown in other troll subspecies—the light of the sun turns them to solid stone. Rock trolls have stony skin studded with crystals, but otherwise display typical troll characteristics—hunched posture, long arms, a large underbite, and powerful regenerative abilities. Because of the crystalline nature of their skin, however, rock trolls prove more susceptible to sonic damage than other trolls, but they are able to regenerate even wounds dealt by fire. Rock trolls are larger and stronger than normal trolls, typically standing 15 to 16 feet tall in height, and weighing upward of 1,200 pounds.

Rock trolls are fond of humanoid flesh, but eat whatever food they can get their claws on. Most underground creatures go out of their way to avoid rock trolls, as the ravenous creatures will eat anything that passes through their territory, as long as it is at least marginally edible. Rock trolls also occasionally eat rocks and minerals, though such fare seems to do little to soothe their voracious hungers. Instead, these minerals supplement the trolls' diet, strengthening their skin, teeth, and claws. Deposits of certain crystals seem especially tasty to rock trolls, and a rock troll who finds such a collection will often gorge himself on the crystalline delicacies.

TURTLE, SNAPPING

A thick shell encases this reptile's body, from which only its tail, its feet, and a head fitted with powerful jaws emerge.

SNAPPING TURTLE	CR 1/3	

XP 135

N Tiny animal

Init −1; **Senses** low-light vision, scent; Perception +5

DEFENSE

AC 12, touch 11, flat-footed 12 (−1 Dex, +1 natural, +2 size)

hp 5 (1d8+1)

Fort +3, **Ref** +1, **Will** +1

OFFENSE

Speed 10 ft., swim 20 ft.

Melee bite +1 (1d3−3)

Space 2-1/2 ft.; **Reach** 0 ft.

STATISTICS

Str 4, **Dex** 8, **Con** 13, **Int** 1, **Wis** 13, **Cha** 6

Base Atk +0; **CMB** −3; **CMD** 4 (8 vs. trip)

Feats Weapon Finesse

Skills Perception +5, Swim +5

SQ hold breath, shell

ECOLOGY

Environment temperate or warm water or shore

Organization solitary or band (2–5)

Treasure none

SPECIAL ABILITIES

Shell (Ex) As a move action, a snapping turtle can pull its extremities and head into its shell. It cannot move or attack as long as it remains in this state, but its armor bonus from natural armor increases by +4 as long as it does.

Snapping turtles are water-dwelling reptiles known for their propensity to bite anyone they deem threatening. Adult snapping turtles are usually about 1-1/2 feet in diameter. A spellcaster who can acquire a familiar can choose a snapping turtle as a familiar. A snapping turtle familiar grants its master a +2 bonus on all Fortitude saves.

GIANT SNAPPING TURTLE COMPANIONS

Starting Statistics: Size Medium; **Speed** 20 ft., swim 20 ft.; **AC** +10 natural; **Attack** bite (1d6); **Ability Scores** Str 8, Dex 10, Con 9, Int 1, Wis 13, Cha 6; **Special Qualities** low-light vision, hold breath, scent.

7th-Level Advancement: Size Large; **AC** +2 natural; **Attack** bite (1d8), **Ability Scores** Str +8, Dex −2, Con +4; **Special Attack** grab.

TURTLE, GIANT SNAPPING

This lumbering turtle is the size of a house; its head features a powerful, razor-sharp beak.

GIANT SNAPPING TURTLE	CR 9	

XP 6,400

N Gargantuan animal

Init +2; **Senses** low-light vision, scent; Perception +21

DEFENSE

AC 23, touch 4, flat-footed 23 (−2 Dex, +19 natural, −4 size)

hp 115 (11d8+66)

Fort +12, **Ref** +5, **Will** +6

OFFENSE

Speed 20 ft., swim 20 ft.

Melee bite +16 (4d6+16 plus grab)

Space 20 ft.; **Reach** 15 ft.

Special Attacks swallow whole (2d8+16 bludgeoning, AC 23, 22 hp)

STATISTICS

Str 32, **Dex** 6, **Con** 21, **Int** 1, **Wis** 13, **Cha** 6

Base Atk +8; **CMB** +23 (+27 grapple); **CMD** 31 (35 vs. trip)

Feats Improved Initiative, Iron Will, Lunge, Skill Focus (Perception), Toughness, Weapon Focus (bite)

Skills Perception +21, Swim +19

SQ armored stomach, hold breath, shell

ECOLOGY

Environment temperate or warm water or shore

Organization solitary or band (2–5)

Treasure none

SPECIAL ABILITIES

Armored Stomach (Ex) A giant snapping turtle's body is difficult to cut through—its stomach gains a +4 bonus to its AC and has double the normal hit points when determining the success of a creature attempting to cut its way free.

Giant snapping turtles typically grow to diameters of about 35 feet and weigh 20,000 pounds.

Illustration by Dean Spencer

Twigjack

This tiny, vaguely humanoid creature seems to be made completely of bundles of sticks wound with thorny vines.

TWIGJACK	CR 3			

XP 800

CE Tiny fey

Init +3; **Senses** darkvision 60 ft., low-light vision; Perception +10

DEFENSE

AC 17, touch 15, flat-footed 14 (+3 Dex, +2 natural, +2 size)

hp 27 (5d6+10)

Fort +3, **Ref** +7, **Will** +6

Weaknesses vulnerable to fire

OFFENSE

Speed 30 ft.

Melee spear +3 (1d4–1/×3) or

2 claws +7 (1d4–1)

Space 2-1/2 ft.; **Reach** 0 ft. (5 ft. with spear)

Special Attacks sneak attack +2d6, splinterspray

STATISTICS

Str 8, **Dex** 16, **Con** 15, **Int** 11, **Wis** 14, **Cha** 13

Base Atk +2; **CMB** +3; **CMD** 12

Feats Agile Maneuvers, Skill Focus (Stealth), Weapon Finesse

Skills Acrobatics +11, Climb +7, Disable Device +8, Knowledge (nature) +8, Perception +10, Stealth +22

Languages Common, Sylvan

SQ bramble jump, woodland stride

ECOLOGY

Environment temperate forests

Organization solitary, pair, or gang (3–8)

Treasure standard

SPECIAL ABILITIES

Bramble Jump (Su) A twigjack can travel short distances between brambles, shrubs, or thickets as if via *dimension door* as part of a move action. The twigjack must begin and end this movement while in an area of at least light undergrowth. The twigjack can travel in this manner up to 60 feet per day. This movement must be used in 10-foot increments and does not provoke attacks of opportunity.

Splinterspray (Ex) A twigjack can eject a barrage of splinters and brambles from its body three times per day as a standard action. This effect creates a 15-foot conical burst of jagged splinters, dealing 4d6 points of piercing damage to all creatures in the area. A DC 14 Reflex saving throw halves this damage. The save DC is Constitution-based.

Deep in old-growth forests, twigjacks spend their time tormenting intruders and wreaking havoc on settlers. Maladjusted protectors of the wood, these malicious fey constantly threaten any attempts to civilize the wild. Twigjacks delight in breaking wagon wheels from expansionists' caravans, snapping hunters' bows, and sabotaging isolated cabins and villages. Although they possess a keen intellect, few creatures, even other fey, can tolerate these twig-born creatures for long. Treants especially find twigjacks bothersome, and resent any suggestion that they are related. Equally, twigjacks resent being considered plants, and are proud of their fey heritage. Twigjacks sometimes go out of their way to impress dryads, an effort that is rebuffed almost every time. But some spriggans, quicklings, and other evil fey associate with twigjacks, and while goblins fear and distrust the creatures, bugbears often bully them into service.

Gnarled sticks bundled by vines and brambles form a twigjack's entire body. Atop its head, a mossy growth not unlike hair sprouts. The creature's eyes appear as vacant dark knotholes, and its mouth is just a canyon of splintered and broken sticks bisecting its face. Leaves and sprigs of new growth randomly sprout from the creature's body.

UNDINE

This blue-haired, blue-skinned man moves with a liquid grace. His ears are fin-like, and his hands and feet are webbed.

UNDINE	CR 1/2	

XP 200

Undine cleric 1

N Medium outsider (native)

Init +2; **Senses** darkvision 60 ft.; Perception +3

DEFENSE

AC 17, touch 12, flat-footed 15 (+5 armor, +2 Dex)

hp 8 (1d8)

Fort +1, **Ref** +2, **Will** +5

Resist cold 5

OFFENSE

Speed 30 ft.; 20 ft. in armor, swim 30 ft.

Melee trident +0 (1d8)

Ranged sling +2 (1d4)

Special Attacks channel positive energy 7/day (DC 12, 1d6)

Spell-Like Abilities (CL 1st; concentration +3)

1/day—*hydraulic push**

Domain Spell-Like Abilities (CL 1st; concentration +4)

6/day—*dazing touch*

6/day—*icicle* (1d6+1 cold damage)

Cleric Spells Prepared (CL 1st; concentration +4)

1st—*bless, charm person*D, *divine favor*

0 (at will)—*create water, guidance, stabilize*

D Domain spell; **Domains** Charm, Water

STATISTICS

Str 11, **Dex** 14, **Con** 8, **Int** 10, **Wis** 17, **Cha** 14

Base Atk +0; **CMB** +0; **CMD** 12

Feats Extra Channel

Skills Diplomacy +6, Knowledge (religion) +4, Swim +4

Languages Aquan, Common

SQ water affinity

ECOLOGY

Environment any land

Organization solitary, pair, or gang (3–5)

Treasure NPC gear (scale mail, trident, other treasure)

SPECIAL ABILITIES

Water Affinity (Ex) Undine sorcerers with the elemental (water) bloodline treat their Charisma score as 2 points higher for all sorcerer spells and class abilities. Undine clerics with the Water domain cast their Water domain powers and spells at +1 caster level.

Undines are humans whose ancestry includes elemental beings of water, such as marids. This connection with the Plane of Water is most noticeably manifested in their coloration, which tends to mimic that of lakes or oceans—all undines have limpid, blue eyes, and their skin and hair can range from pale blue-white to the deep blue or green of the sea.

UNDINE CHARACTERS

Undines are defined by class levels—they do not possess racial Hit Dice. Undines have the following racial traits.

+2 Dexterity, +2 Wisdom, −2 Strength: Undines are both perceptive and agile, but tend to adapt rather than match force with force.

Speed: Undines have a swim speed of 30 feet.

Darkvision: Undines can see in the dark up to 60 feet.

Spell-Like Abilities: *Hydraulic push** 1/day. (Caster level equals the undine's total Hit Dice.)

Energy Resistance: Undines have cold resistance 5.

Water Affinity: See above.

Languages: Undines begin play speaking Common and Aquan. Undines with high Intelligence scores can choose any of the following bonus languages: Auran, Dwarven, Elven, Gnome, Halfling, Ignan, and Terran.

* This spell is detailed in the *Pathfinder RPG Advanced Player's Guide.*

PATHFINDER

URDEFHAN

This fanged humanoid has hideously transparent skin, revealing the vivid colors of internal organs and ivory bones inside its body.

URDEFHAN		CR 3

XP 800

NE Medium outsider (native)

Init +1; **Senses** darkvision 120 ft.; Perception +7

DEFENSE

AC 16, touch 11, flat-footed 15 (+3 armor, +1 Dex, +2 natural)

hp 25 (3d10+9)

Fort +6, **Ref** +4, **Will** +4

Defensive Abilities negative energy affinity; **DR** 5/good or silver; **Immune** death effects (see below), disease, fear, level drain; **Resist** acid 10; **SR** 14

OFFENSE

Speed 30 ft.

Melee rhoka sword +8 (1d8+6/18–20), bite +2 (1d4+2 plus 2 Str) or bite +7 (1d4+4 plus 2 Str)

Ranged composite longbow +4 (1d8+4/×3)

Special Attacks blood drain (1 Con)

Spell-Like Abilities (CL 3rd;
    concentration +5)
    At will—*feather fall*
    3/day—*align weapon*,
       death knell (DC 14),
       ray of enfeeblement
       (DC 13)

STATISTICS

Str 19, **Dex** 12, **Con** 17, **Int** 14,
    Wis 13, **Cha** 14

Base Atk +3; **CMB** +7; **CMD** 18

Feats Iron Will, Weapon Focus (rhoka sword)

Skills Intimidate +8, Knowledge (dungeoneering) +5, Knowledge (planes, religion) +8, Perception +7, Ride +4, Sense Motive +7, Survival +7

Languages Aklo, Undercommon

SQ daemonic pact

ECOLOGY

Environment any land (Abaddon)

Organization solitary, pair, gang (3–12), or cult (13–30 plus 2–6 fighters of 2nd–4th level, 1–4 necromancer wizards of 3rd–6th level, 1 cleric high priest of 5th–9th level, 8–12 skavelings, and 1–3 ceustodaemons)

Treasure NPC gear (studded leather, rhoka sword, composite longbow (+4 Str) with 20 arrows, other treasure)

SPECIAL ABILITIES

Daemonic Pact (Su) Urdefhans are infused with daemonic energy; as an immediate action, an urdefhan can attempt to allow this energy to consume its soul (50% chance of success per attempt). If it succeeds, the urdefhan dies and releases a

5-foot-radius burst of negative energy that deals 2d6 points of damage (DC 14 Reflex half). The save DC is Con-based.

Strength Damage (Su) An urdefhan's bite drains vitality, turning the skin and muscle around the wound transparent and causing 2 points of Strength damage unless the target succeeds on a DC 14 Fortitude save. The flesh remains transparent until the Strength damage is healed, but this does not have any other effects. The save DC is Constitution-based.

Infused with fell energies from Abaddon, urdefhans are an unsightly race dedicated to war. They have developed many strange weapons, but none are more iconic than the two-bladed rhoka sword. Rhoka swords are exotic one-handed melee weapons—all urdefhans are proficient in their use. With such weapons, an urdefhan seeks to inflict as much death as possible upon the world before it perishes, so that its daemonic lords are pleased. Most male urdefhans are sterile—as a result, the women often turn to conjured daemons for mates. The products of such unions are usually typical urdefhans, but sometimes result in half-fiend urdefhans—these monsters usually rise to positions of great power in their violent society.

VAMPIRIC MIST

A cloud of crimson vapor reeking of fresh blood hangs in the air, reaching out with lashing claws.

VAMPIRIC MIST	CR 3

XP 800

NE Medium aberration (air, water)

Init +8; **Senses** darkvision 60 ft., sense blood; Perception +8

DEFENSE

AC 14, touch 14, flat-footed 10 (+4 Dex)

hp 30 (4d8+12)

Fort +4, **Ref** +5, **Will** +5

Defensive Abilities amorphous; **DR** 5/magic

Weaknesses vulnerable to fire

OFFENSE

Speed fly 50 ft. (perfect)

Melee touch +7 (bleed and blood siphon)

Special Attacks bleed (1d6)

STATISTICS

Str —, **Dex** 19, **Con** 16, **Int** 7, **Wis** 13, **Cha** 10

Base Atk +3; **CMB** —; **CMD** —

Feats Improved Initiative, Weapon Finesse

Skills Fly +12, Perception +8, Stealth +11

Languages Aklo

SQ blood overdose, misty form

ECOLOGY

Environment temperate or warm swamps or underground

Organization solitary, pair, or gang (3–6)

Treasure incidental

SPECIAL ABILITIES

Blood Siphon (Ex) A vampiric mist drains blood with each melee touch attack dealing 1d3 points of Constitution damage. Every time a vampiric mist damages a creature in this way, it heals 1d8 hit points. Hit points healed in excess of its maximum are gained as temporary hit points, to a maximum amount equal to its Constitution score. These temporary hit points last for 1 hour.

Blood Overdose (Su) When a vampiric mist gorges on blood to an extent that it gains temporary hit points, it moves much more quickly. It gains a +2 bonus to its Armor Class and on Reflex saves, and can take one additional move action each round.

Misty Form (Ex) A vampiric mist's body is composed of a semisolid red mist similar in consistency to thick foam. The vampiric mist does not have a Strength score, and it cannot manipulate or wear solid objects. This form grants it the amorphous defensive ability, and allows it to move through areas as small as 1 inch in diameter with no reduction to its speed. The creature can speak in a hissing voice. A vampiric mist cannot enter water or other fluids, and is treated as a creature two size categories smaller than its actual size (Tiny for most vampiric mists) for the purposes of how wind affects it.

Sense Blood (Ex) A vampiric mist can immediately sense the presence of warm-blooded creatures in a 60-foot radius as if by scent. It can detect exposed blood within a mile.

Often mistaken for a vampire in gaseous form or an unusual type of air elemental, the vampiric mist is in fact a strange form of aberrant life. With an amorphous body that consists as much of fluid as it does of air, this creature dwells in swamps or moist underground regions where its vulnerability to heat isn't as much of a concern.

Although somewhat intelligent, vampiric mists do not form societies. They sometimes form into small gangs, but even then they show little interest in working together. Much of a vampiric mist's time is spent seeking prey—a pursuit that the monster often shows great creativity in accomplishing. The creatures' propensity for taking on vague, skeletal forms of the creatures whose blood they drink only further adds to their mystique and fuels rumors that they have connections to the undead. Indeed, many vampiric mists enjoy using this common misconception to their advantage, causing foes to use foolish tactics—such as tricking spellcasters into using positive energy against them as if they were undead monsters.

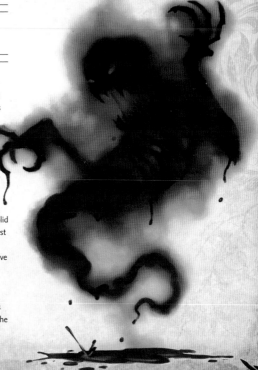

Illustration by Matt Dixon

VEMERAK

This huge monstrosity seems like some alien, clawed insect, with vaguely humanoid features and three tentacular tails.

VEMERAK	CR 14

XP 38,400
CE Huge aberration
Init +7; **Senses** darkvision 60 ft., tremorsense 30 ft.; Perception +23
Aura spore cloud (30 ft.)

DEFENSE

AC 29, touch 11, flat-footed 26 (+3 Dex, +18 natural, –2 size)
hp 195 (17d8+119)
Fort +13, **Ref** +8, **Will** +13
DR 5/—; **Immune** acid, electricity, disease, mind-affecting, poison; **Resist** sonic 20; **SR** 25

OFFENSE

Speed 40 ft., burrow 20 ft., climb 40 ft.
Melee bite +22 (2d6+11), 2 claws +22 (1d8+11 plus grab), 3 tentacles +19 (1d6+5 plus grab)
Space 15 ft.; **Reach** 15 ft.
Special Attacks breath weapon (90-foot line, 14d8 acid damage, DC 24 half, once every 1d4 rounds), constrict (tentacles 1d6+5 or claws 1d8+11), earthquake

STATISTICS

Str 32, **Dex** 17, **Con** 23, **Int** 5, **Wis** 16, **Cha** 22
Base Atk +12; **CMB** +25 (+29 grapple); **CMD** 38 (50 vs. trip)
Feats Awesome Blow, Great Fortitude, Improved Bull Rush, Improved Initiative, Multiattack, Power Attack, Toughness, Weapon Focus (bite), Weapon Focus (claws)
Skills Climb +19, Perception +23
Languages Aklo

ECOLOGY

Environment any underground
Organization solitary
Treasure standard

SPECIAL ABILITIES

Breath Weapon (Su) A vemerak's acidic breath weapon has no effect on inorganic or undead material. If the breath weapon deals damage to a living fleshy creature, the acid creates a transparent cloud of foul-smelling vapor that fills that creature's space and persists for 1 round. Any creature in or passing through the cloud must make a DC 24 Fortitude save or be nauseated for 1d4 rounds. This cloud is a poison effect. The save DCs are Constitution-based.

Earthquake (Su) As a full-round action, a vemerak can burrow its tentacles, legs, and mouth into the ground—this action does not provoke attacks of opportunity. At the start of the next round, it creates an effect identical to an *earthquake* spell (CL 17th). A vemerak can maintain this zone of trembling earth indefinitely, as long as it continues to take full-round actions to maintain the effect.

Spore Cloud (Su) A unique form of magic-resistant mold grows upon the body of a vemerak. This mold is the source of the vemerak's spell resistance. When the vemerak moves, the mold exudes a cloud of spores in a 30-foot radius that acts as a targeted *greater dispel magic* (CL 17th) against the highest caster level magical effect the cloud touches as part of the vemerak's move that turn.

Huge and otherworldly, the vemerak is a monster known as much for its disturbing appearance as its violent and cruel disposition.

A vemerak is 10 feet tall and 20 feet long, its tentacle-like tails adding a further 15 feet to its length. It weighs just over 6 tons. Caverns that serve as lairs to these creatures invariably possess disturbing shrines where the creatures offer up portions of every meal to dark gods that dwell deep below the sane world—as a result, many believe that vemeraks exist as the physical manifestation of the will of a particularly violent and insane deity.

Illustration by Jim Pavelec

VIPER VINE

Large tendrils ending in tiny claws unfurl from the central stalk of this plant, which rises like a serpent ready to strike.

VIPER VINE	CR 13	

XP 25,600

N Large plant

Init +8; **Senses** low-light vision, tremorsense 60 ft.; Perception +13

DEFENSE

AC 27, touch 14, flat-footed 22 (+4 Dex, +1 dodge, +13 natural, −1 size)

hp 190 (20d8+100)

Fort +16, **Ref** +12, **Will** +6

Immune acid, plant traits

Weaknesses cold lethargy

OFFENSE

Speed 10 ft.

Melee bite +23 (2d6+8/19–20 plus 3d6 acid), 4 tentacles +21 (1d6+4 plus grab)

Space 10 ft.; **Reach** 10 ft. (20 ft. with tentacle)

Special Attacks captivating cloud, constrict (1d6+8)

STATISTICS

Str 26, **Dex** 19, **Con** 19, **Int** 1, **Wis** 10, **Cha** 6

Base Atk +15; **CMB** +24 (+28 grapple); **CMD** 39 (can't be tripped)

Feats Combat Reflexes, Dodge, Improved Critical (bite), Improved Initiative, Lightning Reflexes, Multiattack, Power Attack, Toughness, Weapon Focus (bite), Weapon Focus (tentacle)

Skills Perception +13, Stealth +13

ECOLOGY

Environment temperate or warm forests or swamps

Organization solitary

Treasure incidental

SPECIAL ABILITIES

Captivating Cloud (Su) Once per day as a swift action, a viper vine can emit a transparent cloud of pollen in a 60-foot spread that has the power to lull the minds of those that smell it. Once activated, the cloud persists for 5 rounds unless dispersed by moderate or stronger wind. All creatures in the cloud must succeed on a DC 24 Will saving throw each round or become captivated. Once a creature becomes captivated, it takes no actions save to approach the viper vine via the most direct route possible. If this path leads it into a dangerous area, such as through fire or off a cliff, that creature receives a second saving throw to end the effect before moving into peril. A victim that is attacked by the viper vine gets a new saving throw as a free action during each of the vine's attacks to overcome the effect. This is a mind-affecting effect. The save DC is Constitution-based.

Cold Lethargy (Ex) Exposure to any cold effect slows a viper vine (as a *slow* spell) for 1d4 rounds.

A voracious, flesh-eating carnivore, the viper vine has a single enormous bloom arising from a thick, leafy tangle of snake-like vines. When the plant senses the approach of suitable prey through its sensitive, shallowly buried root system, it rises up like an agitated snake and unfurls its brightly colored bloom, an act that releases a cloud of mind-numbing pollen. While stories speaking of the plant's ability to lure prey into its clutches by virtue of its swaying motion persist, this effect is in fact created by this invisible, odorless pollen cloud.

Since viper vines gain nourishment through the consumption of creatures rather than through moisture and soil, they have developed rudimentary locomotion and are able to drag themselves along the ground with their tentacle-like root system. They even possess a form of rudimentary sentience, allowing them to not only discern differences in prey and make limited tactical decisions, but also to avoid creatures that are particularly large or dangerous looking. The area around the hunting grounds of these predators is often strewn with the remains of victims, and it is not unusual to find the rotting corpses of wild animals, ill-fated adventurers, and even giants in their immediate vicinity, along with a scattering of incidental treasure left behind by the plant's victims.

Illustration by Branko Bistrovic

WATER ORM

A reptilian head on a serpentine neck slowly surfaces. Shadows beneath the water hint at a body of considerable size.

WATER ORM	CR 10	

XP 9,600

N Huge magical beast (aquatic)

Init +7; **Senses** darkvision 120 ft., low-light vision; Perception +11

AC 24, touch 11, flat-footed 21 (+3 Dex, +13 natural, −2 size)

hp 136 (13d10+65)

Fort +13, **Ref** +13, **Will** +7

Defensive Abilities elusive; **Immune** cold; **Resist** fire 20

Speed 20 ft., swim 50 ft.

Melee bite +19 (4d6+8/19–20 plus grab), tail slap +14 (2d8+4)

Space 15 ft.; **Reach** 15 ft. (20 ft. with bite)

Special Attacks swallow whole (3d6+12 bludgeoning damage, AC 16, 13 hp)

Str 26, **Dex** 16, **Con** 21, **Int** 4, **Wis** 13, **Cha** 11

Base Atk +13; **CMB** +23 (+27 grapple); **CMD** 36 (40 vs. trip)

Feats Improved Critical (bite), Improved Initiative, Improved Iron Will, Iron Will, Lightning Reflexes, Power Attack, Skill Focus (Stealth)

Skills Perception +11, Stealth +14, Swim +16; **Racial Modifiers** +4 Perception

Languages Aquan (cannot speak)

SQ water travel

Environment any lakes

Organization solitary

Treasure none

Elusive (Su) Water orms are rarely discovered except by their own choice. As a full-round action while in water, a water orm can move up to its run speed (200 ft.) without leaving any trace of its passage (identical in effect to *pass without trace*). An elusive water orm gains a +40 circumstance bonus to its Stealth check. In addition, when not in combat, a water orm is considered to be under the effects of a *nondetection* spell. These effects function at caster level 20th and cannot be dispelled.

Water Travel (Su) As a full-round action once per day, a water orm can dissolve into water, appearing only as a long, dark, serpentine stretch of water that looks similar to the passage of a school of fish when viewed from above the water. While in this form, the water orm swims at a speed of 600 feet per round (60 mph) and gains a +40 bonus on all Swim checks. It cannot attack or take any action other than swimming in this form, and can remain in this form for up to 8 hours at a time. A water orm can revert to its solid form from this state as a free action. Water orms are unable to pass into or through salt water when using this ability.

Just as sailors tell stories of sea serpents, so do denizens on the shores of remote lakes whisper of strange, secretive monsters lurking in the depths of these large bodies of water. Like sea serpents, proof of their existence is as elusive as the beasts themselves. Known as water orms and believed by some to be a strange link between linnorms and sea serpents, most locals refer to any such local monster (real or imagined) by a pet name or the name of the lake it calls home. Water orms are craftier than sea serpents, and generally inclined toward curiosity rather than violence. Nevertheless, a water orm does not hesitate to attack any creature it views as a threat to itself or its lake.

Water orms are extremely long-lived. Several different variants have been reported. With sightings rare and unverifiable, it is unclear whether these are variations within a single species, or several unrelated creatures. Some are described as long-necked aquatic reptiles, some as fresh-water sea serpents, others as bizarrely elongated seals or whales, and still others as impossibly large sea horses. Most are 40 to 45 feet in length, and weigh 2,000 to 3,000 pounds.

Illustration by Adam Vehige

WENDIGO

This hideous shape has the head of a feral elk with jagged teeth and sharp antlers. Its humanoid legs end in blackened, burnt stumps.

WENDIGO — **CR 17**

XP 102,400
CE Large outsider (cold, native)
Init +13; **Senses** blindsight 60 ft., darkvision 60 ft., low-light vision; Perception +26

DEFENSE
AC 32, touch 18, flat-footed 23 (+9 Dex, +14 natural, −1 size)
hp 279 (18d10+180); regeneration 15 (fire)
Fort +21, **Ref** +22, **Will** +11
DR 15/cold iron and magic; **Immune** cold, fear; **SR** 28
Weaknesses vulnerability to fire

OFFENSE
Speed fly 120 ft. (perfect)
Melee bite +26 (2d8+9/19–20 plus 4d6 cold and grab), 2 claws +26 (2d6+9/19–20 plus 4d6 cold)
Space 10 ft.; **Reach** 10 ft.
Special Attacks dream haunting, howl, rend (2 claws, 1d8+13 plus 4d6 cold plus 1d4 Cha damage), wendigo psychosis
Spell-Like Abilities (CL 18th; concentration +25)
At will—*wind walk* (DC 23; see below)
1/day—*control weather* (as druid), *nightmare* (DC 22)

STATISTICS
Str 29, **Dex** 29, **Con** 31, **Int** 26, **Wis** 20, **Cha** 24
Base Atk +18; **CMB** +28 (+32 grapple); **CMD** 47
Feats Ability Focus (howl), Critical Focus, Flyby Attack, Improved Critical (bite, claws), Improved Initiative, Lightning Reflexes, Persuasive, Tiring Critical
Skills Acrobatics +30, Bluff +28, Diplomacy +9, Fly +36, Intimidate +32, Knowledge (arcana, geography, nature, religion) +26, Knowledge (planes) +29, Perception +26, Sense Motive +26, Spellcraft +29, Stealth +26, Survival +26
Languages Aklo, Common, Giant; telepathy 1 mile
SQ no breath

ECOLOGY
Environment any cold
Organization solitary
Treasure none

SPECIAL ABILITIES
Dream Haunting (Su) When a wendigo uses its *nightmare* spell-like ability, the victim is also exposed to wendigo psychosis.
Howl (Ex) Three times per day as a standard action, a wendigo can emit a forlorn howl that can be heard up to a mile away. Any who hear the howl must make a DC 28 Will save to avoid becoming shaken for an hour. Creatures within 120 feet become panicked for 1d4+4 rounds, and those within 30 feet cower with fear for 1d4 rounds. This is a mind-affecting fear effect. The save DC is Charisma-based.
Wendigo Psychosis (Su) Curse—*Nightmare* or *wind walk*; *save* Will DC 26; *onset* 1 minute; *frequency* 1/day; *effect* 1d4 Wis drain (minimum Wis 1); *cure* 3 consecutive saves.

When a victim's Wisdom reaches 1, he seeks an individual of his race to kill and devour. After completing this act, the afflicted individual takes off at a run, and in 1d4 rounds sprints up into the sky at such a speed that his feet burn away into jagged stumps. The transformation into a wendigo takes 2d6 minutes as the victim *wind walks* across the sky. Once the transformation is complete, the victim is effectively dead, replaced by a new wendigo. *True resurrection*, *miracle*, or *wish* can restore such a victim to life, yet doing so does not harm the new wendigo. The save is Charisma-based.

Wind Walk (Sp) If a wendigo pins a grappled foe, it can attempt to *wind walk* with the target by using its spell-like ability—it automatically succeeds on all concentration checks made to use *wind walk*. If the victim fails to resist the spell, the wendigo hurtles into the sky with him. Each round, a victim can make a new DC 23 Will save to turn solid again, but at this point he falls if he cannot fly. Eventually, the wendigo strands the victim in some rural area, usually miles from where it began. A creature that *wind walks* with a wendigo is exposed to wendigo psychosis. The save DC is Charisma-based.

Beings of ancient evil, wendigos haunt the minds of mortals, driving them to desperation and, ultimately, cannibalistic madness. They enjoy whittling down prey before they strike, trailing victims for days, even weeks, while plaguing their journeys with nightmares and foul weather.

Tribal humanoids sometimes worship wendigos as gods, bringing them live sacrifices or attempting to appease the creatures by engaging in ritual cannibalism. They mark a wendigo's territory with fetishes and dress in the furs and hides of whatever animal it most closely resembles. Wendigos take little interest in the practices of their worshipers, and view them only as an ample supply of victims.

Illustration by Tyler Walpole

281

WHALE

This immense whale moves slowly through the water with a grace that seems incongruous, given its immense size.

WHALE	CR 10

XP 9,600

N Gargantuan animal

Init +2; **Senses** blindsight 120 ft., low-light vision; Perception +23

DEFENSE

AC 22, touch 4, flat-footed 22 (–2 Dex, +18 natural, –4 size)

hp 157 (15d8+90)

Fort +17, **Ref** +7, **Will** +7

OFFENSE

Speed swim 40 ft.

Melee tail slap +21 (4d6+21) or bite +21 (4d6+21)

Space 20 ft.; **Reach** 20 ft.

Special Attacks capsize

STATISTICS

Str 38, **Dex** 6, **Con** 23, **Int** 2, **Wis** 11, **Cha** 5

Base Atk +11; **CMB** +29; **CMD** 37 (can't be tripped)

Feats Diehard, Endurance, Great Fortitude, Improved Bull Rush, Improved Initiative, Iron Will, Power Attack, Skill Focus (Perception)

Skills Perception +23, Swim +30; **Racial Modifiers** +4 Perception

SQ hold breath

ECOLOGY

Environment any oceans

Organization solitary, pair, or pod (3–16)

Treasure none

SPECIAL ABILITIES

Capsize (Ex) A whale can attempt to capsize a boat or ship by ramming it as a charge attack and making a CMB check. The DC of this check is 25, or the result of the captain's Profession (sailor) check, whichever is higher. For each size category the ship is larger than the whale's size, the whale takes a cumulative –10 penalty on this CMB check.

Whales are frequently hunted for their meat and the valuable oil in their blubber. Baleen whales have no teeth and attack with a tail slap; toothed whales like sperm whales instead attack with a bite. Whale companions are smaller species—rules for such companions are the same as those for orcas (see page 88 of the *Pathfinder RPG Bestiary*.)

WHALE, GREAT WHITE

This immense whale has an enormous, box-shaped head over a massive, toothy maw. Its rough white hide is laced with scars.

GREAT WHITE WHALE	CR 14

XP 38,400

N Colossal animal

Init –2; **Senses** blindsight 120 ft., low-light vision; Perception +13

DEFENSE

AC 28, touch 0, flat-footed 28 (–2 Dex, +28 natural, –8 size)

hp 225 (18d8+144)

Fort +21, **Ref** +9, **Will** +8

OFFENSE

Speed swim 40 ft.

Melee bite +25 (6d6+20/19–20), tail slap +20 (3d6+10)

Space 30 ft.; **Reach** 30 ft.

Special Attacks capsize, smashing breach

STATISTICS

Str 50, **Dex** 6, **Con** 27, **Int** 2, **Wis** 11, **Cha** 5

Base Atk +13; **CMB** +41; **CMD** 49 (can't be tripped)

Feats Critical Focus, Diehard, Endurance, Great Fortitude, Improved Bull Rush, Improved Critical (bite), Iron Will, Power Attack, Staggering Critical

Skills Perception +13, Swim +39

SQ hold breath

ECOLOGY

Environment any oceans

Organization solitary, pair, or pod (3–16)

Treasure none

SPECIAL ABILITIES

Smashing Breach (Ex) As a full-round action, a great white whale can make a special charge attack against creatures on the surface of the water. At the end of its charge, the whale breaches, then slams down onto the target with incredible force. Any Huge or smaller creatures in the whale's space must make a DC 27 Reflex save or take 4d8+30 points of bludgeoning damage and be forced into the nearest square that is adjacent to the whale. This breach automatically attempts to capsize any boats caught wholly or partially in this area. The save DC is Constitution-based.

Legendary in size and temper, great white whales are far more aggressive than their smaller kin.

Winterwight

Human-sized and of a deathly blue color, this long-taloned skeletal creature is partially encased in jagged sheets of ice.

WINTERWIGHT	CR 17

XP 102,400

CE Medium undead (cold)

Init +10; **Senses** darkvision 60 ft.; Perception +27

Aura cold (10 ft.)

DEFENSE

AC 32, touch 16, flat-footed 26 (+6 Dex, +16 natural)

hp 270 (20d8+180); fast healing 10

Fort +15, **Ref** +14, **Will** +16

Defensive Abilities channel resistance +4; **DR** 15/bludgeoning and good; **Immune** cold, undead traits; **SR** 28

Weaknesses vulnerability to fire

OFFENSE

Speed 30 ft.

Melee bite +30 (2d8+15 plus blightfire), 2 claws +30 (2d6+15 plus blightfire)

Special Attacks rend (2 claws 2d8+22)

Spell-Like Abilities (CL 17th; concentration +26)

Constant—*air walk*

At will—*cone of cold* (DC 24), *dimension door, greater dispel magic, sleet storm, wall of ice*

3/day—*polar ray*

1/day—*control weather*

STATISTICS

Str 40, **Dex** 23, **Con** —, **Int** 11, **Wis** 18, **Cha** 29

Base Atk +15; **CMB** +30; **CMD** 46

Feats Blind-Fight, Combat Reflexes, Critical Focus, Greater Vital Strike, Improved Initiative, Improved Vital Strike, Lightning Reflexes, Power Attack, Staggering Critical, Vital Strike

Skills Acrobatics +26, Intimidate +32, Perception +27, Stealth +29

Languages Common

ECOLOGY

Environment any cold land

Organization solitary, pair, or incursion (3–6)

Treasure standard

SPECIAL ABILITIES

Aura of Cold (Su) Winterwights are surrounded by a 10-foot radius of deathly chill. Any creatures within this area during the winterwight's turn takes 2d10 points of cold damage. All creatures of the cold subtype within this area (including the winterwight) are treated as having fast healing 10.

Blightfire (Su) Whenever a winterwight damages a creature with a bite or claw, the wound erupts with tongues of black fire. For the next 5 rounds, the victim must make a DC 29 Fortitude saving throw at the start of its turn or take 1d6 points of Constitution

drain. The winterwight gains 10 temporary hit points each time the creature fails a saving throw against blightfire. A creature cannot be affected by more than one instance of blightfire at a time. The save DC is Charisma-based.

The winterwight is an undead horror born from the coldest depths of the negative energy plane. Infused with the dark, cold magic that permeates this realm of death, the winterwight takes the form of a skeleton coated in armor of jagged ice.

Though it resembles an ordinary skeleton from a distance, the winterwight's frame is much sturdier than the average humanoid's, its frozen armor intertwining with its bone structure to form an incredibly hardy chassis. Sometimes called hatewraiths because of their insatiable lust for suffering, these frozen horrors are often found in areas that suffer from magical cold or frozen climates.

Winterwights are 7 feet tall and weigh 250 pounds.

Illustration by Alberto Dal Lago

WITCHFIRE

Bathed in sickly green flames, this insubstantial specter of a beautiful young woman floats just off the ground.

WITCHFIRE	CR 9	

XP 6,400

CE Medium undead (incorporeal)

Init +10; **Senses** darkvision 60 ft.; Perception +16

DEFENSE

AC 24, touch 24, flat-footed 17 (+7 deflection, +6 Dex, +1 dodge)

hp 115 (10d8+70)

Fort +10, **Ref** +11, **Will** +10

Defensive Abilities incorporeal, witchflame; **Immune** fire, undead traits

OFFENSE

Speed fly 50 ft. (perfect)

Melee incorporeal touch +13 (8d6 fire plus witchflame)

Ranged witchflame bolt +13 (8d6 fire plus witchflame)

Spell-Like Abilities (CL 9th; concentration +16)

At will—*dancing lights, disguise self, ghost sound* (DC 17), *invisibility, pyrotechnics* (DC 19), *ray of enfeeblement* (DC 18)

1/day—*summon* (level 4, 2 will-o'-wisps 50%)

STATISTICS

Str —, **Dex** 22, **Con** —, **Int** 17, **Wis** 16, **Cha** 25

Base Atk +7; **CMB** +13; **CMD** 31

Feats Combat Reflexes, Dodge, Improved Initiative, Lightning Reflexes, Mobility

Skills Bluff +17, Fly +14, Intimidate +20, Knowledge (any two) +13, Perception +16, Sense Motive +16, Stealth +19

Languages Auran, Common, Giant

SQ sound mimicry (animal noises)

ECOLOGY

Environment any swamps or woodlands

Organization solitary or coven (3 witchfires and hags; see below)

Treasure standard

SPECIAL ABILITIES

Witchflame (Su) Any creature damaged by the incorporeal touch or ranged bolt attacks of a witchfire must succeed on a DC 22 Will save or become engulfed in sickly green flames. While these eerie flames deal no additional damage, the affected creature glows as per *faerie fire* and becomes sickened. While under the effects of the witchflame, the victim gains vulnerability to fire and takes half again as much damage (+50%) from fire attacks of any sort. This effect persists for 10 minutes. The supernatural flames can only be extinguished before this duration expires by a *break enchantment, miracle, remove curse,* or *wish* spell—the effective caster level of the witchflame is equal to the witchfire's HD (CL 10th for most witchfires). Any creature entering the same square as a witchfire or striking it with a melee attack must succeed on a DC 22 Will save or begin burning with witchflame, even if the attack would not otherwise harm the witchfire because of its incorporeal nature. A bolt of witchflame has a range of 60 feet with no range increment. The save DCs are Charisma-based.

When an exceptionally vile hag or witch dies with some malicious plot left incomplete, or proves too horridly tenacious to succumb to the call of death, the foul energies of these wicked old crones sometimes spawn incorporeal undead known as witchfires. These ghostly creatures appear much as they did in life, although the grotesque undead energy that births them makes them appear young and attractive and wreathes their insubstantial bodies in a powerful aura of sickly green flame, a ghostly fire referred to as "witchflame" in local legends.

Strings of will-o'-wisps are often found in the immediate vicinity of witchfires and are typically led by the undead, leading scholars to speculate that the creatures feed off of a witchfire's flames and fury.

WITCHFIRE COVENS

Witchfires occasionally join or subjugate existing hag covens (see page 167 of the *Pathfinder RPG Bestiary*). A hag coven that includes a witchfire gains the following additional coven spell-like abilities: 3/day—*blight, create undead, fire storm* (DC 21), *nightmare* (DC 18), *waves of exhaustion* (DC 20). All abilities function at CL 9th, and save DCs are based on a Charisma score of 16. The use of these abilities functions identically to other coven abilities. Such covens must have at least one living hag, as covens of three witchfires gain no coven-related abilities.

Illustration by Concept Art House

Witchwyrd

This gray-skinned humanoid wears fine red robes. The being has four arms, each ending in a three-fingered hand.

WITCHWYRD	CR 6

XP 2,400

LN Medium monstrous humanoid

Init +6; **Senses** darkvision 60 ft., *detect magic*; Perception +8

DEFENSE

AC 19, touch 12, flat-footed 17 (+4 armor, +2 Dex, +3 natural)

hp 68 (8d10+24)

Fort +7, **Ref** +8, **Will** +9

Defensive Abilities absorb force; **DR** 5/magic

OFFENSE

Speed 30 ft.

Melee ranseur +11/+6 (2d4+4/×3), 2 slams +6 (1d4+1 plus grab) or 4 slams +11 (1d4+3 plus grab)

Space 5 ft.; **Reach** 5 ft. (10 ft. with ranseur)

Special Attacks force bolt

Spell-Like Abilities (CL 8th; concentration +13)

Constant—*detect magic, floating disk, mage armor, resist energy* (one at a time), *unseen servant*

3/day—*dispel magic, displacement, suggestion* (DC 18)

1/day—*dimension door, resilient sphere* (DC 19)

STATISTICS

Str 16, **Dex** 15, **Con** 17, **Int** 18, **Wis** 13, **Cha** 20

Base Atk +8; **CMB** +11 (+15 grapple); **CMD** 23

Feats Deflect Arrows[B], Great Fortitude, Improved Initiative, Iron Will, Persuasive

Skills Appraise +12, Bluff +13, Diplomacy +11, Intimidate +18, Knowledge (arcana) +12, Knowledge (geography) +12, Knowledge (planes) +12, Perception +8, Sense Motive +5, Use Magic Device +9

Languages Common, Draconic, one or more planar languages; *tongues*

ECOLOGY

Environment any land

Organization solitary, entourage (1 witchwyrd and 2–5 humanoid guards), or enclave (2–5 witchwyrds and 11–20 humanoid guards)

Treasure double

SPECIAL ABILITIES

Absorb Force (Su) Once per round, a witchwyrd can use a free hand to "catch" a *magic missile* fired at it. This absorbs the missile and manifests as a glowing nimbus around that hand (which is no longer considered free). The energy lasts 6 rounds or until it is used to create a force bolt. To use this ability, the witchwyrd must be aware of the incoming *magic missile* and cannot be flat-footed.

Force Bolt (Su) A witchwyrd can "throw" a *magic missile* (1d4+1 damage) from each free hand as a free action (maximum of two per round). If it has absorbed a *magic missile*, it can throw an additional force bolt that round, expending the absorbed energy (maximum of two additional bolts per round).

Alien merchants that travel between planets and planes, witchwyrds stand 7 feet tall, weigh 300 pounds, and are covered in hairless blue-gray skin. Witchwyrds new to a market or eager to avoid identification during an important business deal fold their second sets of flexible arms behind their backs and dress in robes, the better to pass as a less-infamous humanoid race. Witchwyrds tend to prefer the driest, warmest regions of the areas they visit—perhaps an indicator of their mysterious home world.

Illustration by Christopher Burdett

WORM THAT WALKS

Although this robed wizard stands and moves like a man, his body is a writhing mass of squirming, slippery worms.

WORM THAT WALKS	CR 14	

XP 38,400

Human worm that walks conjurer 13

NE Medium vermin (augmented human)

Init +8; **Senses** blindsight 30 ft., darkvision 60 ft.; Perception +22

DEFENSE

AC 23, touch 17, flat-footed 18 (+6 armor, +4 Dex, +1 dodge, +2 insight)

hp 113 (13d6+65); fast healing 14

Fort +11, **Ref** +12, **Will** +13

Defensive Abilities worm that walks traits; **DR** 15/—; **Immune** critical hits, disease, paralysis, poison, sleep

OFFENSE

Speed 30 ft.

Melee slam +10 (1d4–1 plus grab)

Special Attacks discorporate, grab (Large), squirming embrace

Arcane School Spell-Like Abilities (CL 13th; concentration +18)

At will—dimensional steps (390 feet/day)

8/day—acid dart (1d6+6 acid)

Conjurer Spells Prepared (CL 13th; concentration +18)

7th—*plane shift* (DC 22), *project image*

6th—*acid fog, disintegrate* (DC 21), *summon monster VI*

5th—*cloudkill* (DC 20), *dismissal* (DC 20), *shadow evocation* (DC 20), *telekinesis* (DC 20), *teleport*

4th—*black tentacles, confusion* (DC 19), *dimension door* (2), *phantasmal killer* (DC 19), *summon monster IV*

3rd—*dispel magic, fly, protection from energy, slow* (DC 18), *stinking cloud* (DC 18), *summon monster III*

2nd—*acid arrow, detect thoughts* (DC 17), *fog cloud, glitterdust* (DC 17), *invisibility, summon swarm*

1st—*charm person* (DC 16), *feather fall, grease* (DC 16), *obscuring mist, protection from good, reduce person* (DC 16), *shield*

0 (at will)—*detect magic, mage hand, prestidigitation, read magic*

Opposition Schools Evocation, Necromancy

STATISTICS

Str 8, **Dex** 18, **Con** 17, **Int** 20, **Wis** 12, **Cha** 10

Base Atk +6; **CMB** +5 (+13 grapple); **CMD** 26

Feats Arcane Armor Training, Combat Casting, Combat Reflexes, Craft Magic Arms and Armor, Craft Wondrous Item, Diehard[B], Dodge, Improved Initiative, Light Armor Proficiency, Scribe Scroll, Toughness, Weapon Finesse

Skills Craft (alchemy) +21, Fly +20, Intimidate +13, Knowledge (arcana, dungeoneering, planes) +21, Perception +22, Sense Motive +9, Spellcraft +21, Stealth +12; **Racial Modifiers** +8 Perception, +8 Sense Motive, +8 Stealth

Languages Abyssal, Aklo, Common, Infernal

SQ arcane bond (staff), summoner's charm (6 rounds)

Illustration by Eric Belisle

ECOLOGY

Environment any

Organization solitary

Treasure NPC Gear (+4 leather armor, cloak of resistance +4, staff of charming)

When a powerful spellcaster with a strong personality, a lust for life, and a remorselessly evil soul dies and is buried in a graveyard infused with eldritch magic, a strange phenomenon sometimes occurs. The flesh of the decaying body fats and instructs the very worms that gnaw, and these graveworms quicken not only on corruption but upon the spellcaster's memories and magical power. The spellcaster's very soul is consumed in this vile process, only to be split apart to inhabit each of the individual chewing worms in so many fragments. The result is a hideous hive mind of slithering life known as a worm that walks—a mass of worms that clings to the vague shape of the body that granted it this new existence, and can wield the powers and magic the spellcaster had in life. A worm that walks retains memories of its life as a spellcaster before its death, but is not undead—it is a hideous new form of undulant life.

CREATING A WORM THAT WALKS

"Worm that walks" is a template that can be added to any evil spellcasting creature. A worm that walks retains all the base creature's statistics and abilities except as noted here.

CR: Same as the base creature +2.

Alignment: Any evil.

Type: The base creature's type changes to vermin. It gains the augmented subtype. Do not recalculate BAB, saves, or skill ranks. Worms that walk are intelligent and do not possess the standard mindless trait of most vermin. Note that while a worm that walks has the ability to discorporate into a swarm, and while its body is made up of countless wriggling worms, it does not itself gain the swarm subtype.

Size: Although the worms that make up the worm that walks's body are Fine creatures, the worm that walks is treated as a creature the same size as the base creature.

Senses: As the base creature, plus darkvision 60 feet and blindsight 30 feet.

AC: The worm that walks loses any natural armor bonus the base creature may have had, but gains an insight bonus to its AC equal to its Wisdom bonus (minimum of +2).

Hit Dice: Change the base creature's racial HD to d8s. All HD derived from class levels remain unchanged.

Defensive Abilities: A worm that walks retains all of the base creature's defensive abilities and special qualities. It also gains the following additional defensive abilities.

Worm that Walks Traits: A worm that walks has no discernible anatomy, and is not subject to critical hits or flanking.

Reducing a worm that walks to 0 hit points causes it to discorporate (see below)—a worm that walks at 0 hit points is staggered, and one at negative hit points is dying. Worms that walk are immune to any physical spell or effect that targets a specific number of creatures (including single-target spells such as *disintegrate*), with the exception of such spells and effects generated by the worm that walks itself, which treat the worm that walks as one single creature if it so chooses. Mind-affecting effects that target single creatures function normally against a worm that walks, since the creature's individual components share a hive mind. A worm that walks takes half again as much damage (+50%) from damaging area effects, such as *fireball* and splash weapons. Worms that walk are susceptible to high winds—treat a worm that walks as a Fine creature for the purposes of determining wind effects.

Damage Reduction: A worm that walks loses any damage reduction possessed by the base creature and gains damage reduction 15/—.

Fast Healing: A worm that walks gains fast healing equal to its CR.

Immunities: Worms that walk are immune to disease, paralysis, poison, and sleep effects.

Melee Attacks: A worm that walks loses any natural attacks the base creature had, but gains a slam attack that deals damage based on its size (see Table 3–1: Natural Attacks by Size, on page 299). This slam has the grab ability and affects creatures up to one size larger than the worm that walks. A worm that walks retains any weapon proficiencies the base creature had.

Special Attacks: A worm that walks retains all of the base creature's special attacks. It also gains the following additional special attacks.

Discorporate (Su) A worm that walks can collapse into a shapeless swarm of worms as a free action. All held, worn, and carried items fall and its Strength score drops to 1. The worm that walks functions as a true swarm while discorporated, with a reach of 0 feet (its space remains unchanged). While discorporated, the worm that walks loses all of its defensive abilities and gains all of the standard swarm traits. It loses its slam attacks and all special abilities and special attacks, but can make a swarm attack that deals damage equal to its engulf attack. A worm that walks can reform into its true form (including equipping all gear in reach) as a full-round action as long as it has at least 1 hit point.

Squirming Embrace (Ex) If a worm that walks grapples a foe, as a swift action, it can cause a swarm of worms to squirm over the grappled creature. These worms deal automatic swarm damage with no attack roll needed (see the table below). If a creature takes damage from the swarm, it is also subject to the swarm's distraction ability, and must make a Fortitude save or be nauseated for 1 round. The save DC equals 10 + 1/2 the worm that walks's HD + its Con modifier).

A worm that walks can only have one embraced target at a time, but it does not have to continue grappling in order to maintain the embrace. If the worm that walks moves more than 5 feet from the swarm or dismisses the swarm (a free action), the swarm dies. Any area attack that damages the swarm or any severe or stronger wind effect that affects the swarm's target kills it.

Tenacious (Ex) A worm that walks gains a +4 racial bonus on CMB checks made to grapple and a +4 racial bonus to its CMD.

Abilities: Dex +4, Con +4.

Skills: Worms that walk gain a +8 racial bonus on Perception, Sense Motive, and Stealth checks.

Feats: Worms that walk gain Diehard as a bonus feat.

ENGULF DAMAGE

HD	Engulf Damage
1–5	1d6 + 1.5 Str bonus
6–10	2d6 + 1.5 Str bonus
11–15	3d6 + 1.5 Str bonus
16–20	4d6 + 1.5 Str bonus
21 or more	5d6 + 1.5 Str bonus

XACARBA

This towering, three-tailed, six-eyed beast seems like three rune-backed serpents partially melded together into one body.

XACARBA	CR 15

XP 51,200

CE Gargantuan outsider (chaotic, evil, extraplanar)

Init +9; **Senses** *arcane sight*, darkvision 120 ft., *detect good*, low-light vision, scent, *true seeing*; Perception +29

DEFENSE

AC 31, touch 12, flat-footed 25 (+5 Dex, +1 dodge, +19 natural, −4 size)

hp 210 (20d10+100)

Fort +17, **Ref** +13, **Will** +20

DR 10/good; **Immune** electricity, poison; **Resist** acid 10, cold 10, fire 10; **SR** 26

OFFENSE

Speed 40 ft., climb 20 ft.

Melee bite +25 (3d8+9 plus poison), 3 tail slaps +20 (2d8+4 plus grab)

Space 20 ft.; **Reach** 15 ft.

Special Attacks constrict (2d6+9), redirect spell

Spell-Like Abilities (CL 18th; concentration +25)

Constant—*arcane sight*, *detect good*, *true seeing*

At will—*detect thoughts* (DC 19), *greater teleport* (self plus 50 lbs. of objects only), *invisibility*, *suggestion* (DC 20)

3/day—*charm monster* (DC 21), *mass suggestion* (DC 23), *scrying* (DC 21), *symbol of pain* (DC 22), *touch of idiocy*, *vision*

1/day—*summon* (level 5, 1 hezrou or 1d4 succubi, 50%)

STATISTICS

Str 29, **Dex** 21, **Con** 21, **Int** 26, **Wis** 22, **Cha** 24

Base Atk +20; **CMB** +33 (+37 grapple); **CMD** 49 (can't be tripped)

Feats Combat Reflexes, Dodge, Improved Initiative, Improved Iron Will, Improved Vital Strike, Iron Will, Lightning Reflexes, Mobility, Spring Attack, Vital Strike

Skills Acrobatics +25 (+29 jump), Bluff +30, Climb +17, Diplomacy +27, Disguise +27, Intimidate +27, Knowledge (arcana) +31, Knowledge (any two) +31, Linguistics +28, Perception +29, Sense Motive +29, Spellcraft +31, Stealth +16, Use Magic Device +27

Languages Abyssal, Common, Draconic; telepathy 100 ft.

SQ change shape (any humanoid as a swift action, but always retains one serpentine trait that negates the bonus to Disguise checks; *alter self*)

ECOLOGY

Environment any land (Abyss)

Organization solitary

Treasure standard

SPECIAL ABILITIES

Poison (Su) Bite—injury; *save* Fort DC 25; *frequency* 1/round for 6 rounds; *effect* one chosen by the xacarba from three options; *cure* 2 consecutive saves. The save DC is Constitution-based.

Fiendish Bile: effect 1d4 Str damage (good-aligned creatures also take 2d8 points of damage).

Mysterious Blood: effect 1d4 Dex and 1d4 Wis damage plus confusion for 1 round.

Vile Disjunction: effect targeted *greater dispel magic* (CL 18th) on the creature.

Redirect Spell (Su) Any creature that attempts to cast a spell within 30 feet of a xacarba must cast the spell defensively. If the caster fails the concentration check to do so (or if the caster opts to not cast defensively), the xacarba can choose the target of the spell as a immediate action. The new target must be a legal target—if there's no legal alternative target to choose from, this ability cannot be used.

Fiends hailing from the darkest reaches of the Abyss, xacarbas are manipulation and destruction intertwined. With their infamous ability to redirect spells, these serpentine goliaths wreak havoc on the mind as well as the body, turning allies against one another and reveling in the destruction doing so produces.

Illustration by Tyler Walpole

XTABAY

This patch of vines is ornamented with beautiful crimson and violet flowers, the petals of which seem to bear tiny faces.

XTABAY	CR 1/2	

XP 200

N Small plant

Init +1; **Senses** low-light vision, tremorsense 30 ft.; Perception +1

DEFENSE

AC 12, touch 12, flat-footed 10 (+1 Dex, +1 size)

hp 8 (1d8+4)

Fort +6, **Ref** +1, **Will** +1

Immune acid, plant traits

OFFENSE

Speed 5 ft.

Melee 2 stings +0 (1d3–1 plus 1d2 acid)

Special Attacks devour, soporific pollen

STATISTICS

Str 8, **Dex** 13, **Con** 19, **Int** —, **Wis** 12, **Cha** 11

Base Atk +0; **CMB** –2; **CMD** 9 (can't be tripped)

ECOLOGY

Environment any land

Organization solitary, pair, copse (3–5), or garden (6–12)

Treasure none

SPECIAL ABILITIES

Devour (Ex) While a creature is under the effects of a xtabay's soporific pollen, the plant may, as a full-round action, occupy the same square as the sleeping creature and slowly sap the life from it. Every round the xtabay uses this ability, the affected creature must make a DC 14 Fortitude save or take 1d2 Con damage. This feeding is curiously painless, and normally isn't enough to waken a foe put to sleep by the plant. Each round this feeding continues, the sleeping victim can attempt a new DC 14 Will save to awaken. This save DC is Constitution-based.

Soporific Pollen (Ex) As a standard action, a xtabay can release sleep-inducing pollen into the air around it. Each creature within a 10-ft.-radius burst centered on the xtabay must make a DC 14 Will save or fall asleep for 1d3 minutes. A creature that succeeds on the Fortitude save cannot be affected by the same xtabay's soporific pollen for 24 hours. A creature put to sleep by this pollen can be awakened by vigorously shaking the sleeper (a standard action) or by damaging it. This is a mind-affecting sleep effect. The save DC is Constitution-based.

Known for their potent—and ultimately deadly—scent, xtabays are a floral hazard to the unwary. As fast-spreading as ivy, a xtabay's vines are sturdy and adaptive, making the plant a potential threat nearly everywhere—from gardens to wells to forest groves.

Attractive flowers blossom from the vines of xtabays, emitting the spores that mean a slow death for their victims. The strange, face-like patterns that grow on the petals are disturbing but seem to have no real function. Hermits or other reclusive types have been known to surround their territory with xtabays, warding off pesky creatures and adventurers alike. Instances of xtabays of larger-than-usual size have also been reported. These massive plants possess tendrils as thick as tree limbs and flowers that can fell even the hardiest of warriors with their overwhelming perfume. Underground, xtabays thrive in the wet, dark environment, covering the walls and floors of entire caverns and anesthetizing whole dens of subterranean creatures.

Nomadic plants, xtabays traverse large expanses of land until they sense nearby life, at which point they lie dormant and take on the guise of harmless flowers while releasing their deceptive aroma. Once a creature is subdued, the beast-like plant wastes no time in devouring it, disregarding creatures unaffected by its aroma. Because of their carnivorous nature, xtabays only rarely run short on nutrients, consuming the entirety of a victim's body over the course of several days following the initial process of draining its blood. Xtabays are able to devour creatures thanks to their lengthy roots, which produce a corrosive acid that breaks down and absorbs flesh and bone.

Illustration by Alberto Dal Lago

YRTHAK

This flying reptile has large, leathery wings and a vibrantly colored crest on its horned, narrow-snouted head.

YRTHAK	CR 9

XP 6,400

N Huge magical beast

Init +6; **Senses** blindsight 120 ft.; Perception +18

DEFENSE

AC 23, touch 11, flat-footed 20 (+2 Dex, +1 dodge, +12 natural, −2 size)

hp 114 (12d10+48)

Fort +12, **Ref** +12, **Will** +8

Immune gaze attacks, visual effects and illusions, sight-based attacks, sonic

Weaknesses blind

OFFENSE

Speed 20 ft., fly 60 ft. (average)

Melee bite +17 (2d6+7), 2 claws +17 (1d8+7)

Ranged sonic lance +12 ranged touch (8d6 sonic)

Space 15 ft.; **Reach** 10 ft.

Special Attacks explosion

STATISTICS

Str 24, **Dex** 14, **Con** 18, **Int** 7, **Wis** 15, **Cha** 11

Base Atk +12; **CMB** +21; **CMD** 34 (38 vs. trip)

Feats Dodge, Flyby Attack, Improved Initiative, Iron Will, Lightning Reflexes, Skill Focus (Perception)

Skills Fly +7, Perception +18; **Racial Modifiers** +4 Perception

Languages Draconic

ECOLOGY

Environment temperate deserts, hills, or mountains

Organization solitary, pair, or clutch (3–6)

Treasure incidental

SPECIAL ABILITIES

Blind (Ex) A yrthak sees and senses exclusively through its blindsight ability, which is based on sound and movement—beyond 120 feet, it is considered blind. A deaf yrthak is effectively blinded as well except against adjacent foes—its weak eyesight functions enough for it to attack targets this close, although in such cases these creatures still gain the benefit of concealment (20% miss chance) because of the creature's poor vision. It is invulnerable to all sight-based effects and attacks, including gaze attacks.

Explosion (Ex) As a standard action, a yrthak can fire its sonic lance at the ground, a large rock, a stone wall, or a similar nonmagical object within 60 feet to create an explosion. This attack deals 2d6 points of piercing damage to all within 10 feet of the effect's center.

Sonic Lance (Ex) Once per round, a yrthak can focus sonic energy in a 60-foot ray that deals 8d6 sonic damage to one target.

Swift, cunning, and perpetually ravenous, the yrthak terrorizes the barren wastelands in which it makes its home, swooping down from on high to blast prey with bursts of pure sound. Though technically blind, as its eyes are tiny and barely capable of vision beyond a few feet, the yrthak senses its surroundings via acute hearing and echolocation. While its powerful jaws and claws are equally capable of taking down opponents, the yrthak generally prefers to wheel through the sky on its membranous wings, firing bolt after bolt of sound into its prey, and exulting in the thrill of the hunt. An adult yrthak is 20 feet long and weighs 1,500 pounds.

Yrthaks spend most of their time aloft—a yrthak hunt often lasts several days, with the yrthak skimming roughly 100 feet over the ground in its wide-ranging search for live prey, only resorting to grazing on carrion in direst need. While they have near-human intelligence, yrthaks generally do not seem interested in forming societies of their own—although the sight of a clutch of yrthaks tormenting a captured morsel might seem to indicate otherwise.

Illustration by Mike Corriero

ZOMBIE, JUJU

This wretched human figure has tight leathery skin, sunken eyes, and an emaciated frame, yet it moves with eerie alacrity.

HUMAN JUJU ZOMBIE   CR 2

XP 600

Human juju zombie rogue 2

NE Medium undead (augmented human)

Init +8; **Senses** darkvision 60 ft.; Perception +6

DEFENSE

AC 18, touch 15, flat-footed 13 (+4 Dex, +1 dodge, +3 natural)

hp 15 (2d8+3)

Fort +0, **Ref** +7, **Will** +1

Defensive Abilities channel resistance +4; evasion, DR 5/magic and slashing; **Immune** cold, electricity, *magic missile*, undead traits; **Resist** fire 10

OFFENSE

Speed 30 ft.

Melee mwk short sword +6 (1d6+4/19–20) or slam +5 (1d6+6)

Special Attacks sneak attack +1d6

STATISTICS

Str 18, **Dex** 19, **Con** —, **Int** 8, **Wis** 13, **Cha** 10

Base Atk +1; **CMB** +5; **CMD** 19

Feats Dodge, Improved Initiative[B], Toughness[B], Weapon Finesse

Skills Acrobatics +8, Climb +16, Disable Device +8, Intimidate +5, Perception +6, Sleight of Hand +9, Stealth +8, Survival +3, Swim +8, Use Magic Device +5; **Racial Modifiers** +8 Climb

Languages Common

SQ rogue talents (combat trick), trapfinding +1

ECOLOGY

Environment any land

Organization solitary

Treasure NPC gear (masterwork short sword, other treasure)

A juju zombie is an animated corpse of a creature, created to serve as an undead minion, that retains the skills and abilities it possessed in life.

CREATING A JUJU ZOMBIE

"Juju zombie" is an acquired template that can be added to any living corporeal creature, referred to hereafter as the base creature.

CR: As base creature +1.

Alignment: Any evil.

Type: The creature's type changes to undead. It retains any subtype except for alignment subtypes and subtypes that indicate kind.

Armor Class: A juju zombie gains a +3 bonus to its natural armor over the base creature's natural armor bonus.

Hit Dice: Change all the creature's racial Hit Dice to d8s. All Hit Dice derived from class levels remain unchanged. As undead, juju zombies use their Charisma modifiers to determine bonus hit points (instead of Constitution).

Defensive Abilities: Juju zombies gain channel resistance +4, DR 5/magic and slashing (or DR 10/magic and slashing if it has 11 HD or more), and fire resistance 10. They are immune to cold, electricity, and *magic missile*.

Speed: A winged juju zombie's maneuverability drops to clumsy. If the base creature flew magically, its fly speed is unchanged. Retain all other movement types.

Attacks: A juju zombie retains all the natural weapons, manufactured weapon attacks, and weapon proficiencies of the base creature. It also gains a slam attack that deals damage based on the juju zombie's size, but as if it were one size category larger than its actual size.

Abilities: Increase from the base creature as follows: Str +4, Dex +2. A juju zombie has no Con score; as an undead, it uses its Charisma in place of Constitution when calculating hit points, Fortitude saves, or any special ability that relies on Constitution.

Feats: A juju zombie gains Improved Initiative and Toughness as bonus feats.

Skills: A juju zombie gains a +8 racial bonus on all Climb checks.

Illustration by Scott Purdy

APPENDIX 1: MONSTER CREATION

Pathfinder RPG Bestiary 2 provides all the information you need to use and quickly modify the monsters presented in this book. For information on creating new monsters, see the *Pathfinder RPG Bestiary*. Table 1–1: Monster Statistics by CR on the following page is an expanded (up to CR 25) version of the table presented in the original *Bestiary*.

APPENDIX 2: MONSTER ADVANCEMENT

The following rules allow you to adjust monsters, increasing (or even decreasing) their statistics and abilities while still creating a balanced and fun encounter.

TEMPLATES

A template is a set of rules that you apply to a monster to transform it into a different monster. It gives precise directions on how to change the original monster's statistics to transform it into the new monster.

Acquired Templates: This kind of template is added to a creature well after its birth or creation.

Inherited Templates: This kind of template is part of a creature from the beginning of its existence. Creatures are born or created with these templates already in place, and have never known life without them.

Celestial Creature Defenses

Hit Dice	Resist Acid, Cold, and Electricity	DR
1–4	5	—
5–10	10	5/evil
11+	15	10/evil

Entropic Creature Defenses

Hit Dice	Resist Acid and Fire	DR
1–4	5	—
5–10	10	5/lawful
11+	15	10/lawful

Fiendish Creature Defenses

Hit Dice	Resist Cold and Fire	DR
1–4	5	—
5–10	10	5/good
11+	15	10/good

Resolute Creature Defenses

Hit Dice	Resist Acid, Cold, and Fire	DR
1–4	5	—
5–10	10	5/chaotic
11+	15	10/chaotic

SIMPLE TEMPLATES

Simple templates can be applied during the game with minimal effort. All simple templates have two categories of changes. The "quick rules" present a fast way to modify die rolls made in play to simulate the template's effects without actually rebuilding the stat block—this method works well for summoned creatures. The "rebuild rules" list the exact changes you make to the base stat block if you have the time to completely rebuild it—this method works best when you have time during game preparation to build full stat blocks. The two methods result in creatures of similar, if not identical, abilities.

Advanced Creature (CR +1)

Creatures with the advanced template are fiercer and more powerful than their ordinary cousins.

Quick Rules: +2 on all rolls (including damage rolls) and special ability DCs; +4 to AC and CMD; +2 hp/HD.

Rebuild Rules: AC increase natural armor by +2; **Ability Scores** +4 to all ability scores.

Celestial Creature (CR +0 or +1)

Celestial creatures dwell in the higher planes, but can be summoned using spells such as *summon monster* and *planar ally*. A celestial creature's CR increases by +1 only if the base creature has 5 or more HD. A celestial creature's quick and rebuild rules are the same.

Rebuild Rules: Senses gains darkvision 60 ft.; **Defensive Abilities** gains DR and energy resistance as noted on the table; **SR** gains SR equal to new CR +5; **Special Attacks** smite evil 1/day as a swift action (adds Cha bonus to attack rolls and damage bonus equal to HD against evil foes; smite persists until the target is dead or the celestial creature rests).

Entropic Creature (CR +0 or +1)

Creatures with the entropic template live in planes where chaos is paramount. They can be summoned using spells such as *summon monster* and *planar ally*. An entropic creature's CR increases by +1 only if the base creature has 5 or more HD. An entropic creature's quick and rebuild rules are the same.

Rebuild Rules: Senses gains darkvision 60 ft.; **Defensive Abilities** gains DR and energy resistance as noted on the table; **SR** gains SR equal to new CR +5; **Special Attacks** smite law 1/day as a swift action (adds Cha bonus to attack rolls and damage bonus equal to HD against lawful foes; smite persists until the target is dead or the entropic creature rests).

Fiendish Creature (CR +0 or +1)

Creatures with the fiendish template live in the Lower Planes, such as the Abyss and Hell, but can be summoned using spells such as *summon monster* and *planar ally*.

Table 1-1: Monster Statistics by CR

CR	Hit Points	Armor Class	High Attack	Low Attack	Average Damage High	Average Damage Low	Primary Ability DC	Secondary Ability DC	Good Save	Poor Save
1/2	10	11	1	0	4	3	11	8	3	0
1	15	12	2	1	7	5	12	9	4	1
2	20	14	4	3	10	7	13	9	5	1
3	30	15	6	4	13	9	14	10	6	2
4	40	17	8	6	16	12	15	10	7	3
5	55	18	10	7	20	15	15	11	8	4
6	70	19	12	8	25	18	16	11	9	5
7	85	20	13	10	30	22	17	12	10	6
8	100	21	15	11	35	26	18	12	11	7
9	115	23	17	12	40	30	18	13	12	8
10	130	24	18	13	45	33	19	13	13	9
11	145	25	19	14	50	37	20	14	14	10
12	160	27	21	15	55	41	21	15	15	11
13	180	28	22	16	60	45	21	15	16	12
14	200	29	23	17	65	48	22	16	17	12
15	220	30	24	18	70	52	23	16	18	13
16	240	31	26	19	80	60	24	17	19	14
17	270	32	27	20	90	67	24	18	20	15
18	300	33	28	21	100	75	25	18	20	16
19	330	34	29	22	110	82	26	19	21	16
20	370	36	30	23	120	90	27	20	22	17
21	400	37	31	24	130	98	27	20	23	18
22	440	39	32	25	140	105	28	21	23	18
23	480	40	33	26	150	113	29	22	24	19
24	520	42	35	27	165	124	30	23	25	20
25	560	43	36	28	180	135	30	24	26	21

A fiendish creature's CR increases by +1 only if the base creature has 5 or more HD. A fiendish creature's quick and rebuild rules are the same.

Rebuild Rules: Senses gains darkvision 60 ft.; **Defensive Abilities** gains DR and energy resistance as noted on the table; **SR** gains SR equal to new CR +5; **Special Attacks** smite good 1/day as a swift action (adds Cha bonus to attack rolls and damage bonus equal to HD against good foes; smite persists until target is dead or the fiendish creature rests).

Giant Creature (+1)

Creatures with the giant template are larger and stronger than their normal-sized kin. This template cannot be applied to creatures that are Colossal.

Quick Rules: +2 on all rolls based on Str or Con, +2 hp/HD, –1 penalty on all rolls based on Dex.

Rebuild Rules: Size increase by one category; **AC** increase natural armor by +3; **Attacks** increase dice rolled by 1 step; **Ability Scores** +4 size bonus to Str and Con, –2 Dex.

Resolute Creature (CR +0 or +1)

Creatures with the resolute template live in planes where law is paramount. They can be summoned using spells such

as *summon monster* and *planar ally*. A resolute creature's CR increases by +1 only if the base creature has 5 or more HD. A resolute creature's quick and rebuild rules are the same.

Rebuild Rules: Senses gains darkvision 60 ft.; **Defensive Abilities** gains DR and energy resistance as noted on the table; **SR** gains SR equal to new CR +5; **Special Attacks** smite chaos 1/day as a swift action (adds Cha bonus to attack rolls and damage bonus equal to HD against chaotic foes; smite persists until target is dead or the resolute creature rests).

Young Creature (CR –1)

Creatures with the young template are immature specimens of the base creature. You can also use this simple template to easily create a smaller variant of a monster. This template cannot be applied to creatures that increase in power through aging or feeding (such as dragons or barghests) or creatures that are Fine-sized.

Quick Rules: +2 on all Dex-based rolls, –2 on all other rolls, –2 hp/HD.

Rebuild Rules: Size decrease by one category; **AC** reduce natural armor by –2 (minimum +0); **Attacks** decrease damage dice by 1 step; **Ability Scores** –4 Strength, –4 Con, +4 size bonus to Dex.

APPENDIX 3: GLOSSARY

This appendix includes the Universal Monster Rules, Creature Types, and Creature Subtypes.

UNIVERSAL MONSTER RULES

The following rules are standard and are referenced (but not repeated) in monster stat blocks. Each rule includes a format guide for how it appears in a monster's listing and its location in the stat block.

Ability Damage and Drain (Ex or Su) Some attacks or special abilities cause ability damage or drain, reducing the designated ability score by the listed amount. Ability damage can be healed naturally. Ability drain is permanent and can only be restored through magic. *Format*: 1d4 Str drain; *Location*: Special Attacks or individual attacks.

All-Around Vision (Ex) The creature sees in all directions at once. It cannot be flanked. *Format*: all-around vision; *Location*: Defensive Abilities.

Amorphous (Ex) The creature's body is malleable and shapeless. It is immune to precision damage (like sneak attacks) and critical hits. *Format*: amorphous; *Location*: Defensive Abilities.

Amphibious (Ex) Creatures with this special quality have the aquatic subtype, but they can survive indefinitely on land. *Format*: amphibious; *Location*: SQ.

Attach (Ex) The creature automatically latches onto its target when it successfully makes the listed attack. The creature is considered grappling, but the target is not. The target can attack or grapple the creature as normal, or break the attach with a successful grapple or Escape Artist check. Most creatures with this ability have a racial bonus to maintain a grapple (listed in its CMB entry). *Format*: attach; *Location*: individual attacks.

Bleed (Ex) A creature with this ability causes wounds that continue to bleed, dealing the listed damage each round at the start of the affected creature's turn. This bleeding can be stopped by a successful DC 15 Heal skill check or through the application of any magical healing. The amount of damage each round is determined in the creature's entry. *Format*: bleed (2d6); *Location*: Special Attacks and individual attacks.

Blindsense (Ex) Using nonvisual senses, such as acute smell or hearing, a creature with blindsense notices things it cannot see. The creature usually does not need to make Perception checks to pinpoint the location of a creature within range of its blindsense ability, provided that it has line of effect to that creature. Any opponent the creature cannot see still has total concealment against the creature with blindsense, and the creature still has the normal miss chance when attacking foes that have concealment. Visibility still affects the movement of a creature with blindsense. A creature with blindsense is still denied its Dexterity bonus to Armor Class against attacks from creatures it cannot see. *Format*: blindsense 60 ft.; *Location*: Senses.

Blindsight (Ex) This ability is similar to blindsense, but is far more discerning. Using nonvisual senses, such as sensitivity to vibrations, keen smell, acute hearing, or echolocation, a creature with blindsight maneuvers and fights as well as a sighted creature. Invisibility, darkness, and most kinds of concealment are irrelevant, though the creature must have line of effect to a creature or object to discern that creature or object. The ability's range is specified in the creature's descriptive text. The creature usually does not need to make Perception checks to notice creatures within this range. Unless noted otherwise, blindsight is continuous, and the creature need do nothing to use it. Some forms of blindsight, however, must be triggered as a free action. If so, this is noted in the creature's description. If a creature must trigger its blindsight ability, the creature gains the benefits of blindsight only during its turn. *Format*: blindsight 60 ft.; *Location*: Senses.

Blood Drain (Ex) The creature drains blood at the end of its turn if it grapples a foe, inflicting Constitution damage. *Format*: blood drain (1d2 Constitution); *Location*: Special Attacks.

Blood Rage (Ex) When the creature takes damage in combat, on its next turn it can fly into a rage as a free action. It gains +2 Constitution and +2 Strength, but takes a –2 penalty to its AC. The rage lasts as long as the battle or 1 minute, whichever is shorter. It cannot end its rage voluntarily. *Format*: blood rage; *Location*: Special Attacks.

Breath Weapon (Su) Some creatures can exhale a cone, line, or cloud of energy or other magical effects. A breath weapon attack usually deals damage and is often based on some type of energy. Breath weapons allow a Reflex save for half damage (DC 10 + 1/2 the breathing creature's racial HD + the breathing creature's Con modifier; the exact DC is given in the creature's descriptive text). A creature is immune to its own breath weapon unless otherwise noted. Some breath weapons allow a Fortitude save or a Will save instead of a Reflex save. Each breath weapon also includes notes on how often it can be used, even if this number is limited in times per day. *Format*: breath weapon (60-ft. cone, 8d6 fire damage, Reflex DC 20 for half, usable every 1d4 rounds); *Location*: Special Attacks; if the breath is more complicated than damage, it also appears under Special Abilities with its own entry.

Burn (Ex) A creature with the burn special attack deals fire damage in addition to damage dealt on a successful hit in melee. A creature affected by the burn ability must also succeed on a Reflex save or catch fire, taking the listed damage at the start of its turn for an additional 1d4 rounds (DC 10 + 1/2 the attacking creature's racial HD + the attacking creature's Con modifier). A burning creature can attempt a new save as a full-round action. Dropping and rolling on the ground grants a +4 bonus on this save.

Creatures that hit the monster with natural weapons or unarmed attacks take fire damage as though hit by the monster's burn attack and must make a Reflex save to avoid catching on fire (see page 444 of the *Pathfinder RPG Core Rulebook*). *Format*: burn (2d6, DC 15); *Location*: Special Attacks and individual attacks.

Change Shape (Su) A creature with this special quality has the ability to assume the appearance of a specific creature or type of creature (usually a humanoid), but retains most of its own physical qualities. The creature cannot change shape to a form more than one size category smaller or larger than its original form. This ability functions as a polymorph spell, the type of which is listed in the creature's description, but the creature does not adjust its ability scores (although it gains any other abilities of the creature it mimics). Unless otherwise stated, it can remain in an alternate form indefinitely. Some creatures, such as lycanthropes, can transform into unique forms with special modifiers and abilities. These creatures do adjust their ability scores, as noted in their descriptions. *Format*: change shape (wolf, *beast form I*); *Location*: SQ, and in Special Abilities for creatures with a unique listing.

Channel Resistance (Ex) A creature with this special quality (usually an undead) is less easily affected by channeled negative or positive energy. The creature adds the listed bonus to saves made to resist the effects of channel energy, including effects that rely on the use of channel energy (such as the Command Undead feat). *Format*: channel resistance +4; *Location*: Defensive Abilities.

Compression (Ex) The creature can move through an area as small as one-quarter its space without squeezing or one-eighth its space when squeezing. *Format*: compression; *Location*: Special Qualities.

Constrict (Ex) A creature with this special attack can crush an opponent, dealing bludgeoning damage, when it makes a successful grapple check (in addition to any other effects caused by a successful check, including additional damage). The amount of damage is given in the creature's entry and is typically equal to the amount of damage caused by the creature's melee attack. *Format*: constrict (1d8+6); *Location*: Special Attacks.

Construct Traits (Ex) Constructs are immune to death effects, disease, mind-affecting effects (charms, compulsions, phantasms, patterns, and morale effects), necromancy effects, paralysis, poison, sleep, stun, and any effect that requires a Fortitude save (unless the effect also works on objects, or is harmless). Constructs are not subject to nonlethal damage, ability damage, ability drain, fatigue, exhaustion, or energy drain. Constructs are not at risk of death from massive damage. *Format*: construct traits; *Location*: Immune.

Curse (Su) A creature with this ability bestows a curse upon its enemies. The effects of the curse, including its save, frequency, and cure, are included in the creature's description. If a curse allows a saving throw, it is usually a Will save (DC 10 + 1/2 the cursing creature's racial HD + the creature's Cha modifier; the exact DC is given in the creature's descriptive text). Curses can be removed through *remove curse* and similar effects. *Format*: **Curse Name (Su)** Slam—contact; *save* Will DC 14, *frequency* 1 day, *effect* 1d4 Str drain; *Location*: Special Attacks and individual attacks.

Curse of Lycanthropy (Su) A natural lycanthrope's bite attack in animal or hybrid form infects a humanoid target with lycanthropy (Fortitude DC 15 negates). If the victim's size is not within one size category of the lycanthrope's size, this ability has no effect. *Format*: curse of lycanthropy; *Location*: individual attacks.

Damage Reduction (Ex or Su) A creature with this special quality ignores damage from most weapons and natural attacks. Wounds heal immediately, or the weapon bounces off harmlessly (in either case, the opponent knows the attack was ineffective). The creature takes normal damage from energy attacks (even nonmagical ones), spells, spell-like abilities, and supernatural abilities. A certain kind of weapon can sometimes damage the creature normally, as noted below.

The entry indicates the amount of damage ignored (usually 5 to 15 points) and the type of weapon that negates the ability.

Some monsters are vulnerable to piercing, bludgeoning, or slashing damage. Others are vulnerable to certain materials, such as adamantine, alchemical silver, or cold-forged iron. Attacks from weapons that are not of the correct type or made of the correct material have their damage reduced, although a high enhancement bonus can overcome some forms of damage reduction.

Some monsters are vulnerable to magic weapons. Any weapon with at least a +1 magical enhancement bonus on attack and damage rolls overcomes the damage reduction of these monsters. Such creatures' natural weapons (but not their attacks with weapons) are treated as magic weapons for the purpose of overcoming damage reduction.

A few very powerful monsters are vulnerable only to epic weapons—that is, magic weapons with at least a +6 enhancement bonus. Such creatures' natural weapons are also treated as epic weapons for the purpose of overcoming damage reduction.

Some monsters are vulnerable to good-, evil-, chaotic-, or lawful-aligned weapons, such as from an *align weapon* spell or the *holy* magical weapon property. A creature with an alignment subtype (chaotic, evil, good, or lawful) can overcome this type of damage reduction with its natural weapons and weapons it wields as if the weapons or natural weapons had an alignment (or alignments) that matched the subtype(s) of the creature.

When a damage reduction entry has a dash (—) after the slash, no weapon negates the damage reduction.

A few creatures are harmed by more than one kind of weapon, such as "cold iron or magic." A weapon that inflicts damage of either of these types overcomes this damage reduction.

A few other creatures require combinations of different types of attacks to overcome their damage reduction (such as "magic and silver"), and a weapon must be both types to overcome this type of damage reduction. A weapon that is only one type is still subject to damage reduction. *Format*: DR 5/silver; *Location*: Defensive Abilities.

Disease (Ex or Su) A creature with this ability causes disease in those it contacts. The effects of the disease, including its save, frequency, and cure, are included in the creature's description. The saving throw to negate the disease is usually a Fort save (DC 10 + 1/2 the infecting creature's racial HD + the creature's Con modifier; the exact DC is given in the creature's descriptive text). Disease can be removed through *remove disease* and similar effects. *Format*: **Disease Name (Ex)** Bite—injury; *save* Fort DC 15, *onset* 1d3 days, *frequency* 1 day, *effect* 1 Con damage, *cure* 2 consecutive saves; *Location*: Special Attacks and individual attacks.

Distraction (Ex) A creature with this ability can nauseate the creatures that it damages. Any living creature that takes damage from a creature with the distraction ability is nauseated for 1 round; a Fortitude save (DC 10 + the 1/2 creature's HD + the creature's Con modifier) negates the effect. *Format*: distraction (DC 14); *Location*: Special Attacks.

Earth Glide (Ex) When the creature burrows, it can pass through stone, dirt, or almost any other sort of earth except metal as easily as a fish swims through water. If protected against fire damage, it can even glide through lava. Its burrowing leaves behind no tunnel or hole, nor does it create any ripple or other sign of its presence. A *move earth* spell cast on an area containing the burrowing creature flings it back 30 feet, stunning it for 1 round unless it succeeds on a DC 15 Fortitude save. *Format*: earth glide; *Location*: Speed.

Energy Drain (Su) This attack saps a living opponent's vital energy and happens automatically when a melee or ranged attack hits. Each successful energy drain bestows one or more negative levels (the creature's description specifies how many). If an attack that includes an energy drain scores a critical hit, it bestows twice the listed number of negative levels. Unless otherwise specified in the creature's description, a draining creature gains 5 temporary hit points for each negative level it bestows on an opponent. These temporary hit points last for a maximum of 1 hour. Negative levels remain until 24 hours have passed or until they are removed with a spell such as *restoration*. If a negative level is not removed before 24

hours have passed, the affected creature must attempt a Fortitude save (DC 10 + 1/2 the draining creature's racial HD + the draining creature's Cha modifier; the exact DC is given in the creature's descriptive text). On a success, the negative level goes away with no harm to the creature. On a failure, the negative level becomes permanent. A separate saving throw is required for each negative level. *Format*: energy drain (2 levels, DC 18); *Location*: Special Attacks and individual attacks.

Engulf (Ex) The creature can engulf creatures in its path as part of a standard action. It cannot make other attacks during a round in which it engulfs. The creature merely has to move over its opponents, affecting as many as it can cover. Targeted creatures can make attacks of opportunity against the creature, but if they do so, they are not entitled to a saving throw against the engulf attack. Those who do not attempt attacks of opportunity can attempt a Reflex save to avoid being engulfed—on a success, they are pushed back or aside (target's choice) as the creature moves forward. Engulfed opponents gain the pinned condition, are in danger of suffocating, are trapped within the creature's body until they are no longer pinned, and may be subject to other special attacks from the creature. The save DC is Strength-based. *Format*: engulf (DC 12, 1d6 acid and paralysis); *Location*: Special Attacks.

Entrap (Ex or Su) The creature has an ability that restricts another creature's movement, usually with a physical attack such as ice, mud, lava, or webs. The target of an entrap attack must make a Fortitude save or become entangled for the listed duration. If a target is already entangled by this ability, a second entrap attack means the target must make a Fortitude save or become helpless for the listed duration. The save DCs are Constitution-based. A target made helpless by this ability is conscious but can take no physical actions (except attempting to break free) until the entrapping material is removed. The target can use spells with only verbal components or spell-like abilities if it can make a DC 20 concentration check. An entangled creature can make a Strength check (at the same DC as the entrap saving throw DC) as a full-round action to break free; the DC for a helpless creature is +5 greater than the saving throw DC. Destroying the entrapping material frees the creature. *Format*: entrap (DC 13, 1d10 minutes, hardness 5, hp 10); *Location*: special attacks and individual attacks.

Fast Healing (Ex) A creature with fast healing regains hit points at an exceptional rate, usually 1 or more hit points per round, as given in the creature's entry. Except where noted here, fast healing is just like natural healing. Fast healing does not restore hit points lost from starvation, thirst, or suffocation, nor does it allow a creature to regrow lost body parts. Unless otherwise stated, it does not allow lost body parts to be reattached. Fast healing continues to function (even at negative hit points) until a creature dies, at which point the effects of fast healing end immediately. *Format*: fast healing 5; *Location*: hp.

Fast Swallow (Ex) The creature can use its swallow whole ability as a free action at any time during its turn, not just at the start of its turn. *Format*: fast swallow; *Location*: Special Attacks.

Fear (Su or Sp) Fear attacks can have various effects.

Fear Aura (Su) The use of this ability is a free action. The aura can freeze an opponent (as in the case of a mummy's despair) or function like the *fear* spell. Other effects are possible. A fear aura is an area effect. The descriptive text gives the size and kind of the area.

Fear Cone (Sp) and Ray (Su) These effects usually work like the *fear* spell. If a fear effect allows a saving throw, it is a Will save (DC 10 + 1/2 the fearsome creature's racial HD + the creature's Cha modifier; the exact DC is given in the creature's descriptive text). All fear attacks are mind-affecting fear effects.

Format: fear aura (30 ft., DC 17); *Location*: Aura.

Format: fear cone (50 ft., DC 19); *Location*: Special Attacks.

Ferocity (Ex) A creature with ferocity remains conscious and can continue fighting even if its hit point total is below 0. The creature is still staggered and loses 1 hit point each round. The creature still dies when its hit point total reaches a negative amount equal to its Constitution score. *Format*: ferocity; *Location*: Defensive Abilities.

Flight (Ex, Sp, or Su) A creature with this ability can cease or resume flight as a free action. If the creature has wings, flight is an extraordinary ability. Otherwise, it is spell-like or supernatural, and it is ineffective in an antimagic field; the creature loses its ability to fly for as long as the antimagic effect persists. *Format*: fly 30 ft. (average); *Location*: Speed.

Freeze (Ex) The creature can hold itself so still it appears to be an inanimate object of the appropriate shape (a statue, patch of fungus, and so on). The creature can take 20 on its Stealth check to hide in plain sight as this kind of inanimate object. *Format*: freeze; *Location*: Special Qualities.

Frightful Presence (Ex) This special quality makes a creature's very presence unsettling to foes. Activating this ability is a free action that is usually part of an attack or charge. Opponents within range who witness the action may become frightened or shaken. The range is usually 30 feet, and the duration is usually 5d6 rounds. This ability affects only opponents with fewer Hit Dice than the creature has. An opponent can resist the effects with a successful Will save (DC 10 + 1/2 the frightful creature's racial HD + the frightful creature's Cha modifier; the exact DC is given in the creature's descriptive text). On a failed save, the opponent is shaken, or panicked if it has 4 Hit Dice or fewer. An opponent that succeeds on the saving throw is immune to that same creature's frightful presence for 24

hours. Frightful presence is a mind-affecting fear effect. *Format*: frightful presence (60 ft., DC 21); *Location*: Aura.

Gaze (Su) A gaze attack takes effect when foes look at the attacking creature's eyes. The attack can have any sort of effect; petrification, death, and charm are common. The typical range is 30 feet. The type of saving throw for a gaze attack is usually a Will or Fortitude save (DC 10 + the 1/2 gazing creature's racial HD + the gazing creature's Cha modifier; the exact DC is given in the creature's text). A successful saving throw negates the effect. A monster's gaze attack is described in abbreviated form in its description. Each opponent within range of a gaze attack must attempt a saving throw each round at the beginning of his or her turn in the initiative order. Opponents can avoid the need to make the saving throw by not looking at the creature, in one of two ways.

Averting Eyes: The opponent avoids looking at the creature's face, instead looking at its body, watching its shadow, tracking it in a reflective surface, etc. Each round, the opponent has a 50% chance to avoid having to make a saving throw against the gaze attack. The creature with the gaze attack, however, gains concealment against that opponent.

Wearing a Blindfold: The foe cannot see the creature at all (also possible to achieve by turning one's back on the creature or shutting one's eyes) and does not have to make saving throws against the gaze. However, the creature with the gaze attack gains total concealment against the opponent.

A creature with a gaze attack can actively gaze as an attack action by choosing a target within range. That opponent must attempt a saving throw but can try to avoid this as described above. Thus, it is possible for an opponent to save against a creature's gaze twice during the same round, once before the opponent's action and once during the creature's turn.

Gaze attacks can affect ethereal opponents. A creature is immune to the gaze attacks of others of its kind unless otherwise noted. Allies of a creature with a gaze attack might be affected; these allies are considered to be averting their eyes from the creature with the gaze attack, and have a 50% chance to not need to make a saving throw against the gaze attack each round. The creature can also veil its eyes, thus negating its gaze ability.

Format: gaze; *Location*: Special Attacks.

Grab (Ex) If a creature with this special attack hits with the indicated attack (usually a claw or bite attack), it deals normal damage and attempts to start a grapple as a free action without provoking an attack of opportunity. The creature has the option to conduct the grapple normally, or simply to use the part of its body it used in the grab to hold the opponent. If it chooses to do the latter, it takes a –20 penalty on its CMB check to make and maintain the grapple, but does not gain the grappled condition itself.

A successful hold does not deal any extra damage unless the creature also has the constrict special attack. If the creature does not constrict, each successful grapple check it makes during successive rounds automatically deals the damage indicated for the attack that established the hold. Otherwise, it deals constriction damage as well (the amount is given in the creature's descriptive text).

Creatures with grab receive a +4 bonus on combat maneuver checks made to start and maintain a grapple.

Unless otherwise noted, grab works only against opponents no larger than the same size category as the creature. If the creature can use grab on sizes other than the default, this is noted in the creature's Special Attacks line.

Format: grab; *Location*: individual attacks.

Format: grab (Colossal); *Location*: Special Attacks.

Heat (Ex) The creature generates so much heat that its mere touch deals additional fire damage. The creature's metallic melee weapons also conduct this heat. *Format*: heat (1d6 fire); *Location*: Special Attacks.

Hold Breath (Ex) The creature can hold its breath for a number of minutes equal to 6 times its Constitution score before it risks drowning. *Format*: hold breath; *Location*: Special Qualities.

Immunity (Ex or Su) A creature with immunities takes no damage from listed sources. Immunities can also apply to afflictions, conditions, spells (based on school, level, or save type), and other effects. A creature that is immune does not suffer from these effects, or any secondary effects that are triggered due to an immune effect. *Format*: **Immune** acid, fire, paralysis; *Location*: Defensive Abilities.

Incorporeal (Ex) An incorporeal creature has no physical body. It can be harmed only by other incorporeal creatures, magic weapons or creatures that strike as magic weapons, and spells, spell-like abilities, or supernatural abilities. It is immune to all nonmagical attack forms. Even when hit by spells or magic weapons, it takes only half damage from a corporeal source. Although it is not a magical attack, holy water affects incorporeal undead. Corporeal spells and effects that do not cause damage only have a 50% chance of affecting an incorporeal creature (except for channel energy). Force spells and effects, such as from a *magic missile*, affect an incorporeal creature normally.

An incorporeal creature has no natural armor bonus but has a deflection bonus equal to its Charisma bonus (minimum +1, even if the creature's Charisma score does not normally provide a bonus).

An incorporeal creature can enter or pass through solid objects, but must remain adjacent to the object's exterior, and so cannot pass entirely through an object whose space is larger than its own. It can sense the presence of creatures or objects within a square adjacent to its current location,

but enemies have total concealment (50% miss chance) from an incorporeal creature that is inside an object. In order to see beyond the object it is in and attack normally, the incorporeal creature must emerge. An incorporeal creature inside an object has total cover, but when it attacks a creature outside the object it only has cover, so a creature outside with a readied action could strike at it as it attacks. An incorporeal creature cannot pass through a force effect.

An incorporeal creature's attacks pass through (ignore) natural armor, armor, and shields, although deflection bonuses and force effects (such as *mage armor*) work normally against it. Incorporeal creatures pass through and operate in water as easily as they do in air. Incorporeal creatures cannot fall or take falling damage. Incorporeal creatures cannot make trip or grapple attacks, nor can they be tripped or grappled. In fact, they cannot take any physical action that would move or manipulate an opponent or its equipment, nor are they subject to such actions. Incorporeal creatures have no weight and do not set off traps that are triggered by weight.

An incorporeal creature moves silently and cannot be heard with Perception checks if it doesn't wish to be. It has no Strength score, so its Dexterity modifier applies to its melee attacks, ranged attacks, and CMB. Nonvisual senses, such as scent and blindsight, are either ineffective or only partly effective with regard to incorporeal creatures. Incorporeal creatures have an innate sense of direction and can move at full speed even when they cannot see.

Format: incorporeal; *Location*: Defensive Abilities.

Jet (Ex) The creature can swim backward as a full-round action at the listed speed. It must move in a straight line while jetting, and does not provoke attacks of opportunity when it does so. *Format*: jet (200 ft.); *Location*: Speed.

Keen Scent (Ex) The creature can notice other creatures by scent in a 180-foot radius underwater and can detect blood in the water at ranges of up to a mile. *Format*: keen scent; *Location*: Senses.

Lifesense (Su) The creature notices and locates living creatures within 60 feet, just as if it possessed the blindsight ability. *Format*: lifesense; *Location*: Senses.

Light Blindness (Ex) Creatures with light blindness are blinded for 1 round if exposed to bright light, such as sunlight or the *daylight* spell. Such creatures are dazzled as long as they remain in areas of bright light. *Format*: light blindness; *Location*: Weaknesses.

Light Sensitivity (Ex) Creatures with light sensitivity are dazzled in areas of bright sunlight or within the radius of a *daylight* spell. *Format*: **Weaknesses** light sensitivity; *Location*: Weaknesses.

Lycanthropic Empathy (Ex) In any form, natural lycanthropes can communicate and empathize with animals related to their animal form. They can use

Diplomacy to alter such an animal's attitude, and when so doing gain a +4 racial bonus on the check. Afflicted lycanthropes only gain this ability in animal or hybrid form. *Format*: lycanthropic empathy (bears and dire bears); *Location*: Special Qualities.

Multiweapon Mastery (Ex) The creature never takes penalties on its attack rolls when fighting with multiple weapons. *Format*: multiweapon mastery; *Location*: Special Attacks.

Natural Attacks Most creatures possess one or more natural attacks (attacks made without a weapon). These attacks fall into one of two categories, primary and secondary attacks. Primary attacks are made using the creature's full base attack bonus and add the creature's full Strength bonus on damage rolls. Secondary attacks are made using the creature's base attack bonus –5 and add only 1/2 the creature's Strength bonus on damage rolls. If a creature has only one natural attack, it is always made using the creature's full base attack bonus and adds 1-1/2 times the creature's Strength bonus on damage rolls. This increase does not apply if the creature has multiple attacks but only takes one. If a creature has only one type of attack, but has multiple attacks per round, that attack is treated as a primary attack, regardless of its type. Table 3–1 lists some of the most common types of natural attacks and their classifications.

Some creatures treat one or more of their attacks differently, such as dragons, which always receive 1-1/2 times their Strength bonus on damage rolls with their bite attack. These exceptions are noted in the creature's description.

Creatures with natural attacks and attacks made with weapons can use both as part of a full attack action (although often a creature must forgo one natural attack for each weapon clutched in that limb, be it a claw, tentacle, or slam). Such creatures attack with their weapons normally but treat all of their available natural attacks as secondary attacks during that attack, regardless of the attack's original type.

Some creatures do not have natural attacks. These creatures can make unarmed strikes just like humans do. See Table 3–1 for typical damage values for natural attacks by creature size.

Format: bite +5 (1d6+1), 2 claws +5 (1d4+2), 4 tentacles +0 (1d4+1); *Location*: Melee and Ranged.

Natural Invisibility (Ex or Su) This ability is constant—the creature remains invisible at all times, even when attacking. As this ability is inherent, it is not subject to the *invisibility purge* spell. *Format*: natural invisibility; *Location*: Defensive Abilities.

Negative Energy Affinity (Ex) The creature is alive but is healed by negative energy and harmed by positive energy, as if it were an undead creature. *Format*: negative energy affinity; *Location*: Defensive Abilities.

No Breath (Ex) The monster does not breathe, and is immune to effects that require breathing (such as inhaled poison). This does not give immunity to cloud or gas attacks that do not require breathing. *Format*: no breath; *Location*: Special Qualities.

Paralysis (Ex or Su) This special attack renders the victim immobile. Paralyzed creatures cannot move, speak, or take any physical actions. The creature is rooted to the spot, frozen and helpless. Paralysis works on the body, and a character can usually resist it with a Fortitude saving throw (DC 10 + 1/2 the paralyzing creature's racial HD + the paralyzing creature's Con modifier; the DC is given in the creature's description). Unlike *hold person* and similar effects, a paralysis effect does not allow a new save each round. A winged creature flying in the air at the time that it is paralyzed cannot flap its wings and falls. A swimmer can't swim and may drown. The duration of the paralysis varies and is included in the creature's description. *Format*: paralysis (1d4 rounds, DC 18); *Location*: Special Attacks and individual attacks.

Plant Traits (Ex) Plants are immune to all mind-affecting effects (charms, compulsions, morale effects, patterns, and

Table 3-1: Natural Attacks by Size

	Base Damage by Size*									Damage	Attack
Natural Attack	Fine	Dim.	Tiny	Small	Med.	Large	Huge	Garg.	Col.	Type	Type
Bite	1	1d2	1d3	1d4	1d6	1d8	2d6	2d8	4d6	B,P, and S	Primary
Claw	—	1	1d2	1d3	1d4	1d6	1d8	2d6	2d8	B and S	Primary
Gore	1	1d2	1d3	1d4	1d6	1d8	2d6	2d8	4d6	P	Primary
Hoof, Tentacle, Wing	—	1	1d2	1d3	1d4	1d6	1d8	2d6	2d8	B	Secondary
Pincers, Tail Slap	1	1d2	1d3	1d4	1d6	1d8	2d6	2d8	4d6	B	Secondary
Slam	—	1	1d2	1d3	1d4	1d6	1d8	2d6	2d8	B	Primary
Sting	—	1	1d2	1d3	1d4	1d6	1d8	2d6	2d8	P	Primary
Talons	—	1	1d2	1d3	1d4	1d6	1d8	2d6	2d8	S	Primary
Other	—	1	1d2	1d3	1d4	1d6	1d8	2d6	2d8	B, P, or S	Secondary

* Individual creatures vary from this value as appropriate.

phantasms), paralysis, poison, polymorph, sleep, and stun. *Format*: plant traits; *Location*: Immune.

Poison (Ex or Su) A creature with this ability can poison those it attacks. The effects of the poison, including its save, frequency, and cure, are included in the creature's description. The saving throw to resist a poison is usually a Fort save (DC 10 + 1/2 the poisoning creature's racial HD + the creature's Con modifier; the exact DC is given in the creature's descriptive text). Poisons can be removed through *neutralize poison* and similar effects. *Format*: **Poison Name (Ex)** Sting—injury; *save* Fort DC 22, *frequency* 1/round for 6 rounds, *effect* 1d4 Con, *cure* 2 consecutive saves; *Location*: Special Attacks and individual attacks.

Pounce (Ex) When a creature with this special attack makes a charge, it can make a full attack (including rake attacks if the creature also has the rake ability). *Format*: pounce; *Location*: Special Attacks.

Powerful Charge (Ex) When a creature with this special attack makes a charge, its attack deals extra damage in addition to the normal benefits and hazards of a charge. The attack and amount of damage from the attack is given in the creature's description. *Format*: powerful charge (gore, 4d8+24); *Location*: Special Attacks.

Pull (Ex) A creature with this ability can choose to make a free combat maneuver check with a successful attack. If successful, this check pulls an opponent closer. The distance pulled is set by this ability. The type of attack that causes the pull and the distance pulled are included in the creature's description. This ability only works on creatures of a size equal to or smaller than the pulling creature. Creatures pulled in this way do not provoke attacks of opportunity and stop if the pull would move them into a solid object or creature. *Format*: pull (tentacle, 5 feet); *Location*: Special Attacks and individual attacks.

Push (Ex) A creature with the push ability can choose to make a free combat maneuver check with a particular successful attack (often a slam attack). If successful, this check pushes an opponent directly away as with a bull rush, but the distance moved is set by this ability. The type of attack that causes the push and the distance pushed are included in the creature's description. This ability only works on creatures of a size equal to or smaller than the pushing creature. Creatures pushed in this way do not provoke attacks of opportunity and stop if the push would move them into a solid object or creature. *Format*: push (slam, 10 feet); *Location*: Special Attacks and individual attacks.

Rake (Ex) A creature with this special attack gains extra natural attacks under certain conditions, typically when it grapples its foe. In addition to the options available to all grapplers, a monster with the rake ability gains two free claw attacks that it can use only against a grappled foe. The bonus and damage caused by these attacks is included in the creature's description. A monster with the rake ability must begin its turn already grappling to use its rake—it can't begin a grapple and rake in the same turn. *Format*: rake (2 claws +8, 1d4+2); *Location*: Special Attacks.

Regeneration (Ex) A creature with this ability is difficult to kill. Creatures with regeneration heal damage at a fixed rate, as with fast healing, but they cannot die as long as their regeneration is still functioning (although creatures with regeneration still fall unconscious when their hit points are below 0). Certain attack forms, typically fire and acid, cause a creature's regeneration to stop functioning on the round following the attack. During this round, the creature does not heal any damage and can die normally. The creature's descriptive text describes the types of damage that cause the regeneration to cease functioning.

Attack forms that don't deal hit point damage are not healed by regeneration. Regeneration also does not restore hit points lost from starvation, thirst, or suffocation. Regenerating creatures can regrow lost portions of their bodies and can reattach severed limbs or body parts if they are brought together within 1 hour of severing. Severed parts that are not reattached wither and die normally.

A creature must have a Constitution score to have the regeneration ability.

Format: regeneration 5 (fire, acid); *Location*: hp.

Rend (Ex) If it hits with two or more natural attacks in 1 round, a creature with the rend special attack can cause tremendous damage by latching onto the opponent's body and tearing flesh. This attack deals an additional amount of damage, but no more than once per round. The type of attacks that must hit and the additional damage are included in the creature's description. The additional damage is usually equal to the damage caused by one of the attacks plus 1-1/2 times the creature's Strength bonus. *Format*: rend (2 claws, 1d8+9); *Location*: Special Attacks.

Resistance (Ex) A creature with this special quality ignores some damage of the indicated type each time it takes damage of that kind (commonly acid, cold, electricity, or fire). The entry indicates the amount and type of damage ignored. *Format*: **Resist** acid 10; *Location*: Defensive Abilities.

Rock Catching (Ex) The creature (which must be of at least Large size) can catch Small, Medium, or Large rocks (or projectiles of similar shape). Once per round, a creature that would normally be hit by a rock can make a Reflex save to catch it as a free action. The DC is 15 for a Small rock, 20 for a Medium one, and 25 for a Large one. (If the projectile provides a magical bonus on attack rolls, the DC increases by that amount.) The creature must be aware of the attack in order to make a rock catching attempt. *Format*: rock catching; *Location*: Defensive Abilities.

Rock Throwing (Ex) This creature is an accomplished rock thrower and has a +1 racial bonus on attack rolls with thrown rocks. The creature can hurl rocks up to two categories smaller than its size; for example, a Large hill giant can hurl Small rocks. A "rock" is any large, bulky, and relatively regularly shaped object made of any material with a hardness of at least 5. The creature can hurl the rock up to five range increments. The size of the range increment varies with the creature. Damage from a thrown rock is generally twice the creature's base slam damage plus 1-1/2 times its Strength bonus. *Format*: rock throwing (120 ft.); *Location*: Special Attacks (damage is listed in Ranged attack).

Scent (Ex) This special quality allows a creature to detect approaching enemies, sniff out hidden foes, and track by sense of smell. Creatures with the scent ability can identify familiar odors just as humans do familiar sights.

The creature can detect opponents within 30 feet by sense of smell. If the opponent is upwind, the range increases to 60 feet; if downwind, it drops to 15 feet. Strong scents, such as smoke or rotting garbage, can be detected at twice the ranges noted above. Overpowering scents, such as skunk musk or troglodyte stench, can be detected at triple normal range.

When a creature detects a scent, the exact location of the source is not revealed—only its presence somewhere within range. The creature can take a move action to note the direction of the scent. When the creature is within 5 feet of the source, it pinpoints the source's location.

A creature with the scent ability can follow tracks by smell, making a Wisdom (or Survival) check to find or follow a track. The typical DC for a fresh trail is 10 (no matter what kind of surface holds the scent). This DC increases or decreases depending on how strong the quarry's odor is, the number of creatures, and the age of the trail. For each hour that the trail is cold, the DC increases by 2. The ability otherwise follows the rules for the Survival skill. Creatures tracking by scent ignore the effects of surface conditions and poor visibility.

Format: scent; *Location*: Senses.

See in Darkness (Su) The creature can see perfectly in darkness of any kind, including that created by *deeper darkness*. *Format*: see in darkness; *Location*: Senses.

Sound Mimicry (Ex) The creature perfectly imitates certain sounds or even specific voices. The creature makes a Bluff check opposed by the listener's Sense Motive check to recognize the mimicry, although if the listener isn't familiar with the person or type of creatures mimicked, it takes a –8 penalty on its Sense Motive check. The creature has a +8 racial bonus on its Bluff check to mimic sounds (including accents and speech patterns, if a voice mimic) it has listened to for at least 10 minutes. The creature cannot duplicate the effects of magical abilities (such as bardic performance or a harpy's captivating song), though it may be able to mimic the sound of those abilities. This ability does not allow the creature to speak or understand languages it doesn't know. *Format*: sound mimicry (voices); *Location*: Special Qualities.

Spell-Like Abilities (Sp) Spell-like abilities are magical and work just like spells (though they are not spells and so have no verbal, somatic, focus, or material components). They go away in an *antimagic field* and are subject to spell resistance if the spell the ability is based on would be subject to spell resistance.

A spell-like ability usually has a limit on how often it can be used. A constant spell-like ability or one that can be used at will has no use limit; unless otherwise stated, a creature can only use a constant spell-like ability on itself. Reactivating a constant spell-like ability is a swift action. Using all other spell-like abilities is a standard action unless noted otherwise, and doing so provokes attacks of opportunity. It is possible to make a concentration check to use a spell-like ability defensively and avoid provoking an attack of opportunity, just as when casting a spell. A spell-like ability can be disrupted just as a spell can be. Spell-like abilities cannot be used to counterspell, nor can they be counterspelled.

For creatures with spell-like abilities, a designated caster level defines how difficult it is to dispel their spell-like effects and to define any level-dependent variables (such as range and duration) the abilities might have. The creature's caster level never affects which spell-like abilities the creature has; sometimes the given caster level is lower than the level a spellcasting character would need to cast the spell of the same name. If no caster level is specified, the caster level is equal to the creature's Hit Dice. The saving throw (if any) against a spell-like ability is 10 + the level of the spell the ability resembles or duplicates + the creature's Charisma modifier.

Some spell-like abilities duplicate spells that work differently when cast by characters of different classes. A monster's spell-like abilities are presumed to be the sorcerer/wizard versions. If the spell in question is not a sorcerer/wizard spell, then default to cleric, druid, bard, paladin, and ranger, in that order.

Format: At will—*burning hands* (DC 13); *Location*: Spell-Like Abilities.

Spell Resistance (Ex) A creature with spell resistance can avoid the effects of spells and spell-like abilities that directly affect it. To determine whether a spell or spell-like ability works against a creature with spell resistance, the caster must make a caster level check (1d20 + caster level). If the result equals or exceeds the creature's spell resistance, the spell works normally, although the creature is still allowed a saving throw if the spell would normally permit one. *Format*: SR 18; *Location*: Defensive Abilities.

Split (Ex) The creature splits into two identical copies of itself if subject to certain attacks or effects. Each copy has half the original's current hit points (rounded down). A creature reduced below the listed hit points cannot be further split and can be killed normally. *Format*: split (piercing and slashing, 10 hp); *Location*: Defensive Abilities.

Stench (Ex) A creature with the stench special ability secretes an oily chemical that nearly every other creature finds offensive. All living creatures (except those with this ability) within 30 feet must succeed on a Fortitude save (DC 10 + 1/2 the stench creature's racial HD + the stench creature's Con modifier; the exact DC is given in the creature's descriptive text) or be sickened. The duration of the sickened condition is given in the creature's descriptive text. Creatures that successfully save cannot be affected by the same creature's stench for 24 hours. A *delay poison* or *neutralize poison* spell removes the effect from the sickened creature. Creatures with immunity to poison are unaffected, and creatures resistant to poison receive their normal bonus on their saving throws. *Format*: stench (DC 15, 10 rounds); *Location*: Aura.

Strangle (Ex) An opponent grappled by the creature cannot speak or cast spells with verbal components. *Format*: strangle; *Location*: Special Attacks.

Summon (Sp) A creature with the summon ability can summon other specific creatures of its kind much as though casting a *summon monster* spell, but it usually has only a limited chance of success (as specified in the creature's entry). Roll d%: On a failure, no creature answers the summons. Summoned creatures automatically return from whence they came after 1 hour. A creature summoned in this way cannot use any spells or spell-like abilities that require material components costing more than 1 gp unless those components are supplied, nor can it use its own summon ability for 1 hour. An appropriate spell level is given for each summoning ability for purposes of Will saves, caster level checks, and concentration checks. No experience points are awarded for defeating summoned monsters. *Format*: 1/day—summon (level 4, 1 hezrou 35%); *Location*: Spell-Like Abilities.

Sunlight Powerlessness (Ex) If the creature is in sunlight (but not in an area of *daylight* or similar spells), it cannot attack and is staggered. *Format*: sunlight powerlessness; *Location*: Weaknesses.

Swallow Whole (Ex) If a creature with this special attack begins its turn with an opponent grappled in its mouth (see Grab), it can attempt a new combat maneuver check (as though attempting to pin the opponent). If it succeeds, it swallows its prey, and the opponent takes bite damage. Unless otherwise noted, the opponent can be up to one size category smaller than the swallowing creature. Being swallowed causes a creature to take damage each round. The amount and type of damage varies and is given in the creature's statistics. A swallowed creature keeps the grappled condition, while the creature that did the swallowing does not. A swallowed creature can try to cut its way free with any light slashing or piercing weapon (the amount of cutting damage required to get free is equal to 1/10 the creature's total hit points), or it can just try to escape the grapple. The Armor Class of the interior of a creature that swallows whole is normally 10 + 1/2 its natural armor bonus, with no modifiers for size or Dexterity. If a swallowed creature cuts its way out, the swallowing creature cannot use swallow whole again until the damage is healed. If the swallowed creature escapes the grapple, success puts it back in the attacker's mouth, where it may be bitten or swallowed again. *Format*: swallow whole (5d6 acid damage, AC 15, 18 hp); *Location*: Special Attacks.

Telepathy (Su) The creature can mentally communicate with any other creature within a certain range (specified in the creature's entry, usually 100 feet) that has a language. It is possible to address multiple creatures at once telepathically, although maintaining a telepathic conversation with more than one creature at a time is just as difficult as simultaneously speaking and listening to multiple people at the same time. *Format*: telepathy 100 ft.; *Location*: Languages.

Trample (Ex) As a full-round action, a creature with the trample ability can attempt to overrun any creature that is at least one size category smaller than itself. This works just like the overrun combat maneuver, but the trampling creature does not need to make a check, it merely has to move over opponents in its path. Targets of a trample take an amount of damage equal to the trampling creature's slam damage + 1-1/2 times its Str modifier. Targets of a trample can make an attack of opportunity, but at a –4 penalty. If targets forgo an attack of opportunity, they can attempt to avoid the trampling creature and receive a Reflex save to take half damage. The save DC against a creature's trample attack is 10 + 1/2 the creature's HD + the creature's Str modifier (the exact DC is given in the creature's descriptive text). A trampling creature can only deal trampling damage to each target once per round, no matter how many times its movement takes it over a target creature. *Format*: trample (2d6+9, DC 20); *Location*: Special Attacks.

Tremorsense (Ex) A creature with tremorsense is sensitive to vibrations in the ground and can automatically pinpoint the location of anything that is in contact with the ground. Aquatic creatures with tremorsense can also sense the location of creatures moving through water. The ability's range is specified in the creature's descriptive text. *Format*: tremorsense 60 ft.; *Location*: Senses. **Trip (Ex)** A creature with the trip special attack can attempt to trip its opponent as a free action without provoking an attack of opportunity if it hits with the specified attack. If the attempt fails, the creature is not tripped in return. *Format*: trip; *Location*: individual attacks.

Undead Traits (Ex) Undead are immune to death effects, disease, mind-affecting effects (charms, compulsions, morale effects, phantasms, and patterns), paralysis, poison, sleep, stun, and any effect that requires a Fortitude save (unless the effect also works on objects or is harmless). Undead are not subject to ability drain, energy drain, or nonlethal damage. Undead are immune to damage or penalties to their physical ability scores (Strength, Dexterity, and Constitution), as well as to fatigue and exhaustion effects. Undead are not at risk of death from massive damage. *Format*: undead traits; *Location*: Immune.

Undersized Weapons (Ex) The creature uses manufactured weapons as if it were one size category smaller than the creature's actual size. *Format*: undersized weapons; *Location*: Special Qualities.

Unnatural Aura (Su) Animals do not willingly approach the creature unless the animal's master makes a DC 25 Handle Animal, Ride, or wild empathy check. *Format*: unnatural aura (30 ft.); *Location*: Aura.

Vulnerabilities (Ex or Su) A creature with vulnerabilities takes half again as much damage (+50%) from a specific energy type, regardless of whether a saving throw is allowed or if the save is a success or failure. Creatures with a vulnerability that is not an energy type instead take a –4 penalty on saves against spells and effects that cause or use the listed vulnerability (such as spells with the light descriptor). Some creatures might suffer additional effects, as noted in their descriptions. *Format*: vulnerability to fire; *Location*: Weaknesses.

Web (Ex) Creatures with the web ability can use webs to support themselves and up to one additional creature of the same size. In addition, such creatures can throw a web up to eight times per day. This is similar to an attack with a net but has a maximum range of 50 feet, with a range increment of 10 feet, and is effective against targets up to one size category larger than the web spinner. An entangled creature can escape with a successful Escape Artist check or burst the web with a Strength check. Both are standard actions with a DC equal to 10 + 1/2 the creature's HD + the creature's Con modifier. Attempts to burst a web by those caught in it take a –4 penalty.

Web spinners can create sheets of sticky webbing up to three times their size. They usually position these sheets to snare flying creatures but can also try to trap prey on the ground. Approaching creatures must succeed on a DC 20 Perception check to notice a web; otherwise they stumble into it and become trapped as though by a successful web attack. Attempts to escape or burst the webbing gain a +5 bonus if the trapped creature has something to walk on or grab while pulling free. Each 5-foot-square section of web has a number of hit points equal to the Hit Dice of the creature that created it and DR 5/—. A creature can move across its own web at its climb speed and can pinpoint the location of any creature touching its web. *Format*: web (+8 ranged, DC 16, 5 hp); *Location*: Special Attacks.

Whirlwind (Su) Some creatures can transform themselves into whirlwinds and remain in that form for up to 1 round for every 2 HD they have. If the creature has a fly speed, it can continue to fly at that same speed while in whirlwind form; otherwise it gains a fly speed equal to its base land speed (average maneuverability) while in whirlwind form.

The whirlwind is always 5 feet wide at its base, but its height and width at the top vary from creature to creature (minimum 10 feet high). A whirlwind's width at its peak is always equal to half its height. The creature controls the exact height, but it must be at least 10 feet high.

The whirlwind form does not provoke attacks of opportunity, even if the creature enters the space another creature occupies. Another creature might be caught in the whirlwind if it touches or enters the whirlwind, or if the whirlwind moves into or through a creature's space. A creature in whirlwind form cannot make its normal attacks and does not threaten the area around it.

A creature that comes in contact with the whirlwind must succeed on a Reflex save (DC 10 + 1/2 the monster's HD + the monster's Strength modifier) or take damage as if it were hit by the whirlwind creature's slam attack. It must also succeed on a second Reflex save or be picked up bodily and held suspended in the powerful winds, automatically taking the indicated damage each round. A creature that can fly is allowed a Reflex save each round on its turn to escape the whirlwind. The creature still takes damage that round but can leave if the save is successful.

Creatures trapped in the whirlwind cannot move except to go where the whirlwind carries them or to escape the whirlwind. Trapped creatures can otherwise act normally, but must succeed on a concentration check (DC 15 + spell level) to cast a spell. Creatures caught in the whirlwind take a –4 penalty to Dexterity and a –2 penalty on attack rolls. The whirlwind can have only as many creatures trapped inside at one time as will fit inside the whirlwind's volume. As a free action, the whirlwind can eject any carried creatures whenever it wishes, depositing them in its space.

If the whirlwind's base touches the ground, it creates a swirling cloud of debris. This cloud is centered on the creature and has a diameter equal to half the whirlwind's height. The cloud obscures all vision, including darkvision, beyond 5 feet. Creatures 5 feet away have concealment, while those farther away have total concealment. Those caught in the cloud of debris must succeed on a concentration check (DC 15 + spell level) to cast a spell.

Format: whirlwind (3/day, 10–30 ft. high, 1d6+6 damage, DC 15); *Location*: Special Attacks.

CREATURE TYPES

Each creature has one type, which broadly defines its abilities. Some creatures also have one or more subtypes, as described on pages 305–310. A creature cannot violate the rules of its subtype without a special ability or quality to explain the difference—templates can often change a creature's type drastically. For full information on creature types and subtypes (such as for the purpose of advancing or creating new monsters), see the *Pathfinder RPG Bestiary*.

ABERRATION

An aberration has a bizarre anatomy, strange abilities, an alien mindset, or any combination of the three.

ANIMAL

An animal is a living, nonhuman creature, usually a vertebrate with no magical abilities and no innate capacity for language or culture. Animals usually have additional information on how they can serve as companions. An animal has an Intelligence score of 1 or 2 (no creature with an Intelligence score of 3 or higher can be an animal).

CONSTRUCT

A construct is an animated object or artificially created creature. A construct has the following traits.

- No Constitution score. Any DCs or other statistics that rely on a Constitution score treat a construct as having a score of 10 (no bonus or penalty).
- Immunity to all mind-affecting effects (charms, compulsions, morale effects, patterns, and phantasms).
- Immunity to bleed, disease, death effects, necromancy effects, paralysis, poison, sleep effects, and stunning.
- Cannot heal damage on its own, but often can be repaired via exposure to a certain kind of effect (see the creature's description for details) or through the use of the Craft Construct feat. Constructs can also be healed through spells such as *make whole*. A construct with the fast healing special quality still benefits from that quality.
- Not subject to ability damage, ability drain, fatigue, exhaustion, energy drain, or nonlethal damage.
- Immunity to any effect that requires a Fortitude save (unless the effect also works on objects, or is harmless).
- Not at risk of death from massive damage. Immediately destroyed when reduced to 0 hit points or fewer.
- A construct cannot be raised or resurrected.
- A construct is hard to destroy, and gains bonus hit points based on its size (included in its stat block).
- Constructs do not breathe, eat, or sleep.

DRAGON

A dragon is a reptile-like creature, usually winged, with magical or unusual abilities.

FEY

A fey is a creature with supernatural abilities and connections to nature or to some other force or place. Fey are usually human-shaped.

HUMANOID

A humanoid usually has two arms, two legs, and one head, or a human-like torso, arms, and a head. Humanoids have few or no supernatural or extraordinary abilities, but most can speak and usually have well-developed societies. They are usually Small or Medium (with the exception of giants). Every humanoid creature also has a specific subtype to match its race, such as human, dark folk, or goblinoid.

Humanoids with 1 Hit Die exchange the features of their humanoid Hit Die for the class features of a PC or NPC class. Humanoids with more than 1 Hit Die (such as giants) are the only humanoids who make use of the features of the humanoid type.

MAGICAL BEAST

Magical beasts are similar to animals but can have Intelligence scores higher than 2 (in which case the creature knows at least one language, but can't necessarily speak). Magical beasts usually have supernatural or extraordinary abilities, but are sometimes merely bizarre in appearance or habits.

MONSTROUS HUMANOID

Monstrous humanoids are similar to humanoids, but with monstrous or animalistic features. They often have magical abilities as well.

OOZE

An ooze is an amorphous or mutable creature, usually mindless. An ooze has the following traits.

- Mindless: No Intelligence score, and immunity to all mind-affecting effects (charms, compulsions, phantasms, patterns, and morale effects). Mindless creatures have no skills or feats. An ooze with an Intelligence score loses this trait.
- Blind (but have the blindsight special quality), with immunity to gaze attacks, visual effects, illusions, and other attack forms that rely on sight.
- Immunity to poison, sleep effects, paralysis, polymorph, and stunning.
- Oozes eat and breathe, but do not sleep.

OUTSIDER

An outsider is at least partially composed of the essence (but not necessarily the material) of some plane other than the Material Plane. An outsider has the following traits.

- Unlike most living creatures, an outsider does not have a dual nature—its soul and body form one unit. When an outsider is slain, no soul is set loose. Spells that restore souls to their bodies, such as *raise dead*, *reincarnate*, and *resurrection*, don't work on an outsider. It takes a different magical effect, such as *limited wish*, *wish*, *miracle*, or *true resurrection*, to restore it to life. An outsider with the native subtype can be raised, reincarnated, or resurrected just as other living creatures can be.

- Outsiders breathe, but do not need to eat or sleep (although they can do so if they wish). Native outsiders breathe, eat, and sleep.

PLANT

This type comprises vegetable creatures. Note that regular plants, such as one finds growing in gardens and fields, lack Intelligence, Wisdom, and Charisma scores; even though plants are alive, they are objects, not creatures. A plant creature has the following traits.

- Immunity to all mind-affecting effects (charms, compulsions, morale effects, patterns, and phantasms).
- Immunity to paralysis, poison, polymorph, sleep effects, and stunning.
- Plants breathe and eat, but do not sleep.

UNDEAD

Undead are once-living creatures animated by spiritual or supernatural forces. An undead creature has the following traits.

- No Constitution score. Undead use their Charisma score in place of their Constitution score when calculating hit points, Fortitude saves, and any special ability that relies on Constitution (such as when calculating a breath weapon's DC).
- Immunity to all mind-affecting effects (charms, compulsions, morale effects, patterns, and phantasms).
- Immunity to bleed, death effects, disease, paralysis, poison, sleep effects, and stunning.
- Not subject to nonlethal damage, ability drain, or energy drain. Immune to damage to its physical ability scores (Constitution, Dexterity, and Strength), as well as to exhaustion and fatigue effects.
- Cannot heal damage on its own if it has no Intelligence score, although it can be healed. Negative energy (such as an *inflict* spell) can heal undead creatures. The fast healing special quality works regardless of the creature's Intelligence score.
- Immunity to any effect that requires a Fortitude save (unless the effect also works on objects or is harmless).
- Not at risk of death from massive damage, but is immediately destroyed when reduced to 0 hit points.
- Not affected by *raise dead* and *reincarnate* spells or abilities. *Resurrection* and *true resurrection* can affect undead creatures. These spells turn undead creatures back into the living creatures they were before

becoming undead.

- Undead do not breathe, eat, or sleep.

VERMIN

This type includes insects, arachnids, other arthropods, worms, and similar invertebrates. Vermin have the following traits.

- Mindless: No Intelligence score, and immunity to all mind-affecting effects (charms, compulsions, morale effects, patterns, and phantasms). Mindless creatures have no feats or skills. A vermin-like creature with an Intelligence score is usually either an animal or a magical beast, depending on its other abilities.
- Vermin breathe, eat, and sleep.

CREATURE SUBTYPES

Some creatures have one or more subtypes. Subtypes add additional abilities and qualities to a creature.

Aeon Subtype: Aeons are a race of neutral outsiders who roam the planes maintaining the balance of reality. Aeons possess the following traits.

- Immunity to cold, poison, and critical hits.
- Resistance to electricity 10 and fire 10.

Envisaging (Su) Aeons communicate wordlessly, almost incomprehensibly. Caring little for the wants and desires of other creatures, they have no need to engage in exchanges of dialogue. Instead, aeons mentally scan beings for their thoughts and intentions, and then retaliate with flashes of psychic projections that emit a single concept in response to whatever the other being was thinking. The flash is usually a combination of a visual and aural stimulation, which displays how the aeon perceives future events might work out. For instance, an aeon seeking to raze a city communicates this concept to non-aeons by sending them a vivid image of the city crumbling to ash. An aeon's envisaging functions as a non-verbal form of telepathy. Aeons cannot read the thoughts of any creature immune to mind-affecting effects.

Extension of All (Ex) Through an aeon's connection to the multiverse, it gains access to strange and abstruse knowledge that filters through all existence. Much of the knowledge is timeless, comprised of events long past, present, and potentially even those yet to come. Aeons gain a racial bonus equal to half their racial Hit Dice on all Knowledge skill checks. This same connection also binds them to other aeons. As a result, they can communicate with each other freely, over great distances as if using telepathy. This ability also works across planes, albeit less effectively, allowing the communication of vague impressions or feelings, not specific details or sights. Due to the vast scope of the aeon race's multiplanar concerns, though, even the most dire reports of a single aeon rarely inspire dramatic or immediate action.

Void Form (Su) Though aeons aren't incorporeal, their forms are only a semi-tangible manifestation of something greater. An aeon's void form grants it a deflection bonus equal to 1/4 its Hit Dice (rounded down).

Agathion Subtype: Agathions are beast-aspect outsiders native to Nirvana. They have the following traits.
- Low-light vision
- Immunity to electricity and petrification.
- Resistance to cold 10 and sonic 10.
- Lay on hands as a paladin whose level equals the agathion's Hit Dice.
- +4 racial bonus on saving throws against poison.
- Except where otherwise noted, agathions speak Celestial, Infernal, and Draconic.
- *Speak with Animals (Su)* This ability works like *speak with animals* (caster level equal to the agathion's Hit Dice) but is a free action and does not require sound.
- *Truespeech (Su)* All agathions can speak with any creature that has a language, as though using a *tongues* spell (caster level equal to angel's Hit Dice). This ability is always active.

Air Subtype: This subtype is usually used for outsiders with a connection to the Elemental Plane of Air. Air creatures always have fly speeds and usually have perfect maneuverability. Air creatures treat Fly as a class skill.

Angel Subtype: Angels are a race of celestials, or good outsiders, native to the good-aligned Outer Planes. An angel possesses the following traits.
- Darkvision 60 feet and low-light vision.
- Immunity to acid, cold, and petrification.
- Resistance to electricity 10 and fire 10.
- +4 racial bonus on saves against poison.
- *Protective Aura (Su)* Against attacks made or effects created by evil creatures, this ability provides a +4 deflection bonus to AC and a +4 resistance bonus on saving throws to anyone within 20 feet of the angel. Otherwise, it functions as a *magic circle against evil* effect and a *lesser globe of invulnerability*, both with a radius of 20 feet (caster level equals angel's HD). The defensive benefits from the circle are not included in an angel's stat block.
- *Truespeech (Su)* All angels can speak with any creature that has a language, as though using a *tongues* spell (caster level equal to angel's Hit Dice). This ability is always active.

Aquatic Subtype: These creatures always have swim speeds and can move in water without making Swim checks. An aquatic creature can breathe water. It cannot breathe air unless it has the amphibious special quality. Aquatic creatures always treat Swim as a class skill.

Archon Subtype: Archons are a race of celestials, or good outsiders, native to lawful good-aligned Outer Planes. An archon possesses the following traits.
- Darkvision 60 feet and low-light vision.

- *Aura of Menace (Su)* A righteous aura surrounds archons that fight or get angry. Any hostile creature within a 20-foot radius of an archon must succeed on a Will save to resist its effects. The save DC varies with the type of archon, is Charisma-based, and includes a +2 racial bonus. Those who fail take a –2 penalty on attack rolls, on saves, and to AC for 24 hours or until they successfully hit the archon that generated the aura. A creature that has resisted or broken the effect cannot be affected again by the same archon's aura for 24 hours.
- Immunity to electricity and petrification.
- +4 racial bonus on saves against poison.
- *Teleport (Sp)* Archons can use *greater teleport* at will, as the spell (caster level 14th), except that the creature can transport only itself and up to 50 pounds of carried objects.
- *Truespeech (Su)* All archons can speak with any creature that has a language, as though using a *tongues* spell (caster level 14th). This ability is always active.

Augmented Subtype: A creature receives this subtype when something (usually a template) changes its original type. Some creatures (those with an inherited template) are born with this subtype; others acquire it when they take on an acquired template. The augmented subtype is always paired with the creature's original type.

Azata Subtype: Azatas are a race of celestials, or good outsiders, native to chaotic good-aligned Outer Planes. An azata possesses the following traits.
- Darkvision 60 feet and low-light vision.
- Immunity to electricity and petrification.
- Resistance to cold 10 and fire 10.
- *Truespeech (Su)* All azatas can speak with any creature that has a language, as though using a *tongues* spell (caster level 14th). This ability is always active.

Chaotic Subtype: This subtype is usually applied to outsiders native to the chaotic-aligned Outer Planes. Most creatures that have this subtype also have chaotic alignments; however, if their alignments change, they still retain the subtype. Any effect that depends on alignment affects a creature with this subtype as if the creature had a chaotic alignment, no matter what its alignment actually is. The creature also suffers effects according to its actual alignment. A creature with the chaotic subtype overcomes damage reduction as if its natural weapons and any weapons it wields are chaotically aligned.

Cold Subtype: A creature with the cold subtype has immunity to cold and vulnerability to fire.

Daemon Subtype: Daemons are neutral evil outsiders that eat souls and thrive on disaster and ruin. They have the following traits unless otherwise noted.
- Immunity to acid, death effects, disease, and poison.
- Resistance to cold 10, electricity 10, and fire 10.

- *Summon (Sp)* Daemons share the ability to summon others of their kind, typically another of their type or a small number of less powerful daemons.
- Telepathy.
- Except where otherwise noted, daemons speak Abyssal, Draconic, and Infernal.

Dark Folk Subtype: Dark folk are reclusive subterranean humanoids with an aversion to light.

Demon Subtype: Demons are chaotic evil outsiders from the Abyss. Demons have the following traits.

- Immunity to electricity and poison.
- Resistance to acid 10, cold 10, and fire 10.
- *Summon (Sp)* Demons share the ability to summon others of their kind, typically another of their type or a small number of less powerful demons.
- Telepathy.
- Except where otherwise noted, demons speak Abyssal, Celestial, and Draconic.

Devil Subtype: Devils are lawful evil outsiders that hail from the plane of Hell. Devils possess the following traits.

- Immunity to fire and poison.
- Resistance to acid 10 and cold 10.
- See in darkness.
- *Summon (Sp)* Devils can summon others of their kind, typically another of their type or a small number of less powerful devils.
- Telepathy.
- Except when otherwise noted, devils speak Celestial, Draconic, and Infernal.

Earth Subtype: This subtype is usually used for outsiders with a connection to the Elemental Plane of Earth. Earth creatures usually have burrow speeds, and most earth creatures can burrow through solid rock. Earth creatures with a burrow speed possess tremorsense.

Elemental Subtype: An elemental is a being composed entirely from one of the four classical elements: air, earth, fire, or water. An elemental has the following features.

- Immunity to bleed, paralysis, poison, sleep effects, and stunning.
- Not subject to critical hits or flanking. Does not take additional damage from precision-based attacks, such as sneak attack.
- Elementals do not breathe, eat, or sleep.

Evil Subtype: This subtype is usually applied to outsiders native to the evil-aligned Outer Planes. Evil outsiders are also called fiends. Most creatures that have this subtype also have evil alignments; however, if their alignments change, they still retain the subtype. Any effect that depends on alignment affects a creature with this subtype as if the creature has an evil alignment, no matter what its alignment actually is. The creature also suffers effects according to its actual alignment. A creature with the evil subtype overcomes damage

reduction as if its natural weapons and any weapons it wields are evil-aligned.

Extraplanar Subtype: This subtype is applied to any creature when it is on a plane other than its native plane. A creature that travels the planes can gain or lose this subtype as it goes from plane to plane. Monster entries assume that encounters with creatures take place on the Material Plane, and every creature whose native plane is not the Material Plane has the extraplanar subtype (but would not have it when on its home plane). Every extraplanar creature in this book has a home plane mentioned in its description. Creatures not labeled as extraplanar are natives of the Material Plane, and they gain the extraplanar subtype if they leave the Material Plane. No creature has the extraplanar subtype when it is on a transitive plane, such as the Astral Plane, the Ethereal Plane, or the Plane of Shadow.

Fire Subtype: A creature with the fire subtype has immunity to fire and vulnerability to cold.

Giant Subtype: A giant is a humanoid creature of great strength, usually of at least Large size. Giants have racial Hit Dice and never substitute such Hit Dice for class levels like some humanoids. Giants have low-light vision, and treat Intimidate and Perception as class skills.

Gnome Subtype: This subtype is applied to gnomes and creatures related to gnomes. Creatures with the gnome subtype have low-light vision.

Good Subtype: This subtype is usually applied to outsiders native to the good-aligned Outer Planes. Most creatures that have this subtype also have good alignments; however, if their alignments change, they still retain the subtype. Any effect that depends on alignment affects a creature with this subtype as if the creature has a good alignment, no matter what its alignment actually is. The creature also suffers effects according to its actual alignment. A creature with the good subtype overcomes damage reduction as if its natural weapons and any weapons it wields are good-aligned.

Grippli Subtype: Gripplis are frog-like humanoids. Creatures with the grippli subtype have darkvision.

Incorporeal Subtype: An incorporeal creature has no physical body. An incorporeal creature is immune to critical hits and precision-based damage (such as sneak attack damage) unless the attacks are made using a weapon with the *ghost touch* special weapon quality. In addition, creatures with the incorporeal subtype gain the incorporeal special quality (see page 298).

Inevitable Subtype: Inevitables are construct-like outsiders built by the axiomites to enforce law. They have the following traits.

- Low-light vision.
- *Constructed (Ex)* Although inevitables are living outsiders, their bodies are constructed of physical components,

and in many ways they function as constructs. For the purposes of effects targeting creatures by type (such as a ranger's favored enemy and *bane* weapons), inevitables count as both outsiders and constructs. They are immune to death effects, disease, mind-affecting effects, necromancy effects, paralysis, poison, sleep, stun, and any effect that requires a Fortitude save (unless the effect also works on objects, or is harmless). Inevitables are not subject to nonlethal damage, ability damage, ability drain, fatigue, exhaustion, or energy drain. They are not at risk of death from massive damage. They have bonus hit points as constructs of their size.

- *Saves*: An inevitable's good saving throws are Fortitude and Will.
- *Skills*: In addition to the class skills all outsiders have, inevitables have Acrobatics, Diplomacy, Intimidate, and Survival as class skills.
- *Regeneration (Ex)* Inevitables have regeneration/chaotic. The regeneration amount varies by the type of inevitable.
- *Truespeech (Su)* An inevitable can speak with any creature that has a language, as if using a *tongues* spell (caster level 14th). This ability is always active.

Lawful Subtype: This subtype is usually applied to outsiders native to the lawful-aligned Outer Planes. Most creatures that have this subtype also have lawful alignments; however, if their alignments change, they still retain the subtype. Any effect that depends on alignment affects a creature with this subtype as if the creature had a lawful alignment, no matter what its alignment actually is. The creature also suffers effects according to its actual alignment. A creature with the lawful subtype overcomes damage reduction as if its natural weapons and any weapons it wields are lawful-aligned.

Native Subtype: This subtype is applied only to outsiders. These creatures have mortal ancestors or a strong connection to the Material Plane and can be raised, reincarnated, or resurrected just as other living creatures can be. Creatures with this subtype are native to the Material Plane. Unlike true outsiders, native outsiders need to eat and sleep.

Nightshade Subtype: Nightshades are monstrous undead composed of shadow and evil. They have the following traits.

- Low-light vision.
- *Desecrating Aura (Su)* All nightshades have a 30-foot-radius emanation equivalent to a *desecrate* spell centered on a shrine of evil power. Undead within this radius (including the nightshade) gain a +2 profane bonus on attack and damage rolls and saving throws, as well as +2 hit points per die, and the save DC of channeled negative energy is increased by +6 (these adjustments are included for the nightshades in their

entries). This aura can be negated by *dispel evil*, but a nightshade can reactivate it on its turn as a free action. A desecrating aura suppresses and is suppressed by *consecrate* or *hallow*; both effects are negated within any overlapping area of effect.

- *Channel Energy (Su)* A nightshade can channel negative energy as cleric of a level equal to its base CR. It can use this ability a number of times per day equal to 3 + its Charisma modifier.
- *Darksense (Ex)* Nightshades gain *true seeing* in dim light and darkness. Regardless of light conditions, they can detect living creatures and their health within 60 feet, as blindsense with *deathwatch* continuously active. *Mind blank* and *nondetection* prevent the latter effect but not the nightshade's *true seeing*.
- *Light Aversion (Ex)* A nightshade in bright light becomes sickened—the penalties from this condition are doubled when the nightshade is in natural sunlight.
- *Summon (Sp)* Nightshades can summon undead creatures. They can be summoned only within areas of darkness, and summoned undead cannot create spawn. The exact type and number of undead they can summon vary according to the nightshade in question, as detailed in each nightshade's entry.

Protean Subtype: Proteans are serpentine outsiders of pure chaos. They have the following traits.

- Blindsense (distance varies by protean type).
- Immunity to acid.
- Resistance to electricity 10 and sonic 10.
- Constrict and grab as special attacks.
- Supernatural flight.
- *Freedom of Movement (Su)* A protean has continuous *freedom of movement*, as per the spell.
- *Amorphous Anatomy (Ex)* A protean's vital organs shift and change shape and position constantly. This grants it a 50% chance to ignore additional damage caused by critical hits and sneak attacks, and grants it immunity to polymorph effects (unless the protean is a willing target). A protean automatically recovers from physical blindness or deafness after 1 round by growing new sensory organs to replace those that were compromised.
- *Change Shape (Su)* A protean's form is not fixed. Once per day as a standard action, a protean may change shape into any Small, Medium, or Large animal, elemental, giant, humanoid, magical beast, monstrous humanoid, ooze, plant, or vermin. A protean can resume its true form as a free action, and when it does so, it gains the effects of a *heal* spell (CL equal to the protean's HD).

Qlippoth Subtype: Qlippoth are chaotic evil outsiders from the deepest reaches of the Abyss. They have the following traits.

- Immunity to cold, mind-affecting effects, and poison.

- Resistance to acid 10, electricity 10, and fire 10.
- *Horrific Appearance (Su)* All qlippoth have such horrific and mind-rending shapes that those who gaze upon them suffer all manner of ill effects. A qlippoth can present itself as a standard action to assault the senses of all living creatures within 30 feet. The exact effects caused by a qlippoth's horrific appearance vary by the type of qlippoth. A successful Will save (DC 10 + 1/2 the qlippoth's Hit Dice + the qlippoth's Charisma modifier) reduces or negates the effect. This ability is a mind-affecting gaze attack.
- Telepathy.
- Except where otherwise noted, qlippoth speak Abyssal.

Shapechanger Subtype: A shapechanger has the supernatural ability to assume one or more alternate forms. Many magical effects allow some kind of shapeshifting, and not every creature that can change shape has the shapechanger subtype.

Swarm Subtype: A swarm is a collection of Fine, Diminutive, or Tiny creatures that acts as a single creature. A swarm has the characteristics of its type, except as noted here. A swarm has a single pool of Hit Dice and hit points, a single initiative modifier, a single speed, and a single Armor Class. A swarm makes saving throws as a single creature. A single swarm occupies a square (if it is made up of nonflying creatures) or a cube (of flying creatures) 10 feet on a side, but its reach is 0 feet, like its component creatures. In order to attack, it moves into an opponent's space, which provokes an attack of opportunity. A swarm can occupy the same space as a creature of any size, since it crawls all over its prey. A swarm can move through squares occupied by enemies and vice versa without impediment, although the swarm provokes an attack of opportunity if it does so. A swarm can move through cracks or holes large enough for its component creatures.

A swarm of Tiny creatures consists of 300 nonflying creatures or 1,000 flying creatures. A swarm of Diminutive creatures consists of 1,500 nonflying creatures or 5,000 flying creatures. A swarm of Fine creatures consists of 10,000 creatures, whether they are flying or not. Swarms of nonflying creatures include many more creatures than could normally fit in a 10-foot square based on their normal space, because creatures in a swarm are packed tightly together and generally crawl over each other and their prey when moving or attacking. Larger swarms are represented by multiples of single swarms. The area occupied by a large swarm is completely shapeable, though the swarm usually remains in contiguous squares.

Swarm Traits: A swarm has no clear front or back and no discernible anatomy, so it is not subject to critical hits or flanking. A swarm made up of Tiny creatures takes half damage from slashing and piercing weapons. A swarm composed of Fine or Diminutive creatures is immune to all weapon damage. Reducing a swarm to 0 hit points or less causes it to break up, though damage taken until that point does not degrade its ability to attack or resist attack. Swarms are never staggered or reduced to a dying state by damage. Also, they cannot be tripped, grappled, or bull rushed, and they cannot grapple an opponent.

A swarm is immune to any spell or effect that targets a specific number of creatures (including single-target spells such as *disintegrate*), with the exception of mind-affecting effects (charms, compulsions, morale effects, patterns, and phantasms) if the swarm has an Intelligence score and a hive mind. A swarm takes half again as much damage (+50%) from spells or effects that affect an area, such as splash weapons and many evocation spells.

Swarms made up of Diminutive or Fine creatures are susceptible to high winds, such as those created by a *gust of wind* spell. For purposes of determining the effects of wind on a swarm, treat the swarm as a creature of the same size as its constituent creatures. A swarm rendered unconscious by means of nonlethal damage becomes disorganized and dispersed, and does not reform until its hit points exceed its nonlethal damage.

Swarm Attack: Creatures with the swarm subtype don't make standard melee attacks. Instead, they deal automatic damage to any creature whose space they occupy at the end of their move, with no attack roll needed. Swarm attacks are not subject to a miss chance for concealment or cover. A swarm's stat block has "swarm" in the Melee entries, with no attack bonus given.

A swarm's attacks are nonmagical, unless the swarm's description states otherwise. Damage reduction sufficient to reduce a swarm attack's damage to 0, being incorporeal, or other special abilities usually give a creature immunity (or at least resistance) to damage from a swarm. Some swarms also have acid, blood drain, poison, or other special attacks in addition to normal damage.

Swarms do not threaten creatures, and do not make attacks of opportunity with their swarm attack. However, they distract foes whose squares they occupy, as described below.

Swarms possess the distraction universal monster rule. Spellcasting or concentrating on spells within the area of a swarm requires a caster level check (DC 20 + spell level). Using skills that involve patience and concentration requires a DC 20 Will save.

Water Subtype: This subtype is usually used for outsiders with a connection to the Elemental Plane of Water. Creatures with the water subtype always have

swim speeds and can move in water without making Swim checks. A water creature can breathe underwater and can usually breathe air as well. Water creatures treat the Swim skill as a class skill.

APPENDIX 4: MONSTERS AS PCS

For simple rules on using monsters as player characters, see page 313 of the *Pathfinder RPG Bestiary*.

APPENDIX 5: MONSTER FEATS

Most of the following feats apply specifically to monsters, although some player characters might qualify for them (particularly Craft Construct).

Ability Focus

One of this creature's special attacks is particularly difficult to resist.

Prerequisite: Special attack.

Benefit: Choose one of the creature's special attacks. Add +2 to the DC on all saving throws against the special attack on which the creature focuses.

Special: A creature can gain this feat multiple times. Its effects do not stack. Each time the creature takes the feat, it applies to a different special attack.

Awesome Blow (Combat)

This creature can send opponents flying.

Prerequisites: Str 25, Power Attack, Improved Bull Rush, size Large or larger.

Benefit: As a standard action, the creature may perform an awesome blow combat maneuver. If the creature's maneuver succeeds against a corporeal opponent smaller than itself, its opponent takes damage (typically slam damage plus Strength bonus) and is knocked flying 10 feet in a direction of the attacking creature's choice and falls prone. The attacking creature can only push the opponent in a straight line, and the opponent can't move closer to the attacking creature than the square it started in. If an obstacle prevents the completion of the opponent's move, the opponent and the obstacle each take 1d6 points of damage, and the opponent is knocked prone in the space adjacent to the obstacle.

Craft Construct (Item Creation)

You can create construct creatures like golems.

Prerequisites: Caster level 5th, Craft Magic Arms and Armor, Craft Wondrous Item.

Benefit: You can create any construct whose prerequisites you meet. The act of animating a construct takes 1 day for each 1,000 gp in its market price. To create a construct, you must use up raw materials costing half of its base price, plus the full cost of the basic body created for the construct. Each construct has a special section that summarizes its costs and other prerequisites. A newly created construct has average hit points for its Hit Dice.

Empower Spell-Like Ability

One of this creature's spell-like abilities is particularly potent and powerful.

Prerequisite: Spell-like ability at caster level 6th or higher.

Benefit: Choose one of the creature's spell-like abilities, subject to the restrictions below. The creature can use that ability as an empowered spell-like ability three times per day (or less, if the ability is normally usable only once or twice per day).

When a creature uses an empowered spell-like ability, all variable, numeric effects of the spell-like ability are increased by half (+50%). Saving throws and opposed rolls are not affected. Spell-like abilities without random variables are not affected.

The creature can only select a spell-like ability duplicating a spell with a level less than or equal to 1/2 its caster level (round down) – 2. For a summary, see the table in the description of the Quicken Spell-Like Ability feat on page 311.

Special: This feat can be taken multiple times. Each time it is taken, the creature can apply it to a different spell-like ability.

Flyby Attack

This creature can make an attack before and after it moves while flying.

Prerequisite: Fly speed.

Benefit: When flying, the creature can take a move action and another standard action at any point during the move. The creature cannot take a second move action during a round when it makes a flyby attack.

Normal: Without this feat, the creature takes a standard action either before or after its move.

Hover

This creature can hover in place with ease and can kick up clouds of dust and debris.

Prerequisite: Fly speed.

Benefit: A creature with this feat can halt its movement while flying, allowing it to hover without needing to make a Fly skill check.

If a creature of size Large or larger with this feat hovers within 20 feet of the ground in an area with lots of loose debris, the draft from its wings creates a hemispherical cloud with a radius of 60 feet. The winds generated can snuff torches, small campfires, exposed lanterns, and other small, open flames of nonmagical origin. Clear vision within the cloud is limited to 10 feet. Creatures have concealment at 15 to 20 feet (20% miss chance). At

25 feet or more, creatures have total concealment (50% miss chance, and opponents cannot use sight to locate the creature).

Normal: Without this feat, a creature must make a Fly skill check to hover and the creature does not create a cloud of debris while hovering.

Improved Natural Armor

This creature's hide is tougher than most.

Prerequisites: Natural armor, Con 13.

Benefit: The creature's natural armor bonus increases by +1.

Special: A creature can gain this feat multiple times. Each time the creature takes the feat, its natural armor bonus increases by another point.

Improved Natural Attack

Attacks made by one of this creature's natural attacks leave vicious wounds.

Prerequisite: Natural weapon, base attack bonus +4.

Benefit: Choose one of the creature's natural attack forms (not an unarmed strike). The damage for this natural attack increases by one step on the following list, as if the creature's size had increased by one category. Damage dice increase as follows: 1d2, 1d3, 1d4, 1d6, 1d8, 2d6, 3d6, 4d6, 6d6, 8d6, 12d6.

A weapon or attack that deals 1d10 points of damage increases as follows: 1d10, 2d8, 3d8, 4d8, 6d8, 8d8, 12d8.

Multiattack (Combat)

This creature is particularly skilled at making attacks with its natural weapons.

Prerequisite: Three or more natural attacks.

Benefit: The creature's secondary attacks with natural weapons take only a –2 penalty.

Normal: Without this feat, the creature's secondary attacks with natural weapons take a –5 penalty.

Multiweapon Fighting (Combat)

This multi-armed creature is skilled at making attacks with multiple weapons.

Prerequisites: Dex 13, three or more hands.

Benefit: Penalties for fighting with multiple weapons are reduced by –2 with the primary hand and by –6 with off hands.

Normal: A creature without this feat takes a –6 penalty on attacks made with its primary hand and a –10 penalty on attacks made with all of its off hands. (It has one primary hand, and all the others are off hands.) See Two-Weapon Fighting in the *Pathfinder RPG Core Rulebook*.

Special: This feat replaces the Two-Weapon Fighting feat for creatures with more than two arms.

Quicken Spell-Like Ability

This creature can use one of its spell-like abilities with next to no effort.

Prerequisite: Spell-like ability at CL 10th or higher.

Benefit: Choose one of the creature's spell-like abilities, subject to the restrictions described in this feat. The creature can use the chosen spell-like ability as a quickened spell-like ability three times per day (or fewer, if the ability is normally usable only once or twice per day).

Using a quickened spell-like ability is a swift action that does not provoke an attack of opportunity. The creature can perform another action—including the use of another spell-like ability (but not another swift action)—in the same round that it uses a quickened spell-like ability.

The creature can only select a spell-like ability duplicating a spell with a level less than or equal to 1/2 its caster level (round down) – 4. For a summary, see the table below.

A spell-like ability that duplicates a spell with a casting time greater than 1 full round cannot be quickened.

Normal: The use of a spell-like ability normally requires a standard action (at the very least) and provokes an attack of opportunity.

Special: This feat can be taken multiple times. Each time it is taken, the creature can apply it to a different one of its spell-like abilities.

EMPOWERED AND QUICKENED SPELL-LIKE ABILITIES

Spell Level	Caster Level to Empower	Caster Level to Quicken
0	4th	8th
1st	6th	10th
2nd	8th	12th
3rd	10th	14th
4th	12th	16th
5th	14th	18th
6th	16th	20th
7th	18th	—
8th	20th	—
9th	—	—

Snatch

This creature can grab other creatures with ease.

Prerequisite: Size Huge or larger.

Benefits: The creature can start a grapple when it hits with a claw or bite attack, as though it had the grab ability. If it grapples a creature three or more sizes smaller, it squeezes each round for automatic bite or claw damage with a successful grapple check. A snatched opponent held in the creature's mouth is not allowed a Reflex save against the creature's breath weapon, if it has one.

The creature can drop a creature it has snatched as a free action or use a standard action to fling it aside. A flung creature travels 1d6 × 10 feet, and takes 1d6 points of damage per 10 feet traveled. If the creature flings a snatched opponent while flying, the opponent takes this amount or falling damage, whichever is greater.

Wingover

This creature can make turns with ease while flying.

Prerequisite: Fly speed.

Benefits: Once per round, the creature can turn up to 180 degrees as a free action without making a Fly check. This turn does cost the creature any movement.

Normal: A flying creature can turn up to 90 degrees by making a DC 15 Fly check and expending 5 feet of movement. A flying creature can turn up to 180 degrees by making a DC 20 Fly check and expending 10 feet of movement.

APPENDIX 6: MONSTER COHORTS

The Leadership feat (see page 129 of the *Pathfinder RPG Core Rulebook*) allows a character to gain a loyal cohort. With the GM's approval, this cohort can be a similarly aligned monster. Monsters on the following list all work well as cohorts (be they assassins, bodyguards, mounts, etc.)—their effective cohort "level" corresponds to the level available to the PC as afforded by his Leadership score. Use these monsters as guidelines when determining cohort levels for other monsters.

For more information on monster cohorts, see page 316 of the *Pathfinder RPG Bestiary*.

MONSTER COHORTS

Monster	Level	Monster	Level
Aranea	8th	Dragon horse	16th
Avoral	15th	Howler	7th
Axiomite	14th	Leonal	17th
Azer	5th	Leucrotta	9th
Blink dog	4th	Redcap	10th

APPENDIX 7: ANIMAL COMPANIONS

The following list indexes all additional animal companions found in this book, along with the page numbers on which they can be located.

ANIMAL COMPANIONS

Animal	Page	Animal	Page
Allosaurus	90	Megaloceros	187
Arsinoitherium	186	Megatherium	187
Baboon	212	Parasaurolophus	91
Gar	128	Ram	154
Glyptodon	186	Snapping turtle	273
Hippopotamus	157	Stingray	232
Manta ray	232	Tylosaurus	91

APPENDIX 8: MONSTERS BY TYPE

Listed below are all of the monsters in this book, organized alphabetically by type.

Aberration: akata, charybdis, decapus, destrachan, dust digger, faceless stalker, fungal crawler, grick, grindylow, gug, neh-thalggu, reefclaw, scylla, seugathi, sinspawn, tentamort, vampiric mist, vemerak

(Air): belker, cloud dragon, dragon horse, ice elemental, jabberwock, lightning elemental, mihstu

Animal: allosaurus, arsinoitherium, baboon, badger, behemoth hippopotamus, camel, compsognathus, dire badger, emperor cobra, giant anaconda, giant gar, giant snapping turtle, giant toad, glyptodon, great white whale, hippopotamus, manta ray, megaloceros, megatherium, monkey swarm, monstrous gar, parasaurolophus, ram, snapping turtle, stingray, tylosaurus, whale

(Aquatic): bunyip, charda, charybdis, devilfish, draugr, freshwater merrow, giant dragonfly nymph, giant gar, grindylow, hippocampus, jellyfish swarm, kelpie, locathah, manta ray, monstrous jellyfish, nereid, nightwave nightshade, reefclaw, saltwater merrow, scylla, sea drake, stingray, water orm

(Cold): frost drake, frost worm, ice elemental, glacier toad, ice troll, wendigo, winterwight

Construct: adamantine golem, alchemical golem, carrion golem, clockwork golem, glass golem, mithral golem, necrophidius, scarecrow, soulbound doll

Dragon: brine dragon, cloud dragon, crystal dragon, flame drake, forest drake, frost drake, jabberwock, magma dragon, sea drake, umbral dragon

(Earth): crysmal, crystal dragon, magma elemental, mud elemental, pech, rock troll, sandman, thoqqua

Fey: brownie, forlarren, gremlins, grig, kelpie, korred, leprechaun, lurker in light, nereid, pech, quickling, redcap, twigjack

(Fire): azer, jabberwock, magma dragon, mamga elemental, magma ooze, rast, thoqqua, thrasfyr

(Giant): athach, freshwater merrow, ice troll, marsh giant, rock troll, rune giant, saltwater merrow, taiga giant, wood giant

Humanoid: athach, dark slayer, dhampir, freshwater merrow, grippli, ice troll, locathah, marsh giant, ogrekin, rock troll, rune giant, saltwater merrow, skulk, spriggan, taiga giant, werebear, wereboar, weretiger, wood giant

(Incorporeal): animate dream, banshee, poltergeist, witchfire

Magical Beast: amphisbaena, aranea, aurumvorax, blindheim, blink dog, bunyip, catoblepas, chupacabra, death worm, devilfish, dragon horse, frost worm, glacier toad, gray render, gryph, hippocampus, hippogriff, krenshar, leng spider, leucrota, mobat, peryton, shantak, siren, slurk, thrasfyr, thunderbird, water orm, yrthak

Monstrous Humanoid: charda, lamia matriarch, mongrelman, mothman, serpentfolk, witchwyrd

Ooze: amoeba swarm, carnivorous blob, giant amoeba, magma ooze, slime mold, slithering tracker

Outsider: aeons, d'ziriak, gloomwing, jyoti, mercane, sceanduinar, soul eater, tenebrous worm

Outsider (air): belker, ice elemental, lightning elemental, mihstu

Outsider (chaotic): azata, chaos beast, demons, denizen of Leng, Elysian titan, howler, proteans, qlippoth, Thanatotic titan, xacarba

Outsider (cold): ice elemental, wendigo

Outsider (earth): crysmal, magma elemental, mud elemental, sandman, thoqqua

Outsider (elemental): belker, ice elemental, lightning elemental, magma elemental, mihstu, mud elemental, sandman, thoqqua

Outsider (evil): achaierai, daemons, demons, denizen of Leng, devils, hellcat, hound of Tindalos, howler, qlippoth, shining child, Thanatotic titan, xacarba

Outsider (extraplanar): aeons, agathions

Outsider (fire): azer, magma elemental, rast, thoqqua

Outsider (good): agathions, angels, archons, azatas, Elysian titan

Outsider (lawful): achaierai, archons, axiomite, devils, hellcat, inevitables

Outsider (native): fetchling, ifrit, oread, sylph, triton, undine, urdefhan, wendigo

Outsider (water): ice elemental, mud elemental, triton

Plant: hangman tree, mandragora, moonflower, mu spore, phycomid, quickwood, sard, tendriculos, viper vine, xtabay

(Shapechanger): aranea, faceless stalker, imentesh protean, keketar protean, lamia matriarch, naunet protean, voidworm protean, wereboar, werebear, weretiger

(Swarm): amoeba swarm, flesh-eating cockroach swarm, jellyfish swarm, monkey swarm, mosquito swarm, tick swarm

Template: juju zombie, lycanthrope, ogrekin, petitioner, ravener, worm that walks

Undead: attic whisperer, banshee, bodak, crawling hand, crypt thing, draugr, dullahan, giant crawling hand, juju zombie, nightshades, poltergeist, ravener, revenant, skaveling, totenmaske, winterwight, witchfire

Vermin: cave scorpion, colossal black scorpion, flesh-eating cockroach swarm, giant bee, giant black widow spider, giant dragonfly, giant dragonfly nymph, giant fly, giant maggot, giant mosquito, giant queen bee, giant solifugid, giant tarantula, giant tick, giant whiptail centipede, goliath stag beetle, jellyfish swarm, monstrous jellyfish, monstrous roach, mosquito swarm, sicuel solifugid, slicer beetle, tick swarm, titan centipede, worm that walks

(Water): brine dragon, ice elemental, mud elemental, nereid, triton

APPENDIX 9: MONSTERS BY CR

The following section lists all monsters included in this book, alphabetically by CR. Variant monsters (such as the alternate versions of the magma ooze and the various giant vermin of alternate sizes) are not included in this list—an index of these monsters appears instead in Appendix 11: Variant Monster Index. In the case of templates, like ogrekin and raveners, only the sample creature presented with a full stat block at the start of the template's entry in this book is included. Similarly, for dragons, only those that have full stat blocks presented in this book are listed on the following tables (young, adult, and ancient dragons)—dragons of other age categories are not included on these lists.

CR 1/2

baboon, badger, crawling hand, dhampir, fetchling, giant maggot, grindylow, grippli, ifrit, locathah, monstrous roach, oread, pugwampi, snapping turtle, stingray, sylph, undine, xtabay

CR 1

akata, amoeba swarm, brownie, camel, cave scorpion, compsognathus, giant amoeba, giant bee, giant fly, giant gar, giant solifugid, giant tick, grig, gryph, hippocampus, ice elemental (Small), jinkin, krenshar, lightning elemental (Small), magma elemental (Small), manta ray, mongrelman, mud elemental (Small), ram, reefclaw, skulk, vexgit

CR 2

arbiter, azer, blindheim, blink dog, cacodaemon, cassisian, cythnigot, dire badger, draugr, flesh-eating cockroach swarm, forlarren, giant toad, hippogriff, juju zombie, leprechaun, lyrakien, monkey swarm, nuglub, ogrekin, paracletus, silvanshee, sinspawn, slime mold, slurk, soulbound doll, thoqqua, triton, voidworm, wereboar

CR 3

accuser devil, bunyip, chupacabra, crysmal, dark slayer, d'ziriak, freshwater merrow, fungal crawler, giant black widow spider, giant dragonfly nymph, giant whiptail centipede, grick, howler, ice elemental (Medium), lightning elemental (Medium), magma elemental (Medium), mobat, mosquito swarm, mud elemental (Medium), necrophidius, pech, quickling, sandman, spriggan, twigjack, urdefhan, vampiric mist

CR 4

amphisbaena, aranea, attic whisperer, carrion golem, decapus, devilfish, dust digger, faceless stalker, forest drake, giant dragonfly, gloomwing, ice troll, kelpie, korred, mandragora, megaloceros, parasaurolophus, peryton, phycomid, poltergeist, scarecrow, serpentfolk, sicuel solifugid, slicer beetle, slithering tracker, tentamort, werebear, weretiger

CR 5

achaierai, crypt thing, emperor cobra, flame drake, giant crawling hand, giant queen bee, hippopotamus, ice elemental (Large), leucrota, lightning elemental (Large), lurker in light,

magma elemental (Large), megatherium, mercane, mud elemental (Large), rast, siren, skaveling

CR 6
belker, ceustodaemon, death worm, giant mosquito, glacier toad, glyptodon, jellyfish swarm, monstrous gar, mothman, redcap, revenant, rock troll, saltwater merrow, sea drake, seugathi, tendriculos, vulpinal, witchwyrd, wood giant, young crystal dragon

CR 7
allosaurus, arsinoitherium, chaos beast, charda, dullahan, frost drake, hangman tree, hellcat, hound of Tindalos, ice elemental (Huge), lightning elemental (Huge), magma elemental (Huge), magma ooze, monstrous jellyfish, mud elemental (Huge), naunet, sceaduinar, shoggti, soul eater, theletos, totenmaske, young brine dragon

CR 8
animate dream, axiomite, bodak, denizen of Leng, destrachan, giant tarantula, glass golem, goliath stag beetle, gray render, hydrodaemon, lamia matriarch, marsh giant, mihstu, moonflower, neh-thalggu, quickwood, shantak, tenebrous worm, tylosaurus, young magma dragon

CR 9
alchemical golem, aurumvorax, avoral, dragon horse, giant snapping turtle, ice elemental (greater), jyoti, leukodaemon, lightning elemental (greater), magma elemental (greater), mud elemental (greater), tick swarm, titan centipede, witchfire, young cloud dragon, yrthak, zelekhut

CR 10
adult crystal dragon, behemoth hippopotamus, giant anaconda, gug, imentesh, kalavakus, movanic deva, nereid, nyogoth, piscodaemon, shield archon, water orm, whale, young umbral dragon

CR 11
adult brine dragon, ice elemental (elder), lightning elemental (elder), magma elemental (elder), meladaemon, mud elemental (elder), thunderbird

CR 12
adult magma dragon, akhana, athach, catoblepas, chernobue, clockwork golem, derghodaemon, frost worm, kolyarut, leonal, monadic deva, omox, shining child, taiga giant

CR 13
adult cloud dragon, banshee, carnivorous blob, charybdis, thanadaemon, viper vine

CR 14
adult umbral dragon, augnagar, great white whale,

handmaiden devil, leng spider, nightwing, vemerak, worm that walks

CR 15
ancient crystal dragon, cetaceal, colossal black scorpion, marut, xacarba

CR 16
ancient brine dragon, astradaemon, belier devil, bythos, mithral golem, nightwalker, scylla, shemhazian

CR 17
ancient magma dragon, brijidine, keketar, rune giant, thrasfyr, wendigo, winterwight

CR 18
ancient cloud dragon, nightcrawler nightshade, purrodaemon, thulgant qlippoth

CR 19
adamantine golem, ancient umbral dragon, immolation devil, sard, star archon, vrolikai

CR 20
draconal, iathavos, lhaksharut, nightwave, olethrodaemon, pleroma

CR 21
Elysian titan, mu spore

CR 22
Thanatotic titan, wyrm red dragon ravener

CR 23
jabberwock

APPENDIX 10: MONSTERS BY TERRAIN
The following lists group all of the monsters in this book into their respective terrains. Note that there can be a certain amount of crossover on these lists, especially between climate bands, similar terrains, or a planar terrain and the Material Plane. For example, although death worms are normally encountered in warm deserts, it's certainly possible to encounter one in a temperate desert (but much less likely to find one in a cold desert). Likewise, while aurumvoraxes usually limit their hunts to hilly terrain, it wouldn't be unusual to find one in the mountains or even on a plain. Creatures listed under planar terrains can usually be encountered anywhere on the Material Plane as well, but are only very rarely encountered on planes other than the one associated with them. In short, use these lists as a guide, not as shackles—if your adventure works better with a colossal black scorpion encountered in a cold forest, by

all means, go for it! Just keep in mind that you should also probably come up with an in-game reason to explain the monster's presence there.

ANY TERRAIN

adamantine golem, akata, alchemical golem, amoeba swarm, banshee, carnivorous blob, carrion golem, clockwork golem, crawling hand, denizen of Leng, dhampir, dragon horse, dullahan, flesh eating cockroach swarm, giant amoeba, glass golem, hound of Tindalos, ifrit, juju zombie, lamia matriarch, leng spider, lurker in light, mercane, mithral golem, monstrous roach, moonflower, mothman, necrophidius, neh-thalggu, ogrekin, oread, peryton, petitioner, poltergeist, ravener, revenant, scarecrow, shining child, skulk, soulbound doll, sylph, thrasfyr, totenmaske, umbral dragon, undine, winterwight, witchwyrd, worm that walks, xtabay

COASTLINE

denizen of Leng, draugr, giant snapping turtle, reefclaw, scylla, sea drake, snapping turtle, undine

DESERT (TEMPERATE)

yrthak

DESERT (WARM)

camel, colossal black scorpion, death worm, dust digger, giant solifugid, sicuel solifugid

FOREST (COLD)

forest drake, giant tarantula, jabberwock, mandragora, sard, taiga giant, werebear, wereboar, witchfire

FOREST (TEMPERATE)

aranea, aurumvorax, badger, blink dog, brownie, decapus, dire badger, forest drake, forlarren, giant tarantula, giant tick, giant toad, giant whiptail centipede, grig, gryph, hangman tree, jabberwock, korred, krenshar, leprechaun, leucrota, mandragora, megaloceros, megatherium, quickling, quickwood, redcap, sard, slicer beetle, slime mold, spriggan, tendriculos, titan centipede, twigjack, viper vine, werebear, wereboar, witchfire, wood giant, xtabay

FOREST (WARM)

allosaurus, baboon, compsognathus, forest drake, giant mosquito, giant solifugid, giant tarantula, giant whiptail centipede, goliath stag beetle, grippli, hangman tree, jabberwock, leucrotta, megaloceros, megatherium, monkey swarm, mosquito swarm, parasaurolophus, sard, sicuel solifugid, tendriculos, tick swarm, titan centipede, viper vine, werebear, wereboar, witchfire

HILLS (COLD)

glacier toad, thunderbird

HILLS (TEMPERATE)

amphisbaena, athach, aurumvorax, hippogriff, leucrota, redcap, siren, thunderbird

HILLS (WARM)

chupacabra, leucrota, pugwampi, siren, thunderbird

MOUNTAINS (COLD)

frost drake, frost worm, glacier toad, ice troll, magma dragon, rune giant, shantak, thunderbird

MOUNTAINS (TEMPERATE)

flame drake, magma dragon, ram, redcap, thunderbird, yrthak

MOUNTAINS (WARM)

magma ooze, magma dragon, thunderbird

OCEAN (COLD)

brine dragon, charda, charybdis, devilfish, draugr, great white whale, grindylow, kelpie, nereid, reefclaw, scylla, triton, whale

OCEAN (TEMPERATE)

brine dragon, bunyip, charybdis, devilfish, draugr, great white whale, grindylow, hippocampus, jellyfish swarm, kelpie, locathah, monstrous jellyfish, nereid, reefclaw, saltwater merrow, scylla, triton, whale

OCEAN (WARM)

brine dragon, bunyip, charybdis, devilfish, draugr, nereid, great white whale, grindylow, jellyfish swarm, kelpie, locathah, manta ray, monstrous jellyfish, reefclaw, scylla, stingray, triton, tylosaurus, whale

PLAINS (COLD)

frost worm, glacial toad, taiga giant, wereboar, weretiger

PLAINS (TEMPERATE)

arsinoitherium, aurumvorax, blink dog, brownie, forlarren, giant bee, giant queen bee, giant toad, glyptodon, krenshar, megaloceros, wereboar, weretiger

PLAINS (WARM)

allosaurus, chupacabra, compsognathus, giant bee, giant queen bee, giant solifugid, giant toad, goliath stag beetle, parasaurolophus, sicuel solifugid, wereboar, weretiger

PLANAR (ABADDON—NEUTRAL EVIL)

astradaemon, ceustodaemon, cacodaemon, derghodaemon, hydrodaemon, leukodaemon, meladaemon, olethrodaemon, piscodaemon, purrodaemon, thanadaemon

PLANAR (ASTRAL)

astradaemon, dragon horse, pleroma aeon

PLANAR (ABYSS—CHAOTIC EVIL)

augnagar qlippoth, bodak, chernobue qlippoth, cythnigot qlippoth, iathavos qlippoth, kalavakus demon, nyogoth qlippoth, omox demon, shemhazian demon, shoggti qlippoth, Thanatotic titan, thulgant qlippoth, vrolikai demon, xacarba

PLANAR (ELYSIUM—CHAOTIC GOOD)

brijidine azata, Elysian titan, lyrakien azata

PLANAR (ETHEREAL PLANE)

animate dream, belier devil, dragon horse, hound of Tindalos, monadic deva

PLANAR (HEAVEN—LAWFUL GOOD)

shield archon, star archon

PLANAR (HELL—LAWFUL EVIL)

accuser devil, achaierai, belier devil, handmaiden devil, hellcat, immolation devil

PLANAR (LIMBO—CHAOTIC NEUTRAL)

chaos beast, howler, imentesh protean, keketar protean, naunet protean, voidworm protean

PLANAR (NIRVANA—NEUTRAL GOOD)

avoral agathion, cassisian angel, cetaceal agathion, draconal agathion, leonal agathion, monadic deva, movanic deva, silvanshee agathion, vulpinal agathion

PLANAR (NEGATIVE ENERGY PLANE)

movanic deva, sceaduinar

PLANAR (PLANE OF AIR)

belker, cloud dragon, dragon horse, ice elemental, lightning elemental, mihstu, monadic deva

PLANAR (PLANE OF EARTH)

crysmal, magma elemental, mud elemental, monadic deva, pech, sandman

PLANAR (PLANE OF FIRE)

azer, magma elemental, monadic deva, rast, thoqqua

PLANAR (PLANE OF SHADOW)

d'ziriak, fetchling, gloomwing, nightcrawler nightshade, nightwalker nightshade, nightwave nightshade, nightwing nightshade, tenebrous worm

PLANAR (PLANE OF WATER)

ice elemental, monadic deva, mud elemental

PLANAR (POSITIVE ENERGY PLANE)

jyoti, movanic deva

PLANAR (PURGATORY—NEUTRAL)

akhana aeon, bythos aeon, paracletus aeon, pleroma aeon, soul eater, theletos aeon

PLANAR (UTOPIA—LAWFUL NEUTRAL)

arbiter inevitable, axiomite, kolyarut inevitable, lhaksharut inevitable, marut inevitable, zelekhut inevitable

RIVERS/LAKES

behemoth hippopotamus, brine dragon, bunyip, devilfish, draugr, freshwater merrow, giant dragonfly nymph, giant gar, giant snapping turtle, hippocampus, hippopotamus, kelpie, locathah, monstrous gar, nereid, snapping turtle, tylosaurus, water orm

SWAMP (COLD)

catoblepas, faceless stalker, tentamort, weretiger, witchfire

SWAMP (TEMPERATE)

catoblepas, emperor cobra, faceless stalker, giant dragonfly, giant fly, giant mosquito, giant toad, giant maggot, gray render, grippli, marsh giant slurk, snapping turtle, tentamort, vampiric mist, viper vine, weretiger, witchfire

SWAMP (WARM)

catoblepas, emperor cobra, faceless stalker, giant anaconda, giant dragonfly, giant fly, giant maggot, giant mosquito, giant toad, grippli, mosquito swarm, snapping turtle, tentamort, viper vine, weretiger, witchfire

UNDERGROUND

amoeba swarm, amphisbaena, blindheim, cave scorpion, charda, crypt thing, crysmal, crystal dragon, dark slayer, decapus, destrachan, faceless stalker, fungal crawler, giant amoeba, giant black widow, giant crawling hand, giant solifugid, giant whiptail centipede, glacier toad, grick, gryph, gug, ice troll, jinkin, magma ooze, mercane, mobat, mongrelman, mu spore, necrophidius, nuglub, pech, phycomid, redcap, rock troll, serpentfolk, seugathi, sicuel solifugid, sinspawn, skaveling, skulk, slime mold, slithering tracker, slurk, tentamort, titan centipede, totenmaske, urdefhan, vampiric mist, vemerak, vexgit

URBAN

attic whisperer, flesh-eating cockroach swarm, jinkin, nuglub, revenant, soulbound doll, vexgit, witchwyrd

APPENDIX 11: VARIANT MONSTER INDEX

Not all of the monsters presented in this book have their own stat blocks. Many of them are merely variants on a theme, such as the various kinds of sinspawn or alternate versions of the chupacabra. Monster variants use the standard monster's stats but with specific changes, as outlined in the text.

The following list indexes all of the monster variants in this book that are associated with rules changes (creatures that are only mentioned in passing, such as the agathion leaders, primal inevitables, or protean lords, are not indexed here).

APPENDIX 12: ABILITY INDEX

The monsters detailed in this book have a wide range of special attacks, defenses, and qualities—and only in the case of relatively unique abilities are rules given in a monster's actual entry. Other abilities are detailed in the universal monster rules, in shared abilities for that creature's type, or even as class abilities or other features detailed in the *Pathfinder RPG Core Rulebook*. Use the following ability index to track down full rules for monster abilities not detailed in a monster's entry.

Note: Entries listed in bold are usually class abilities, and thus the page number listed refers to a page in the *Pathfinder RPG Core Rulebook*. Page numbers prefixed with a *B* (such as *B-92*) refer to dragon abilities described in the *Pathfinder RPG Bestiary*. All other page number references point to pages in the *Pathfinder RPG Bestiary 2*.

APPENDIX 13: MONSTER ROLES

The following lists categorize all of the monsters in this book into their roles. These roles indicate what types of character classes are treated as key classes for each monster.

Combat monsters are good at ranged and melee combat. Spell monsters have an inherent ability to cast magic spells. Skill monsters are particularly adept at ambushing prey, use sneak attacks, or have bard-like powers. Special monsters have no key classes—their focus is on unique tactics and abilities.

Creatures listed as having "Any Role" do not use special rules when advancing via class level—they lack racial Hit Dice, and thus advance in level normally, as detailed in the *Pathfinder RPG Core Rulebook*. All of the PC races listed in that book fit into this category as well.

Creatures listed in the "No Role" category have no key classes—these are generally any creatures that are mindless or have an Intelligence score of 2 or lower. Creatures in this category cannot gain class levels at all, and must advance using other methods. If a creature in this category gains an Intelligence score of 3 or higher, the creature becomes a Combat Role monster.

Note that monster templates are not listed in this appendix—with the exception of skeletons and zombies (which lose their intelligence and thus have no key classes), a templated monster's key class is the same as the base creature's key classes.

If you add levels in a key class to a monster, increase its CR by +1 for every level in a key class. For more information on adding class levels to a monster, see pages 296, 297, and 323 of the *Pathfinder RPG Bestiary*.

ANY ROLE
azer, dhampir, fetchling, grippli, ifrit, locathah, oread, serpentfolk, sylph, undine

COMBAT ROLE
accuser devil, achaierai, akata, animate dream, arbiter, astradaemon, athach, attic whisperer, augnagar, avoral, axiomite, belier devil, belker, blindheim, blink dog, bodak, brijidine, brine dragon, bythos, cacodaemon, catoblepas, cetacean, ceustodaemon, chaos beast, charda, charybdis, chernobue, chupacabra, cloud dragon, crypt thing, crysmal, crystal dragon, cythnigot, death worm, decapus, derghodaemon, destrachan, devilfish, draconal, dragon horse, draugr, dullahan, d'ziriak, Elysian titan, flame drake, forest drake, forlarren, freshwater merrow, frost drake, glacier toad, gray render, grick, grindylow, gug, handmaiden devil, hangman tree, hellcat, hippocampus, hound of Tindalos, howler, hydrodaemon, iathavos, ice elemental, ice troll, imentesh, immolation devil, jabberwock, jyoti, kalavakus, keketar, kelpie, kolyarut, korred, krenshar, lamia matriarch, leng spider, leonal, leukodaemon, lhaksharut, lightning elemental, lurker in light, magma dragon, magma elemental, mandragora, marsh giant, marut, meladaemon, mercane, mihstu, mobat, monadic deva, mongrelman, moonflower, movanic deva, mu spore, mud elemental, naunet, nightcrawler, nightstalker, nightwave, nightwing, nuglub, nyogoth, olethrodaemon, omox, pech, peryton, poltergeist, pugwampi, purrodaemon, quickwood, rast, ravener, redcap, reefclaw, revenant, rock troll, rune giant, saltwater merrow, sandman, sard, sceaduinar, scylla, sea drake, seugathi, shantak, shemhazian, shield archon, shining child, shoggti, silvanshee, sinspawn, skaveling, slithering tracker, slurk, soul eater, star archon, taiga giant, tendriculos, thanadaemon, Thanatotic titan, theletos, thoqqua, thrasfyr, thulgant, thunderbird, totenmaske, triton, twigjack, umbral dragon, urdefhan, vampiric mist, vemerak, voidworm, vrolikai, water orm, wendigo, winterwight, witchfire, witchwyrd, wood giant, xacarba, yrthak, zelekhut

NO ROLE
adamantine golem, alchemical golem, allosaurus, amoeba swarm, amphisbaena, arsinoitherium, aurumvorax, baboon, badger, behemoth hippopotamus, bunyip, camel, carnivorous blob, carrion golem, cave scorpion, clockwork golem, colossal black scorpion, compsognathus, crawling hand, dire badger, dust digger, emperor cobra, flesh-eating cockroach swarm, frost worm, fungal crawler, giant amoeba, giant anaconda, giant bee, giant black widow spider, giant crawling hand, giant dragonfly, giant dragonfly nymph, giant fly, giant gar, giant maggot, giant mosquito, giant queen bee, giant snapping turtle, giant solifugid, giant tarantula, giant tick, giant toad, giant whiptail centipede, glass golem, gloomwing, glyptodon, goliath stag beetle, great white whale, gryph, hippogriff, hippopotamus, jellyfish swarm, magma ooze, manta ray, megaloceros, megatherium, mithral golem, monkey swarm, monstrous gar, monstrous jellyfish, monstrous roach, mosquito swarm, necrophidius, parasaurolophus, phycomid, ram, scarecrow, sicuel solifugid, slicer beetle, slime mold, snapping turtle, stingray, tenebrous worm, tentamort, tick swarm, titan centipede, tylosaurus, viper vine, whale, xtabay

SKILL ROLE
dark slayer, denizen of Leng, faceless stalker, grig, jinkin, nereid, paracletus, siren, skulk, spriggan, vexgit, vulpinal

SPECIAL ROLE
akhana, banshee, cassisian, leucrota, mothman, quickling, soulbound doll

SPELL ROLE
aranea, brine dragon, brownie, cloud dragon, crystal dragon, draconal, lamia matriarch, leprechaun, lyrakian, magma dragon, monadic deva, movanic deva, neh-thalggu, pleroma, ravener, star archon, umbral dragon, worm that walks

PATHFINDER
ROLEPLAYING GAME

Fearsome Foes Await!

MYTH AND MAGIC FROM ACROSS THE SEA!

PATHFINDER BESTIARY 3

AVAILABLE NOW!

paizo
PUBLISHING LLC

PAIZO.COM/PATHFINDER